A Dictionary of
European History and Politics 1945–1995

A Dictionary of

European History and Politics 1945–1995

Derek W. Urwin

LONGMAN

LONDON AND NEW YORK

Addison Wesley Longman Limited
Edinburgh Gate, Harlow
Essex CM20 2JE, England
and Associated Companies throughout the world.

*Published in the United States of America
by Longman Publishing, New York*

First published 1996

ISBN 0 582 25874X PPR

British Library Cataloguing-in-Publication Data
A catalogue record for this book is
available from the British Library

Library of Congress Cataloging-in-Publication Data
Urwin, Derek W.
   A dictionary of European history and politics, 1945–1995 / Derek W. Urwin.
     p. cm.
   Includes index.
   ISBN 0–582–25874–X
   1. Europe – History – 1945 – Dictionaries. I. Title.
IN PROCESS
940.55'03 – dc20   95–46452
                            CIP

Set by 3 in Times and Melior
Produced through Longman Malaysia, VVP

Preface

This dictionary is an attempt to depict, in a concise and summary format, the most significant features of European history and politics in the tumultuous period since the end of the Second World War in 1945. The entries broadly fall into four categories: events and issues; territories (states, regions, and disputed areas); organizations – both national and international; and individuals. Their inclusion has been based upon an assessment of whether the subjects have been significant in a national and/or international context. Inevitably, this means that a larger number of entries are devoted to the larger European states, but not, it is hoped, to the total detriment of their smaller neighbours. Clearly, no compilation of this nature can hope or claim to be comprehensive, and this dictionary is no exception. Social and political change is an ongoing and complex process, often not immediately apparent and never easily amenable to simple itemization. The dictionary purports to do no more than attempt to provide a succinct and accurate account of complex issues, although in the last resort the final selection of what should be included is inevitably dependent upon personal judgment and interests.

The scope of the book is based upon a generous interpretation of what constitutes Europe, the definition of which is often a term of convenience and never as simple as might be imagined. This is particularly relevant for the post-1989 period and a coverage of the successor states to the former Soviet Union. A conscious decision was to incorporate Armenia, Azerbaijan and Georgia, excluding only those successor states which clearly lie in the heartlands of Asia. The entries, which are listed alphabetically, are intended to be self-contained, but more complex organizations, particularly the European Union/European Communities and the North Atlantic Treaty Organization, have been disaggregated into their numerous component parts. However, cross-references have been included throughout. These are printed in small capitals at the end of entries and elsewhere when directing the reader to consult another entry, but in bold type when names and terms with their own entries are discussed in passing within another entry. These will hopefully enable the reader to relate events and issues more readily with each other. Personal and place names are given in the form commonly employed in English, but on occasions the original version has been retained where there is no obvious or accepted Anglicized equivalent.

A

Abatement. The term used in the **European Union (EU)** to describe the mechanism whereby a member state receives back a proportion of its budget contribution. It was originally adopted by the **European Communities (EC)** to satisfy **United Kingdom** complaints about its budget contribution. It applies in situations where a state's budget contribution is greater than the funds it receives from various EC/EU bodies.

Abkhazia. An ethnically distinctive region of **Georgia**. Before the disintegration of the **USSR** it had the status of an autonomous republic within Georgia. In 1989 conflict broke out in the province between the ethnic majority and the Georgian minority over discrimination in higher education, and Abkhazian leaders demanded the transfer of the region to the Russian Federation or its constitution as a Soviet republic. Tension increased after the 1990 election victory in Georgia of an ultra-nationalist coalition led by **Gamsakhurdia**, leading to the outbreak of sporadic acts of violence. Abkhazian rebels began a full-scale war against Georgian troops in July 1993. With material support from **Russia**, they defeated their opponents within a few months, declaring independence and expelling the Georgian population from the province. In 1994 a trilateral agreement between Abkhazia, Georgia and Russia provided for the return of refugees and the presence of a Russian peace-keeping force.

Abrene. A district of **Russia** bordering on **Latvia**. Part of Latvia before 1940, it was ceded to the Russian Federation by the **USSR** in 1944. The annexation was not recognized by the independent Latvian state after 1991.

Accord for Europe. An alliance of conservative and nationalist parties in **Russia** founded in 1994. Its objective was to put forward a single candidate to challenge for the presidency in 1996.

Acheson, Dean Gooderham. (1893–1971) USA Secretary of State 1949–53. After a distinguished legal career he was appointed Assistant Secretary of State in 1941, before serving as Under-Secretary of State 1945–47. In February 1947 he presented an outline of what became the **Truman Doctrine**, and the following May he was the first American official publicly to advocate an economic aid programme for Europe. He was a strong supporter of Western Europe security, actively working for the creation of the **North Atlantic Treaty Organization (NATO)**. In the early 1950s he urged the strengthening of NATO, especially the rearmament of the **Federal Republic of Germany**.

Acquis Communautaire. A collective phrase describing all the secondary legislation passed by the **Commission** and the **Council of Ministers** under the provisions of the **founding treaties** of the **European Communities (EC)** and their subsequent amendments. Countries which become members of the **European Union (EU)** have to accept, and are bound by, the body of acquis communautaire built up since 1958.

Acquis Politiques. A collective phrase describing all the decisions and resolutions adopted by the member states of the **European Union (EU)** in the field of foreign policy. *See* EUROPEAN POLITICAL CO-OPERATION, COMMON FOREIGN AND SECURITY POLICY.

Action Committee for a United States of Europe (ACUSE). An interest group of influential political and economic leaders established by **Monnet** in 1955 to work for a renewal of the momentum for European integration after the failure in 1954 of the proposed **European Defence Community (EDC)**. Its membership was deliberately elite-based, though drawn from across the whole democratic political spectrum, and it argued for a more intensive structure of integration that would embrace as many European countries as possible.

Action Committee for Democracy and Pension Justice. *See* FIVE-SIXTHS ACTION COMMITTEE.

Action Directe. A terrorist group in **France** formed in 1979 and combining Maoist organization and anarchist doctrines. Its targets were public and government buildings. Two of its leaders, Jean-Marc Rouillan and Nathalie Ménigon, were arrested in September 1980, but were released in 1981 under a general amnesty declared by the newly elected President **Mitterrand**. After stepping up its bombing campaign it was proscribed by the government. By 1983 it had divided into two factions, one based in Lyons which concentrated on bank and armoured car robberies, and one in Paris led by Rouillan which in 1985, in conjunction with the West German **Red Army Faction (RAF)**, declared its target would be the **North Atlantic Treaty Organization (NATO)**. It was responsible for a number of assassination attempts of political and military leaders 1985–86. Four of its leaders, including Rouillan, were captured in February 1987, and sentenced to life imprisonment in January 1989. Most of the Lyons faction were also arrested, receiving life sentences in June 1989.

Action Party. (*Partito d'Azione – Pd'A*) A political party in **Italy** founded in 1944 upon the democratic principles espoused by the **Resistance movements**. Under the leadership of Ferruccio Parri, it sought to establish itself as a broad church for both liberals and socialists. It briefly led a coalition government in 1945, but was forced to resign after a few months when its partners withdrew their support. It failed to develop any kind of mass base and disappeared after a disastrous electoral performance in 1946.

Additionality. A term employed in the **European Communities (EC)**, referring to the allocation of money from the **European Regional Development Fund (ERDF)**. It means that ERDF funding is additional to that provided by national and local authorities, and was designed to ensure that the latter contributed to the financing of infrastructural projects.

Additional Member System. An electoral system combining elements of **first past the post** and **proportional representation**. Based upon single-member constituencies, the composition of the legislature is completed by additional members drawn from party lists or from those defeated constituency candidates who received the highest percentage of votes. Its supporters claim that it retains the important linkage between representative and constituency, while also bringing some proportionality to the allocations of seats across the political parties. A version of the system is employed in national and regional elections in the **Federal Republic of Germany**.

Adenauer, Konrad. (1876–1967) Chancellor of the **Federal Republic of Germany** 1949–63. A leading member of the Catholic Centre Party before 1933, he presided over the Prussian State Council 1920–33, and served as Mayor of Cologne 1917–33. Dismissed by the Nazis, he was briefly arrested in 1934, and again in 1944. In 1945 he was reinstated as Mayor of Cologne, but was soon dismissed by the British military administration for alleged inefficiency. He was a founding member and subsequently first national leader of the **Christian Democratic Union (CDU)**. In 1948 he chaired the Parliamentary Council that drew up a new constitution for the new republic, becoming its first premier in 1949. Despite an autocratic leadership style which in part reflected his distrust of mass participation, that critics labelled **Chancellor Democracy**, he oversaw the economic growth and democratic consolidation of West Germany.

His major interests were in foreign policy, where he sought the reunification of Germany and its international rehabilitation. He believed that reunification could come only through a policy of strength, a demonstration that the Federal Republic was politically and economically superior to the Communist-led **German Democratic Republic (DDR)**, and that any offers from the **USSR** for a united but neutral Germany had to be rejected. He looked to the USA and Western Europe for support, committing himself to Western defence and to all endeavours in European integration. He demanded the isolation of the DDR and the refusal by the West to accept its legitimacy. The credibility of his DDR policy (the **Hallstein Doctrine**) was finally destroyed by the erection in 1961 of the **Berlin Wall**, at the same time as his style of leadership came under increasing fire, even from within his own party. Worried by the American response to the Berlin Wall, he established closer relations with the French President, **de Gaulle**, signing a **Treaty of Friendship** in 1963 shortly before he was forced to give up the premiership.

While his foreign policy may have contributed to the hardening of the **Cold War**, the rehabilitation of the Federal Republic as a western democracy was successful, and it was doubtful whether, given the international climate, any West German government would have been able to steer a different course.

Advisory Committee on Safety, Hygiene and Health Protection At Work. A consultative agency of the **European Communities (EC)**, established in 1974 to consider problems of, and make recommendations on, industrial health and safety. Its role was strengthened by the 1987 **Single European Act (SEA)** which removed the requirement that proposals on safety and health needed the unanimous approval of the member states.

Aegean Sea. Part of the Mediterranean separating **Greece** from **Turkey**, and disputed by the two countries. The six-mile limit for territorial waters applied before 1940 had given Greece some 35 per cent of the Sea, and Turkey 9 per cent. Under the provisions of the 1958 United Nations Law of the Sea Convention, Greece would have received some 64 per cent, and Turkey 10 per cent. Turkey refused to ratify the Convention and argued that a unilateral extension of its limits by Greece would be a cause for war. The two states had different conceptions of what constituted territorial waters, and their dispute grew after 1969 because of the possibility of oil reserves on the seabed and a Greek attempt to offer exploration licences beyond its six-mile limit. On–off talks between the two sides after 1970 were complicated by the issue of **Cyprus** and that of airspace jurisdiction, and generated arguments over command and control arrangements for the reintegration of Greece within the **North Atlantic Treaty Organization (NATO)**. A serious argument over oil-drilling in March 1987 threatened to spill over into open hostility, but a series of meetings in Davros, **Switzerland**, between the leaders of the two countries, **Andreas Papandreou** and **Özal**, resulted in an agreement to explore ways of lessening tension and resolving more minor issues through a hotline, reciprocal visits, summit meetings and binational committees. The consultation process began in 1989, but made little progress towards the resolution of problems.

AETR Judgment. A 1971 ruling by the **Court of Justice** that where the **European Communities (EC)** have explicit internal competence, they also have a parallel external competence. It meant that in such areas the Member States cannot act independently of the EC.

AFCENT. Allied Forces Central Europe, one of the major command structures of the **North Atlantic Treaty Organization (NATO)**. Directly responsible to **SACEUR**, it consisted of two major forces guarding the **Central Front**. The more northerly group was **NORTHAG**, the more southerly CENTAG (Central Army Group, Central Europe) consisting mainly of American forces.

Afghanistan. A state in Asia, historically a buffer between the British and Russian empires. A monarchy from 1929–73, it subsequently collapsed into violence and armed conflict. Soviet troops invaded the country in September 1979 to support an ailing socialist regime. During the next decade Mujaheddin religious guerillas fought a bloody war against government forces totally dependent upon Soviet support. The Soviet involvement led to a hardening of attitudes in the **Cold War**. The cost of the conflict to the **USSR** in terms of equipment and deaths was enormous. It was a war the USSR could not win. After 1985 the new Soviet leader, **Gorbachev**, began to seek disengagement, and the USSR finally withdrew in February 1989. Involvement in Afghanistan did much to weaken the domestic credibility of the Soviet regime.

AFNORTH. *See* NORTHERN FLANK.

African, Caribbean and Pacific (ACP) States. The collective title used after the 1975 **Lomé Convention** for those developing countries which entered into an **Association Agreement** with the **European Communities (EC)**. Before 1975 the ACP participants were known as the Associated African States and Madagascar (AASM). The ACP states, currently numbering 70, are nearly all ex-colonies of EC Member States, and were given duty-free access to the EC market for most of their products on a non-reciprocal basis, as well as eligibility for grants and loans from EC institutions.

Aggregate Measure of Support (AMS). The calculation of the costs to taxpayers and consumers in the **European Communities (EC)** of domestic farm support and export subsidies provided by the **Common Agricultural Policy (CAP)**.

Agonizing reappraisal. A threat of a shift in American foreign and defence policy. It was made in 1954 by **Dulles** as a reaction to the reluctance of **France** to ratify the **European Defence Community (EDC)** treaty. It probably stiffened French hostility towards the EDC, and no significant changes in American policy followed from the eventual French rejection of the treaty.

Agrarian Democratic Party of Romania. (*Partidul Democrat Agrar din România – PDAR*) A political party in **Romania** founded in 1990. A conservative group that attempted to claim defence of farm interests and demand agricultural modernization, it was dominated by ex-Communists, but failed to establish itself as a meaningful party.

Agrarian Party. (*Zemědělská Strana – ZS*) A political party in the **Czech**

Republic. It was founded in 1990 as a centrist movement that would act as a voice for farm interests, but failed to establish a large electoral base.

Agreement Regarding International Trade in Textiles. *See* MULTI-FIBRE ARRANGEMENT (MFA).

Agusta affair. A political and financial scandal in **Belgium**. It involved allegations of bribery, money-laundering, blackmail and murder. Leading members of the country's two Socialist parties, in **Flanders** and **Wallonia**, were alleged to have accepted money from the Italian helicopter manufacturer, Agusta, which in 1985 was seeking to persuade the Belgian army to purchase 46 of its attack and reconnaissance craft. The judicial investigation, which began in 1991, escalated in 1994, with several leading Flemish Socialists placed under investigation, and forcing the resignation of three government ministers from the French-speaking party.

Ahlen Programme. A policy manifesto produced by the West German **Christian Democratic Union (CDU)** in 1947. Strongly influenced by ideas of Christian Socialism, it included a condemnation of capitalism as something which had contributed to Nazism, and argued for the adoption of some form of communal economy. It marked the high point of economic radicalism within the party and was abandoned as soon as the CDU began to experience electoral success. By 1949 the CDU, under the influence of **Adenauer** and **Erhard**, had adopted a new programme which gave priority to the notion of the **social market economy**.

Airbus Industrie. A cross-national consortium of West European governments and aeronautics manufacturers to produce the European Airbus passenger plane. Despite some initial difficulties, it was a successful cooperation. The first planes were in service by the late 1970s, proving themselves to be commercially competitive.

Air Exclusion Zone. A ban on military flights in the airspace of **Bosnia-Hercegovina** imposed by the United Nations (UN) in October 1992. It was implemented the following April when the UN requested the **North Atlantic Treaty Organization (NATO)** to provide air patrols to enforce the ban. The first action occurred in February 1994 when NATO planes shot down four Serb aircraft. This was the first ever combat action undertaken by NATO.

Ajuria Enea Pact. An agreement in **Spain** on the principles of political activity signed in January 1988 by all bar one of the main parties in the Basque region. The signatories rejected the use of violence as a political weapon in the region, and reaffirmed their support for the 1979 Statute that established an autonomous community for the area. The radical **Herri Batasuna (HB)** refused to endorse the pact.

Åland Islands. (Ahvenanmaa) An archipelago of some 6,000 islands in the Gulf of Bothnia. Swedish until 1809, they then passed to **Russia**. After the collapse of the Tsarist Empire in 1917 they were claimed by **Finland**, which used German army units to evict Swedish troops who had occupied them, even though in a plebiscite the islanders had voted to rejoin **Sweden**. In 1921 the League of Nations supported Finnish sovereignty, a decision accepted by both countries. Finland conceded considerable autonomy to the islands, which are almost totally Swedish-speaking. In September 1945 the islands' assembly's call for reunion with Sweden was not supported by the latter. In 1951 the islands were given greater autonomy over their internal affairs and economic policy, and Swedish was confirmed as the official language, effectively denying Finnish speakers any linguistic rights in the islands. The degree of constitutional autonomy, including the right of the islands to decide, independent of Finland's decision, to join the **European Communities**, was extended in 1991, taking effect in 1993.

Albania. Part of the Ottoman Empire from the fifteenth century until the 1912 Balkan War, when it became an independent Muslim principality. After internecine warfare from 1917–21, a regency council, backed by **Greece**, **Italy** and **Yugoslavia**, ruled the country until 1924. In 1925 it became a republic after a successful rebellion led by a large landowner, Ahmed Bey Zogu, who declared himself King Zog I in September 1928. Albania was invaded by Italy in 1939 and remained occupied until 1944, although partisan resistance forces, whose leaders included **Hoxha**, controlled the mountains. With the retreat of German forces, Hoxha established a republican government in November 1945, which was recognized by the Allies. Elections the following month established a Communist People's Republic under Hoxha's leadership. The new regime faced pressure for absorption from its large neighbour, Yugoslavia, with several leading Communists headed by Hoxha's chief lieutenant and rival, Koçi Xoxe, also favouring a union of the two states.

After the 1948 rift between **Tito** and **Stalin**, Albania became a favoured client state of the **USSR**. Xoxe and his followers were dismissed from their government positions in October 1948, and after a massive purge of the party, which was completed by the following June, Xoxe was executed for treason. Hoxha refused to accept the denunciation of Stalin by **Khrushchev** in 1956, and was attacked by the USSR for deviationism. Albania was subsequently expelled from the **Warsaw Pact** and the **Council for Mutual Economic Asssistance (Comecon)** in 1961. Remaining rigidly Stalinist, it developed a close relationship with China until the death of Mao Zedong in 1976. After 1956 Albania cut its diplomatic links with most countries and became a closed state, with little economic development or trade, until Hoxha's death in 1985. Although his widow, Nexhmije, retained a strong influence, the new leader, **Aliá**, began to re-establish diplomatic links with neighbouring states, and in February 1988 travelled to Belgrade to participate in a Balkan conference. In April 1990 he declared a wish to have diplomatic links with the USA and USSR, to have a relationship with the **European Communities (EC)**, and to join the **Conference on Security and Co-operation in Europe (CSCE)**. However, he spurned domestic reform.

Albania was the last Eastern European state to witness mounting popular pressure against the Communist regime, but in May 1990 the government was forced to introduce a wide-ranging reform package: propaganda against the state was no longer a capital offence; the holding of religious services was legalized; and foreign travel was permitted. Protests and demonstrations continued, and many Albanians sought asylum in foreign embassies or in Italy. In December 1990 opposition political parties were legalized, and the country's first-ever democratic election was held the following March. It was won by the reconstructed **Party of Labour**, although there were several allegations of unfairness. The new leaders of what was Europe's poorest country struggled to introduce some market economy reforms against a background of economic decline and heightened social and political instability. The opposition democratic forces won the parliamentary elections of 1992, and Aliá resigned as President. The new democratic government, however, continued to struggle to overcome severe economic problems and political instability.

Algerian War of Independence. (1954–62) A guerilla war fought by the Algerian *Front de Libération Nationale (FLN)* against the French military and administrative agencies in Algeria. Regarded by **France** as a civil war, because Algeria was constitutionally defined as being part of the metropolitan territory, it was a classic decolonization struggle. Outbreaks of violence had occurred since the late 1940s, but a full-scale war began in November 1954. It was exceptionally savage, with both sides committing atrocities against combatants and civilians. The French army was determined not to suffer a repetition of the humiliation experienced in **French Indo-China**. Backed by the white settler population, the largest in Africa outside South Africa, it was given full police powers in 1957. As costs and casualties rose, French public opinion began to turn against the war. Fearing that France would negotiate a peace with the FLN, the army and settlers became more hostile. When an offer of reconciliation was made in May 1958, the army seized power in Algiers and the military insurrection soon spread to **Corsica**. The army leaders called for **de Gaulle** to assume power in Paris. Initially supportive of the new **Fifth French Republic**, the army and settlers turned against de Gaulle when he accepted that the only solution to the conflict was to give Algeria a free choice between independence and a form of association with France. Insurrections broke out in January 1960 and again in April 1962, with an attempt by the **Organisation de l'Armée Secrète (OAS)**, led by General **Salan** and other senior officers, to overthrow the French government. The war was ended with the **Évian Agreements** of March 1962 and a plebiscite in Algeria in which 99 per cent voted in favour of independence.

Aliá, Ramiz. (1925–) President of **Albania** 1982–92. Active in the national liberation movement during the Second World War as a student, he joined the Communist Party in 1943. He rose quickly through the organization to be admitted to the **Politburo** in 1956. In 1982 he was made President of the Republic, and in 1985 succeeded **Hoxha** as party leader and effective head of government. He cautiously began to relax some of the rigid policies and practices of his predecessor, but in 1990 was unable to quell the mounting popular pressure for reform and was forced to concede multi-party elections and democratization. In May 1991 he gave up his party positions under the terms of the interim constitution. Although he remained neutral in the first democratic parliamentary elections in March 1992, the defeat of the reformed Communists led to his resignation from the presidency the following month. In September 1992 he was placed under house arrest and charged with having misused state funds and with abuse of power. In July 1994 he was sentenced to nine years' imprisonment.

Aliyev, Geidar. (1924–) President of **Azerbaijan** from 1993. A career **KGB** officer since 1949 and a long-serving Communist functionary who became party leader in the former **USSR** province in 1969, he was dismissed in 1987 for tolerating local corruption, though retaining considerable local influence and popularity. In 1992 he founded the New Azerbaijan party (*Yeni Azerbaijan*), but was defeated by a coalition of nationalist forces. He was invited to return the following year after popular disillusion with the failure to stem the loss of territory in the war with **Armenia** led to the removal of the government in a military coup. Strongly pro-Russian in orientation, he reversed the nationalist emphasis upon closer links with **Turkey** and sought realignment with **Russia**.

Alliance 90. (*Bündnis 90*) A coalition of citizens' rights groups in the **German Democratic Republic (DDR)**. It was formed in early 1990 as an intellectual-led association, but in the several elections of 1990 formed a pact with a new Green formation and soon disintegrated.

Alliance for Equality and Justice. (*Samtök um Jafnrétti og Felagshyggju*) A small liberal party in **Iceland** formed in 1987. It was the result of a secession from the centrist **Progressive Party** and campaigned primarily on the need to provide more economic assistance for the regions, but failed to gain much electoral support.

Alliance for Germany. (*Allianz für Deutschland*) A centre-right electoral pact in the **German Democratic Republic (DDR)**. It was formed in February 1990 by the **Christian Democratic Union (CDU)**, **German Social Union (DSU)** and **Democratic Departure (DA)**, three reconstructed or new organizations established after the disintegration of the Communist regime. It won the largest number of votes in the March election, with the CDU leader, **de Maizière**, becoming prime minister. Its victory ensured a speedy continuation of the process of German reunification.

Alliance for Poland. (*Przymierze dla Polski – PdP*) An electoral alliance in **Poland** formed in 1994 by five right-wing parties with strong conservative positions on social and moral issues. It agreed that leadership of the alliance would rotate across the parties.

Alliance of Free Democrats. (*Szabad Demokraták Szsövetsége – SzDSz*) A political party in **Hungary**. Founded as an opposition group in November 1988, it emerged out of the intellectual-based Democratic opposition of the late 1970s which later shifted ground to support principles of classic liberalism. Strongly pro-Western in orientation, it brought together liberal and social democratic groups. In the Triangular Discussions on constitutional reform in 1989, it rejected any continuing role for the **Hungarian Socialist Workers' Party**. It was the second largest party in the 1990 multi-party election and subsequently formed the major opposition to the first democratic government. After the sweeping electoral victory in 1994 of the reconstructed Communists, the Hungarian Socialist Party, it agreed to join the latter in a coalition government.

Alliance of Independents. (*Landesring der Unabhängigen/Alliance des Indépendents – LdU/AI*) A small conservative party in **Switzerland** formed in 1935. It espoused social liberalism and the free market, and evolved as a middle class consumers' party. Given that government formation in Switzerland has not been dependent upon election outcomes, it has often been the largest party not in government and the closest thing in the country to an official opposition.

Alliance of Left and Progressive Forces. (*Synaspismós*) A coalition in **Greece** formed in 1989 by the **Communist Party of Greece (KKE)**, the Eurocommunist Greek Left (*Elliniki Aristera – EAR*) and the centre-left Democratic Socialist Party (*Komma Dimokratikou Sosialismou*). Originally an electoral alliance intended to sustain a continued radical presence in the legislature, it soon created a unified structure. Dominated by the ex-KKE, which had been strongly pro-Moscow in orientation, it had difficulty in coming to terms with the collapse of Communism in Eastern Europe and more or less collapsed in 1991 when the hardline Communists left to re-form as a separate organization.

Alliance of the Democratic Left. *See* POLISH UNITED WORKERS' PARTY.

Alliance of Young Democrats. (*Fiatal Demokratá Szsövetsége – Fidesz*) An opposition political movement in **Hungary**. It was formed in March 1988 as an alternative independent youth movement, but was soon banned by the Communist regime. It re-emerged to participate in the 1989 Triangular Discussions on political reform, but refused to sign the agreements because of its hostility to their acceptance of a continued role for the **Hungarian Socialist Workers' Party**. Until 1993 only those aged under 35 were eligible for membership. Its limited influence in the new democratic system was weakened further by internal factionalism and secessions in 1993.

Alliance Party. A small centrist party in **Northern Ireland**. Founded in 1970 on a non-confessional basis, it sought the re-establishment of autonomy for the province on the basis of the sharing of power between the Protestant and Catholic communities. It is the only party to have gained support from both religious groups, but the polarized nature of the province's politics prevented it from developing into a major political force.

Allied Command Europe (ACE). The central element of the tripartite command structure (along with Allied Command Atlantic and Allied Command Channel) of the **North Atlantic Treaty Organization (NATO)**. It was set up to be the primary command structure for air and land operations in the event of a war with the **USSR** and the **Warsaw Pact**. Under the command of **SACEUR**, it was based at Casteau in **Belgium** after 1966, moving there from Versailles when **France** withdrew from NATO's integrated command structure. Member states that contribute military forces to NATO (all bar France, **Iceland** and **Spain**) have maintained a Permanent Military Representative to ACE, who liaises between SACEUR and his own national Chiefs-of-Staff. ACE has also provided a stand-by unit, the ACE Mobile Force, formed of units from member countries, that could respond quickly in more localized disputes and trouble spots within the NATO area of operations. Its role and purpose were made more questionable with the ending of the **Cold War** and the demise of the USSR and Warsaw Pact.

Allied Commission. *See* ALLIED CONTROL AUTHORITY.

Allied Control Authority. The body established in 1945 by the wartime allies to administer the military occupation of Germany. Each occupying power was largely sovereign in its own zone of occupation, but the four allies – **France**, **United Kingdom**, USA and **USSR** – were expected to work for the re-establishment of a unified democratic Germany. Co-ordination was to be achieved through the Control Authority. At its apex the supreme decision-making body was the Allied Control Council, formed by the four Military Governors. The small province of the **Saarland** and the capital, **Berlin**, were excluded from the arrangements. The Saar was administered directly by France, while Berlin was given a separate quadripartite structure of military administration, the **Allied Kommandatura**. Although it had been previously agreed that Germany was to be treated as a single economic unit and that the Authority would deal with matters affecting the whole country, the zones soon became separate economic units, and there was little agreement on what constituted all-German issues. Each Governor possessed a veto in the Council. The USA and Britain began to merge their zones in 1946, but France and the USSR resisted integration. The Authority's effectiveness had already largely ceased when the Soviet commander walked out of the Council in March 1948 as a response to fears that the Western allies, themselves exasperated by Soviet obstruction, were planning to create an independent German state from their zones. The collapse of the Authority was a major turning point in the **Cold War**, leading to the establishment of two German states in 1949. After the Soviet walk-out, the Western allies reformed as a tripartite Allied Commission. Their relationship with the new **Federal Republic of Germany** was formalized by the Occupation Statute of April 1949, with a civilian Allied High Commission replacing military government. The period of Western occupation formally ended with the Paris Agreements of 1954. Similar Allied Control Authorities were established in the other defeated Axis countries (except **Italy**). **Austria** was also divided into four zones, with Vienna having its own quadripartite division, but an elected national government was permitted. Full sovereignty was returned by the 1955 **Austrian State Treaty**. Western influence was negligible in the Control Authorities established in **Bulgaria**, **Hungary** and **Romania**, which were wholly in the Soviet sphere of influence.

Allied Control Council. *See* ALLIED CONTROL AUTHORITY.

Allied High Commission. *See* ALLIED CONTROL AUTHORITY.

Allied Kommandatura. The military government structure established in 1945 by the war-time allies to administer **Berlin**. Because the city fell within the Soviet zone of occupation and because of its symbolic importance as the German capital, each ally wished a presence in it, and it was excluded from the zonal arrangement for Germany. It was divided into four sectors – American, British, French and Soviet – and each ally had full authority in its own sector. Overall authority was vested in the Kommandatura, headed by the four sectoral military commanders. Each ally had the right to have its military personnel visit any sector, and the three Western allies were guaranteed land and air access to the city through the Soviet zone. The principles governing the activities of the Kommandatura were the same as those for the **Allied Control Authority**, as were the problems it faced. The **USSR** withdrew from the Kommandatura in June 1948. Its departure coincided with the launch of the Soviet-imposed **Berlin Blockade**. While the Kommandatura ended in 1948, Berlin remained apart from the two new German states. The Western Allies insisted that it was still under four-power military rule, but the East Berlin suburb of Pankow was declared capital of the Communist-led **German Democratic Republic (DDR)**. The **Quadripartite Agreement** of 1971 confirmed the rights of the Western Allies in the city. With the demolition of the **Berlin Wall** in 1989 and German reunification in 1990, the occupying powers disbanded their military structures, with the last troops leaving the city in 1994.

Alpen-Adria. A regional association established in 1978 by provincial authorities in **Austria**, the **Federal Republic of Germany**, **Hungary**, **Italy**, and **Yugoslavia**. Its objective was to encourage cross-regional co-operation in tourism, transport, energy and environmental protection. Authorities in **Croatia** and **Slovenia** maintained their membership after the disintegration of Yugoslavia in 1991.

Alps Convention. The more common name of the Agreement on the Protection of the Alps, an international convention signed in November 1991 by states with territory in or adjacent to the Alpine region. It contained protocols on minimum standards for environmental protection with regard to various forms of economic activity. To be adopted, any proposal would require the consent of all signatories.

Alsace-Lorraine. Two provinces of **France** bordering Germany. Ceded to Germany after the 1871 Franco-Prussian War, they were returned to France in 1918 by the Treaty of Versailles. In 1940 Germany re-annexed the provinces. They returned to France in 1945, since when they have become more linguistically and culturally integrated, with France for a long time allowing few concessions in education and other cultural areas to the Alsatian Germanic dialect. There was no occurrence after 1945 of the demands for autonomy that were a feature of inter-war Alsatian politics. The largest city in the region, **Strasbourg**, became after 1950 one of the major symbols of European co-operation and integration.

Alto Adige. The Italian name for the predominantly German-speaking Alpine province of South Tyrol, ceded to **Italy** in 1919 by the Treaty of St Germain. Large-scale Italian settlement in the area was encouraged by the Mussolini regime. An accord on autonomy and equality for German-speaking citizens reached between **Austria** and Italy in 1946 was obviated when the **de Gasperi** government merged the province with Trentino in 1948, thereby guaranteeing an Italian majority in any devolved structure. The German speakers mobilized behind the conservative and Catholic South Tyrolean People's Party (*Südtiroler Volkspartei*), which became the largest political force in the region. Frustration over the failure to gain concessions from Rome, despite strong support from neighbouring Austria, led to sporadic violence and mass demonstrations in the 1950s and 1960s. The dispute was resolved by a 1969 settlement, embodied in an Austro-Italian treaty in July 1971 and endorsed by the International Court of Justice. The settlement was a complex package of specific measures, usually known as the *Proporzpaket*, which catered for a proportional sharing of, and equal access to, public goods and services for both language communities. It has been widely regarded as one of the more successful solutions to an inter-ethnic conflict. In May 1988 Italy proposed an extended autonomy package for the region. While the extent of devolution alarmed many Italian speakers, placing the arrangement under potentially greater strain, the package was approved by the Austrian and Italian parliaments in 1992.

Amato, Giuliano. (1938–) Prime Minister of **Italy** 1992–93. A professor of constitutional law and a member of the **Italian Socialist Party (PSI)**, his earlier political activities had earned him the nickname of the subtle doctor (*dottore sottile*). A critic of the authoritarian leadership style of **Craxi**, he later joined forces with the PSI leader and held offices in PSI-led coalition governments after 1983. As the wave of corruption charges swept over Italy in 1992, he was appointed Prime Minister in June. He struggled to hold together what was left of the **pentapartito**, but while he restored some confidence in the economy, he failed to stem the tide of popular discontent with the traditional style of government, and was forced to resign the following April.

Anarchism. A political philosophy which rejects the state and other forms of coercive authority and seeks their replacement by a social order based upon voluntary regulation and co-operation among individuals. It developed two distinctive traditions: an extreme libertarian strand which emphasized the individual, and a communitarian strand which praised the virtues of co-operative communities. It was popularly associated with terrorism and chaos as a result of violent actions adopted by some anarchist groups to achieve their goals. Prominent in some Socialist movements in the late nineteenth and early twentieth centuries, especially in **France**, **Italy** and **Spain**, it was marginalized after 1945. It re-emerged in the 1960s as one of the guiding elements of several peace and environmentalist movements.

Andorra. A small territorial enclave in the Pyrenees. Most of its population is Spanish, with few native-born Andorrans. The official language is Catalan. Joint sovereignty was held by the Kings (and later the Presidents) of **France** and the Spanish Bishops of Urgel, a co-suzerain system (the *Pareatges*) established in 1278. However, the first meeting of the co-suzerains after 1278 did not occur until 1973. Until 1981 the government was led by the First Syndic-General, or President of the General Council of the Valleys. A new Executive Council was established in 1981, separating the executive from the legislature. Andorra had no defined international status, and was not affiliated to any international organization. The co-suzerains represented it at the inter-national level and were jointly responsible for its external security. When **Spain** joined the **European Communities (EC)** in 1986, Andorra had to seek an arrangement with the EC. The September 1989 agreement on a **customs union** was its first international treaty for 700 years. In June 1990 a commis-sion was established to draft a constitution that would define and limit the co-

suzerains' powers. In 1993 a referendum endorsed the constitutional proposals and full sovereignty, and the ending of the co-suzerains' executive
powers. Later in the year Andorra joined the United Nations (UN).

Andreotti, Giulio. (1919–) Prime Minister of **Italy** 1972–73, 1976–79,
1987, 1989–92. Entering the legislature in 1948 for the **Christian Democratic Party** (DC) after previously serving as a personal aide to **de Gasperi**,
he rose rapidly to prominence, serving continuously in government
1954–92. His first premiership was as head of a centrist coalition in 1972.
His return to the premiership in 1976 was marked by an extension of the
coalition, through the **historic compromise**, to include the **Italian Communist Party (PCI)** as an informal member. After a brief caretaker spell in
1987, he was re-appointed premier in 1989, with his party already in disarray
and decline. He refused to carry through proposals for party and political
system reform, preferring to continue to rely upon the traditional brokerage
role of all previous DC leaders. In the reformist mood that swept the country
in the 1990s in the wake of revelations of financial and political corruption,
he was identified with the old regime and became a main target of criticism.
His political power base was severely weakened by the collapse of the DC,
and his reputation was challenged by allegations of maladministration,
corruption and links with the **Mafia**. In 1993 he was indicted on charges of
corruption and was found guilty in November 1994. In November 1995 he
was further indicted for murder.

Andropov, Yuri Vladimirovich. (1914–1984) Secretary-General of
the **Communist Party of the Soviet Union** 1982–84. After joining the
party's youth organization, the Komsomol, he became a party administrator
in 1944. After 1953 he worked mainly as a diplomat, serving *inter alia* as
ambassador to **Hungary** 1954–57. In 1961 he was promoted to membership
of the party's Central Committee, but was admitted to the **Politburo** only in
1973. In 1967 he was appointed head of the **KGB**, overhauling and
improving the organization, and serving until becoming Soviet leader in
1982. As his health was poor, his period of effective leadership was for only
a few months, with his last public appearance being in August 1983.
Although his long tenure at the KGB gained him the reputation of being a
hard-liner, he had earlier come into contact with reformist tendencies in
Eastern Europe, especially during the 1956 **Hungarian Revolution**. As
Soviet leader he began a process of reform, within a strictly Communist
framework, against the corruption and inertia of the **Brezhnev** years, which
after 1985 was resumed by his protégé, **Gorbachev**.

Anglo-Irish Agreement. An agreement on **Northern Ireland** by the
United Kingdom and **Ireland**, also known as the Hillsborough Accord. It
was signed by the two premiers, **Thatcher** and **Fitzgerald**, in November
1985. It granted Ireland a right to be consulted on and involved in political,

legal and security matters relating to Northern Ireland. In return the Irish government accepted that Irish reunification could only be achieved with the consent of a majority of the population of Northern Ireland. Although both sides continued to accept its basic principles, there were several strains and disagreements in subsequent years, and it was rejected by many in the Protestant community. *See also* DOWNING STREET DECLARATION.

Another Europe. *See* NATIONS OF EUROPE.

Antall, Jozsef. (1932–1993) Prime Minister of **Hungary** 1990–93. Son of the founder of the pre-war Independent Smallholders' Party, he became a schoolteacher. He was imprisoned after the 1956 **Hungarian Revolution**. After his release, he was banned from resuming a teaching career, and in 1960 became a librarian. In 1964 he joined the staff of a medical history museum in Budapest, becoming its director in 1974. He was a founder member of the dissident **Hungarian Democratic Forum** in September 1987, becoming its leader in 1989. He attempted initially to tone down its stress on populist nationalism, but after 1990 some of his remarks on the situation of Hungarian minorities alarmed governments of neighbouring states. He broadly developed the Forum as a centre-right party, which won the first democratic election in 1990. As prime minister he continued a programme of democratization and a transition to a market economy. He died suddenly in office.

Antici Group. The name given to the informal grouping of the personal assistants to the Permanent Representatives of the Member States of the **European Union**. In practice they form an important element of the **Committee of Permanent Representatives (Coreper)**.

Anticlericalism. Ideological hostility to the social and political power of organized religion. In Europe it originated in the French Revolution and became a radical opposition to the political role of the Catholic Church, with its principles being accepted by many liberal and socialist parties. After 1945 it declined sharply as a political issue and organizing force, partly because of the secularization of society, but it resurfaced on occasions when issues with a moral content, such as abortion, divorce or education, became politicized. It was more pronounced after 1945 in the Communist regimes of Eastern Europe where organized religion was at best discouraged and at worst persecuted.

Anti-nuclear movements. Mass organizations in Western Europe seeking the abandonment of nuclear weapons. They took their inspiration from the 1955 Pugwash Manifesto drawn up by Bertrand Russell and Albert Einstein. The first major movement was the British **Campaign for Nuclear Disarmament (CND)**, founded in 1958. During the 1970s, opposition to nuclear armaments and nuclear power became a major concern of emerging Green movements. The hardening of the **Cold War** after the late 1970s led to an increase in activity, and an umbrella **European Nuclear Disarmament**

(END) was formed, with widespread protest and direct action occurring throughout Western Europe. END attempted, without much success, to enter into dialogue with and recruit the support of **Charter 77** and other Eastern European dissident groups. While they were active and prominent, the movements failed to have a decisive impact upon government policy, and their numbers and activity were in decline even before the ending of the Cold War.

Anti-party group. The name given in July 1957 by **Khrushchev** and his allies to those members of the Soviet Praesidium who had demanded his resignation as Soviet leader. The group opposed Khrushchev's **De-Staliniza-tion** policy and was critical of his attempts at administrative reform and his reconciliation with **Tito** and **Yugoslavia**. Khrushchev successfully out-manoeuvred the group, and they were moved from their party positions to minor administrative posts. The group included **Bulganin**, **Malenkov** and **Molotov**. Khrushchev's victory removed the major obstacles to his personal rule of the **USSR**.

Anti-Revolutionary Party. (*Anti-Revolutionaire Partij – ARP*) A political party in the **Netherlands**. Formed in 1879 in opposition to the liberal trends associated with the French Revolution, it was closely aligned with the Orthodox Reformed (*Gereformeerde*) churches, and gained little electoral support from outside these religious communities. A conservative party, it tended to collaborate closely with the other major Dutch religious parties. Although it was relatively unaffected by the wave of secularization that swept Dutch politics after the early 1960s, it agreed to join the **Christian Democratic Appeal (CDA)** in 1975.

Anti-semitism. Sustained hostility towards Jews and Judaism. It has a long history in Europe, growing rapidly in strength in the nineteenth century. Systematic persecution of Jews climaxed with the Nazi Holocaust. It survived after 1945, mainly in reaction to the state of Israel and Zionism. It was most evident and systematic in the **USSR**. In the 1960s and 1970s there were several accusations that Soviet Jews had been imprisoned for seeking the right to emigrate to Israel, with reports in 1962–63 of Jews being executed for 'economic crimes'. In 1978 Jewish dissidents of the **Helsinki Human Rights Group** were given heavy prison sentences. After democrat-ization in 1989 there were allegations that anti-semitism had become more overt and widespread throughout Eastern Europe. Sporadic outbursts of anti-semitic activity also occurred in Western Europe where the associated sentiments were most apparent among extreme right-wing political groups, which grew in size and activity after the 1980s. There is no generally agreed explanation of why such strong racial antagonism should persist over time, but jealousy would seem to be common to most explanations that have been advanced.

Anti-Terrorist Liberation Group. (*Grupos Antiterroristas de Liberación – GAL*) A secret organization in **Spain**, founded in 1983 to combat the **Euskadi ta Askatasuna (ETA)** death squads. Allegedly funded by a government agency, and held responsible for several killings in both **France** and Spain, it was accused of running a 'dirty war' in the 1980s against Basque separatists, especially ETA activists. After a three-year investigation, three senior Ministry of the Interior officials were arrested in 1994 and charged with founding and running the group. Several police officers were also convicted for GAL-related activities. The scandal was one of several that threatened the integrity and survival of the **González** government.

Apollo. A joint venture between the **European Space Agency (ESA)** and the **Commission** of the **European Communities (EC)** to encourage closer collaboration within Europe in high-volume data transmission by satellite. The objective was to develop equipment and a market in ground stations and receiving antennae in order to enable Europe to establish a strong position in an important area of technological development.

Apparatchik. A full-time member of staff in a party, state or other public organization in a Communist country. The term was more usually employed to refer to the party bureaucracy at both national and local levels. In theory subordinate to elected committees and politicians, the party bureaucracy exercised enormous influence over policy and played a dominant role in the political system.

Apparentement. An electoral device which permits political parties to declare an alliance for the purpose of counting votes and allocating seats, while still contesting the election as separate organizations. The votes cast for parties making such a prior declaration are treated as if cast for a single list of candidates. The device was usually intended to encourage co-operation among moderate parties and strengthen the political centre. It has been particularly associated with French electoral politics.

Approximation. The process within the **European Communities (EC)** of removing unwarranted or undesired differences in national legislation in order to achieve the full potential of the **internal market** in terms of the free movements of goods, services, labour and capital. It is similar to, but more limited in scope than, **harmonization**, not requiring identical legislation across the member states.

Aragonese Regionalist Party. (*Partido Aragonése Regionalista – PAR*) A centre-right regionalist party in **Spain** founded in 1978 to seek extensive autonomy for Aragon beyond that on offer from the central government. It enjoyed some electoral success, and in June 1987 its leader became head of the regional government. In February 1990 it renamed itself the Aragonese Party (*Partido Aragonés*).

Arge-Alp. The Association of the Central Alps, a cross-national association of ten Alpine provinces. It was founded in 1972 to promote co-operation in economic, environmental and cultural affairs.

Ariane. A French-designed rocket launcher system used widely by the **European Space Agency (ESA)**. Partially funded by the **European Investment Bank (EIB)**, it was successfully tested in 1979. In 1980 ESA established the Arianespace company to market the launcher commercially. Its facilities were made available to all, with over 50 launches by 1994.

Armed Forces Movement. (*Movimento das Forças Armadas – MFA*) A group of junior military officers who carried out the coup (the **Carnation Revolution**) on 25 April 1974 that overthrew the authoritarian regime in **Portugal** established by **Salazar**. Mainly from lower-class backgrounds, they had become frustrated by the lack of success in the colonial wars in Africa and alarmed by government plans for military reform. After the coup the MFA acquired an aura of progressive populism and saw itself as the guardian of a new Portugal. It laid down strict conditions for a transfer of power to civilian authority, and played a central role in the construction of the 1976 Constitution. Its overall authority was weakened by severe factionalism and by 1976 its more radical elements had been marginalized within the movement. It dissolved itself soon after its pact with the political parties that produced the Constitution.

Armed Phalange. (*Falange Armata*) A shadowy right-wing terrorist group in **Italy** which after 1990 claimed responsibility for several bomb attacks and assassinations, including the murder of a senior judge, Giovanni Falcone, in May 1992. It revealed little about its motivations and objectives, but was believed to have connections with extreme right-wing elements in the security services and with organized crime.

Armed Revolutionary Nuclei. A shadowy right-wing terrorist group in **Italy**. It claimed responsibility for several terrorist episodes, including the bombing of the Bologna railway station in 1980, but the extent of its activities, strength and organization remained unclear.

Armenia. A region covering parts of north-eastern **Turkey** and the ex-**USSR**. In the late nineteenth and early twentieth centuries agitation for independence was met by massacres and deportations. An independent Transcaucasian Federal Republic of Armenia survived briefly from 1918 to 1920, when the Russian areas were made a Soviet republic. By 1923 the remainder had been totally absorbed by Turkey. After 14 years as part of a Transcaucasian Soviet Republic, Armenia became a separate Soviet Republic in 1936. Many Armenians remained in the **Nagorno-Karabakh** region of neighbouring **Azerbaijan**, and their situation became a source of increasing tension between the two republics after 1985. As a result of the liberalization policies of **Gorbachev**, non-Communist parties were formed and, headed by the Armenian Pan-National Movement of **Ter-Petrosian**, they won a majority in the 1990 regional elections. In March 1991 the new government declared its independence from the USSR. The Communist Party later dissolved itself, and was reconstituted in 1993 as the Armenian Democratic Party. Post-independence politics were characterized by fragmentation, uncertainty and high instability. The ongoing conflict with Azerbaijan over Nagorno-Karabakh, while largely successful in terms of territorial gains, further disrupted a fragile economy. President Ter-Petrosyan's room for manoeuvre was further limited because the military leaders of the campaign mostly adhered to the more radical nationalist party, Dashnak.

Arms Control. The policy or process whereby attempts are made to negotiate international agreements on limiting or reducing the stockpiling and deployment of weapons systems. The core element of discussions was strategic nuclear arms control. After the 1970s an equal emphasis was placed on limiting intermediate and theatre nuclear weapons and conventional arms. Discussions primarily involved the USA and **USSR**, but they were a major European concern because it was in Europe that the two super-powers and their allies were in direct confrontation. The history of arms control talks was complex and littered with setbacks. The most striking successes were the two Strategic Arms Limitation Talks (SALT) treaties of 1972 and 1979 between the USA and USSR over the deployment of strategic nuclear weapons. Talks on removing all intermediate nuclear forces (INF) from Europe began in Vienna after the USA had agreed in 1979 to provide INF weapons to its European allies in response to their fears of a Soviet military build-up on the continent, but they made little headway.

Possibilities of agreement first emerged in the **Double Zero Option** suggested in the 1986 Reykjavik summit meeting between **Gorbachev** and President Ronald Reagan, but an effective reduction and abandonment of INF deployment did not begin until after 1989 and the subsequent dissolution of the **Warsaw Pact**. Serious general discussions on arms control between the **North Atlantic Treaty Organization (NATO)** and the Warsaw Pact first began in 1973. Discussions in Vienna on **Mutual and Balanced Force Reductions (MBFR)** were aimed first at reducing proportionally American and Soviet troops in the European theatre, and then those of their European allies. The talks had little success until the 1990s when their original purpose was made redundant by the disintegration of the USSR and Warsaw Pact. In the 1980s a supplementary round of talks on **Confidence-Building Measures (CBMs)**, sponsored by the **Conference on Security and Co-operation in Europe (CSCE)** and aimed at reducing the risk of surprise attacks, led quickly to some agreements.

Arms control in Europe was also concerned with securing a complete and enforceable ban on the production, stockpiling and deployment of chemical weapons. Negotiations on a **Chemical Warfare Convention (CWC)** were held more or less continuously after 1967, with the **Forty Nations Conference on Disarmament (CD)** in **Geneva** being the major forum after 1982. The major problem in all arms control negotiations was verification. Both sides had doubts about how far they could trust each other short of visual inspection of the opponent's sites. NATO and the USSR held different conceptions of what would constitute acceptable and effective verification. A breakthrough occurred only in 1991 with the **Open Skies Agreement**. The ending of the **Cold War** did not realize the dreams of arms control negotiators. While levels of armaments and forces in Europe were reduced, the demise of the USSR and its control over Eastern Europe raised new problems. In particular, it created three states – **Russia**, **Ukraine** and Kazakhstan – with a nuclear capacity, and therefore a new urgency to secure an agreement on nuclear weapons.

Article Six Committee. An expert group established by the **Commission** to oversee the implementation of the Financial Protocols relating to the agreements signed by the **European Communities (EC)** with several countries around the Mediterranean.

Assembly of European Regions (AER). An intergovernmental organ ization, founded in 1985 as the Council of the European Regions. It was established to serve as a discussion and research forum for its members, representatives from regional government authorities in **Council of Europe** countries.

Assent Procedure. A method of decision-making in the **European Communities (EC)** whereby specified categories of decisions taken by one EC institution require the approval of another.

Associated African States and Madagascar (AASM). *See* AFRICAN, CARIBBEAN AND PACIFIC (ACP) STATES, YAOUNDÉ CONVENTION.

Associated List of Social Democrats. (*Združena Lista Socialdemokratov*) A left-wing political party in **Slovenia** formed in 1993 by a merger of some smaller groupings with the Social Democratic Reform Party which, constituted in 1990 with a programme aimed at achieving social justice and a market-based economy, had been established as the successor to the Slovenian wing of the **League of Communists of Yugoslavia**.

Association Agreements. Agreements signed between the **European Communities (EC)** and other European states which at the time had indicated a wish to seek full EC membership at some unspecified point in the future. The first Agreement was with **Greece** in 1961. It served as a model for the Agreements with **Turkey** (1964), **Malta** (1970) and **Cyprus** (1972). In February 1991 the EC began negotiations on similar **Europe Agreements** with the new democratic governments of **Czechoslovakia**, **Hungary** and **Poland**. The general principle of Association Agreements was that they established reciprocal arrangements for imports and exports within a form of

21

customs union. Each Agreement has been supervised by an Association Council made up of representatives from the EC and the contracting state. Where consensus between the two sides proves impossible, the issue may be referred to arbitration or to the **Court of Justice**.

Association for the Republic – Republican Party of Czechoslovakia. (*Sdružení pro Republika – Republikánská Strana Československa – SPR-RSČ*). An extreme right-wing populist party in **Czechoslovakia**, founded in 1990. It survived into the Czech Republic as a vehicle for protest and youth alienation.

Association of European Border Regions (AEBR). A collective body encouraging collaboration among organizations from over 50 border regions in continental Western Europe. Founded in 1971, it has acted as a clearing house for information on cross-frontier problems, and has sought to sponsor cross-border proposals that will aid regional development.

Atanasov, Georgi. (1933–) Prime Minister of **Bulgaria** 1986–90. A historian, he was elected to the Central Committee of the **Bulgarian Communist Party (BKP)** in 1965, serving as a senior planning administrator until becoming premier in 1986. He was the last orthodox BKP premier, being replaced in February 1990 by a reformer. In November 1992 he was sentenced to ten years' imprisonment for embezzlement of public funds while in office, but in August 1994 was pardoned on health grounds.

Atlantic Alliance. A popular alternative name for the **North Atlantic Treaty Organization (NATO)**.

Atlantic Arc Commission. An intergovernmental association of regional authorities from littoral states in the British Isles and Iberia, founded in 1989. Its main objectives were to secure **European Communities (EC)** funding for infrastructural developments for the poorer, more peripheral areas of the EC.

Atlantic Nuclear Force (ANF). A British proposal of the early 1960s whereby the nuclear guarantee provided by the **North Atlantic Treaty Organization (NATO)** to Western Europe would be shared by its member states. The idea reflected, in part, European worries that their security was ultimately dependent upon weapons solely under American control. It also reflected British concerns about the continued viability of its own independent nuclear deterrent. The ANF was an alternative to the American proposal for a **Multilateral Force (MLF)**. Like several similar ideas of the period, it came to nothing.

Atomic Demolition Munitions. Nuclear mines buried by the **North Atlantic Treaty Organization (NATO)** in areas which **Warsaw Pact** forces would have to cross in any invasion of Western Europe, or where they would destroy vital communications nodes or equipment. They were first developed after NATO developed the strategy of **massive retaliation**.

Regarded by many military tacticians as possessing minimal value, they were removed in the late 1980s.

Attila Line. *See* GREEN LINE.

Attlee, Clement Richard. (1883–1967) British Prime Minister 1945–51. He entered Parliament in 1922 as a **Labour Party** representative. He served as a junior minister 1930–31 and was elected party leader in 1935. In the war-time coalition he was effectively Deputy Prime Minister under **Churchill**. His attention to detail and ability to expedite business was impressive. When the Labour Party won the 1945 election on a programme of social and economic change, he headed a government which embarked upon an ambitious reform proogramme. A welfare state was established through an implementation of the 1942 **Beveridge Report**. Public ownership was considerably expanded, with the nationalization of public utilities and other key industries. While critical economic shortages enforced a severe rationing policy, full employment was sustained through the relocation of industry and the establishment of new towns. Overseas, Attlee was concerned with the development of the **Commonwealth of Nations**, beginning the process of decolonization with the granting of independence to India, Pakistan and Burma in 1947. His efforts to maintain friendly relations with the **USSR** were unsuccessful, and his government was active in seeking a continued American presence in Europe. Despite growing tension between left and right, he maintained a firm leadership which kept the party well-disciplined. He was returned to power in the 1950 election, but with a wafer-thin majority which, combined with his growing ill-health, reduced his effectiveness. The party was defeated in the 1951 election, but he remained party leader until 1955, attempting to maintain a balance between the party's left and right wings. Upon retiring as leader, he went to the House of Lords as Earl Attlee.

Audit Board. Established in 1957 under the terms of the **Treaty of Rome** as a body which would examine the accounts of revenue and expenditure of the **European Economic Community (EEC)**. Its powers were limited, and in 1977 it was replaced by a more authoritative **Court of Auditors**.

Auriol, Vincent. (1884–1966) President of **France** 1947–53. He first entered politics in 1914 as a **Socialist Party** (SFIO) deputy, and was Minister of Finance and of Justice in the 1936 Popular Front government. During the Second World War he escaped from internment to join **de Gaulle** and the Free French Movement in Britain. Upon returning to France he served in de Gaulle's 1945–46 provisional government and played a prominent role in the formation of the **Fourth French Republic**. Widely respected in Parliament, he was elected as the Republic's first President. He adopted a strict non-partisan position, but within those restraints he used the limited authority of a largely ceremonial office to commit France to a

Western alliance and to encourage some order at a time of great instability in French politics.

Aussiedler. (Resettlers) A collective German word for ethnic Germans residing outside Germany, the descendants of colonists of earlier centuries, who have settled, or wish to settle, in the **Federal Republic of Germany**. After 1948 they were originally given an unrestricted right to resettle, as distinct from other asylum seekers and migrants, but as their numbers rose sharply after the ending of the **Cold War**, posing severe problems of economic and political assimilation for Germany, the eligibility rules were tightened, obliging potential emigrants first to submit an application for resettlement in their country of residence.

Austria. The first independent Austrian state was formed in 1918 as a Germanic rump of the Habsburg Empire that no one else wanted, but it was not allowed to unite with Germany, as most of its population wished. Dominated by two mutually hostile mass parties, Catholic and Socialist, whose enmity resulted in a civil war in 1934, it was taken over by Hitler in the 1938 Anschluss. In 1945 it was militarily occupied by the Allies and divided into four zones of occupation. Vienna, which lay within the Soviet zone, was treated separately and divided into four distinct occupation sectors. A Second Austrian Republic was established in December 1945 on the basis of the 1920 Constitution, and full sovereignty was regained in 1955 with the signing of the **Austrian State Treaty**. The two major pre-war parties reconstituted themselves as the **Austrian People's Party (ÖVP)** and the **Socialist Party** of Austria (SPÖ). Memories of the bitter pre-war past and the need to present a united front against the occupying forces led them to form a **grand coalition** backed by over 90 per cent of the electorate. The coalition helped to stabilize politics and transformed the country into an effective democracy, a change aided by rapid industrialization and sub-stantial economic development. The coalition was based first upon a proportional system (*proporz*) of the sharing between the two parties of public goods and offices that extended beyond government positions to the whole public sector, and second upon the development of a **social partner-ship**, a corporatist society based upon a series of agreements between government, employers and trade unions.

The grand coalition ended in 1966 after an electoral victory by the ÖVP. In 1970 government power was gained by the SPÖ and under the leadership of **Kreisky** the social partnership was intensified, enabling Austria to weather the economic problems of the 1970s better than most democracies. The *proporz* system also survived the end of the grand coalition. The SPÖ lost its overall majority in 1983, but continued in office in alliance with the small **Freedom Party of Austria (FPÖ)**. In 1986 it renewed a grand coalition with a declining ÖVP. The new coalition was the result of several factors: (1) a series of political scandals and controversies affecting both parties, including the election of **Waldheim** as President, the **Reder Handshake** and the **Lucona Affair**; (2) a rise in **anti-semitism** and a more vocal right-wing populist sentiment expressed by **Haider**, the dynamic new star of the FPÖ, who also attacked the whole patronage system of *proporz* and social partnership; (3) a worsening economic situation and the need to reform the domination of public ownership and state direction in the economy; and later (4) the more uncertain situation in Eastern Europe that followed the relaxation of Soviet hegemony.

In the 1990s pressure on the coalition intensified with increasing electoral gains for the more right-wing FPÖ. In international affairs Austria carefully observed the conditions of the 1955 Treaty which obliged it to remain neutral in the East–West conflict. It did join the **Council of Europe** and was a founder member of the **European Free Trade Association (EFTA)**. In 1989 it applied to join the **European Communities (EC)**, a move previously rejected because of the view that the **USSR** would regard an application as a violation of the Treaty. In November 1990 Austria declared several elements of the Treaty to be void, effectively bringing its importance to an end. A popular referendum in 1994 gave a large majority in favour of EC membership, which began in January 1995.

Austrian People's Party. (*Österreichische Volkspartei – ÖVP*) The major conservative party in **Austria**, founded in 1945 as a successor to the pre-war Christian Social Party, but, unlike its predecessor, independent of the Catholic Church. It won an absolute majority in the 1945 election, but its leader, **Figl**, chose to govern in a **grand coalition** with the rival **Socialist Party** of Austria (SPÖ). In the 1945–66 grand coalition the ÖVP always provided the Chancellor (Figl 1945–53, **Raab** 1953–61, Alfons Gorbach 1961–64, Josef Klaus 1964–66). After winning an absolute majority in 1966 it chose to form a single-party government, but after losing the 1970 election it remained in opposition until 1986, with a declining electoral support making victory more improbable. It returned to government as the junior partner of the SPÖ in a renewed grand coalition. Its effectiveness was further reduced because of persisting factionalism between left and right groups and between reformers and those who wished to retain the party's federal structure of semi-autonomous leagues based mainly upon occupational groups. Its prestige was further damaged after 1986 by its adoption of **Waldheim** as its presidential candidate. The increasing popularity after the late 1980s of the more right-wing **Freedom Party of Austria (FPÖ)** placed it under further strain.

Austrian State Treaty. A document formally recognizing the sovereignty of **Austria** signed by **France**, the **United Kingdom**, USA and **USSR** on 15 May 1955. It brought to an end the post-war military occupation of the country, with foreign troops leaving by the end of the year. Austria was prohibited from possessing major offensive weapons, seeking the restoration of the Habsburg dynasty, or attempting any union with Germany. It also agreed to pay reparations to the USSR and to amend its Constitution to include a commitment to permanent neutrality. The Western allies had hoped that the USSR's willingness to accept the Treaty would also mark a relaxation of Soviet control elsewhere in Central and Eastern Europe. However, the Treaty coincided with the establishment of the **Warsaw Pact**, which formalized Soviet military control over its satellite states. With the ending of the **Cold War**, in November 1990 the Austrian government declared several items of the Treaty relating to the country's neutral status void.

Autonomous Province of Western Bosnia. A state proclaimed within **Bosnia-Hercegovina** by Muslims in the Bihać region in the north-west of the country. The Bihać pocket was isolated from the main territory controlled by the Bosnian government, and its leaders were forced to reach an informal accommodation with the Serb- and Croat-controlled areas surrounding it. In September 1993 a dissident group declared the foundation of the Autonomous Province, but was immediately opposed by forces loyal to the central Bosnian government. The rebel forces were finally defeated in August 1994.

Avis. The statement issued by the **Commission** on the acceptability of a formal application by a state for membership of the **European Communities (EC)**.

Azerbaijan. An ancient Mongol territory steadily taken over by Persian and Russian armies in the eighteenth and nineteenth centuries. By 1914 it was the largest oil-producing area in the world. It was conquered by Soviet forces in 1920, and a Soviet Republic was established. It became formally part of the **USSR** in 1936. The majority Muslim population was opposed by an Armenian minority centred mainly in the **Nagorno-Karabakh** region, and antagonism between the two communities was not eliminated by Soviet control, also because the western Azerbaijani province of Nakhichevan was separated from the rest of the country by Armenian territory. Tensions erupted into outbreaks of sporadic violence in the late 1980s after the liberal reforms introduced in the USSR by **Gorbachev**. In January 1990 several Armenians were killed in a pogrom in the capital, Baku, and Soviet troops were sent in to restore order. Azerbaijani demands for more autonomy and a right to secede from the USSR were met by the imposition of a state of emergency, and Soviet troops were used to break up a strike in Baku. With the break-up of the USSR in 1991 Azerbaijan declared its independence, but its politics and ailing economy were dominated by a war with **Armenia** over the Nagorno-Karabakh enclave. In 1992 the Communist rulers were replaced by a nationalist government backed by **Turkey**, headed by Abulfaz Elchibey and his Popular Front of Azerbaijan. By 1993 a series of military reversals had resulted in Armenian control of Nagorno-Karabakh and other considerable areas of the country. Popular discontent led to the overthrow of the nationalist government in June 1993 by military forces linked to the old Communist leadership and possessing a more pro-Russian outlook. Previous ex-Communists, under the leadership of **Aliyev**, were reinstalled in Baku, with Elchibey and the defeated nationalists continuing to assert their legitimacy from western Azerbaijan.

Aznar, José María. (1953–) Spanish politician. A tax inspector, he joined the conservative **Popular Party (PP)**, eventually to head the regional government of Castile-Léon 1987–89. In April 1990 he was elected party leader, and continued his predecessor's efforts to consolidate the PP as the major alternative to left-wing government. He survived an assassination attempt in 1995.

B

Baader–Meinhof Group. The popular name given by the media to the West German anarchist group that coalesced after 1968 and later called itself the Red Army Faction (*Rote Armee Faktion – RAF*). The name derived from two of its original leaders, Andreas Baader (1943–1977) and Ulrike Meinhof (1934–1976). The group was dedicated to the violent overthrow of capitalist society, claiming a heritage from both nineteenth century **anarchism** and the student protest movement of the 1960s, especially the **Extra-Parliamentary Opposition (APO)**. The group was held responsible for several murders, bomb attacks and bank robberies. Several of its leaders, including Baader and Meinhof, were arrested in 1972. Meinhof was found dead in her prison cell in 1976: officially her death was reported as suicide. In April 1977 Baader and two of his associates were sentenced to life imprisonment. An attempt to free them six months later in return for the release of hostages failed with the successful **Mogadishu Raid** by West German police commandos. On 18 October 1977 it was announced that Baader and his associates had committed suicide in prison. The deaths of Baader and Meinhof were as controversial as their brief reign as terrorists. The arrest of most of its leading participants throughout the 1970s reduced the coherence and effectiveness of the RAF. The wave of terrorism, which had escalated after the arrests of Baader and Meinhof, peaked in 1977. Although the RAF remained active in the 1980s and 1990s, it seemed to possess a less cohesive structure and integrated leadership, operating more as several relatively unco-ordinated cells. After German reunification it was revealed that the **German Democratic Republic (DDR)** trained and sheltered RAF members in the 1970s and 1980s, and several former activists living in the ex-DDR were later arrested.

Bad Godesberg Programme. A radical revision of the aims of the West German **Social Democratic Party (SPD)** in 1959. It was the result of three successive and progressively more emphatic electoral defeats. The reform movement in the party was particularly associated with the influential *Bürgermeister* group of regional and local politicians. It argued that the party had to change if it wished to lose its negative image and be seen as a credible alternative to the dominant **Christian Democratic Union (CDU)**. The programme, the first restatement of the party's aims since 1925, rejected its

Marxist heritage and the notion of a class party. It set out a broad definition of democratic socialism based upon the Christian ethic as the platform for the SPD becoming a party of the whole society (*Volkspartei*). While all that the programme destroyed was a set of revolutionary myths, it was widely credited with helping the emergence of a new party image, style and acceptability that culminated in electoral victory of 1969.

Bahr, Egon. (1922–) West German politician. A member of the **Social Democratic Party (SPD)** since 1957, he pursued a career in radio and journalism from 1950–60 before becoming the press and information director in West **Berlin** and a close associate of **Brandt**, the party leader. In 1963 he gave a speech on foreign policy which signalled that the SPD was reappraising its policy on the **German Democratic Republic (DDR)** and Eastern Europe, since it was regarded as a reflection of Brandt's views. It foreshadowed the initiatives that after 1969 were described as the **Ostpolitik** process. After the formation of the 1966 **grand coalition**, Bahr became head of the policy and planning staff in the foreign ministry under Brandt from 1967–69. After 1969 he was Brandt's principal representative in negotiations with the DDR, the **USSR** and other Eastern European countries, and was acknowledged as the major architect of Ostpolitik. After 1973 he served briefly as a Minister without Portfolio until Brandt's resignation as Chancellor. He later served as Party General Secretary 1976–81, becoming strongly identified with the SPD left, and opposed several aspects of the foreign policy pursued by **Schmidt**.

Balance of Power. A classic strategic concept describing an international situation where no one country or group of allied countries can exercise a military strength so great that the liberty and independence of other countries are threatened. It became a major element of European diplomacy in the eighteenth and nineteenth centuries. Its main virtue was held to be its ability to ensure peace. Despite its common application as a description of post-1945 Europe, the **Cold War** era did not satisfy its conditions. The USA and **USSR** were so dominant in their respective alliances that no shift in strategy or alignment by any third country could significantly affect the relative influence of either super-power. The balance of power was essentially bipolar rather than multipolar, a situation indicated by the alternative phrase of a 'balance of terror'. The latter phrase, however, was used more to describe a frozen situation where the probability of total destruction inhibited recourse to war, whereas war was accepted as an element sometimes essential for the maintenance of a balance of power.

Balkan Federation. A proposed federation of Balkan and Danubian states suggested in 1947 by **Dimitrov** and **Tito**. Shortly after they had endorsed the idea, the two were summoned to Moscow where **Stalin** voiced his strong opposition to the plan and ordered them to abandon it.

Balkanization. A process whereby the territory of a state is divided into smaller independent or autonomous political units. It was coined in the early twentieth century to describe the disintegration of the Ottoman Empire, and was later applied to several similar situations, including the post-1991 fragmentation of the **USSR** and **Yugoslavia**. The term has generally held negative connotations, implying that disintegration is the result of a mutual hostility between groups that continues to express itself in conflict between the newly created territorial units.

Balkan Pact. An agreement on mutual military assistance in the event of external aggression against any one of the signatories. It was signed in August 1954 by **Greece**, **Turkey** and **Yugoslavia**. It was part of the effort of **Tito** to consolidate the non-aligned status of Yugoslavia vis-à-vis the Soviet bloc. Its value ended only a few months later because of hostility between Greece and Turkey over **Cyprus**, although it was never formally renounced. A broader attempt at Balkan co-operation was made in February 1988 with a meeting in Belgrade of foreign ministers from all the Balkan states, but the discussions ended without any agreement.

Balladur, Edouard. (1929–) Prime Minister of **France** 1993–95. A bureaucrat and diplomat, he served as an adviser to **Pompidou** from 1966–68, but did not become involved in party politics until 1986 when he entered Parliament for the **Rally for the Republic (RPR)**. As Economy and Finance Minister 1986–88, he was the principal architect of the privatization programme of the **Chirac** government. Chirac, as leader of the RPR, chose not to nominate himself as premier after the RPR electoral victory of 1993, putting forward Balladur's name instead. Balladur adopted a firm economic policy which despite generating high unemployment proved politically popular, making him a rival to Chirac for the leadership of the French right. He was defeated in the 1995 presidential election and resigned as premier when his conservative rival, Chirac, became President.

Balladur Memorandum. A French government document of February 1988. Named after **Balladur**, it outlined reforms of the **European Monetary System (EMS)** deemed necessary for the **European Communities (EC)** to complete the planned **internal market**. It demanded that all Member States join the **Exchange Rate Mechanism (ERM)** where identical margins of permissible currency fluctuations would be strictly maintained.

Balladur Plan. A proposal advanced by **Balladur**, and adopted by the **European Union (EU)**, in 1994 for the construction of a framework for bilateral treaties among Eastern European countries that would aid in the prevention of tensions and issues within and between the states breaking out into violence and armed conflict.

Baltic Assembly. Established in 1991 as a forum for representatives of the legislatures of the three **Baltic states**. It first met in 1992 and recommended the establishment of a Baltic **common market** that would be compatible with the possible future integration of the states into European economic organizations.

Baltic Council. Established in May 1990 by the three **Baltic states** to co-ordinate policy-making, especially with regard to the **USSR** from which at that time they were attempting to secede. They were particularly concerned to adopt a common front on negotiations to secure the removal of all Soviet troops from their territories. After independence, its aims were extended to embrace economic co-operation and the integration of the countries into European structures.

Baltic Marine Environment Protection Commission. *See* CON-VENTION ON THE PROTECTION OF THE BALTIC SEA AREA.

Baltic Sea. A section of the Atlantic Ocean in Northern Europe encircled by Germany, **Poland**, the **USSR** and Scandinavia. Because of its importance as a naval location, it was regarded as strategically vital by both the **North Atlantic Treaty Organization (NATO)** and the **Warsaw Pact**, but the most serious military controversies occurred in the 1980s with persistent allegations from neutral **Sweden** that its territorial waters had been violated by Soviet submarines. In 1989 the USSR declared it would withdraw its Golf Class submarines from the Baltic, and repeated its willingness, previously rejected by the West, to incorporate the sea into a northern **nuclear-free zone**. Other disputes have been over fishing rights and the assumed presence of oil. These intensified in 1978 when the littoral states extended their fishing limits on the principle of the median line between their respective base lines. There were four major disputes: between **Denmark** and Poland, the two Germanies, Denmark and Sweden, and the USSR and Sweden. The latter two were the most contentious, with Denmark and Sweden reaching a provisional agreement only in 1983, and the USSR and Sweden not until 1988. Despite the various disputes, there was after 1960 a general willingness to collaborate on environmental measures to combat growing marine pollution and degradation. In addition to several bilateral agreements, all the states signed the **Convention on the Protection of the Baltic Sea Area** (also known as the Helsinki Convention) in 1974. An enforcing Commission was established in 1980 when the Convention began to operate.

Baltic States. A collective name for the three countries of **Estonia**, **Latvia** and **Lithuania**. Part of the Russian Empire until 1917, they were independent from 1918 to 1940 when they were reincorporated into the **USSR**. Nationalist sentiment survived despite strong Russification policies, and their annexation by the USSR was never recognized by Western countries. Pressures for autonomy emerged after 1988, with the relaxation of Soviet centralization. In 1990 the three republics declared their wish to secede from the USSR. Despite some military skirmishes and economic pressure, Soviet attempts to quell the discontent were not whole-hearted, and in August 1991 their independence was recognized just before the USSR itself collapsed.

Banco Ambrosiano Scandal. The collapse of a Milan-based bank in August 1982, precipitated by the death in June of its president, Roberto Calvi, whose body was found hanging on Blackfriars Bridge in London. In February 1989 his death was ruled to be a case of murder. Calvi had been a member of the **Propaganda Due (P2)** secret Masonic lodge and had been at liberty pending appeal against a fine of over $13 million and a four-year prison sentence for violation of foreign exchange regulations in the 1970s. The bank's collapse, which shook the Italian banking system, was attributed by a Milan court to its failure to recover a loan of some $1400 million to Panamanian front companies, which had been made on the basis of letters of patronage issued by the **Vatican** bank, the *Istituto per le Opere di Religione (IOR)*. The resulting argument strained relations with the Vatican, especially when **Italy** sought the extradition from the Vatican of the IOR President, Archbishop Paul Marcenkus. In May 1984, after a new concordat between the papal see and the **Craxi** government, the IOR, while denying culpability, agreed to pay substantial 'moral compensation' to creditor banks. Trials of individuals connected with the scandal continued for some years, and Licio Gelli, a close friend of Calvi and Grand Master of P2, was extradited from **Switzerland** in February 1988. Several of the accused were eventually sentenced to imprisonment in 1992. The episode was one of the many scandals of the 1980s and 1990s that undermined the credibility of the Italian elite, and was directly linked to the party funding scandals (*see* TANGENTO-POLI) that broke in the 1990s.

Bank for International Settlements. A joint venture of European national central banks established in 1930 originally to aid a solution to the problem of German reparations and to handle their transfer under the proposed Young Plan. Its founders also hoped it would provide facilities for international monetary co-operation and financial operations. Based in Basel in **Switzerland**, it extended its activities to hold deposits for some 80 national central banks and managing some 10 per cent of the world's foreign exchange reserves. Until the establishment of the **European Monetary Institute** it served as the headquarters of the **Committee of the Governors of the Central Banks** and acted on behalf of the **European Communities (EC)** as their agent for the **European Monetary Co-operation Fund (EMCF)**.

Bank of Crete Scandal. *See* KOSKOTAS AFFAIR.

Barcelona Convention. An international convention, formally the Convention for the Protection of the Mediterranean Sea against pollution, adopted in Barcelona in 1976 by the Mediterranean littoral states of Europe, North Africa and the Middle East. The signatories agreed to take measures to prevent the pollution of the Mediterranean through the dumping of waste. Further protocols were added in 1980 and 1982. In 1980 a Mediterranean Action Plan was adopted, under the aegis of the United Nations (UN) Environment Programme, to administer the convention and its provisions.

Barents Euro-Arctic Council. A co-operative arrangement to foster the development of trade and economic collaboration in the **Barents Sea** region. It was established in January 1993 by a meeting of the foreign ministers of **Russia** and the Nordic states. It was agreed that the Council would also include a representative of the Sami (Lapp) population, and that Sami welfare and environment protection would be major concerns of the Council.

Barents Sea. An outlying section of the Arctic Ocean to the north of **Norway** and the **USSR**. It was of great strategic value because it provided access to the open oceans from the Soviet ports and military centres of Murmansk and Arkhangelsk. There were several protracted disputes on boundary delimitations between Norway and the USSR, especially after 1976 when both established 200-mile exclusion zones which overlapped with each other. The two reached an interim fisheries agreement in 1978, but found it more difficult in the 1980s to concur on oil exploration. In 1989 there were two accidents involving Soviet nuclear submarines, raising serious concern about radioactive fallout, and in December they reached an agreement to exchange information on all accidents outside their territorial waters. In February 1990 they established a special hotline for notification of oil spills and other pollution problems, and in June 1991 reached agreement in principle on most of the disputed ocean area.

Barre Plan. A strategy for **Economic and Monetary Union (EMU)** advanced after the December 1969 **Hague Summit** of the **European Communities (EC)**. Named after its proposer, **Barre**, it outlined a monetarist approach to EMU with the the immediate introduction of fixed exchange rates preceding and being necessary for any economic **harmonization**. (*See also* SCHILLER PLAN, WERNER REPORT).

Barre, Raymond. (1924–) Prime Minister of **France** 1976–81. An economist and university professor, he was appointed to the **Commission** of the **European Communities (EC)** in 1967 before returning to France to serve as Economics and Finance Minister. He joined the Central Union (*Union Centraliste*) of **Giscard d'Estaing**, but entered Parliament only in 1976 when he was subsequently appointed premier. A loyal supporter of the President but without a personal power base, he pursued a rigorous programme of economic austerity which was highly unpopular among the electorate.

Barzel, Rainer. (1924–) West German politician. He joined the **Christian Democratic Union (CDU)** after 1945 and became a protégé of **Adenauer**.

He entered Parliament in 1957, becoming a government minister in 1962. He led the CDU parliamentary group from 1964–71 and served as chairman of the party organization 1970–73. In 1971 he became party leader. His strong opposition to **Ostpolitik** was a factor that contributed to the resignation of the **Brandt** government in 1972, but a heavy CDU defeat in the subsequent election weakened his authority, already under challenge because of his attempts to modernize and centralize the party. He was replaced as party leader in 1976 by **Kohl**. When the CDU returned to power in 1982 he became President (Speaker) of the Bundestag, but was forced to resign in October 1984 after being implicated in the **Flick Affair**.

Basket of Currencies. A description of the national currencies which collectively determined the value of the **European Currency Unit (ECU)**. The basket and the ECU were created in 1979 as part of the **European Monetary System (EMS)**. Depending upon its gross national product (GNP), trade and short-term credit quotas, each country's currency received a weighting in the basket, expressed as a percentage of the whole. The weights were made subject to review every five years, but requests for a review were permitted at any time when market pressures induce significant appreciation or depreciation of a single currency. The basket consisted of the currencies of the Member States of the **European Communities (EC)**. After the 1991 agreement to form a **European Economic Area (EEA)**, several members of the **European Free Trade Association (EFTA)** linked their currencies to the ECU. The basket was intended to be a provisional step en route to **Economic and Monetary Union (EMU)**, the deadline for which and for a single currency was set by the **Treaty on European Union** for 1999.

Basque Homeland and Liberty. *See* EUZKADI TA ASKATASUNA (ETA).

Basque Left. (*Euzkadiko Ezkerra – EE*) An electoral coalition of left-wing Basque parties formed in the late 1970s. The main element was the Basque Revolutionary Party (*Euskal Iraultzarako Alderdia – EIA*), which dissolved itself in 1981. In the same year a secession from the Basque section of the **Communist Party of Spain (PCE)** briefly boosted its flagging membership, but it failed to progress beyond being a minor force in Basque politics, and in 1993 it merged with the Basque Socialist Party, the regional wing of the **Spanish Socialist Workers' Party (PSOE)**. A small minority, rejecting the merger, reformed itself as a new and tiny EE.

Basque Nationalist Party. (*Eusko Alderdi Jeltzalea/Partido Nacionalista Vasco – EAJ/PNV*) A Christian Democrat-oriented party favouring extensive Basque autonomy within **Spain** and opposed to the strategy of violence pursued by **Euskadi ta Askatasuna (ETA)**. Formed in 1895, the PNV was banned during the **Franco** regime, but survived in exile. It was re-established in Spain after Franco's death and gained considerable success in the 1977 national election. It argued for and accepted the regional autonomy statute for the Basque area. After the first regional election in 1980 it formed the regional government, but its overall majority was due to the refusal of the radical **Herri Batasuna** to take up its seats in the provincial assembly. In 1986 a faction led by the former PNV leader and regional premier, Carlos Garaikoetxea, seceded from the party. While remaining the largest party after the 1986 regional election, the PNV lost its majority, remaining in office only through a coalition with the Basque section of the **Spanish Socialist Workers' Party (PSOE)**. After 1978 it often employed the strategy of warning Madrid that failure to accept its 'reasonable' demands might result in Spanish governments being confronted with a much more radical nationalist government in the Basque region.

Basques. A race of some three-quarters of a million people settled in the Pyrenees region. A small number live in **France**, with the vast majority living in the Spanish provinces of Álava, Guipúzcoa, Navarra and Vizcaya. They speak a unique language, and they enjoyed, as a society, collective rights respected by **Spain** until abrogated in 1839. Nationalist sentiment developed with the industrialization of Guipúzcoa and Vizcaya in the late nineteenth century. Strongly Catholic, the Basques nevertheless supported the Republican government in the 1930s in return for a promise of autonomy. A Basque Republic (Euskadi) was inaugurated in October 1936, but five months later the region was occupied by the Nationalist forces of General **Franco**. Under the Franco regime Basque culture was actively suppressed, with use of the language penalized. Nationalist opposition re-emerged as a clandestine force after the later 1950s with the establishment of **Euskadi ta Askatasuna (ETA)**. In 1974 the refusal of Spain to release political prisoners led to terrorist attacks and a general strike in the region.

Tensions lessened with the accession of **Juan Carlos I** in November 1975 and the installation of a democratic regime in Madrid. Basque political organizations were permitted, and in December 1977 the Spanish government promised autonomy to the region, which had become radicalized and alienated from the Spanish state. Autonomy was granted under the 1979 Statute of Guernica, with a Basque Parliament established in March 1980, but the degree of autonomy failed to satisfy radical nationalists, including ETA, who demanded self-determination. Terrorist activity continued sporadically after 1980. One of the major problems facing the region was the considerable Spanish-speaking settlement which left native Basque speakers almost a minority in their own homeland. Equally, Basque terrorism, although seemingly in decline, remained a challenge to the government of Spain. In February 1990 the Basque Parliament approved a resolution proclaiming the right of self-determination. It was supported by all but one of the Basque parties and opposed by the Basque sections of national Spanish parties.

Basque Solidarity. (*Eusko Alkartasuna – EA*) A centre-left Basque nationalist party formed in 1986 after a secession from the **Basque Nationalist Party (PNV)**. Led by the former PNV leader and regional premier, Carlos Garaikoetxea, it established itself as a considerable force, but refused to collaborate with the more moderate PNV. It advocated independence for the region and, along with the radical **Herri Batasuna**, refused to sign the November 1987 anti-terrorist pact between the other Basque parties and the main Spanish parties.

Bastian, Gert. (1923–1992) West German politician. Joining the German military in 1942, he subsequently rose through the ranks of the West German army (*Bundeswehr*) to become major-general. He was forcibly retired from the army in 1980 for criticizing the deployment by the **North Atlantic Treaty Organization (NATO)** of a new generation of American intermediate nuclear missiles. He had previously formed an association with environmentalist movements and, under the influence of **Kelly**, he joined the **Green Party**. He was the author of the **Krefeld Appeal** and in 1983 was elected to Parliament as a Green representative. Although retaining his seat until 1987, he resigned from the party in 1984 in protest against its insistence that President Reagan and the USA were solely responsible for the **Cold War**. His military reputation had been invaluable in giving the Greens some respectability, but he played little role in Green politics after 1984. In October 1992 he and his long-time partner, Kelly, were found shot dead in their apartment in Bonn.

Bavaria. A region of the **Federal Republic of Germany**. An independent kingdom until incorporated into the German state in 1870, Bavaria successfully maintained a distinctive sense of identity, with its politics generally of a highly conservative nature. In 1949 it rejected the proposed West German Constitution as creating a too centralized political system. After 1950 economic development made it one of the richest German states (*Länder*), and since 1960 its politics have been dominated by the conservative **Christian Social Union (CSU)**.

Bayar, Maymud Celâl. (1884–1986) President of **Turkey** 1950–60. A member of the Young Turk movement after 1908, he became an associate of Mustafa Kemal Atatürk, the founder of modern Turkey, serving regularly in government during the next two decades. In 1945 he formed the **Democratic Party (DP)** and led it to electoral victory in 1950. Becoming President, he advocated a programme of developing private enterprise. Re-elected in 1954 and 1957, he was deposed and arrested after a military coup in 1960. Imprisoned for alleged crimes against the state, he was released in 1964 and retired to private life.

Belarus. A successor state of the ex-**USSR**. Previously known as Byelorussia (White Russia), the area had never previously experienced any
significant period of independence, and had only low levels of national
consciousness. It was a founder republic of the USSR in 1919, and after
1945, along with **Ukraine**, had separate representation in the United Nations.
During the **Gorbachev** period it remained largely unaffected by the nationalist sentiments that emerged elsewhere in the USSR. The Belarussian Popular
Front (*Belaruski Narodny Front – BNF*), founded in 1988, was limited in
activity, and was forced to hold its first congress in 1989 in neighbouring
Lithuania. In 1990 it captured less than 10 per cent of the region's seats in
the Soviet legislature. Reaction against the USSR arose primarily as
economic protest against Moscow's policies, with a general strike declared
in April 1991. Several of the region's Communist leaders supported the
attempt in August 1991 to overthrow Gorbachev, but were ousted from
office when the coup failed. With USSR authority failing, the legislature
suspended the Communist Party and declared independence. However, after
the establishment of independence the new state collaborated closely with
Russia in many policy areas. Even so, discontent over economic decline
resulted in 1994 in a largely unreformed Communist Party being returned to
office on a platform of much closer political and economic collaboration
with Russia. In 1995 Russian was confirmed as an official language of the
state.

Belgium. A state in Western Europe formed in 1830 when the provinces of
Flanders and **Wallonia** seceded from the **Netherlands**. It was established as
a centralized parliamentary monarchy, a structure which remained until 1970
when a process of federalization began. Although linguistic tensions always
existed between the two provinces, until 1960 political competition revolved
around a religious cleavage moderated to a large extent by class divisions.
Each of the major political parties had its own sub-cultural network of
institutions and organizations across almost all aspects of social life. This
organizational density kept the linguistic divide in check, although the latter
occasionally broke through to polarize politics, as with the royal crisis over
Leopold III after 1945. Stability was further buttressed by a high degree of
elite collaboration across the major parties in a behavioural pattern that was
said to be typical of **consociational democracy**. The stable picture began to
crumble after 1958 with the rise of linguistic parties pressing for extensive
decentralization and even independence. The immediate catalyst was the
removal of religion as a political issue through the 1958 **Schools Pact**.
Governments in the 1960s attempted to respond positively to decentralizing
demands from the two provinces, but failed to neutralize the pressure, and by
the 1970s all the parties had split into independent Flemish and Walloon
organizations. Constitutional revisions in 1970 and 1980 created an institu-

tional structure of federalism which, although a compromise between various interests, was largely acceptable to all. The major difficulty in implementing the revisions completely related to disputes over **Brussels**, a mainly French-speaking city located in historic Flemish territory and claimed by both sides. By 1993 most of the changes had been endorsed and implemented, with a formal federal structure in operation in which the central government retained only very limited powers and policy competences.

Belgo-Luxembourg Economic Union. An agreement by **Belgium** and **Luxembourg** in 1921. It began in March 1922 as a **customs union**, later developing many of the characteristics of an economic union. After 1944 it became part of the **Benelux Economic Union**. The 1921 treaty was to last for 50 years, and after 1971 it was renewed on a decennial basis. Despite the long collaboration, problems still occurred, most seriously in 1982 when Belgium devalued without consulting its partner. In 1990 the two moved closer together with the abolition of a dual exchange rate within their monetary union which had previously distinguished between financial and current commercial transactions.

Belgrade Declaration. A joint statement by **Yugoslavia** and the **USSR** in June 1955. It was issued during a state visit to Yugoslavia by **Khrushchev** who formally apologized to **Tito** for the policy pursued by **Stalin** after 1948. It asserted that domestic concerns were a matter solely for the people of the country concerned. Despite the later adoption by the USSR of the **Brezhnev Doctrine**, Yugoslavia insisted upon the re-endorsement of the Declaration by the USSR in 1971 and 1972 on the occasion of reciprocal state visits.

Benelux Economic Union. An economic association between **Belgium**, the **Netherlands** and **Luxembourg**. The first attempts by the three countries at economic collaboration in 1919 and 1932 were not successful. In 1944 their governments in exile in London agreed to establish an economic unit after the war. The Benelux Customs Union was formed in January 1948 with the introduction of a **common external tariff** and the abolition of internal customs duties. With a few exceptions, internal trade was mostly tariff-free by 1956. The three also began to present a common front in international economic discussions, beginning in 1947 with a single delegation to the meeting that established the **General Agreement on Tariffs and Trade (GATT)**. In January 1960 the customs union was expanded by treaty into an economic union. It developed an elaborate institutional structure which reflected and paralleled that of the **European Communities (EC)**, within which it survived as a distinctive structure. Its significance as a distinct entity declined after the EC established its **internal market**.

Beneš, Edvard. (1884–1948) President of **Czechoslovakia** 1935–38, 1945–48. During the First World War he was a leader in exile of the Czech nationalist movement. After independence, he served as Foreign Minister from 1918–35, and then as President until 1938. Refusing to accept the Munich Agreement, he resigned his office and went into voluntary exile. During the Second World War he formed a government in exile in London. Upon his return to Czechoslovakia in 1945 he was reappointed President. For three years he struggled in vain to ensure the impartial observance of the constitution and his office in the face of expanding Communist influence in government and administration. Finding it impossible to maintain a neutral presidency, he refused to sign the new constitution proposed by the Communist leader, **Gottwald**. He resigned in June 1948, dying three months later.

Bérégovoy, Pierre Eugène. (1925–1993) Prime Minister of **France** 1992–93. Born of an Ukrainian immigrant father, he was largely self-taught and served in the **Resistance Movement**. A long-time ally of **Mitterrand**, he worked primarily as a party bureaucrat. With Mitterrand's presidential victory in 1981, he was appointed Secretary-General in the President's Office, before becoming a government minister 1982–86. He first entered Parliament for the **Socialist Party (PS)** in 1986. He re-entered government in 1988 with the PS electoral victory. His brief tenure as Prime Minister was unhappy and contentious, and he committed suicide in May 1993, one month after his resignation.

Beria, Lavrenti Pavlovich. (1899–1953) Soviet commissar. Born in **Georgia**, he joined the Bolsheviks as a student in 1917. He quickly rose to head the secret police (*Cheka*) in Georgia 1921–31, also becoming First Secretary of the Georgian Communist Party. Brought to Moscow in 1938 by **Stalin**, he was put in charge of the **NKVD** secret police with the title of Commissar of Internal Affairs, a position of great power which he held until after Stalin's death in 1953. Greatly feared by other leading Communists, he was a victim of the power struggle that followed Stalin's death. His opponents believed that he had hastened the death to realize his own ambitions to succeed Stalin. In July 1953 he was dismissed from office and charged with conspiracy. His exact fate is unknown. It was announced in December 1953 that he had been tried in secret and executed for treason, but it is possible that he had been killed several months earlier without the benefit of a trial.

Berisha, Sali. (1944–) President of **Albania** from 1992. A cardiologist, he had joined the ruling **Party of Labour** but did not hold any political office or play an active political role. He first rose to prominence during the December 1990 student demonstrations demanding the establishment of a democratic multi-party system. The same month he was a co-founder of the Democratic Party (*Partia Demokratike të Shqipërisë – PDSh*), becoming its leader. The PDSh became the centre of the opposition movement and after its electoral victory in 1992, he was elected by the legislature as President. He and his party sought to strengthen Albanian democracy and its rapid transition to a market economy through greater contacts with the West. While also seeking Balkan co-operation, he was concerned about the situation of the Albanian minorities in **Serbia** and **Macedonia**.

Berlaymont. The headquarters of the **Commission** of the **European Communities (EC)** custom-built in 1969. In 1992 it had to be evacuated for extensive renovation (not to be completed until 1998) because of asbestos used in the original construction. The word has often been used as a shorthand term to describe the Commission and the EC administration, frequently employed to symbolize bureaucracy, rigidity and red tape.

Berlin. The capital city of Germany, under Allied Military occupation 1945–90, making it the most prominent symbol of the **Cold War** and the divided nature of Europe. Berlin was not part of any military zone of occupation after 1945. It had been divided into four sectors of occupation: American, British, French and Soviet. Each power had full political and military authority within its own sector. Co-ordination of all-city affairs was the responsibility of the **Allied Kommandatura**, working in conjunction with a democratically elected city government. The Kommandatura system was ineffective. The **USSR** withdrawal from it in June 1948 coincided with the imposition of the **Berlin Blockade**, sealing off the Western sectors of the city. While movement between the Soviet sector (East Berlin) and the Western sectors (West Berlin) was possible after the blockade was called off in May 1949, Berlin had become two cities. The all-city government relocated itself in West Berlin, and a separate Communist administration was established in East Berlin. The USSR claimed that East Berlin was the capital of the **German Democratic Republic (DDR)**, but the Western view was that without a peace treaty with a united Germany, the city still remained under four-power military jurisdiction. West Berlin was not allowed constitutionally to become part of the **Federal Republic of Germany**, but the two closely co-ordinated policy activities.

In the 1950s Berlin was a centre of tension in the East–West dispute and also the only exit to the West through which East Germans could freely pass. In August 1961 the erection of the **Berlin Wall** finally sealed the two halves of the city from each other. The existing situation and the rights of all four Allies were formalized in the 1971 **Quadripartite Agreement**. Despite increased collaboration between the two Germanies, the status of Berlin remained unchanged until the withdrawal by **Gorbachev** of the Soviet guarantee of unswerving support for the Eastern European Communist regimes, a relaxation that led to the disintegration of the DDR after October 1989. As it collapsed, the regime opened most of the access points in the Wall, without restriction. Negotiations between the Allies and the German government produced agreement on the withdrawal of the occupying military forces from the capital, with the last troops leaving in 1994. In 1991 the German Parliament voted that Berlin should be re-established as the country's capital, with the seat of government moving to the city by 1995. The date of transferral was later moved to 2000.

Berlin Airlift. *See* BERLIN BLOCKADE.

Berlin Blockade. The Soviet reaction in June 1948 to the decision of the Western Allies to introduce currency reform and to create an independent West German state from their occupation zones. The **USSR** closed all West Berlin's land borders, sealing its road and rail links with western Germany. Power and food from its hinterland were also blocked. West Berlin was accessible only by air, and even though there were severe doubts as to whether sufficient planes could be found or the adequate basic needs of Berliners met, the West responded with a massive airlift of essential material, fuel and food. With planes eventually landing at a rate of one every two minutes, the airlift successfully defeated the Soviet objective of starving the city into submission. The USSR conceded defeat and abruptly ended the blockade in May 1949. The blockade and airlift was the first major trial of strength between East and West after 1945, and set some important precedents for the future: the USSR was not prepared to use military force to gain control of the whole city, and the Western response indicated that while only military force would make them abandon Berlin, they were equally unwilling to assert their rights in the city by military means.

Berlinguer, Enrico. (1922–1984) General Secretary (leader) of the **Italian Communist Party (PCI)** 1972–84. Joining the PCI shortly before the Second World War, he became a member of its Central Committee in 1945 and of the Executive Committee in 1948. He was placed in charge of its youth organization in 1949, and was appointed to the Secretariat in 1958, with responsibility for party organization. He did not enter Parliament until 1968, one year before becoming deputy party leader. In 1972 he was elected party leader. He attempted to push the PCI to the right to make it more respectable as a potential government party. Drawing a lesson from the failure of the Allende Marxist government in Chile, he advocated the **historic compromise**, and between 1976 and 1979 placed the PCI as part of the government majority. He simultaneously swung the party behind **Euro-communism** and stressed that the PCI accepted **Italy's** membership of both the **European Communities (EC)** and the **North Atlantic Treaty Organiz-ation (NATO)**. His strategy failed to bring the promised rewards: the party was not invited to become part of a coalition government, and after 1976 its electoral support began to decline. Despite these setbacks, he remained firmly in control of the party. A highly respected political figure, who commanded immense personal loyalty, he died suddenly during the 1984 election campaign for the **European Parliament (EP)**.

Berlin Wall. A barrier of concrete, barbed wire and mined 'no man's land' constructed in August 1961 by the **German Democratic Republic (DDR)** to encircle the enclave of West Berlin. Only a few access points between the two halves of the city were left. The Wall was a response to the huge flow of East Germans who could easily pass to the West through **Berlin**, a flow which had severely damaged the DDR economy. It was heavily guarded and many people were killed, wounded or arrested trying to cross it. In 1989 the DDR regime, suddenly faced with massive popular discontent and lacking support from the **USSR**, abruptly opened the access points on 9 November, without conditions. In the first day of free movement since 1961 some 40,000 people crossed into West Berlin, though few chose not to return. The Wall was already being dismantled by a host of 'volunteers' when the DDR regime collapsed. On 22 November the historic Brandenburg Tor was reopened, and plans were announced for the complete demolition of the most visible symbol of the **Cold War**.

Berlusconi, Silvio. (1936–) Prime Minister of **Italy** 1994. A media and business tycoon, he suddenly declared an intention to enter politics in 1993 as the post-war Italian political system began to collapse under the weight of scandals such as **Tangentopoli**. His hastily formed **Forza Italia** emerged as the largest party in the 1994 elections and he was appointed to lead a coalition government. The coalition was an unruly one, with a lack of clear policy direction. Political mistakes and the fact that he and his family faced allegations of corruption denuded his authority. After only a few months in office he resigned rather than face a vote of no confidence, and in 1995 faced further investigations for fraud.

Bernadotte, Count Folke. (1895–1948) Swedish international mediator. A nephew of King Gustavus V and trained as a soldier, he began to work for the Swedish Red Cross during the First World War, and continued with the organization after 1918. In February 1945 he was asked by Heinrich Himmler to act as an intermediary with the Western Allies about a possible German surrender to the USA and the **United Kingdom** (but not the **USSR**). As President of the Swedish Red Cross he was asked in May 1948 by the United Nations Secretary-General, **Lie**, to act as a mediator in Palestine. He was assassinated by Israeli terrorists on 17 September 1948.

Berne Convention. *See* INTERNATIONAL COMMISSION FOR THE PRO-TECTION OF THE RHINE.

Berufsverbot. *See* RADIKALENERLASS.

Bessarabia. A region in Eastern Europe lying between the Pruth and Dniester rivers, historically disputed by **Romania** and **Russia** after 1856, and changing hands between them on several occasions. In March 1944 most of the region was incorporated into the **USSR** as the Moldavian Soviet Socialist Republic, but tensions between the Romanian majority and Russian minority continued to be a strain in the post-Stalin period. With the disintegration of the USSR in 1991 the Romanian majority in the province declared its independence as the state of **Moldova**. In turn, this was rejected by the minority who set up a state of **Trans-Dnestria**.

Bevan, Aneurin. (1897–1960) British politician and founder of the National Health Service. From a Welsh mining background, he entered Parliament in 1929 as a member of the Independent Labour Party, joining the **Labour Party** in 1931. He was a skilled, fiery and impressive orator in the radical tradition. He was appointed Minister of Health in the 1945 Labour Government and was responsible for the establishment of the National Health Service. In January 1951 he was made Minister of Labour, but resigned from office in April in protest against the introduction of health service charges to meet rising defence costs. He headed a radical group 1951–57 within the party (popularly described as the Bevanites) in opposition to the dominant reformist wing, and was particularly critical of defence expenditure. He made a bid for the party leadership after the retirement of **Attlee**, but was defeated by the moderate **Gaitskell** in December 1955. He was reconciled with Gaitskell in 1956 and became party spokesman on foreign affairs. He shifted ground in 1957, attacking left-wing demands for unilateral British nuclear disarmament. With his health already failing, he became deputy party leader in 1959, but died the following year.

Beveridge Report. A British report of 1942 proposing a comprehensive scheme of social welfare to combat poverty and unemployment. Entitled *A Report on Social Insurance and Allied Services*, it was prepared by a commission headed by the academic economist, Sir William Beveridge. The report formed the basis of the British welfare state structure introduced after 1945 by the **Labour Party**, and many of its ideas were taken up by other European governments.

Bevin, Ernest. (1881–1951) British Foreign Secretary 1945–51. A prominent trade union leader in the 1920s and 1930s, he was recruited into the wartime coalition government in May 1940 as Minister of Labour. Appointed to the Foreign Ministry in 1945, he was allowed a fairly free hand in foreign policy by the premier, **Attlee**. He represented British scepticism about federalism and supranationalism in Europe. He accepted the importance of the **Commonwealth** and a strong relationship with the USA as a back-up to his ultimately abortive attempts to build an Anglo-French leadership in Western Europe. He resisted proposals for a European federal union, and successfully watered down the original plans for the **Council of Europe**. While cautiously welcoming the **Schuman Plan**, he stressed that Britain would not participate in it. His more negative attitude to integration was offset by a positive commitment to collaborative security, being early aware of Britain's reduced military capacity and the potential threat of the **USSR**. To a large extent, he saw the **Treaty of Dunkirk** and the **Treaty of Brussels** not only as safeguards against any future German aggression, but also as embryonic anti-Soviet holding operations until the USA became actively involved in European defence. He welcomed the **Marshall Plan** and played a leading role in the creation of the **Organization for European Economic Co-operation (OEEC)** and the **North Atlantic Treaty Organization (NATO)**.

Bidault, Georges. (1899–1982) Prime Minister of **France** 1946, 1949–50, 1958. A leading activist in the **Resistance** during the Second World War, he helped to found the **Popular Republican Movement (MRP)**, France's first Christian Democrat party, in 1944. He served as Prime Minister and Foreign Minister in the **Fourth French Republic** on several occasions. Along with **Bevin**, he worked for the establishment of an effective collective security system in Western Europe. He became more right-wing in the 1950s because of the **Algerian War of Independence**. While strongly supporting the return to power of **de Gaulle** in 1958, he was later a bitter critic of de Gaulle's increasingly conciliatory policy in Algeria, eventually identifying with the extremist **Organisation de l'Armée Secrète (OAS)**. In danger of being arrested for treason, he fled to Brazil in 1963. He returned to France in 1968 after de Gaulle declared a general amnesty, but played no further political role.

Bielecki, Jan Krzysztof. (1951–) Prime Minister of **Poland** 1991. An academic economist, he acted as an economic adviser to **Solidarity** in 1980. After the 1981 declaration of martial law he was banned from his previous occupation, and established a timber haulage company. He entered Parliament in 1989 on the Solidarity list, but then founded the right-wing Liberal Democratic Congress. As premier in January 1991 he pursued a policy of rapid economic reform, but his policies and their severe economic consequences were rejected at the general election the following October.

Bierut, Boleslaw. (1892–1956) President of **Poland** 1945–52. Joining the Communist Party in 1920, he spent much of the next 20 years abroad or in prison. He went to Moscow in 1938, returning to Poland in 1943. A loyal supporter of **Stalin**, he organized the Communist plans to take over the country in 1944, becoming President the following year. In 1948 he also became the general secretary of the party. In 1952 he supervised a reorganization of the party and constitution, abolishing the presidency in favour of a collective Council of State. He continued to serve as Prime Minister until 1954. He died in Moscow while attending the **Twentieth Party Congress** of the Soviet Communist Party.

Bildt, Carl. (1949–) Prime Minister of **Sweden** 1991–94. A professional politican, he worked as an administrator for the **Moderate Unity Party** before being appointed Party Secretary in 1973. He was a government minister 1976–81, but did not enter Parliament until 1979. He became party leader in 1986. After becoming premier in 1991 he declared the **Swedish Model** dead and attempted an ambitious programme of radical tax and public sector reforms, but his policies were only partially successful because of monetary pressures and the effects of the most severe depression since the 1930s. In foreign policy he worked for a softening of Swedish neutrality and formally submitted an application to join the **European Communities (EC)**. His austerity programme was unpopular and he lost the 1994 election. In 1995 he succeeded **Owen** as the **European Union (EU)** mediator in the former **Yugoslavia**.

Bill of Rights. A constitutionally guaranteed list of citizens' rights specifically protected against state and government actions, revocable only by some extraordinary constitutional amendment process. All charters have drawn upon the archetypes of the American Constitution and the 1789 French Declaration of the Rights of Man and the Citizen. The liberal-democratic values and rights have been included in most modern European constitutions, most prominently in the **Federal Republic of Germany**, where they cannot be revoked by constitutional process. After 1945 several Communist regimes in Eastern Europe included a bill of rights in their constitutions, but these stressed socialist and collective rights relating to economic welfare rather than rights of individuals.

Bizonia. The economic and administrative unit formed in December 1946 by the merging of the American and British zones of military occupation in Germany. German administrative officials were involved in the negotiations, and the merger gave a boost to German economic recovery and political life. By 1948 Bizonia had developed an elaborate structure of representative and administrative institutions, a framework which largely served as a basis for the 1949 Basic Law of the **Federal Republic of Germany**.

Black Legion. (*Crna Legija*) A Croat paramilitary group operating in **Croatia** and **Bosnia-Hercegovina**. A volunteer force established in 1991, and operating in practice as an independent unit, it was an ultra-nationalist defender of Croat interests, modelling itself on the **Uštaše**.

Black Sea Economic Co-operation (BSEC). An agreement proposed in 1989 and signed in July 1991 by **Bulgaria**, **Romania**, **Turkey** and the **USSR**. The development of its plans were initially disrupted by the break-up of the USSR and by differences of opinion between some of the successor states, though those located next to the Black Sea affirmed their interest in adhering to the principles of the agreement. After 1992 a lead in furthering collaboration was taken by Turkey, and by 1994 a high degree of co-operation had been achieved, including an agreement to form a joint bank for trade and development along with an intergovernmental structure modelled in part on the **European Communities (EC)**. The foreign ministers meet regularly, with the presidency rotating among the members.

Black Wednesday. A term popularized by the media to describe the 1992 currency speculation unleashed on the world's financial markets against currencies within the **Exchange Rate Mechanism (ERM)**. The speculation, which returned again in 1993, exposed the weaknesses of the ERM and threatened the intention of the **European Communities (EC)** to establish **Economic and Monetary Union (EMU)** by 1999. Several countries were forced to devalue their currencies, and the British pound and the Italian lira were taken out of the ERM.

Blair House Agreement. A proposed agreement on a trans-Atlantic agricultural trade structure within the **Uruguay Round** of the **General Agreement on Tariffs and Trade (GATT)**. Named after the Washington DC mansion where the meeting took place in 1993, it was an attempt to break the farm deadlock between the USA and the **European Communities (EC)** which had been a major factor in the stalled GATT negotiations. The agreement was denounced by **France** which threatened to use a veto within the EC unless the agreement was withdrawn or radically amended. While some changes were subsequently made, the Agreement opened the way to a resolution of the GATT Round.

Bloc of Expellees and Disenfranchised. (*Bund der Heimatver-triebenen und Entrechteten – BHE*) A political movement in the **Federal Republic of Germany**. It was founded in 1950 by refugee groups from previously German territories in Eastern Europe. They had earlier proclaimed a Charter of the Expellees which asserted, *inter alia*, the right to live in one's homeland, and there were fears that the expellees and refugees, some 20 per cent of the West German population, might provide a large nucleus for a right-wing extremism. The BHE became a national political party in 1951, but saw its constituency rapidly decline as economic recovery helped the social integration of the refugees, and it was absorbed by the **Christian Democratic Union (CDU)** in the late 1950s.

Block Exemptions. Categories of agreements between the **European Communities (EC)** and other countries which have been accepted by the EC as being exempt from the general prohibition on restrictive trade agreements.

Blue Zone. The popular name given to the demilitarized buffer areas in **Croatia** which after 1991 separated government-controlled territory from that held by rebel Serb forces, and patrolled by United Nations (UN) troops.

Blum, Léon. (1872–1950) Prime Minister of **France** 1936, 1946–47. A distinguished leader of the **Socialist Party (SFIO)**, he had become France's first Socialist premier in 1936, heading a Popular Front government. In 1940 he was arrested by the Vichy Government, but the trial was abandoned in 1942. After the German occupation of Vichy France he was interned in

Germany 1943–45. After the war he headed an economic mission to the USA before returning briefly to serve as Prime Minister. Accepted as a kind of elder statesman, he was influential in the drafting of the constitution of the **Fourth French Republic.**

Boban, Mate. (1940–) Bosnian Croat politician. An economist, he became the dominant leader of the Bosnian Croats soon after the eruption of civil war in **Bosnia-Hercegovina** in March 1992. He sought the partition of Bosnia and the incorporation of its Croat-controlled areas into **Croatia**. His influence declined after military defeats and because of international pressure, and was replaced in February 1994 by a less hard-line leadership.

Bologna Station Bombing. A terrorist act in **Italy** in August 1980. The bombing of the railway station at Bologna was the greatest single cause of deaths and injuries during the country's period of political violence. It later became a judicial and political scandal. In 1988 13 people were convicted of involvement in the atrocity. Most were sympathizers of extreme right-wing causes, but they also included senior members of the security and intelligence agencies, and of the banned **Propaganda Due (P-2)**. All bar two were acquitted on appeal in 1990. Later evidence suggested that the act had been part of an extreme right-wing strategy of political destabilization. The judges at the original trial were placed under investigation for corruption, and a new trial of the same defendants was ordered in October 1993.

Bonn Agreement. A treaty signed in June 1969 whereby eight littoral countries agreed to develop and co-ordinate policies designed to remove and prevent pollution of the North Sea by oil and other harmful substances.

Bonnefous Plan. *See* EUROPEAN CONFERENCE OF MINISTERS OF TRANSPORT.

Boross, Péter. (1928–) Prime Minister of **Hungary** 1993–94. A lawyer and businessman, his activities during the 1956 **Hungarian Revolution** cost him his job with the Budapest city council. He later joined a catering company, directing it from 1971–89. A prominent human rights activist in the 1980s, he became a minister in the 1990 **Hungarian Democratic Forum (MDF)** government, though remaining politically unaffiliated. He joined the MDF in October 1992, and in December 1993 succeeded as leader and premier after the death of **Antall**. He failed to stem the growing unpopularity of the government's economic policies, and resigned after the heavy MDF electoral defeat in May 1994.

Bosnia-Hercegovina. A region of the Balkans incorporated in 1918 into the Kingdom of Serbs, Croats and Slovenes, later (1929) **Yugoslavia**. In January 1946 it became one of the federated Communist republics of Yugoslavia. Much of the indigeneous population had historically converted to Islam under its long domination by the Ottoman Empire, but large parts of the territory were increasingly populated by Croats and Serbs in a confusing ethnic distribution. When Yugoslav unity began to fray under separatist pressures from **Croatia** and **Slovenia**, similar demands for autonomy and independence were raised in Bosnia, and in regional elections in December 1990 the Communists were defeated by a coalition of three nationalist parties. After 1990 the Bosnian government tried to remain neutral in the conflict between Croatia and **Serbia**, but its own declaration of independence, made in December 1991, was inevitable. The consequence was a collapse of territorial control as Muslims, Serbs and Croats fought a three-sided civil war in the province, which soon degenerated into a conflict dominated by local guerilla groups. Efforts by the United Nations, the **European Communities (EC)** and other countries to develop peace initiatives that would also confirm an independent Bosnia-Hercegovina all failed. By 1993 the Bosnian government controlled only a fraction of the province. Although it subsequently signed a confederal accord with Bosnian Croats, some form of partition into separate Muslim, Croat and Serb territories seemed to be the only possible outcome, though Muslims and Serbs still sought resolution through war. In a peace conference at Dayton, Ohio in November 1995, Bosnia, Croatia and Serbia agreed to a territorial settlement which acknowledged a unitary Bosnian state, but one which would effectively be divided between separate Serb and Croat–Muslim administrations.

Bossi, Umberto. (1941–) Italian politician. A former medical student and one time rock musician, he was a co-founder of the **Lombardy League** in 1984. A right-wing and free market radical populist, it was never clear whether he stood for a federalization of **Italy** or a secession of the richer Northern provinces. He entered Parliament in 1987 and became leader of the **Northern League** alliance in 1990. In 1994 he took the Northern League into the coalition government of **Berlusconi**, after which he seemed to modify his views on the Italian state. His subsequent withdrawal from the coalition contributed to the government's fall and split the League. His prestige was further weakened in 1994 when he was investigated on suspicion of fraud and defamation.

Brandt, Willy. (1913–1992) Chancellor of the **Federal Republic of Germany** 1969–74. Born Herbert Ernst Karl Frahm in Lübeck, he became a member of the **Social Democratic Party (SPD)**. He fled from Germany in the 1930s to Scandinavia, eventually taking Norwegian citizenship and assuming the name of Willy Brandt. Returning to Germany after 1945, he resumed a political career in the SPD. Elected to the West **Berlin** city council in 1951, he served as mayor 1957–66 during a period of great crisis in the divided city's history. He was one of the forces behind the 1959 **Bad Godesberg Programme** under which the SPD renounced its Marxist heritage. He was nominated as the party's candidate for the Chancellorship in 1961, effectively becoming party leader. His major interest was in foreign policy and relations with the **German Democratic Republic (DDR)**. By the 1960s he was convinced that the **Hallstein Doctrine** and **Adenauer's** policy of strength had to be abandoned. He served as Foreign Minister in the **grand coalition** government of 1966–69, becoming Chancellor when the SPD headed a coalition government after the 1969 election. He accepted that the division of Germany was likely to remain for some time, but wished to ensure the survival of an all-German awareness, an attitude he expressed as 'two states, one nation'. These beliefs, which involved the recognition of the DDR, were the basis of the 1970–72 **Ostpolitik** negotiations, which recognized the **Oder-Neisse Line**, the special status of West Berlin, and several measures to facilitate exchanges between the two Germanies. He became the first West German leader to visit the DDR, and when he travelled to Warsaw in 1970 to sign the Ostpolitik treaty with **Poland** he knelt at the memorial of the 1943 Jewish uprising in the Warsaw ghetto against Nazi occupation. His concern with an effective Eastern policy did not weaken his commitment to Western European collective defence and integration, but he favoured a European collaboration greater than that of the existing **European Communities (EC)**. After 1972 his control of government began to weaken and he was obliged to resign as Chancellor in 1974 as a consequence of a spy scandal involving one of his own personal assistants (*see* GUIL-LAUME). Awarded the Nobel Peace Prize in 1971, he became very much an elder statesman of Germany and Europe after his resignation, although playing an active role in SPD politics where he became more and more identified with the party's left-wing. He also accepted an invitation to chair the Independent Commission on International Development Issues, whose conclusions were published in 1980 as the *Brandt Report*. He remained highly popular in his adopted city of Berlin, no more so than in 1989 when the **Berlin Wall** was demolished and the process of German reunification begun.

Bratteli, Trygve Martin. (1910–1984) Prime Minister of **Norway** 1971–72, 1973–76. He worked as an editor for **Labour Party** (DNA) journals 1934–40, and was imprisoned during the German occupation of Norway 1942–45. He entered Parliament in 1950 and served in various government ministries 1951–64. In 1965 he was elected party leader, and in 1971 became Prime Minister of a minority Labour government after a non-socialist coalition government resigned because of internal disagreements over **European Communities (EC)** membership. He took over the negotiations with the EC and promised to honour the earlier all-party agreement to hold a consultative referendum once the terms of entry were known, but warned that if the vote was negative he would treat the decision as binding, break off all negotiations with the EC, and resign. He carried out his promises after the negative result of the September 1972 referendum. Although the Labour Party lost much support in the 1973 election, primarily because of internal divisions over the EC issue, it remained the largest party. With no other alternative possible, he returned as head of a minority government. Ill-health forced his retirement in 1976 and he was succeeded as premier and party leader by Oddvar Nordli.

Brazauskas, Algirdas Mykolas. (1932–) President of **Lithuania** from 1993. Trained as a hydraulic engineer and economist and a Communist activist since 1959, he was appointed to the regional government in Lithuania in 1965, becoming First Secretary in 1988. In December 1990 he declared the Communist Party of Lithuania independent of the **Communist Party of the Soviet Union** in an attempt to enable the party to resist the growing pressure of Lithuanian nationalists. It was one of the first cracks in the facade of Soviet Communist unity, and a major one. He restructured the party as the Democratic Labour Party. Although losing the 1990 open elections, he was swept back to power in the 1992 elections, subsequently being appointed President and resigning his party offices.

Bretton Woods Agreement. An agreement by 44 countries in July 1944 to support, for 25 years, an international monetary system of stable exchange rates, with the American dollar and British sterling as supporting reserve currencies. The objectives were to make national currencies convertible on current account, encourage multilateral world trade, and avoid disruptive devaluations and financial crashes. Problems of economic reconstruction in Europe prevented the system from becoming more or less fully operational until the late 1950s. After 1960 it faced increasing difficulties, especially because of a growing USA balance of payments deficit and pressure on the reserve currencies. Already in some considerable disarray, it effectively ended in 1971 when President Richard Nixon devalued the dollar and unilaterally suspended its convertibility against gold. It was replaced by a world of floating currencies which led to much uncertainty at the international level. The **Smithsonian Agreement** and subsequent European **Snake** were two attempts to recreate some of the stability provided by Bretton Woods. The 1979 **European Monetary System (EMS)** was a more limited but successful attempt to produce a more stable exchange rate system in Western Europe.

Brezhnev Doctrine. *See* BREZHNEV, LEONID ILYICH.

Brezhnev, Leonid Ilyich. (1906–1982) First Secretary of the Soviet Communist Party 1964–82. Trained as an engineer, he worked in agricultural conservation before becoming a Communist Party official in 1938. A political commissar from 1941–45, he was elected to the Supreme Soviet in 1950, the Party Central committee in 1953, and the **Politburo** in 1957. He replaced the rather erratic **Khrushchev** as Soviet leader in 1964, returning the **USSR** to a position of conservative Communist orthodoxy. Although the excesses of the **Stalin** period were not repeated, there was severe repression of all forms of dissent, a strengthened and deadening bureaucratization accompanied by nepotism and corruption, and a stifling of necessary economic adaptation and innovation. Abroad he sought to expand the global influence of the USSR within a framework of **détente** with the USA. He did not see détente as incompatible with super-power competition, continuing to build up Soviet military power. Relations with the USA deteriorated in the late 1970s, provoking a harder line from President Ronald Reagan in 1981. He pushed the USSR into a series of adventurist policies around the world, most notably and disastrously intervening militarily in **Afghanistan** in 1979. In 1968 he declared the Brezhnev Doctrine, that the USSR had the right and duty to intervene abroad to preserve Socialism against internal and foreign threats. The Doctrine was formulated to justify the **Warsaw Pact** invasion of **Czechoslovakia** to crush the **Prague Spring** of the **Dubček** regime. While little more than a reiteration of central tenets of Soviet policy, the Doctrine alarmed many in the West because it implied a greater Soviet willingness to provide aid for supporters of the USSR in the non-Communist world, a view which seemed to gain credence from the more adventurist policies of his later years. The rigidity of the Brezhnev regime and its refusal to con-template internal change contributed to the difficulties of the USSR in the 1980s.

Britain. *See* UNITED KINGDOM.

British Army of the Rhine (BAOR). The title of the British army of occupation in Germany after 1945. After the formation of the **North Atlantic Treaty Organization (NATO)** in 1949, it was retained to describe the British contribution to NATO's land forces. Its responsibility was to defend the northern section of the **Central Front** in any engagement with **Warsaw Pact** forces. It was Britain's largest military commitment, some one-third of total troop strength. In 1954 its presence in Germany was insisted upon by **France** as an essential element of **Western European Union (WEU)**. Although there was no formal bilateral treaty between Britain and the **Federal Republic of Germany**, the two had a long-standing agreement on the size of the British forces. With the ending of the **Cold War**, agreement was reached on a significant reduction in the size of BAOR.

Brittany. A region of north-western **France** covering the four departments of Finistère, Ille et Vilaine, Morbihan and Côtes du Nord. Formally integrated into France in 1547, it retained its own distinctive Celtic culture and language, which on occasions spawned nationalist movements seeking autonomy within France or even independence. Breton nationalist move-ments have occasionally been prone to violence, but typically they have been short-lived and susceptible to factionalism, with almost no record of success in achieving their aims. The most important movement has been the Breton Democratic Union (*Union Démocratique Brétonne/Unvaniezh Demokratel Breizh – UDB*), founded in 1964 as a moderate left-wing party.

Brokdorf. The site of a proposed nuclear energy plant in Schleswig-Holstein in the **Federal Republic of Germany**. It became a focus of environmental opposition after work on the site began in 1975. Court action stopped construction in 1976, and it resumed again only in 1981. The **Social Democratic Party (SPD)** regional government refused an operating licence in 1988, but this was overruled by the national government. It was the scene of several massive anti-nuclear demonstrations in 1975–76, and again in 1981 when construction work recommenced.

Brookeborough, Lord. (1888–1973) Prime Minister of **Northern Ireland** 1943–63. Born Basil Stanlake Brooke, a scion of an old Anglo-Irish family, he succeeded to the baronetcy in 1907. He served as Commandant of the Special Constabulary in Fermanagh from 1922 before entering the Northern Ireland Parliament in 1929. He became a member of the government in 1933. He was a strong supporter of the Protestant ascendancy in the province, and the later sectarian troubles were in part due to the immobility of his lengthy premiership during which Catholics were excluded from responsibility and participation. He was a strong critic of the overtures between the two Irelands that emerged after 1963.

Bruges Group. A name given to a group of British **Conservative Party** politicians opposed to further political and economic union within the **European Communities (EC)**. It was derived from a speech by the British Prime Minister, **Thatcher**, in Bruges in September 1988 attacking the EC **Commission** for attempting to impose a bureaucratic and unrepresentative centralization upon the EC. The Group declared it would set in motion a Campaign for a Europe of Sovereign States, but its major concern was domestic party politics. It made little effort, and failed to have an impact, outside the **United Kingdom**.

Brundtland, Gro Harlem. (1939–) Prime Minister of **Norway** 1981, 1986–89, and from 1990. She entered politics from a medical background in 1974, being invited by the **Labour Party** (DNA) government to become Minister of the Environment (1974–79). Upon the resignation of Oddvar Nordli, she became party leader and prime minister in 1981, but her governments were always minority administrations. Her interests were in gender equality, health and the environment. In 1986 her government was the first in the world to have 50 per cent of the positions reserved for women. In 1985 she led a United Nations World Commission on Environment and Development. The Brundtland Report was published in 1988. She chaired the follow-up Earth Summit on the environment held in Brazil, but her reputation was slightly dented in 1993 when she announced that Norway would defy a world ban and resume whaling. She was a supporter of proposals for a **nuclear-free zone** in Northern Europe, but argued that it should include the Kola Peninsula, a heavily militarized Arctic area of the **USSR**. In 1988 she took the lead in arguing for a closer relationship between the **European Free Trade Association (EFTA)** and the **European Communities (EC)** in a **European Economic Area (EEA)**, but later accepted that Norway should consider re-applying for EC membership. However, her attempt to take Norway into the EC was defeated in a 1994 referendum.

Brussels. The capital city of **Belgium** and the home of several European organizations. In 1966 it became the political and administrative head-quarters of the **North Atlantic Treaty Organization (NATO)** and in 1957 the location of the executive and administrative offices of the **European Communities (EC)**. Because of the concentration of EC decision-making in the city, it is often popularly used as a term describing the EC as a whole. Occasionally suggestions have been made that the city, as 'capital-elect' of a potential European union, should become a 'European district' along the lines of Washington DC.

Bukovina. A region of **Ukraine**. Formerly part of the principality of Moldavia after the fourteenth century, it became part of **Romania** in 1918. Northern Bukovina was annexed by the **USSR** in 1940. Although the population is predominantly Ukrainian, after 1990 nationalist groups in Romania demanded its return.

Bulganin, Nikolai. (1895–1975) Prime Minister of the **USSR** 1955–58. He joined the Communist Party in 1917, serving in the Cheka secret police 1918–22. He was chairman of the Moscow Soviet 1931–37, and during the Second World War helped to organize the defence of the city. For his achievements he was appointed a Marshal of the Soviet Union, taking over from **Stalin** as Minister of Defence in 1946, but in March 1949 he was replaced as head of the armed forces. After Stalin's death he served as Vice-Premier under **Malenkov** until February 1955. Promoted to the premiership and Chairman of the Council of Ministers, he shared authority with **Khrushchev**, the Party Secretary. By late 1956 it was apparent that he was little more than a mouthpiece for Khrushchev, who replaced him as Prime Minister in March 1958. Five months later he was dropped from the Party Praesidium and his name added to the offenders of the **Anti-party group**. He later became Chairman of the Soviet State Bank.

Bulgaria. The modern independent state dates from 1908. In both world wars it aligned itself with Germany. Inter-war politics were turbulent and violent: a virtual peasant dictatorship under Alexandur Stamboliisky was followed by a series of short-lived civilian and military dictatorships under royal nominees. Soviet forces invaded Bulgaria in September 1944. The monarchy was abolished and a Communist-dominated **Fatherland Front** led by **Dimitrov** established a republican regime. A Communist republic was declared in 1946. After Dimitrov's death in 1949, a power struggle within the **Bulgarian Communist Party (BKP)** between Moscow-trained and 'home-grown' Communists such as Anton Yugov was won by his brother-in-law, **Chervenkov**, who faithfully followed Stalinist principles until removed from office in 1956. Although Yugov was rehabilitated in 1956 and made premier, effective power had been seized by **Zhivkov**, the Party Secretary. Yugov was dismissed from office in 1962 and also from the party central committee, allegedly for violating socialist equality through personal dishonesty and incompetence. Zhivkov, who made himself Prime Minister in 1962 and President in 1971, ruled unchallenged until 1989. Under him Bulgaria was the **USSR**'s most loyal ally in the **Warsaw Pact**. The BKP leadership pursued a policy of comprehensive state ownership, agricultural **collectivization** and central economic planning. Opposition to Zhivkov's economic policy and his attempts to enforce **Bulgarization** on the country's Turkish minority (some 10% of the population) began to emerge in the 1980s, and in 1987 he offered a series of reforms, including more self-management in industry.

In 1989 the disturbances elsewhere in Eastern Europe led to a massive anti-government demonstration on 3 November, fuelled also by a declining economic situation. One week later Zhivkov was dismissed. His successor, **Mladenov**, promised democratic reforms and an amnesty for political prisoners. After a huge demonstration in January 1990 the National Assembly voted to remove the BKP's monopoly of power. Zhivkov was arrested and the secret police disbanded. The BKP renamed itself the Bulgarian Socialist Party (BSP) before the first competitive election, held in June. The BSP narrowly won in a seven-party contest which was generally regarded as having been conducted fairly, but the new BSP government soon ran into difficulties. Mladenov, earlier elected President by the National Assembly, resigned and the BSP was forced into coalition with the **Union of Democratic Forces (SDS)** in December. After losing support in the November 1991 election, the BSP left office. It was replaced by a fragile coalition headed by the SDS which also saw its candidate, **Zhelev**, narrowly win the January 1992 presidential election. However, continuing economic problems and weak government policies resulted in an impressive electoral victory for the BSP in 1994.

Bulgarian Agrarian People's Union. (*Bŭlgarski Zemedelski Naroden Soyuz – BZNS*) A political party in **Bulgaria**. The successor of the largest pre-war party, it joined the **Fatherland Front** in 1943, but later withdrew and opposed the Communists. In 1947 it was effectively taken over by the

Bulgarian Communist Party (BKP) and used as an auxiliary organization to aid Communist control over the countryside. It was the only party, other than the BKP, permitted to exist. After the disintegration of BKP control and the dismissal of **Zhivkov**, its attempt to reassert itself as an independent democratic organization was hindered by its association with the previous regime and in 1990 it split into several factions, with most agreeing to reunite in November 1992.

Bulgarian Communist Party. (*Bŭlgarska Komunisticheska Partiya – BKP*) The Communist party of **Bulgaria**, founded in 1903 and adopting the title in 1919. It enjoyed considerable mass popularity in the inter-war period, but was forced to operate underground after 1923. The dominant element in the **Fatherland Front** after 1943, it gradually consolidated its power and had established an effective one-party system by 1947. A power struggle after the death of **Dimitrov** was won by **Chervenkov** who undertook a purge of his rivals 1949–50 with over 90,000 people being expelled from the party. The party maintained a monopoly of power until 1989 when internal factionalism began to appear. A reformist wing gained ascendancy and in 1990 it recognized the right of internal party pluralism, and reorganized itself as the Bulgarian Socialist Party (*Bulgarska Sotsialicheska Partiya*) to maintain a high degree of unity and mass support in multi-party democratic elections, managing to stay in power until 1991. It regained a parliamentary majority in 1994.

Bulgarization. The process of forced assimilation of ethnic and religious minorities pursued at intervals after 1945 in **Bulgaria**. It increased in intensity during the later years of the **Zhivkov** regime, and the severe policies pursued against the Turkish minority after 1984 were widely condemned abroad.

Bundesbank. The central bank of the **Federal Republic of Germany**. It was established in 1957 to issue banknotes, regulate the circulation of money, supply and credit control, and regulate the reserve levels of West German banks. It was unique as a central bank in its degree of autonomy from government. Its autonomy led it on occasions into disputes with the government. Because of the importance of the German economy, it came to have a substantial influence on Western European economic policy and activity, especially when the latter conflicted with its central policy concern of controlling German inflation. The most publicized dispute occurred in 1992–93 when its insistence upon high German bank rates led to severe financial and monetary strains throughout Western Europe and contributed to the disruption of the **European Monetary System (EMS)**.

Burden-Sharing. A term describing the costs of **North Atlantic Treaty Organization (NATO)** defence expenditure borne by each member state. It was perhaps the most contentious issue within NATO, primarily because the members could never agree on a formula for sharing costs. Accusations of unfairness were most prominent in the USA. It had been accepted in 1949 that the USA would bear the greatest burden because of the economic weakness of its allies, but as Western Europe recovered economically after the early 1950s it tended to reject American proposals that it should take on more of the costs of NATO. The arguments became more acrimonious after the late 1970s, and the ending of the **Cold War** did not resolve the problem. Although there was a general assumption that defence could be scaled down, the post-1989 discussions on the future and role of NATO repeated the problems of burden-sharing and the debates over the level of, and an equitable distribution between, the contributions of the member states.

Business Co-operation Centre (BCC). A liaison office established by the **Commission** of the **European Communities** (**EC**) to provide an industrial and commercial information service for both the Commission and European companies. Its major purpose was to provide to companies details of regulations passed by the EC and its Member States, and to place companies in contact with each other, but without itself seeking to persuade them to collaborate.

Butler, Richard Austen. (1902–1982) British politician. He entered Parliament in 1929, representing the **Conservative Party**, and held junior government offices 1932–40. He was responsible for the 1944 Education Act which provided the framework for the post-war English free secondary education system. Regarded as being on the moderate left of the party, he worked from 1945–51 to persuade it to accept the principles of a welfare state. Between 1951 and 1964 he served in several senior government positions, and was deputy Prime Minister 1962–64. In 1957 and 1963 he put himself forward as a contender for the party leadership, but lost on both occasions. He retired from active politics in 1965 and was made a life peer, Lord Butler of Saffron Walden.

Butskellism. A term introduced into British politics in the early 1960s. Referring to the prominent Conservative politician, **Butler**, and the Labour leader, **Gaitskell**, it was used by those who argued that there existed a huge area of common ground between the two major British parties and hence a lack of proper debate over political principles and policies.

Butter Mountain. A term that became part of the folklore of the **European Communities** (**EC**). It was popularly and critically employed to symbolize the large surpluses of produce created by the price guarantee system of the **Common Agricultural Policy** (**CAP**). Overproduction had been most pronounced in the dairy sector, and the butter surplus was one of the first to come to popular attention.

Byelorussia. *See* BELARUS.

Byrnes, James Francis. (1879–1972) USA Secretary of State 1945–47. An active supporter of the United Nations (UN), he believed that the USA and its allies should attempt to establish a working relationship with the **USSR** within the UN rather than engage in a policy of confrontation. While stressing an American commitment to Germany, he did not favour a division of the country. He was reluctant to endorse the **Truman Doctrine**, and in January 1947 he was replaced by **Marshall**.

C

Caetano, Marcello José Das Neves Alves. (1904–1981) Prime Minister of **Portugal** 1968–74. A long-term lieutenant of **Salazar**, he helped to draft the 1933 Constitution and the 1944 law integrating the overseas territories with metropolitan Portugal. He was appointed Deputy Prime Minister in 1955, but left government in 1959 to become rector of Lisbon University. He returned to politics in 1969 after the stroke which incapacitated Salazar. He attempted a limited degree of constitutional reform and liberalization, but was unwilling to consider extensive democratization, and in Africa he continued to pursue a repressive colonial policy. In 1974 he and the regime were overthrown by a military coup, the **Carnation Revolution**, and he went into exile in Brazil.

Callaghan, Leonard James. (1912–) British Prime Minister 1976–79. He was elected to Parliament in 1945 for the **Labour Party**. After 1964 he served as Chancellor of the Exchequer 1964–67 and Home Secretary 1967–70, and later as Foreign Secretary 1974–76. In 1963 he stood unsuccessfully for the party leadership. When **Wilson** suddenly announced his retirement in March 1976, Callaghan was elected party leader and became premier. Lacking an overall majority, he entered into a pact with the **Liberal Party**. Partly to satisfy Liberal demands and partly to block a nationalist challenge to his own party in those areas, he attempted to introduce devolution for **Scotland** and **Wales**. His premiership was a period of great turmoil. He had to wrestle with severe economic problems, an increasingly militant trade union movement, and the radicalization of his own party. Lukewarm towards the **European Communities (EC)**, his government was deeply divided over defence policy, with a strong minority demanding unilateral nuclear disarmament. His weak position deteriorated with the collapse of the pact with the Liberals and the widespread strikes of the 1978–79 **Winter of Discontent**. Defeated in the 1979 election, he resigned as party leader in October 1980, but remained in the House of Commons, publicly attacking his party's defence policy in the 1983 election campaign. In 1987 he accepted a life peerage, becoming Lord Callaghan of Cardiff.

Camorra. A crime syndicate in **Italy**, based in Naples and the surrounding

Campania region. Although active for over a century, it seemingly acquired an effective organization only in the 1970s, developing a close alliance with the **Mafia**. In May 1993 its alleged leader, Michele Zaza, was arrested, and investigations into political corruption revealed the existence of close links between the Camorra and senior figures within the ruling **Christian Democratic Party (DC)**.

Campaign for Nuclear Disarmament (CND). A British organization founded in 1958 to work for the abandonment of nuclear weapons and a substantial reduction in British defence spending. It grew rapidly in the 1960s to become the largest British movement of the twentieth century, attracting wide publicity through its annual Easter march and receiving support from sections of the trade unions and **Labour Party**. In 1960 the latter approved a unilateral disarmament motion, but this was ignored by the 1964–70 Labour government, and CND lost much of its impetus. It experienced a resurgence after 1977 with the **Euromissile** issue and the decision by the **North Atlantic Treaty Organization (NATO)** to install intermediate nuclear missiles in Europe. After 1979 it wielded considerable influence in the Labour Party, which in 1983 adopted unconditional unilateral disarmament as official party policy. Labour's disastrous electoral performance in 1983 was widely blamed on its unilateral stance. CND's influence waned rapidly after 1983 to the point of effective extinction. It continued to argue for full disarmament after the ending of the **Cold War** but, greatly weakened, its uncompromising opposition to Western intervention in the 1990 Gulf Crisis between Iraq and Kuwait cost it much of whatever credibility it retained.

Canary Islands. Two Spanish provinces in the Atlantic Ocean. In 1983 they became one of **Spain's** 17 autonomous regions. After democratization in 1975 they were dominated by the **Spanish Socialist Workers' Party (PSOE)**, and regional nationalist sentiment failed to develop any great strength. In 1985 three small centre-right regionalist parties formed a new alliance, the **Independent Grouping of the Canaries**, which was able to establish an electoral presence. Other nationalists joined a smaller Majority Assembly (*Asamblea Majoriera*), and a more left-wing alliance, the Canary Coalition (*Coalición Canaria*) was founded in 1992. A direct action group demanding outright independence, the Movement for the Self-Determination and Independence of the Canary Archipelago (*Movimiento para la Autodeterminación y Independencia del Archipilago Canario*) was founded in 1961. It engaged sporadically in terrorist activity, but found little popular support.

Carinthia. A province of **Austria** situated on the border with **Yugoslavia** (later **Slovenia**). Its location and the presence in it of an ethnic Slav minority contributed to a powerful conservative and nationalist sentiment in its politics. Its regional governments resisted for some time an acceptance of any linguistic provision for the ethnic minority. It was the region which launched the political career of **Haider**, and remained his major power base.

Caritas Affair. A fraudulent pyramid-selling scheme in **Romania**. Established by a businessman, Ion Stoica, in March 1992, it attracted many small investors as well as support and funding from several political parties. By the end of 1993 Caritas was unable to pay off its investors or its debts, collapsing the following May. Stoica was arrested and charged with fraud in August 1994.

Carlsson, Ingvar. (1934–) Prime Minister of **Sweden** 1986–91, and from 1994. A member of the **Social Democratic Labour Party (SAP)**, he served in several party administrative and government positions after 1958, though entering Parliament only in 1965. He was elected as deputy party leader and deputy premier in 1982. He succeeded to the premiership after the assassination of **Palme**. He had to cope with growing economic problems and accepted the need to limit or scale down Sweden's huge public sector and welfare state, an argument which created problems with members of his own party. After 1989 and the collapse of Communism in Eastern Europe he cautiously began to encourage an open discussion on a revision of foreign policy that would place less emphasis upon the traditional concept of neutrality, and in 1990 he announced an intention to apply for membership of the **European Communities (EC)**. Economic discontent led to SAP defeat in the 1991 election, and he led the party into opposition for only the second time since 1933. In opposition, he swung back to adopt a more traditional SAP economic line, and won the 1994 election.

Carmona, António Oscar de Fragoso. (1869–1951) President of **Portugal** 1927–51. A military officer promoted to general in 1922, he participated in the 1926 military coup and was appointed Prime Minister. Elected President in 1927, he helped to adopt the 'New State' constitution of 1933. He retained the presidency until his death, but was very much a figurehead of the **Salazar** regime.

Carnation Revolution. A popular name for the military coup of April 1974 in **Portugal** which overthrew the **Caetano** government. The name came from the flower worn by the revolutionary officers.

Car Party. (*Auto Partei/Parti Automobiliste – AP/PA*) A small right-wing party in **Switzerland**. It was formed in 1985 to represent the interests of motorists. Despite its specialized interests, it developed a broader right-wing populist protest profile, and in 1994 renamed itself the Freedom Party of Switzerland (*Freiheitspartei der Schweiz/Parti suisse de la Liberté – FPS/PSL*).

Carpathian Euroregion. An inter-governmental association established in February 1993 by **Hungary**, **Poland** and **Ukraine** to develop co-operation on cultural, economic and environmental issues, especially through the involvement of local councils.

Carrero Blanco, Luis. (1903–1973) Spanish politician. Joining the naval academy in 1918, he rose through the ranks to become an admiral. After 1940 he became a close ally and adviser of **Franco**. He joined the government in 1951 and became Vice-President of the Council of Ministers in 1969, taking over the responsibility of running the country. An austere individual closely associated with the technocrat wing of **Opus Dei**, he rejected all forms of liberalization and adopted a hard line on dissidence, especially in **Catalonia** and among the **Basques**. Under his direction, after 1967 censorship became stricter, judicial sentences more severe, and more organizations were declared illegal. Widely regarded as Franco's chosen political heir, he was assassinated by **Euskadi ta Askatasuna (ETA)** terrorists in 1973.

Carrillo, Santiago. (1915–) Leader of the **Communist Party of Spain (PCE)** 1956–82. An active Communist since the 1930s, he returned clandestinely to **Spain** after the death of **Franco** to urge the legalization of the PCE. He abandoned an orthodox pro-Soviet line to argue for national Communism. One of the leading proponents of **Eurocommunism**, his attempt to argue for a specific Spanish route towards Communist goals did not bring electoral success for the PCE. He was ousted as party leader in 1982, and in 1985 was expelled from the party's central committee, ostensibly because of the rigid internal control he had maintained over it. Leaving the PCE he formed two dissident groups, Communist Unity in 1985 and the Workers' Party of Spain-Communist Unity in 1986. Neither group was successful, and they refrained from participating in the **United Left** alliance formed in 1986.

Carrington, Lord. (1919–) British politician and Secretary-General of the **North Atlantic Treaty Organization (NATO)** 1984–88. A member of the **Conservative Party**, he inherited his title in the House of Lords in 1938. He served in a variety of government positions from 1951–64, and was appointed Foreign Secretary in 1979. The senior Conservative politician in the House of Lords, and much respected, he resigned from the government in 1982 after the Falklands War, accepting that his ministry had failed to detect the storm signals. In 1984 he served a four-year term as an effective political leader of NATO.

Cassis de Dijon. The popular name of a ruling (*Rewe-Zentral AG v. Bundesmonopolverwaltung für Branntwein*) by the **Court of Justice** in 1979. The decision confirmed that where a product is legally manufactured and on sale in one member state of the **European Communities (EC)**, another member state cannot prohibit its import and sale, except on grounds of risk to public health.

Catalonia. An autonomous region of **Spain**. Historically independent and economically significant, it maintained its own identity and language despite centralizing pressures. Catalan nationalism became a mass movement at the turn of the century. It was conceded extensive autonomy by the Second Republic in 1931, but the **Franco** regime removed all privileges and sought to destroy all manifestations of Catalan culture. This hardened anti-Spanish feeling, but protest rarely took on violent forms. After democratization the Spanish premier, **Suárez**, began negotiations with the previously exiled leader of the 1930s Catalan government (*Generalitat*). Autonomy was restored in 1979, with extensive legislative competence. Unlike the 1930s, Catalan nationalism now presented a united political front through **Convergence and Union (CiU)**, a broad centre-left alliance which formed the regional government in 1980. The CiU leader and regional premier, **Pujol i Soley**, continued to press for more concessions from Madrid. The strength of nationalism forced regional sections of Spanish parties to include 'Catalan' in their title and operate in a semi-autonomous manner. In 1993 a minority Socialist government in Madrid was sustained in office only with CiU support.

Catholic People's Party. (*Katholieke Volkspartij – KVP*) A political party in the **Netherlands**. It was formed in 1945 as a successor to the Catholic Electoral League (formed in 1897) and its later (1926) reorganization as the Catholic States Party. It represented the Catholic minority and enjoyed close ties with the Catholic Church. Often the largest party in the country and central in most post-war governments, it suffered an exceptional electoral decline after the mid-1960s, and in 1975 threw in its lot with the two major Dutch Protestant parties to form the **Christian Democratic Appeal (CDA)**.

Cavaco Silva, Aníbal. (1939–) Prime Minister of **Portugal** 1985–95. An academic and banker, he was appointed Minister of Finance and Planning in 1980. A member of the centrist **Social Democratic Party (PSD)**, he was elected party leader in May 1985, becoming Prime Minister of a minority government after the October election. In July 1987 he led the PSD to the first absolute parliamentary majority since 1979. He successfully brought the factional tendencies of the party under control and used his authority to pursue a policy of economic liberalization and modernization.

Ceauşescu, Nicolae. (1918–1989) President of **Romania** 1967–89. Joining the banned Communist Party in 1936, he was responsible for organizing its youth section. With the establishment of a Communist republic, he became a protégé of **Gheorghiu-Dej**. After the latter's death in 1965, he succeeded his mentor as Party Secretary. Defeating a challenge from the pro-Soviet chief of the security forces, he was elected head of state in 1967, and re-elected when the constitution was amended in 1974. He was a strong critic of Soviet policy. Stressing the national sovereignty of each Communist state, he refused to participate in and denounced the Soviet occupation of **Czechoslovakia** in 1968. In 1984 he refused to follow the **USSR** boycott of the Los Angeles Olympic Games, but despite his criticisms he made no effort to leave the **Council for Mutual Economic Assistance (Comecon)** or the **Warsaw Pact**. His criticism of the USSR made him, for a while, a popular figure in the West where Romania received favoured nation status. His nationalistic line revived Romanian national pride, but he increasingly tolerated abuse of the 1952 constitutional guarantees to ethnic minorities. The Magyar communities of **Transylvania** were a particular target of oppression. His rule became increasingly personalized and idiosyncratic, and by the 1980s he and his family had turned Romania into a personal fiefdom characterized by brutal oppression, an extremely callous secret police, nepotism, and extravagant monuments of personal aggrandizement. Initially, Romania remained calm in the unrest which swept Eastern Europe in 1989, but massive protests suddenly erupted in December, toppling the regime almost overnight. He and his wife were seemingly surprised by the sudden turn of events. They fled from Bucharest, but were arrested and summarily executed on Christmas Day. The full extent of his regime's brutality and extravagance only emerged after his death.

Cecchini Report. Published in 1988 by a committee of experts under the chairmanship of Paolo Cecchini on the problems facing the **European Communities (EC)** in establishing an **internal market**. Entitled *1992: The European Challenge – Benefits of a Single Community*, it was based upon an analysis of economic and financial data bases and interviews with some 11,000 companies across the EC. It outlined the obstacles – national practices, regulations and standards – that would need to be removed, and estimated that they cost the EC some 5 per cent of its gross domestic product (GDP).

Celtic League. A cultural and political organization founded in 1961 to foster the exchange of ideas and to promote co-operation among Celtic nationalist associations and societies. Its objective was to campaign on issues affecting Celtic culture and society in **France**, **Ireland** and the **United Kingdom**, and to support non-violent movements that sought political autonomy.

Central Committee for the Navigation of the Rhine. Europe's oldest international organization, founded originally in 1816 to implement the principle of free navigation of Europe's international rivers adopted by the 1815 Congress of Vienna. More specific rules restricting rights to the riparian states were laid down in the 1831 Mainz Convention and the 1868 Mannheim Convention. Based in **Strasbourg**, it has powers of binding arbitration in disputes among users of the river.

Central European Co-operation Committee. *See* VISEGRAD TRI-
ANGLE.

Central European Free Trade Agreement. *See* VISEGRAD TRI-
ANGLE.

Central European Initiative. *See* PENTAGONALE.

Central Front. The major confrontation line between the forces of the
North Atlantic Treaty Organization (NATO) and the **Warsaw Pact**, and
the most intense concentration of weapons and troops in the world.
Essentially the border between the two Germanies, it was the one place
where American and Soviet troops directly faced each other. NATO
contingents were drawn from all member states of the alliance, and were
under the command of **SACEUR**. The Warsaw Pact forces were made up
primarily of the **Group of Soviet Forces, Germany (GSGF)**, supported by
the East German army. While the Warsaw Pact held a numerical advantage,
it was insufficient to guarantee victory. One of NATO's problems was that it
lacked strong defensive fortifications along the Front due to the reluctance of
the **Federal Republic of Germany** to allow anything that might undermine
its view that the two Germanies were two halves of a single country. With
German reunification in 1990, the disbanding of the Warsaw Pact, and the
phased withdrawal of Soviet forces from German soil, the Front ceased to
exist.

Centre Alliance. (*Porrozumienie Centrum*) A Christian Democratic party
in **Poland**, founded in 1990 by members of **Solidarity**. Originally a
supporter of **Wałęsa**, it broke with him in 1992. With little mass base of its
own, it agreed in 1994 to form part of the **Alliance for Poland**.

Centre Democrats. (*Centrumsdemokraterne – CD*) A small centrist party
in **Denmark**. It was formed in 1973 as a result of a right-wing secession
from the **Social Democratic Party (SD)**. It objected to the leftward drift of
the Social Democrats and a perceived left-wing influence in the public
sector, especially in communications and the media. Without a clear
programme, the nature of its mass support changed at each election, making
it more a receptacle for protest or floating votes. While generally moderate
right in sympathy, it was not averse to supporting left-wing parties on
specific issues.

Centre Democrats. (*Centrum-Democraten – CD*) A small right-wing
party in the **Netherlands**. It was formed in 1980 as a breakaway group from
the Centre Party (*Centrumpartij*), which it soon replaced as the major voice
of the extreme right. It campaigned almost exclusively on an uncompromising anti–immigration programme.

**Centre for Co-operation with European Economies in Transi-
tion (CCEET).** A body established in 1990 by the **Organization for
Economic Co-operation and Development (OECD)** to serve as a link

between the OECD and the new democracies of Eastern Europe. It was intended to provide and assist in relaying advice, training and technical expertise in a range of economic and financial areas to the new regimes in order to help the development of market economies and pluralist democratic systems. *See also* GROUP OF TWENTY-FOUR, OPERATION PHARE.

Centre for Information and Documentation (CID). An agency of the **European Atomic Energy Community (EURATOM)**. It was established to act as a clearing house for the collection, collation and dissemination of information on developments and practices within the field of nuclear energy.

Centre for the Development of Industry (CDI). An agency of the **European Communities (EC)** established under the terms of the third **Lomé Convention** of 1984. Located in **Brussels**, its brief was to assist the Third World signatories of the Convention (the **African, Caribbean and Pacific (ACP) States**) to develop an industrial strategy, and to sponsor joint initiatives between ACP states and European countries.

Centre of Social Democrats. (*Centre des Démocrates Sociaux – CDS*) A centrist Christian Democratic party in **France**, founded in 1976. It agreed in 1978 to form a moderate electoral alliance, the **Union for French Democracy**, along with other non-Gaullist parties. Although always willing to consider co-operation, it was wary of losing its identity within a broad centrist grouping, and in 1988 its leader, Pierre Méhaignerie, insisted on forming a separate centrist group, the Union of the Centre (*Union du Centre – UDC*), in the National Assembly.

Centre Party. (*Keskustapuolue – KP*) The major centrist party in **Finland**. Founded in 1906 as the Agrarian League, its primary objective was the defence of farming interests. It changed its name in 1965 to signal an attempt to broaden its electoral base as a response to a decline of the agricultural population, a strategy which brought some modest success. It participated in and frequently led coalition governments. It occupied a strategic position in the centre of the political spectrum, and was willing to entertain co-operation with parties both to its left and its right. It also benefited from the view that it accepted post-1945 realities and was trusted by the **USSR**, a perception helped by the long presidential rule of one of its leaders, **Kekkonen**. It suffered an electoral blow in 1962 with the secession of the **Finnish Rural Party**, but more or less held its ground until 1980, after which it went into decline and largely lost its role as the hinge of the political system, although regaining some of the lost ground after 1990.

Centre Party. (*Senterpartiet – SP*) A small agrarian party in **Norway**, founded in 1920 and changing its name to SP in 1959 as a response to the decline in the size of the agricultural electorate. A centrist movement which had some interests in common with the leading **Labour Party (DNA)**, it moved after the mid-1950s more to the right and to consider more seriously co-operation with the other non-socialist parties. It served in coalition governments in 1963 and again from 1965–71 when its leader, Per Borten, was Prime Minister. It opposed Norwegian membership in the **European Communities (EC)**. In 1981 it supported a minority **Conservative Party** government, formally becoming part of the administration in 1983. After the late 1970s it generally allied itself with the Conservatives, but its greater interest in public funding for agriculture made it wary of too close an association and was a source of tension between the two. In the 1990s it again strongly opposed EC membership, taking the lead in the campaign which culminated in the 1994 referendum, a stand which brought it major electoral gains in 1993.

Centre Party. (*Centerpartiet – C*) A centrist party in **Sweden** formed in 1910 as the Farmers' Union Party to defend agrarian interests. Its change of name in 1957 reflected its concern about relying only upon a declining agricultural base for electoral support, and it did achieve some limited success in attracting urban voters. From the 1930s to the 1960s it was an occasional junior partner of **Social Democratic Labour Party (SAP)** governments. It later moved to the right, and in 1976–82 led a three-party non-socialist coalition. The three were uneasy partners, with particular tension over the Centre's strong opposition to any form of nuclear power. Its level of support declined after 1982, but it remained generally in favour of non-socialist co-operation.

Centre Union. (*Unione di Centro – UDC*) A small moderate party in **Italy**. It was formed in 1993 by reformist elements of several centrist secular parties in the wake of the disintegration of the traditional party system caused by corruption scandals. In 1994 it agreed to form part of the **Freedom Alliance**.

Ceuta and Melilla. Two separate enclaves on the North African coast retained by **Spain** when Morocco gained independence in 1956. They have repeatedly been claimed by Morocco. The devolutionary structure adopted by Spain after 1975 did not extend to the enclaves which remained part of the Cadiz (Ceuta) and Málaga (Melilla) provinces. Tensions increased in 1985 because of an aliens law which required all foreigners in Spain to register with the authorities, and in 1986 there began demonstrations demanding greater autonomy.

Chaban-Delmas, Jacques. (1915–) Prime Minister of **France** 1969–72. A leader in the **Resistance movement**, he served as a minister in **de Gaulle's** 1945 government. He entered Parliament in 1946 as a **Radical Republican and Radical Socialist** deputy, and was elected mayor of Bordeaux in 1947. He led the rump Gaullist group (*Républicains Sociaux*) in Parliament 1953–56 after the demise of the **Rally of the French People**, and served in coalition governments in 1954–55 and 1956–58. He realigned himself with de Gaulle after the establishment of the **Fifth French Republic**, and served as President of the National Assembly 1958–69. On the liberal wing of the Gaullist movement, he was appointed Prime Minister by **Pompidou** in 1969, but was not permitted to take over the party leadership. He was dismissed in 1972 because of worries that his liberalizing programme was going too far. In 1974 he unsuccessfully contested the presidential election.

Chancellor Democracy. A term coined in the 1950s to describe a perceived deviance in the **Federal Republic of Germany** from the norms of parliamentary democracy. It was used critically to express fears that too much power was concentrated in the hands of the Chancellor. Subsequent developments demonstrated that the fears were exaggerated. The term was appropriate, if at all, only for the first part of the **Adenauer** era, and arose from a particular set of circumstances: Adenauer's own autocratic personality and its appeal for the electorate of the day, his total domination of his own party, and the opportunities which the weak international status of West Germany gave him to act as a statesman.

Channel Islands. A group of islands in the English Channel, close to the French coast. They are dependencies of the British Crown, though not part of the **United Kingdom**. They are politically constituted as two bailiwicks (Guernsey and Jersey) and have their own constitutions, legislatures and legal–administrative systems. The British monarch appoints a lieutenant-governor as the royal representative in each bailiwick, and the British government has accepted responsibility for defence and foreign affairs.

Channel Tunnel Treaty. Signed by **France** and the **United Kingdom** on 12 February 1986 at Canterbury. It provided for government collaboration on the construction of a rail link under the English Channel. Ideas for a land-link between Britain and France date back to 1802, and the Treaty represented the 27th scheme since 1881. It was ratified in July 1987, with completion scheduled for June 1993. The project was plagued by technical problems, rising costs and, in Britain, public objections to the planned new rail links to the tunnel. Although the first engine to pass completely through the tunnel did so in June 1993, the completion date was delayed by a year and a full service began only in late 1994.

Charter 77. A human rights movement in **Czechoslovakia**. Inspired by the 1975 agreement of the **Conference on Security and Co-operation in Europe (CSCE)** on human rights, the Charter was signed in January 1977 by some 250 academics, clergy and intellectuals. It appealed to the Czech government to respect the United Nations Declaration of Human Rights as well as the CSCE agreement. Over the next decade its members were persecuted and imprisoned by the state. In the 1980s it extended its critique from human rights to address broad social, political and economic issues.

Although never developing a mass base, it survived to help inspire the democratization of Czechoslovakia. Its members helped found **Civic Forum** in November 1989, which spearheaded the **Velvet Revolution** that ended the Communist system of government. It agreed to dissolve itself in 1992, stating that its historic role had been completed.

Charter for a New Europe. *See* CHARTER OF PARIS.

Charter of Fundamental Social Rights. Prepared in 1989 by the **Commission** as part of the plans for an **internal market** for the **European Communities (EC)**. Later more popularly known as the Social Charter, it was intended to codify in general terms what the EC had already initiated plus what the Commission argued would be desirable new goals in the area of social and employment policy. It outlined a code of practice aimed primarily at the rights of workers. It was not a particularly revolutionary document and was generally welcomed by all Member States bar the **United Kingdom**, which objected to several of its provisions. Because of British objections, it was made, as the Social Chapter, only a Protocol of the **Treaty on European Union**, with Britain winning the right to opt out of its key provisions, an unsatisfactory arrangement that many thought would be unworkable.

Charter of Paris. A document, also known as the Charter for a New Europe, signed at the meeting of the **Conference on Security and Co-operation in Europe (CSCE)** in Paris in November 1990. The signatories, declaring that 'the era of confrontation and division of Europe has ended', agreed to support the promotion and defence of democracy, human rights and a free market economy. It also established new CSCE structures for settling disputes by peaceful means. The document was formally held to mark the end of the **Cold War**.

Chechnya. A region of **Russia**, and home of a Muslim ethnic group, located on the country's southern border. The Chechens were deported to Asian Kazakhstan in 1944 by **Stalin**, who accused them of collaborating with Nazi Germany. Their return to their Caucasian homelands was sanctioned in 1957, but not completed until 1966. In November 1991, during the last months of the **USSR**, it unilaterally declared its independence under the leadership of Dzhokar Dudayev, a former Soviet bomber pilot, who had been elected President in October in a poll regarded as illegal by the USSR. When Russian troops were sent in to restore order, the Chechens threatened terrorist retaliation in Moscow, and the troops were withdrawn. Boycotted by Russia, and with war-torn **Georgia** its only other neighbour, the region's economy collapsed, but despite the refusal of international organizations to recognize it, it continued to refuse to renounce its declaration of independence. In December 1994 the Russian President, **Yeltsin**, sent armed forces back into the province, after attempts to engineer a coup from inside had failed. The Chechens offered strong resistance, prolonging the conflict and making it more bloody.

Chemical Warfare Convention (CWC). A major objective of the **Forty Nations Conference on Disarmament (CD)**. Linked to the United Nations, but separate from other bodies or organizations, the CD first met in **Geneva** in 1983 to seek agreement on a CWC that would ban all preparations for and use of chemical warfare. While broad agreement was reached in principle, little progress on the finer details was achieved until 1992, with problems of verification remaining a stumbling block. With the ending of the **Cold War**, a *de facto* agreement in Europe was widely assumed to exist.

Chernenko, Konstantin Ustinovich. (1911–1985) Secretary-General of the Soviet Communist Party 1984–85. He joined the party in 1931 and pursued a career as a party administrator, mainly in propaganda and agitation. He was moved to Moscow in 1950, joining the party's Central Committee in 1965, the Secretariat in 1976 and the **Politburo** in 1978. An associate of **Brezhnev** since 1950, his later advancement was largely due to Brezhnev's backing and patronage. After 1978 he was widely seen as Brezhnev's favoured successor as Soviet leader but did not succeed to the position until after the not unexpected death of **Andropov** in February 1984. The oldest man elected as Soviet leader, his age and colourless character made him very much a transitional choice that might maintain some stability and continuity, and a compromise between the supporters and opponents of Andropov's reform programme. With little experience of leadership, and suffering from ill-health, he made few positive contributions to Soviet life, although the process of reform was largely stalled. He made his last public appearance in December 1984, dying three months later.

Chernobyl. The location in **Ukraine** of a Soviet nuclear power station, some 80 miles north of the capital, Kiev. It was the scene of the world's worst nuclear disaster when a steam turbine went out of control on 26 April 1986, resulting in the overheating and destruction of a graphite-moderated reactor. Large quantities of radiation were also released. Some 250 people died as a direct result of the accident, and some 130,000 were evacuated from the surrounding areas, where the land was permanently contaminated. An international volunteer force of doctors flew in to help the victims. Radioactive fallout affected much of Europe, especially Scandinavia and upland regions of Britain, and it extended into Siberia and Asia Minor. In July 1987 the senior executives of the plant were found guilty of criminal negligence and sentenced to imprisonment with hard labour. The accident was a major blow to the claims for, and prestige of, Soviet science and technology, and severely disrupted the nuclear energy programme of the Soviet bloc. More generally, it stimulated a wider debate on nuclear safety, and persuaded many European governments to review their nuclear development plans. In 1994 the **European Union (EU)** agreed to provide Ukraine with technical and financial aid to close down its remaining reactors, and to construct more modern Western-designed reactors elsewhere.

Chervenkov, Vulko. (1900–1980) Prime Minister of **Bulgaria** 1950–56. A founder member of the **Bulgarian Communist Party (BKP)**, he fled to the **USSR** in 1925, becoming a member of the Soviet security police network. He returned to Bulgaria in 1946. Immediately joining the **Politburo**, he was the chief instigator, after the death of **Dimitrov,** of the trial and execution of **Kostov**. The most loyal lieutenant of **Stalin** in Eastern Europe, he became both Party General Secretary and Prime Minister, using his absolute control to enforce a rigid policy of Stalinization and to purge the party of 'home grown' Communists. As a result of the new emphasis on collegiality in the USSR after the death of Stalin, he was forced to give up the party secretariat in 1954, handing it over to **Zhivkov**. He misjudged the shifting power balance in Moscow, patronizing **Malenkov** rather than **Khrushchev**. Two months after the latter's denunciation of Stalin, he was obliged to resign the premiership in April 1956, despite remaining relatively popular within the BKP. His successor was his rival and home-grown Communist, Anton Yugov. He nevertheless retained government and party positions, but in November 1961 was stripped of all appointments after being accused of Stalinist 'mistakes and vicious methods', and of fostering a personality cult. In November 1962 he was expelled from the party. His party membership was restored without fanfare in 1969, but he lived in obscurity until his death.

Cheysson, Claude. (1920–) French diplomat and politician. After serving as a long-time career diplomat, he was appointed to the **Commission** of the **European Communities (EC)**, serving 1973–81 and 1985–88, responsible respectively for development aid and for Mediterranean policy and North–South relations. On both occasions he was heavily involved in the development of the **Lomé Conventions**. A highly respected figure, he also served as French Foreign Minister 1981–84. After his second term of office in **Brussels**, he was elected to the **European Parliament (EP)**.

Cheysson Facility. A Financial Co-operation Scheme established by the **European Communities (EC)**. Named after the French Commissioner, **Cheysson**, responsible for its inauguration, it was set up to offer venture capital for EC industrial companies wishing to expand their operations in Asia and Latin America. To qualify, companies had to present a detailed plan that incorporated a commitment to co-operate with Asian or Latin American enterprises.

Chirac, Jacques René. (1932–) Prime Minister of **France** 1974–76, 1986–88, and President from 1995. From a civil service background, he became a member of President **Pompidou's** personal staff. In 1974 he was selected by the new President, **Giscard d'Estaing**, to form a government. He also became leader of the Gaullist Union of Democrats for the Republic (UDR) after the poor performance of the Gaullist candidate, **Chaban-Delmas**, in the 1974 presidential election. He resigned as premier in 1976, claiming that Giscard d'Estaing would not allow him the freedom to do the job properly, and set about reorganizing the UDR as the **Rally for the Republic (RPR)**. In 1977 he gained a further power base when he was elected mayor of Paris. When Giscard lost the 1981 presidential election, he was left more or less unchallenged as the leading spokesman of the French right, with the RPR as the largest non-socialist party. When the RPR won a majority in the 1986 parliamentary election, he was appointed Prime Minister by **Mitterrand**. The 1986–88 period of **cohabitation** was an uneasy one, not least because the two men were rivals, with Chirac intending to challenge Mitterrand for the presidency in 1988. When Mitterrand won the election, he immediately dissolved the legislature, and in the resulting parliamentary election the RPR lost its majority. In opposition, Chirac still claimed to be the major voice of the right, but when the RPR and its allies won the 1993 parliamentary election, he declined to consider government office, fearing that a repeat performance of what had happened in 1986–88 – which he believed had demonstrated that the prime minister could not compete in prestige and power with the presidency – might damage his chances in the 1995 presidential contest. However, in supporting the nomination of his colleague, **Balladur**, for the premiership, he created a potential rival for the leadership of the French right and its presidential nomination. He successfully overcame Balladur's challenge and went on to win the presidency in 1995.

Christian Democracy. A political ideology seeking to combine liberal conceptions of political democracy and individual rights with Christian views on social and economic justice. It has been primarily, but not exclusively, associated with the Catholic Church. It emerged in the nine-teenth century as a reaction to individualism, laissez-faire economics and **anticlericalism**. With the Catholic hierarchy playing an active organiz-ational and directive role in many countries, it sought the establishment of religious socio-economic organizations, especially trade unions, and the formation of political parties for religious defence. A centrist force, it combined traditional conservative values on family life and moral issues with more progressive views on social welfare programmes and state intervention in the economy. It received an additional boost after 1945 as a reaction to Fascism and an ideological counterweight to Communism. It acquired considerable electoral strength and dominated government in many countries in Western Europe. Decline began in the 1960s as a result of a general erosion of political ideologies, secularization and international stability. The rate of decline seemed to stabilize around 1980, but by then most parties had begun the process of projecting themselves as moderate and pragmatic centre-right movements in which Christian Democratic ideology would have a place, but not a dominant one.

Christian Democratic Appeal. (*Christen Democratisch Appel – CDA*) The major centre-right party in the **Netherlands**. It was founded in 1975 as an electoral alliance of the three largest confessional parties, the **Catholic People's Party**, **Anti-Revolutionary Party** and **Christian Historical Union**, all of which had suffered electoral decline since the early 1960s. In 1980 the three agreed to merge in a single party. The strategy worked: electoral support was stabilized, and the CDA continued the tradition of its predecessors by participating in, and usually dominating, all government coalitions from 1980 to 1994.

Christian Democratic Community Party. (*Kristdemokratiska Samhällspartiet – KdS*) A small centre-right party in **Sweden**. It was founded as the Christian Democratic Union (*Kristen Demokratisk Samling*) in 1964 as a protest against permissive legislation and a proposed reduction in the level of religious education in schools. Associated to some extent with more fundamentalist elements within the state Lutheran Church, it enjoyed only limited electoral success, but in 1991 was invited to support a non-socialist coalition government.

Christian Democratic Movement. (*Krest'ansk-demokratické Hnutie – KDH*) A small political party in **Slovakia**, founded in 1990 and forming part of the subsequent coalition government. Its support declined considerably after 1992.

Christian Democratic National Peasants' Party. (*Partidul Naţional Ţărănesc-Creştin şi Democrat*) A political party in **Romania**, founded in 1990 by a merger of the historic National Peasants' Party (formed in 1869 and banned 1947–89) and a new Christian Democrat formation. Broadly centre-right in orientation, it claimed to represent agrarian interests.

Christian Democratic Party. (*Křesťansko-Demokratická Strana – KDS*) A political party in the **Czech Republic**. It was formed in 1989 as a broadly Christian Democrat social party, but with a strong free market economy programme. Its success was limited and in 1992 it aligned itself with the Civic Democratic Party (*see* CIVIC FORUM).

Christian Democratic Party. (*Partito della Democrazia Cristiana – DC*) The largest party in **Italy** from 1945 to 1993. Founded in 1945 on the basis of the pre-Mussolini Popular Party, it was strongly backed by and could use the vast organizational network of the Catholic Church. Under the skilful leadership of **de Gasperi**, it quickly established itself as the major bulwark against the large **Italian Communist Party (PCI)**, acceptable to moderates, conservatives and practising Catholics. It was a perpetual member of government after 1945, dominating every administration, and on only two occasions, 1981–82 and 1983–87, not providing the premier. However, it never succeeded in winning an absolute majority of votes or seats, and its best performance was in 1948. It was in essence an alliance of several principled and personal factions, and to a great extent it was the factional competition which decided at any one time the external orientation of the party and the partners in government it sought. Its long tenure of office blurred the distinction between party and public office, with **clientelism**, **lottizzazione** and **partitocrazia** being prominent features. Attempts by several party secretaries in the 1970s and 1980s to modernize and reform the party were all blocked by entrenched interests. In the 1970s it began to distance itself from the Catholic Church as a result of ongoing secularization and its humiliating defeat in the 1970 referendum on the legalization of divorce, and in 1976 many of its leaders were prepared to consider the PCI offer of a **historic compromise**. Its strength continued to decline in the 1980s and it was obliged to accept non-DC premiers in 1981 and 1983. The reformist attack on the immobility and corruption of the political system that swept Italy in the 1990s inevitably had the DC as one of its major targets, and with the ending of the **Cold War** it was unable to use the anti-Communist card. Several of its leading personalities and supporters were indicted for fraud and corruption, and as its support collapsed in local elections in 1993, it sought a programme of internal reform and changed its name to the Popular Party (*Partito Populare*). In the 1994 election, however, the new party was reduced to a tiny fragment of its former strength. A right-wing faction opposed the reconstruction, and formed the Christian Democratic Centre (*Centro Cristiano Democratico – CCD*).

Christian Democratic Party. (*Krikščionių Demokratų Partija – KDP*) A small political party in **Lithuania**. Originally founded in 1904, it was proscribed from the 1920s to 1989. Highly conservative, it had only limited electoral success.

Christian Democratic People's Party. (*Kereszténydemokrata Néppárt – KDNP*) A political party in **Hungary**. Formed in 1989, it claimed to be the successor of the moderate Democratic People's Party, proscribed by the Communist regime in 1949. Conservative in orientation, it aligned itself with centre-right alliances after 1990.

Christian Democratic People's Party. (*Christlich-demokratische Volkspartei/Parti Démocrate-Chrétien*) A major centre-right party in **Switzerland**. Founded in 1912 as the Catholic Conservative Party, it retitled itself the Conservative Christian Social Party in 1957 before adopting the current name in 1971. Essentially a Catholic party, its historical roots and much of its present strength have lain in the more rural German-speaking areas.

Traditionally an advocate for the defence of cantonal rights, it has been in government since the turn of the century, a member since 1945 of the semi-permanent four-party coalition that has governed the country.

Christian Democratic Union. *See* CZECHOSLOVAK PEOPLE'S PARTY.

Christian Democratic Union. (*Christlich Demokratische Union – CDU*) The major centre-right party in the **Federal Republic of Germany**. Regional Christian Democratic parties had been licensed by the occupying Allies in 1945, but these did not formally merge into the CDU, forming Germany's first cross-denominational religious party, until 1950, one year after the formation of the republic. Although the bulk of its electorate was initially Catholic, Protestants were prominent within the party leadership and organization. Under **Adenauer** it rapidly established itself as a conservative party committed to a free market economy, and in 1957 became the first and only German party to win an absolute majority. It was the dominant element in coalition governments 1949–69 and again after 1982. It reflected its regional federalist origins for some time, although in the 1950s these were partially concealed by the authority of Adenauer. His successors after 1963 experienced difficulties in controlling the party, but greater discipline was achieved after 1976 under the leadership of **Kohl**. The religious basis of its support began to decline in the 1960s as it steadily became a more mainstream conservative party. Strongly committed to the Western alliance, it was hostile to the **German Democratic Republic (DDR)**, upholding the **Hallstein Doctrine** until 1969 and initially opposing the **Ostpolitik** process. In power when the DDR collapsed in 1989, its leadership pushed strongly for immediate German reunification. This brought its rewards in the ex-DDR territories in the 1990 all-German election, although its support in the old Federal Republic declined. The later economic problems caused by reunification led to it forfeiting much support in both parts of Germany, and it clung on only narrowly in the 1994 election. A separate CDU survived in the DDR as an auxiliary adjunct to the **Socialist Unity Party (SED)**. It reasserted its independence after November 1989, and after successes in the 1990 DDR election merged with the western party.

Christian Democratic Union of Latvia. (*Latvijas Kristīgo Demokrātu Savienība – LKDS*) A small political party in **Latvia**, founded in 1991. More conservative than most Christian Democratic parties, it enjoyed only limited electoral success.

Christian Historical Union. (*Christelijk-Historische Unie – CHU*) A Protestant political party in the **Netherlands** formed in 1908. It drew its support primarily from more conservative elements of the Dutch Reformed Church, but was never as successful as its religious competitors – with whom it often collaborated in government – in mobilizing support from its religious group. Its support, already small, began to collapse after the early 1960s, and in 1975 it became part of the inter-confessional **Christian Democratic Appeal**.

Christian National Union. (*Zjednoczenie Chrześcijańsko Narodowe – ZChN*) A political party in **Poland**. Formed in 1991, and originally entitled the Catholic Electoral Action (*Wyborcza Akcja Katolicka*), it represented conservative Catholicism and traditional Polish nationalism. Although it was close to, and semi-officially endorsed by, the Catholic Church, its electoral success fell markedly after 1991, and in 1994 it joined the **Alliance for Poland**.

Christian People's Party. (*Christelijke Volkspartij – CVP*) The major party in **Flanders**. It was previously the Flemish branch of the federal Belgian **Christian Social Party**, which split into distinct Flemish and French-speaking organizations in 1968. Larger and generally more con-servative than its Walloon counterpart, it had been the major component of the largest political grouping in **Belgium**. While it aggressively defended Flemish interests and worked for greater autonomy for Flanders within Belgium, it simultaneously tended to dominate in national governments, providing the leadership of most coalition governments after 1968.

Christian People's Party. (*Kristeligt Folkeparti – KrF*) A small centre-right party in **Denmark**. It was formed in 1970 as a reaction to permissive legislation, specifically opposing the decriminalization of abortion and pornography. With roots in the Evangelical Lutheran Church and non-conformist sects, it succeeded after 1973 in consolidating a presence in the Parliament, where its behaviour was pragmatic and issue-oriented as long as its basic religious and moral concerns were not involved, and it was a supporter of most non-socialist governments on at least an *ad hoc* basis.

Christian People's Party. (*Kristelig Folkeparti – KF*) A religious party in **Norway**. Founded in the western part of the country in 1933, it established itself as a national organization after 1945. Strongly concerned with moral issues, reflecting its base in more fundamentalist elements of the Lutheran Church, it was wary of losing its independence and only slowly began to entertain the idea of formal collaboration with other non-socialist parties. It served in non-socialist coalition governments after 1963, but after 1986 relationships with its potential partners became more strained.

Christian Social Party. *Parti Social Chrétien – PSC*) A Catholic-based party in **Belgium**. It was founded in 1945 as a successor to the pre-war Catholic Party. The largest party in the country 1945–68, it headed coalition governments throughout the period, except for 1954–58. Its defence of religious interests ended with the 1958 **Schools Pact** which largely gave the Church what it wished. The PSC was organized federally, with autonomous organizations in **Flanders** and **Wallonia**. The degree of autonomy increased in 1965 as a result of growing regional and linguistic pressures. In 1968 a dispute over Leuven (Louvain) University served as a linguistic catalyst that split the PSC into two separate bodies. The French-speaking Walloon section retained the PSC title. The diminished PSC found itself considerably weaker than its Flemish counterpart, the **Christian People's Party**, and in an inferior position in Wallonia. Although its potential for influence in both national and regional politics was limited, it continued to be a pragmatic party, dropping its commitment to a unitary state and accepting the need for greater regional autonomy and willing to entertain collaboration. It served in several government coalitions.

Christian Social People's Party. (*Chrëschtlech-Sozial Vollekspartei/ Parti Chrétien Social – CSV/PCS*) The major conservative party in **Luxembourg**. Formed as the Party of the Right in 1914, it adopted its present title in 1945. Consistently the largest party in the country, it has been the dominant partner in every government coalition since 1919, except for a brief period in opposition 1974–79, and providing all premiers bar one since 1945.

Christian Social Union. (*Christlich-Soziale Union – CSU*) A conservative party in **Bavaria**. Formed in 1945 under licence by the occupation Allies, it refused to merge into the **Christian Democratic Union (CDU)** national party structure in 1950. Strongly defensive of Bavarian interests within the **Federal Republic of Germany**, in national politics it coordinated its activities with the CDU, serving in every CDU-led government after 1949. In return the CDU refrained from fielding candidates in Bavaria. Because the CSU was more conservative than its partner, there was occasionally tension between the two, most seriously in 1976 when its leader, **Strauss**, threatened to turn it into a national conservative party in competition with the CDU. It established itself as the leading party in Bavaria after 1945, always forming the regional government apart from a brief spell in the 1950s. After 1960 it became totally dominant, successfully combining economic modernization policies with the protection of Bavarian interests and identity. Long dominated by and associated with the personality of Strauss, it suffered some internal conflicts and loss of support after his death in 1988.

Churchill, Winston Leonard Spencer. (1874–1965) British Prime Minister 1940–45, 1951–55. Elected to Parliament in 1900, he had a long and distinguished parliamentary and ministerial career before becoming Prime Minister of the war-time coalition government in 1940. Since the 1930s he had commented upon the necessity and value of European cooperation. His war-time speeches on the theme made him a symbol to and inspiration for those who believed that post-war reconstruction had to mean European union. After his **Conservative Party** was defeated in the 1945 election, he continued to stress the needs of the future Europe. He warned of the dangers of an aggressive **USSR**, and urged an integrated defence of Western Europe to which the USA would be fully committed. His 1946 phrase '**iron curtain**', became the standard description of the division of Europe. While active in the **Congress of Europe** and supportive of the **European Movement**, he did not see the **United Kingdom** as part of a united Europe. Like the 1945–51 **Labour Party** government, he gave greater priority to the American relationship and the **Commonwealth of Nations**. His views and policy did not change when he returned as Prime Minister in 1951. Although not particularly interested in domestic policy, his second premiership coincided with a significant recovery of the economy. In failing health and suffering a stroke in 1953, he reluctantly retired from political life in 1955. He was knighted in 1953, the same year that he received the Nobel Prize for Literature for his historical writings. In 1963 he was uniquely granted honorary American citizenship by the USA Congress. He was also honoured with a state funeral in recognition of his war-time leadership.

Church Tax. A tax paid in the **Federal Republic of Germany** by all members of a church. It is levied as a surcharge upon income tax, collected by regional (*Land*) tax authorities, and distributed to churches on the basis of the denominational affiliation of taxpayers. People who are not members of a church are exempt from the tax. The amount of income involved has been substantial and the tax has been controversial partly because the sums involved are affected by changes in fiscal policy and partly because it has made the churches dependent upon the state.

Ciampi, Carlo Azeglio. (1921–) Prime Minister of **Italy** 1993–94. He had served as the Governor of the Bank of Italy since 1979, successfully establishing its independence from government and developing a reputation for honesty and integrity. As the reformist movement gained momentum and toppled the **Amato** government, he was invited to become premier. Italy's first non-party Prime Minister of the twentieth century, he formed a broad coalition government, bringing into it members of the Democratic Party of the Left (formerly the **Italian Communist Party**). While he successfully stabilized the economy, he stressed that his major priority was electoral reform, something that was widely regarded as a step that would decisively change the face and structure of Italian politics. He stepped down after the 1994 election produced a very different parliamentary constellation of parties.

Çiller, Tansu. (1946–) Prime Minister of **Turkey** from 1993. A former professor of economics, she joined the conservative **True Path Party** in 1990, entering parliament the following year. She attempted to embark upon an ambitious programme of economic privatization and modernization. Her strategy was hindered by increasing unpopularity due to economic problems, which forced her to accept a coalition with more left-wing parties. Her attempts to move Turkey more towards the European mainstream were further hindered by Western disapproval of her strong policy of repression against the country's Kurdish minority.

CINCHAN. The more commonly used acronym of Commander-in-Chief Channel, the overall commander of Allied Command channel within the **North Atlantic Treaty Organization (NATO)**. In practice subordinate to **SACEUR**, though nominally equal in status, the office was always held by a British admiral operating from British naval headquarters in London.

Citizen initiatives. Movements outside established political parties and interest groups which seek to influence governments and decision-makers on a specific policy area or issue. They became prominent in Western Europe in the late 1960s, and were particularly associated with objections to planning decisions that affected a locality or neighbourhood, especially environmental issues such as new roads or nuclear power stations. They were most visible in the **Federal Republic of Germany** in the 1970s, where they provided a basis for the future **Green Party**. They tended to be short-lived because of their specific issue orientation, spontaneous in nature with little organization, and reluctant to develop regularized relationships with political organizations.

Citizens' Charter. *See* SĄJŪDIS.

Citizens Europe Advisory Service. A facility established by the **Commission** in January 1990 to advise individuals in the **European Communities (EC)** of their rights, and to provide information on social benefits within the EC such as medical treatment, housing and pensions. It was part of a series of initiatives, known collectively as Citizens' Europe, begun in the mid-1980s to strengthen the identity, image and legitimacy of the EC among the citizens of the Member States.

Citizens' Party. (*Borgaflokkurinn*) A small centre-right populist party in **Iceland**. It was formed in 1987 by Albert Gudmundsson, a former leader of the **Independence Party**, who had been obliged to resign from the government because of alleged tax irregularities. It survived his retirement in 1989 to maintain a limited electoral presence.

Civic Alliance. (*Aliantei Civice*) An action group in **Romania**, formed in 1990 to press for extensive political and economic reforms. It turned itself into a political party in 1991, and the following year opted to become part of the **Democratic Convention of Romania**.

Civic Democratic Union-Public Against Violence (CDU-VPN). A liberal democratic group in **Slovakia**. It was formed in 1991 after a split in the leading **Public Against Violence** Slovak nationalist party.

Civic Forum. (*Občanské Forum*) An opposition movement in **Czechoslo-**

vakia. It was founded in November 1989 after a series of student demonstrations against the Communist regime, bringing together a number of dissident groups. It defined itself as an association of citizens seeking political reform and democratization. With **Havel** as its leading spokesman, it was invited to join the government in December, and later turned itself into a political party although several members objected to this change. Its strength was concentrated in the Czech provinces, and in Slovakia it was weaker than a rival group, **Public Against Violence**. It fragmented into several groups in February 1991 after bitter internal disputes over the pace of economic reform, but most factions agreed to retain an 'umbrella' structure until the 1992 elections. The largest successor group was the Civic Democratic Party (*Občanské Democraticka Strana – ODS*) headed by **Klaus**, which sought a rapid transition to a market economy, major **privatization**, and a reduction in the level of social benefits. After 1992 it became the largest party in the Czech Republic. The other meaningful factions were the centre-left Civic Movement, which after failing electorally reformed as the Free Democrats (*Svobodní Demokraty*), and the pro-market conservative Civic Democratic Alliance (*Občanská Demokratická Aliance*).

Claes, Willy. (1938–) Secretary-General of the **North Atlantic Treaty Organization (NATO)** from 1994–95. A Belgian politician, he was elected to Parliament in 1968 for the **Flemish Socialist Party**, serving in five governments 1972–94. The Foreign Minister of **Belgium** after 1992, and with a reputation as a conciliator, he was a compromise choice in 1994 for NATO's senior political position. His tenure was placed in doubt in 1995 when his name surfaced in the allegations surrounding the **Agusta Affair**, and he resigned the office in October after being stripped of his parliamentary immunity.

Clay, Lucius D. (1897–1978) American Military Governor in Germany 1947–49. A distinguished military general, he was appointed deputy military governor in Germany in 1945, before taking over as Governor in 1947. He was the most powerful man in Germany during the period of military occupation. In 1945 his major responsibility was to take charge of American administration, but in practice it was he who formulated American occupation policy from the outset, being given a fairly free hand by his political masters in Washington. He quickly moved to reverse the original punitive, and what he saw as an unrealistic, German policy, and actively supported a policy of reconstruction and political democratization as a way of improving the economy and removing the danger of future German militarism. In 1948 he took the decision to launch the airlift that overcame the **Berlin Blockade**. His positive actions made him almost as popular in Germany as he was powerful. He surrendered his functions in May 1949 after the signing of the Basic Law that established the **Federal Republic of Germany**. After retiring from the military he became a businessman, but in 1961 was appointed by President John Kennedy as his personal representative in **Berlin** shortly after the building of the **Berlin Wall**.

Clean Hands. (*Mani Pulite*) The code-name, later popularized by the media, of the original investigation of political corruption and illegal party funding in Milan in 1992. It began with the arrest of a Socialist administrator, but rapidly escalated into a national investigation of **Tangentopoli** and other alleged scandals.

Clientelism. An informal power relationship between individuals and groups in unequal positions, linked by the exchange of benefits between them. The higher status partner acts as a patron, controlling political organizations and distributing public goods (jobs, social benefits, etc.) to clients who in turn deliver their votes to the patron and the patron's organization. The most conspicuous example of mass clientelism in post-1945 Europe was in **Italy** where the ruling **Christian Democratic Party** used its control of government to maintain a huge patronage system, particularly in the more impoverished southern half of the country, as a means of retaining electoral and political dominance. *See also* LOTTIZZA-ZIONE, PARTITOCRAZIA.

Club for the Support of Glasnost and Democracy. A dissident group in **Bulgaria**. It was founded in 1989 by a group of intellectuals alarmed by the attack on reformist tendencies within the **Bulgarian Communist Party (BKP)** by **Zhivkov**. Subjected to harassment during the closing months of Zhivkov's regime, it survived to become a major component of the **Union of Democratic Forces**.

Cockfield, Lord Francis. (1916–) British appointee to the **Commission** 1985–89. He was given the responsibility and portfolio of preparing for the implementation by the **European Communities (EC)** of an **internal market** by the end of 1992. In March 1985 he produced a White Paper listing some 300 measures that would need to be taken, with a programme and timetable for each. While most items were non-contentious, there was particular opposition to ending all frontier controls within the EC, the harmonization of excise duties, and the approximation of Value-Added Tax (VAT). His sternest critic was the British premier, **Thatcher**, who had appointed him to the Commission. Because of its objections to some of his proposals, the British government did not nominate him for a second term of office in 1989, despite his desire to continue on the Commission.

Codecision Procedure. *See* CONCILIATION PROCEDURE.

Codetermination. (*Mitbestimmung*) A system introduced in the **Federal Republic of Germany** whereby trade unions and workers were represented on the supervising boards of industrial companies. Parity representation, first introduced in the British zone of military occupation, was extended in 1951 to all coal, iron and steel industries. In 1952 a more limited form of codetermination was introduced for other industrial companies. After many years of struggle by the unions, near parity worker representation for all larger companies was established in 1976. Complaints by employers were rejected by the Federal Constitutional Court in 1979, which upheld the constitutionality of the measure. Similar systems of institutionalized participation in management by trade unions were introduced in **Austria**, the **Netherlands** and Scandinavia. A form of codetermination was the aspect of the **Charter of Fundamental Social Rights** to which the **United Kingdom** objected most strongly.

Cod War. The popular name given to the 1972–76 dispute between **Iceland** and the **United Kingdom** (and to a lesser extent the **Federal Republic of Germany**) over fishing rights in the Atlantic. The cause was Iceland's unilateral decision to extend its territorial fishing limits from 12 to 50 miles as a protective measure against overfishing. The war was characterized by a series of incidents between British trawlers, escorted by Royal Navy vessels, and Icelandic gunboats. A compromise agreement, but largely in Iceland's favour, was reached in 1976. Iceland's action sparked off a major revision of national claims over territorial waters in the Atlantic, with significant negative consequences for many European fishing industries.

Coexistence. (*Együttélés/Spolužitie/Wspólnata/Soužití* – *ESWS*) A political group in **Slovakia**, founded in 1990. Its objective was to work for equal rights for all ethnic minorities in the country. In 1992 it aligned itself with the **Hungarian Christian Democratic Party**, and enjoyed some modest electoral success.

Cohabitation. A phrase describing the 1986–88 situation in **France** when politicians of opposing political parties held the offices of President and Prime Minister. In 1958 the Constitution of the **Fifth French Republic** created a divided executive, but with ambiguity on the exact division of authority between the two offices. Before 1986 no problem had arisen because the President's party or coalition had also dominated the parliament. The 1986 parliamentary election was won by a centre-right alliance and the **Socialist Party (PS)** President, **Mitterrand**, had to accept **Chirac** as Prime Minister. Chirac was not prepared to accept a secondary role and argued that effective decision-making was constitutionally his province. He introduced a programme of liberalization and **privatization**, and legislation that would permit the government to rule by decree on some socio-economic issues. Mitterrand asserted his right in foreign and defence policy, and refused to sign legislation he thought contrary to his own party's objectives and previous achievements. Chirac counteracted by introducing a guillotine procedure on the time available for the President to delay signing approved legislation. Despite the previous concerns and the clear tensions, cohabitation produced a fairly clear division of labour, indicating that constitutional ambiguity was not necessarily a drawback. There was no great crisis: much of the difficulty was created by personal antagonism, as both men planned to be presidential candidates in 1988. But Mitterrand gained the advantage. By detaching himself more from domestic issues, he avoided being criticized for growing economic problems, which helped him win the 1988 election, after which he dissolved Parliament. In the ensuing election victory went to his own PS. In 1993 Mitterrand had to accept another period of cohabitation when the centre-right again won a parliamentary majority, but this time it was accepted as a normal part of politics, with little speculation on a possible constitutional or political crisis.

Cohesion. A policy of the **European Communities (EC)** that seeks to reduce the structural and socio-economic disparities between the richest and poorest states and regions. Always a declared EC objective, it was formalized further in the **Treaty on European Union** through the establishment of a specific Cohesion Fund to help the poorest Member States, especially, to adapt to the requirements for **Economic and Monetary Union (EMU)**. It involves taking regional disparities into account in the formulation of common policies, and joint action through EC institutions and programmes.

Cold War. The ideological, political and diplomatic conflict after 1945 between the USA and **USSR**, and between Western and Eastern Europe, with the two blocs facing each other on the continent as regional military and security alliances. The phrase was first used in April 1947 by Bernard Baruch, an American presidential adviser, in the context of the declaration of the **Truman Doctrine**. It was soon extended beyond Europe to describe the global competition between the super-powers, but it was generally acknowledged that Europe was the heart of the Cold War. It was perhaps the determination of **Stalin** to maintain political and military hegemony over Eastern Europe that escalated tension. Suspicious of the West and its intentions, he wished to create a buffer zone between the USSR and potential enemies. Equally, the West was alarmed by what it believed to be a Soviet bid for European hegemony. A Communist coup in **Czechoslovakia**, the **Berlin Blockade**, attempts by the native Communist parties to destabilize **France** and **Italy**, the treaty imposed upon **Finland** – all seemed to confirm Western fears. Equally, the Western decision to press ahead with the creation of a West German state fuelled Soviet fears, and the Cold War was definitely in place by 1948.

It is doubtful whether either side seriously contemplated or was prepared to risk outright war. Collectively or singly, the Western European countries were no military match for the USSR. What they wanted was a major American presence in Europe. Soviet control of Eastern Europe was paralleled by a series of American commitments: the political Truman Doctrine, the economic **Marshall Plan**, and the military **North Atlantic Treaty Organization (NATO)**. With the formation of NATO and, later, the **Warsaw Pact**, the lines of engagement and the security alliances were firmly drawn for the next four decades. The unparalleled concentration of armaments, along with thermonuclear parity, stabilized the situation and precluded a direct military confrontation. From the mid-1950s there was a debate on changes in the intensity of the Cold War. **Détente**, peaceful coexistence and thaw were phrases used to describe periods when relationships seemed less glacial. They reflected initiatives intended to bring the two sides to agree on measures to prevent what neither wanted: a full-scale war in Europe. These initiatives were most fully institutionalized in the **Conference on Security and Co-operation in Europe (CSCE)**. Phrases such as the Second Cold War, employed in the early 1980s, indicated periods of greater tension, but in general, with the possible exception of the 1962 Cuban Missile Crisis, neither the USA nor the USSR was prepared to risk direct and total confrontation. Both developed a common interest in ensuring that they would not be forced into war through the uncontrolled actions of a third party. While each side interpreted détente differently, the stalemate, parity and rules of the game in Europe were so absolute that for the continent the decades of the Cold War were decades of peace. With the withdrawal by **Gorbachev** of the Soviet military guarantee to the Communist regimes of Eastern Europe in the late 1980s, the Cold War entered its final phase. Between 1989 and 1991, with the democratization of Eastern Europe, German reunification, the disbanding of the Warsaw Pact, and the disintegration of the USSR, there emerged a consensus that the Cold War had come to an end.

Collective Security. A concept and formula for achieving peace in international relations. It first gained prominence, as a better option than the traditional **balance of power**, at the end of the First World War. It implied that states would enter into mutual binding agreements to respect boundaries and to renounce the use of force to resolve international disputes, with signatories pledged to aid any pact member suffering from external threat or attack. The League of Nations and its post-1945 successor, the United Nations (UN), were intended to be the major agencies of collective security. The crystallization of bipolar super-power competition after 1945 and the **Cold War** meant that the UN had to function more within a pseudo-balance of power situation, especially in Europe where a balance was sustained by two regional security systems, the **North Atlantic Treaty Organization (NATO)** and the **Warsaw Pact**. After the ending of the Cold War after 1989, European discussions on stability focused upon seeking a new form of collective security, perhaps through a revision of the role and purpose of

NATO and its possible geographical extension, with the main forum of discussions being the **Conference on Security and Co-operation in Europe (CSCE)**.

Collectivization. The process by which privately owned land is expropriated by the state in order to create large collective, or co-operative, farm units whose profits are shared by all the member cultivators. It has been particularly associated with Communist ideology. It was introduced in the **USSR** in the 1930s where it led to great hardship, destitution and starvation, but consistently failed to generate an economically efficient and productive agriculture. After 1945 it was imposed upon much of Eastern Europe by the new Communist regimes. Never popular or effective, it was quickly abandoned in some countries.

College of Europe. *See* CONGRESS OF EUROPE.

Colombo, Emilio. (1920–) Prime Minister of **Italy** 1970–72. A member of the dominant **Christian Democratic Party (DC)**, he entered Parliament in 1946, serving in a variety of government positions after 1948 before being appointed premier in 1970. In 1976 he was elected to the **European Parliament (EP)**, serving as its President (Speaker) 1977–79. Returning to Italian politics he became Foreign Minister 1979–83. In 1981 he supported and lent his name to the proposals by the West German Foreign Minister, **Genscher**, for a Draft European Act and declaration on economic integration for the members of the **European Communities (EC)**. The document, more commonly known as the Genscher–Colombo Plan, was submitted to the **European Council** for discussion.

Columbus. Western Europe's planned contribution to the development of an International Space Station. Originally linked to the abortive **Hermes** space shuttle project, it was sponsored by the **European Space Agency (ESA)**. Adopted in 1988, the planning stage was completed only in 1990.

COMECON. *See* COUNCIL FOR MUTUAL ECONOMIC ASSISTANCE.

COMINFORM. *See* COMMUNIST INFORMATION BUREAU.

Comitology. A phrase describing the method of implementing legislation in the **European Union (EU)** through a process of delegation where the implementation of decisions taken by the **Commission** is passed to committees composed of officials from the member states.

Command Economy. A form of economic and political organization in which the state seeks to establish as complete a control as possible over all aspects of economic activity. It has been particularly associated with Communist regimes. No Communist party has been able to maintain itself in power without a command economy, and apart from war-time conditions no non-Communist regime has sought to adopt a command economy. The model was the Stalinist economy of the **USSR** 1929–53, copied later by several other Communist regimes, but there were considerable variations in the degree of effective economic control achieved. Outside the USSR, the most prolonged post-war example of a sustained and rigid command economy was perhaps **Romania** under the **Ceaușescu** regime.

Commission. The highest administrative organ and one of the two executive institutions of the **European Communities (EC)**. It was intended to represent the supranational element of the EC, and the title has been used to refer both to the whole administrative apparatus based in **Brussels** and to the set of individual Commissioners who head it. It was made responsible by the **Treaty of Rome** for the initiation, supervision and implementation of EC policies, sharing decision-making with the **Council of Ministers**. Where it is dissatisfied with what it regards as the failure of other institutions and the member states to fulfil their constitutional obligations, it can submit a complaint to the **Court of Justice**. It was given general responsibility for the financial management of the EC, preparing the draft budget and overseeing the administration of the EC's structural funds, and it has had particular autonomy of action in agriculture, competition policy, and coal and steel. It represents the EC and the member states in several international organizations, as well as in external trade negotiations with non-member countries.

The Commissioners are appointed by the Council of Ministers upon nomination by the national governments: the larger states have each been entitled to two nominees, the others to one each. On entering office a Commissioner must swear an oath of loyalty to the EC, agreeing not to take or seek instructions from any national government or other body. Appointment is for a renewable four-year term, and since 1957 about one-half have been reappointed for at least one further term of office, providing it with a strong degree of continuity. One Commissioner is appointed as President and has potentially a great deal of influence, but without the ability to appoint or dismiss. Commission decisions have usually been by majority vote, with all members thereafter expected to obey the principle of collective responsibility. It was intended in 1957 to be the motor force of integration, but its success has been dependent upon how much of a free rein the Council of Ministers was prepared to give it. EC consolidation after 1957 was due to a vigorous Commission, but only because national governments were not too assertive. In 1965 its activism was curbed by **de Gaulle**, and until the 1980s it was less innovative than the **European Council**. It became more active after 1985 under the leadership of **Delors**, strengthened by constitutional and institutional changes which gave it greater leeway and autonomy in planning for the future, but this in turn led to increased complaints about its undemocratic nature and tendency to ignore national distinctiveness. With the implementation of the **Treaty on European Union** after November 1993, it became formally known as the European Commission.

Committee for a People's Europe. A body established by the

European Council in 1984 to explore ways of strengthening popular identity with the **European Communities (EC)** and of improving the image of the EC. In 1985 it submitted two reports containing a series of recommendations for EC activities and on how the rights and freedoms of EC citizens might be improved.

Committee for European Economic Co-operation (CEEC). *See* ORGANIZATION FOR EUROPEAN ECONOMIC CO-OPERATION.

Committee for the Creation of European Monetary Union. An interest group formed in February 1988. It was an initiative of the former French and West German leaders, **Giscard d'Estaing** and **Schmidt**, who argued that the successful 1979 **European Monetary System (EMS)** should move to a second stage of development. With a target membership among leading politicians, financiers and industrialists, it was intended to be an influential and expert body that would persuade governments to expand the EMS into an instrument of economic union. Many of its suggestions were to be found in the proposals for **Economic and Monetary Union (EMU)** advanced by the **Commission** after 1989, and in the text of the **Treaty on European Union**.

Committee for the Defence of the Unjustly Persecuted (VONS). A human rights group in **Czechoslovakia**. It was formed in 1978, one year after **Charter 77**, and sought to persuade the Czechoslovak government to honour the commitment to human rights it made in signing the **Helsinki Final Act**. Its membership remained small and largely confined to the Czech provinces. It was persecuted by the government, and many of its members were imprisoned.

Committee for the Defence of Workers. (*Komitet Obrony Robotników – KOR*) A dissident protest group in **Poland**. It was formed in 1976 by intellectuals and professionals to provide legal advice and aid for workers charged with participating in strike activity that had been provoked by the **Gierek** government's announcement of immediate rises in food prices. Basically libertarian, it was interested more broadly in human rights, and in the late 1970s was a spearhead of the 'self-organization' process in Poland that sought to parallel the Communist regime. It played a leading role in integrating the 1980 wave of protests which enabled **Solidarity** to claim to represent more than the shipyard workers in **Gdansk**, or even workers in general. Later calling itself the Committee for Social Self-Defence, it disbanded itself in September 1981.

Committee of Agricultural Organizations in the European Community. (*Comité des Organisations Professionelles Agricoles – COPA*) A transnational federation of farming unions and associations within the **European Communities (EC)**. Its influence upon EC policy has been greater than the political or economic importance of agriculture would warrant. The structure of the **Common Agricultural Policy (CAP)** and its centrality to the EC meant that in practice COPA engaged in wage negotiations for the whole farming sector in the annual CAP price review process.

Committee of Permanent Representatives. (*Comité des Représentants Permanent – COREPER*) The heads of the delegations, or permanent representatives (*see* PERMANENT REPRESENTATION) that each member state of the **European Communities (EC)** maintains in **Brussels**. Its members have senior ambassadorial status. Formed in 1953, it was formally acknowledged in 1965 after the merger of the executives of the EC. As the workload increased, the term came to refer more broadly to the totality of the delegations. A service agent and gatekeeper for the **Council of Ministers**, it examines material awaiting Council decisions, prepares recommendations, and draws up the agenda for Council meetings. If COREPER makes an unanimous recommendation, the Council usually approves it without discussion or a vote. Its centrality to the EC decision-making process has occasioned much criticism, particularly because it has strengthened the role of national governments and has lacked accountability within the EC constitutional framework. In 1991 it was given formal recognition in the **Treaty on European Union**.

Committee of the Governors of the Central Banks. The heads of the central banks of the member states of the **European Communities (EC)**, established in 1964. Although all except the **Bundesbank** have been subject to direction from their national governments, its combined expertise has given its views some weight. It elects its own President annually, and meets monthly in Basel at the headquarters of the **Bank for International Settlements**.

Committee of the Regions. An agency of the **European Communities (EC)** established under the terms of the 1991 **Treaty on European Union**. It was intended to involve representatives of elected regional authorities in EC decision-making, but the member states were willing to give it only a consultative and advisory role. Its inauguration was delayed until 1994. It must be consulted on training, infrastructure networks, public health and cultural issues, but may express an opinion on any matter which it believes to have regional implications.

Committee of Three Wise Men. The popular title of a three-man body appointed in 1978 by the **European Council** to review the institutional machinery of the **European Communities (EC)**, even though it had not yet discussed the 1976 **Tindemans Report** which covered the same theme. The group reported in 1979, recommending a strengthening of the supranational institutions of the EC and a curtailment of national sovereignty. No action was taken by the Council on the recommendations.

Common Agricultural Policy (CAP). A policy of the **European Communities (EC)**. It is one of the few areas where the EC was able early on to establish a common policy. Its history has been controversial and contentious. The general principles of the CAP were provisionally accepted in January 1962, but in 1965 the need to finalize the financial arrangements was a major ingredient of the dispute between **de Gaulle** and the EC which led to the **empty chair crisis**. A more detailed framework was contained in the 1968 **Mansholt Plan**. This was watered down in the version accepted in 1972. In practice the CAP contained three major elements: a single market for agricultural products, with common prices; a **common external tariff** levied upon imports; and common financial responsibility. Its core was to be a guaranteed price system. Because of interest group pressure, the prices set each year for farm products have invariably been at high levels determined more by political factors rather than by market calculations. The major consequence was overproduction, since for farmers there was no inverse link between costs, prices and production. The surplus was bought by the EC at the fixed price and stored or exported, with exporters receiving subsidies (restitutions) to cover the difference between the high purchase price and the lower selling prices on the world markets. It resulted in high prices for European consumers. By the early 1980s the CAP had expanded to consume some two-thirds of the EC budget. The only major critic was the **United Kingdom**, for whom CAP costs were linked to the level of its net budget contribution. External criticism was more vocal. Third World countries regarded it as detrimental to the development of their own export agriculture, while the USA and other major food producers attacked it for its protectionism, price distortion and the dumping of stored surpluses on world markets, sometimes at cut-rate prices. With the CAP threatening to outstrip the EC's financial resources, a more critical approach was adopted in the late 1980s, and several reforms were introduced, most importantly in 1992. However, debates remained acrimonious, with strong opposition from several member states to any radical overhaul.

Common Carrier Legislation. Rules set by the **European Communities (EC)** which require transmission systems that carry energy between any third party supplier and the consumer to do so at a reasonable tariff.

Common Course. (*Fælles Kurs*) A small left-wing populist party in **Denmark**, formed in 1986 by Preben Moeller Hansen, the leader of the seamen's union. It adopted a left-wing populist and isolationist line, demanding Danish withdrawal from both the **European Communities (EC)** and the **North Atlantic Treaty Organization (NATO)**. It also urged strict curbs on immigration and a more significant progressive taxation. Briefly successful, it faded from the political scene after 1988.

Common European Home. A phrase associated with the Soviet leader,

Gorbachev. He used it on several occasions in 1989–90 in discussions with Western leaders and in a major speech to the **Council of Europe**. The context of the phrase varied, and it is unclear what he took it to mean. On some occasions it was Europe-specific; on others he mentioned the USA and Canada. To some extent a reaction to the crumbling Communist control in the **USSR** and Eastern Europe, it could be taken to mean the creation of a new European-wide security system that would aid his own domestic authority and also accommodate a European house with many rooms, where countries with different political and socio-economic systems could coexist with each other within a framework of common European values.

Common external tariff (CET). An essential element of a **customs union**, with participating states having a single tariff system for goods imported from countries outside the union. A CET was a major objective of the **Treaty of Rome**, and was introduced by the **European Economic Community (EEC)** in the early 1960s. Since then the CET of the **European Communities (EC)** has been reduced on several occasions in line with agreements reached within the **General Agreement on Tariffs and Trade (GATT)**.

Common Fisheries Policy (CFP). A policy of the **European Communities (EC)**. The first proposals for a CFP were made in 1966, with agreement in 1970. The scheme was controversial because it coincided with the negotiations on terms of entry to the EC with **Denmark**, **Ireland**, **Norway** and the **United Kingdom**, all major fishing states which believed that the CFP was being rushed through without taking their interests into account. The issue was widely believed to have contributed to Norway's rejection of membership in 1972. The extension of exclusive national fishing zones in the Atlantic in the 1970s (*see* COD WAR) disrupted the CFP. EC deep-sea vessels, barred from many traditional fishing grounds, were forced back into EC waters, with consequent fierce competition and overfishing. A new CFP was adopted in 1983 after much argument, and was to last until 2003. It set guidelines on access to and preservation of stock. It opened EC waters to all EC vessels within a 200 mile limit, allowing states a national exclusion zone of only 12 miles. Most of its measures related to conservation. The central element was the **Total Allowable Catch (TAC)**, an annual quota for different species of fish permitted to be caught in EC waters, with each state receiving a share of each TAC. An inspectorate answerable to the **Commission** was set up to monitor the system. Other measures, including guide prices and compensation payments, were modelled upon the price guarantee system of the **Common Agricultural Policy (CAP)**. The system proved to be contentious, with disagreements over TAC levels, verification and enforcement, and an interim review in 1993 failed to resolve the disputes.

Common Foreign and Security Policy (CFSP). One of the parallel pillars of the **European Union (EU)** set up by the 1991 **Treaty on European Union**. It was established only as a structure of intergovernmental co-operation, and so was not made subject to the normal decision-making procedures of the **European Communities (EC)**. It replaced the earlier **European Political Co-operation (EPC)**, but was given an additional stress upon security in anticipation of the EU developing a common defence policy. Direction of the CFSP was given to the **European Council**, with implementation through the **Council of Ministers**, and its objectives were to safeguard the common values, interests and security of the EU through the promotion of peace, international security and co-operation, and the development of democracy, the rule of law and respect for human rights. Although the Treaty referred to a future common defence policy, defence and security issues were excluded from CFSP procedures. The defence and security element, involving the absorption of **Western European Union (WEU)** by the EU, was scheduled to be fully reviewed before 1998.

Common market. An economic agreement which extends co-operation beyond a **customs union** to provide for the free movement of capital and labour as well as goods. The term became popular in the late 1950s as an alternative title for the **European Economic Community (EEC)**. While relatively neutral when first coined, it later acquired political overtones, often being used by those who rejected political integration and who believed that the **European Communities (EC)** should be content with the economic goal of a common market.

Commonwealth of Independent States (CIS). (*Sodruzhestvo Nezavisimykh Gosudarstv*) A loose association of the former constituent republics (bar the **Baltic states**) of the **USSR**. It was established in December 1991 at a meeting where the republics declared that the USSR no longer existed, and abolished central authority from Moscow. It grew out of an earlier decision in Minsk by the three Slavic republics – **Belarus**, **Russia** and **Ukraine** – to form a Slavonic Commonwealth. Apart from the Baltic states, only **Georgia** originally refused to join the CIS. There was agreement on setting up a headquarters in Minsk, the capital of Belarus, and on twice-yearly meetings of heads of state. Its immediate objective was to manage a negotiated divorce between the republics and to serve as a forum where common problems could be discussed and resolved. These aims did not meet with much success, with major arguments over the disposal of Soviet resources, especially military material. Tensions were particularly acute between the two major successor states, Russia and Ukraine, and between the Slavic and Asiatic republics. All were suspicious of Russia, by far the largest member. Tensions were exacerbated in 1993 when the three Slavic states declared an intention to collaborate more closely in economic matters, but in September all reached an agreement on building a framework for the construction of an economic union.

Commonwealth of Nations. An international grouping of the **United Kingdom** and former members of its empire. The British monarch is accepted as head of the Commonwealth and symbol of the association. Its character changed dramatically after decolonization, and in 1975 it was accepted that the relationships between its members should remain informal and unstructured. There are regular meetings of national leaders, and an international secretariat in London which seeks to encourage political, economic and cultural co-operation. These have helped to maintain links and unity among its members, which contain about one-quarter of the world's population.

Communal Liberation Party. (*Toplumcu Kurtuluş Partisi – TKP*) A centre-left party in the self-styled **Turkish Republic of Northern Cyprus**. It was founded in 1976. Its regular participation in government coalitions reflected its pragmatic style and willingness to collaborate with other parties. It sought a confederal solution to the island's ethnic problems.

Communism. A political ideology developed in the nineteenth century which argued that all people are equal, that they should all work for the common good of society, and that all property and authority belonged to the community as a whole. Ultimately, it believed that when a true classless society was established, the state, which it claimed was a device utilized by the property-owning class to maintain power, would 'wither away'. The first Communist state was established in the **USSR** in 1917. Communist regimes were established, and Communist principles claimed to have been introduced, in Eastern Europe after 1945. Practical experience indicated that it was the state, rather than the people, which gained enormously in power, and that this in turn produced a different kind of inegalitarian society.

Communist Information Bureau (Cominform). An international organization of the governing Communist parties of the **USSR** and Eastern Europe, along with those of **France** and **Italy**. It was established in October 1947 and widely regarded by Western countries as a replacement for the Third or Communist International (Comintern) dissolved by **Stalin** in 1943. It established a headquarters in Belgrade to co-ordinate Communist activities throughout Europe. Its first decision was to confirm the supremacy of the Soviet party and to reject the possibility of distinctive national paths to socialism. In June 1948 it upheld Stalin's condemnation of **Tito** for 'national deviancy', expelling **Yugoslavia** from the organization. Its headquarters were then removed to Bucharest. It became largely dormant after 1948, with little activity and no clear purpose. It was already moribund when **Khrushchev** dissolved it in April 1956. For Khrushchev it was a cost-free gesture of a willingness to discuss **détente** with the West.

Communist Party of Austria. (*Kommunistische Partei Österreichs – KPÖ*) A small party in **Austria**, without any political influence after 1945. In

1991 its leadership resigned after a refusal by many party functionaries to accept any form of liberalization. Hundreds of members subsequently left the party, leaving it a hollow shell.

Communist Party of Czechoslovakia. (*Komunistická Strana Česko-slovenska – KSČ*) The government party of **Czechoslovakia** 1948–89. Founded in 1921 it enjoyed high levels of support in the inter-war period. Its opposition to Nazism increased its appeal and prestige in 1945, and it emerged as the largest party in the 1946 election. Supported by other left-wing groups, it gained parliamentary approval in 1948 for its seizure of power, abandoning its previous commitment to a distinctive Czech road to socialism and pursuing a strict Stalinist ideology under the leadership of **Gottwald** and **Novotný**. Attempts by **Dubček** in 1968 to liberalize the party were prevented by the **USSR** and **Warsaw Pact** occupation of the country. The reassertion of orthodoxy under **Husák** after 1968 froze it in inertia, and it failed to respond to the mood of reform in Eastern Europe in the late 1980s. In 1989 its monopoly of power was ended, and it was swept aside in the subsequent democratic elections. In 1990 it was reconstituted in the Czech Republic as the Communist Party of Bohemia and Moravia (*Kommunistická Strana Čech a Moravy*) as a left socialist party. In 1993 a reformist wing seceded to form the Democratic Left Party (*Strana Demokratické Levice*).

Communist Party of Greece. (*Kommounistiko Komma Ellados – KKE*) A major party in **Greece**. It waged a civil war against royal government forces after 1945, a campaign which ended in defeat in 1949. Outlawed in 1947, it operated only in exile until relegalized in 1974. With a leadership committed to strict Marxist-Leninist orthodoxy, it suffered from severe internal tension, leading to the secession in 1968 of the Communist Party of Greece-Interior (*KKE-Esoterikou*), a wing which differed only in its willingness to accept a more gradualist approach to disentanglement from pro-Western commit-ments. A reformist wing left the party in 1991 in protest against the insistence on orthodoxy, leaving the KKE as a small fringe party.

Communist Party of Luxembourg. (*Kommunistisch Partei vu Letze-burg/Parti Communiste Luxembourgeoise – KPL/PCL*) A small left-wing party in **Luxembourg**. Founded in 1921, its first parliamentary seat in 1934 was annulled by the legislature, and in 1937 it survived a referendum proposal to ban it. Although it has been consistently represented in Parliament since 1945, its political influence has been minimal.

Communist Party of Malta. (*Partit Komunista Malti*) A small left-wing party in **Malta**. Founded in 1969 by ex-members of the **Labour Party**, it declared itself loyal to Marxist-Leninist principles and supported Maltese non-alignment. Until 1987 it refused to contest elections on the grounds that this would split the left-wing vote and increase the chances of a conservative victory.

Communist Party of Slovakia. (*Komunistická Strana Slovenska*) The semi-autonomous Slovakian section of the **Communist Party of Czechoslovakia**. After the 1938 Munich Agreement resulted in an autonomous **Slovakia**, it was recognized as a separate party by the Communist International (Comintern) in 1939, retaining a distinctive organizational structure until 1948 and the imposition of a rigid Stalinism. In the 1960s it began more openly to express Slovakian complaints about over-centralization, and in January 1968 supported the removal of **Novotný**. Its demands for a federal system of government as a means of gaining a more equitable treatment for Slovakia were conceded by the **Dubček** government, and was the one reform of the **Prague Spring** not reversed after the reimposition of Soviet-style orthodoxy, although with a more authoritarian form of government and with policies moderated to some extent by the federal structure, its influence upon national politics declined after 1969. In 1991 the KKS reformed itself as a left socialist Democratic Left Party (*Strana Demokratickej L'avice – SDL*) and proved more successful in retaining support than its Czech counterpart.

Communist Party of Spain. (*Partido Communista de España – PCE*) A left-wing party in **Spain**. Founded in 1920, it became part of the republican Popular Front in the 1930s. It played a prominent role during the Civil War, placing a higher priority on military victory over the forces of **Franco** than a socialist revolution. Banned during the Franco regime, it maintained an organizational structure in exile. Under the leadership of **Carrillo** it re-established itself in Spain in 1975 in advance of its legalization in 1977. Carefully avoiding any revolutionary rhetoric or action, it collaborated with other parties and played a positive role in the transition to democracy. At home and abroad it praised the virtues of **Eurocommunism**. The moderate line did not bring it great electoral success and it was outstripped by the rival **Spanish Socialist Workers' Party (PSOE)**. Discontent grew over Carrillo's rigid internal control of the party, and Eurocommunist and pro-Soviet factions began to vie with each other more openly. Turmoil grew further after a disastrous electoral performance in 1982, in contrast to a great victory for the PSOE. Carrillo was forced to resign, but the arguments continued. In 1985 Carrillo and his supporters were forced off the central committee, eventually departing to form a rival party. The PCE joined the **United Left** in 1986, but without any benefit, and the factional disputes continued.

Communist Party of the Netherlands. (*Communistische Partij van Nederland – CPN*) A small left-wing party in the **Netherlands**. Founded in 1918 it has enjoyed no real political influence, though always succeeding to obtain a minimal parliamentary representation. Briefly popular in 1945 because of its war-time record of resistance, it soon became marginalized. In an attempt to revive its flagging fortunes, it agreed in 1989 to join three other small left parties in a **Green Left** alliance.

Communist Party of the Soviet Union. (*Kommunisticheskaya Partiya Sovetskogo Soyuza – KPSS/CPSU*) The single legal party of the **USSR**. Formed by Lenin in 1919 out of the triumphant Bolshevik party, it followed his precepts in stressing that it had the 'leading role' in social and political development. It built a hierarchical organizational structure which paralleled that of the state institutions of the USSR, with at each level the party organ essentially supervising and monitoring the activities of the relevant state agencies. The secretary-general of the party was always the true ruler of the USSR, although after the domination of **Stalin** it possessed some attributes of a collective leadership. Despite its domination of the society, it was not a mass organization. Potential applicants had to be sponsored by existing and long-standing members, and if accepted were admitted only on a probationary basis in the first instance. In 1986 it reaffirmed that it was the 'tried and tested militant vanguard of the Soviet people, which unites, on a voluntary basis, the more advanced, politically more conscious section of the working class, collective farm peasantry and intelligentsia'. In practice, particularly at the top of its hierarchy, it became more like a closed shop of a privileged caste. Many members resisted the call by **Gorbachev** after 1986 for **glasnost** and **perestroika**, which also saw a more limited role for the party in directly managing public affairs. However, in 1988 it accepted the proposal that there should be a choice of candidates in elections to all public offices, and in the 1990s it dropped the claim for a leading role, insisting rather that it should have a consolidating and unifying role. These concessions did not halt the pressures for change, and in 1991 its reputation was damaged further by allegations that it had been implicated in the plot to remove Gorbachev from power. Its frayed authority and unity ended with the collapse of the USSR, which it proved powerless to prevent. While many party members were able to pursue a political career in the successor states, the party itself largely ceased to exist even where it was not proscribed, making a slow comeback in some of the successor states only after 1992.

Communist Refoundation. *See* ITALIAN COMMUNIST PARTY.

Communists and Allies. One of the original transnational **party groups** in the **European Parliament (EP)**. Formed in 1973, it consisted of members of national Communist parties. After the first direct elections to the EP in 1979, it also included a few independents elected on a Communist list. It was dominated by representatives from **France** and **Italy**, but the two national parties had followed different brands of Communism, the Italians presenting a distinctive national version, the French remaining perhaps the most Stalinist party in Western Europe. This fracture was repeated in the EP group, making it one of the least cohesive and effective in the assembly. The tensions climaxed in 1989, partly as a result of developments in Eastern Europe, and after the 1989 direct elections it split into two party groups, the

Italian-dominated **Group for the European Unitarian Left** and the more orthodox French-dominated **Left Unity**.

Community Method. A term frequently used to describe policy-making procedures applied by the supranational institutions of the **European Communities (EC)**. It is different from those practices pursued through intergovernmental structures and mechanisms.

Community Programme in Education and Training for Technology (COMETT). A **European Communities (EC)** programme launched in 1986 to sponsor policy initiatives in research and technology development. It was designed to promote the training of engineers and technicians in new technology at a European level through collaboration between industrial companies and universities. Students would obtain work experience during their studies through job placements in companies based in another EC country. In April 1990 the scheme was extended to the members of the **European Free Trade Association (EFTA)**.

Comparability of Transaction. A phrase that originated within the **European Coal and Steel Community (ECSC)**. It refers to the principle that all purchasers of material who produce similar goods or perform the same function should have the right of equal access to the sources of production.

Comprehensive Test Ban Treaty (CTBT). A major objective of **arms control** negotiations since the early 1960s. The first step was in 1963 when the **United Kingdom**, USA and **USSR** signed the Partial Test Ban Treaty (PTBT) which limited nuclear testing to underground sites. It was perhaps more a reaction to concerns about atmospheric fall-out than a major interest in arms limitation. Since 1963 over 100 states have signed the PTBT, though two nuclear powers, China and **France**, declined to do so. In 1974 a Threshold Test Ban Treaty (TTBT) proposed kiloton limitations on underground tests by the USA and USSR. Although not ratified by the USA Senate, its terms were largely accepted by both countries. The final stage of a CTBT proved to be more elusive, but by the 1990s there was a general informal moratorium on testing by the major nuclear powers apart from China, although renewed testing was announced by the new **Chirac** presidency in France in 1995.

Concerted Action. (*Konzertierte Aktion*) A system of annual tripartite discussions between government, business and trade union leaders in the **Federal Republic of Germany**. It was initiated by the **Brandt** government after 1969 as a forum for reviewing general economic conditions and policy, specifically setting guidelines for wages, prices and economic growth. It failed to survive the emergence of recession and growing unemployment. The trade unions withdrew from the formal processes in 1977, and participated only informally in subsequent meetings.

Conciliation Procedure. A mechanism introduced into the **European Communities (EC)** by the **Treaty on European Union**. It replaced and extended the earlier co-operation and codecision procedures governing relationships between key EC institutions in the decision-making process. In response to the granting by the treaty of greater powers to the **European Parliament (EP)** to block legislation, it also created a Conciliation Committee to aid the resolution of legislative conflict between the EP and the **Council of Ministers**.

Concord. (*Omónoia*) A political and cultural organization in **Albania** established in 1989, as an underground body, to represent the interests of the Greek ethnic minority. In 1991 it established a party, the Democratic Union of the Greek Minority. It reconstituted itself in 1992 as the Party for the Defence of Human Rights (*Énosi Anthrópikon Dikaiomáton*) as a result of legislation banning parties based on ethnic groups.

Concordat. A bilateral agreement between **Italy** and the Roman Catholic church in February 1984, coming into operation the following January. It revised key provisions of the 1929 Lateran Treaty, most importantly removing the designation of Catholicism as the state religion. It did not affect the status of the **Vatican City**.

Condominium. Shared rule or sovereignty over a territory by two or more external authorities. The term literally means co-ownership or joint tenancy. The major European example has been **Andorra** where sovereignty has been shared by the French presidency and the Spanish bishopric of Urgel. It was sometimes advocated as a solution for territories where ownership is in dispute, such as **Northern Ireland**. By granting **Ireland** a consultative right in the domestic affairs of the province, the 1985 **Anglo-Irish Agreement** represented a move in the direction of a condominium.

Conducator. A Romanian word meaning leader. It was adopted by **Ceaușescu** and indicated the personal nature of his dictatorial regime, bringing back memories of Mussolini's title of *duce* and Hitler's title of *führer*.

Confederal European United Left. A **party group** in the **European Parliament (EP)**. It was formed after the 1994 elections as a grouping of former Communists and representatives of other left-wing parties.

Confederation of Family Organizations in the European Community. *See* CONSUMERS' CONSULTATIVE COMMITTEE.

Conference of Local and Regional Authorities in Europe. Established in 1957 to discuss and study common social problems and issues facing local government authorities in Western Europe. It was sponsored by the **Council of Europe**, and meets in **Strasbourg**.

Conference on Disarmament (CD). *See* FORTY NATIONS CONFERENCE ON DISARMAMENT.

Conference on Security and Confidence-Building Measures and Disarmament in Europe (CDE). A series of discussions seeking to achieve a greater degree of mutual trust among the European states engaged in the broader forum of the **Conference on Security and Co-operation in Europe (CSCE)**. The initiative came from the **North Atlantic Treaty Organization (NATO)**, and at the Madrid sessions of the CSCE, 1980–83, it was agreed to set up parallel talks on trust between the security blocs of NATO and the **Warsaw Pact**. The first meeting was in Stockholm in January 1984, with the same membership as CSCE, but unlike the CSCE or the **Mutual and Balanced Force Reduction (MBFR)** it did not discuss reduction of armed forces in Europe. Its theme was the movement of forces and the formulation of rules to prevent possible misinterpretation of intent or a surprise attack by one side on the other, and to develop the CSCE principles on the exchange of information on planned military exercises. These were regarded as important **confidence-building measures (CBMs)**. The first agreement, the 1986 **Stockholm Accord**, covered verification and aerial inspection of exercises by observers from the other side. It was the first time that the **USSR** had been willing to open its exercises to inspection. The ending of the **Cold War** increased the importance of the CDE. NATO in particular was concerned that the post-1989 changes in Eastern Europe might generate localized conflicts that could spark off a major war.

Conference on Security and Co-operation in Europe (CSCE). A series of international conferences on European collaboration on security, economics, science and technology, environmental issues, and human rights. It first convened in Helsinki in July 1973 and was attended by all European countries except **Albania**, as well as by the USA and Canada. It was the outcome of a Soviet proposal, accepted by the West on condition of American and Canadian participation, for a security forum that might also endorse post-1945 boundaries, which no peace treaty had ratified. Its launch was therefore a result of both the Soviet desire for formal recognition by the West of the European *status quo*, and the Western concern to involve the **Warsaw Pact** in a dialogue on reducing tensions. The first sessions (held in **Geneva** September 1973–July 1975) ended with the participants signing the Helsinki Final Act in August 1975. It reflected agreement on three themes: economic, scientific and technological co-operation; closer contacts between different peoples and a reaffirmation of human rights; and a lessening of tension through an exchange of military information. Follow-up meetings were to monitor progress on the provisions.

Several problems remained unresolved. East and West held very different views on human rights. Western countries had a very wide interpretation of what constituted security, which the **USSR** wished to restrict to military bases and troop levels. The West also rejected the Soviet desire for confirmation of the inviolability of post-1945 boundaries because of its commitment to German reunification and long-standing refusal to recognize the Soviet incorporation of the **Baltic states**. Follow-up sessions were held at frequent but irregular intervals, and the formal meetings were accompanied by a host of more specialized sessions of experts on **arms control**, **disarmament** and **confidence-building measures**. The first sessions in Belgrade and Madrid were strained, even acrimonious, but by 1983 some progress had been made, indicating that all participants had a vested interest in the survival of the CSCE. Its greatest successes were in the military and security spheres. Progress in economic co-operation was hindered by the different nature of the Eastern and Western economic systems. The greatest difficulties were with human rights, where the USSR and its allies regarded Western concerns as an unwarranted intrusion into their own domestic affairs, pursuing a rigorous crackdown on dissidents after 1976. By the time of the Vienna meetings, 1986–89, the climate had changed, making it easier to secure agreements, especially on reducing conventional land forces. The events of 1989–91 gave greater urgency to the need for the CSCE to continue as a pan-European forum which would also include the successor states of the USSR and **Yugoslavia**. The participants signed the **Charter of Paris** in 1990, also endorsing German reunification and a cut in arms levels, and the following year agreed to establish a permanent headquarters and an inter-governmental organization with the aim of constructing a pan-European security system. In 1992 the members adopted the Helsinki Document, which reinforced the institutional framework and created new bodies for conflict prevention and crisis management. In 1994 it renamed itself the Organization for Security and Co-operation in Europe.

Confidence-building measures (CBMs). Agreements to create a greater level of mutual trust between the members of the **North Atlantic Treaty Organization (NATO)** and the **Warsaw Pact**. The need to secure CBMs was incorporated into the 1975 Helsinki Final Act of the **Conference on Security and Co-operation in Europe (CSCE)**. Accepting that it was difficult to secure arms reductions, CBMs were designed to achieve a form of **arms control** within existing armaments levels. They were mainly developed in the area of conventional weapons, chiefly involving advance warning to all CSCE members of planned large-scale military exercises, as well as allowing these to be observed by CSCE members. These provisions were included in the final documents of the 1986 **Conference on Security and Confidence-Building Measures and Disarmament in Europe (CDE)**. Agreement on nuclear CBMs was more difficult. Some progress on limited verification procedures was reached after 1989, and an **Open Skies Agreement** was signed in 1992.

Congress of Europe. An assembly of representatives of political organizations committed to European integration and union. It met at The Hague in May 1948, and was organized by the **International Committee of the Movements for European Union**. There were over 750 delegates from 16 countries, including a group from Germany, plus observers from the USA, the **Commonwealth** and Eastern Europe. **Churchill** was appointed General President of the Congress. It adopted several resolutions calling for a European union or federation with its own institutions, a charter of human rights linked to a European court, a **common market**, monetary union, the promotion of European education, and the establishment of a European cultural centre. Despite the presence of many leading politicians, it did not speak for or represent governments, which paid it little heed. One resolution was realized: the establishment of a **European Movement** as a cross-national federation of groups that would co-ordinate activities and press the cause of integration. Other initiatives that were eventually realized were a European Cultural Centre in **Geneva** and a postgraduate educational College of Europe in Bruges, Belgium.

Conscription. Compulsory enlistment for national service in the military. First introduced by **France** in 1793 with the *levée en masse*, it was widely adopted for continental armies during the nineteenth century. The **United Kingdom** employed it in 1916–20 and again after 1939. After 1945 conscription was commonplace throughout Europe. Britain was the first country to rely only upon professional volunteer forces, abandoning conscription in 1960. Although military technology increasingly reduced the value of large conscript armies, very few countries followed the British example. The length of service was generally too short for conscripts to receive a thorough military training. Most Western European countries gradually became more sympathetic to pacifists and other conscientious objectors, permitting some form of civilian or community service in lieu of conscription.

Conservative Party. (*Høyre*) The major right-wing party in **Norway**. Founded in 1884 it resisted the introduction of parliamentarianism and the dissolution of the Union with **Sweden**. By the 1930s it had become marginalized with the rise to domination of the **Labour Party**. It began to moderate its position on several issues in the 1950s as a way of seeking collaboration with other non-socialist parties. It served in coalition governments in 1963 and 1965–71. Its strong support for **European Communities (EC)** membership alienated it from its partners. Its support increased substantially after 1973, making it the leading non-socialist party, heading coalition governments 1981–86 and 1989–90, when it introduced a degree of **privatization**. After 1989 it lost some of its effectiveness, and that, coupled with the re-emergence of the EC question, resulted in a loss of votes in 1993.

Conservative Party. (*Partia Konserwatywa – PK*) A political party in **Poland**, founded in 1992 as a merger of several small right-wing parties. Still relatively weak in a fragmented party system, it formed part of the Homeland alliance, and later of the **Eleventh of November Alliance** in 1993.

Conservative Party. The major right-wing party in the **United Kingdom**, traditionally linking strong imperialism with moderate reform and respect for established institutions. After 1945 it was in government 1951–64, 1970–74, and since 1979. The first post-war leader was **Churchill**, who retired in 1955. His successor, **Eden**, was discredited by the **Suez Crisis**. The resulting leadership contest was won by **Macmillan** who reinvigorated the party to win the 1959 election. By 1963 he was beset by several problems, including the **Profumo Affair**. The way in which his successor, **Douglas-Home**, had been appointed increased criticism of the way leaders were chosen by a small group of party grandees, and a new system of election by Members of Parliament was introduced. The first new-style contest, in July 1965, was won by **Heath**, who became Prime Minister in 1970. A series of conflicts with the trade unions contributed to defeat in two elections in 1974. Heath's failure led to demands for a change of leadership. He was defeated in a contest in February 1975 by **Thatcher** who went on to lead the party to three successive electoral victories before being forced to resign as a result of internal discontent over her style of leadership. She was replaced by **Major**. Until the 1970s the party, after an initial hostility in the 1940s to the socio-economic programme of the **Labour Party**, pursued a pragmatic, generally socially conscious conservatism and consensual politics, accepting the welfare state. It became more ideologically right-wing under Thatcher, emphasizing neoliberalism, individual responsibility and the importance of the market, and attacking the widespread system of state support, subsidy and benefits. Under Major this ideological emphasis was slightly modified, but at the cost of heightened internal factionalism.

Conservative People's Party. (Konservativ Folkeparti – KF) A right-wing party in **Denmark**. Formed in 1915, and traditionally an urban and suburban party, it became the leading non-socialist party after 1968. Before 1981 it was an infrequent partner in government coalitions (only 1950–53 and 1968–71). After 1973 it co-operated with **Social Democratic Party** minority governments, but was able steadily to increase its support. In 1982 **Schlüter** became the first KF prime minister since the 1920s, skilfully leading a series of minority governments until the party was damaged by the 1993 **Tamilgate** scandal.

Consociational democracy. A style of government claimed to be appropriate for societies that are deeply divided by religious, linguistic or other cultural differences into distinctively separate segments. It possesses four major principles: executive power-sharing by the segments in a **grand coalition**; a high degree of autonomy for each segment in the management of its own affairs; the **proportional representation** of all segments in decision-making and representative institutions; and the right of each segment to exercise a veto on proposed policies. **Austria**, **Belgium**, the **Netherlands** and **Switzerland** have been claimed to be examples of consociational democracy.

Constantine (Konstantinos) II. (1940–) King of the Hellenes 1964–73. He spent his childhood in exile, and succeeded his father in 1964. His sporting achievements – an Olympic gold medal in yachting in 1960 – made him initially a popular heir. He inherited a situation where Greek politics were dominated by tension over **Cyprus** and by military hostility to left-wing politicians. When the junta of **Greek Colonels** overthrew the civilian regime in August 1967, he initially collaborated with the new military government. In December he attempted to organize a counter-coup. When it failed, he went into voluntary exile in Rome. In 1973, alleging that he was still plotting against them, the colonels declared **Greece** a republic. He returned to Greece after the overthrow of the military regime in 1974, but the position of and support for the monarchy had been weakened. In a referendum the electorate voted overwhelmingly against its restoration, and he returned into exile. A private visit to Greece in 1993 and a declaration of his willingness to resume the throne if asked to do so reawakened hostility and suspicion of his intentions, and in 1994 the legislature voted to revoke his citizenship and to confiscate his remaining property in the country.

Consumers' Consultative Committee. An advisory body of the **European Communities (EC)** established in 1973. Its members were to be appointed by the **Commission** from the membership of four consumers' associations: the Confederation of Family Organizations in the European Community (COFACE); the European Community Consumer Co-operatives (EUROCOOP); the European Bureau of Consumers' Unions (BEUC); and the **European Trade Union Confederation (ETUC)**. It has to be consulted by the Commission on any proposed initiative that might affect consumer interests.

Contact Group. The name of a body formed in April 1994 by the **Federal Republic of Germany**, **France**, **Russia**, the **United Kingdom** and USA to co-ordinate discussions and strategy on a settlement to the armed conflicts in **Bosnia-Hercegovina**. It buttressed and broadened the mediation efforts pursued by the United Nations (UN) and the **European Union (EC)** by directly involving Russia and the USA. It sought, without immediate success, to secure a ceasefire and to establish a territorial settlement that would broadly divide the country along ethnic lines. The different perspectives and national interests of its members hindered its effectiveness.

Containment. The policy of the USA towards the **USSR** and **Communism** after the 1947 **Truman Doctrine**. It was intended to block what were believed to be the expansionist aims of **Stalin**. The immediate European consequence was the American commitment to defence through the **North Atlantic Treaty Organization (NATO)**, with additional military and financial aid to countries experiencing Soviet pressure. In the 1950s the defensive objectives of containment were redefined by the Eisenhower administration as the doctrine of **massive retaliation**. Until the disintegration of the USSR in 1991, the policy was never officially renounced.

Controlled shock. The name given in **Poland** to the radical reform programme introduced after 1989 to introduce a market-based economy as soon as possible. While its economic objectives were quickly established, output and incomes fell while unemployment rose sharply. Although the negative effects had been foreseen, the time it would take to turn the economy around was underestimated, and it led to deep popular discontent.

Conventional Defence Initiative (CDI). An American proposal designed to persuade the European members of the **North Atlantic Treaty Organization (NATO)** to co-operate on increasing defence expenditure. It arose from the concern that the **Warsaw Pact** was greatly superior to NATO in conventional arms. The USA, which bore the brunt of NATO expenditure, had constantly urged Western Europe to take on more of the costs. With the CDI the USA offered Western Europe the possibility of some co-operation on defence procurement. Although Western Europe had always resisted this kind of American pressure, it did respond to the CDI because of alarm over demands in the USA that American forces be withdrawn from Europe unless its allies spent more on defence. A motion calling for withdrawal failed in the American Senate in 1984 by only one vote. After the ending of the **Cold War**, the CDI became redundant as attention switched to reducing defence expenditure.

Conventional Forces in Europe (CFE). A framework of discussions between the **North Atlantic Treaty Organization (NATO)** and the **Warsaw Pact** on the reduction of conventional armaments in Europe. Originally called the Conventional Stability Talks (CST), they were held in conjunction with the 1989 sessions of the **Conference on Security and Co-operation in Europe (CSCE)** in Vienna. Agreement was reached on three issues: verification of levels by the other side; the exchange of military information; and an asymmetric reduction in armaments to take account of superior Warsaw Pact levels. The issue of verification was finalized in 1990 in an **Open Skies Agreement**, and a final CFE treaty was signed. It planned for a considerable reduction in the arms surplus created by the ending of the **Cold War**, with NATO planning to scrap its surplus material on the **Central Front** or transfer it to its poorer southern members.

Conventional Stability Talks. *See* CONVENTIONAL FORCES IN EUROPE.

Convention for the Prevention of Marine Pollution by Dumping from Ships and Aircraft. *See* OSLO CONVENTION.

Convention for the Prevention of Marine Pollution from Land-Based Sources. *See* PARIS CONVENTION.

Convention for the Protection of the Mediterranean Sea against Pollution. *See* BARCELONA CONVENTION.

Convention on Long-Range Transboundary Air Pollution. An international agreement, also known as the Geneva convention, signed in November 1979 by 29 European states as well as the USA and Canada. It was prepared under the aegis of the **Economic Commission for Europe**, coming into force in March 1983. It committed the signatories to a series of measures to limit, reduce and prevent air pollution. Stricter conditions were set by the Helsinki Protocol of 1985, with further requirements being added in 1988 and 1991.

Convention on the Conservation of European Wildlife and Natural Habitats. *See* EUROPEAN INFORMATION CENTRE FOR NATURE CONSERVATION.

Convention on the Protection of the Baltic Sea Area. The first international agreement on protection of the Baltic marine environment against pollution. Signed in Helsinki by all the littoral states, it became operational in May 1980. A Baltic Marine Environment Commission (the Helsinki Commission) was established to implement and supervise the terms of the Convention. In 1992 a second convention added further and more wide-ranging measures.

Convergence. A phrase used to describe the objective and process of encouraging the member states of the **European Communities (EC)** to work more closely together in the area of economic policy, especially with regard to inflation, deficits and interest rates. It was applied most importantly to the preconditions set after 1989 for **Economic and Monetary Union (EMU)** by 1999.

Convergence and Union. (*Convergència i Unió – CiU*) A nationalist party in **Catalonia**. Formed in 1979 through a merger of the Democratic Convergence party and a smaller Democratic Union, it quickly established itself as the largest party in the province, forming the regional government since the granting of autonomy by **Spain** in 1980. Centre-right in socio-economic orientation and in favour of further decentralization and ultimately independence, it agreed in 1993 to support a minority left-wing government in Madrid in return for further concessions.

Cooking Oil Affair. A political and commercial scandal in **Spain**. In 1981 some 600 people died and up to 25,000 suffered some form of permanent injury after consuming contaminated rapeseed oil meant for industrial use. The oil had been imported from **France** and sold as olive oil by door-to-door salespeople. Those responsible were not sentenced until 1989, and in 1994 several former government officials were indicted for professional negligence for authorizing the use of a drug-removing agent on the waste and for granting an import licence without instituting proper controls. The victims, however, received very little compensation.

Cools Case. The assassination of André Cools, a senior Belgian politician. A member of the **Socialist Party (PS)** who had earlier held a number of government posts, he was shot dead in Liège in July 1991. His murder was variously attributed to personal and party jealousy, extreme right-wing protest against his role in developing a federal structure for the country, and the **Agusta Affair**, but the assassin was never apprehended.

Co-operation Agreements. Bilateral agreements signed by the **European Communities (EC)** with countries outside Western Europe. They were similar to, but less comprehensive and liberal than, **Association Agreements**. They were signed with the Mashreq states of the Middle East, the Maghreb states of North Africa, Israel and the Andean Pact countries. Before 1989 there were similar agreements with some Eastern European countries.

Co-ordinating Committee for Multilateral Export Controls (COCOM). An association of Western democracies formed in 1949 to regulate the flow of equipment and technology of potential military significance to the **USSR** and its allies. Beginning in 1950 as a secretive body, it lacked any formal treaty or structure, and did not have any relationship with any other international agreement. Although an informal grouping, there was since the 1950s tension between the USA, which sought a more extensive embargo list, and its European allies. Controls were relaxed slightly in the 1970s during a period of super-power **détente**, but were made more stringent again, upon American insistence, after the Soviet invasion of **Afghanistan**. It was widely believed that the lengths to which the USSR went to obtain controlled items by illegal means indicated the importance and effectiveness of the association. After the ending of the **Cold War** its members agreed in 1990 to create a more selective core list of embargoed items. In 1993 it discussed extending an invitation of membership to **Russia** and other former Soviet bloc countries in order to strengthen the ability to prevent technology reaching what were deemed to be potentially aggressive states elsewhere in the world, but in March 1994 it was formally dissolved.

COREPER. *See* COMMITTEE OF PERMANENT REPRESENTATIVES.

Corporatism. A system of functional representation where organizations representing socio-economic interests possess a privileged institutionalized position with regard to public decision-making bodies and the formulation of public policy. Traditionally associated with Fascist and authoritarian regimes, a liberal variety developed in all European democracies to a greater or lesser extent after 1945, where it formed a network outside the formal system of democratic control by elections and legislatures. It typically involves close and formalized collaboration between government and major socio-economic interests such as employers' federations and trade unions. **Austria** has often been quoted as the best example of liberal corporatism, but its elements were also strongly present in the Nordic countries.

Corsica. An island in the Mediterranean belonging to **France** since 1768. Constituted as a separate region in 1970, it received the special status of a 'territorial collectivity' in 1982, with a directly elected assembly and substantial administrative powers. This was a limited response to years of demands by islanders for more autonomy within France. The agreement was never fully implemented, giving further ammunition to groups which sought independence. A series of terrorist acts led to the proscription of several nationalist groups, most notably the Corsican National Liberation Front (*Front Libération Nationale de la corse – FLNC*) and the Corsican Movement for Self-Determination (*Mouvement Corse pour l'Autodétermination – MCA*). After the MCA was banned, the political wing of the FLNC, the Nationalist Council (*Cuncolta Nazionalista*) campaigned for the recognition of the national rights of Corsicans and supported 'public struggles, including electoral ones' to obtain its objectives. In May 1988 the FLNC expressed a willingness to suspend operations in order to permit discussions with the French government on economic development and the provision of language teaching. The truce was broken by an FLNC bombing campaign in November 1989. Earlier in 1989 the island had been crippled by a general strike which demanded an 'insularity bonus' to compensate for the higher costs of living on the island. A government mediator's report in September contained little innovation, and the arguments over whether Corsica should have a special autonomous status and attention continued. Although some greater autonomy in specified policy areas was granted in 1991, the FLNC and other groups continued to insist upon direct action and independence.

Cosgrave, Liam. (1920–) Prime Minister of **Ireland** 1973–77. The eldest son of William Cosgrave, the first President of the Executive Council of the Irish Free State in 1922, he entered Parliament in 1943 as a member of **Fine Gael**. He held minor offices in the coalition governments of 1948–51 and 1954–57. He was elected party leader in 1965. His coalition government failed to come to grips with the economic problems of the mid-1970s, and economic discontent led to its defeat in the 1977 election. He retired from politics in 1981.

Cossiga, Francesco. (1928–) President of **Italy** 1985–92. An academic lawyer, he joined the **Christian Democratic Party (DC)** in 1945, serving in a variety of party positions before entering parliament in 1958. He first became a government minister in 1974, and served briefly as a stop-gap Prime Minister 1979–80. Elected to the presidency in 1985, he used the office to comment widely on Italian politics and policies. He criticized the judiciary for inefficiency and attacked the party system for failing to offer the electorate a meaningful choice between alternative governments. His more activist role was resented by many politicians, and during his last years in office he was engaged in a constant feud with his own party. In 1992 his repeated threats to dissolve parliament because of disputes between the parties and a growing stalemate over policies alienated him from almost all leading politicians. His resignation at the same time as that of the **Andreotti** government created a constitutional dilemma as without a president there was no one with the authority to appoint a new prime minister. After 1992 he aligned himself with the reformist tendency in Italian politics.

Costa v. ENEL. A 1964 ruling by the **Court of Justice** which established the primacy of **European Communities (EC)** law, and confirmed that it cannot be overruled.

Costello, John. (1891–1976) Prime Minister of **Ireland** 1948–51, 1954–57. A lawyer who had served as Attorney General in the 1920s, he was a compromise choice by his **Fine Gael** party to head a coalition government in 1948. His tenure in office was notable for the **Mother and Child Affair** and his decision in 1948 to take Ireland out of the **Commonwealth**.

Coty, René. (1882–1962) President of **France** 1954–58. He was first elected to Parliament in 1923 as a Republican Independent. Although generally respected by his fellow deputies, he was relatively unknown outside the legislature. He was elected to the presidency in 1954 on the 13th ballot, very much as a safe compromise choice. He took a more circumspect view of the presidency than his predecessor, **Auriol**, refraining from putting forward any personal views and accepting all government policies and enactments. As France drifted towards possible civil war in 1958 because of the **Algerian War of Independence**, he took the initiative to send for **de Gaulle** and threatened to resign if Parliament rejected his nomination of de Gaulle for the premiership. Although his action was strongly resented, it met little effective opposition. After de Gaulle became Prime Minister, Coty remained in office for seven months before resigning two years before his term was due to end, and effectively withdrew from politics.

Coudenhove-Kalergi, Richard. (1894–1972) Austrian diplomat and publicist of European unity. Born into a wealthy aristocratic family, his **Pan-European Union** of 1923 became a leading organization arguing the case for European integration in the inter-war period. During the war he lived in exile in the USA as a university professor, but after his return to Europe in 1946 he found that his influence had faded and he had little impact upon post-war debates. Breaking with the Union, he attempted to establish a

European Parliamentary Union as a new kind of lobby for integration. It remained almost still-born, and collapsed in the early 1950s. He became reconciled with the Pan-European Union, but by then it had shrunk to a minor body restricted largely to **Austria**.

Council for Cultural Co-operation (CCC).

A body established in 1962 by the **Council of Europe** to help realize the aims of the **European Cultural Convention**. It assimilated the other cultural bodies sponsored by the Council and became the principal agency for European cultural co-operation. Its major interest has been in education.

Council for Mutual Economic Assistance (COMECON/ CMEA).

An organization established by the **USSR** in January 1949 as part of its strategy for maintaining hegemony over Eastern Europe, subsequently developing into an agency of economic co-ordination and co-operation for the Communist bloc. In 1949 **Stalin** seemed to have no clear purpose in mind for it except perhaps as a counter-gesture to the **Marshall Plan**. It had a small secretariat and a Session of the Council in Moscow, but these had few resources and there was no constitution or defining document. While the satellite states were encouraged to develop heavy industries, this occurred on a national level without any attempt at international co-ordination. Its only immediate objective seems to have been to stress the expulsion of **Tito** from the **Communist Information Bureau (COMINFORM)** and to help the Eastern European countries to cope with the economic consequences of the boycott of **Yugoslavia**. After three meetings in 1949–50, it became more or less dormant until after Stalin's death. Twelve standing commissions were created 1955–60, and a constitution drafted. This produced an international executive by 1962, and regular meetings to work for joint planning, investment and co-operation. Yugoslavia and China were admitted as observers, and its membership expanded to include non-European states: Mongolia (1962), Cuba (1972) and Vietnam (1978). **Albania** was expelled in 1961, but was readmitted in 1971. In 1962 **Khrushchev** sought to fit it more closely to the dictates of a **command economy**, with centralized planning of production. A Basic Plan of International Socialist division of Labour proposed that each state other than the USSR should concentrate on only one or two economic specializations prescribed by COMECON, and that these products would be exchanged for Soviet primary products, especially oil. There were objections from Eastern Europe, most notably **Romania**, and the scheme was modified in 1963.

COMECON developed as essentially a semi-barter system where trade exchanges were calculated on the value of produced goods rather than money transfers. It was inefficient and produced two tiers: the internal market was dominated by poor quality goods, with the better products reserved for export to the West, but because COMECON currencies were non-convertible, Western trade was also semi-barter. The 1971 Complex Programme for the Development of Socialist Economic Integration called for long-term planning to deal with some of these problems, partly through adjusting to a common currency or convertible rouble by 1980. Talks with the **European Communities (EC)** began in 1976, but no progress had been made when they were ended in 1980 because of Western hostility to the Soviet invasion of **Afghanistan**. They were resumed in 1986, producing an agreement on mutual recognition in June 1988 and a series of trade agreements.

The collapse of the Communist regimes in 1989 called COMECON's viability into question. The new democratic governments accepted the difficulties of disentanglement, but were critical of its performance and record. In 1991 they proposed its replacement by a two-year interim body based upon market economy principles, the Organization for International Economic Co-operation. They also called for Western aid to convert themselves into market economies. With the fragmentation of the USSR at the end of 1991, COMECON effectively ceased to exist.

Council of Baltic Sea States. Established in March 1992 by all the Baltic littoral states and **Norway**, after a joint Danish–German initiative. The major objectives were to foster economic growth in the region and to create a mechanism for channelling aid from its Western members to the poorer East. The first agreements were for the funding of transport construction projects and the development of an anti-pollution resource plan for the **Baltic Sea**. It did not establish any institutional infrastructure, but agreed to hold annual summit meetings.

Council of Europe. An inter-governmental consultative body established in 1949 as Western Europe's first post-war political organization. It came indirectly out of the 1948 **Congress of Europe** and a blueprint drawn up by the **European Movement**. Its structure was a compromise between those countries which wanted it to be an agency of integration, and the **United Kingdom** and the Nordic states which refused to concede sovereignty and wanted only voluntary inter-governmental co-operation. It was established by the Treaty of Westminster, and was to be concerned with European co-operation (but not integration) in all areas bar defence. **France** provided permanent offices in **Strasbourg**, and English and French were adopted as its official languages. There were two major institutions: a Committee of Ministers and an Assembly. The Committee was to be a conference of foreign ministers meeting twice yearly, but after 1952 they usually attended only for highly symbolic occasions or issues, and the Committee has normally consisted of diplomats. It can only make recommendations to the member states, which are free to ignore them, and each country was given a veto in the Committee. The Assembly was given few substantive powers, able only to forward recommendations to the Committee which could ignore or reject them. The Assembly, whose delegates are appointed by or from national legislatures, has always supported European union, and in 1974 symbolically retitled itself the Parliamentary Assembly.

Until the formation of the **European Economic Community (EEC)** in 1957, the Council was the most important forum for discussions of integration, but could not itself serve as a base because of the negative attitudes of some of its members. Instead it sought broad organizational co-operation in a variety of less controversial areas, producing some 135 non-binding conventions or agreements. It also attempted to secure some co-ordination in economic policy areas. In 1960 its competence was extended by taking over from the **Western European Union (WEU)** the cultural responsibilities WEU had inherited from the 1948 **Treaty of Brussels**. Its formation in 1949 was a watershed, marking the end of the willingness of those who wished integration to compromise their objectives in order to carry with them more sceptical countries. It grew to incorporate all non-Communist states by the 1980s, and after 1989 it began to accept Eastern European countries as members. Its broad membership and weak powers enabled it to remain a forum where a variety of ideas and views could be discussed without prejudice or commitment, and it developed into a kind of clearing house for inter-governmental communication and information, receiving and reviewing reports from a variety of European and world organizations.

Council of European Municipalities and Regions (CEMR).
Established in **Geneva** in January 1951 as the Council of European Municipalities (CCE), changing its name in 1985. It was set up to be a forum for local mayors and regional officials within the member states of the **Council of Europe** as a forum for strengthening and promoting the activities of local and regional communities and authorities, especially in regional economic development and cross-border collaboration.

Council of Ministers. The essential decision-making authority of the **European Communities (EC)**, representing the national governments of the member states. While most proposals originate from the **Commission**, and though it may have to consult or deal with other bodies, the Council was given the authority to adopt proposals and legislate for the EC. Apart from one representative per state, it has no fixed membership. Its responsibility for a wide range of policy areas has meant that in practice there are several Councils, which can meet simultaneously in parallel sessions, and whose membership at any one session is determined by the specific policy agenda. The most important meetings are those of the foreign ministers, known as the **General Affairs Council**, who supervise and co-ordinate the several Council activities, as well as taking responsibility for broader or more sensitive issues. It has its own secretariat in **Brussels**. Its major supports are the permanent representatives (*see* PERMANENT REPRESENTATION) who meet regularly as the **Committee of Permanent Representatives (COREPER)**. The direction of the Council rotates across the member states every six months. The foreign minister who holds the presidency is expected to take the lead in securing Council agreement on issues, press for new initiatives, and advance causes beneficial to his or her country, but direction can be constrained by the pattern of voting in the Council. Where it is not presented with an unanimous recommendation from COREPER (when no vote is taken), the matter can be decided by a simple majority, qualified majority, or unanimously. Simple majority voting has generally been restricted to minor questions, often procedural in nature. With qualified voting, each state has an indivisible bloc of votes roughly proportionate to its population size, and a qualified majority has been two-thirds of the total. The **Treaty of Rome** anticipated a gradual increase in the use of majority voting, but this was blocked by **de Gaulle** in 1965 and the consequent **Luxembourg Compromise**. The 1987 **Single European Act (SEA)** significantly expanded the number of areas to which qualified majorities would apply, but the states failed to agree upon a meaningful extension of the system in the **Treaty on European Union**. The voting system, and the general preference of many states to operate by unanimity wherever possible, partly explain the relatively slow progress of much proposed EC legislation.

Court of Auditors. An agency which examines all accounts of revenue and expenditure of all **European Communities (EC)** institutions, publishing an annual report of its findings. It was created in 1977, replacing a more limited **Audit Board**. It has acted as a watchdog and critic of wasteful expenditure and, sometimes, financial mismanagement and fraudulent claims. Its members are appointed by the **Council of Ministers**, with one appointee per Member State. Appointees are expected to have had previous experience of the external audit section of their own national administration. Based in **Luxembourg**, it elects its own president from its membership for a renewable three-year term.

Court of First Instance. Established in September 1989 by the **European Communities (EC)** to lessen the workload of the **Court of Justice**. It was set up to take over the jurisdiction of some policy areas and some of the more minor categories of cases, but soon attempted to broaden its areas of competence.

Court of Justice. The organ of the **European Communities (EC)** with responsibility for EC law and ensuring that EC institutions and member states conform with the provisions of the **Treaty of Rome** and subsequent amending treaties. Based in **Luxembourg**, it soon became potentially the most significant EC institution. It has no direct links with national court systems and no control over how they apply and interpret national laws, but takes precedence over them since EC law takes precedence over national law. Within its area of competence it is supreme, with no appeal against its rulings. It hears three different types of cases. Opinions are given on international agreements to which the EC is party. Referrals are preliminary rulings on cases and points of EC law brought before it from national court systems: they have been used to ensure the pre-eminence of EC law and its uniform application across countries. Disputes have occupied most of its time: they have been between the EC and member states, between EC institutions, between member states, or between individuals and corporate bodies and the EC. Any one of these categories can seek to initiate Court proceedings. Most actions have been protests by individuals and companies against EC regulations, but the most active plaintiff and defendant has been the **Commission**. All member states have been the subject of charges brought by the Commission for failure to carry out EC obligations. In declaring both for and against EC institutions and member states, the Court has been very important in the consolidation and **harmonization** of EC law.

Couve de Murville, Maurice Jacques. (1907–) Prime Minister of **France** 1968–69. A career diplomat since 1930 and loyal Gaullist, he served **de Gaulle** as a faithful Foreign Minister 1958–68 before taking over briefly as Minister of Justice after the **May Events** of 1968. He replaced **Pompidou** as Prime Minister in July, entering Parliament for the first time. He lacked any individual power base or authority within the **Union for the New Republic (UNR)**, and when Pompidou became President in 1969 he was not included in the new government, and his attempt to return to Parliament failed with his defeat in a by-election. He was later elected to the Senate in 1986.

Craxi, Benedetto. (1934–) Prime Minister of **Italy** 1983–87. A member of the **Italian Socialist Party (PSI)**, he entered Parliament in 1968 and rose to become party leader in 1976. He continued to accept collaboration in centre-left coalitions with the **Christian Democratic Party (DC)**, and undertook a reform of the PSI which enabled him to bring the several factions under his control. His major objective was to establish the PSI as a government alternative to the DC. A weakened DC, which recorded its lowest ever vote in 1983, was forced to accept him as Prime Minister of a five-party (**pentapartito**) coalition government. He effectively led the coalition for almost five years. When it finally collapsed in March 1987 it had become the longest serving government since 1945. In 1992 his name surfaced in the widespread judicial investigation (**Clean Hands**) of political corruption originating in Milan, his political power base. Severely damaged by the allegations, which he strongly denied, he was forced to resign his party offices in 1993 as attempts were made to indict him. In 1994 he was found guilty of corruption in connection with the **Banco Ambrosiano Scandal**, and faced further court proceedings relating to illegal party funding.

Cresson, Edith. (1934–) Prime Minister of **France** 1991–92. A consultant economist, her political career began in the Republic Centre before joining the **Socialist Party (PS)** in 1975. Elected to the **European Parliament (EP)** in 1979, she returned to France to join the government in 1981, but entered Parliament only in 1986. Widely seen as a protégé of **Mitterrand**, her appointment as premier was meant to flag a leftward shift in PS policy-making towards more interventionism and protectionism. Her leadership style was contentious within the party and unpopular among the electorate, forcing her replacement after a year. In 1995 she was appointed to the **Commission** of the **European Communities (EC)**.

Crimea. A region of the **USSR**. Part of the Russian Empire since 1783, it was transferred from the Russian Federation to the **Ukraine** in 1954 by **Khrushchev**. Its major port, Sevastopol, was the base of the important Soviet Black Sea fleet, and its population remained largely Russian. These two factors created problems after the disintegration of the USSR. **Russia** and Ukraine held long and acrimonious arguments over the disposition of the fleet, and both laid claim to the territory. In 1993 the Russian Parliament demanded that the region be returned to Russian jurisdiction, but the claim was rejected out of hand by Ukraine. In 1994, Russian nationalists in the Crimea defied the Ukrainian government by establishing their own assembly, and after strong electoral support declared an intention to establish an autonomous republic in the region.

Crna Gora. *See* MONTENEGRO.

Croatia. One of the successor states and former region of **Yugoslavia**. Briefly independent in the tenth century, it was incorporated into **Hungary** until 1918. A separate republic was proclaimed in October 1918, but in 1921 it became part of the Kingdom of Serbs, Croats and Slovenes (later renamed Yugoslavia). The Croats, Catholic and more economically developed, objected to perceived Serb domination in the new state. In 1941 Germany established a puppet Croatia under Fascist terrorists led by Ante Pavelić who waged a war of atrocities against Serbs. In 1946 the region became a Socialist People's Republic within Yugoslavia. Although **Tito** was a Croat, the mutual antipathy between Serbs and Croats remained, albeit suppressed, and exiled Croat nationalists committed several terrorist attacks abroad. A new movement for autonomy and independence emerged in the 1980s after Tito's death, and a non-Communist regional government, headed by the Croatian Democratic Union (*Hrvatska Demokratska Zajednica – HDZ*) was elected in 1990. The HDZ quickly gained control of most institutions in the republic. In June 1991 Croatia followed the example of **Slovenia** and formally seceded from Yugoslavia. The new state fought with Serbian units for control of areas populated largely by Serbs. Croatia lost much of this territory in **Krajina** and **Slavonia** before an uneasy peace was arranged. In 1993 it became involved in the civil war in **Bosnia-Hercegovina**, where there was a substantial Croat population. Politics revolved around nationalism, with the dominant HDZ facing attacks from more rightist nationalist parties and groups, especially the Croatian Party of Rights (*Hrvatska Stranka Pava – HSP*). Discontent with HDZ domination led after 1992 to greater support for more moderate forces, led by the centrist Croatian Social Liberal Party (*Hrvatska Socijalno Liberalna Stranka – HSLS*), but the moderates remained fragmented and left-wing politics were almost totally absent. Western Slavonia was recaptured by Croat forces in 1995.

Croatian Republic of Herzeg-Bosnia. A state proclaimed by representatives of the Croat population of **Bosnia-Hercegovina**. Originally established as a 'community' in July 1992, shortly after the outbreak of the Bosnian war, it declared itself a republic in August 1993. The following February it agreed to a ceasefire and one month later it negotiated an agreement with the Bosnian government to form a Muslim–Croat Federation.

Crocodile Group. The colourful name of a group of Members of the European Parliament (MEPs) founded in 1980 by **Spinelli**. It took its name from the **Strasbourg** restaurant where the MEPS met. Its aim was to persuade the first directly elected **European Parliament (EP)** to develop a plan for a radical reform of the **European Communities (EC)** and a strategy for political union. The activities of the group led to the **Draft Treaty on European Union**.

Cruise Missiles. Intermediate range nuclear missiles developed by the USA. They were part of the armoury which the **North Atlantic Treaty Organization (NATO)** agreed to install in Western Europe after 1979 to counter what was perceived as a dangerous Soviet military build-up They became a popular symbol of the subsequent debates between NATO supporters and a regenerated disarmament movement.

CSCE. *See* CONFERENCE ON SECURITY AND CO-OPERATION IN EUROPE.

Cunhal, Alveiro Barreirinhas. (1913–) Portuguese politician. Joining the **Portuguese Communist Party** in 1931, he undertook a substantial reorganization of the party after 1941, establishing a large clandestine network throughout the country. Arrested first in 1937, and spending altogether 14 years in prison, often in solitary confinement, he became party leader in 1961. After the **Carnation Revolution**, he returned to **Portugal** and attempted to use the party as a springboard for a radical socialist revolution. He served in four provisional governments 1974–75, but as democracy reasserted itself, he and his party were pushed to the political sidelines. He resigned as party leader in 1992 but remained the most influential figure in the organization.

Curzon Line. The frontier between **Poland** and the **USSR** after 1945. It had first been proposed by the British Prime Minister, David Lloyd George, in 1920 as a possible boundary for the new Polish state. The subsequent negotiations were handled by the British Foreign Secretary, Lord Curzon, but the line was rejected by Poland. In 1939 it was used by Germany and the USSR to define their separate areas of occupation of Poland, and in 1945 Poland accepted that the areas east of the line were Soviet territory.

Customs union. An economic association of countries based upon an agreement to eliminate tariffs and other obstacles to trade within their union, but with a common trade policy towards third countries, usually through a **common external tariff (CET)** on goods imported into the union. The CET distinguishes a customs union from a **free trade area**, but the degree of co-ordination is less than in a **common market**. The first post-1945 union was **Benelux**, and a Nordic union was established later. The **European Communities (EC)** had a customs union largely in place by 1968, and later entrants to the EC have had to accept it immediately, but all were given a short transition period in which to adjust to its requirements.

Cyprus. An island in the Eastern Mediterranean disputed by **Greece** and **Turkey** because of its ethnically mixed population. Part of the Ottoman Empire 1571–1879, it was formally annexed by Britain in 1914, becoming a crown colony in 1925. Greek speakers, some 80 per cent of the population, wished for union (**enosis**) with Greece, and there were serious riots in 1931. They rejected a new constitution offered by Britain in 1948 because it did not provide for institutional links with Greece. By contrast, Turkish Cypriots favoured a form of partition. In 1951 and 1953 Britain rejected Greek proposals for a special status for the island within a form of enosis. Discontent crystallized in the **National Organization of Cypriot Fighters (EOKA)** terrorist movement led by **Grivas**, which conducted an extensive sabotage campaign over the rest of the decade. The unrest strained Anglo-Greek relations and intensified Turkey's concerns about the Turkish Cypriot minority. In 1959 Britain offered **Commonwealth** status to the island, and this was accepted by the Greek Cypriot leader, **Makarios**. A government was formed in 1960 with Makarios as President and the Turkish Cypriot leader, Fazil Kachuk, as Vice-President. Relations between the two language communities worsened and after extensive violence in 1963 a United Nations (UN) peace-keeping force was sent in the following year to maintain order.

By 1970 Turkish Cypriots had rejected the legality of the national government, accusing it of discrimination and establishing ther own unofficial assembly in northern Cyprus. In 1974 the military junta (the **Greek**

Colonels) in Athens engineered a coup and declared enosis, with Makarios fleeing into exile. Turkey's response was to invade the island, occupying some two-fifths of its territory and establishing a Turkish Federated State. Although the coup brought about the fall of the Greek junta, Cyprus was effectively partitioned into Greek and Turkish areas. Talks in **Geneva** between the interested parties and the **United Kingdom** failed, but Makarios returned in 1975 as President of Greek Cyprus. Further attempts at reconciliation foundered in 1977 with the death of Makarios. In November 1983 the Turkish Federated State unilaterally declared its independence as the **Turkish Republic of Northern Cyprus**, but this was recognized only by Turkey. The deadlock and partition persisted, with the Turkish Cypriot region ostracized by the rest of Europe. In 1987 the Greek Cypriot government signed an **Association Agreement** with the **European Communities (EC)**, and in 1990 submitted an application to join the EC, acts which it hoped would aid the reunification of the island.

Czechomoravian Centre Party. (*Českomoravská Strana Středu – ČMSS*) A political party in **Czechoslovakia** founded in 1990 as the Movement for Self-Governing Democracy of Moravia and Silesia, changing its name in January 1994. It claimed to represent the interests of the two smaller regions against possible domination by Bohemia, and after the formation of the Czech republic it argued that the new state should be reconstituted as a Czechomoravian Republic.

Czechoslovakia. A republic created in 1918 from the Western Slavonic provinces of the Habsburg Empire, incorporating Bohemia, Moravia-Silesia, **Slovakia** and **Ruthenia**. It contained a large German minority, and under the 1938 Munich Agreement was forced to cede territory to Germany, **Poland** and **Hungary**. Hitler annexed the Czech provinces in March 1939, with Slovakia remaining autonomous under German supervision. A provisional government in exile was formed by **Beneš** in July 1940. After liberation a post-war coalition government was established under Beneš. Ruthenia, with a largely Ukrainian population, was ceded to the **USSR** in July 1945, and the large German minority in the **Sudetenland** was expelled. The Communists became the largest party after the May 1946 election and dominated a coalition government headed by **Gottwald**.

By 1948 Communist popularity was in decline, partly because of its rejection, under Soviet pressure, of the **Marshall Plan**, and partly because of their attempts to dominate the police and army. Fearing defeat in the May election, Gottwald, supported by a workers' militia and the police, undertook a government reorganization that effectively was a coup, and proceeded to establish a Stalinist system of control, ruthlessly repressing dissidents and non-Communists. After his death in 1953 the system was maintained by **Novotný** until 1968. In 1966 discontent began to be openly expressed about the country's economic exploitation by the USSR, and the less-developed Slovakia voiced complaints about over-centralized government. Intellectuals attacked Novotný in June 1967, and four months later students demonstrated against the regime.

In January 1968 **Dubček** replaced Novotný as party leader. The new government presented a reform programme in April and proposed constitutional amendments – 'socialism with a human face' – to permit greater individual freedom and an element of political democracy. The USSR was not satisfied by Dubček's assurances that Czechoslovakia would remain a loyal ally, and on 20 August Soviet troops, backed by token forces from other **Warsaw Pact** state (except **Romania**), invaded the country to end the **Prague Spring**. The USSR justified its action by the **Brezhnev Doctrine**, claiming it had been necessary to forestall a counter-revolution directed from within the **Federal Republic of Germany**. Most of the planned reforms were immediately abandoned, but a federal state with separate Czech and Slovak republics was retained. Dubček was dismissed from office in April 1969. His successor, **Husák**, who also became President in 1975, reintroduced a hard-line policy, and Soviet troops remained in the country. Although relatively bloodless, the invasion hardened anti-Soviet feeling.

Dissidence continued in the 1970s, especially after the formation of **Charter 77**. Some limited reforms were introduced in the 1980s by the long-time (1970–88) prime minister, Lubomir Strougal. These were blocked when Husák resigned as Party Secretary in December 1987, to be replaced by another hard-liner, Milos Jakeš. Discontent broke out in January 1989 with a week of continuous protest countered by strong police action. After further protests, 12 opposition groups came together in November to form **Civic Forum**, with **Havel** as its leading spokesman. The Communists were forced to share power, and Jakeš and the **Politburo** resigned on 24 November, the day when Dubček returned to Prague. The Prime Minister, Ladislav Adamec, announced the end of the Communist monopoly of power four days later, and within two weeks Husák had resigned as President. The transition, known as the **Velvet Revolution**, was orderly and peaceful. Havel was nominated as President and Dubček as Chairman of the Federal Assembly pending free elections. The secret police and death penalty were abolished in 1990. Havel was elected as President of what was to be the Czech and Slovak Federative Republic. The new government planned a cautious and slow transition to a market economy, but this worried many in less prosperous Slovakia, where a renewed Slovak nationalism had proved electorally popular, and ethnic tensions began to increase. Despite Havel's efforts to maintain unity, Slovak demands for independence became louder, and they were not totally opposed by many Czech politicians. A timetable was agreed for a formal divorce to occur in January 1993 when Czechoslovakia ceased to exist.

Czechoslovak People's Party. (*Československá Strana Lidová*) A Catholic party, originally founded in 1919, included after 1948 in the **National Front of the Czechoslovak Socialist Republic**. It was allowed to operate only as an auxiliary of the **Communist Party of Czechoslovakia**, with the function of tying Christian groups more closely to the regime. In November 1989 it reorganized itself, replaced its leadership, and announced its intention to operate as an independent Christian Democratic Union (*Kresťansko Demokratická Unie – KDU*).

Czechoslovak Socialist Party. (*Československá Strana Socialistická*) A non-Communist party included after 1948 in the **National Front of the Czechoslovak Socialist Republic**. It was the successor to the historic National Socialist party founded in 1897, whose membership had been purged by the Communists. It operated only as an ancillary Communist organization. It was reconstituted in 1990 as the Czechoslovak Social Democratic Party (*Československá Strana Sociálně Demokratická*), changing its name in 1993 to the Liberal National Social Party (*Liberální Strana Národně Sociální*).

Czech Republic. One of the successor states of **Czechoslovakia**. Coming into existence in January 1993, it consisted of the provinces of Bohemia and Moravia-Silesia.

D

Dafiment and Jugoskandić Affair. A financial and political scandal in **Yugoslavia**. In 1991 the country's two largest private banks, Dafiment and Jugoskandić, attracted deposits from millions of small investors who saw the very high interest rates on offer as a protection against the current hyperinflation. A dubious financial scheme, it was endorsed by the **Milošević** government as a way of limiting social unrest in a time of economic uncertainty. The banks overextended themselves and both collapsed within a few weeks of each other in March 1993. Several senior politicians were arrested on charges of fraud, and the following year it was alleged that many more politicians, judges and bureaucrats had benefited from financial irregularities arising from the schemes.

Danube Group. *See* DONAULÄNDER.

Danzig. *See* GDANSK.

Davignon Report. A document prepared in 1970 by the foreign ministers of the **European Communities (EC)** outlining how further progress in integration could be maintained in the context of the impending enlargement of the EC's membership. Named after Vicomte Étienne Davignon of **Belgium**, it proposed that the EC should look first at policy areas where the states already possessed an identifiable commonality of interest, and recommended that the first steps should be in foreign policy. The report was put into effect more or less immediately, with the first ministerial foreign policy meeting held in November 1970. A second Davignon Report in 1973 argued that the system had been successful and should be continued. *See also* EUROPEAN POLITICAL CO-OPERATION.

Debré, Michel. (1912–) Prime Minister of **France** 1959–62. A lawyer and long-time ally and supporter of **de Gaulle** during the **Fourth French Republic**, he served in the Senate 1948–58. He was de Gaulle's chief constitutional adviser in 1958 and the major architect of the constitution of the **Fifth French Republic**, which he sought to tailor to de Gaulle's perceptions and needs. He later became the first premier of the new republic. After his resignation in 1962 he continued to serve as a minister in subsequent governments.

Decommunization. A term used to describe the process in Eastern

Europe after 1989 of removing from positions of authority officials and other public figures associated with the former Communist regimes. Members of the former security services were priority targets. The process was only in some instances placed on a formal legislative and legal basis, but often led to the prosecution of those accused for abuse of power and human rights, and misuse of public funds.

Decoupling. A concept relating to the nature of the linkage between American nuclear forces and the defence of Western Europe. In accepting in the 1950s that it could not match the conventional strength of the **Warsaw Pact**, the **North Atlantic Treaty Organization (NATO)** placed its faith in the American nuclear deterrent, but no American guarantee was given in the form of an explicit assurance. This created doubts as to whether the USA would use nuclear weapons in the event of a Warsaw Pact attack, that it might 'decouple' itself from Europe. It was one factor that led Western Europe to argue after 1977 for the **Euromissile** deployment in order to tie the USA more closely to Europe and to deter the **USSR** from risking an adventurist policy on the continent.

Deficiency Payments. A technique for ensuring that producers receive a fair price for their products and labour when the costs of the latter are higher than the prices for their produce obtainable on the open market. Deficiency payments, in the form of compensation subsidies, have been employed within the **Common Agricultural Policy (CAP)** as an integral part of the price guarantee system.

De Gasperi, Alcide. (1881–1954) Prime Minister of **Italy** 1945–53. Born in Trentino, then a Habsburg province, he was elected to the Vienna Parliament in 1911. After 1918 he joined the Italian People's Party and was a parliamentary deputy 1919–25. Briefly imprisoned by Mussolini in 1926, he lived in the **Vatican** 1929–43, forging links with Catholic **Resistance movement** groups. He was a founder of the **Christian Democratic Party (DC)** in 1945, and the first and longest-serving premier of the post-war republic, highly successful in maintaining authority over the heterogeneous DC. His governments established a programme of economic reconstruction and supported a Western security alliance. He welcomed an American commitment to Italian democracy in 1948 in the face of widespread rumours of a possible impending Communist coup, and he withstood Communist attempts to use general strikes as a means of bringing down the government. He also strongly supported European integration, believing that it and a security alliance would strengthen Italy against domestic extremist challenges, as well as helping its economic development. His actions and policies largely set the agenda of Italian foreign policy and domestic government strategy until the 1990s, when the ending of the **Cold War** and an escalation of political scandals brought the whole institutional and party framework into question.

De Gaulle, Charles André Joseph Marie. (1890–1970) President of **France** 1958–69. A career army officer, he refused to accept the surrender of France in 1940, fleeing to London and assuming leadership of the Free French forces. After the liberation of France in 1944, he became the head of a provisional government. In 1946, disillusioned by what he regarded as the selfish activities of the political parties and disliking the weak authority given to government by the constitution of the **Fourth French Republic**, he retired from politics. He remained a focal point and symbol for those conservative forces opposed to the Republic and desiring strong political leadership. He attempted a political comeback in 1947, forming the **Rally of the French People (RPF)**. Its initial electoral successes had little effect, and he had already distanced himself from it when he disbanded it in 1953.

A second comeback opportunity came in 1958 with a constitutional crisis and threat of military intervention occasioned by the **Algerian War of Independence**. Invited back to restore order and stability, he formed a government of national safety in May. He was able to dictate the terms on which he would assume office, and four months later a constitution for a new **Fifth French Republic** reflected his own views on government authority. He was elected President in December 1958. His first concern was to end the war in Algeria. His policy pushed right-wing army officers into rebellion, and he survived three assassination attempts. By 1962 he had curbed the army, and the **Évian Agreements** had given independence to Algeria. His style of government was highly personal and autocratic, with a major interest in foreign policy where he sought to restore French prestige. He specifically sought French leadership of the **European Communities (EC)**, strong links with the **Federal Republic of Germany** and the **USSR**, and less reliance on and subservience to the USA. He developed an independent French nuclear capability and in 1966 withdrew France from the integrated military command structure of the **North Atlantic Treaty Organization (NATO)**, demanding the removal from French soil of all NATO installations within a year.

On several visits to Eastern Europe after 1966 he proposed a Europe stretching from the Atlantic to the Urals, but this provoked little positive response from other countries, especially the USSR. He accepted the value of integration as long as it served French interests, but was hostile to the supranational implications of the **Treaty of Rome**. To preserve French influence in Europe, in 1963 and again in 1967 he vetoed the application by the **United Kingdom** for EC membership on the grounds that it was not a European nation. In 1965 he provoked a crisis in the EC to block moves that would have limited national sovereignty. In the short run he won all these disputes, but although the economy flourished under his presidency, there emerged a growing resentment of his autocratic style and the priority given to defence expenditure over social concerns. Student demonstrations in May 1968 were followed by the most sustained industrial strikes in French history, and he was forced to make economic and other concessions. He resigned in 1969 following an adverse referendum result on proposed institutional reform. He was the most prominent European politician of the 1960s, with much of the Western European political agenda revolving around him, but in the end he failed to push Europe totally in his desired directions.

Delegation for Nordic Economic Co-operation, *See* NABOLAND BOARDS.

Delgado, Humberto. (1906–1965) Portuguese politician. Born into a military family, he pursued a career in the air force, rising to the rank of general. He entered politics in 1958 by putting himself forward as a candidate for the presidency, the first ever opposition candidate to the **Salazar** regime. The campaign was stormy and violent, and after his substantial defeat he complained about the restrictions placed upon his campaign and that the results had been rigged. His actions made him the most prominent opponent of the regime, but six months later he sought political asylum in the Brazilian embassy. Stripped of his military rank, he subsequently left for exile in Brazil and Algeria. In 1964 he broke with other opposition politicians who resented his authoritarian manner. His murdered body was discovered in **Spain** in April 1965.

Delors, Jacques Lucien Jean. (1925–) President of the **Commission** 1985–1994. His earlier career was in economics and finance. He joined the French **Socialist Party (PS)** in 1974, and in 1979 was elected to the **European Parliament (EP)**. During his long leadership of the Commission, he had overall responsibility for implementing the **internal market** agreed upon by the **European Communities (EC)**, but his vision went beyond an economic market, arguing also for monetary and political integration. A powerful figure who dominated the Commission, his aim was to turn the EC into an effective political union. His important initiatives included the endorsement of the **Charter of Fundamental Social Rights**, the 1987 proposals for EC budgetary reform, and the 1988 proposals for **Economic and Monetary Union (EMU)**, all items which he argued must be included in the planned **Treaty on European Union**. His arguments were resisted most strongly by the **United Kingdom**, especially during the **Thatcher** premiership. Although many other countries had by 1990 indicated a wish to join the EC sooner or later, he insisted that his plans for closer union must take priority over enlargement. The outcome and aftermath of the 1991 Maastricht treaty indicated that his vision would not be totally implemented. After the results of the 1992 French and Danish referendums on the Treaty, he had to moderate his position slightly, but still insisted that if the EC were to be enlarged, it would survive only if national parity was abandoned and more authority given to its supranational institutions. Although widely courted and seen as a Socialist replacement for **Mitterrand**, in December 1994 he announced that he would not be a candidate for the French presidency.

De Maizière, Lothar. (1940–) Prime Minister of the **German Democratic Republic** 1990. A lawyer, he joined the East German **Christian Democratic Union (CDU)** in 1956, becoming its leader in November 1989. In the same month he was recruited into the **Modrow** government after the Communist regime had opened up the **Berlin Wall**. As party leader he sought to distance it from the dominant **Socialist Unity Party (SED)**, though rejecting demands from the West German Chancellor, **Kohl**, not to collaborate with the SED. After the CDU's success in the free elections of March 1990, he formed a coalition government which began to prepare the way for reunification. In the 1990 all-German elections, the East German CDU again proved highly popular. Made deputy leader of the integrated CDU, he resigned as an interim minister in the all-German government in December 1990 as a result of accusations that he had been a **Stasi** informant. He was exonerated by a government inquiry in February 1991, but the following September resigned his party posts and retired from politics.

Demirel, Süleyman. (1924–) President of **Turkey** from 1993. An electrical and hydraulic engineer after 1949, he was co-founder, in 1961, and leader of the **Justice Party** 1964–80, serving as Prime Minister on several occasions, 1965–71, 1975–77, 1977–78, 1979–80, and 1991–93. After the 1980 military coup, he and other senior politicians were banned from political activity for ten years. The ban was ignored long before it was lifted in 1987, and after the ending of military rule in 1982 he formed the **True Path Party** as a successor to the Justice Party. A highly paternalistic figure, he resigned as premier and gave up his party offices after his election to the presidency in 1993.

De Mita, Luigi Ciriaco. (1928–) Prime Minister of **Italy** 1988–89. Elected to Parliament in 1963 as a member of the **Christian Democratic Party (DC)**, he served in a variety of party and government positions after 1973. In March 1979 he was appointed vice-secretary of the party, becoming secretary in 1982. Chosen to bring some order and reform to the faction-ridden and scandal-prone DC, his efforts to impose authority and overhaul the structure were not entirely successful, and his control of the party was already on the wane when he became Prime Minister in 1988. The DC backed his bid only on the condition that he give up the party secretaryship. He chose to move to become the party's president in February 1989, but three months later internal party tensions brought his government down. In 1990 he resigned the party presidency after continuing internal DC arguments, and his faction withdrew from all leadership posts. Invited to head a commission on constitutional reform in September 1992, he resigned the following March after his brother was charged with fraud. In May 1993 he was accused of involvement in the embezzlement of public funds allocated for the rebuilding of the region around Naples devastated by an earthquake in 1980.

Democratic Action Party. (*Stranka Demokratske Akcije – SDA*) A major political party in **Bosnia-Hercegovina**. Centre-right on socio-economic issues, it was the major representative of the Muslim community, leading coalition governments after 1990. Originally committed to the retention of a unitary state in Bosnia, the consequences of the civil war forced it to moderate its position and accept that some form of partition was inevitable.

Democratic Alliance. (*Alleanza Democratica – AD*) A political party in **Italy**. Formed in 1992 as an 'honest alternative' to the discredited traditional party system, it turned itself into a party in May 1993. Despite its claims, it contained many members of the old secular parties of the collapsed **pentopartito**.

Democratic Alternative. (*Demokraattinen Vaihtoehtie – Deva*) The electoral organization of the orthodox Marxist-Leninist group (Finnish Communist Party – Unity) within the **Finnish Communist Party (SKP)** until both groups were dissolved in April 1990. It was established in 1986, after a decade of internal disputes, by opponents of the SKP adoption of **Eurocommunism**. With little support or success, it dissolved itself in 1990 to join in a new **Left-Wing Alliance**.

Democratic and Social Centre. (*Centro Democrático y Social – CDS*) A liberal reformist party in **Spain**. It was founded in 1982 by **Suárez** as a successor to his **Union of the Democratic Centre**, and was intended to be a moderate centre-left alternative to the **Spanish Socialist Workers' Party (PSOE)**. It failed to establish itself as a meaningful force. Its leadership was unable to prevent local organizations acting independently, many of them preferring to forge alliances with the right-wing **Popular Party**, and in 1993 it collapsed completely.

Democratic Centralism. The organizing principle of the **Communist Party of the Soviet Union**, and adopted by other Communist parties. It referred to the election of leaders and free discussion of an issue at all levels of the party until a decision was reached, at which point all discussion had to cease with all members accepting the decision without reservation. In practice, because of the strict internal hiararchy within the parties of a military-style chain of command, it meant that decisions were formulated at the top of the structure and transmitted downwards, with little opportunity for or approval of general discussion and grass-roots initiatives or criticisms.

Democratic Convention of Romania. (*Conventie Democraţie din România – CDR*) A loose alliance of some 20 parties in **Romania** opposed to the **National Salvation Front** government after 1989. Formed in 1990, its frequent change of name and composition reflected the fragmented nature of party politics. Mainly urban in nature, its cohesion rested mainly on a common commitment to a market economy and extensive political reforms.

Democratic Deficit. A phrase used critically within the **European Communities (EC)** to describe a perceived lack of democratic participation in and control over the decision-making institutions of the EC. The way to resolve the problem is usually claimed to be providing the **European Parliament (EP)** with more effective authority over the **Commission**, and reducing the influence of the **Council of Ministers** and the national governments.

Democratic Departure. (*Demokratischer Aufbruch – DA*) A centre-right party in the **German Democratic Republic (DDR)**. A new opposition formation established in 1989, it participated in the **Round Table** talks on the future of the DDR and in 1990 agreed to enter the electoral **Alliance for Germany**. The prospects of it establishing itself as a significant political force were severely damaged when its founder and leader, Wolfgang Schur, admitted that he had been forced to collaborate with the **Stasi**.

Democratic Front. (*Fronti Demokratik*) A front organization of the Albanian **Party of Labour**. Nominally, all adult Albanians were supposed to belong to it, but in practice it was indistinguishable from the party organization. Its major function was supposed to be that of drawing up the single list of candidates for national and local elections.

Democratic Front of Francophones. (*Front Démocratique des Francophones – FDF*) A regional party in **Belgium** claiming to represent the interests of **Brussels**. It was founded in 1965 as a reaction to pressures for decentralization of power to the provinces of **Flanders** and **Wallonia**. While seeking to preserve the French-speaking character of Brussels, it demanded that the city be treated as a distinct third element in any devolutionary process. Enjoying considerable electoral success in the 1970s, it later lost substantial amounts of its support.

Democratic Left Party. (*Demokratik Sol Partisi – DSP*) A political party in **Turkey** founded in 1985 by **Ecevit** supporters as a successor to the historic **Republican People's Party** banned by the military in 1980. Ecevit took over the leadership in 1986, but resigned the following year after a poor electoral performance.

Democratic Left Party. *See* COMMUNIST PARTY OF CZECHOSLO-VAKIA.

Democratic Left Party. *See* COMMUNIST PARTY OF SLOVAKIA.

Democratic Left Party. *See* WORKERS' PARTY.

Democratic Movement of Serbia. (*Demokratska Pokret Srbije –* *DEPOS*) A loose political alliance in **Serbia** formed in 1992 by a variety of groups opposed to the **Milošević** government, ranging in orientation from centre-left to right-wing. Its stance became more conservative and it became dominated by the ultra-nationalist Serbian Renewal Movement (*Srpski Pokret Obnove – SPO*) which advocated the incorporation of all the historic lands into a Greater Serbia, and the restoration of the monarchy.

Democratic Party. (*Dimokratikó Kómma – DIKO*) A centre-right party in **Cyprus**. It was formed in 1976 after the Turkish occupation of northern Cyprus, winning its first election with an absolute majority. Its leader, **Kyprianou**, was elected President in 1977, but in 1981 it could continue in office only in coalition. Its popularity waned further in the 1980s. Its control of government ended in 1985 when its coalition partners objected to Kyprianou's handling of the intercommunal negotiations on ending the partition of the island, and in 1988 it also lost the presidency. Prone to internal factionalism, it was more willing than most Greek Cypriot parties to accept that Turkish Cypriot concerns had to be taken into account in any solution to the island's problems.

Democratic Party. (*Parti Démocratique – PD*) A centrist party in **Luxembourg**. Founded in the 1840s as a conservative party, it is the smallest of the country's three major parties. After 1945 it participated as a junior partner in most government coalitions, but went into opposition in 1984. Its electoral support began to decline after 1980.

Democratic Party. (*Stronnictwo Demokratyczne*) A political party in **Poland**. Formed during the Second World War, it was a member of the first post-war coalition government, but in 1946 joined the Communist-led Democratic Bloc against the Peasant Party. It soon fell under Communist domination and until 1989 was no more than an ancillary of the **Polish United Workers' Party (PUWP)**, with the task of mobilizing white collar groups in support of the regime. It broke with the PUWP in 1989 and declared itself in favour of democratization, but its past history militated against it after the establishment of a democratic regime.

Democratic Party. *See* NATIONAL SALVATION FRONT.

Democratic Party. (*Demokrat Partisi – DP*) A political party in **Turkey**. Founded as a centre-right organization in 1945, under the leadership of **Menderes** it formed the government of 1950–60. Fearing that it was moving to accept Muslim ideas, the military seized power in 1960. Menderes was executed and the party banned. In 1961 it was reconstituted as the **Justice Party**.

Democratic Party. (*Demokrat Parti – DP*) A political party in the **Turkish Republic of Northern Cyprus**. It was founded in 1992 as a secession from the ruling **National Unity Party** by those who opposed the policy of refusing to consider the possibility of reunification of the island through a federal or confederal solution. Supported by **Denktash**, it became a major force after 1993, absorbing several other movements, including the **New Dawn Party**.

Democratic Party of Albania. *See* BERISHA, SALI.

Democratic Party of the Left. *See* ITALIAN COMMUNIST PARTY.

Democratic Peasants' Party. (*Demokratische Bauernpartei Deutschlands – DBD*) A political party in the **German Democratic Republic (DDR)**. It was one of two parties founded in 1948 by the **Socialist Unity Party (SED)** to mobilize specific social groups in support of the regime. The DBD's targets were the peasantry and agricultural workers, and it played a major role in the **collectivization** programme of the late 1950s.

Democratic Rally. (*Dimokratikós Synagermós – DISY*) A conservative party in **Cyprus**. Formed in 1976 as a merger of two smaller groupings opposed to **Makarios**, it became the leading right-wing political group after 1981. Led by **Klerides** 1976–93, it was reluctant to consider a federal solution to the partition of the island.

Democratic Renewal. (*Dimokratikis Ananeosis*) A centre-right party in **Greece**. It was formed in 1985 by Kostis Stefanopoulos and other rebel deputies from **New Democracy**, who seceded in protest against the pursuance by the latter's leaders of party advantage rather than the public interest. It failed to secure a mass base, and after 1990 its sole remaining parliamentary deputy collaborated closely with New Democracy.

Democratic Renewal Party. (*Partido Renovador Democrático – PRD*) A centre-left party in **Portugal**. It was founded in 1975 by supporters of **Eanes** and was intended to be a personal vehicle for him. It largely reflected his views, but its personalized character prevented it from becoming an important force in its own right, and after 1985 it declined rapidly in significance. Eanes led it only briefly from 1986–87.

Democratic Russia. A political party in **Russia**. An alliance of most of the reformist groups that after 1991 brought **Yeltsin** to power, it suffered from severe internal factionalism, and in 1993 it was reduced to an ineffectual rump, especially after the formation of **Russia's Choice** and **Russian Unity**.

Democratic Social Centre-People's Party. (*Centro Democrático Social-Partido Popular – CDS-PP*) A political party in **Portugal**. Founded in 1974 as a Christian Democrat organization which participated in the first democratic governments, it moved to the right after 1980, when its support began to decline.

Democratic Union. (*Unia Demokratyczna*) A political party in **Poland**. Formed after 1989 as a union of several organizations, all coming out of the earlier **Solidarity** movement, it emerged as the largest party in the 1991 election, but with only some 12 per cent of the vote. Centrist in orientation, it was severely divided between left and right factions on many issues. In 1994 it abandoned independence and merged with other groups in the Freedom Union (*Unia Wolości*) led by **Mazowiecki**.

Democratic Unionist Party (DUP). A Protestant party in **Northern Ireland**. Founded in 1971 as a split from the **Ulster Unionist Party**, it challenged the **Official Unionist Party** as the voice of the Protestant community under its outspoken and controversial hard-line leader, **Paisley**. Conservative on socio-economic issues, it demanded the restoration of substantial autonomy to the province, but rejected the notion of Irish unity and any compromise with **Ireland**. It endorsed the peace initiative of 1994 only with great reluctance and suspicion.

Democrats 66. (*Democraten 66 – D66*) A liberal party in the **Netherlands**. Founded in 1966 by young radical activists, it called for a revolutionary overhaul of Dutch politics, a breaking of the domination of religious parties and a refocusing on socio-economic issues. It saw itself as a party of the new generations, and at the beginning most of its voters were aged under 35. It matured in the 1970s to become more centrist, and increasingly willing to enter coalition governments with the more conservative **Christian Democratic Appeal (CDA)**, though continuing to advocate a more decentralized form of decision-making and a greater concern for the environment. It renamed itself the Liberal Democratic Party in 1994.

Denktash, Rauf. (1924–) President of the **Turkish Republic of Northern Cyprus** from 1983. A lawyer, he worked for various Turkish Cypriot organizations after 1958, leading the Turkish Cypriot communal legislature in 1960. In exile 1963–68, he became Vice-President of **Cyprus** 1973–75. The leader of the **National Unity Party (UAP)**, he headed the Turkish Federated State of Cyprus in 1975 after the Turkish invasion of the island. After the creation of the republic, he was made President and won re-election on several occasions, though breaking with the UAP in 1992.

Denmark. A constitutional monarchy since 1849, in the early twentieth century it pursued a policy of neutrality. It was invaded and occupied by Germany in 1940. From 1945 to the early 1970s its politics were dominated by four parties, divided into a left and right alliance. Under the leading **Social Democratic Party**, it built up an extensive welfare state. The party system fragmented in 1973, after which governments, either single party or coalitions, have rarely had a parliamentary majority. The consequences have been an increase in the influence of parliament over policy, especially in foreign affairs, and the need for governments to shop around for a majority on an *ad hoc* policy-by-policy basis: the increased likelihood of government failure on specific issues has meant that resignation is not regarded as a necessary response to parliamentary defeat. To ensure its security, Denmark joined the **North Atlantic Treaty Organization (NATO)** in 1949 as a founder member, but it imposed limitations upon its involvement, in particular refusing to allow allied troops or nuclear weapons on its territory. It has often been regarded as a reluctant member of NATO. In 1960 it was a founder member of the **European Free Trade Association (EFTA)**, but in 1973 resigned when it became a member of the **European Communities (EC)**. Since 1945 it has been generally sceptical of integration endeavours and suspicious of supranationalism. Its motives for joining the EC were economic, and there has persisted a strong opposition to membership. This became more manifest in the late 1980s with problems in ratifying the **Single European Act (SEA)**. In 1992 a referendum rejected the **Treaty on European Union**, and extensive negotiations had to be held before a second referendum the following year approved ratification of changes which permitted Denmark to opt out of several of the major objectives of the treaty.

Derogation. A term used within the **European Communities (EC)** which refers to a decision to exempt one or more of the member states from some specified provisions of EC legislation. In theory, the exemptions are intended to be temporary, to allow governments time to adapt to the legislative requirements, but in practice there has been a tendency for them to become permanent. *See also* OPT OUT.

Der Spiegel Affair. A political scandal and civil rights issue in the **Federal Republic of Germany** in 1962. The government ordered a raid on the offices of the news magazine, *Der Spiegel*, and arrested its editors. The journal was alleged to have illegally obtained and published secret defence documents. The action was strongly criticized in the country at large, the small **Free Democratic Party (FDP)** threatened to withdraw from the coalition, and the Minister of Justice, who had not been informed in advance of the raid, resigned. The Minister of Defence, **Strauss**, who had sanctioned the action (and who had been the subject of investigations by the magazine), was forced to resign, and the government indictment was later quashed in the courts. The affair contributed to the weakening of the authority of **Adenauer** and effectively destroyed the national political ambitions of Strauss.

De-Stalinization. The official process in the **USSR** of reversing the cult of personality associated with the **Stalin** dictatorship. It began with the 1956 attack on Stalin by **Khrushchev** and was heightened in 1961 by such symbolic acts as renaming Stalingrad Volgograd and the removal of the dictator's embalmed body from the Red Square mausoleum in Moscow. Further and more extensive critical evaluations and indictments of the regime were undertaken under **Gorbachev** after 1985.

Détente. A term broadly used since the mid-1950s to describe a lessening of tension in the **Cold War**. More recently, it was used to refer more specifically to the reduction of antagonism between the super-powers in the early 1970s, after the 1972 visit of President Nixon to Moscow and the successful conclusion of the bilateral Strategic Arms Limitation Talks (SALT I). It was a highly subjective and rather misleading term since the super-powers never ceased their competition and rivalry. Each side had a different definition and understanding of détente. Insofar as it was real, it related less to military agreements than to the recognition of a stalemate and a mutual economic interdependence and interest in agreeing to some degree of **arms control**. Its importance for Europe was more psychological. It related to perceptions of a lessening of tension and risk of a continental war.

Deterrence. Any policy or strategy designed to persuade a potential aggressor not to attack. After 1945 it was particularly associated with nuclear deterrence, to prevent aggression by making the costs to an assailant greater than any benefits that might come from military success. It was a primary function of the **North Atlantic Treaty Organization (NATO)**, with **massive retaliation** seen as more cost-effective than conventional forces for the protection of Western Europe. Deterrence lay at the heart of Western security, often being used interchangeably with defence. But the two terms did mean different things. When the USA adopted the principle of massive retaliation, it was because nuclear deterrence was cheaper than conventional defence, and this remained unchanged after the adoption of the principle of **flexible response**. The difficulty was that to be credible in deterring aggressors, the deterrent had to be employed in the last resort. The key issue was that while NATO forces would respond to any invasion by the **Warsaw Pact**, it was always uncertain whether the USA would sanction the nuclear option should the conventional forces appear to be in danger of being overwhelmed.

De Valéra, Éamonn. (1882–1975) Prime Minister 1932–48, 1951–54, 1957–59, and President 1959–73 of **Ireland**. Born in New York of an Irish mother and Spanish father, he joined **Sinn Féin** and was a leader of the 1916 Easter Rising. Reprieved from the death penalty because of his American citizenship, he later became President of the rebel independent assembly (*Dáil Éireann*) established by Sinn Féin in 1919. He repudiated the 1922 agreement for an Irish Free State, but in 1926 abandoned direct action and founded **Fianna Fáil**. His long tenure as Prime Minister, which led to him being regarded as the father of modern Ireland, was marked by a determination to gain full political and economic independence from Britain and to achieve Irish reunification. He decided to retire from active politics in 1959, and ran for the ceremonial presidency. His previous popularity began to erode in the 1960s and he barely won the 1966 presidential election.

Developed Socialism. An official doctrine adopted by the **USSR** during the **Brezhnev** regime. It purported to describe the stage of social development reached by the USSR by the late 1960s.

Dien Bien Phu. A remote but strategic village in **French Indo-China** and scene of the decisive battle between French forces and Communist nationalist insurgents. Seized by French troops in November 1953 as part of a strategy to force the Viet-Minh guerillas into a set-piece battle, it was besieged from 13 March to 7 May 1954, with its position increasingly untenable. The siege ended with the surrender of the French forces, and within two months the defeat had led to an armistice and the end of French rule in Indo-China. It greatly weakened the **Fourth French Republic** and helped to alienate the army, which believed that it had not received sufficient political support from Paris. It buttressed the military's determination, in the subsequent **Algerian War of Independence**, not to suffer a similar humiliation.

Die Wende. (The Turning Point) A German phrase widely used to describe the transitional period from the collapse of the Communist regime in the **German Democratic Republic (DDR)** in November 1989 through to the formal reunification of the two German states the following October.

Dimitrov, Georgi. (1882–1949) Prime Minister of **Bulgaria** 1946–49. Joining and organizing the Communist Party in 1917, he fled to Moscow in 1923. After 1929 he headed the Bulgarian section of the Third International (Comintern) in **Berlin**, where he was arrested and tried in 1933 for complicity in the Reichstag fire. Deported back to the **USSR**, he returned to Bulgaria in 1945 as head of a Soviet-sponsored provisional government. In 1946 he established the Bulgarian People's Republic, introducing a ruthless policy of Stalinization, but attempted to develop close relations with **Yugoslavia**. He was a personal friend of **Tito**, but with his health failing, he played little part in the denunciation by **Stalin** of revisionism which followed the dispute between the USSR and Yugoslavia. He died in Moscow while visiting the USSR for medical treatment.

Di Pietro, Antonio. (1950–) Italian public prosecutor. A police officer who rose to the rank of commissioner, he subsequently acquired qualifications in law and transferred to the public prosecutors' office. In 1985 he was moved to Milan where he became the leading investigator in the **Clean Hands** operation, becoming also a national symbol of the exposure of the political corruption that seemingly pervaded the whole system.

Diplock Courts. The popular name for special courts established in **Northern Ireland** in 1974. They were for the trial of individuals accused of offences relating to political and sectarian violence where it was normally difficult to secure unbiased or unintimidated witnesses. They were distinctive because they involved a single judge sitting without a jury, and with more diffuse rules on admissable evidence and the rights of defendants. Named after Lord Kenneth Diplock, who chaired the commission which recommended their introduction, they were controversial and the subject of strong criticism from human rights organizations.

Direct Information Access Network for Europe (Euronet-Diane). One of the first information networks in Europe, initiated by the **European Communities (EC)** to encourage cross-national collaboration in telecommunications. It began operations in 1980 as a joint venture between the EC and the national postal and telephone authorities which enabled users to tap the resources of some 750 data bases. The control and management centre was located in London, with regional nodes set up in other European cities.

Disarmament. An objective of peace movements, focusing after 1945 on nuclear weapons. While countries subscribed to the principle, little progress was made on general or complete disarmament, with doubts persisting about the value or success of agreements on weapons-specific disarmament. The major problem was that the technology of warfare, once invented, cannot be unmade. No disarmament movement met with success, and governments preferred instead to work for policies of **arms control.**

Djilas, Milovan. (1911–1995) Yugoslav Communist and dissident. A Montenegran intellectual who became a Communist in 1929, he was imprisoned for his beliefs in 1933–36. He became a supporter and close ally of **Tito**, being appointed Vice-President in 1946, and in 1948 issued an ideological defence of the 'Yugoslav road to socialism' after the split with the **USSR** . In 1953 he declared the Leninist state obsolete and attacked the party leadership for corruption and abuse of power. He was dismissed from government and expelled from the party. In prison 1956–61, he was re-arrested in 1962 for continuing dissent. He was released in 1966, but in 1969 was banned from travelling abroad. The ban was only lifted in 1988, and in 1989 he was rehabilitated by the party. A committed socialist, he was a persistent critic of the way in which **Communism** had produced party oligarchies which perpetuated privilege, and consistently warned that because of this they carried the seeds of their own destruction.

Dobrudja. A coastal region of the Black Sea around the mouth of the Danube. South Dobrudja was disputed by **Bulgaria** and **Romania** after 1878, changing hands several times. The 1947 **Paris Peace Treaties** confirmed Bulgaria's right to the area, and Romania later formally abandoned its claim on the territory.

Doctors' Plot. An accusation levelled by **Stalin** in January 1953 against a group of doctors in Moscow. They were accused of having conspired to murder members of the Soviet leadership, beginning with Stalin himself, on behalf of Zionist and imperialist interests. The accusations reflected the intense **anti-semitism** of Stalin's later years. The charges were clearly fabricated, and those accused were liberated in April following the dictator's death.

Dodecanese. A group of islands in the eastern **Aegean Sea**. Part of the Ottoman Empire after the sixteenth century, they were seized by **Italy** in 1912, though claimed by **Greece**. In 1947 they were ceded to Greece which in 1954 agreed to the demilitarization of Leros, less than 30 miles from **Turkey**, but the Greek presence on the islands and claims on the surrounding sea-bed continued to strain Greek–Turkish relations.

Donauländer. An association of regions along the Danube, established after an Austrian initiative in May 1990. Several regional authorities from **Bavaria** in the west to **Moldova** in the east agreed to collaborate on reviving the river as a major trade route in order to help develop commerce in Eastern Europe, and to sponsor cultural links. The agreement did not resolve all conflicts over rights of access to the river.

Dooge Committee. An *ad hoc* group of 'personal representatives' of the leaders of the Member States of the **European Communities (EC)**, also known as the Committee on Institutions, established in 1984. Chaired by James Dooge of **Ireland**, it was charged with examining the possibility of institutional reform in the EC in the light of the **Draft Treaty on European Union** issued by the **European Parliament (EP)**. Its final report, which included several recommendations for change that primarily involved strengthening the supranational elements of the EC, was published in June 1985. Several of its ideas were later incorporated into the treaty revisions of 1987 and 1991.

Double Zero Option. The proposed removal of all short- and intermediate-range nuclear missiles from Europe. It arose during the 1986 Reykjavik summit between **Gorbachev** and USA President Reagan. In 1981 Reagan had called for a **Zero Option**, the withdrawal of intermediate-range missiles from the European theatre. His allies gave the call a guarded welcome, concerned that it might leave them at a disadvantage because of **Warsaw Pact** superiority in short-range missiles. The Double Zero Option was meant to allay these worries. It was not a complete nuclear ban: it did not cover battlefield nuclear weapons nor the deployment of ballistic missile submarines. Both sides accepted its principles, but its objectives were not met until after the ending of the **Cold War**.

Douglas-Home, Alexander Frederick. (1903–1995) British Prime Minister 1963–64. Entering Parliament for the **Conservative Party** in 1931, he succeeded as Earl of Home in 1951, moving to the House of Lords. He served in various government positions, eventually as Foreign Secretary 1960–63. He was the surprise and controversial choice of **Macmillan** to be his successor as premier, an event which persuaded the party to change its method of selecting its leader. He disclaimed his peerage in order to return to the House of Commons. As premier he pursued a high-risk policy of monetary expansion, but lost the 1964 election. He led the party for a further nine months before being replaced by **Heath**. He served again as Foreign Secretary 1970–74 before being made a life peer, Lord Home of the Hirsel.

Downing Street Declaration. A declaration issued in 1993 by the Prime Ministers of **Ireland** and the **United Kingdom**. It declared their intention to launch a new initiative on **Northern Ireland** – though mostly restating principles set down in the 1985 **Anglo-Irish Agreement** – which could involve discussions among all interested groups if terrorist activities were called off. It led by the end of 1994 to a military truce being accepted by the terrorist groups and discussions, *inter alia*, between British diplomats and representatives of **Sinn Féin**.

Draft European Act. *See* GENSCHER–COLOMBO PLAN.

Draft Treaty on European Union. A proposal that the **European Communities (EC)** form a political union, approved overwhelmingly by the **European Parliament (EP)** in February 1984. The groundwork was begun in 1980 by **Spinelli** and the **Crocodile Group**, and in 1981 the EP appointed an Institutional Committee to prepare a blueprint. The Treaty sought increased powers for the EC's supranational institutions and a severe reduction in the influence of national governments, but it was largely ignored by the latter. Some of its ideas were incorporated into the discussions of the late 1980s on the future progress and objectives of the EC which culminated in the **Treaty on European Union**.

Dubček, Alexander. (1921–1992) Secretary of the Czechoslovakian Communist Party 1968–69. Brought up in the **USSR**, he returned to **Slovakia** in 1938, joining the Party in 1939. He held various party offices after 1945 before becoming principal secretary of the Slovak party in Bratislava in 1958. He was nominated to succeed **Novotný** in January 1968, even though he had not played a prominent role in the criticisms of Novotný's leadership. He wished to reduce the authoritarian nature of Communism and during the **Prague Spring** he and a number of reformist colleagues set in motion a programme of economic and political liberalization, while still attempting to assure an alarmed USSR that the country would remain a loyal ally. His pledges failed to satisfy **Brezhnev** and other **Warsaw Pact** leaders. On 20 August Soviet and Pact forces occupied **Czechoslovakia**. Dubček and his fellow liberals were taken to Moscow and forced to renounce the reform programme. Dismissed from office in 1969, he was sent briefly as ambassador to **Turkey**. Recalled the following year he was expelled from the party. For the next 20 years he was allowed to hold only minor administrative positions in Slovakia. He returned to Prague in 1989 after Communist rule collapsed. Treated as a hero, he was elected

Speaker of the National Assembly and played a supporting role in the democratization process until his death in a car accident.

Dublin Convention on Asylum. A **European Communities (EC)** document signed in 1990 outlining common formal arrangements and asylum procedures throughout the EC. Most important, it stipulated that when individuals have been refused asylum in one Member State, they cannot seek it in another signatory state, and confirmed that the Member State where the refugee arrives is responsible for dealing with the asylum request.

Dulles, John Foster. (1888–1959) USA Secretary of State 1953–59. With a career in diplomatic and government service since 1919, after his appointment by President Eisenhower in 1953, he pursued a hard anti-Communist line. He emphasized the strategy of **massive retaliation**, pressed hard for West German rearmament, and stressed the rights of the Western Allies in **Berlin**. He was sometimes exasperated by Western European caution, being particularly irritated by the reluctance of **France** to accept the **European Defence Community (EDC)**, when he threatened an **agonizing reappraisal** of American policy. After 1955 he disagreed with the British and French position and actions in the **Suez Crisis**, condemning the invasion of Egypt in 1956.

Dušan. A paramilitary organization in the former **Yugoslavia**. Formed in 1991, it took its name from Stefan Dušan, King of **Serbia** 1331–55, and advocated the creation of a Greater Serbia. It was alleged to have participated in massacres of Muslims and Croats, and also to have had connections with organized crime in Serbia.

Dutschke, Rudi. (1940–1979) West German radical. A refugee from the **German Democratic Republic (DDR)**, he rose to prominence during the 1966 student demonstrations in the **Federal Republic of Germany** against the American war in Vietnam. For the next three years he was the most prominent representative of a radical student-based movement opposed to the existing structure of the West German state. He demanded the creation of an **extra-parliamentary opposition (APO)** which would seek to establish a form of direct democracy that would transform the socio-economic structure through continual agitation. Students were to be the shock troops that would overthrow what he called the oppressive exploitative state. His influence had already begun to wane when he was seriously wounded in an assassination attempt in **Berlin** in April 1968. He never regained his previous influence after recovering from his injuries, which eventually contributed to his death in 1979.

E

Eanes, Antônio dos Santos Ramalho. (1935–) President of **Portugal** 1976–86. A professional soldier who rose through the ranks to become a General and Army Chief of Staff, he had served in Portugal's African colonies after 1962. Supportive of the **Carnation Revolution**, he was opposed to the radical tendencies of the **Armed Forces Movement**, and was cleared of being involved in the abortive March 1975 counter-coup led by **Spinola**. His more moderate views, austere personality and reputation for honesty led to him being backed by the major moderate parties as a non-party candidate for the presidency in 1976. He rigorously upheld the constitution and worked to bring the military more firmly under civilian control, giving up his position as Chief of Staff only in 1981. His relationship with the politicians deteriorated during his second term of office after 1981, and he did not present himself for re-election in 1986. He briefly headed the **Democratic Renewal Party**, but retired from politics in 1987.

East Berlin Uprising. A large-scale workers' protest in East Berlin in June 1953. It began as a spontaneous demonstration by construction workers against a government decree imposing an increase in work output. It spread rapidly into a protest against the Communist regime and to other cities. Although the Prime Minister, **Grotewohl**, was forced to rescind the decree, it took Soviet troops to quell the protest.

EC. *See* EUROPEAN COMMUNITIES.

Ecevit, Bülent. (1925–) Prime Minister of **Turkey** 1974, 1977, 1978–79. A journalist, he joined the **Republican People's Party**, serving as a government press officer 1944–50. He entered Parliament in 1957, serving as general secretary of the party 1966–71, before being elected as its leader 1972–80. He was first appointed to government office in 1961. Under his leadership the RPP swung more to the left, contributing to the heightened instability of the 1970s, although military hostility towards him was fuelled as much by his alliance with the right-wing pro-Islam National Salvation Party (*Milli Selamet Partisi*). After the 1980 military coup, like other politicians he was barred from public life, and in 1981 was briefly imprisoned for criticizing the military regime. He became leader of the

135

Democratic Left Party in 1986 but resigned the following year after a severe electoral defeat, returning to Parliament only in 1991.

Ecoglasnost. (*Ikoglasnost*) An opposition group of dissidents in **Bulgaria**. It was formed in 1989 to agitate for more government openness and greater concern for environmental issues. It was denied formal recognition and was harassed by the Communist regime, but successfully organized a mass demonstration in Sofia in October. After the dismissal of **Zhivkov**, it continued to act as a pro-democracy interest group.

Ecologist Alternative. (*Oikologia Anallaktiki*) A loose alliance of green and alternative candidates and groups in **Greece**. It was formed for the 1989 election and campaigned on decentralization and the banning of private cars from Athens.

Ecology Generation. (*Génération Écologie*) A green party in **France**. Founded in 1990 as a more pragmatic alternative to the radical **Greens**, it neverthless was willing after 1993 to contest elections jointly with its rival in order to maximize the potential environmental vote.

Ecology Party. (*Parti Ecologiste – Ecolo*) A green party in **Belgium**. Founded as a French-speaking party in **Wallonia** in 1978, it was willing after 1981 to collaborate with its Flemish counterpart, **Live Differently**. While possessing many characteristics typical of green parties, such as a collective leadership, it pursued a more pragmatic political strategy, entering into coalition governments at the regional and local level.

Ecology Party – The Greens. (*Miljöpartiet de Gröna – MP*) An environmental party in **Sweden**. Founded in 1981 it won its first parliamentary representation in 1988, but later suffered from internal disputes over strategy and policy, which contributed to electoral defeat in 1991. Returning to Parliament in 1994, it agreed to support a left-wing government.

Economic and Financial Council of Ministers (ECOFIN). The meetings of the economics and finance ministers of the Member States of the **European Communities (EC)**. It was set up to review both broad and detailed issues affecting the EC and its place in the international economy. The same ministers meet to discuss related problems in the different guises of the EC's Monetary Policy Committee and the Economic Policy Committee.

Economic and Monetary Union (EMU). The integrative stage beyond a **common market**, with economic co-ordination, unification of economic policy, an integrated budgetary policy, and a monetary union based upon either an unconditional fixed exchange rate with full currency convertibility or a single currency. EMU has been on the agenda of the **European Communities (EC)** since 1969 when they agreed to set 1980 as the completion date. The 1980 timetable set by the **Werner Report** was destroyed by the economic turmoil of the 1970s, and EMU was more or less abandoned. The **European Monetary System (EMS)** of 1979 was a first step back on the road, but EMU did not figure prominently in EC thinking until the 1989 report by a committee headed by **Delors**, which outlined a three-stage sequence for full EMU within the context of the 1992 **internal market**. The 1991 **Treaty on European Union** committed the EC to establishing full EMU by 1999 at the latest, but set strict conditions that the economies of the Member States would have to meet. Subsequent problems afflicting the national economies, difficulties over ratifying the Treaty, the disruption of the **Exchange Rate Mechanism (ERM)** in 1992–93, the granting of **opt out** clauses for **Denmark** and the **United Kingdom**, and popular unhappiness with several aspects of the Treaty all weakened the chances of success for EMU and its timetable, and by 1995 it was accepted that only a partial EMU was possible by 1999.

Economic and Social Committee (ESC). A central institution of the **European Communities (EC)**. While it was granted only an advisory function, the **Commission** and the **Council of Ministers** were required to consult it on a wide range of issues, and in practice the degree of consultation became intense. Its members, all with a part-time commitment, have been drawn from national interest groups of employers, trade unionists and other occupational groups. While much of its work has been done in specialist sub-groups, it has often been divided politically along left–right lines, which has hindered its effectiveness. On serious economic matters its members have often preferred to seek to influence the EC through lobbying their own national governments.

Economic Commission for Europe (ECE). A regional agency of the United Nations (UN) established in 1947. Its origins lay in the Allied war-time plans for post-war economic reconstruction in the German-occupied territories. Three bodies, the so-called E-Organizations, had been established: the European Central Inland Transport Organization (ECITO) in London in September 1941, replacing an earlier Technical Advisory Committee on Inland Transport (TACIT) set up by an Inter-Allied Committee on Post-War Requirements; the European Coal Organization (ECO) in London in 1945, replacing the Solid Fuels Section of SHAEF (Supreme Headquarters Allied Expeditionary Forces); and the more all-purpose Emergency Economic Committee for Europe (EECE) set up also in London in May 1945. These three bodies and their predecessors were concerned with ensuring adequate fuel and transport resources after the conclusion of peace. By the end of 1945 it was felt that more was needed to cope with long-term reconstruction, and negotiations on a replacement began in February 1946, with an ECE being proposed by **Czechoslovakia** in the UN in August. Because of objections by the **USSR**, the ECE was delayed until March 1947. During the following year it absorbed the obligations and duties of the

E-Organizations. It was created on the assumption that economic problems would be treated on a continental basis, but it soon fell victim to the bipolarization of the **Cold War**. Agreements were difficult because decisions had to be unanimous, and its terms of reference precluded it from interfering in any country without the consent of that state. It did consider East–West trade, but failed to establish a broad multilateral system, and it was unable to consider long-term economic planning. It retained some value as the only European body until the 1970s where the states of East and West met on a regular basis. It assisted in exchanges of information and produced a series of economic surveys. In the 1980s its annual meetings, which had English, French and Russian as working languages, became rather more productive through looking at less politically contentious areas, especially cross-boundary environment problems.

Economic Co-operation Administration (ECA). *See* MARSHALL PLAN.

Economic Policy Committee. *See* ECONOMIC AND FINANCIAL COUN-CIL OF MINISTERS.

ECSC. *See* EUROPEAN COAL AND STEEL COMMUNITY.

ECU. *See* EUROPEAN CURRENCY UNIT.

Eden, Robert Anthony. (1897–1977) British Prime Minister 1955–57. Elected to Parliament in 1923 for the **Conservative Party**, his main interest was in foreign affairs. He served in a variety of government positions, including Foreign Secretary 1935–38, 1940–45 and 1951–55. After 1940 he was widely accepted as the natural successor to **Churchill** as Conservative leader. His health had already begun to fail when he finally took over from Churchill in 1955. His term of office was disappointing, and dominated by the **Suez Crisis**. His opposition to appeasement in the 1930s led him to draw analogies between Adolf Hitler and the Egyptian leader, Gamel Nasser, and persuaded him to intervene militarily in the Middle East. His hard line cost him the support of the USA and most **Commonwealth** leaders. There was widespread unease in the country, and he was unable to withstand the pressures on him. His health collapsed and he resigned from office in January 1957, retiring completely from politics. He was knighted in 1954 and created Earl of Avon in 1961.

Edinburgh Summit. A 1992 meeting of the **European Council** held in the aftermath of the referendum rejection by **Denmark** of the **Treaty on European Union**. The Council agreed on a number of **opt outs** for Denmark from various elements of the Treaty, and sought further to clarify the meaning of **subsidiarity**.

EEC. *See* EUROPEAN ECONOMIC COMMUNITY.

EFTA. *See* EUROPEAN FREE TRADE ASSOCIATION.

Egmont Pact. A 1977 agreement between the political parties in **Belgium**

on a solution to the issues raised by the country's linguistic disputes. It was a complex plan for institutional reform, and its importance lay in the fact that it was the first realistic attempt to produce a coherent response which accepted that extensive devolution was central to any resolution of the problem. Some of the parties soon became alarmed by some of its implications, and the schedule for its legislative implementation was abandoned. Many of its ideas, however, were subsequently incorporated into the 1980 and 1993 constitutional reforms that turned Belgium into a federal state.

Eichmann, Adolf. (1906–1962) Nazi administrator. He joined the Austrian Nazi Party in 1932 and after the 1938 *Anschluss* supervised anti-Jewish activities in Vienna and Prague. In 1941 he was made head of the Gestapo section responsible for Jewish affairs, and in 1942 organized the logistics for the transport of Jews to the death camps. Arrested by American troops in 1945, he subsequently escaped from custody and fled to South America. In May 1960 he was kidnapped in Argentina by Israeli agents. Put on trial in Jerusalem for crimes against the Jewish people, he was found guilty and executed in May 1962.

Einaudi, Luigi. (1874–1961) President of **Italy** 1948–55. A distinguished academic and economist, he was appointed Governor of the Bank of Italy in 1945, and later Minister of the Budget in 1947. He was largely credited with the success of the deflationary measures that stabilized the Italian economy. In May 1948 he was elected as the first post-war President. Although the post lacked power and influence, he worked closely with the premier, **de Gasperi**, and established a presidential style followed by his successors through to the 1980s. He was defeated in the 1955 election.

ELAS. *See* NATIONAL PEOPLE'S LIBERATION ARMY.

Elbe. A river in Central Europe. After 1945 it constituted, for much of its length, the border between the two German states. There was an unresolved dispute between them over the exact boundary, whether it should follow the eastern bank (the Western view) or the centre of the river (the Eastern argument).

Eleventh of November Alliance. (*Porozumienie Jedenastego Listopada – PJL*) A right-wing political organization in **Poland**, founded in December 1993 as a further attempt to rationalize the highly fragmented nature of post-Communist politics. It consisted of five parties, most of which had earlier in the year formed the Homeland (*Ojczyzna*) alliance, with an agreement that leadership would rotate across the five. The name derives from the date in 1918 which marked the restoration of an independent Polish state.

Emergency Economic Committee for Europe (EECE). *See* ECONOMIC COMMISSION FOR EUROPE.

Empty chair crisis. The period of seven months from June 1965 when

France boycotted meetings of the **Council of Ministers** of the **European Communities (EC)** apart from those dealing with minor or routine business. The French action was the result of the hostility of **de Gaulle** to a package of proposals which would have strengthened the supranational institutions of the EC at the expense of the sovereignty of the member states. The argument was resolved by the 1966 **Luxembourg Compromise**.

Encyclicals. Circular letters sent by a Catholic prelate to all churches within his province, but usually used to describe major statements by Popes. The major social and political theory of Catholicism, rejecting socialism and excessive free competition while stressing social justice, was contained in *Rerum Novarum* (1891) and *Quadragesimo Anno* (1931). In July 1961 **John XXIII** issued *Mater et Magistra* which accepted that in some instances a form of socialism could benefit the common good. Other major post-1945 encyclicals include *Humani Generis* (**Pius XII**, 1950) condemning existentialist philosophy, *Acterna Dei* (John XXIII, 1961) on prospects of Christian unity, *Pacem in Terris* (John XXIII, 1963) attacking nuclear weapons and urging peace, *Humanae Vitae* (**Paul VI**, 1968) condemning contraception, *Laborem Exercens* (**John Paul II**, 1981) on the mutual obligations of employers and workers, *Mulieris Dignitatem* (John Paul II, 1988) on the right of women to participate fully in church life, but reiterating the tradition of a male priesthood, and *Veritatis Splendor* (John Paul II, 1993) on absolute moral values.

Enimont Affair. A political and financial scandal in **Italy**. Enimont was a joint trading venture between the Montedison chemicals company and the state-owned ENI (*Ente Nazionale Idrocarburi*) energy concern. Established in January 1989, it would have had almost a total monopoly of the Italian petrochemicals industry, but was wound up in November 1990 after sustaining heavy losses. It was subsequently proved in 1993 that large bribes had been paid to senior members of the **pentapartito** parties, first to gain approval for the venture, and later to persuade the government to buy out Montedison. Although only one financier was arrested and charged, it was the largest single case of bribery and illegal party funding that came to light in the 1990s and was seen as a symbolic indictment of the political elite.

Enlargement. A term used to describe the process of the admission of states as members of the **European Communities (EC)**.

Enosis. A Greek word meaning union, used to describe a campaign in **Cyprus** for union with **Greece**. First employed in the nineteenth century, it was the objective and slogan of the terrorist campaign waged by **Grivas** and his **National Organization of Cypriot Fighters (EOKA)** 1954–59. It remained a clarion call until the clumsy 1974 coup attempt engineered by the **Greek Colonels** regime in Athens which provoked a Turkish invasion of the island. The subsequent partition of the island effectively removed it from the political agenda.

EOKA. *See* NATIONAL ORGANIZATION OF CYPRIOT FIGHTERS.

E-Organizations. *See* ECONOMIC COMMISSION FOR EUROPE.

Eppelmann, Rainer. (1943–) East German dissident. Imprisoned as a conscientious objector, he studied theology and became a leading critic of the Communist regime. His church in **Berlin** became known as a refuge for opponents of the regime. He was a co-founder of an opposition group, Democratic Renewal, becoming its chairman in 1990, and acting as its representative in the 1989–90 round of talks with the **Modrow** government. In February 1990 he entered the government as Minister without Portfolio, becoming in March Minister of Defence and Disarmament in the **de Maizière** government. In 1992 he was appointed to head a parliamentary commission charged with assessing the methods and legacy of the former East German regime.

Equal Rights. (*Līdztiesība/Ravnopraviye*) A political party in **Latvia**. Emerging out of the Communist party which had been banned in 1991, its objective was to secure equal rights for the large ethnic Russian minority, most of whom had been denied citizenship in the newly independent state.

Erhard, Ludwig. (1897–1977) Chancellor of the **Federal Republic of Germany** 1963–66. An economist, he was recruited after 1945 to be the head of the industrial reconstruction programme in **Bavaria**, in 1948 becoming chairman of the Economic Executive Council for the American and British occupation zones. He was the architect of the 1948 currency reform and the **social market economy** widely credited for West Germany's rapid economic recovery. He joined the **Christian Democratic Union (CDU)** in 1949, entering Parliament the same year and serving as Minister of Economic Affairs until 1963. Although Deputy Chancellor after 1957 and widely regarded as the natural heir to **Adenauer**, the two men were not close and Adenauer did not wish Erhard to be his successor. But when Adenauer retired in 1963, he failed to block Erhard's succession. Erhard was less skilled politically, especially in foreign affairs and in controlling a relatively decentralized party, but it was his handling of domestic policy that caused his downfall. In 1966 he demanded a number of tax increases to counter a possible economic recession. The proposals divided the CDU, and he opted for resignation and retirement from politics later in the year.

Erlander, Tage Fritiof. (1901–1985) Prime Minister of **Sweden** 1946–68. Entering Parliament in 1933 for the **Social Democratic Labour Party**, he held various party and governmental offices before succeeding Albin Hansson as party leader and premier. He continued the reform programme of his predecessor, building up an extensive welfare state that included a massive extension of benefits and educational provision. His preferred style of leadership was consensual, and he sought wherever possible to obtain all-party support for his policies, sometimes modifying or abandoning those strongly opposed by other parties. He insisted upon the retention of neutrality for Sweden, but in 1948–49 attempted to construct a Nordic defensive alliance that would be non-aligned in the **Cold War**.

ERTA Judgment. A 1971 ruling by the **Court of Justice** that the **European Communities (EC)** had external jurisdiction wherever they had internal jurisdiction. It had important implications for the development of EC external and foreign policy.

Estonia. The most northerly of the three **Baltic states**. Non-Slavic and speaking a language akin to Finnish, it was annexed by **Russia** from **Sweden** in 1709. It gained independence in 1918, withstood a Communist uprising in 1924, and from 1934 to 1939 was governed by an agrarian autocracy under Konstantin Paets. Under the terms of the 1939 Nazi-Soviet Pact it was occupied by the **USSR** in June 1940, and in 1944 became a constituent Soviet republic, but its incorporation into the USSR was never recognized by the West. Large numbers of the population were deported by **Stalin** to the Soviet east, and Russian immigration was encouraged. It was one of the more economically developed regions of the USSR, and its population enjoyed a comparatively higher standard of living. It was politically quiescent until 1990 when a mass rally, inspired by similar actions in **Lithuania**, demanded negotiations with the USSR on the restoration of independence. The demand was supported by the Estonian Supreme Soviet which abrogated the Communist Party's monopoly of power and declared the 1940 incorporation illegal. In May 1990 the 1920 Constitution was reinstated, and talks began on creating a special relationship with the USSR. The efforts of **Gorbachev** to hold on to the country, backed by the threat of possible military force, proved futile, and in 1991 the USSR accepted its secession. Large numbers of Soviet troops remained in the country until 1994, forcing the new democratic government to tread warily. There was also a large Russian minority which wished to remain part of Russia. Under pressure from national sentiment, the government passed a very limited prescription for citizenship, which excluded most of the Russian population. The citizenship law was strongly criticized by Russia and in the West, and communal-ethnic differences remained a major political problem.

Estonian National Independence Party. (*Eesti Rahvasliku Sõltumatuse Partei – ERSP*) A political party in **Estonia**, founded in 1988. Centre-right on socio-economic issues, it was strongly nationalistic on the relationship with **Russia** and on the status of the ethnic Russian minority in the country.

Estonian People's Centre Party. *See* POPULAR FRONT.

Estonian Royalist Party. (*Eesti Rojalistlik Partei – ERP*) A small right-wing party in **Estonia**, founded in 1988, which sought the establishment of a constitutional monarchy.

ETA. *See* EUSKADI TA ASKATASUNA.

Ethnic Cleansing. A phrase that came into popular use after the outbreak of civil war in **Bosnia-Hercegovina** in March 1992. It referred to the enforced expulsion from their home territories of members of one ethnic group by members of another in order to establish ethnically homogeneous areas. The term was first used by Croat nationalists in the 1940s.

EU. *See* EUROPEAN UNION.

Euclid. *See* INDEPENDENT EUROPEAN PROGRAMME GROUP.

Eupen-Malmédy. Two small German-speaking provinces of **Belgium**, incorporated from Germany in 1919. The discussions on and problems of language between **Flanders** and **Wallonia** after 1960 stimulated the emergence of political movements demanding German language rights. In 1972 a separate Cultural Council for German speakers was created, with the same powers as those for the Flemish and French-speaking communities, but in the final constitutional settlement no devolved political and administrative powers were granted or really expected, the provinces remaining part of Wallonia. On the other hand, there was no pressure for reunion with Germany.

EURATOM. *See* EUROPEAN ATOMIC ENERGY COMMUNITY.

Eurocities. An intergovernmental association of city administrators from **European Union (EU)** countries, founded in 1986. Incorporating most of the major cities in the EU, its major objective was to encourage co-operation on urban economic and environmental problems.

Euro-Citizens Action Service (ECAS). An intergovernmental body representing voluntary non-governmental organizations within the **European Union (EU)**. Established in 1990, it was intended to act as both a lobby for its members within the EU, and to provide them with an information service on their rights.

Eurocommunism. A phrase describing the increased dissent within Western European Communist parties in the 1970s against the position and arguments of the Soviet party. It was first coined by a Yugoslav journalist in June 1975. It was most strongly espoused by **Carrillo**, the Spanish Communist leader, who attempted to give it a theoretical basis rooted in Marxist-Leninism. In practice it was the **Italian Communist Party (PCI)**, which had followed an independent line vis-à-vis the **USSR** since **Togliatti** developed his ideas of polycentrism in 1953, which most clearly followed Eurocommunism, most notably in its espousal in 1976 of a **historic compromise**. The more hard-line **French Communist Party (PCF)** briefly flirted with it before reverting to a more orthodox position. In **Finland** the acceptance of Eurocommunist ideas by a majority of the party led in the 1980s to the expulsion of the Stalinist minority and the creation of two separate parties. The principles of Eurocommunism were expressed first in a joint statement by the Italian and Spanish parties in July 1975. They rejected the notion of an 'official state ideology' and accepted the necessity of a 'plurality of parties' and 'individual and collective freedom'. The parties had hoped that this more flexible doctrine would, by catering to different national cultures, benefit them electorally and make them more acceptable as potential coalition government partners. Because no benefits accrued from it, it had been more or less abandoned as a strategy by the mid-1980s, before the policies of **Gorbachev** made it irrelevant.

Eurocorps. An integrated military unit formally inaugurated in November 1992 and due to be fully operational by 1995. Its origins lay in the joint Franco-German brigade formed in 1991 under the auspices of the **Franco-German Defence Council**. Its supporters hoped that it would become the nucleus of a European army at the centre of a reformed **Western European Union (WEU)** and the military-security element of the **European Union (EU)**, an objective spelled out in the **Treaty on European Union**. In 1993 the aims of its supporters were boosted by the intention of some other EU states to participate in it.

Eurocrat. A colloquial term used to describe a bureaucrat or administrator employed by the **European Communities (EC)**.

Eurofighter 2000. *See* EUROPEAN FIGHTER AIRCRAFT PROGRAMME.

Eurogroup. The more widely used term for the Informal Group of NATO Defence Ministers within the **North Atlantic Treaty Organization (NATO)**. They agreed to meet regularly to review developments and initiatives that were more specifically of European, rather than Western, concern. Its formation initially eased some problems for the **European Communities (EC)** where defence discussions were inhibited by the presence of neutral **Ireland**. It also aided co-operation with **France** and (after 1986) **Spain**, neither part of the integrated NATO command.

Euromissile. A media-invented term used to describe the nuclear missiles which in the 1980s were the subject of **arms control** discussions between the USA and the **USSR**, and the object of strong campaigning by disarmament movements. In general, the term referred more specifically to intermediate-range nuclear missiles stationed in Europe with programmed targets also located within the continent.

Europa Nostra. Also known as the International Federation of Non-Governmental Associations for the Protection of Europe's Cultural and Natural Heritage, a cross-national environment group founded in Paris in 1963. It set itself the objective of persuading governments and international institutions to preserve historical buildings and sites of natural beauty.

Europe Agreements. Agreements signed by the **European Communities (EC)** with Eastern European countries subsequent to their democratization after 1989. Similar to **Association Agreements**, the first ones were signed in 1991.

Europe à la carte. A phrase used by those who argue that the strategy of integration pursued by the **European Communities (EC)** and **European Union (EU)** should be sufficiently flexible to allow member states to participate in or decline to to join common programmes or policies according to their own wishes or requirements. It was first used in 1979 by the German sociologist, Ralf Dahrendorf. *See also* TINDEMANS REPORT; VARIABLE GEOMETRY.

European Agricultural Guidance and Guarantee Fund (EAGGF). The structural fund of the **European Communities (EC)** established to service the financial requirements of the **Common Agricultural Policy (CAP)**. Its Guidance Section was intended to support restructuring and modernization, but has consumed only some 5 per cent of the CAP budget. The remainder has been taken by the Guarantee Section which was given the responsibility for maintaining the price support structure which provided farmers with guaranteed prices for their products irrespective of market conditions. Because of soaring costs, it was agreed in 1988 that maximum permissible increases in EAGGF funding would be pegged to the rate of growth of the EC's gross national product (GNP), and several other measures to reduce the costs of the CAP were also introduced.

European Anthem. The official anthem adopted by both the **Council of Europe** and the **European Communities (EC)**, and played on ceremonial occasions. It consists of the words of Schiller's *Ode to Joy* as set to music in the final movement of Beethoven's Ninth Symphony.

European Atomic Energy Community (EURATOM). A core institution of the **European Communities (EC)** established in 1957 to promote the development of nuclear energy for peaceful purposes. It was not an unqualified success. Technical problems, costs, and public concerns about the safety of nuclear fuels hindered its aims, and it found it difficult to control and integrate national developments and policies. After the merger of the EC executives in 1967, responsibility for it passed to the **Commission**, which can call for the co-ordination of national programmes and recommend concentration of resources on particular programmes. It can also receive details of all patents sought or obtained, and has the power (as yet unused) to seek licences to use them through a compulsory purchase order. It developed its own Supply Agency for the acquisition of ores and materials for the member states, which retained responsibility for the regular monitoring of nuclear installations.

European Atomic Forum. An association founded in Paris in 1960 to promote the economic development of peaceful uses of nuclear energy as a way of developing the world's energy resources and raising living standards.

European Bank for Reconstruction and Development (EBRD).

An initiative of the **European Communities (EC)** to aid the economic reconstruction of Eastern Europe after the collapse of the Communist regimes in 1989. It was proposed by **Mitterrand** in November 1989. The EC took a 51 per cent stake in the enterprise, the remainder being provided by states from other parts of the world. In 1992 membership was extended to all the successor states of the ex-**USSR**, and it was agreed to direct some 40 per cent of its funding towards members of the **Commonwealth of Independent States (CIS)**. It began operations in March 1991 under the leadership of Jacques Attali, a close associate of Mitterrand, with its work checked by an international board of governors. It was embroiled in scandal in 1993 when it was disclosed that it had spent more on furnishing its headquarters in London and on expense accounts than it had advanced in loans, and Attali was forced to resign in July. The EBRD was meant to work in conjunction with the International Monetary Fund (IMF) and the World Bank, but many critics argued that it could only duplicate their work, and its creation seemed in part a political gesture rather than the establishment of a body that would provide a service not available from the IMF or World Bank.

European Broadcasting Union (EBU). A cross-national federation of state broadcasting authorities founded in 1950 to encourage collaboration between countries and the development of European broadcasting. It was not given any authority to control or direct the policy, strategy or content of national broadcasting networks, but has tried to persuade countries to raise the share of the European content of national network programming.

European Bureau of Consumers' Unions (BEUC). *See* CONSUMERS' CONSULTATIVE COMMITTEE.

European Bureau of Lesser Used Languages. An organization established in 1982 and based in Dublin. Its objective was to preserve and promote minority non-state languages and to support their use and tuition in them in national education systems.

European Central Bank. A blueprint for a proposed body that would issue a single European currency and control monetary policy within **Economic and Monetary Union (EMU)**. The **Treaty on European Union** confirmed that it would be established in the third stage of EMU, between 1997 and 1999. To be located in Frankfurt, it would be preceded by a **European Monetary Institute**.

European Central Inland Transport Organization (ECITO). *See* ECONOMIC COMMISSION FOR EUROPE (ECE).

European Centre for Regional Development (CEDRE). An association of technical co-operation intended to assist the development of regional economic initiatives. It was established in **Strasbourg** in January 1985 by representatives of regions in Western Europe.

European Centre for the Development of Vocational Training

(CEDEFOP). A service agency of the **Commission** established in 1975 and located in **Berlin**. Its task was to encourage and advance vocational and in-service training for adults within the **European Communities (EC)**. It later turned to emphasizing the employment problems of women, especially those returning to the labour market after a long absence.

European Charter for Regional or Minority Languages. An international agreement signed in 1992 under the aegis of the **Council of Europe**. Its objectives were to persuade states to adopt measures to preserve some 50 identifiable minority languages, and to promote their use in education and public life.

European Civil Aviation Conference (ECAC). A standing conference of governmental experts and representatives of European airlines. Established in 1955 and based in **Strasbourg**, it was set up by the **Council of Europe** to develop the co-ordination and more effective utilization of European air transport.

European Coal and Steel Community (ECSC). Established in April 1951 by the **Treaty of Paris** as the first European organization to involve the ceding by countries of some sovereignty to a supranational authority. Based upon the 1950 **Schuman Plan**, it became operational in July 1952 with a membership of six countries. Its principal objective was to 'foster economic expansion, growth of employment and a rising standard of living' through the creation within five years of a **common market** in the coal and steel industries. The supranational element was the executive High Authority whose members, though appointed by national governments, were independent of state control or influence. The interests of the governments were represented by a Council of Ministers. There was also an advisory Assembly drawn from the national legislatures, a Court of Justice with powers of interpretation and arbitration, and a Consultative Committee representing national interest groups. This institutional framework was the model adopted in 1957 for the broader **European Economic Community (EEC)**. The ECSC executive met in **Luxembourg**, while the Assembly shared the **Council of Europe** building in **Strasbourg**.

The ECSC claimed success in expanding coal and steel output, but this was due in part to the favourable world economic conditions of the 1950s. Able to cope with eliminating tariffs and quotas, it had difficulty with the wide array of other national discriminatory practices, and in 1959 failed to resolve a major crisis of coal overproduction and shrinking demand. One major problem was to achieve co-ordination in only two economic sectors which could not easily be divorced from either political considerations or the broader national economies. When the EEC and the **European Atomic Energy Community (EURATOM)** were established in 1957, a common set of institutions was created, with the three executives finally merging as the

Commission in 1967. The ECSC continued to be semi–independent, retaining the separate sources of revenue granted in 1951, a direct levy on national coal and steel producers. Most of the funds were spent on restructuring, rationalization and retraining and redeployment programmes. It also retained powers of direction and control greater than those given to the EEC, and in coal and steel the Commission was able to act more independently in directing and punishing national interests. At the extreme it was given the authority to seek a state of manifest crisis whereby it is given almost dictatorial powers over production levels and prices. A state of manifest crisis was declared in the steel industry in 1980 to cope with growing surplus capacity. It was not lifted until 1988 when the Commission was satisfied that a greatly slimmed down industry was economically viable and competitive.

European Coal Organization (ECO). *See* ECONOMIC COMMISSION FOR EUROPE (ECE).

European Commission. *See* COMMISSION.

European Commission of Human Rights. A semi-judicial body that examines charges of infringements of human rights as defined in the **European Convention of Human Rights**. It was established in 1953, operating under the aegis of the **Council of Europe**. It was given both a judicial and conciliatory function, able to act on its own initiative or in response to complaints from states or by individual petition. It can attempt a resolution or conciliation, or refer the case, along with its recommendation, to the **European Court of Human Rights** for adjudication. Each country which has ratified the Convention is entitled to one representative on the Commission, and the nominations must be approved by the Assembly of the Council of Europe. Candidates must be judges or otherwise similarly qualified in law. They serve for six years and are expected to act as individuals, not as representatives of states. Procedures intended to increase the rate at which cases were heard were introduced in April 1994.

European Communities (EC). The collective body, also sometimes known by the singular of the term, that resulted in July 1967 from the merger of the administrative networks and structures of the **European Atomic Energy Community (EURATOM)**, **European Coal and Steel Community (ECSC)**, and **European Economic Community (EEC)**. Membership expanded from six states in 1957 to 15 by 1995, with more applications to join pending. After German reunification in 1990 it automatically absorbed the former **German Democratic Republic (DDR)**. Its objectives were set down in the 1957 **Treaty of Rome**, with more specific targets and amendments listed in the 1987 **Single European Act (SEA)** and the 1991 **Treaty on European Union**. It has developed into a highly complex network of institutions, but its principal structures have remained a dual executive – the supranational **Commission** and a **Council of Ministers** representing the Member States, a directly elected (since 1979) **European Parliament (EP)**, and a **Court of Justice**. These are buttressed by a mass of support agencies and administrative and advisory bodies. In 1974 the **European Council** was established as a forum for the heads of government of the member states. Under the terms of the Treaty on European Union the EC became the central of the three pillars that constituted the **European Union**. The Treaty also specified that the singular of the term would be the new official title of the EEC.

European Community Action Scheme for the Mobility of University Students (ERASMUS).

A **European Communities (EC)** programme whereby students can spend an integral part of their studies at a university in another EC country. It was launched in 1987, and widened in 1991 to incorporate students from the member states of the **European Free Trade Association (EFTA)**. It had originally been hoped that by 1992 some 10 per cent of the EC student population would be participants within some kind of cross-national course credit transfer scheme. While successful, funding limitations and linguistic obstacles prevented the target from being reached.

European Community Consumers' Co-operatives (EURO-COOP).

See CONSUMERS' CONSULTATIVE COMMITTEE (CCC).

European Community Visitors' Programme (ECVP).

A scheme established by the **Commission** and **European Parliament (EP)** to raise the international profile of the **European Communities (EC)**. It was intended to offer young people from other parts of the world the opportunity to travel to Europe and meet with various representatives of the EC so as to acquire a better understanding of its operation and purposes.

European Company for the Financing of Railway Rolling Stock (EUROFIMA).

Established in 1955 by the **European Conference of Ministers of Transport (ECMT)** and based in Basel, it was set up to aid national railway companies to rationalize their systems through a common procurement of rolling stock of a standard type and performance.

European Confederation of Iron and Steel Companies (EURO-FER).

An association of most of the steel producers in the **European Communities (EC)**. Founded in 1956, it was reorganized in 1977 upon an initiative by the **Commission** in an attempt to resolve a persisting crisis of overcapacity. It was intended to take the lead in raising productivity, achieving a more effective utilization of capacity, and restructuring and reducing the labour force. Its success was limited because it could not prevent individual companies from acting unilaterally or force national governments to accept its proposals. In 1980 the Commission had to intervene directly, imposing strict compulsory controls upon the industry.

European Conference of Ministers of Transport (ECMT). An inter-governmental institution established in **Brussels** in October 1953 by the **Organization for European Economic Co-operation (OEEC)**. In 1961 it was taken over by the **Organization for Economic Co-operation and Development (OECD)**. In the early 1950s a co-ordinated transport plan was thought to be essential for European reconstruction and development, and in August 1950 was proposed by Edouard Bonnefous of **France** in the **Council of Europe**. The Bonnefous Plan called for a supranational authority to rationalize and direct the inland transport system, but this was rejected by many governments which were nevertheless prepared to accept an ECMT with only advisory powers. It consists of the European members of OECD, with other OECD states having observer status. Some Eastern European countries were given observer status after 1989. The ministers meet twice yearly, and have extended their discussions to include inland waterways and oil pipelines.

European Conference of Postal and Telecommunications Administrations (ECPT). An association of Western European organizations established in June 1956 at Montreux. It was set up to work for the co-ordination of practices and the exchange of information. A liaison office was established in Berne, with the effective administration rotating annually across its members.

European Convention on Human Rights. The shortened and more well-known version of the European Convention for the Protection of Human Rights and Fundamental Freedoms, the first initiative undertaken by the **Council of Europe**. Signed in Rome in November 1950, it came into operation in September 1953. Rather than being a statement of principles, it set down detailed definitions of specific rights. Its watchdog is the associated **European Commission of Human Rights**, with the ultimate arbiter of alleged infringements being the **European Court of Human Rights**. Not all the signatories of the Convention have recognized the right of individuals to lodge complaints with the Commission, nor the compulsory jurisdiction of the Court. It has acquired a powerful moral authority throughout Western Europe, and observance of its principles has been taken by the Council of Europe as the essential criterion which applicant countries must meet.

European Convention on the Suppression of Terrorism. An international agreement sponsored by the **Council of Europe** in 1977, and in force in 1978. Its objectives were to facilitate the extradition and prosecution of people suspected of committing acts of political terrorism. By listing a series of offences that would not merit special treatment for extradition purposes, it offended a convention of international criminal law which held that political offences should be excluded from extradition treaties and agreements.

European Convention on Transfrontier Broadcasting. Adopted
by the **Council of Europe** in March 1989 as a result of telecommunications
and satellite developments which brought into sharper focus the different
natures of national broadcasting systems and rules. It was particularly
concerned with the proportion of non-European programmes permitted and
national rules governing advertising. It set down principles on programme
standards, advertising and sponsorship, protection against excessive violence, pornography and incitement of racial or religious hatred, and urged
that wherever practical a majority of programmes on any one channel should
be of European origin.

**European Co-operation in the Field of Scientific and Techni-
cal Research (COST).** A Western European framework for the prepara-
tion and implementation of transnational European projects in applied
scientific research, established in 1971. A concept rather than an institution
or integrated programme, it emerged from the desire to ensure that European
industries would remain competitive in rapidly changing and potentially
profitable areas. Its secretariat was attached to the **European Communities
(EC)**, and the **Commission** was made largely responsible for the technical
management of established projects. To be approved, a project must involve
collaboration between enterprises from at least two countries.

European Correspondent. *See* POLITICAL DIRECTORS.

European Council. The collective organ of the heads of government of
the Member States of the **European Communities (EC)**, formed in 1975.
There were no provisions in the **Treaty of Rome** for the formal involvement
of heads of government in the EC, and at first they met only rarely. After a
series of problems in the 1960s had indicated that their involvement was
needed to give the EC a firmer direction, they met frequently on an *ad hoc*
basis 1969–74. In 1974 **Giscard d'Estaing** proposed that the meetings
should be placed on a more formal and regular footing. The new Council first
met in Dublin in March 1975, convening thereafter three times a year with its
presidency rotating across the national capitals every six months. The
Council met in the country currently occupying the presidency, with the third
annual meeting in **Brussels**. This third annual meeting was dropped after
December 1985. The principle of rotation underlined the equal status of the
Member States, with each having the opportunity once every few years to be
a centre of European and world diplomacy. The governments preferred the
fact that the Council had no legal recognition within the EC. Its more
informal atmosphere and restricted number of supporting participants gave
them a flexibility to range over broad questions of policy without necessarily
having to keep to a timetable or arrive at a decision.

Its activities made it central to the EC, and after 1975 virtually all major
advances were the result of Council initiatives or endorsements, with its

151

decisions normally taken on the basis of unanimity: this occasionally caused resentment at the fact that progress towards further co-operation and integration was limited to the pace of the most reluctant members. Its position within the EC was formally acknowledged by the 1987 **Single European Act (SEA)** which confirmed that when it deals with matters in a way which conforms to the constitutional requirements of the Treaty of Rome, it is essentially another and superior version of the **Council of Ministers**. Its other initiatives have been framed as broad principles and then passed to the **Commission** and Council of Ministers for further consideration and discussion. Under the 1991 **Treaty on European Union** it became the only body with authority across the pillars of the **European Union**.

European Council for the Village and Small Town (ECO-VAST). An organization established in 1984 to work for the protection of the socio-economic and cultural vitality of rural communities in Western Europe.

European Court of Human Rights. The final arbiter of the **European Convention on Human Rights** and of cases arising from its provisions, based in **Strasbourg**. It is elected by the Assembly of the **Council of Europe**, but in practice candidates have been nominated by national governments. Members serve for nine years. Cases alleging infringement of the Convention can be brought by individual petition, interest groups or the **European Commission of Human Rights**. Its decisions are final, but it was not given the power to compel governments to implement its rulings, and some signatories have refused to recognize its compulsory jurisdiction. It has acted as much as a moral as a judicial authority, and in most instances governments have felt obliged to accept its recommendations.

European Court of Justice. *See* COURT OF JUSTICE.

European Cultural Centre. *See* CONGRESS OF EUROPE.

European Cultural Convention. Sponsored by the **Council of Europe** in 1954, it stressed the need to preserve and strengthen both the diversity and unity of European culture. In 1962 the Council established a **Council for Cultural Co-operation** to encourage further collaboration. Some Eastern European countries signed the Convention after 1989.

European Currency Unit (ECU). Created in 1979 as a book-keeping device for, and the potential common currency of, the **European Communities (EC)**, replacing the **European Unit of Account (EUA)**. It was established as the basic denominator of the **Exchange Rate Mechanism (ERM)**, the basic indicator determining the divergence of national currencies from their central rates in the **European Monetary System (EMS)**, the unit of account for the ERM intervention system, and the reserve instrument for the national central banks and the means by which they would make settlements between themselves. Its value is based upon a weighted **basket**

of currencies. In December 1991 the **Treaty on European Union** accepted that the ECU would become the only currency of the EC and its Member States within a decade.

European Defence Community (EDC). An unsuccessful attempt of the early 1950s in **sectoral integration**. Its background lay in the Western concern that with the Korean War the **USSR** was seeking to escalate the **Cold War**. The USA responded by extending its policy of **containment**, but arguing that its additional global commitments prevented it from providing the increase in support necessary to boost Western European defence that all thought desirable. When the European members of the **North Atlantic Treaty Organization (NATO)** declined to increase their own expenditure on the grounds that their economies were still too weak to bear the strain, the USA suggested in September 1950 that a stronger defence could be achieved by rearming the **Federal Republic of Germany** and incorporating it into NATO. The proposal was disquieting to Western Europe, but the French premier, **Pleven**, suggested the establishment of a European army which would include a West German contingent. The Pleven Plan took its inspiration from the **European Coal and Steel Community (ECSC)**, and was the blueprint for the EDC. Pleven envisaged a limited West German rearmament with no national unit in the European army being larger than a battalion. Only the six states of the ECSC were interested, although **France** had wanted British participation. The EDC treaty was signed in Paris in May 1952. It was so controversial in France that governments, all weak and concerned primarily with survival rather than policy, did not dare submit it to the legislature for ratification. It was only in August 1954, after the defeat of the French army at **Dien Bien Phu**, that a new reformist government under **Mendès-France** invited Parliament to discuss the treaty. The request was refused, and although this was only a technical vote on whether to discuss the treaty, it was taken to mean rejection, and the EDC was abandoned. It was a setback for European integration, and reopened the defence debate. It was too sensitive a subject for sectoral integration and would have restricted West Germany so much that it could not have been an association of equals. The USA still wanted a stronger NATO, with West German rearmament if necessary, and with no other alternative in sight this had to be accepted by France. To satisfy French concerns, the projected members of the aborted EDC accepted a proposal from the British Prime Minister, **Eden**, for a **Western European Union (WEU)** modelled upon the 1948 **Treaty of Brussels**.

European Democratic Alliance (RDE). A cross-national **party group** in the **European Parliament (EP)**. A rather artifical creation formed in 1973 and originally called the Progressive Democratic group, it was a marriage of convenience between representatives of the Gaullist **Rally for**

the Republic (RDR) and the Irish **Fianna Fáil** who felt that in terms of ideology and political orientation they could not accommodate themselves within the other party groups being formed. After 1973 they were joined on occasions by representatives from other countries. Despite the lack of cohesiveness, it was able to develop a consistent policy line in several areas.

European Democratic Group (DE). A cross-national **party group** in the **European Parliament (EP)** formed in 1973 by representatives of the British and Danish Conservative parties. They had rejected membership of the leading conservative group, the **European People's Party (PPE)**, because of its Christian Democratic (and mainly Catholic) tradition and strong endorsement of a federal Europe. It was dominated by its British members, and joined by representatives from other countries only in 1987–89. In 1989 it asked for a merger with the PPE. The application was rejected on the grounds that the British **Conservative Party** was ideologically too right-wing and insufficiently committed to integration, but an agreement on a merger was reached in 1992 and the DE effectively came to an end.

European Democratic Union. Founded in Salzburg in 1978 upon the signature of the Klessheim Declaration by representatives of Christian Democrat, Conservative and similar minded non-socialist parties and organizations. Its objective was to develop common programmes and guidelines in European foreign policy.

European Development Fund (EDF). Established by the **European Economic Community (EEC)** in 1963 as part of the **Yaoundé Convention**, and retained in the 1975 **Lomé Convention** with the **African, Caribbean and Pacific (ACP) States**. It was set up to provide grants to the ACP states for development programmes and projects. After 1984 it gave priority to rural and agricultural projects.

European Economic Area (EEA). A trading bloc agreed upon in 1991 by the **European Free Trade Association (EFTA)** and the **European Communities (EC)**. In the late 1980s non-EC states became concerned that the EC decision to create a single **internal market** by 1992 might have a negative effect upon their own exports to the EC. In Oslo in March 1989 the EFTA countries sought a joint approach to the EC, using the phrase European Economic Space (EES) to describe the kind of structured partnership they wanted. The term was taken up by the **Commission** which depicted the space as a series of concentric rings. The EC would be at the centre, and each of the rings would be distinguished by the kind of economic arrangements other countries would have with it, with the EFTA countries forming the innermost circle. The Commission saw this as a way of delaying applications for EC membership until after the internal market and the proposals for further union had been realized. Negotiations with EFTA began in June 1990, but the democratization of Eastern Europe had already challenged the Commission's strategy, for the new governments indicated that they wanted EC membership in the medium term. Some EFTA states also concluded that an EEA would be less valuable than membership, and formally applied to join the EC. These events and developments coloured the negotiations, which were completed in November 1991, with an agreement on a **common market** in all but agriculture, and largely on EC terms. Ratification was delayed by a query from the **Court of Justice** about the constitutional compatibility of the proposed arbitration procedures with the **Treaty of Rome**, and EFTA had to agree that all disputes would be resolved by the Court. A further complication arose when a referendum in **Switzerland** in 1992 effectively rejected the EEA, but without Swiss participation it came into existence in January 1994.

European Economic Community (EEC). An organization established in 1957 to create a **common market** based upon free trade, common social and financial policies, the abolition of restrictive trading practices, and the free movement of labour and capital. It marked the end of **sectoral integration** as a strategy and the beginning of a new kind of co-operation. It was planned at the 1955 **Messina Conference** of the six members of the **European Coal and Steel Community (ECSC)**. The Belgian foreign minister, **Spaak**, was commissioned to prepare a report which became the basis of the **Treaty of Rome**. The EEC was given its own executives, but shared its assembly and judicial functions with the ECSC and the **European Atomic Energy Community (EURATOM)**. The executive and administrative networks were merged in 1967, creating the **European Communities (EC)**. The EEC's target was a common market within 12 years, but its initial economic successes created problems. Its viability persuaded other countries to seek membership, and there were concerns that **enlargement** would change its character and its objectives. The demands for closer integration by **Hallstein** led to opposition from **de Gaulle** against any weakening of national sovereignty. These developments prevented a common market being reached by 1969. The 1991 **Treaty on European Union** decreed that the EEC would hitherto be known as the European Community.

European Economic Space (EES). *See* EUROPEAN ECONOMIC AREA.

European Energy Charter. A legal and financial agreement signed at The Hague in December 1991 by energy ministers from Europe, Japan and the USA. First proposed by the Dutch premier, **Lubbers**, and developed further by the **Commission**, its purpose was to make European energy supplies more secure by linking the natural resources of Eastern Europe with the West through a grid of electricity networks and pipelines. In return for the supply of energy, Eastern Europe would receive Western investment. As part of the plan, the **European Communities (EC)** proposed to extend its Organizations for the Promotion of Energy Technologies (OPET), a scheme for the cross-national transfer of energy-efficient and environmentally friendly technologies, to Eastern Europe and the **Commonwealth of Independent States (CIS)**. A secondary purpose was to strengthen the Eastern democracies by easing their balance of payments problems and to offer **Russia** an alternative to membership of the oil producers' cartel, the Organization of Petroleum Exporting Countries (OPEC). Negotiations on a formally binding treaty were completed in June 1994.

European Environment Agency. Established in March 1990 by the **European Communities (EC)** to collect detailed information on environmental questions and problems, with membership to be open also to non-EC states. Its inauguration was blocked by **France** which refused to allow it to begin until the EC confirmed that **Strasbourg** would be recognized as the permanent home of the **European Parliament (EP)**. Although the EP issue was not totally resolved, the way ahead was opened in November 1993 when it was agreed to locate the agency in Copenhagen.

European Federalist Movement. The major federalist movement since the mid-1950s. It succeeded the **European Union of Federalists** and was led by **Spinelli** until 1962. It had little direct influence upon governments, but some of its views were received more sympathetically by the **European Parliament (EP)** and fed into the debates of the 1980s on further integration within the **European Communities (EC)**.

European Federation of Mayors. A consultative association founded in 1977 to enable national associations of mayors and equivalent local government leaders to collaborate on and co-ordinate responses to common problems.

European Fighter Aircraft Programme. The first major joint European armaments project, designed to replace aircraft due to be obsolete by the mid-1990s. The agreement was made in 1985 by the arms procurement directors of the **Federal Republic of Germany, Italy, Spain**, and the **United Kingdom**. Finalized in May 1988, the first 750 planes were intended to be in service by 1997. Rising costs, technical problems, and the desire for defence cuts after the ending of the **Cold War** created doubts about its continued viability and schedule. In 1992 and again in 1995 there were strong indications in Germany of a wish to withdraw from the project because of strains on its economy. After 1992 the programme was scaled down in size, and renamed Eurofighter 2000.

European Flag. A standard adopted by the **European Communities (EC)** in 1986, consisting of a crown of 12 five-pointed stars set against an azure background. The design had already been used by the **Council of Europe** since 1955. It is flown over EC headquarters in **Brussels** and the Council of Europe buildings (shared by the **European Parliament**) in **Strasbourg**. It has been used at national and international meetings and ceremonies where the EC have been formally represented.

European Foundation for the Improvement of Living and Working Conditions. An agency of the **Commission** established in 1975 to advise on and propose policies relating to the betterment of the working environment of employees. Based in Dublin, it concentrated mainly on health and safety aspects of employment.

European Free Trade Association (EFTA). An organization founded in 1960 by seven Western European countries which for various reasons were unwilling or unable to accept the supranational principles of the **European Economic Community (EEC)**. It was created after the breakdown of the **Maudling Committee** negotiations on the creation of a broader and looser **free trade area**. After several discussions in 1959, EFTA was established by the **Stockholm Convention** of January 1960. It planned an elimination of tariffs on most industrial goods within seven years. There was no agreement on agriculture, and no **common external tariff (CET)**. It had only a skeletal institutional structure, with a Council of Ministers meeting two or three times a year. Its decisions have tended to be made on the basis of unanimity. It looked a rather makeshift body, assembled hastily and bringing together a disparate group of countries bound together mainly by rejection of the implications of the **Treaty of Rome** and a belief that unity would give them a more advantageous bargaining position with the EEC than separate negotiations. The free trade area was in place by 1966, but EFTA was not able to compete successfully with the EEC. Collaboration began in the 1970s, and led to a free trade agreement in industrial products in January 1984. **Denmark** and the **United Kingdom** left EFTA to join the **European Communities (EC)** in 1973. The other EFTA countries negotiated **Special Relations Agreements** with the EC. In 1991 the EC and EFTA agreed to establish a **European Economic Area (EEA)** under which EFTA would have to accept a range of EC decisions and make a financial contribution to the economic development of the poorer Southern members of the EC. Several EFTA states, however, became full members of the EC in 1995, placing the future of EFTA in doubt.

European Greens. A loose international association of national environmentalist parties in Western Europe, established in 1984.

European Information Centre for Nature Conservation. Established in 1967 to assist in the co-ordination of national policies on nature conservation. The initiative came from an expert Committee for the Conservation of Nature and Natural Resources appointed by the **Council of**

Europe. It has sponsored a range of activities, developed a set of comprehensive guidelines, and provided some of the groundwork for the 1979 Convention on the Conservation of European Wildlife and Natural Habitats.

European Investment Bank (EIB). An institution of the **European Communities (EC)**. Based in **Luxembourg**, it was set up to finance capital investment in order to aid economic development, with some 5 per cent of its reserves allocated to non-EC programmes. While the member states have subscribed collectively to its capital, it has raised most of its funds on international capital markets, where it soon gained the highest credit rating. Funds have been given as loans at a fixed rate of interest for between seven and 20 years. It has never totally funded a project, and its contributions have normally had to be matched by equivalent sums from other sources. Its level of lending has almost equalled that of the World Bank.

European Investment Fund (EIF). A **European Union (EU)** programme drafted in December 1992 and inaugurated in June 1994. Its objective was to promote economic growth and reduce unemployment by providing financial aid for major infrastructural projects, and for capital investments by smaller companies, through a system of loan guarantees. Its administration was to be handled by the **European Investment Bank (EIB)**.

European Launcher Development Organization (ELDO). Formed in 1964 as a cross-national effort to establish a European presence in space research and development. Its purpose was to design and build a European launcher for placing a heavy satellite in orbit. Development of the satellite was to be the responsibility of the parallel **European Space Research Organization (ESRO)**. It was plagued with financial and technical difficulties. Each country had a specialized role in the project, but this led to disputes between the participants, with the Secretariat, with no real authority, unable to exercise effective cost control. The problems led to political doubts about its viability. Some major countries withdrew from the operation in the early 1970s, and it was abandoned with the establishment of the **European Space Agency (ESA)** in 1975.

European League for Economic Co-operation (ELEC). An organization founded in March 1947 in **Brussels** to work for the establishment of a **customs union** in Western Europe. It sought to recruit economic experts and people in positions of authority rather than building a mass membership, and did not set down any political objectives. Two months later it renamed itself the League for Economic Co-operation in Europe, but failed to make a mark on political developments.

European Liaison Committee. *See* INTERNATIONAL COMMITTEE OF THE MOVEMENTS FOR EUROPEAN UNITY.

European Medicines Evaluation Agency. Founded by the **European Union (EU)** and located in London, it began operations in 1994. It was intended to be responsible for the licensing of all drugs throughout the EU and for monitoring their effectiveness and efficacy.

European Meteorological Satellite Organization (EUMET-SAT). An association of the national meteorological associations of Western Europe, established in 1986. Its formation was stimulated by the launch in 1975 of the first European meteorological satellite by the **European Space Agency (ESA).** A protocol was signed in 1977 whereby ESA would operate satellites from its operational centre in Darmstadt, but a proper programme was developed only in 1981, and EUMETSAT agreed upon in 1985. Funded by the national authorities, it has worked closely with ESA.

European Monetary Agreement. *See* EUROPEAN PAYMENTS UNION.

European Monetary Co-operation Fund (EMCF). Established in 1973 by the **European Communities (EC)** as part of the **Snake** and their plans for **Economic and Monetary Union (EMU).** It survived the collapse of the Snake and in 1979 was incorporated into the **European Monetary System (EMS)** as a reserve fund. Member States were expected to deposit 20 per cent of their gold and dollar reserves with the EMCF which in return would issue **European Currency Units (ECUs)** to the national central banks. Its business in practice is transacted by the **Bank for International Settlements.** It was dissolved at the end of 1993 in anticipation of the establishment of the **European Monetary Institute.**

European Monetary Institute. Founded in 1994 under terms of the **Treaty on European Union** as a central organ in the second stage of **Economic and Monetary Union (EMU).** Based in Frankfurt, it was charged with strengthening co-operation between the national central banks, co-ordinating monetary policies, and monitoring the **European Monetary System (EMS).** It also took over several functions previously handled by the **Bank for International Settlements.** In the third stage of EMU it would be replaced by a **European Central Bank.**

European Monetary System (EMS). A regulated exchange rate system established by the **European Communities (EC)** in 1979 after the failure of attempts to establish full **Economic and Monetary Union (EMU).** The EMS was originally a less ambitious attempt at monetary co-operation, aiming to build a zone of monetary stability in Western Europe. It contained two fundamental elements. An **Exchange Rate Mechanism (ERM)** would link national currencies together in a structure that imposed limits on how far each currency could fluctuate against its counterparts, and a **European Currency Unit (ECU)** would be developed as a common European currency. It contributed to a reduction in currency level fluctuations and in levels of inflation in the 1980s. It had been seen as a first step towards EMU, which was readopted as a goal by the EC in 1989. The 1991 **Treaty on European Union** endorsed this view and set 1999 as the deadline for full monetary integration. Intensive currency speculation against the ERM in 1992–93 and heightened political doubts disrupted the EMS and placed a question mark against its longer term goals.

European Monitoring Centre for Drugs and Drug Addiction. An agency of the **European Communities (EC)** established in 1991. Its purpose was to collect and collate information to help the Member States take effective steps to reduce the production, consumption and trafficking in drugs.

European Movement. An umbrella organization of national groups and associations working for and dedicated to European union. It was founded by the 1948 **Congress of Europe** and several statesmen, including **Churchill** and **de Gasperi**, became its official patrons. Responding to an invitation from **Spaak** to consider and draft proposals for a European institution, it put forward an outline of what was to become the **Council of Europe**. Its influence after 1950 was more limited but, based in **Brussels**, it survived as a body and information dissemination service with a wide membership, including recruits from Eastern Europe after 1989.

European NATO. A collective term referring generally to all European members of the **North Atlantic Treaty Organization (NATO)**. It has sometimes been taken to mean, with the addition of the **Federal Republic of Germany**, only the founding members of NATO, including **France** which has been only a partial member since 1966. It did not develop an institutional framework and was more an expression of the fact that there was a European pillar of NATO that shared some common defence and security concerns and interests different from those of the USA. *See also* EUROGROUP, INDE-PENDENT EUROPEAN PROGRAMME GROUP, WESTERN EUROPEAN UNION.

European Nuclear Disarmament (END). A cross-national organiz-ation in Western Europe founded in 1980 to co-ordinate opposition to the deployment of nuclear weapons and to work for the designation of Europe as a **nuclear-free zone (NFZ)**. It arose out of the **Euromissile** debate and the decision by the **North Atlantic Treaty Organization (NATO)** to deploy intermediate-range nuclear missiles in Western Europe. NATO's plans met with vocal opposition in all the countries, bar **Italy**, that were to house the missiles. END was intended to co-ordinate this opposition across national boundaries. Its structure and strategy were largely inspired by the British **Campaign for Nuclear Disarmament (CND)**, and its central direction was based in the **United Kingdom**. To achieve its goal of an NFZ, it sought to establish links with peace movements in Eastern Europe, but because these were largely state-sponsored and because of the strong Soviet support for Western anti-nuclear sentiment, it was to some extent discredited in the Western public mind. It had no leverage or significant influence upon any Western government, and the weapons were deployed without too much difficulty, after which END collapsed, fragmenting back into national groups.

European Nuclear Energy Agency (ENEA). An autonomous agency established by the **Organization for European Economic Co-operation (OEEC)** in December 1957 to encourage the peaceful utilization and application of nuclear research and to promote collaboration between national research bodies. Its major focus was on safety standards. After 1961 it was taken over by the **Organization for Economic Co-operation and Development (OECD)** which in 1972 replaced it with the **Nuclear Energy Agency (NEA)**.

European Organization for Nuclear Research (CERN). A cross-national venture founded in 1954 out of the 1952 European Council for Nuclear Research to finance and develop joint scientific non-military nuclear research across Western Europe. Very much a showpiece of European scientific co-operation, it has been concerned with the theoretical basis of nuclear and particle physics, rather than being an applied science institution. Based near **Geneva**, its funding has come from the subscribing national governments, including after 1989 some from Eastern Europe.

European Organization for the Safety of Air Navigation (Eurocontrol). Established by an International Convention Relating to Co-operation for the Safety of Air Navigation signed in **Brussels** in December 1960, and amended by Protocol in 1981, to work for a common structure of air traffic services in upper air space and to persuade countries to assign to it control of similar services in their lower air space. In 1981 a multilateral agreement provided for route changes, and in 1988 the **European Civil Aviation Conference (ECAC)** increased its capacity to control air space, but national governments proved reluctant to give up all authority over their own air space.

European Parliament (EP). The directly elected assembly of the **European Communities (EC)**. Its origins lie in the **Strasbourg** advisory assembly of the **European Coal and Steel Community (ECSC)**, which was amended in 1957 to be a single body serving also the **European Atomic Energy Community (EURATOM)** and the **European Economic Community (EEC)**. Its members were appointed by the national legislatures from among their own ranks. Direct elections were introduced in 1979, to take place at regular five-year intervals. Its seats have been allocated among the Member States in rough proportion to their population size. It was charged with supervising the **Commission** and **Council of Ministers** and with participating in the legislative and budgetary processes of the EC. It was always dissatisfied with its secondary and supportive role, and early adopted the title of EP as a symbol of what it hoped to become. Amendments to the original treaty have augmented its authority, but its role in EC legislation has remained negative and counteractive rather than positive. Two structural problems further inhibited its effectiveness. It conducts its business in 11 official languages, entailing huge translation costs, and its activities have been scattered across three countries. For historical reasons its plenary home has been Strasbourg. Most of its committees have preferred to meet in **Brussels**, to be close to the EC executives and administration. Much of the supporting secretariat has been located in **Luxembourg**, moving itself and the necessary documentation to Strasbourg only when the EP met in plenary session. The EP declared a wish to make Brussels its permanent home and in 1993 work began on a new building for it. However, **France** and Luxembourg have strongly resisted any suggestion of a concentration in Brussels.

European Parliamentary Union. A short-lived association of parliamentarians established in 1947 by **Coudenhove-Kalergi**. It was the outcome of his circulation of a questionnaire to several thousand European legislators soliciting their views on European union. It had only a limited appeal, and only about 110 representatives attended the inaugural meeting in Gstaad. Never prominent, it collapsed within a few years.

European Patent Organization (EPO). Established by the adoption in Munich in 1973 of the European Patent Convention. A Western European body, it also developed close links with similar national offices in Eastern Europe. Based in Munich, with sub-offices in **Berlin** and The Hague, its main task was to grant and register European patents and to disseminate information on national patent policies. It eliminated the costly procedure of having to apply for patent protection in each country, but where infringements of protection occurred, plaintiffs still had to pursue complaints separately in each country where the offences allegedly took place.

European Payments Union (EPU). An institution established in 1950 under the auspices of the **Organization for European Economic Co-operation (OEEC)** to facilitate further economic development once the **Marshall Plan** had ended, through provision of a system of reciprocal credits in intra-European trade. It was a more effective alternative than foreign exchange markets as an official clearing mechanism and surrogate bank for multilateral trade and payments. It helped to ease exchange controls and balance of payments difficulties, and gave Western Europe valuable experience in inter-governmental co-operation. The major problem was that it discriminated against the dollar in financial settlements, but this the USA accepted as the price for raising European economic prospects. By the late 1950s the change in economic conditions was such that the discrimination, which violated the **Bretton Woods Agreement**, could end. In 1958 the USA proposed the introduction of full currency convertibility and, endorsed by the OEEC, the EPU was dismantled in December. It was replaced by a more stringent European Monetary Agreement which served essentially the same purposes.

European People's Party (PPE). A **party group** in the **European Parliament (EP)**. Deputies from the national Christian Democratic parties had dominated the early EP. In anticipation of the introduction of direct elections, they formed the PPE in 1976. The decision to constitute a party rather than a federation of representatives was deliberate. The PPE has always argued for more powers to be given to the supranational institutions of the **European Communities (EC)**, and for the transformation of the EC into a federal political union. Generally moderately conservative in orientation, it has also included several radical strands.

European Police Office (EUROPOL). An agency founded by the **European Communities (EC)** in 1993 to co-ordinate national police activities in combatting major international crime such as drug trafficking, terrorism and money laundering. It was intended to be an intelligence agency rather than an integrated police force, but its operationalization was delayed by the objection of some countries to the loss of national control over police activity.

European Political Community (EPC). An attempt in the early 1950s to achieve political integration, arising from the decision to create a European army within a **European Defence Community (EDC)**. One problem with the EDC was that ideally it would require a correspondingly unified foreign policy. This flaw in the EDC concept led to proposals for an EPC. At the time the EDC treaty had not been ratified. An Article of the treaty would require its Common Assembly to consider ways of establishing federal institutions. **Spaak** suggested that the **European Coal and Steel Community (ECSC)** Assembly could be convened as an *ad hoc* EDC Common Assembly to consider the format of the EPC. It convened in September 1952 and proposed in a draft treaty six months later that the EPC should be a comprehensive federation that would subsume both the ECSC and EDC. The EPC discussions attracted little argument because attention was focused upon the difficulties of the EDC treaty, where ratification by **France** was highly unlikely. The inaction over EPC confirmed that it would stand or fall with the ratification or rejection of the EDC, and the refusal of France in August 1954 to discuss EDC ratification also ended the hopes for the EPC. Political union along the lines of the EPC was not seriously considered again until the late 1980s.

European Political Co-operation (EPC). A concept rather than a formal structure or institution, more narrowly describing the efforts of the members of the **European Communities (EC)** to collaborate on foreign policy issues. It developed from the recommendations of the **Davignon Report**. It was conceived as basically an inter-governmental operation co-ordinated at its apex by regular meetings of the national foreign ministers, backed up by a Political Committee of the **Political Directors** of the national foreign ministries. EC ambassadors in foreign capitals and at the United Nations (UN) also consulted regularly, and the foreign ministries often issued common instructions to their representatives abroad. In 1992 some Member States agreed to share an embassy and the related duties in some of the successor states of the ex-**USSR**. EPC focused primarily upon three kinds of broad initiatives: the adoption of common foreign policy statements and policies by the **European Council**; sanctions against undemocratic regimes; and adoption of a single representation in international forums and conferences, most successfully in the UN. The 1991 Gulf War and the post-1991 problems in the former **Yugoslavia** illustrated that the reconciliation of national positions was not an easy process. With the **Treaty on European Union** EPC was replaced by the **Common Foreign and Security Policy (CFSP)** pillar of the **European Union (EU)**.

European Productivity Agency (EPA). Established by the **Organization for European Economic Co-operation (OEEC)** in 1953 because of concerns about the low level of Western European productivity. Its task was to co-ordinate the work of national productivity centres that had been recommended by an OEEC committee in 1952. It extended its competence to include applied research and technological help for countries experiencing particular development problems, and built up close links with industrial enterprises and trade unions.

European Programme for High Technology Research and Development. *See* EUROPEAN RESEARCH CO-ORDINATION AGENCY.

European Public Health Committee. Established by the **Council of Europe** in 1966. Consisting of the heads of national public health departments, health experts and representatives of the European offices of the World Health Organization (WHO) and the League of Red Cross Societies, it was charged with facilitating the exchange of health information and cross-national collaborative research. It sponsored a European Blood Bank and a European Pharmacopoeia.

European Radical Alliance. A cross-national **party group** in the **European Parliament (EP)**. It was formed in 1994 by newcomers to the EP and survivors of the **Rainbow Group** as a moderate left of centre grouping.

European Recovery Programme (ERP). *See* MARSHALL PLAN, ORGANIZATION FOR EUROPEAN ECONOMIC CO-OPERATION.

European Regional Development Fund (ERDF). A structural fund of the **European Communities (EC)** and the key element of their regional policy, established in 1975. The bulk of its funding has gone to specific projects for regional infrastructural developments proposed by Member States, but it normally has been prepared to advance only one-half of the projected costs. When it began, each state received a fixed quota from the fund, so that its beneficiaries were the weakest areas of each country and not the EC's poorest regions. The system was changed in 1985 with each state eligible to receive a percentage range of the budget against which it can bid for funds. A new set of priorities were set after 1989, with the major targets being regions with weak economic development, industrial decline, or problems of rural development.

European Reparations Commission. *See* REPARATIONS.

European Research Co-ordination Agency (EUREKA). Established in 1983 to stimulate and finance a European Programme for High Technology Research and Development. It was a consequence of widespread concern that Western Europe was falling behind in technology development. Based in **Brussels**, EUREKA was a joint venture of the **European Communities (EC), European Free Trade Association (EFTA)** and **Turkey**, sponsoring over 100 collaborative international projects across a wide range of research areas. It raised most of its funding from non-governmental sources and the capital markets. In 1990 it agreed to involve the new democracies of Eastern Europe in its activities.

European Right (DR). A cross-national **party group** in the **European Parliament (EP)**. It was formed in 1984 by representatives of three extreme right-wing parties who because of their views were not welcomed as potential partners or members by other party groups. It remained isolated within the EP because no other group was willing to be associated with it. It lost its status after the 1994 elections because under the rules of the EP it lacked sufficient members to be recognized as an official party group.

European Romany Parliament. A Gypsy political organization founded in August 1992 by some 20 national Gypsy or Romany organizations. Its objectives were to defend the cultural and legal interests of the gypsy communities, and to combat discrimination against them.

European Schools. Educational institutions established by the **Commission**. Nine schools were set up in five of the member states of the **European Communities (EC)**. They were meant primarily for the children of EC employees, especially those working in a country other than their own, but if places are available they have been opened to other pupils. They provide an international syllabus: the teachers have been of different nationalities, and tuition has been given in several EC languages.

European Social Charter. A document sponsored and drafted by the

Council of Europe in 1955 and signed in Turin in 1961. It came into force in 1965. Its objective was to improve the standard of living and promote the welfare of European peoples by the protection of 19 specified human rights, later extended in number by a 1988 Protocol. It was designed to be a supplement to the **European Convention on Human Rights**, setting minimum standards which the signatories would implement. Several Eastern European countries signed it in 1991.

European Social Fund (ESF). A structural fund of the **European Communities (EC)**, established in 1958 and specifically concerned with employment and training. Its operations were minimal until the 1970s and the increase in unemployment levels. It has generally been concerned with assistance for the retraining of workers made redundant, but in the 1980s narrowed its focus more specifically to young people and the most economically disadvantaged areas of the EC.

European Space Agency (ESA). The second Western European attempt to establish co-operation in space research and development, founded in 1975. The first space ventures, the **European Space Research Organization (ESRO)** and the **European Launcher Development Organization (ELDO)**, were in difficulties by the late 1960s, with tension between them and the absence of an overall policy compounding technical problems and soaring costs. In 1971 a supervisory European Space Conference was established to review the situation and propose action. It recommended a coherent unified package of programmes rather than continuing to allow countries the freedom to choose which options they would support, and in 1973 proposed the establishment of ESA to promote space co-operation and technology for peaceful purposes, to develop a long-term space policy, and to co-ordinate national space programmes. The Convention formally establishing it only came into force in 1980, and the national ministerial representatives did not convene between 1977 and 1985, with spending on space research barely increasing in real terms during the first decade. ESA launched the first European communications satellite (ESC1) by **Ariane** in 1983, and a space probe, Giotto, was sent to rendezvous with Halley's Comet in 1985. It was the realization by governments of the communications value of satellites that increased their interest in ESA, with a promise to increase its science budget annually. In 1988 it announced Programme 2000, the development of crewed European space flight through construction of the **Hermes** space shuttle and **Columbus** space station. In 1991 the time span of the project was extended because of budget cuts, and the plan was damaged further with the abandonment of Hermes in 1993.

European Space Conference (ESC). *See* EUROPEAN SPACE AGENCY.

European Space Research Organization (ESRO). A multi-purpose agency established in 1962 to supervise and carry out collaborative research, and to design and develop European space satellites. A parallel body, the **European Launcher Development Organization (ELDO)**, was set up to develop a booster rocket system. It suffered from immediate problems. The Member States resisted collaboration when it conflicted with their own national interests and priorities, with considerable disputes also between the scientists. Escalating costs forced severe budget cuts in 1968, although two small satellites had been launched using American facilities. By 1971 there was consensus on the need for a new start, and a European Space Conference led to the establishment of the **European Space Agency (ESA)**, which took over ESRO's activities.

European System of Central Banks. A structure scheduled under the **Treaty on European Union** to come into existence in 1997 with the onset of the third stage of **Economic and Monetary Union (EMU)**. It would be a supportive body of the **European Central Bank** in the development of a common monetary policy for the **European Union (EU)**.

European Telecommunications Satellite Organization (EUTELSAT). An association of national Posts, Telegraphs and Telephone (PTT) organizations, established in 1977 to work on the development of a European communications satellite in conjunction with the **European Space Agency (ESA)**. Funded by the participating PTTs, its responsibilities were the procurement, operation and maintenance of the space segment of the European regional telecommunications and data transmission system. It has leased and used ESA satellites.

European Trade Union Confederation (ETUC). The major umbrella organization for national trade union federations in Western Europe. It was established in February 1973 by the International Confederation of Free Trade Unions (ICFTU) out of the latter's European section. In May 1974 it was joined by the European segment of the Christian Democrat-oriented World Congress of Labour (WCL). Based in **Brussels** and sharing its headquarters with the ICFTU, it has worked closely with both world bodies in seeking to co-ordinate trade union activities and their interests across national boundaries in the face of the internationalization of business and manufacturing. It has been formally involved with advising the **European Communities (EC)** in a variety of ways.

European Training Foundation (ETF). An institution formed to develop vocational training and retraining, and to assist in the financing of training programmes and projects. Established in 1990 by the **Council of Ministers**, it was a response to the economic problems of the **European Communities (EC)** and the democratization of Eastern Europe. It was specifically charged with emphasizing projects that involved Eastern European countries. Membership was not restricted to EC states.

European Union (EU). The structure created by the 1991 **Treaty on European Union**. It was intended to extend citizen rights across the **European Communities (EC)** and lay 'the foundations for a Union citizenship which will complement national citizenship without replacing it'. Coming into force in November 1993 it essentially consisted of the EC, which was flanked by two parallel pillars of inter-governmental decision-making, one dealing with a **Common Foreign and Security Policy (CFSP)**, the other with co-operation on **Justice and Home Affairs (JHA)**. Since the two new pillars were formally outside the EC structure, no complaints against their policies or actions would be able to be pursued in the **Court of Justice**, and the role of major EC institutions – the **Commission** and the **European Parliament (EP)** – in them was restricted to a consultative role. Only the **European Council** had authority across the pillars. Despite the impressive title, it remained restricted to the Member States of the EC, which remained the only legal entity, although in its stress upon citizenship it could be said to provide a further foundation for a future political union.

European Union of Christian Democrats. A cross-national organization of Christian Democrat parties. It began in 1947 as the *Nouvelles Équipes Internationales (NEI)* based in **Brussels**, Paris and eventually Rome after 1964. In 1965 the member parties of NEI formed the European wing of the Christian Democratic International and adopted the present name. In 1976 its members from the **European Communities (EC)** founded the **European People's Party (PPE)** as a transnational organization, with a membership eventually extending to some 30 countries.

European Union of Federalists (UEF). A cross-national umbrella organization of national associations which advocated a federal union of Europe after 1945. Established in Basel in December 1946, it set up a provisional secretariat in Paris, and plans were made to develop a headquarters in **Geneva**. It wished for a neutral federal state, not aligned militarily with either the USA or the **USSR**. Its popularity peaked in 1947 and it lost much of its impetus and limited influence after 1948 with the establishment of the **European Movement**. After 1949 it became increasingly riddled with internal disputes over doctrine and strategy, and it disintegrated in 1956.

European Unit of Account (EUA). A book-keeping device created by the **European Communities (EC)** for recording the relative value of payments into and from EC accounts. After the **European Currency Unit (ECU)** was established in 1979, it replaced the EUA in EC book-keeping in 1981.

European University Institute (EUI). A postgraduate research and training centre in history and the social sciences founded in 1976 by the **European Communities (EC)** and based in Florence. Students, funded by national governments, are also expected to have competence in more than one EC language. Staff are seconded to it for fixed terms of between three and seven years.

European Venture Capital Association (EVCA). An agency for promoting the management and investment of venture capital, and development of a European capital market. It was formed in 1973 as a **European Communities (EC)** initiative, with membership also from other states. It focused in particular upon sponsoring the development of small- and medium-sized companies.

European Youth Forum. Established by the **European Communities (EC)** in the mid-1970s to foster and promote a EC educational policy. Its membership was to consist of the leaders of national student and youth organizations. Its impact has been limited, not least because of the transient nature of its membership.

Europe Day. *See* SCHUMAN, ROBERT.

Europe of Nations. An international organization formed in April 1994 by members of national legislatures within the **European Union (EU)** and other individuals who argued that European co-operation should be based on sovereign nation states. It declared its objectives were to resist the centralizing trends of the EU and to secure a reversal of the process of integration outlined in the **Treaty on European Union**.

Europe of the Regions. A phrase in common usage in the 1980s, employed by those who wished local and regional authorities to have a greater input into **European Communities (EC)** discussions and policies. Its objectives were partially realized by the establishment of the **Committee of the Regions** by the **Treaty on European Union**.

EUROPOL. *See* EUROPEAN POLICE AGENCY.

Eurosceptic. A phrase used, especially in the **United Kingdom**, to describe those people who opposed the **Treaty on European Union** and the attempts by the **European Communities (EC)** to introduce further political integration.

Euskadi. *See* BASQUES.

Euskadi ta Askatasuna. (**ETA**, *Basque Homeland and Liberty*) A Basque terrorist organization. It was formed in 1959 by young activists who rejected a moderate approach to the **Franco** regime, and broke away from the **Basque Nationalist Party (PNV)**. Stronger repressive measures in the Basque territories in the 1960s stiffened its resolve and gave it greater popular appeal. Becoming the visible vanguard of Basque resistance, its anti-Franco activities peaked with the assassination of Franco's chosen heir, **Carrero Blanco**, in 1973. In 1974 it split into 'political-military' and 'military' factions. It rejected any compromise with the democratic Spanish governments after 1975, and the autonomous structure of government granted to the Basque region in 1979, continuing a campaign of kidnapping, violence and intimidation. Its impact weakened after 1980, partly because of internal conflicts between 'purer' nationalists and Marxists, and partly because of more effective anti-terrorist measures introduced by the Spanish and Basque governments. While retaining a hard core of popular support, its continuing intransigence led by 1993 to more visible public expressions of opposition among the Basque population against its insistence upon continuing an armed struggle.

Evangelical People's Party. (*Evangelische Volkspartei/Parti Évangelique Populaire – EVP/PEP*) A small Christian Democratic party in **Switzerland** founded in 1919. It advocates policies consistent with Protestant principles, and its appeal and support have been largely confined to the Protestant population.

Évian Agreements. A series of agreements in March 1962 at Évian-les-Bains in **France** which ended the **Algerian War of Independence**. They were the outcome of secret negotiations begun in **Switzerland** in December 1961 between French representatives led by **Pompidou** and representatives of the Algerian revolutionaries. Mohammed Ahmed Ben-Bella, the Algerian leader, was secretly released from internment to participate in the discussions. An immediate cease-fire in Algeria was accepted, and France agreed to hold a plebiscite on Algeria's future. Referendums in France in April and in Algeria in June overwhelmingly supported the option of independence. The Agreements were attacked by the extremist secret organization of army officers and white settlers, the **Organization de l'Armée Secrète (OAS)**, led by **Salan**.

Exchange Rate Mechanism (ERM). A key component of the **European Monetary System (EMS)** established by the **European Communities (EC)** in 1979. It was to be the tool by which the EMS would stabilize exchange rates and limit currency fluctuations. Before 1988 it was a fairly flexible arrangement, easily accommodating several currency realignments. The rules were tightened in 1988 in anticipation of the establishment of **Economic and Monetary Union (EMU)**, a goal endorsed by the **Treaty on European Union**. With currencies of different strengths and no economic harmonization, the more rigid ERM came under intense pressure from currency speculation in September 1992, forcing several involuntary devaluations and the withdrawal of **Italy** and the **United Kingdom** from the system. The return of pressure in August 1993 resulted in the broadening of the permissible range of currency fluctuation to such an extent that the ERM effectively ceased to be a regulatory mechanism, casting doubts upon the EC aim and timetable for monetary union.

Extra-parliamentary opposition. (*Ausserparlamentarische Opposition – APO*) A loose alliance of radicals in the **Federal Republic of**

Germany 1966–69. It arose during the period of the **grand coalition** between the two major parties. It argued that the coalition had left parliamentary opposition too weak and feeble, and that the only effective opposition had to come from outside. Its core lay in the Socialist German Student Association (SDS), a body disowned some years previously by the **Social Democrat Party (SPD)** because of its extreme radical views, and its mass base lay in university students who were pressing, through protests and demonstrations, for major reforms to an archaic higher educational system. The APO hoped through direct action to secure a radical reform and democratization of the state institutions, and that its case would be supported by the trade unions and the working class. It found allies in some of the many local **citizen initiatives** groups that were beginning to emerge, and attacked the emergency laws and loyalty tests for state employees passed by the government. Regarding itself as part of a world revolutionary movement, it supported the 1968 **May Events** in **France** and vociferously opposed American involvement in Vietnam. Always an uneasy alliance of radical democrats and Marxists of various persuasions, it failed to win support among the trade unions and began to fragment in 1969, losing much of its mass base after the government initiated reforms in higher education. Some of its supporters opted to seek future political influence within the SPD or public service through a 'long march through the institutions'. Others, emphasizing various aspects of Marxist purity, turned to environmental causes or resorted to terrorism, with the **Baader–Meinhof Group** having its roots in the APO.

F

Fabius, Laurent. (1946–) Prime Minister of **France** 1984–86. A civil servant, he joined the **Socialist Party (PS)** in 1974, becoming an economics adviser to **Mitterrand**. Elected to Parliament in 1978 he served in various government positions after 1981 before taking over the premiership. Regarded as a potential PS leader, he attempted to introduce a more technocratic style of government in order to increase prime ministerial authority, but was only partially successful. On the right of the party, he adopted policies that might attract votes from the political centre, but his influence within the PS declined markedly after he lost the 1986 parliamentary election. He was elected PS leader in January 1992, but resigned after a heavy electoral defeat in April 1993.

Factortane Judgment. (R v. Secretary of State for Transport, ex parte Factortane Ltd) A 1990 ruling by the **Court of Justice** which confirmed that within the **European Communities (EC)** national legislation which is found to be in conflict with EC law must be suspended.

Falange. (*El Falange Española*) The Spanish fascist party and, renamed the Falangist Movement and Syndicalist Juntas of the National Offensive (*Falange Española Tradicionalista y de las Juntas de Ofensiva Nacional-Sindicalista*), the only party officially permitted under the **Franco** dictatorship. Founded in 1933, its Grand Council acted as the main legislative authority in **Spain** 1939–42, but its influence then declined rapidly as Franco preferred to rule by more autocratic methods. It opposed his plans to restore the monarchy, but by 1945 had become marginalized, thereafter being little more than a historical curiosity.

Falcone and Borsellino murders. The murder of two senior magistrates by the **Mafia** in May and June 1992. Giovanni Falcone had been the leading prosecutor in the largest mass trial of Mafia members 1986–87, and was widely expected to be appointed as the head of a new anti-Mafia investigation unit. Paolo Borsellino was the senior public prosecutor in Palermo, Sicily. Both were killed by car bombs. Their deaths caused a huge public outrage, and a new series of police and judicial measures were introduced to combat organized crime.

Falklands War. A military confrontation between the **United Kingdom**

and Argentina over the Falkland (*Malvinas*) Islands, a British colony since 1832, but occupied by Argentina, April–June 1982. Negotiations over Argentina's claims to the islands were begun under United Nations (UN) auspices in 1965, but no satisfactory agreement was reached. On 2 April 1982 Argentina militarily occupied the islands. A hastily assembled British task force sailed to the South Atlantic and began its counter-attack on 1 May. The Argentinian forces surrendered on 14 June. The military operation did much to enhance the prestige at home and abroad of the British premier, **Thatcher**.

Fälldin, Thorbjörn. (1926–) Prime Minister of **Sweden** 1976–78, 1979–82. Entering Parliament in 1958 for the **Centre Party**, he was elected its leader in 1971. In 1976 he headed the first non-socialist government since 1932. The coalition, an uneasy alliance of three parties, failed to make a great impact, essentially following the policies of its social democratic pre-decessors, but the major factor contributing to its final collapse was Fälldin's strong espousal of environmental issues, especially his opposition to a nuclear energy programme. He continued as party leader until 1985 before retiring from politics.

Fanfani, Amintore. (1908–) Prime Minister of **Italy** 1954, 1958–59, 1960–62, 1962–63, 1982–83, 1987. A founder member of the **Christian Democratic Party (DC)**, he entered Parliament in 1945, serving in various ministerial capacities after 1947. He was an energetic Party Secretary 1954–59, building up the party organization and membership. Identified as belonging to the moderate left of the party, he was a supporter of the idea of an 'opening to the left', the negotiation of an alliance with the **Italian Socialist Party (PSI)** as the best way of guaranteeing stable coalition government under DC direction. He successfully began the process of rapprochement after 1960, after the failure of the DC right to extend its coalition to include parties of the extreme right. The PSI supported his 1960 and 1962 governments by a policy of 'benevolent abstention'. He was elected to the Senate in 1968 and made a Senator for life in 1972. A Party grandee and father figure in the 1970s and 1980s, he returned briefly to centre stage in the 1980s, heading two stop-gap or caretaker administrations pending renegotiation of party alliances, but not putting forward any vigorous or positive government programme.

Farmers Union of Latvia. (*Latvijas Zemnieka Savienība* – *LZS*) A political party in **Latvia**. First formed in 1917, it had been a leading political force before the Second World War. It was reconstituted in 1989 as a right-wing agrarian party, but was only a shadow of its former self.

Faroe Islands. A group of islands in the North Atlantic, and a self-governing unit of **Denmark**. A Danish possession since 1380, the islands, which possess their own language, were granted self-government in 1948.

173

Denmark retained responsibility for foreign policy, defence, justice, finance and law and order. The islands were given their own legislature and government, while still electing representatives to the Danish parliament. After 1948 Denmark was represented in the Faroes by an appointed commissioner. The economy of the islands is heavily dependent upon fishing: economic problems and fears for the industry led to the islands leaving the **European Free Trade Association (EFTA)** in 1972, and one year later they voted not to follow Denmark into the **European Communities (EC)**.

Fascism. An authoritarian revolutionary ideology that emerged in the early twentieth century, appealing in particular to middle-class elements of society. Derived from the Italian *Fascismo*, itself coming from the Latin *Fasces*, an insignia of the consuls of ancient Rome, it took root to a greater or lesser extent throughout Europe in the inter-war period, though taking a great variety of political formats, of which German Nazism was the most extreme version. After 1945 the word has been used so widely in a pejorative manner that it has lost much of its value and meaning. New varieties of extreme right-wing politics emerged after 1945, and made an appearance in Eastern Europe after 1989. Often referred to as being neo-Fascist, there is a debate over whether they reflect the same phenomenon, ideology and causes as the inter-war movements.

Fatherland. (*Isamaa*) A political alliance in **Estonia**. It was formed in 1992 by the five main right-wing parties that emerged after 1988. Although it has been electorally successful, internal disagreements between its autonomous units strained its cohesion and effectiveness.

Fatherland Front. (*Otechestven Front*) A Popular Front organization in **Bulgaria**. It was formed in 1943 to co-ordinate opposition to the pro-German regime. Control of it was gradually seized by the **Bulgarian Communist Party (BKP)**. After 1948 it consisted of the only two parties legally permitted in the country, the BKP and the **Bulgarian Agrarian National Union**, but operated as a single organization that claimed to possess a mass membership greater than that of the two parties. In practice it was a centrally directed body controlled by the BKP. It collapsed in 1989.

Fatherland Front. (*Vaterländische Union – VU*) A conservative party in **Liechtenstein**. Originally populist, it became a defender of the dynasty and constitutional monarchy. Founded in 1914 as the Christian Social People's Party, it changed its name after merging with the *Heimatdienst* movement in the early 1930s. The largest party since then, it has, in alliance with the **Progressive Citizens' Party**, been continuously in government since 1938.

Faulkner, Arthur Brian Deane. (1921–1977) Prime Minister of **Northern Ireland** 1971–72, and a Unionist member of the **Stormont** parliament since 1949. His premiership coincided with an escalation of sectarian violence in the province. His introduction of internment for suspected terrorists in August 1971 hardened Catholic opposition, and in March 1972 the British government imposed direct rule of the province from Westminster. Despite his support for internment, he had sought reconciliation between the two communities in the province and some collaboration with **Ireland**, promoting the idea of a Council of Ireland. However, his conciliatory stance alienated him from major elements of his own party, and he resigned as leader in January 1974. He was made Baron Faulkner of Downpatrick and retired from political life in 1976.

Faure, Edgar. (1908–1988) Prime Minister of **France** 1952, 1955–56. Entering Parliament in 1946 as a Radical deputy, he was a somewhat surprising choice as premier in 1952. Leftward-leaning, he favoured co-operation with the Socialist Party (SFIO), but found it hard to sustain. His second ministry in 1955 was more long-lived and successful, building up France's fiscal reserves. Defeated by a Parliament increasingly paralysed by the **Algerian War of Independence**, he dissolved it in 1956, as a result of which he was expelled from the party. In 1959 he was elected to the Senate and, moving to the right, became a strong supporter of **de Gaulle**.

Federal Republic of Germany. A state originally formed in 1949 out of the American, British and French zones of military occupation, though not granted full sovereignty by the Allies until 1955. Its creation had been part of the Western reaction in the **Cold War** to their concerns about the territorial ambitions in Europe of the **USSR**. Under the leadership of the **Christian Democratic Union (CDU)** 1949–69, it rapidly rebuilt its economy to become the major economic power on the continent. Under **Adenauer** and his successors, it became an integral part of Western security, joining the **North Atlantic Treaty Organization (NATO)** in 1955, and was a participant in all European integration initiatives after 1950. Involvement in Western defence was regarded as essential for West German security, and it formed a particularly close relationship with the USA in the 1950s. In turn, it vocally attacked the Communist regime in the **German Democratic Republic (DDR)**, denying the latter's existence through the **Hallstein Doctrine** and claiming to be the only legitimate successor to the pre-war German state. Equally, its participation in integration processes was seen as a way of rehabilitating the country with its neighbours and allaying their fears about any possible political resurgence of German military power. It successfully demonstrated its political maturity and democratic credentials in its reaction to the first major resurgence of extreme-right wing politics, the **National Democratic Party (NPD)** in the 1960s, and to the terrorist activities of the **Baader–Meinhof Group** in the 1970s.

After 1969 the **Brandt** government sought through the **Ostpolitik** process a reconcilation and relationship with the DDR. When the Communist regime of the DDR crumbled in November 1989, the **Kohl** government moved quickly to press for German reunification. The way forward was cleared by the **Two Plus Four Talks** of June 1990. A Treaty of Unification was signed and later in the year the Federal Republic expanded to incorporate the DDR, with all-German elections held in October, and the war-time Allies formally abrogating their rights in the country. With reunification, the new Parliament decreed that **Berlin** should be reinstated as the capital of the state. After 1990 there was strong resentment in the former DDR over 'Western takeovers', and despite huge capital transfers living standards in the eastern territories remained well below those of Western Germany. The economic discontent contributed to social tensions which were reflected, *inter alia*, in resentment at and attacks upon immigrants and refugees. The pressure and fear of large-scale immigration from Eastern Europe led the government to modify the liberal asylum laws in 1993.

Federal Union. An international committee formed to argue the case for a federal state of Europe after the end of the Second World War. Its detailed proposals were contained in memoranda produced in July 1943 and in a proposed Declaration of Solidarity between governments. Its strongest advocates were from Eastern Europe. It had little impact and faded away completely during 1945.

Federal Union of European Nationalities (FUEN). An organization founded in Paris in 1949 to work for the preservation of the culture and language of national minorities. It drew its membership from ethnic minority organizations in Western Europe, but failed to develop as a strong body, primarily perhaps because there was no single target to which it could address its demands.

Federation of Bosnia-Hercegovina. A state proclaimed by Bosnian Muslims and Bosnian Croats in March 1994, intended to end the conflict between the two groups. The participants agreed to set up a decentralized state built upon ethnically based local units and with power-sharing at the national level. Implementation of the proposed structure was delayed until agreement could be reached with the Bosnian Serbs, who controlled much of the territory claimed by the new Federation.

Federation of Green Lists. (*Federazione delle Liste Verdi*) An electoral alliance in **Italy** founded in 1984. More moderate than most green movements, it brought together several environmental groups, but failed to weld them into a coherent organization or gain much political support until after the **Tangentopoli** political crisis, when it agreed to enter into a broad left-wing alliance headed by the Party of Democratic Socialism, the reconstructed successor to the **Italian Communist Party (PCI)**.

Federation of the Democratic and Socialist Left. (*Fédération de la Gauche Démocratique et Socialiste*) A broad moderate left-wing alliance of several parties in **France**. It was formed in September 1965 by **Mitterrand** to serve as a vehicle for his presidential challenge against **de Gaulle**. It demanded constitutional reforms, especially curbs on the powers of the presidency, and attacked de Gaulle's nationalistic foreign policy. It survived to contest the 1967 and 1968 parliamentary elections in alliance with the **French Communist Party (PCF)**, but collapsed after its heavy defeat in the 1968 election.

Felvidék. The Hungarian name for the predominantly Magyar-speaking areas of southern **Slovakia** and **Ruthenia** taken by **Hungary** from **Czechoslovakia** by the Vienna awards of 1938. After **USSR** forces occupied the region during the winter of 1944–45, the pre-1938 frontiers were restored in an armistice concluded with the provisional Hungarian republican government in January 1945. The following June, the USSR took the whole of Ruthenia for itself, incorporating it into the Ukrainian Soviet Socialist Republic as Transcarpathia. After the democratization of Eastern Europe in 1989, Hungary expressed concern about the future of the Magyar minority in the newly independent Slovakia, giving rise to some tension between the two states.

Feminism. A movement demanding the social and economic, as well as political, equality of women with men. Although campaigns for the rights of women date back to the nineteenth century, the term more usually refers to activities, organizations and demands since the 1960s, especially women's liberation movements. It was divided by several strands of thought. Liberal feminism argued for equality of individual rights. Socialist feminism adopted a Marxist framework and blamed capitalism for forcing women into specific roles in child-bearing and employment. Radical feminism maintained that the two sexes were different and incompatible, and at the extreme argued for a separate female society maintained by artifical means of reproduction. Feminist movements developed throughout Western Europe, but not in Eastern Europe. By the end of the 1970s they were split into several different associations in most countries. The success of feminist movements varied from country to country. While most states accepted legislation outlawing gender discrimination in employment and other areas of social activity, women's advancement to high political and economic positions was more varied and limited. The movements were perhaps most successful in Scandinavia, with a separate party, the **Women's Alliance**, being founded in **Iceland**.

Fenech Adami, Edward. (1934–) Prime Minister of **Malta** from 1987. A lawyer and journalist, he joined the **Nationalist Party** in 1961, entering Parliament in 1969 and becoming party leader in 1977. In 1987 he led the party back to government after 16 years in opposition. As Prime Minister he sought to bring Malta closer to Western Europe, reversing the more aggressive non-aligned stance of the previous **Labour Party** governments.

Fianna Fáil. (Soldiers of Destiny) The largest political party in **Ireland**. It was founded in 1926 by **de Valéra** to campaign for a united republican and totally independent Ireland. It won its first electoral victory in 1932, and has been in government for most of the time since, often as a single party majority administration. It has regarded itself as a left of centre party, but has enjoyed good relations with the Catholic Church and has been strongly conservative on moral issues. It claimed for itself the inheritance of Irish nationalism and adopted a strong nationalistic stance, modified only in the late 1980s, with regard to **Northern Ireland** and the question of Irish reunification.

Fifth French Republic. The system of government established in **France** in 1958 by and for **de Gaulle**. It was radically different from the previous **Fourth French Republic** in its emphasis upon a strong presidency and its curbing of parliamentary authority and powers, turning France into a semi-presidential regime. The President, elected for seven years, nominates the Prime Minister, can rule by decree, and seek popular support for policies through referendums. It survived initial tensions over the question of Algeria and possible military intervention to consolidate itself in the economic growth of the 1960s and afterwards. It similarly survived the departure of de Gaulle in 1969 and the first experiment in **cohabitation** in 1986–88. After the first decade critics of the system no longer sought to replace it, but argued that some constitutional powers should be shifted from the presidency to the Parliament.

Fighting Communist Cells. (*Cellules Communistes Combattantes*) A left-wing urban terrorist group in **Belgium**. It waged an intensive bombing campaign 1984–86 against **North Atlantic Treaty Organization (NATO)** installations and supplies, and against the offices of non-socialist parties. It declined after several of its leaders were arrested in 1986 and sentenced to life imprisonment with hard labour two years later, but continued to claim responsibility for sporadic acts of violence.

Fighting Communist Nuclei. *See* RED BRIGADES.

Fighting Communist Party. *See* RED BRIGADES.

Figl, Leopold. (1902–1965) Chancellor of **Austria** 1945–53. Politically active in the Austrian Farmers' League after 1927 and a leading member of the pre-war Christian Social Party, he had urged resistance to annexation by Germany in 1938, as a result of which he was interned in a concentration camp, apart from a brief period in 1943–44, until 1945. A co-founder of the **Austrian People's Party (ÖVP)**, he led it until 1951. Although winning a majority in the 1945 election, he chose to construct a **grand coalition** in order to present a united front against the occupying Allies, introducing the system of **proporz** as a means of lessening the acute distrust which had characterized pre-war party politics. After choosing to resign as premier in 1953, he served as Foreign Minister until 1959.

Filesa. A bogus holding company which became the synonym of a major political scandal in **Spain**. It erupted in 1992 when it was revealed that two dummy companies had been set up to channel money to the governing **Spanish Socialist Workers' Party (PSOE)**, which had been suffering severe funding problems. The companies obtained commissions from leading enterprises for fictitious consultancy work. A report issued by the official investigators in 1993 showed that the PSOE had received over $2 million for election expenses and the maintenance of its Madrid headquarters, while several of the donors had later been awarded government contracts. The scandal and the judicial investigation overturned a parliamentary inquiry which, following a tacit agreement by parties that they would not pry into each other's finances, had accepted that no rules had been broken. The number of people charged with crimes in connection with Filesa ran into the thousands, and the episode was one of several that cast a cloud over PSOE and government probity. It was one of several scandals involving illegal party funding, especially by the PSOE.

FINEFTA. An agreement between **Finland** and the **European Free Trade Association (EFTA)**. Finland had participated in the discussions that led to the formation of EFTA, but because of its proximity to and relationship with the **USSR** felt that it could not join the organization. Under FINEFTA it received associate status, but possessed more or less the same rights as a full EFTA member. It became a full member of EFTA in 1986.

Fine Gael. (United Ireland) A centre-right party in **Ireland**. Founded in 1922 as Cumann na nGaedheal and supporting the 1921 Anglo-Irish Treaty which created the Irish Free State, it changed its name in 1933 after losing government power. Since 1932 it has been Ireland's second largest party, but lagging far behind the rival **Fianna Fáil**. Since 1945 it has headed five government coalitions for short periods. Like other parties it has claimed adherence to Irish nationalism, but usually with a more moderate emphasis, accepting that a united Ireland should only be achieved peacefully.

Finland. A Baltic state independent since 1917. Part of **Sweden** from the early Middle Ages until 1809, it then became a Grand Duchy within **Russia**. Left-wing groups opposed the declaration of independence, and there was a bloody civil war 1917–18, and the Communist Party was banned in 1930. During the Second World War Finland fought two military campaigns against the **USSR**. Totally outnumbered, it sued for peace in August 1944 and under the terms of the peace treaty ceded territory to the USSR together with fleet facilities at the port of Porkkala, and agreed to pay reparations. In 1948 it signed a **Treaty of Friendship, Co-operation and Mutual Assistance** with the USSR, which effectively constrained its foreign policy and permitted Soviet influence upon and possible intervention in Finnish domestic affairs. The first two post-war presidents, **Paasikivi** and **Kekkonen**, pursued a careful policy of neutrality, seeking to maintain links with the West while cultivating Soviet friendship and trust. Porkkala was returned in 1955, and gradually Finland felt able to associate itself more with Western Europe in non-defence areas, joining the **Nordic Council** in 1956 and linking up with the **European Free Trade Association (EFTA)** as an associate member in 1961. Its neutral position made it a good location for dialogue between the two European power blocs.

After 1981 the new president, **Koivisto**, began to follow a more independent foreign policy line. A welfare state was gradually constructed after 1945, and the country benefited economically also from having a 'favoured nation' status in trade with the USSR. Until the 1960s governments revolved mainly around a red-green coalition, a collaboration between the **Finnish Social Democratic Party** and the **Centre Party**. From the mid-1960s until the early 1980s governments were mainly centre-left with, under indirect Soviet pressure, Communist participation. The electoral rise after the late 1970s of the conservative **National Coalition Party** and internal Communist conflict led to the formation of more centrist coalitions. The treaty with the USSR was revised in 1991 with the deletion of its military aspects, but by the end of the year had been unilaterally ended by Finland. In 1992 it signed a new agreement with **Russia** which contained no references to defence or security. Also in 1992 it applied to join the **European Communities (EC)**, formally becoming a member in 1995 after a strong positive endorsement in a referendum the previous year.

Finlandization. The accommodation by a small state of the interests of a larger neighbour while still retaining a significant degree of independence. The phrase was coined to describe the relationship of **Finland** with the **USSR** after 1944 and the way in which the 1948 treaty between the two countries obliged Finland in practice to take account of Soviet strategic and ideological interests in its policy formulation, especially in foreign affairs, as the price for continued independence. In return, the USSR agreed that it would not interfere in domestic Finnish economic and political matters. The term was sometimes used in a derogatory sense in the West, being likened to little more than appeasement of the USSR. Others used it to describe a purposeful Soviet strategy which it would wish to enforce on other countries.

Finnbogadóttir, Vigdis. (1930–) President of **Iceland** from 1980. The first woman elected as head of state in Europe, her victory reflected the impact of **feminism** in Iceland, which had also produced a **Women's Alliance** at the same time. Previously a tourist guide and theatre manager who had never been a member of a political party, she became a highly popular and respected figure.

Finnish Christian Union. (*Suomen Kristilliinen Liitto – SKL*) A small fundamentalist Christian party in **Finland**, formed in 1958. A fringe party that exhorted the application of Christian ideals in public life, it first gained greater appeal and representation after 1970, in part because of its strong opposition to permissive legislation passed by left-wing governments.

Finnish Communist Party. (*Suomen Kommunistinen Puolue – SKP*) A major left-wing party in **Finland** until its dissolution in April 1990. Founded in 1918 by Socialist opponents of the declaration of independence from the **USSR**, it experienced severe discrimination in the 1920s and was outlawed in 1930–44. After its legalization in 1944 it was by far the dominant element in the **Finnish People's Democratic League (SKDL)**. It entered coalition governments in 1966, but the behaviour of its members was erratic and it tended to ignore the conventions of collective responsibility. After 1969 the majority of the party began increasingly to espouse the ideas of **Euro-communism**. The resulting internal disputes between Eurocommunists and Stalinists contributed to electoral decline, a return to opposition in 1984, and the eventual split in the party with the expulsion of the Stalinist wing. It dissolved itself in 1990 when it and the SKDL elected to join a new **Left-Wing Alliance**.

Finnish Communist Party – Unity. *See* DEMOCRATIC ALTERNATIVE.

Finnish People's Democratic League. (*Suomen Kansan Demokraattinen Liitto – SKDL*) A broad Communist-dominated left-wing alliance in **Finland**. Formed in 1944, it was to all intents and purposes the electoral organization of the **Finnish Communist Party (SKP)**. In April 1990 it disbanded itself to become part of a new **Left-Wing Alliance**.

Finnish Rural Party. (*Suomen Maaseudun Puolue – SMP*) A small populist party in **Finland**. It was formed in 1959 by Veikko Vennamo as a breakaway group from the **Centre Party**. Its formation was a reaction in the poorer north to the plans by a Centre Party-led coalition government to amalgamate small farms as a programme of agricultural rationalization. Very much a vehicle for Vennamo who led it until 1979, when he was succeeded by his son, it was a typical protest movement with fluctuating support, although it succeeded in extending its appeal beyond the small farmers of the north. It surprisingly entered a coalition government 1983–87, where it was criticized for persisting with its tradition of dissident behaviour. A splinter broke away in 1972 to form a Finnish People's Unification Party (*Suomen Kansan Yhtenäiyyden Puolue*).

Finnish Social Democratic Party. (*Suomen Sosialdemokraattinen Puolue – SDP*) A major left-wing party in **Finland**. Founded in 1903, by 1907 it was the most successful Socialist party in Europe, but it was split by the declaration of independence in 1917, facing thereafter a powerful challenge from the Communists to its left. In the 1930s it began to collaborate with the Agrarian Union (later the **Centre Party**) in red–green alliances, which lasted until the 1960s. Memories of 1917 and the role its leaders played in the wars against the **USSR** in the 1940s made it suspect in Soviet eyes, and after 1945 some of its leaders were imprisoned, upon Soviet insistence, for war crimes. After the 1960s it was the major and a consistent element of government coalitions, and successfully retained its level of electoral support in a period of substantial political change.

First of October Anti-Fascist Resistance Group. (*Grupo de Resistencia Antifascista Primero de Octubre – GRAPO*) An extreme left-wing terrorist group in **Spain**. Claiming a Marxist ideology, it emerged in 1975 with the objective of establishing a revolutionary Communist regime through a campaign of bombings and assassinations. Overt the next decade most of its leaders were arrested and imprisoned. Some of these staged a hunger strike in prison in 1989, after which the organization seemed to be reactivated, with a new campaign of bombings and murders occurring.

First past the post. The popular name given to the simple majority, single member electoral system as employed in the **United Kingdom**. Its supporters argued that by penalizing fringe parties it offers a clear choice to the electorate and guarantees strong majority government. Its critics argue that it is essentially unrepresentative, discriminating against smaller parties that nevertheless receive a substantial number of votes, allowing the election of candidates who have failed, sometimes substantially so, to gain a majority of the votes in a constituency, and producing majority governments which have nevertheless failed to win a majority of votes in the country.

Fitzgerald, Garret. (1926–) Prime Minister of **Ireland** 1981–82, 1982–87. A lawyer and academic who was first elected to Parliament for **Fine Gael** in 1965, he served as Foreign Minister in the 1973–77 coalition government. He became party leader in 1977. As Prime Minister he sought a more conciliatory and realistic policy towards **Northern Ireland** and the issue of Irish reunification, signing the **Anglo-Irish Agreement** in 1985. He resigned the party leadership and withdrew from active party politics after losing the 1987 election on economic issues.

Fiume. (Rijeka) An Adriatic port of the Habsburg Empire, claimed in 1919 by both **Italy** and **Yugoslavia**. In 1924 Yugoslavia accepted Italian incorporation of most of the area, but renewed its claim after 1945. The **Paris Peace Treaties** formally ceded the territory to Yugoslavia.

Five-Sixths Action Committee. An interest group in **Luxembourg** turned political party in 1989. It campaigned solely for the extension of the pension rights of civil servants, who received pensions worth five-sixths of final salary, to all citizens of retirement age. It later broadened its platform to defend the interests of the elderly in general, and renamed itself the Action Committee for Democracy and Pension Justice.

Flanders. A linguistically cohesive province of **Belgium**. Loyally Catholic, in the nineteenth century its economic development lagged well behind that of neighbouring **Wallonia**, and its language was discriminated against, with French used as the language of state. Flemish nationalism first emerged around 1900, but its expansion was hindered by its association with Germany in both World Wars. After 1950, the province, already possessing a majority of the Belgian population, experienced dramatic economic growth to become the richer, more advanced part of the country. At the same time a new nationalist party, the **People's Union**, emerged, and the resolution of the **Schools Pact** opened the way for language divisions to dominate Belgian politics. The linguistic issue, resolved eventually in 1993 by the establishment of a federal structure, was driven by Flemish demands for greater autonomy. The creation of a federal state was accepted in principle in 1970: one of the stumbling blocks which delayed its formalization was Flemish claims to **Brussels**, a city on Flemish territory but possessing a large French-speaking majority. In the 1980s a more extreme version of nationalism emerged, demanding independence and focusing on the issue of immigration.

Flanking Measures. A term used in the **European Union (EU)** to describe measures or actions intended to support the implementation and objectives of a specific common policy or programme, but not themselves integral to it.

Flemish Bloc. (*Vlaams Blok*) An extreme right-wing party in **Belgium**. It was formed in 1979 after an alliance the previous year between two small groups, the Flemish People's Party (*Vlaamse Volkspartij*) and the Flemish National Party (*Vlaams Nationale Partij*). It rejected the devolution proposals accepted by the major Belgian parties in 1978 and attacked as betrayal the constitutional concessions made by the **People's Union (VU)** on Flemish autonomy. Demanding full independence for **Flanders**, it was hostile to all forms of immigration and in the 1990s found some popular support for its extreme stand on the compulsory repatriation of all 'ethnic' immigrants, although it denied that its programme was racialist.

Flemish Socialist Party. (*Socialistische Partij*) The Flemish segment of the former Belgian Socialist Party (PSB), formed in 1978. Very much the smaller of the two linguistic successors to the PSB, it was also a minority party within **Flanders**. A moderate social democratic party, it was forced to support extensive devolution and was willing to enter into coalitions with other parties. In 1994 several of its leaders were investigated for fraud in connection with the **Agusta Affair**.

Flexible response. A doctrine adopted by the **North Atlantic Treaty Organization (NATO)** in 1967 as a modification of the policy of **massive retaliation**. In 1961 the Kennedy administration had decided that massive retaliation was untenable as the only option against a **Warsaw Pact** invasion of Western Europe. But if a massive strike was rejected, the only alternative would be huge expenditure to bring NATO conventional forces up to Warsaw Pact levels. No NATO government was willing to accept such expenditure, especially as massive retaliation had originally been adopted because of its cost-effectiveness. **European NATO** was at first unwilling to accept the modification of flexible response which stated that NATO would respond to any attack with a level of force appropriate for meeting the particular nature of the challenge, subsequently escalating the response if more was required, if necessary up to the extreme of massive retaliation. It did not mean the end of the American nuclear guarantee to Western Europe, but NATO never defined clearly what it would involve. To some extent it was satisfied with the uncertainty such vagueness might create for Warsaw Pact planning. Flexible response was a political compromise that satisfied both the American fear of placing its own population at risk in the event of a nuclear war, and European fears of a large-scale conventional conflict like the Second World War.

Flick Affair. A political scandal in the **Federal Republic of Germany**. It arose from the common practice of political parties seeking to circumvent the regulations of the 1967 Party Law on financial contributions to political organizations which granted the parties tax immunity on only very small amounts of money. In the late 1970s it had become accepted that immunity should extend to large corporate donations as part of a reform of the law. In 1981 investigations revealed a complex series of suspicious financial arrangements between the giant Flick industrial corporation and leading figures in all the political parties. As part of the reform process, the government proposed an amnesty for all those allegedly involved in previous political fund tax evasion, but was forced to back down because of public protest. In June 1984 the Economics Minister, **Lambsdorff**, was obliged to resign after being arraigned, to be followed in October by the President (Speaker) of the Parliament, **Barzel**. Although the politicians were acquitted in the trials which did not begin until 1987, and while the whole affair had been exaggerated by the media, it weakened public respect for the parties and the political system.

Fontainebleau Summit. A scheduled meeting of the **European Council** in June 1984. Hosted by **Mitterrand**, it was a significant meeting which resolved several major issues facing the **European Communities (EC)**: the complaints by the **United Kingdom** about the size of its contribution to the EC budget relative to its economic strength, the admission of **Portugal** and **Spain**, funding the EC budget, limiting the costs of the **Common Agricultural Policy (CAP)**. It also endorsed initiatives for further action which led towards the **internal market** and the later momentum towards greater integration.

Force de frappe. The name given to the independent French nuclear force first developed and deployed under **de Gaulle** 1964–66. Because of its relatively small size, it suffered from a credibility problem for some two decades.

For Fatherland and Freedom. (*Tēvzemei un Brīvībai – TUB*) A political alliance in **Latvia**. It was formed in 1993 as a merger of several extreme right-wing and nationalist movements.

Forlani, Arnaldo. (1925–) Prime Minister of **Italy** 1980–81. Following an administrative career within the **Christian Democratic Party (DC)**, he first entered Parliament in 1958, serving in several government positions as well as Party Secretary-General 1969–73 before being appointed premier. His coalition government was forced to resign in 1981 because of the **Propaganda Due** scandal. He later became DC Secretary-General in 1989, resigning in 1992 to make a bid for the presidency. Like many of his DC colleagues, his political career was halted by the aftermath of the **Tangentopoli** scandal, and in 1993 he was placed under investigation, and on trial the following year, for alleged bribery and abuse of the law on party finance.

Former Yugoslav Republic of Macedonia. *See* MACEDONIA.

Fortress Europe. A term widely used in the late 1980s to describe the concern of many countries about the possible negative consequences for their own economies of the implementation of a single **internal market** by the **European Communities (EC)**. Their fear was that the EC might adopt a more protectionist policy towards imports. Concern was widespread in the Third World, but it was most explicitly stated by the USA which had long argued that the EC was unduly protectionist. The major focus of attack was the **Common Agricultural Policy (CAP)**. The EC's insistence upon retention of the CAP principles was one factor that disrupted and stalled the **Uruguay Round** of international trade negotiations.

Forty Nations Conference on Disarmament (CD). A gathering of representatives from 40 countries in **Geneva** in the 1980s under the auspices of the United Nations (UN). Officially known as the Conference on Disarmament, its particular concern was to secure agreement for a global ban on chemical weapons. Although not possessing a specifically European focus, it operated in tandem with the **Conference on Security and Confidence-Building Measures and Disarmament in Europe (CDE)**.

Forum for Security Co-operation (FSC). An intergovernmental body formed in September 1992 under the auspices of the **Conference on Security and Co-operation in Europe (CSCE)**. It was intended to meet in continuous session and negotiate on confidence and security-building measures, **arms control**, and **disarmament**.

Forza Italia. A political party in **Italy**. Taking its name (Come On Italy) from a popular football slogan, it was hastily assembled in 1993 by

Berlusconi in the wake of the collapse of the traditional party system caused by the series of political and financial scandals and allegations levelled against the political elite. Essentially a centre-right alliance that favoured a free market economy, it headed a broad Freedom Alliance (*Polo della Libertà*) and emerged as the largest party in the 1994 elections, forming a brief coalition government. With an inexperienced political leadership which also by 1994 had had allegations of corruption levelled against it, its long-term future was placed in doubt.

Fouchet Plan. A draft treaty for a union of states produced in 1961. President **de Gaulle** had proposed such a union to the other five members of the **European Economic Community (EEC)** as a way of achieving greater political unity. A committee led by a French diplomat, Christian Fouchet, considered the proposal. The Plan deviated strongly from the ideas of the **Treaty of Rome** and was opposed by the three smaller members of the EEC. It was abandoned in 1962, and this contributed to a growing rift between **France** and its partners which culminated in 1965.

Founding Treaties. A collective phrase referring to the three documents that established the **European Communities (EC)**: the 1951 **Treaty of Paris** and the two **Treaties of Rome** of 1957.

Fourons. *See* VOEREN.

Fourth French Republic. The system of government in **France** between December 1946 and October 1958. In October 1945 a provisional government headed by **de Gaulle** held a referendum which rejected a return to the pre-war Third Republic. In the debates on what should replace it, de Gaulle was defeated in his desire for a strong presidency. A first draft constitution was rejected by referendum in May 1946, but a second draft was approved by a narrow majority on a very low turnout. It established a strong legislature, a government with limited powers, and a ceremonial presidency. Its political character differed little from that of the Third Republic in its structural weaknesses and undisciplined political parties. There were 23 coalition governments in less than 12 years, though the continuity in government of individual politicians was substantial. It did have a successful European policy, especially during the foreign ministry of **Schuman** (1948–53). It laid the foundations for subsequent economic growth, and it defied the challenge of the Stalinist **French Communist Party (PCF)**, but it never commanded great popular support or legitimacy. It was further weakened by the military humiliation of **Dien Bien Phu**, and collapsed in 1958 when faced with a threat of civil war arising from army discontent in Algeria and domestic political paralysis.

Fraga Iribarne, Manuel. (1922–) Spanish politician. A lawyer, after an academic career, he entered the diplomatic service in 1945. In 1962 he was appointed Minister of Information and Tourism by **Franco**, permitting some limited liberalization of the censorship laws. He was dismissed in 1969 for criticizing the Matesa scandal which had involved government ministers associated with **Opus Dei**. Ambassador to the **United Kingdom** 1973–75, he returned as Minister of the Interior in the government of Carlos Arias Navarro, where he argued against political reform. After the collapse of the Arias Navarro government in 1976 and the launch of democratization, he formed the Popular Alliance (*Alianza Popular – AP*) and led it and its successor, the **Popular Party (PD)** until April 1990. Elected to Parliament in 1977, he became, with the collapse of the **Union of the Democratic Centre**, the major conservative figure and opposition leader to the Socialist governments after 1982. In December 1989 he contested the regional elections in **Galicia**, winning an absolute majority and becoming head of the provincial government in February 1990, withdrawing from national politics. He was the most prominent personality of the Spanish right after 1975, but the failure of the AP/PD to gain extensive support was widely attributed to his authoritarian personality and his previous association with the Franco regime.

France. A major state in Western Europe. Defeated and occupied during the Second World War, after 1945 referendums rejected the re-establishment of the pre-war Third Republic and endorsed the formation of a **Fourth French Republic**. The political system was characterized by a fragmented multi-party system and weak government, and was further strained by opposition to it from the left by the powerful **French Communist Party (PCF)** and from the right where several groups supported the symbolic figure of **de Gaulle**. Governments were fragile coalitions whose major concern, although none lasted for long, was survival rather than the initiation of policy. However, it did lay the foundations for economic growth and through support for integration developed a successful European policy. Its Achilles heel was colonial policy where disaster in **French Indo-China** and the post-1954 struggle in Algeria helped politicize the military. The Republic collapsed in 1958, to be replaced by a **Fifth French Republic** dominated by de Gaulle. The new system introduced a presidential and more authoritative style of government. The number of parties declined, although the degree of organization was not greatly improved. During the 1960s de Gaulle set a policy style and objectives which were maintained by his successors, all designed to emphasize French independence in foreign affairs, especially from American influence, and leadership in European integration. A new relationship was forged with the **Federal Republic of Germany** after 1963, and the alliance between the two countries tended, after the 1970s, to dominate the activities of the **European Communities (EC)**. In the 1980s the determination to match German economic strength led to a strong monetary policy which placed great strains upon the French economy. In

1966 de Gaulle took France out of the military wing of the **North Atlantic Treaty Organization (NATO)**, though by the 1980s the degree of collaboration and consultation with NATO had increased significantly.

Franco-German Defence Council. A collaboration on joint defence and military planning by **France** and the **Federal Republic of Germany**. Proposed in 1987, it agreed in 1988 to the formation of a joint Franco-German brigade, which became operational in 1991 and was later called the **Eurocorps**. France saw it as the nucleus of a military component for the **European Communities (EC)** that would reduce reliance upon the USA and the **North Atlantic Treaty Organization (NATO)**.

Francovich Judgment. (Francovich et v. Italy) A 1992 ruling of the **Court of Justice** on accusations that the Italian government had not implemented **European Communities (EC)** rules. The Court's ruling gave individuals the right to appeal against the non-implementation of EC law on the grounds that this infringed individual rights, and indicated that member states of the EC found guilty of non-implementation could be fined.

Franco y Bahamonde, Francisco. (1892–1975) Spanish general and head of state 1939–75. A professional soldier, he became Chief of the General Staff in 1935 and governor of the **Canary Islands** in 1936. After the outbreak of the Civil War, he led troops from Morocco to **Spain** and established a rebel nationalist government in Burgos. After his victory in the Civil War, he assumed dictatorial powers. He remained neutral in the Second World War, although sympathizing with the Axis powers. In the early 1940s he modelled Spain upon Mussolini's corporatist **Italy**, banning all political opposition. In 1947 he was proclaimed head of state (*caudillo*) for life, pending restoration of the monarchy. In 1969 he named Prince **Juan Carlos**, grandson of Alfonso III (who had abdicated in 1931), as both his successor and heir to the throne. His regime was widely condemned and ostracized by Western countries after 1945, but after the consolidation of the **Cold War** his strong anti-Communism and Spain's strategic position brought him back into some favour, and he signed a co-operation treaty with the USA in 1953. In domestic politics he refused to permit any liberalization, pursuing particularly harsh policies towards the Basque and Catalan minorities. His refusal to relax the authoritarian style of government produced increasing opposition in the 1960s from students, workers, the Catholic Church, and, most violently, from Basque terrorists. After his death in November 1975, Spain quickly reverted to constitutional monarchy and democracy.

Free Democratic Party. (*Freie Demokratische Partei – FDP*) A small centrist party in the **Federal Republic of Germany**. Founded in 1948 out of zonal liberal parties licensed by the occupying Allies, it established itself as the third force in West German politics, but since 1949 has been out of government for only eight years. An alliance of conservative and liberal interests, it was dominated by the former until the 1960s. A liberal takeover pushed it to the political centre where it became the hinge party in the contest between the larger **Christian Democratic Union (CDU)** and **Social Democratic Party (SPD)**, because its support was necessary for either to form a government. Although it has switched sides rarely since the 1960s, it has often been accused of opportunism.

Freedom Alliance. *See* FORZA ITALIA.

Freedom and Progress Party. (*Partij voor Vrijheid en Vooruitgant – PVV*) A conservative party in **Belgium**, and the Flemish segment of the former Belgian Liberal Party, which adopted the name in 1961. It was constituted as a separate organization in 1970, in protest against the Liberal leadership's refusal to grant linguistic parity in the party organization in **Brussels**, but it continued to maintain amicable relations and some co-operation with its French-speaking counterpart in **Wallonia**. In 1992 it renamed itself the Flemish Liberals and Democrats (*Vlaamse Liberalen en Demokraten*).

Freedom Party of Austria. (*Freiheitliche Partei Österreichs – FPÖ*) A small conservative party in **Austria**, formed in 1955. It was the eventual successor to pre-1938 pan-German nationalist groups. Because of their association with Nazism, these groups were not permitted by the Allies to contest the 1945 election, but in 1949 they formed a loose Electoral Party of Independents (*Wahlpartei der Unabhängigen*). The FPÖ, formed by a former Nazi, Anton Reinthalle, absorbed the Independents. It first entered a coalition government in 1983, but returned to opposition in 1986. With the election of the populist **Haider** as party leader, it became more explicitly right-wing and nationalist, urging strict controls upon immigration and minorities, attacking the **proporz** system operated by the two major parties, and opposing entry to the **European Communities (EC)**. In 1993 a small group of moderates seceded in protest against the extremist leadership to form the Liberal Forum (*Liberales Forum*). Nevertheless, the FPÖ's strategy seemed to work, and it gained striking electoral successes in 1994.

Freedom Party of Switzerland. *See* CAR PARTY.

Freedom Union. *See* DEMOCRATIC UNION.

Free Galician People's Guerrilla Army. (*Exército Guerrilheiro do Pobo Galego Ceibe*) A revolutionary terrorist group in **Galicia** calling for full independence from **Spain**. It first emerged in 1987 with a bombing campaign against security personnel and government buildings.

Free trade area. A grouping of states that have agreed to abolish tariffs, quotas and other quantitative restrictions on trade and commerce between themselves. There is no **common external tariff (CET)**, unlike a **customs union**. Each state retains control over its own trade policies and tariffs with the rest of the world. The best European example has been the **European Free Trade Association (EFTA)**.

Free Voters' List. (*Freie Wählerliste – FW*) A small alternative organization of radicals and environmentalists in **Liechtenstein**. Formed in 1985, it became in 1986 the first party for over 12 years to contest an election against the governing coalition of the **Fatherland Union** and **Progressive Citizens' Party**, and gained parliamentary representation in 1993.

French Communist Party. (*Parti Communiste Français – PCF*) A major political party in **France**. Formed in 1920, its popularity increased because of its strong involvement in the war-time **Resistance movement**. After 1945 it emerged as one of the strongest parties in the country. Briefly involved in **tripartism** governments 1945–47, under the leadership of **Thorez** it became a rigid Stalinist organization, utterly loyal to the **USSR** and dedicated to the overthrow of the regime, but after 1948 without the capacity to launch a revolution. In 1968 it refused to associate itself with the radicals of the **May Events**. In the 1970s it began an association with the **Socialist Party (PS)**, briefly serving in government after 1981. By then, however, it had been surpassed by the PS as the major left-wing alternative, and in the 1980s entered into a marked downward spiral. Under **Marchais** it continued to uphold Stalinist principles, rejecting, for instance, the reform programme in the USSR and Eastern Europe. Relegated to being a minor party, it was only in 1995 that the leadership admitted that there had been flaws in Soviet policy and ideology, though this was still strongly disputed within the party.

French Community. An association of **France** with its overseas territories and colonies established by **de Gaulle** in 1958 in an attempt to forestall decolonialization. Its members were offered considerable autonomy. It was immediately rejected by Guinea, which opted for independence. Its unpopularity elsewhere led to constitutional revision in 1960, but the following year it collapsed, with most of its members declaring independence.

French Indo-China. A union established by **France** in 1893 of its protectorates and colonial possessions in South-East Asia, covering present-day Cambodia, Laos and Vietnam. Anti-French movements emerged in the 1920s, most notably a Vietnamese Communist Party founded by Ho Chi Minh. French repression strengthened the opposition, and French authority and prestige were destroyed by the Japanese invasion of 1941. A Communist-dominated VietMinh resistance movement was formed and in 1945 Ho Chi Minh declared a Vietnamese republic. After Japan's surrender France attempted to reassert its authority with a policy of repression. In December 1946 full-scale hostilities began between French forces and the VietMinh. It was a war where France had insufficient resources to win. Imposing huge costs upon the French economy, it lasted for eight years, ending with the catastrophic defeat of the French army at **Dien Bien Phu**. The **Geneva Agreements** of July 1954 formally marked the independence of the territories. The Indo-China war greatly weakened the **Fourth French Republic** politically and economically, and contributed to a politicization of the military which felt that it had been betrayed by the politicians in Paris.

French Union. A reorganization of the French Empire in 1946 by the **Fourth French Republic**, in order to support the participatory rights granted to the colonial populations in the 1944 Brazzaville Declaration. It was never accepted by nationalist movements in the colonies and, remaining very much a skeletal structure, was replaced in 1958 by the **French Community**.

Friuli-Venezia Giulia. *See* TRIESTE.

G

Gabčíkovo. A territorial and environmental dispute between **Hungary** and **Slovakia**. In the 1980s a huge hydroelectric project was planned at Gabčíkovo-Nagymáros on the Danube. It was strongly criticized by environmentalists who feared its effects upon the river's ecosystem. Hungary abandoned work on its side of the river in 1990, but the following year work resumed on the Slovakian side, with the final stage of construction planned for October 1992. The issued strained relations between the two states, but in 1993 they agreed to operate a temporary water management scheme while submitting the dispute to the International Court of Justice.

Gagarin, Yuri Alexeyevich. (1934–1968) Soviet cosmonaut. In April 1961 he became the first human to travel in space, orbiting Earth in the satellite of the Vostok spaceship. He was killed in an air accident in March 1968.

Gaillard, Félix. (1919–1970) Prime Minister of **France** 1957–58. A **Resistance** activist, he later joined the French Planning Office under **Monnet**, before entering Parliament in 1947 for the **Radical Republican and Radical Socialist Party**. In 1957 he became the youngest French premier at a time when the **Fourth French Republic** was under severe pressure because of the escalating Algerian problem. The fall of his government effectively marked the end of the Republic, and he retired from active politics, though participating in attempts to build a viable centre-left opposition to **de Gaulle**.

Gaitskell, Hugh Todd Naylor. (1906–1963) British politician. An economist, he entered Parliament in 1945 for the **Labour Party**, holding several government positions 1947–51. As Chancellor of the Exchequer 1950–51 he alienated the party left by introducing charges in the National Health Service. Representing the moderate social democratic wing of the party, he defeated a left-wing challenge to replace **Attlee** as party leader in 1955. His leadership was marked by a struggle against strong left-wing pressure for a commitment to unilateral nuclear disarmament and an ultimately unsuccessful campaign to abandon the commitment in the 1918 party program to large-scale public ownership. He died in 1963 with his efforts to reform the party only partly achieved.

Galicia. An economically poor and linguistically distinctive region in north-western **Spain**. The sense of Galician nationalism, though strong, has not been reflected in votes for nationalist parties. After democratization in 1975 regional politics were dominated by Spanish centre-right parties. Nationalists were less successful because of widespread popular doubts that autonomy could bring the region the same level of economic benefits that it received from Madrid. In the constitutional revisions of 1979 the province did not receive as extensive an autonomous structure as that granted to the **Basques** and **Catalonia**.

Galician Coalition. (*Coalición Gallega – CG*) A moderate nationalist party in **Galicia**. Formed in the early 1980s as a merger of smaller groups, it became the major voice of Galician nationalism, but adopted a pragmatic stance and was willing to collaborate with Spanish parties. After 1987 its moderate behaviour was attacked by a smaller and more extreme Galician Nationalist Bloc (*Bloque Nacionalista Gallego*).

Gamsakhurdia, Zviad. (1939–1994) President of **Georgia** 1991–92. A philologist and anti-Communist dissident after 1972, he co-founded the Georgia Helsinki Watch Group in 1977. He helped to organize anti-state demonstrations in April 1989, and founded a reformist coalition, the Round Table–Free Georgia, for the October 1990 Soviet elections. Winning a majority, he became Chairman of the Georgian Supreme Soviet, and began to work for full independence, becoming President of an independent Georgia in May 1991. His authoritarian style and strong nationalist views caused widespread concern, especially among the country's minorities where he rejected all claims for a form of autonomy from **Abkhazia** and **Ossetia**. Popular discontent at the failure to quell minority revolts led to a brief armed conflict which forced him to flee from the capital. Deposed as President in 1992, he made several abortive military attempts at a comeback before committing suicide in 1994.

Gaullism. A French political movement and loose doctrine based upon the political views of **de Gaulle**. It stressed the nation state as the basis of political life, reflecting internationally both suspicion of supranational integration that involved the giving up of sovereignty and hostility towards American influence in Europe. It favoured a more plebiscitarian form of democracy with a strong authoritative executive linked directly to the electorate. While many of its ideas were enshrined in the constitution of the **Fifth French Republic**, after de Gaulle's death the Gaullist movement, while displaying several differences of opinion, generally adapted to conform more closely to the model of a typical conservative party.

Gdansk. (Danzig) A Baltic city at the mouth of the Vistula river. Part of Prussia until 1919, it was made a Free City, divorced from German territory, by the Treaty of Versailles, in order to give **Poland** an outlet to the sea. Its anomalous position made it ripe for mobilization by the Nazis. It was occupied by Soviet forces in March 1945, and in June the **USSR** handed it to Poland. The German population was expelled, and it was renamed Gdansk. The huge shipyards of the port were later a constant source of opposition to the Polish Communist regime, and the birthplace of the **Solidarity** trade union movement.

Gdansk Agreement. *See* WAŁĘSA, LECH.

General Affairs Council. The meetings of the national foreign ministers of the **European Communities** (**EC**) when they formally assemble as the **Council of Ministers**. It has been regarded as the most important manifestation of the Council because it has been responsible for handling broad and intransigent issues and for reviewing foreign policy collaboration.

General Agreement on Tariffs and Trade (GATT). An agency established in 1947 under the auspices of the United Nations (UN) to develop a set of rules for the conduct of and growth in international trade, and to construct a framework for negotiations on the reduction and elimination of tariffs and other barriers to trade. Its core strategy, the obligation of all contracting parties to adopt a policy of non-discrimination, was not entirely realized, as several areas, including the important commodities of agriculture and textile, were excluded. These and other loopholes relating to customs union were utilized by many European states. There were five GATT rounds of negotiations between 1947 and 1961. Later rounds adopted a broader approach based upon a new set of principles, intended *inter alia*, to go beyond manufactured products to incorporate agriculture, copyright and services, agreed in 1963. These principles served as guidelines for the progressively more difficult to resolve 1964–67 **Kennedy Round**, the 1973–79 Tokyo Round and the 1986–94 **Uruguay Round**. The last eventually concluded with a World Trade Organization, as a replacement for GATT, to begin in 1995.

General Elderly People's Union. (*Algemeen Ouderenverbond – AOV*) A political party in the **Netherlands**, founded in 1993 as a protest group campaigning against cuts in welfare provisions, especially a temporary freeze on state pensions. It subsequently became a party taking up all issues of interest to older people, also demanding strong controls on immigration. In 1995 it was greatly weakened by severe internal factionalism.

Generalized System of Preferences (GSP). A strategy by which industrialized states agree to aid developing economies through the introduction of an element of equity into trade between them. It was first proposed by the United Nations Conference on Trade and Development (UNCTAD) in 1968 to replace the practice of industrial countries giving preference to exports from only some developing countries. The most important European GSP has been that adopted by the **European Communities** (**EC**) in 1971, which applies to Third World countries not otherwise formally associated with the EC. It illustrates the limited value of GSPs since in practice these countries gain preference in the EC market over only a handful of non-European industrialized states.

Geneva. A city in **Switzerland** which has hosted several international conferences and has housed several international organizations. Its prominence is due to the long tradition of Swiss neutrality and to the fact that in 1920 the League of Nations was located in the city. After 1945 it became a favoured venue for meetings on non-European disputes and a neutral ground for meetings of the USA and **USSR**.

Geneva Agreements. The result in July 1954 of a series of negotiations on **French Indo-China** following the French capitulation at **Dien Bien Phu**. Attended by the foreign ministers of China, **France**, the **United Kingdom**, USA and **USSR**, they formally ended French involvement in South-East Asia.

Geneva Conventions. A series of treaties between national governments defining what is permissible in warfare in terms of the effects upon and treatment of military personnel and civilians. The first convention was signed in 1864, the most recent in 1949. Two Protocols on the rights of civilians and combatants in a guerilla war were added in 1977.

Genscher–Colombo Plan. *See* GENSCHER, HANS-DIETRICH.

Genscher, Hans-Dietrich. (1927–) German politician. Brought up in Halle, in 1946 he joined the Liberal Democratic Party in the Soviet zone of occupation. In 1952 he moved to the **Federal Republic of Germany**, joining the **Free Democratic Party (FDP)**, and entered Parliament in 1960. He was Minister of the Interior 1969–74, before becoming a long-serving Foreign Minister 1974–92. Between 1974 and 1985 he also served as FDP leader. A committed supporter of **Ostpolitik**, he worked for closer links between the two Germanies, and in 1990 was one of the major architects of reunification. He also supported closer political and economic union in Western Europe where in 1981 he prepared the outline of the Genscher–Colombo Plan, which took the form of a Draft European Act which he urged the **European Communities (EC)** to accept: several of its ideas could be found in the later documents on further integration developed after the late 1980s. In 1991 he insisted upon the recognition of **Croatia** by the EC, an action which at the time was widely believed to have stimulated the subsequent armed conflict between Croatia and **Serbia**.

Georgia. A successor state of the **USSR**. Part of the Russian Empire, it declared independence in 1918, but was reconquered by Soviet forces and reconstituted as a Soviet Socialist Republic in 1921. In 1922 it was made part of a Transcaucasian Soviet Federal Socialist Republic before being reformed as a separate constituent republic in 1936. It also contained two autonomous republics and one autonomous region, an arrangement which reflected its ethnic diversity. In April 1989 a mass demonstration in favour of independence was brutally broken up by undisciplined Soviet troops, an act which radicalized Georgian politics. The regional Communist leadership and government were replaced, and in November the 1921 incorporation into the **USSR** was declared illegal. The first multi-party elections in October 1990 brought victory to the dissident leader, **Gamsakhurdia**, and his loose Round Table–Free Georgia coalition. After a referendum which supported independence, Georgia seceded from the **USSR**. It later attempted to break all links with the other successor states to the USSR, refusing to join the **Commonwealth of Independent States (CIS)**. After Gamsakhurdia's victory in the 1991 presidential election, the new nationalist regime moved to suppress all internal opposition, especially complaints from the minorities in the autonomous republics of **Abkhazia** and South **Ossetia**. Law and order disintegrated at the end of 1991 and the regime was overthrown by a paramilitary coup. Gamsakhurdia fled to his stronghold in the western part of the country. In March 1992 the former Soviet foreign minister, **Shevardnadze**, was invited to return and take up the presidency. The new government had to face military opposition from pro-Gamsakhurdia forces, as well as continuing unrest in South Ossetia, which sought to join **Russia**, and an armed conflict with separatist forces in Abkhazia. With political turbulence and economic decline continuing, the Shevardnadze government was humiliated when its forces were defeated in and expelled from Abkhazia in 1993. It was forced to turn to Russia for military and economic assistance in restoring some semblance of order, and had to join the CIS.

Gerhardsen, Einar. (1897–1987) Prime Minister of **Norway** 1945–51, 1955–63, 1963–65. He entered local government in 1932 as a **Labour Party** representative. Opposition to German occupation led to internment in a prison camp 1941–45. After liberation he was appointed party leader and headed a provision coalition government until the 1945 election, which produced a Labour majority. In 1951 he resigned the premiership, but was persuaded to return in 1955 after criticism of his successor, Oscar Torp. Under his leadership a welfare state was constructed and economic rebuilding begun. He abandoned Norway's traditional neutrality, joining the **North Atlantic Treaty Organization (NATO)**. After 1961 he remained in office as head of minority Labour administrations. Very much revered as a father figure who had shaped and steered the development of modern Norway, he retired from active politics in 1969.

German Communist Party. (*Deutsche Kommunistische Partei – DKP*) A fringe party in the **Federal Republic of Germany**. Founded in 1968, it was a belated successor to the KPD (*Kommunistische Partei Deutschland*), banned by the Federal Constitutional Court in 1956. Given the divided nature of Germany, its uncritical support before 1989 of the **USSR** and total rejection of **Eurocommunism** effectively kept it in the political wilderness, as did the anti-Comunist sentiment after reunification in 1990.

German Democratic Republic (DDR). A state formed in October 1949 from the Soviet zone of occupied Germany. Led by **Ulbricht** and his **Socialist Unity Party (SED)**, it embarked upon a programme of Socialist reconstruction. Its harsh conditions and the requirement to pay reparations to the **USSR** led to massive protests (the **East Berlin Uprising**) in June 1953, quelled only by Soviet forces. In 1954 it was declared a sovereign state, although not recognized as one by the West, and in 1955 it was a founder member of the **Warsaw Pact**. In the 1950s it experienced a large flow of refugees defecting to the West, primarily through **Berlin**. The **Berlin Wall** was constructed in 1961 to stop the flow. Living standards began to improve, and it was widely regarded as the economic success of the Communist bloc. Its relations with the West improved under Ulbricht's successor, **Honecker**, as a result of the **Ostpolitik** process. In the 1980s it sought to emphasize more its German historical roots as a source of legitimacy, but a wave of discontent emerged in 1988 against the centralized bureaucratic system, elite corruption, and the ruthless secret policy (**Stasi**). In the summer of 1989 many citizens chose to flee to the West via **Hungary** which had opened its borders with **Austria**. In September further demonstrations were spearheaded by a new reform group, **New Forum**. Honecker refused to bow to the pressure, but was forced to resign in October. The new government, still confined to the SED, failed to stem the growing popular pressure for change, and on 9 November it opened the Berlin Wall as a final gesture before it collapsed. The Communist monopoly of power was abandoned, free elections were held in March 1990, and a democratic government under **de Maizière** began to negotiate with the **Federal Republic of Germany** on reunification. This was achieved in October 1990, but it was less a merger of the two Germanies and more the absorption of the DDR by the Federal Republic.

German People's Union. (*Deutsche Volksunion – DVU*) A political party in the **Federal Republic of Germany**. Founded in 1987, it was an extreme right-wing organization that openly praised Hitler and Nazism. Strongly opposed to any form of immigration, it made some limited inroads in regional elections.

German Social Union. (*Deutsche Sozial Union – DSU*) A small party in the **German Democratic Republic (DDR)**. It was founded after the erosion of the Communist regime, in January 1990, as a moderate right-wing movement stressing German unity, federalization within the DDR, and Christian values. Initially endorsed by the Bavarian **Christian Social Union (CSU)**, it joined the **Alliance for Germany** for the March 1990 elections, but failed to establish any significant support. In 1993 it decided to attempt to establish itself as a nation-wide party.

Germany. *See* FEDERAL REPUBLIC OF GERMANY, GERMAN DEMOCRATIC REPUBLIC.

Gheorghiu-Dej, Gheorghe. (1901–1965) President of **Romania** 1961–65. Joining the Communist Party in 1929, he was imprisoned in Dej 1933–44, later adding the hyphenated suffix to his surname to commemorate his incarceration. In March 1945 he was appointed Minister of National Economy in the coalition government established by King Michael, and remained responsible for long-term economic planning when Romania became a Communist republic in 1948. He acquired control of the party administration, and in 1952 was strong enough to purge it of his opponents. Ruler of the country thereafter in all but name, he declared himself President only in 1961. After the death of **Stalin**, he became a close ally of **Khrushchev** and negotiated the withdrawal of Soviet troops from Romania in 1958. He later pursued an independent economic policy which often brought him into dispute with the **USSR**. His actions and individualization of authority laid the foundations for the independent line and personal dictatorship of his protégé and successor, **Ceauşescu**.

Gibraltar. A rocky prominence on the Iberian peninsula overlooking the entrance from the Atlantic to the Mediterranean. Captured by the **United Kingdom** from **Spain** in 1713, it was developed as a major dockyard and naval base, but its strategic importance declined substantially after 1945. A British crown colony, it was claimed by Spain, but a referendum in 1967 voted overwhelmingly in favour of remaining British. Some self-government was introduced in 1964 and extended in 1969, an action which prompted Spain to close its land border with Gibraltar. Anglo-Spanish talks on easing tensions began in 1977, and a further agreement in 1980 led to the relaxation of some frontier restrictions. A full re-opening of the border was postponed in 1982 because of tension over the **Falklands War**, and did not occur until February 1985. Disputes continued and restrictions occasionally re-introduced because Spain refused to renounce its territorial claims which in turn were always rejected by the Gibraltar government and population. The closure of the naval dockyards and reduction of the British military presence after 1984 caused serious economic problems.

Gierek, Edward. (1913–) First Secretary of the **Polish United Workers' Party** 1970–80. Born in Austrian **Silesia**, he emigrated to **France** with his mother in 1923. After joining the **French Communist Party (PCF)** he was arrested in 1934 and deported to **Poland**. He emigrated to **Belgium** in 1937 and during the Second World War worked for the **Resistance movement**. He returned to Poland in 1948, working his way through the party hierarchy to join the **Politburo** in 1956. With a reputation for effective economic management as Communist head of the heavily industrialized Silesian region, he was made party leader and effective leader of Poland after protests in **Gdansk** and other cities had forced the resignation of **Gomulka**. He failed in his promise to re-evaluate economic policy, and lost all popular approval after 1976 because of his attempt, without warning, to impose steep increases in food prices. Economic protests continued to mount and when the **Solidarity** action began in 1980, he was dismissed from office. Expelled also from the party, he was briefly interned 1981–82 by the **Jaruzelski** government.

Gil Robles y Quinoñes, José Maria. (1898–1980) Spanish politician. A prominent conservative Catholic leader in the pre-war Second Republic, he did not actively support **Franco** and the nationalists during the Civil War, leaving **Spain** in 1936. He lived in exile in **Portugal** until 1953, and again 1962–64. He returned to Spain and attempted to found a Christian Democratic party, but neither he nor it had any success in the new democracy after 1975.

Giscard d'Estaing, Valéry. (1926–) President of **France** 1974–81. Entering politics as a Gaullist deputy in 1956, he was appointed Minister of Finance in the 1962 **Pompidou** government. Associating with the political group called the Independent Republicans (RI), he used it to develop his own political objectives and as a springboard for a broad centre-right alliance. After his presidential victory, helped by the failure of the Gaullists to agree upon a single candidate, his strategy was strongly contested by the new Gaullist leader, **Chirac**. His attempts to develop a new technocratic style and more open political life were damaged by allegations of scandals, especially the claim that he had received gifts from the discredited and deposed self-styled Emperor Bokassa of the Central African Republic. In foreign policy he remained loyal to Gaullist perceptions of defence and national sovereignty, but pursued a pragmatic line within the **European Communities (EC)**. The **European Council** was his initiative, and within it he forged a close personal relationship with the West German Chancellor, **Schmidt**: the two men formed an axis which dominated the EC until 1981. After losing the 1981 presidential election, he retired briefly from active politics, re-emerging later to attempt to reinvigorate a moderate conservative alternative to Chirac and the Gaullist **Rally for the Republic**, becoming leader of the **Union for French Democracy** in 1988.

Gladio. A political scandal in **Italy**. A secret paramilitary group, codenamed Gladio, was set up in 1956 to provide armed resistance in the event of an invasion by **Warsaw Pact** forces or an internal Communist coup d'état. It was part of a series of such units created throughout the **North Atlantic Treaty Organization (NATO)** at the height of the **Cold War**. An investigation of its records began in 1990, and in 1992 the published report indicated that in the 1970s it had been involved in plots to discredit left-wing politicians, and had aligned itself with extreme right-wing organizations conducting bombing campaigns as part of a strategy of destabilizing the regime. Although Gladio had been formally disbanded in 1990 after being classified as an illegal armed band, the existence of a successor group, named Scorpion (*Gruppo Scorpioni*), was demonstrated in 1992. The Gladio revelations were a further indictment of political corruption in the country.

Glasnost. A Russian word meaning openness. It was used by **Gorbachev** in February 1986 in a speech to the Soviet Communist Party Congress where he argued that the party had to become less bureaucratic, secretive and elitist, and that it had to liaise with and inform the public. While he used the word in conjunction with domestic politics as part of his strategy to improve the ailing Soviet economy, it was also seen as reflecting what he sought in international politics. To the extent that it enabled the emergence of a new openness in Soviet society, with the voicing of criticism and competing opinions, it contributed to the weakening of Gorbachev's own authority and the eventual disintegration of the **USSR**.

Gligorev, Kiro. (1917–) President of **Macedonia** from 1991. An economist and war-time partisan, he joined the Anti-Fascist Council in 1943. After 1945 he held a variety of party and government posts in **Yugoslavia**, including serving as Vice Prime Minister 1967–69. During the 1980s he concentrated more on academic research, but was elected as leader of the Communist Party in Macedonia. He attempted to steer the region clear of the escalating conflicts elsewhere in the Yugoslav state, but in 1991 declared Macedonia to be independent. Surrounded on almost all sides by states hostile to an independent Macedonia for a variety of reasons, he strove to remedy the consequences for a weak economy and, through seeking Western assistance, to avoid having to take sides in Balkan disputes.

Glistrup, Mogens. (1926–) Danish politician. A lawyer specializing in tax law, he founded the **Progress Party** in 1972 as a right-wing anti-tax, anti-bureaucracy party, remaining its leader until 1985. A critic of almost all aspects of public spending and shunned by other political leaders, he was convicted of tax fraud in 1983 and expelled from Parliament. He was re-elected again in 1984 while on temporary release from prison, only to be expelled again. After he had served his sentence, the party refused to re-accept him as leader, accusing him of having used it for his own purposes. With his political career in decline, he was expelled from the Progress Party in 1991 for forming a new Prosperity Party (*Trivlespartiet*).

Globke, Hans. (1898–1973) German bureaucrat. Joining the bureaucracy in 1929, as a member of the Ministry of the Interior he wrote the commentary to the Nuremberg racial laws which were the basis for Hitler's anti-Jewish legislation. In 1949 he was appointed by **Adenauer** to lead the Chancellor's

Office. Frequently criticized for his past, he retained the strong support of Adenauer, retiring in 1963 along with his political master. His supporters argued that he had not been a Nazi but had done his best to modify the Nuremberg laws: there was never any evidence that he had been involved in the persecution of Jews.

Golden Triangle. A phrase often used to describe what some claim is the economic centre of the **European Communities (EC)**. It refers to the area bounded by Milan, Paris and the Ruhr.

Gomulka, Wladyslaw. (1905–1982) First Secretary of the **Polish United Workers' Party** 1956–70. A founding member of the Polish Communist Party, he was imprisoned on several occasions between 1920 and 1939. In 1943 he became secretary-general of the underground Polish Workers' Party, and in 1945 joined the national unity government of **Bierut**, with responsibility for the territories annexed from Germany. He was dismissed in 1948 for speaking on the historical roots of the Polish labour movement, an act which was interpreted by the **USSR** as deviationist and advocating independence from Moscow, and in 1951 was imprisoned for four years. Rehabilitated as a result of **de-Stalinization**, he was readmitted to the party in August 1956. Two months later, after anti-Soviet riots in Poznań and other cities, and with the endorsement of **Khrushchev**, he was appointed party leader and effective ruler of the country. His task was to reassure the USSR of **Poland's** loyalty while trying to develop a Polish style of socialism that would reconcile the party with the society, especially the powerful Catholic Church. By insisting on retaining defence links with the USSR and allowing Soviet troops to remain in the country, he avoided a repeat of the Soviet intervention in **Hungary**. He reversed the previous policy of agricultural **collectivization** and permitted some limited personal and religious liberty, but some of the reforms were reversed 1962–63 after further unrest. His initial popularity plummeted in the 1960s because of persisting economic problems and his greater emphasis upon autocratic government. A new outbreak of urban unrest over food prices in 1970 finally discredited him and led to his dismissal from office.

González Márquez, Felipe. (1942–) Prime Minister of **Spain** from 1982. A lawyer, he joined the illegal **Spanish Socialist Workers' Party (PSOE)** in 1964, serving on its provincial committee in Seville 1965–69, before joining the national executive in 1970. He became party leader in 1974. When the PSOE was legalized in 1977 he led the party delegation in the negotiations on the transition to democracy, and sought to transform the party into a modern mass-based organization. Elected to Parliament in 1977 he sought to portray the PSOE as a moderate social democratic party, briefly resigning as leader in 1979 (May–September) in protest against a party resolution that described the organization as a Marxist body. As Prime

Minister he pursued a policy of pragmatic economic reform and modernization, with strict control of public resources, a policy which led to frequent
conflicts with the trade unions. His foreign policy was strongly European,
seeing membership of the **European Communities (EC)** and further
integration as the best way of raising the standard of living and guaranteeing
democracy in Spain. To some extent his task was made easier by the lack
after 1982 of a credible alternative to the PSOE, something which continued
to benefit him in the 1990s when he and his government faced a series of
allegations relating to corruption, intimidation and abuse of civil rights, and
illegal party funding.

Gorbachev, Mikhail Sergeyevich. (1931–) Secretary-General of the
Communist Party of the Soviet Union 1985–91, and **USSR** President
1990–91. Joining the party in 1952, he quickly rose through the ranks as a
protégé of **Andropov.** He was brought to Moscow to be Secretary of
Agriculture in 1978, and appointed to the **Politburo** in 1980. He was
Andropov's chief spokesman on reform proposals for the state and party
1982–84, but was passed over for the party leadership after his mentor's
death. He eventually succeeded **Chernenko** in March 1985. He made a
whirlwind arrival on the world scene, calling for a new international
thinking. Advocating **glasnost** and **perestroika**, he allowed a greater degree
of liberty to dissidents, and authorized the release of details of 'crimes
against humanity' committed by the **Stalin** regime. Abroad, the West came
to accept that his wish to lessen the **Cold War** was genuine. In June 1988 he
declared an intention to democratize government, and later effectively
dropped the Soviet guarantee of political and military support for the East
European Communist regimes, urging them to liberalize their systems. In
1989 the regimes were swept away, and in 1990 he had to accept German
reunification and that the two Soviet control organizations in Eastern Europe,
the **Warsaw Pact** and the **Council for Mutual Economic Assistance
(COMECON)** had become moribund.

To a large extent his wish to ease world tension was due to his perception
of the USSR's economic weaknesses and the crippling cost of defence
expenditure, but he wanted economic and political change kept separate. The
party was to be the major agency of change and remain the leading
organization after reconstruction. To strengthen his ability to direct affairs,
he had himself elected President in March 1990 by the newly created
Congress of People's Deputies, the first multi-party legislature in the USSR.
His strategy was resisted by many in the party who either feared that it would
weaken Soviet world influence or their own positions and security. The party
proved incapable of being an agency for change. Relaxation of central
control had encouraged popular pressure for further reforms, and unrest
among the USSR's many national minorities, with several constituent

republics, headed by the **Baltic states**, agitating for greater autonomy or even independence. He was forced into a more and more difficult balancing act between conservatives opposing any change and radicals pressing for ever greater reform. In 1991 he was briefly deposed by a clumsy and abortive hard-line conservative coup, but its failure did little to increase his personal popularity. Upon his re-installation he continued to insist upon the centrality of the party, but was forced to cede independence to the Baltic states, something which was a prelude to the fragmentation of the USSR. By the end of 1991 the presidency was an office with little or no authority. His resignation confirmed the end of the USSR. His brief rule effectively ended the Cold War and decisively transformed the contours of Europe that had been forged out of two world wars.

Goria, Giovanni. (1943–1994) Prime Minister of **Italy** 1987–88. An economist and banker, he entered Parliament for the **Christian Democratic Party (DC)** in 1976, serving as a government minister after 1982. The youngest ever Italian Prime Minister, his term of office was undistinguished. He returned to government in 1991, but resigned in 1993 after being accused of fraud in connection with the collapse of a savings bank in his native region. He was cleared of the charges, but the following February was placed on trial on bribery charges. He died three months later of a lung tumour.

Gottwald, Klement. (1896–1953) President of **Czechoslovakia** 1948–53. Trained as a carpenter, he was conscripted in 1915 and classified as 'politically unreliable'. A founder of the Communist Party in 1921, he became its general secretary in 1929. After the 1938 Munich Agreement, which led to the dismemberment of Czechoslovakia, he went to Moscow, staying in the **USSR** until 1945. Upon his return, he became Prime Minister of a broad coalition government after the 1946 election. He attempted to strengthen Communist control of the country, but fearing that the party faced significant losses in the election due later in the year, in February 1948 he established a one-party government, using the workers' militia and the police to consolidate his control. When **Beneš** resigned in June, he took over the presidency. He introduced a Stalinist programme, including forced labour camps, purges and show trials, with a five-year plan under which Czechoslovak industries would be satellites of the Soviet economy. With the **Slansky Trial** and execution of his major rivals in 1952, he was in sole control of the country, but died of pneumonia contracted while attending the funeral of **Stalin** in March 1953.

Grand coalition. A phrase describing a government composed of all or the most dominant political parties in a country, leaving little in the way of effective parliamentary opposition. The major example after 1945 has been the coalition of the two major parties in **Austria** 1945–66 and since 1986. The two major parties in the **Federal Republic of Germany** formed a grand coalition 1966–69. The semi-permanent four-party government that has ruled for almost the whole of the post-war period in **Switzerland** has also sometimes been described as a grand coalition.

Greater Romania Party. (*România Măre*) An extreme right-wing political party in **Romania**. Formed in 1990, with many of its leading figures having been officials in the **Ceauşescu** regime, it campaigned for restrictions on the rights of ethnic minorities and strong controls on foreign investment.

Greece. A Balkan state gaining independence in 1830 after centuries of Ottoman rule. Because significant Greek populations remained outside the state boundaries, it continued to espouse nationalist aspirations and irredentist policies which largely ended after defeat in Asia Minor by **Turkey** in 1923. Greek politics were highly unstable with several upheavals caused by conflict between republicans and royalists, along with several instances of military intervention. After the Second World War the monarchy was restored in 1946. Between 1946 and 1950 the country was dominated by the **Greek Civil War** between the army and Communist guerillas. Although in theory a democracy, the post-1950 regime was authoritarian and rather repressive, with power resting ultimately with the monarchy and army. Social discontent and demands for democratization strengthened in the 1960s, but the response to the first post-war left-wing parliamentary victory was a military coup in 1967 and the imposition of the regime of the **Greek Colonels**. The monarchy was abolished and opponents of the regime persecuted. It collapsed in 1974 after its abortive attempt to engineer a coup in **Cyprus**. Greece reverted to democracy after 1974, with a pattern of bipolar politics structured as much, however, around the personality of leaders as political organization, and practices of **clientelism**, along with accusations of corruption, remained a widespread feature. Greece was an early member of the **North Atlantic Treaty Organization (NATO)**, but its contribution to the organization was occasionally limited because of its disputes with Turkey over Cyprus and control of the **Aegean Sea**. It was admitted to the **European Communities (EC)** in 1981, where its weaker and slightly different economy, along with a different foreign policy emphasis, has occasionally caused problems. It has vetoed the possibility of Turkish entry to the EC and took a distinctive stance on Balkan problems after 1989, most particularly in its attempts to embargo **Macedonia**.

Greek Civil War. A conflict between the Western-backed royalist government of **Greece** and Communist guerillas 1946–49. During the Second World War the Communist-dominated **Resistance movement**, the National Liberation Front (EAM), had formed a **National People's Army of Liberation (ELAS)**. EAM sought a Communist state in Greece, and conflict between ELAS and royalist forces in 1944 was ended by the Truce of Varkiza of February 1945, which left EAM controlling some two-thirds of the country. In October 1946 the ELAS leader, Markos Vafiades, formed a new Democratic Army of Greece in the north of the country which, with the help of neighbouring Communist regimes, sought to overthrow the government. The Greek royalist army was supported by the **United Kingdom** and then, as a result of the **Truman Doctrine**, the USA. The Democratic Army was defeated in a decisive battle in August 1949: fighting stopped two months later, and in November it announced a cease-fire, effectively disbanding itself. The decisive element in the government victory was American support, although the Communists had also been weakened by popular hostility towards their brutal methods of intimidation and the loss of their bases in **Yugoslavia** after the 1948 rift between **Tito** and **Stalin**. Nevertheless, the Greek Communist Party (*Kommunistiki Komma Ellades – KKE*) remained a potentially significant force in the country, with large popular support for several decades. It began to weaken after long and persisting conflicts between orthodox conservatives and reformers, who eventually split into two separate parties in 1991.

Greek Colonels. A term used to describe the military junta that governed **Greece** 1967–74. The military coup of 20 April 1967 was led by two colonels, **Papadopoulos** and Stylianos Pattakos. The regime was shunned by the West because of its repression and widespread use of imprisonment and torture, with some Western governments bringing charges against it in the **European Court of Human Rights**. It justified martial law by claiming the existence of a Communist threat to the state. In December 1967 an attempt by **Constantine II** to overthrow the regime failed. The king was forced into exile, and Papadopoulos became Prime Minister. In March 1972 he declared himself Regent and, after allegations of a royalist plot in the navy, President of a Greek republic in November 1973. Oppression and economic problems generated riots in Athens, suppressed only by military force, and Papadopoulos resigned in favour of General Gizikis who endorsed a junta attempt to engineer a coup in **Cyprus**. The failure of the attempted coup, which brought about a Turkish invasion of Cyprus, also brought Greece to the brink of civil war. Totally discredited, the army surrendered power on 23 July 1974, and accepted the return of civilian constitutional government. The leaders of the junta were put on trial in August 1975. Papadopoulos and Pattakos were sentenced to death, which was later commuted to life imprisonment.

Green Alliance. (*Vihreä Liitto*) A small environmentalist party in **Finland**. It set up a formal but decentralized structure in 1987 after existing for four years as a loose electoral alliance of disparate groups.

Green Alliance. (*Grünes Bündnis/Alliance Verte – GB/AV*) A small radical environmentalist party in **Switzerland**. It was formed in 1987 as an alliance of several regional movements which were reluctant to associate with the larger **Green Party**, and preferred to collaborate electorally with the left-wing **Progressive Organizations of Switzerland**.

Green Alternative. (*Grüne Alternative*) A small environmentalist party in **Austria**. It was formed in 1987 by a merger of two smaller groupings established in 1982 which had previously refused to collaborate with each other – the radical Austrian Alternative List (ALÖ) and the moderate conservationist United Greens of Austria (VGÖ).

Green Alternative. (*Déi Greng Alternativ*) A small environmentalist party in **Luxembourg**, formed in 1983. A radical dissenting group broke away in 1986 to form the **Green List–Ecological Alternative**, but the two subsequently agreed to form an electoral alliance.

Green Currencies. Artificial price figures introduced into the **Common Agricultural Policy (CAP)** by the **European Communities (EC)** in 1969 as a means of preserving the common price structure when the international system of fixed exchange rates began to collapse. The EC wished to retain the common agricultural prices at their original level. These values, expressed in national currencies, were the green currencies and bore little relationship to actual market prices. To adjust the price structure and green currencies to the real world, a compensation system, Monetary Compensation Amounts (MCAs), were introduced. Green currencies were a focal point of complaints about the CAP, and in 1984 the EC agreed to phase out MCAs by 1989, but their end did not occur until the system was reformed to conform with the principles of the **internal market**.

Greenham Common. An American air force base in the **United Kingdom** and the site of the most visible protest in Britain against nuclear weapons in the 1980s. A women's peace camp was set up outside the base, which was one designated to take the intermediate-range nuclear missiles decided upon by the **North Atlantic Treaty Organization (NATO)** in 1979. The women camped outside the base for more than a decade. Their attempts to disrupt the base's operations were sporadic and mainly unsuccessful, but they did become a major symbol of the peace movement. The camp was disbanded in 1994 when the base closed down as a consequence of the ending of the **Cold War**.

Greenland. A large island in the North Atlantic. A colony of **Denmark** since 1380, it became part of the Danish kingdom in 1953 and was granted internal self-government in 1979. It became part of the **European Communities (EC)** in 1973, although in the 1972 referendum there had been a large majority on the island against membership. There was an increase in nationalist agitation fuelled by concerns that EC membership was detrimental to the economy, especially the vital fishing industry. With internal autonomy in 1979, Denmark retained control only of defence and foreign policy. A 1982 referendum voted narrowly in favour of leaving the EC.

Negotiations on the terms of withdrawal were concluded in 1984, and Greenland left the EC in February 1985, being granted **Overseas Countries and Territories (OCT)** status.

Green Left. (*Groen Links*) A radical electoral alliance in the **Netherlands**. It was a marriage of electoral convenience formed in 1989 by four small left-wing parties: the **Radical Political Party**, the **Pacifist Socialist Party**, the **Communist Party**, and the **Evangelical People's Party**. Although it presented an ecologically oriented programme, it was not joined by Dutch green movements. It was essentially a strategy that sought to improve the chances of the four components winning parliamentary representation.

Green Line. The popular name for the neutral zone established on **Cyprus** in 1974 and patrolled by a United Nations (UN) Peace-Keeping Force, separating Greek Cypriot and Turkish Cypriot territory. The name allegedly derives from the fact that a British general working for the UN used a green pen to denote on a map the ceasefire line which marked the end of the hostilities occasioned by the Turkish invasion of the island. The neutral buffer zone was sometimes also described as the **Attila Line**.

Green List–Ecological Alternative. (*Greng Lescht–Ekologesch Initiativ*) A small radical environmentalist party in **Luxembourg**. It was founded in 1986 by Jup Weber, the former leader of **Green Alternative** after an intra-party conflict. The two groups later agreed to form an electoral alliance.

Green Party. (*Die Grünen*) A small environmentalist party in the **Federal Republic of Germany**, and the most successful green movement in Europe in the 1980s. It was founded in 1979 from a merger of regional groups and local **citizen initiatives** associations. It supported **feminism** and **disarmament** as well as radical changes in the economy to restrict the rate of growth and emphasize the priority of environmental protection. In its own organizational structure, which was largely copied by green parties in other countries, it sought to develop an alternative political ethos which stressed the primacy of the grass-roots base, gender quotas in offices, and a collective and rotating leadership directly controlled by the mass base. It entered a few regional governments as a junior coalition partner. After 1980 it experienced internal tension between the *realo* (realist) wing willing to collaborate with other parties in coalition governments and the *fundi* (fundamentalist) faction which rejected any kind of compromise of green principles. In 1993 it merged with the remnants of **Alliance 90**, which had attempted to become the green party in the former East German territory.

Green Party. (*Grüne Partei der Schweiz/Parti Écologiste Suisse – GPS/PES*) A small party in **Switzerland**, formed in 1983 as a merger of several regional groups to argue the environmentalist cause. Originally called the Federation of Green Parties, it changed its name in 1985.

Green Party. A small environmentalist party in the **United Kingdom**. The oldest European green party, founded in 1973 as the Ecology Party, it changed its name in 1985 but failed to have any political impact other than as the recipient of substantial protest votes in the 1989 elections to the **European Parliament (EP)**.

Greens. (*Les Verts*) A small environmentalist party in **France**. Founded in 1984, it refused to associate itself with other political movements until accepting collaboration with the more moderate **Ecology Generation** in 1993. It suffered from persistent internal tension and factionalism.

Greens of Slovenia. (*Zeleni Slovenije – ZS*) A small environmentalist party in **Slovenia**. Founded in 1989 as an alliance of several groups, after 1990 it rapidly became one of the more successful green parties in Europe, though its support declined after 1992, and the following year a left-wing faction seceded to form an Eco-Social Party.

Grey Wolves. (*Bozkurtlar*) A shadowy terrorist group in **Turkey** linked to the extreme right **National Action Party**. It conducted an assassination campaign against left-wing politicians, journalists and trade unionists in the 1970s, but many of its leaders were subsequently arrested and imprisoned. In the 1990s its attacks were focused more upon the country's Kurdish minority.

Grey Zone. An area in **Bosnia-Hercegovina** disputed between two or more sides in the country's civil war and placed under temporary international administration and United Nations protection in 1993 or later. The grey zones covered the capital, **Sarajevo**, and other strategic towns or corridors.

Grivas, Georgios Theodoros. (1898–1974) Greek soldier and Cypriot terrorist leader. A serving officer in the Greek army, he acquired experience of guerilla warfare during the Second World War. After the army's victory in the **Greek Civil War**, he retired with the rank of colonel. In 1953 he discussed with **Makarios** and **Papagos** the idea of a guerilla campaign in **Cyprus** as a way of gaining independence from **United Kingdom** control and **enosis** with **Greece**. The two men rejected the idea, but he proceeded to form the **National Organization of Cypriot Fighters (EOKA)** which in 1954 began a five-year campaign of violence. After Britain ceded independence to Cyprus, he continued to demand union with Greece. Against the wishes of Makarios, he was given command of the Greek Cypriot National Guard, but his raids on Turkish Cypriot villages in November 1967 were widely condemned, and he was recalled to Athens. Returning secretly to Cyprus in 1971, he attempted to reorganize a guerilla campaign to force the government to accept enosis, but his health was failing rapidly. With little organization left, and hunted by government forces, he died in hiding in January 1974.

Gromyko, Andrei Andreyevich. (1909–1989) Soviet Foreign Minister 1957–85. Born in Byelorussia, he entered the Soviet diplomatic service in 1939, serving as ambassador to the USA 1943–46. He was made Foreign Minister by **Khrushchev** in February 1957. A skilled negotiator, his task was primarily to interpret the policies of the Soviet leadership and insist upon them in international negotiations. He was not fully a member of the Communist inner circle, being admitted to the **Politburo** only in 1973, but tended to be trusted by Khrushchev and **Brezhnev** as someone whose ambitions did not entail a threat to themselves. When **Gorbachev** became Soviet leader in 1985, Gromyko's more negative style of diplomacy became more of a liability, and he was removed to become presidential head of state, a position with no executive authority. He was hostile to Gorbachev's reform programme, as a result of which he was removed from the presidency in September 1988, retiring from public life.

Grósz, Károly. (1930–) Secretary-General of the **Hungarian Socialist Workers' Party** 1988–89. After working as a local party administrator, he was promoted to the national organization in 1961, becoming in 1984 head of the party in Budapest. In 1987 he was appointed Prime Minister and sought to establish a broader process of consultation by involving expert and professional bodies in government discussions. As premier he indicated an interest in reform and displayed a willingness to hear the views of opposition and dissident groups. His commitment to reform lessened after he moved to head the party in 1988, and a growing opposition within the party to his authoritarian style of government forced him in June 1989 to accept a collective party leadership. As the pressure for reform increased, he opposed in October 1989 the transformation of the party into a democratic Hungarian Socialist Party, and chose to resign in order to head a small group of Communists who wished to preserve the old party as a separate organization.

Grotewohl, Otto. (1894–1964) Prime Minister of the **German Democratic Republic (DDR)** 1949–64. A member of the **Social Democratic Party (SPD)** since 1918, he was arrested and briefly imprisoned on two occasions between 1938 and 1945. Having moved to **Berlin**, he was chosen to lead the reconstituted SPD in the Soviet zone of occupation. At a party meeting near Hanover in October 1945 he proposed that the SPD should collaborate with the Communists as a prelude to a merger of the two parties, but this was rejected outright by **Schumacher** and the representatives of the SPD in exile. Returning to Berlin, he broke with the SPD in the Western zones and actively worked for the merger of the two parties into the **Socialist Unity Party (SED)**, hence playing a key role in the development of Communist control. The SED was formed in April 1946, and he became co-chairman of the new organization. Very much subservient to the Communist leader, **Ulbricht**, he became the first premier of the DDR in 1949, faithfully following Communist policy and helping to implement a rigid Stalinist system of control. His actions made him a particular object of hatred among his ex-SPD colleagues who were forced to flee to the West. He died in office.

Group for the European Unitarian Left (GUE). A cross-national **party group** in the **European Parliament (EP)**. It was formed in 1989 as a result of a split in the former **Communists and Allies** group, by those who wished to establish a **Eurocommunism** profile and strategy rather than strict adherence to Marxist–Leninist doctrine. The lead was taken by representatives of the **Italian Communist Party (PCI)** who dominated the new grouping.

Group of Seven (G-7). Formally the meetings of the Finance Ministers of Canada, the **Federal Republic of Germany**, **France**, **Italy**, Japan, the **United Kingdom** and the USA, established in Tokyo in May 1986. The term has been more widely used to describe the summit meetings of the heads of government of the seven countries which began at Rambouillet, France, in 1975. Originally intended to discuss common economic problems, the agendas of the summits became increasingly political, with the finance ministers and experts dealing with more technical economic matters. The President of the **Commission** attends some of the summit sessions, while after 1991 the Soviet, and later the Russian, leader was invited to attend. The position of chair and the responsibility for following through recommendations has rotated annually across its members. Some discontent has been expressed by other countries at being excluded from its meetings.

Group of Soviet Forces, Germany (GSFG). The major Soviet forward-based and battle-ready army at the core of the **Warsaw Pact**, based along the **Central Front**. It consisted of five separate armies supported by a Tactical Air Force. With German reunification in 1990 and the disbanding of the pact, the **Federal Republic of Germany** and the **USSR** agreed that in return for German aid and compensation, Soviet forces would be withdrawn from German territory in a phased operation.

Group of the Greens in the European Parliament. A cross-national **party group** in the **European Parliament (EP)**. It was formed after the 1989 elections, which returned sufficient Green representatives to form a party group as defined in EP rules. The first Greens had been elected to the EP in 1984. Insufficient in number, they had had to choose between sitting as independents and so losing the privileges which members of party groups enjoy, or joining another group. Until 1989 they were aligned with a heterogeneous number of small parties in the **Rainbow Group**.

Group of Twenty-Three. A meeting of the members of the **North Atlantic Treaty Organization (NATO)** and the **Warsaw Pact** in November 1987. The purpose was to review the possibility of holding conventional arms limitation talks and how they could be linked to the **Conference on Security and Co-operation in Europe (CSCE)**. A framework for negotiations on conventional arms was set up as the **Conventional Stability Talks (CST)**.

Group of Twenty-Four. A loose intergovernmental association formed by the member states of the **Organization for Economic Co-operation and Development (OECD)**. It was established in 1989 to facilitate the channelling of economic aid and advice to Eastern European countries that had rejected Communism, and it was agreed that its activities would be co-ordinated by the **Commission** of the **European Communities (EC)**. *See also* CENTRE FOR CO-OPERATION WITH EUROPEAN ECONOMIES IN TRANSITION, OPERATION PHARE.

Guillaume, Günter. (1927–1995) East German spy. An army officer in the **German Democratic Republic (DDR)** and trained as an espionage agent, he fled to West Germany in 1956, claiming to be a political refugee. He set up a courier network in the **Federal Republic of Germany**. The following year he joined the **Social Democratic Party (SPD)** and became a party administrator. He became a personal aide to **Brandt**, and after 1969 occupied a post in the Chancellory which gave him access to secret and sensitive material. In April 1974 he was arrested and later sentenced to 13 years imprisonment on charges of spying for the DDR. His arrest forced the resignation of Brandt as Chancellor the following month. His activities represented one of the most significant espionage coups of the **Cold War**. In 1981 he was released in a spy swap, and returned to live quietly in the DDR.

Gulag. Russian acronym for Chief Administration of Correction Labour Camps. It came into common usage after the publication of **Solzhenitsyn's** *Gulag Archipelago*, to describe both the whole structure and the evils of the vast prison and forced labour system set up by **Stalin** in the 1930s which used convict labour as an integral part of the Soviet economy. Many individuals were arrested and sent to the camps not because they had committed a crime, but in order for the camps to fulfil economic quotas.

Gunaltay, Semseddin. (1883–1961) Prime Minister of **Turkey** 1948–50. A distinguished academic historian and a member of Kemal Atatürk's **Republican People's Party** since 1923. He introduced a number of liberal reforms as premier, most notably the introduction of free elections. The reforms led to his defeat in the 1950 election, and he and his government resigned, the first time the party had gone out of power since the formation of the secular state. He retired from politics in 1954.

Gürsel, Cemal. (1895–1966) President of **Turkey** 1960–66. A serving soldier, who eventually rose to the rank of General, he had associated himself with Kemal Atatürk's nationalist movement in the 1920s. Political conflict in the 1950s between **Menderes** and **Inönü** increasingly forced the army into the role of arbiter. Military officers objected to the repressive policy pursued by the Menderes government and its attempts to use the army to control and suppress opposition. Gürsel endorsed and joined the military coup which seized power in 1960. Although regarded at the time as a mere figurehead, he moved quickly to remove the more radical officers from positions of authority. In 1961 he returned the country to civilian rule and was elected President. He continued to play a moderating role in the debate on how far the army should seek to influence politics. Gravely ill, he died shortly after his resignation from office.

Gymnich Meetings. Informal specialist ministerial meetings usually held in conjunction with sessions of the **European Council**. They were originally intended to be deliberately informal meetings, without any detailed agenda, where exchanges of views and opinions could be discussed without publicity or the need to come to a decision. The name derived from Schloss Gymnich in the **Federal Republic of Germany** where the first meetings were held.

Gysi, Gregor. (1948–) East German politician. A lawyer, he joined the **Socialist Unity Party (SED)** in 1967. He acted as a defence lawyer for several accused dissidents and opponents of the regime, acquiring a reputation for fairness. In 1988 he was elected head of the council of lawyers' associations, and was identified with the reformist group within the SED that in late 1989 forced the resignation of **Krenz** and the old guard SED leadership. In December 1989 he was elected party leader and sought to engineer the survival of the party, changing its name to the Party of Democratic Socialism and emphasizing its commitment to democracy. His efforts ensured the retention of reasonable mass support, which increased after 1993 as reunification failed to bring the expected economic benefits to the population of the ex-**German Democratic Republic (DDR)**. He resigned as party leader in 1993.

H

Hagen, Carl Ivar. (1944–) Norwegian politician. A wealthy business-man, he joined the newly formed **Progress Party** in 1973, and was elected party leader the following year. An effective communicator and organizer, he rapidly transformed it into an effective populist conservative challenger in the 1980s.

Hague Club. A series of agreements in May 1955 by Western European countries on how to handle multilaterally the external financial situation of countries experiencing debt repayment difficulties. Its immediate task was to deal with Brazil's indebtedness to several Western European countries and banks. Its mode of operation and membership was similar to that of the **Paris Club**.

Hague Summit. A meeting in December 1969 of the heads of government of the six members of the **European Communities (EC)**. It was the first summit since the French veto of the British application for membership, the **empty chair crisis**, and the retirement from politics of **de Gaulle**, and its objective was to give the EC a new impetus. Its discussions opened the way for the **enlargement** of the EC, especially a possible renewed bid from the **United Kingdom**. It extended the budgetary powers of the **European Parliament (EP)**, called for the implementation of **Economic and Mone-tary Union (EMU)** by 1980, reconfirmed political union as the ultimate goal for the EC, and established summit meetings as a new style of EC decision-making, institutionalized in 1974 in the **European Council**.

Haider, Jörg. (1950–) Austrian politician. A lawyer, he joined the youth movement of the **Freedom Party of Austria (FPÖ)** in 1964, becoming its national chairman 1970–74. A Member of Parliament 1979–83 and again after 1986, he briefly returned to provincial politics in **Carinthia**, where he brought substantial gains to the FPÖ because of his demands for restrictions on the use of the minority Slovenian language in the region. A radical populist, he became the hero of the party's right wing. His election as party leader in 1986 reinforced the role of nationalist ideology in its actions and statements. His leadership persuaded the **Socialist Party of Austria (SPÖ)** to end its government coalition with the FPÖ. A vigorous champion of small farmers, he attacked the two major parties for their support of the **proporz**

system of patronage, bureaucracy and privilege. While his arguments gained some popular support, he was condemned by other parties for his nationalistic demand to end all immigration and repatriate all non-Austrians, as well as for his ambivalent stance on the Nazi period. In 1989 he had been elected as governor of Carinthia but was dismissed in 1991 after making seemingly favourable comments about the employment policies of the Third Reich. His radical views persuaded some moderate conservatives to break from the party in 1993. However, this did not greatly weaken his power base, and in 1994 he led the party to its greatest electoral triumph, a performance that seemed to many to threaten the stability of the system.

Hainburg Au. The site of a proposed hydro-electric plant in **Austria**. It was occupied in 1984 by demonstrators protesting that its development would destroy one of Central Europe's few remaining areas of wetland forest. The occupation was ended forcibly by police action. The degree of violence employed embarrassed the government and led to a suspension of the plans. The incident was one of several in the 1980s that indicated a fracture in the consensual style of Austrian politics and a growing disenchantment with government.

Hallstein Doctrine. The official policy of the **Federal Republic of Germany** towards the **German Democratic Republic (DDR)** in the 1950s and 1960s. It resulted from the West German claim to be the only legitimate German state with the right to speak for all Germans pending reunification of the two Germanies and a peace treaty with the war-time Allies. It denied the legitimacy and existence of the DDR, and refused diplomatic relations with any state (but excluding the **USSR**) which recognized it. West Germany persuaded its Western allies to accept and apply its position on the DDR. The value and point of the Doctrine weakened after the erection of the **Berlin Wall**, which demonstrated that the USSR was willing to pay a high price to sustain the DDR as a state. It was finally abandoned in 1970 when the **Ostpolitik** process began.

Hallstein, Walter. (1901–1982) President of the **Commission** 1958–67. A close associate of and foreign policy adviser to **Adenauer**, he was the architect of West Germany's policy towards the **German Democratic Republic (DDR)**, the **Hallstein Doctrine**. In January 1958 he left national politics to become the first president of the Commission of the newly-formed **European Economic Community (EEC)**. His selection was largely due to his prominent role in earlier discussions on European integration and his prestige abroad, especially in **France**. He had led the West German delegation in the discussions on the 1950 **Schuman Plan** and at the 1955 **Messina Conference**. He attempted to use the Commission as the driving force for more and rapid political and economic integration within the EEC, declaring that national sovereignty was a thing of the past and that his office could be regarded as a kind of European premiership. His views and strategy brought him into conflict with **de Gaulle** in the mid-1960s. His authority and influence were greatly weakened by and after the **empty chair crisis**. Rather than face the near certainty of a French refusal to accept his re-election for a further term of office, he resigned in 1967 and retired from public life.

Hammarskjöld, Dag Hjalmar Agne Carl. (1905–1961) Secretary-General of the United Nations (UN) 1953–61. A Swedish diplomat and a skilled negotiator, he did much to consolidate and raise the prestige and authority of the UN, but the freezing effect of the **Cold War** prevented him from using his office effectively in European affairs. His efforts to resolve the 1960 Congo (Zaire) civil war irritated the **USSR** which campaigned for limits to be placed upon the authority of the Secretary-General. He was killed in an air crash in Northern Rhodesia (Zambia) in 1961.

Happart, José. (1947–) Belgian politician. A member of the **Socialist Party (PS)** and a militant Francophone, he first emerged to national prominence after his election in 1984 as mayor of **Voeren** (Fourons), a small mainly French-speaking area within **Flanders**. A previous leader of Fourons Action 1978–82, he became a figure of controversy when his appointment was ruled void because of his refusal to take a test of competence in Flemish, the official language of the region. His repeated re-election led ultimately in October 1987 to the resignation of a national government led by **Martens**. Re-elected mayor yet again in October 1988, he was persuaded not to seek appointment in return for the guarantee of a secure leading position on the PS list of candidates for the 1989 election to the **European Parliament (EP)**, but in 1993–94 he returned to the attack on what he regarded as an unjust imposition of a foreign language upon his community.

Hard ECU. A British proposal in 1990 that sought to modify the arguments put forward by the 1989 **Delors** plan for a single currency and a single central bank for the **European Communities (EC)**. It proposed that the **European Currency Unit (ECU)** should not replace national currencies, but exist alongside them within a common framework. The idea was that, in order to retain its value and so remain 'hard', the ECU would never be devalued against national currencies. The proposal failed to gain support from other Member States.

Harmel Report. A document commissioned by the **North Atlantic Treaty Organization (NATO)**. Prepared by Pierre Harmel, the Belgian Foreign Minister and entitled *The Future Tasks of the Alliance*, it was adopted in December 1967. It committed NATO to a dual approach towards the **USSR**, to balance **deterrence** with **détente**, and to seek a more stable relationship that would be conducive to resolving political issues between the two regional security alliances.

Harmonization. A phrase widely used in the **European Communities**

(EC) after the mid-1980s to describe the overall process of the co-ordination and integration of the member states and their policies and practices, especially with regard to the **internal market**, to reduce the degree of variation between them to minimal levels. Some critics have alleged that the EC have often confused it with homogenization and standardization.

Harpsund Democracy. A phrase often used to describe the style of policy-making in **Sweden**. It refers to the regular meetings of government with industry and trade union leaders at the country residence of the Prime Minister, first begun in 1939. By allowing a free discussion between the two sides of industry and allowing them to hear government thinking, it was held to have contributed to the Swedish consensual style of decision-making and, more specifically, to eliminating industrial and economic conflict.

Haughey, Charles James. (1925–) Prime Minister of **Ireland** 1979–81, 1982, 1987–92. A successful businessman and lawyer, he entered Parliament in 1957 as a **Fianna Fáil** representative. Appointed as a government minister in 1961, he was subsequently forced to resign in 1970 after allegations that he had links with Irish terrorist groups. Acquitted of alleged arms smuggling, he returned to government in 1977, and was elected party leader and premier in 1979. A controversial figure and strongly nationalist in outlook, he pursued a more aggressive policy on **Northern Ireland**, especially after 1987, but allegations of scandals and favouritism within his party weakened his authority. His failure to handle economic problems in the 1990s eventually led to party pressure for him to resign, but his departure in 1992 was due more to allegations of his implication in a telephone-tapping scandal.

Havel, Václav. (1936–) President of **Czechoslovakia** 1989–92, and of the **Czech Republic** from 1993. He is a distinguished playwright, but after the reimposition of Communist orthodoxy after 1968 his works were banned in Czechoslovakia as being subversive, although they were published abroad. He became a prominent dissident and critic of the regime, establishing the **Committee for the Defence of the Unjustly Persecuted (VONS)**. He was later a signatory of **Charter 77**. His activities led to a brief imprisonment in 1977, house arrest in 1977–79, and imprisonment again from 1979–83 for sedition. After his release he founded an independent periodical, *Lidove Noviny*, in 1988 which led to his further arrest in January 1989 for incitement and obstruction, although the immediate cause was his participation in the commemoration of the 1969 suicide of **Palach**. Released in May, he helped to form **Civic Forum** in November, rapidly becoming its leading force. When Communist rule began to crumble, he was elected President by the Communist-dominated Parliament as a successor to **Husák**. He was re-elected by popular vote the following year. Committed to the continued integrity of Czechoslovakia, he was nevertheless unable to prevent or deflect Slovak pressures for independence, and in 1992 the strength of Slovak separatists in the Parliament elected in June blocked his election to a second term. After the consequent separation of the country into two distinct states, he was elected as President of the Czech Republic.

Heath, Edward Richard George. (1916–) British Prime Minister 1970–74. Briefly a civil servant and news editor, he entered Parliament for the **Conservative Party** in 1950, serving in government 1961–64. A committed pro-European, he was appointed by **Macmillan** to head the British delegation 1961–63 negotiating entry to the **European Communities (EC)**. In July 1965 he became party leader, winning the first democratic electoral contest for the position. After winning the 1970 election, he successfully negotiated British entry to the EC, but his domestic problems were more severe. He was obliged in 1972 to impose direct rule upon **Northern Ireland**, and his expansionary economic policy helped create serious inflationary and balance of payments problems. His attempts to regulate industrial relations and impose an incomes policy led to a national coal strike in 1972, and widespread industrial action, spearheaded by the miners, in late 1973. Refusing to compromise, he placed industry on a three-day week in January 1974 to conserve energy, and called an election the following month. Failing to gain a majority, he resigned and soon became increasingly isolated within his own party. His leadership was challenged by **Thatcher** and he was defeated in the leadership election of February 1975. Returning to the backbenches, he continued to urge greater involvement in Europe, and in the 1980s and 1990s opposed many of the policies of the Thatcher and **Major** governments.

Hedtoft, Hans. (1903–1955) Prime Minister of **Denmark** 1947–50, 1953–55. Largely self-educated, in 1939 he became the youngest ever leader of the **Social Democratic Party**, but in 1941 was forced to resign because of his outspoken criticism of and opposition to the German occupation. In 1948 he argued forcefully for Denmark to join the **North Atlantic Treaty Organization (NATO)**, abandoning its traditional neutrality. He was the principal actor in the decision to form the **Nordic Council**.

Heinemann, Gustav. (1899–1976) President of the **Federal Republic of Germany** 1969–74. A lawyer and founder member of the **Christian Democratic Union (CDU)** in 1945, he served in the first **Adenauer** government, but resigned in 1952 over the issue of West German rearmament. A committed Christian and pacifist, he formed his own neutralist German People's Party, but without much electoral success, before joining the **Social Democratic Party (SPD)** in 1957. He became the party's chief legal spokesperson. He returned to government in the 1966 **grand coalition** before being overwhelmingly elected as head of state in 1969. His dignified occupancy of the office strengthened both its and his prestige. He retired from public life after completing his term of office.

Heligoland. A small island in the North Sea close to the German coast. Occupied by the **United Kingdom** from 1810 to 1890, it was ceded to Germany which developed it as a military base. It was evacuated in 1946 and used as a bombing practice range. It was subsequently returned to the **Federal Republic of Germany** which in March 1952 decided to resettle the island.

Helsinki Citizens' Assembly. An international association of **citizen initiatives** groups and other organizations concerned with the defence of human rights. With a secretariat based in Prague, its objective has been to safeguard the principles outlined in the Helsinki Final Act signed by the **Conference on Security and Co-operation in Europe (CSCE)** in 1975 through providing a forum for individuals to express views independent of their governments.

Helsinki Convention. *See* CONVENTION ON THE PROTECTION OF THE BALTIC SEA AREA.

Helsinki Document. *See* CONFERENCE ON SECURITY AND CO-OPERATION IN EUROPE.

Helsinki Final Act. *See* CONFERENCE ON SECURITY AND CO-OPERATION IN EUROPE.

Helsinki Human Rights Group. A group of Soviet dissidents formed in May 1976 to demand that the **USSR** fulfil its promises on human rights contained in the 1975 Helsinki Final Act of the **Conference on Security and Co-operation in Europe (CSCE)**. It attempted to monitor infringements of human rights and prison conditions within the USSR. Its founder, Yuri Orlov, was arrested and imprisoned in May 1978 for seven years for anti-Soviet agitation. Other members of the group also received prison sentences. The actions of the Soviet authorities against the Group provoked strong protests abroad and contributed to a hardening of East–West relations.

Helsinki Protocol. *See* CONVENTION ON LONG-RANGE TRANSBOUNDARY AIR POLLUTION.

Helsinki Watch. The European segment of Human Rights Watch, an American-based network established in 1987 to monitor and promote observance by governments of human rights.

Hermes. A planned crewed space shuttle sponsored by the **European Space Agency (ESA)**. Proposed by **France** in 1985, it entered the planning stage in 1988, with completion scheduled for 1998. In 1991 soaring costs led to questions about its viability, and the completion date was put back to 2002. Continuing problems and pressures caused it in 1993 to be downgraded to a potential design: its effective abandonment was a major setback to the European ambition to establish a presence in space developments.

Herri Batasuna (HB). (People's Unity). A radical Basque nationalist party founded in 1978. It broadly supported the armed struggle waged by the terrorist organization, **Euskadi ta Askatasuna (ETA)**, and many people regarded it as the political wing of ETA. In 1980 and 1984 its hard-line stance led it to decline to take up the seats it had won in the regional Parliament, on the grounds that it refused to recognize the legitimacy of either the Spanish state or the Basque regional assembly. It ended its boycott of the national Parliament in 1989, but its members were immediately expelled for refusing to swear allegiance to the Constitution. In June 1990 a legal ruling allowed them to swear an amended oath of allegiance. In 1987, along with **Basque Solidarity (EA)**, it refused to sign the anti-terrorist pact negotiated by the main Spanish and Basque parties, and it persisted with a general policy of non-co-operation. As the popularity of ETA began to wane in the 1990s, HB began a process of distancing itself from the terrorists.

Herzog, Roman. (1934–) President of the **Federal Republic of Germany** from 1994. An academic lawyer, he joined the **Christian Democratic Union (CDU)** in 1970, serving 1978–83 as a minister in the regional government of Baden-Württemberg, before being appointed to the Federal Constitutional Court. In 1987 he became President of the Court. Not initially the party's first choice as its presidential candidate, his later nomination was highly popular, and he won acclaim for his dignified stance during various ceremonies in 1995 commemorating the end of the Second World War.

Hess, Rudolf. (1894–1987) Former deputy leader of the Nazi Party and convicted war criminal. Sentenced to life imprisonment in the 1946 **Nuremberg Trials**, he was sent to **Spandau** prison in **Berlin**. After 1966 he was the sole occupant of Spandau. The **USSR** consistently rejected proposals from the Western allies for his release. A symbol in life and death to extreme right-wing groups, he allegedly committed suicide in August 1987.

Heuss, Theodor. (1884–1963) President of the **Federal Republic of Germany** 1949–59. A distinguished academic and constitutional lawyer, he had been a member of and parliamentary deputy of the pre-1933 Democratic Party. Banned from writing during the Third Reich, he helped to build the **Free Democratic Party (FDP)** in 1946, becoming its leader in 1949. Elected as West Germany's first President in 1949, he did much by his speeches and actions to inspire confidence in the new state and its democratic institutions, emphasizing the need to reject the Nazi past through an awareness of collective shame. He was unanimously elected to a second term of office in 1954.

Hexagonale. *See* PENTAGONALE.

Hillsborough Accord. *See* ANGLO-IRISH AGREEMENT.

Historic compromise. A strategy adopted by the **Italian Communist Party (PCI)** in the 1970s, advocating re-entry of the PCI to the political mainstream through collaboration with other parties, especially the **Christian Democratic Party (DC)**. It was first put forward in 1973 by the PCI leader, **Berlinguer**, who believed that the overthrow of the Marxist Allende regime in Chile indicated that a Communist party would not be able by itself to assume governmental power, and that influence could best be achieved by collaboration. He indicated that the PCI supported the democratic system and would be available as a loyal partner in government. After 1976 the PCI became regarded as part of the government forces, first by abstaining in parliamentary votes and later, after the murder of **Moro**, by voting with the DC-led government. The strategy failed to achieve its objectives. It was rejected by other pro-government parties which feared being squeezed and made unnecessary by a linkage between the two biggest parties in the country, and it was primarily utilized by the DC, especially after Moro's death, merely as a means of reinforcing government stability. Berlinguer's hopes that it would lead to electoral gains was not realized, and the PCI was never invited to become a formal government partner. However, the brief period of solidarity did aid policies designed to combat inflation and the terrorist activities of the **Red Brigades**. Many PCI leaders became disillusioned with the strategy, and Berlinguer abandoned it in 1980.

Holkeri, Harri. (1937–) Prime Minister of **Finland** 1987–91. Making a career as a full-time official of the conservative **National Coalition Party**, he became Party Secretary in 1966 and leader in 1971, entering Parliament in 1970. He contested the presidency in 1982 and 1988 and oversaw a substantial rise in the party's electoral support, to a position where it could not easily be ignored as a potential government partner. In 1987, as head of a four-party coalition government, he became the country's first conservative premier since 1944, something which indicated a weakening of the latent influence of the **USSR** on Finnish government formation.

Homeland. *See* ELEVENTH OF NOVEMBER ALLIANCE.

Homeland Union. *See* SĄJŪDIS.

Honecker, Erich. (1912–1994) Head of state of the **German Democratic Republic (DDR)** 1976–89. Born in the **Saarland**, he joined the German Communist Party in 1929, organizing its youth movement in the early 1930s. Held in a concentration camp 1933–45, he was appointed leader of the Free German Youth in the Soviet zone of Germany in 1946, rising through the **Socialist Unity Party (SED)** until elevated to the **Politburo** in 1956. He was later the principal deputy to **Ulbricht**, who he succeeded as Party Secretary in 1971. As the effective leader of the DDR he was willing initially to seek a more relaxed relationship with the **Federal Republic of Germany** in return for receiving international recognition of the DDR as a sovereign state by the West. He also remained unswervingly loyal to the **USSR**. In 1987 he met with the West German leader, **Kohl**, and pledged that war must never again happen on German soil, but in the 1980s he became more rigid in his attitude, committed to a Stalinist style of rule, unwilling to tolerate any liberalization within the DDR, and seemingly ignoring the recommendations of **Gorbachev** after 1985. A visit to **Berlin** by Gorbachev in October 1989 to celebrate the DDR's fortieth anniversary was a catalyst for large demonstrations against the regime. Ill for much of the summer, Honecker had become remote from the real state of affairs, and totally resisted the pressure for reform, but within two weeks his party colleagues forced him to resign. Faced with arrest, he fled from a Soviet military hospital where he was receiving treatment for liver cancer, and moved to Moscow. Fearing extradition to Germany after the collapse of the USSR, he took refuge in the Chilean embassy, but in July 1992 he was extradited to stand trial on manslaughter charges relating to people killed while trying to escape from the DDR across the **Berlin Wall**, as well as for the misappropriation of state funds. His trial began in November but was abandoned two months later on health grounds. He went into exile in Chile where he died.

Horn, Gyula. (1932–) Prime Minister of **Hungary** from 1994. Brought up in a Marxist family, he completed his studies in the **USSR**, returning to Hungary in 1954 to work as an economist in the Finance Ministry. Subsequently a diplomat and Communist Party official on foreign affairs, he was a convert to the need for a more democratic structure in the 1970s. As Foreign Minister in 1989 he was prominent in the reforms undertaken by the **Hungarian Socialist Workers' Party**, and instrumental in the opening of Hungary's borders with **Austria**. He became leader of the reconstructed Hungarian Socialist Party in 1990, leading it to electoral victory in 1994.

Hoxha, Enver. (1908–1985) First Secretary of the Albanian Communist Party 1945–85. Educated in **France** and a member of the **French Communist Party (PCF)**, he returned to **Albania** in 1936, becoming leader of the **Resistance movement** after the Italian invasion. By 1944 he headed a National Liberation Army that controlled most of the country. In 1945 he led a provisional republican government, but quickly established a dictatorship based upon Stalinist principles, eliminating all opposition to his personal rule, especially party colleagues who were favourable towards the idea of a union with **Yugoslavia**. He spurned all contacts with the West, and in 1960 also attacked **Khrushchev** for his criticisms of **Stalin**, accusing him of revisionism. Breaking with the **USSR**, he formed close links with Mao Zedong and China, but later criticized China's rapprochement with the USA after 1968. During his unchallenged personalized dictatorship, Albania was economically the most backward country in Europe and diplomatically isolated from the rest of the world. In April 1985 he died of diabetes, which he had suffered from since 1968. He was succeeded by **Aliá**.

Hungarian Christian Democratic Party. (*Magyar Keresztényde-mokrata Mozgalom – MKDM*) A political party in **Slovakia**. It was founded in 1989 to represent the ethnic Hungarian minority. In 1992 it aligned itself with the broader **Coexistence** movement.

Hungarian Democratic Forum. (*Magyar Demokrata Fórum*) A centre-right political party in **Hungary**. It was established in 1987 as an open discussion forum by intellectuals, including several who were members of the ruling **Hungarian Socialist Workers' Party**. Criticized by the regime, after the fall of **Kádár** it turned itself in September 1988 into a more overtly political movement that pressed for democratic reform. It successfully maintained a dialogue with the ruling party, and in 1989 decided to contest elections as a distinctive party. It won a convincing victory in the 1990 election and formed a government. Internal disputes and popular discontent with its economic policies led to severe defeat and a return to opposition.

Hungarian Democratic Union of Romania. (*Romániai Magyar Demokraták Szövetsége – RMDSz*) A political party in **Romania**, founded in 1990 to represent the ethnic Hungarian minority in **Transylvania**. Its objectives were to secure rights for all ethnic minorities and some form of self-administration for the predominantly Hungarian districts of the region.

Hungarian Revolution. A popular uprising in **Hungary** in 1956 against Communist rule and Soviet domination. It was the most visible consequence in Eastern Europe of the denunciation of **Stalin** by **Khrushchev** in February 1956. There was a revival of nationalist sentiment, and in an attempt to appease it, Khrushchev forced the hardline Hungarian leader, **Rákosi**, to resign. Aided by economic discontent, the protests continued, with a demand for the withdrawal of Soviet troops from the country. The **USSR** was initially willing to collaborate, and some army units did leave. On 23 October the statue of Stalin in Budapest was pulled down, and the following day two former victims of the Rákosi regime, **Nagy** and **Kádár**, were appointed Prime Minister and Party Secretary respectively. The Nagy government announced a programme of immediate liberalization, legalizing political parties, releasing the Catholic primate, **Mindszenty**, from prison, and declaring an intention to leave the **Warsaw Pact** and adopt neutrality. The proposals were too radical for the USSR, and also alarmed Kádár, who left Budapest to form a rival government in Eastern Hungary. He returned to the capital on 4 November with Soviet tanks and troops, who quickly overcame a brave but mainly unarmed opposition. Nagy was replaced by Kádár. There was no prospect of intervention by the West, which was in any case preoccupied by the simultaneous **Suez Crisis**. Some 200,000 Hungarians fled to exile in the West, and the USSR subsequently reneged on its pledges of safe conduct, handing Nagy and his major supporters over to the new government, which executed them.

Hungarian Social Democratic Party. (*Magyarországi Szocialdemokrata Párt*) A left-wing party in **Hungary**. Founded in 1890, it survived the interwar conservative authoritarian regime to contest the 1945 election, emerging as the second largest party. In 1948 it was forcibly merged with the Hungarian Communist Party, and most of its leaders were subsequently purged. An attempt to relaunch it as an independent entity was briefly made in 1956 shortly before the **Hungarian Revolution**. It finally re-emerged in 1988, being formally constituted as a party the following year. It enjoyed only limited success, with its effectiveness further weakened by disputes between traditional social democrats and pro-Western modernizers.

Hungarian Socialist Workers' Party. (*Magyar Szocialista Munkáspárt*) The ruling party of the Communist regime of **Hungary**. Founded in 1918 as the Hungarian Communist Party, it was banned by the conservative Horthy regime. A leadership nucleus was rebuilt in Moscow during the Second World War under the direction of **Rákosi**. After 1944 it dominated the National Independence Front set up in Budapest by the **USSR**, but it fared badly in the relatively free 1945 election. With Soviet support, it quickly moved to seize a monopoly of power, also enforcing a merger with the Social Democrats in a new body called the Hungarian Workers' Party. Its cohesion was strained by internal disputes over strategy and tactics between the Moscow-trained leadership and 'home-grown' Communists. The latter were largely purged by Rákosi after 1948. Its imposition of a rigid programme of Stalinization was unpopular, and discontent began to emerge after 1953. After the removal of Rákosi in 1956, it renamed itself, and the new leader, **Kádár**, attempted to strike a better balance between moderate and more hard-line elements, introducing a cautious reform programme after 1963. Its internal cohesion began to decay after 1985, and in February 1989 it accepted the principle of a multi-party democracy. During negotiations with opposition groups on how to manage the transition to democracy, it adopted the title of Hungarian Socialist Party (*Magyar Szocialista Párt*) in October, but a minority opted to secede and retain the original title as a separate party (but renaming itself the Hungarian Workers' Party in 1992). It successfully survived the change of regime, and returned to government in 1994 after a convincing electoral victory.

Hungarian Way. (*Magyar Ut*) A cultural and political organization in **Hungary**. Founded in 1992, it developed as an extreme nationalist mass movement, denouncing Jews, Communists and liberals, and demanding 'living space' for a new Hungary, a claim which referred to the annexation of Hungarian areas in neighbouring **Romania**, **Serbia**, and **Slovakia**. It was linked with the extreme right-wing Hungarian Justice and Life Party (*Magyar Igazságés Élet Párt*), formed in 1993.

Hungary. A country in Eastern Europe. Previously part of the Habsburg Empire, but with some self-government after 1867, it was established as an independent state in 1918. After a brief Communist dictatorship under Béla

Kun, it was ruled by a conservative authoritarian regime headed by Admiral Miklós Horthy which aligned itself with Germany during the Second World War. The first post-war election of 1945 produced a multi-party system, but through the use of **salami tactics** the Communists seized effective one-party control by 1948. The last non-Communists were removed from government in 1950. The Communist leader, **Rákosi**, launched a series of purges against his opponents and rivals within the party, and introduced a ruthless policy of Stalinization. After the death of **Stalin**, he rejected pressure from the **USSR** to moderate his course. His position became untenable after the attack upon Stalin by **Khrushchev** in 1956, and his removal was the starting point of the **Hungarian Revolution**.

After the liberal regime of **Nagy** had been quashed, **Kádár** reorganized the party as the **Hungarian Socialist Workers' Party** and completed the programme of agricultural **collectivization**. Apart from the treatment of Nagy, who was executed, control and punishment were less severe than under Rákosi, and some reforms and relaxation were introduced after 1961, with a **New Economic Mechanism** to revitalize the economy through allowing the operation of some market elements introduced in 1968. Attempts by orthodox groups within the party in the 1970s to slow down or reverse reform failed. Instead, they fuelled demands, also within the party, for even more change. Further experiments with reform were accepted in the 1980s, but political pressures and economic problems weakened the authority of the regime after 1985, leading to a radical overhaul of the party leadership and a policy of controlled democratization and market reforms in 1988. Even though opposition groups openly pushed for more radical reform, Hungary was further down the road of political change than most Eastern European countries by 1989 when open dissent within the party and the emergence of new opposition groups accelerated an acceptance of democracy. A programme of political reform was accepted in 'triangular discussions' in September 1989 between all political groups, and a new democratic system of government was established after elections in 1990. The first act of the new legislature was to commemorate the Hungarian Revolution and its victims. Hungary soon announced its desire to join the **North Atlantic Treaty Organization (NATO)** and in 1994 submitted a formal application to become a member of the **European Communities (EC)**. The post-Communist democratic coalition, weakened by splits and blamed for the economic dislocation problems caused by the transition to a market economy, was defeated in the 1994 election. The reconstructed Communists, now the Hungarian Socialist Party, achieved a majority and returned to government.

Husák, Gustav. (1913–1992) First Secretary of the Czechoslovakian Communist Party 1969–87, and President of **Czechoslovakia** 1975–89.

Joining the Communist Party in the 1930s, he was a champion of Slovak rights. In 1950 he was accused of nationalist-bourgeois deviation, and was imprisoned in 1954. Released in 1960, his rehabilitation within the party was slow. After the Soviet invasion of the country he was appointed Secretary of the Party in **Slovakia** and became the main representative of the realist view that the occupation had to be accepted. He replaced **Dubček** as Party Secretary in April 1969 and re-enforced Communist orthodoxy on the country. It was only in the 1980s that he was prepared to tolerate some limited reforms. He consolidated his position in 1975 by also becoming President. He resigned his party position in December 1987, and in 1989 did not play a prominent role in the attempts by party hard-liners to quash the spreading mass anti-regime demonstrations. With the collapse of Communist supremacy, he resigned the presidency in December 1989.

I

Ibarruri, Dolores. (1895–1989) Spanish politician. Joining the Communist Party in 1917, she wrote articles under the pseudonym of *La Pasionaria*, a name by which she was later always known. During the 1936–39 Spanish Civil War her anti-Fascist speeches gave her an international reputation. In 1939 she fled to Moscow where she became acknowledged as the elder stateswoman of exiled Spanish Communists. She was allowed to return to **Spain** only after the death of **Franco**, doing so in 1977, but she played only a limited role in party politics.

Iceland. An island and state in the North Atlantic. Part of **Norway** and, later, **Denmark** after the tenth century, it was granted some limited autonomy in 1874, extended in 1918 to almost full self-government. In 1940 it was occupied by British forces, who were relieved the following year by American troops. After a plebiscite in 1944 it broke the final links with Denmark and became a republic. In 1949 it joined the **North Atlantic Treaty Organization (NATO)**, though not providing any forces to the organization: its main importance was its strategic geopolitical position in the North Atlantic and its provision of facilities for a major American military base. There was an occasional resentment and demonstration against the American presence, and in 1971 a left-wing government restricted the NATO presence to specific areas of the island. Its major economic activity was fishing, and attempts to protect this key industry by extending the geographical range of its jurisdiction over fishing grounds led to prolonged disputes with some European countries (the **Cod War**).

Ideological Delimitation. (*Abgrenzung*) A policy adopted in the **German Democratic Republic (DDR)** in the 1970s by **Honecker**. It was intended to counteract some aspects of the potential impact of the **Ostpolitik** agreements. Fearing that more contacts between the two Germanies would be a destabilizing influence within the DDR, the Honecker strategy stressed the distinctive historical and socio-cultural differences between the two states. It argued that because since 1945 the DDR had developed a progressive working-class culture while its Western neighbour had been dominated by an exploiter class, the gulf between the two states had become unbridgeable.

Iliescu, Ion. (1930–) President of **Romania** from 1990. A hydraulic engineer, he joined the Communist Party in 1944, heading its youth wing 1956–60 and joining its Central Committee in 1969. He lost influence after criticizing the personality cult of **Ceauşescu** and was given only middle-ranking party posts in the 1970s and 1980s. He took a lead in restructuring elements of the party as the **National Salvation Front**, being appointed as interim President. He was confirmed in the position in 1991. His background, and what opponents regarded as an authoritarian style of government, generated considerable criticism at home and abroad.

Independence Party. (*Sjálfstaedisflokkurin – Sj*) A conservative party in **Iceland**. Formed in 1929 as a merger between the Conservative and Liberal parties, it established itself as the country's largest party and the core element of most government coalitions.

Independent European Programme Group (IEPG). An offshoot of the **Eurogroup** within the **North Atlantic Treaty Organization (NATO)**. It was formed in December 1975 to secure a greater level of European NATO collaboration in military research and development and in arms procurement programmes as important steps towards building a viable European defence industry. Opposition by the larger European states to the division of labour and degree of specialization it implied, which they feared would damage their own multi-purpose defence industries, made it largely inoperative for a number of years. Its revival after 1984 coincided with Western European fears that their own interests might be harmed by possible bilateral agreements between the USA and **USSR**, and substantial progress was subsequently made on several armaments projects. In June 1989 the IEPG agreed to a joint programme, code-named Euclid, to promote collaborative research and development among European defence contractors.

Independent Grouping of the Canaries. (*Agrupación Independiente de Canarias – AIC*) A small electoral grouping of several regional parties in the **Canary Islands**. Formed in 1985, it failed to establish much of a presence except in Tenerife until 1993 when it formed a minority regional administration.

Independent Smallholders' Party. (*Független Kisgazdapárt*) A centrist party in **Hungary**. The revival in 1945 of a major pre-war party, it became the largest non-socialist organization, winning the relatively free 1945 election – although its appeal had been enhanced because of a ban on right-wing parties. It was a target of harassment by the Hungarian Communist Party, and it began to disintegrate under the pressure after its leader, Béla Kovács, was arrested by the Soviet occupation authorities in 1947. Its collapse was complete a year later. Some of its leaders reappeared briefly during the 1956 **Hungarian Revolution**, but attempts to reconstitute the party were not made until October 1988, as the Independent Smallholders',

Farmworkers' and Citizens' Party (*Független Kisgazda, Föklmunkás és Polgari Párt*). Formally established the following March with a conservative programme that supported a market economy and the reprivatization of all land, it failed to establish a large mass base and fared badly in later elections, splitting in 1992 over the issue of land reform.

Informal Group of NATO Defence Ministers. *See* EUROGROUP.

Inönü, Ismet. (1884–1974) Prime Minister of **Turkey** 1923–37, 1961–65, and President 1938–50. A career army officer, he was chosen by Mustapha Kemal Atatürk as the first premier of the new secular republic in 1923. He supported Atatürk's policy of enforced Westernization, and succeeded him as president and virtual dictator in 1938. During the Second World War he sympathized with the Allies, but kept Turkey neutral until March 1945. He gradually allowed a degree of liberalization, permitting political parties to form after 1945. After losing the first free election in 1950, he led the **Republican People's Party** in opposition, clashing strongly with the premier, **Menderes**. He returned as prime minister in 1961 in the wake of the 1960 military coup. His election defeat in 1965 was attributed to his cancellation, under strong American pressure, of a proposed invasion of **Cyprus** to protect the island's Turkish minority. He remained titular leader of the opposition until the declaration of martial law in July 1972.

Integrated Mediterranean Programmes (IMPs). A package of measures introduced by the **European Communities (EC)** in 1985 to assist the development of their Mediterranean regions that were still heavily dependent upon agricultural production. They were a consequence of a demand by **Greece** in 1981 for a renegotiation of its terms of entry to the EC and its threat of a veto on the admission of **Portugal** and **Spain**. The first seven-year IMP was initiated in Greece in 1986.

Integrated Operations. A strategy adopted by the **European Communities (EC)** in 1979. They were projects funded from several EC sources for socio-economic development and reconstruction in specifically defined and limited geographical areas regarded as suffering from rapid economic decline or depression because of structural economic change. They served as a model for the more ambitious **Integrated Mediterranean Programmes.**

Intermediate-Range Nuclear Forces (INF). *See* ARMS CONTROL.

Internal Macedonian Revolutionary Organization–Democratic Party for Macedonian National Unity. (*Vnatrešna Makedonska Revolucionerna Organizacija–Demokratska Partija za Makedonska Nacionalno Edinstvo*) A political party in **Macedonia** founded in 1990, taking the same name as an organization that had sought, through direct action, to achieve Macedonian independence in the nineteenth and early twentieth centuries. Strongly nationalistic, it rejected the idea of rights for ethnic minorities.

Internal market. A term describing the end product of the **European Communities (EC)** plan to establish a **common market** by the end of 1992. The **Treaty of Rome** had set it as an objective to be achieved within 15 years, but while quotas and tariff restrictions were quickly removed, the broader goal was not reached, and serious discussions on it were not renewed until 1985. A White Paper prepared by Lord **Cockfield** listed some 300 actions that would need to be taken, and an infrastructure was outlined in the 1987 **Single European Act (SEA)**. Most of the necessary changes were achieved on time, and the internal market officially came into existence in January 1993. Committed integrationists, however, continued to complain that frontier controls and other structures and practices still blocked the establishment of the full free movement integral to the working of a proper internal market.

International Commission for the Protection of the Rhine. A body established in 1965 to carry out and support recommendations of the **Central Committee for the Navigation of the Rhine**. It was the result of the 1963 Berne convention on environment and pollution, and it later endorsed the 1976 Bonn Convention on chemical pollution. Regular ministerial conferences began in 1972, but few positive outcomes were achieved until the mid-1980s.

International Commission on Civil Status (ICCS). An organization established in December 1949 to compile and update aspects of national legislation and jurisprudential documents that related to matters of personal status such as those referring to family or nationality. The arrangements were finalized by a Protocol signed in Berne in September 1950.

International Committee of the Movements for European Unity. An umbrella organization founded in Paris in December 1947 to co-ordinate and act as a link between the several bodies and groups that argued for political and economic integration in Europe. Duncan Sandys (the son-in-law of **Churchill**), who had taken the initiative in July to establish a European Liaison Committee, became its secretary. Its effectiveness was reduced by disputes and rivalry between federalists and those with more modest or pragmatic objectives. It organized the 1948 **Congress of Europe**, after which its role was taken over by the **European Movement**.

International Conference on Former Yugoslavia. Also known as the Geneva Conference, an international meeting seeking a solution to the several conflicts in the former **Yugoslavia**, sponsored by the **European Communities (EC)** and the United Nations (UN). Established in 1992, its objective was to seek agreement on basic principles for regional settlements that would provide guarantees for ethnic minorities. Representatives of the various ethnic groups in Yugoslavia were also participants.

International Conference on the Protection of the North Sea. An inter-governmental organization of the North Sea littoral states. Its objectives were to protect and improve the marine environment of the sea.

International Danube River Conference. A meeting held in Belgrade in August 1948 to discuss navigation rights on the Danube. An earlier proposal by the USA at the **Potsdam Conference** for the internationalization of Europe's inland waterways, which had included an international commission and the principle of free navigation on the Danube, had been rejected by the **USSR**. The meeting was dominated by the USSR and its Eastern European satellites, and the Western participants (the USA, **France** and the **United Kingdom**) were outvoted on every issue. It rejected United Nations (UN) involvement and accepted the Soviet proposal that control should belong solely to the riparian states, with Western countries totally excluded. It essentially confirmed the post-1945 reality whereby control of shipping was largely in Soviet hands through the establishment of joint shipping companies formed by the USSR with each of the Danubian states.

International Energy Agency (IEA). An organization established in November 1974 by the Western industrial democracies as a response to the 1973 oil crisis. It was intended to develop an energy programme that would reduce the West's dependence on imported oil, especially from the Middle East. The measures related to energy conservation, the development of alternative energy sources, and a system of oil allocation in any future emergency that would be both reasonable and equitable. Most objectives had been reached by the 1980s, but whether this was due to IEA activity was a matter of debate. It became an autonomous agency associated with the **Organization for Economic Co-operation and Development (OECD)**.

International Federation of Non-Governmental Associations for the Protection of Europe's Cultural and Natural Heritage. *See* EUROPA NOSTRA.

International Federation of Resistance Movements. *See* RESISTANCE MOVEMENTS.

International Helsinki Federation for Human Rights. An international body established in 1982 to pressure governments to comply with the human rights provisions of the 1975 Helsinki final Act endorsed by the **Conference on Security and Co-operation in Europe (CSCE)**. It set up national committees in most CSCE countries.

International Maritime Satellite Organization (INMARSAT). A collaborative research and communications agency established in 1982. It arose out of conferences held in London in 1975–76 under the auspices of the International Maritime Consultative Organization, a United Nations agency. Although not a specifically European body, it was agreed to base it in London and that it would lease its communications capacity from **European Space Agency (ESA)** satellites.

International Ruhr Authority (IRA). An agency established in April 1949 to supervise coal and steel production in the Ruhr region of Germany. It was a response to the 1948 decision of the Western Allies to create a West German state out of their zones of occupation. A draft agreement the previous January stated that it would take account of essential German needs while ensuring that the Ruhr's resources would not be used for aggressive purposes. The IRA was a compromise between **France** and the other Western allies. In order to prevent future German aggression, France had wanted the Ruhr detached from Germany, but had to settle for some limited form of international control. The operation of the IRA did not satisfy France, while after its establishment the **Federal Republic of Germany** argued that it was unfair for its resources to be subject to international control and that the IRA was exporting coal that was needed at home. The **United Kingdom** and the USA sympathized with the West German position, and were unwilling to accept the French argument for constraints upon Ruhr production. In November 1949 the Petersberg Protocol accepted a halt to the dismantling of West German industrial plants, effectively destroying the IRA's purpose. The failure of the IRA, abandoned in 1950, was one factor which made France look favourably upon the **Schuman Plan** as an alternative strategy for retaining an influence upon West German industrial production.

International Space Station. *See* COLUMBUS.

Iparretarak. (Northerners) A Basque terrorist group in **France**. Founded in 1973, it engaged in a bombing campaign against public buildings and property companies it accused of selling land and property to non-Basques, as part of its objective of securing Basque separatism. Banned in 1987, it was widely regarded as possessing close links with **Euskadi ta Askatasuna (ETA)**.

Ireland. A state in Western Europe. After years of struggle, the 1801 Act of Union between Great Britain and Ireland was dissolved by the Anglo-Irish Treaty of December 1921, and an Irish Free State, with dominion status, was established in 1922. The new state, which excluded six northern counties which formed **Northern Ireland**, was rejected by many republicans led by **de Valéra**. After 1932 there began a progressive elimination of the surviving restrictions upon full independence. A new constitution, which refused to acknowledge the partition of the island, was promulgated in 1937. The state remained neutral in the Second World War, and in 1948 Ireland became a sovereign republic, leaving the **Commonwealth**. The principle of neutrality was maintained after 1945. Economic links with the **United Kingdom** were strengthened after a free trade agreement in 1966, and in 1973 Ireland entered the **European Communities (EC)** along with Britain. Since 1932 Irish party politics and government have been dominated by **Fianna Fáil**, with collaboration between all other parties usually being essential to keep it in opposition. The dominant issue in Irish politics has been partition and reunification. After decades of unspoken hostility, dialogue with Northern Irish politicians began in the 1960s. The 1985 **Anglo-Irish Agreement** recognized the Irish right to be consulted on Northern Irish affairs, establishing an inter-governmental conference and co-operation on terrorism. The 1994 **Downing Street Declaration** set in motion a peace process that seemed to offer the best opportunity for an ending to hostility, if not reunification, since 1921. The 1980s also saw a reaction to the traditional political influence of the Catholic Church. Although efforts to legalize abortion and divorce failed, several political and moral scandals weakened the Church.

Irish Republican Army (IRA). A terrorist organization in **Northern Ireland** seeking Irish reunification. Founded in 1919 by **Sinn Féin** as an armed force in the independence struggle, it rejected the Irish Free State and became a terrorist organization after 1924. Outlawed in **Ireland** 1930–32 and again in 1936, it waged a bombing campaign in the **United Kingdom** 1939–40. After Ireland left the **Commonwealth** in 1948, it concentrated on the issue of reunification, but met with little success until the 1960s.

It declared a resumption of hostilities in 1969 after the emergence of large-scale civil rights demonstrations in Northern Ireland, but internal disputes over the role of violence and strategy soon led to a split between Official and Provisional wings. The Marxist-oriented Officials wanted an all-Irish campaign for a united socialist republic, but soon became dormant in the North. The nationalist Provisionals, whose core was in Northern Ireland, sought guerilla warfare to force British withdrawal from the province as a prelude to reunification, and in 1972 denounced a cease-fire announced by the Officials. The bombing and assassination campaign intensified in 1971, and after 1972 was extended to the British mainland, most significantly in 1984 with the bombing of a hotel in Brighton where the Prime Minister, **Thatcher**, and many of her government were staying for a party conference. The British policy of internment without trial introduced in 1971 produced a further backlash of demonstrations, hunger strikes and claims by detainees that they were entitled to a special political status. The IRA was disowned by Irish governments and lost much support in Ireland, but continued to enjoy considerable popular sympathy in its Northern Irish strongholds as well as abroad, especially in the USA. In Northern Ireland its campaign of violence was counterbalanced by a similar one waged by Protestant paramilitary organizations against Catholics. As a result of the 1994 **Downing Street Declaration**, it announced it would suspend all activities in order to permit all-party discussions on the future of the province to take place. Its armed opposition was paralleled by that of smaller breakaway factions such as the Irish National Liberation Army (which seceded in 1975) and the Irish People's Liberation Organization (which seceded in 1987).

Iron curtain. A term popularly used to describe the divide between the Communist regimes of Eastern Europe and the Western democracies. It was used by **Churchill** in a speech at Fulton, Missouri, in March 1946, though he had employed it earlier in a telegram to President Truman. It signified more specifically the border restraints imposed by the Communist regimes upon freedom of movement. In practice, the Curtain was not rigid, and the blanket phrase also tended to obscure significant national variations in behaviour.

Ismay, Lord. (1887–1965) Secretary-General of the **North Atlantic Treaty Organization (NATO)** 1952–57. Born Hastings Lionel Ismay, he pursued a military career, rising to the rank of general and serving as Chief of Staff 1940–46. He received a peerage after retiring from the army in 1946. In 1951 he was appointed to be the first Secretary-General of NATO where he sought to develop the importance of the permanent representatives and the necessity of a good working relationship between the civilian and military elements of the organization. While urging NATO to be an effective defence structure, he opposed giving it any supranational functions.

Istria. *See* TRIESTE.

Italian Communist Party. (*Partito Comunista Italiano – PCI*) A major left-wing party in **Italy**. Illegal during the Fascist period, its **Resistance** activities helped to transform it into a mass movement after 1945 and the second largest party in the country. Under **tripartism** it served in government 1945–47. After moving into opposition, it attempted to use its control of the trade union movement to bring about a Communist revolution. The strategy failed in 1948 and it gradually shifted ground to portray itself as a democratic opposition party, developing the notion of polycentrism (a forerunner of **Eurocommunism**) to justify the propriety of 'an Italian road to socialism'. Its vote increased in every election from 1946 to 1976 when it announced the **historic compromise**, a willingness to collaborate with the leading **Christian Democratic Party (DC)** in government. Although counted as part of the government majority 1976–79, government membership was not forthcoming and it reverted back to opposition. A declining electoral base, the scandals of the late 1980s, and confusion arising from the ending of the **Cold War** and the political changes in Eastern Europe led it to attempt a complete relaunch in 1991 as the Democratic Party of the Left (*Partito Democratico della Sinistra*). With the decay of the old party system, in 1993 it established itself as the core of a broad left-wing alliance. A minority dedicated to Communist ideals opposed the reforms, and seceded to form the Communist Refoundation (*Rifondazione Comunista*).

Italian Liberal Party. (*Partito Liberale Italiano – PLI*) A small conservative party in **Italy**. A continuous member of government coalitions
1947–62, it went into opposition during the following period of centre-left
collaboration, before returning as part of the **Pentapartito** after 1979. Like
other traditional parties, it was badly damaged and effectively destroyed by
the accusations of political corruption that emerged in the 1990s.

Italian Republican Party. (*Partito Repubblicano Italiano – PRI*) A
small centre-left party in **Italy**, arguing for more representative democracy
and local autonomy. Originally formed in 1895, it was reconstituted in 1945.
Between 1947 and 1991 it was an ever-present member of government
coalitions except for the period of the **historic compromise** in the late
1970s.

Italian Social Democratic Party. (*Partito Socialista Democratico
Italiano – PSDI*) A small centre-left party in **Italy**. It was founded by
Saragat in 1947 as a moderate breakaway group from the **Italian Socialist
Party (PSI)** in protest against the PSI decision to form an electoral alliance
with the **Italian Communist Party (PCI)**. Originally called the Socialist
Party of Italian Workers, it changed its name in 1952. Reconciliation with
the PSI occurred in 1966, but policy disagreements led to its reformation as a
separate party in 1969. An ever-present member of government throughout
most of the period after 1947, it rejected a second overture for a merger from
the PSI in 1989, but was later swept away as the traditional party system
collapsed.

Italian Socialist Party. (*Partito Socialista Italiano – PSI*) A left-wing
party in **Italy**. Founded in 1892, it lost out to the **Italian Communist Party
(PCI)** after 1945 as the major representative of the left. Its close alliance with
the PCI led to the secession of the moderate **Italian Social Democratic
Party (PSDI)** in 1947. In the late 1950s it sought a more moderate
alignment, offering an 'opening to the left' to the ruling **Christian Democratic Party (DC)**, officially supporting the government in 1960 and
entering the coalition in 1962. A merger with the PSDI in 1966 broke down
again in 1969. After **Craxi** became party leader in 1976, it sought more
vigorously to become indispensable to government as a way of supplanting
the PCI as the leading left-wing party, a strategy that brought governmental
but not electoral success. Its prestige and support collapsed after 1991 after
accusations that Craxi and other leaders were heavily implicated in the
political and financial scandals that swept the country.

Italian Social Movement–National Right. (*Movimento Sociale Italiano–Destra Nazionale – MSI–DN*) A neofascist party in **Italy** founded as
the MSI in 1946 as a successor to Mussolini's National Fascist Party. In 1973
it merged with, and effectively took over, the smaller monarchist Democratic
Party of Monarchical Unity. Strongly anti-Communist, it enjoyed pockets of

considerable support in the southern half of the country, but apart from a brief attempt to flirt with the **Christian Democratic Party (DC)** in 1960, it was largely shunned by other parties. With the collapse of the DC in the 1990s because of political and financial scandals, it could lay claim to be the leading representative of the right, and in 1994 provided the core of the electorally successful National Alliance (*Alleanza Nazionale*). In 1995 a party congress accepted a leadership proposal to dissolve itself as a separate organization and to 'leave the future' to the Alliance.

Italy. A state in Southern Europe united as a kingdom under the House of Savoy in 1860. A late belligerent in the First World War on the side of the Entente in 1915, disappointment over the peace settlement and fears of the revolutionary left helped the rise of Fascism and the rule of Benito Mussolini, who aligned himself with Hitler in the 1930s. The Allied invasion of Italy in 1943 led to Mussolini's dismissal by the king, and a new government made peace with the Western Allies. In 1946 King Victor Emmanuel abdicated in favour of his son, but three weeks later a referendum voted in favour of a republic. While the post-war state experienced economic reconstruction and growth, especially in its northern provinces, it was characterized by political instability, with frequent changes of government – some 50 administrations within five decades. The brief period of **tripartism** (1945–47) was followed by decades of dominance by the **Christian Democratic Party (DC)** whose internal factional disputes often determined which coalition partners the party would accept, and what policy thrust there would be. DC supremacy and freedom to manoeuvre were limited by the presence of powerful political extremes, the Communists on the left and Neofascists on the right. However, the system proved sufficiently resilient to withstand the challenges of the **Red Brigades** and other terrorist groups after the early 1970s. The domestic Communist threat was a factor that led to Italy becoming a founder member of the **North Atlantic Treaty Organization (NATO)** and of the **European Communities (EC)**. The weakness of government, long DC domination of government, and its claim to be a bulwark against Communism were all factors that led to politics and policy operating in a system of **clientelism**, or patronage. Allegations of political corruption, never far from the surface, erupted in the late 1980s, and within a few years had swept away the old actors, including most of the leading politicians and political parties, though whether this would be sufficient to reform the system remained to be seen.

Izetbegović, Alija. (1925–) President of **Bosnia-Hercegovina** from 1992. A lawyer and writer, and a Muslim, he had been a leading critic of the former Communist regime in **Yugoslavia**, imprisoned for 'pan-Islamic activities' 1946–49, and for 'counter-revolutionary acts' 1983–88. In May 1990 he was elected leader of the newly formed **Democratic Action Party**

(SDA). When it won the December election, he was appointed President of the republic's collective leadership, and reconfirmed in the position after the declaration of independence in March 1992. He faced a struggle to maintain the integrity of the new republic, and was a bitter critic of both the Western arms embargo and United Nations policy in the Bosnian civil war.

J

Jaanilinn. A small territory disputed by **Estonia** and **Russia**. After the annexation of Estonia by the **USSR**, a small stretch of land east of the Narva river was incorporated into the Russian Federation. The post-1991 democratic government in Estonia regarded the territory, which the Russians call Ivangorod, as Estonian, and extreme nationalist groups demanded its return, although its population had become almost entirely Russian.

Jajce Congress. A meeting of the Anti-Fascist National Liberation Committee of **Yugoslavia** in November 1943 to discuss the future of the country. Dominated by Communists, it resolved to create a federal republic, declared itself to be a provisional government, and conferred the title of Marshall upon **Tito**. The Federal People's Republic was established symbolically on the second anniversary of the congress, in November 1945.

Jan Mayen. A small island in the Arctic Ocean and a possession of **Norway** since 1929. With no permanent settlement, it became the source of disputed territorial claims over the sea-bed by **Denmark, Iceland** and Norway in the 1970s. The conflict was caused by the declaration of 200-mile economic zones around **Greenland**, Iceland and Jan Mayen, which had consequences for fishing interests around the island. Iceland and Norway reached agreement in 1980 on fishing rights, and on mineral exploitation of the continental shelf in 1981. The dispute between Denmark and Norway continued until submitted to the International Court of Justice in 1988, with a settlement being reached in 1993.

Jaruzelski, Wojciech. (1923–) Prime Minister of **Poland** 1981–85, and Head of State 1985–89. A professional soldier, he was placed in charge of the army's political education in 1961. He entered Parliament and was admitted to the **Politburo** in 1964. He was Chief of the General Staff 1965–68, and Defence Minister 1968–83. In 1981 the government was faced with a massive wave of unrest spearheaded by the **Solidarity** trade union movement. Unable to quell the protests, and under pressure from the **USSR** to act more decisively, the Politburo invited him to become premier in February 1981. He quickly consolidated his own authority, becoming secretary of the **Polish United Workers' Party** in September. Three months later he carried through a military coup and imposed martial law, lifted only in July 1983. Although his actions displaced the Communist party from its leading role, they were accepted by the USSR and perhaps avoided direct Soviet intervention in Poland. He skilfully handled the unrest, but sought also to check the security forces and to collaborate with the powerful Catholic Church. He gave up the premiership in November 1985, moving to become head of state (Chairman of the Council of State). He did not stand in the way of democratization 1988–89, eventually retiring from office in December 1990. In 1993 he was indicted for actions taken against a workers' protest in the port of Gdynia during his time as Defence Minister.

Jenkins, Roy Harris. (1920–) President of the **Commission** 1977–81. Elected to the British Parliament in 1948 for the **Labour Party**, he occupied several senior positions in Labour governments 1964–70 and 1974–76, overseeing a number of important social reforms and eliminating a large balance of payments deficit. A strong advocate of British membership of the **European Communities (EC)**, he had defied his party in 1971 to vote in the House of Commons to accept the terms of EC entry negotiated by the **Heath** government. In 1976 he was appointed to the Commission, becoming its President. He inherited a stagnant situation caused largely by the difficult economic climate of the 1970s. Although a vigorous president, he was not wholly successful in giving the EC a new momentum, but did persuade it to establish the **European Monetary System (EMS)**. In 1981 he returned to British politics. On the moderate social democratic wing of his party, he had become disillusioned by its progressive radicalization. In 1981 he and some senior colleagues left it to form the **Social Democratic Party (SDP)**. He became chair of the new party, and represented it in Parliament until 1987, after which he supported its proposed merger with the **Liberal Party**. He was made Lord Jenkins of Hillhead in 1988.

John XXIII. (1881–1963) Pope 1958–63. Born Angelo Giuseppe Roncalli and ordained in 1903, he held various **Vatican** posts after 1918, and was appointed a cardinal in 1953. As Pope he sought greater collaboration with other Christian churches, and pursued more liberal social doctrines for the Catholic Church. In 1962 he summoned the Second Ecumenical Vatican Council as a means of advertising and advocating a revitalization of the Church. The Council's endorsement of more liberal parties weakened Catholic unity. A highly popular figure because of his progressive views, he was succeeded by the more conservative **Paul VI**.

John Paul II. (1920–) Pope from 1978. Born Karol Wojtyla in **Poland**, he was ordained in 1946, becoming a bishop in 1958, Archbishop of Cracow in 1963, and a cardinal in 1967. The first non-Italian Pope since 1522, he travelled more extensively than any of his predecessors, including several visits to his native Poland where his presence strengthened popular Catholic opposition to the Communist regime. He was seriously wounded in an assassination attempt in Rome in May 1981, possibly as part of an international conspiracy, and survived a later attempt on his life in **Portugal**. While he supported certain elements of Liberation Theology and democratic principles, his approach to the pontificate was highly conservative. He opposed abortion, birth control and homosexuality, and limited the regional autonomy of the episcopate.

Joint European Torus (JET). The flagship of the nuclear policy of the **European Communities (EC)**, established in 1984 on the basis of a 1978 decision. Based in the **United Kingdom** and funded primarily by the **Commission**, its objective was to develop nuclear fusion as a safer, cleaner and economic energy source than nuclear fission. It collaborated closely with similar institutions in Japan, **Russia** and the USA.

Joint Research Centre (JRC). A collective name for nine institutes within the **European Communities (EC)**, operating under the direction of the **European Atomic Energy Community (EURATOM)**. They extended their focus from an emphasis upon nuclear research to incorporate safety standards, information technology, and environmental protection.

Juan Carlos I. (1938–) King of **Spain** from 1975. A grandson of Alfonso XIII, the last Spanish king, who had abdicated in 1931, he was born in Rome. He was encouraged by **Franco** to return to Spain in 1960, and in July 1969 he was recognized by Franco as heir to the vacant throne. Proclaimed king in November 1975 after Franco's death, he was a firm supporter of democratization and played a positive role in the transition to democracy and constitutional monarchy. In February 1981 he openly attacked an attempted right-wing coup by dissident military officers, refusing to acknowledge or be identified with their objectives. By the 1980s he had made the monarchy a legitimate and popular institution.

Jugoskandić Affair. *See* DAFIMENT AND JUGOSKANDIĆ AFFAIRS.

June Uprising. *See* EAST BERLIN UPRISING.

Jura. A French-speaking region of the canton of Berne in **Switzerland**. Attached to Berne in 1815, it persistently opposed the annexation, but a more sustained demand for separate cantonal status developed only after 1947. The campaign was headed by the Jura Rally (*Rassemblement Jurassien*) which endorsed or rejected politicians of all persuasions rather than establish itself as a distinctive regional political party. Its efforts attracted considerable public support and led to a series of referendums between 1969 and 1975, resulting in the establishment of a new canton of Jura in 1979. However, the canton consisted only of the heavily Catholic northern districts of the region. The predominantly Protestant southern districts voted to remain part of Berne, and the Jura Rally pledged that it would work to win over the south in order to secure the reunification of the Jura.

Justice and Home Affairs (JHA). A pillar of the **European Union**, established by the 1991 **Treaty on European Union**. It was set up as an intergovernmental body distinct from the **European Communities (EC)**, answerable only to the **European Council** within the EC framework, with its decisions to be implemented by the **Council of Ministers**, not the **Commission**. It was a formalization and extension of intergovernmental co-operation developed earlier within the **TREVI** structure.

Justice Party. (*Retsforbundet*) A small centrist party in **Denmark**. It is unique in Europe as a party based upon American economist Henry George's ideas of a single-tax on land values, and stresses libertarianism and individual freedom. It was able to maintain only an erratic foothold in the Danish Parliament, though briefly entering a government coalition in the early 1960s.

Justice Party. (*Adalet Partisi*) A centre-right party in **Turkey**. It was founded in 1961 as a successor to the **Democratic Party** in the restructuring of party life occasioned by the 1960 military coup. Particularly associated with **Demirel**, who was its leader and dominant personality, it adopted a pro-Western and pro-business stance while still seeking to protect Muslim interests. It was dissolved in 1980 after the military coup. When civilian political life was allowed to resume, the ban on previous parties remained, and Demirel reconstituted it as the **True Path Party**.

Justiciable. A term which, under the treaties of the **European Communities (EC)**, describes those matters under dispute which can be submitted to the EC judiciary for arbitration and resolution.

K

Kádár, János. (1912–1989) Secretary-General of the **Hungarian Social Workers' Party** 1956–88, Prime Minister of **Hungary** 1956–58, 1961–65, and President 1988–89. Joining the illegal Workers' Party (Communist) in 1932, he was imprisoned on several occasions before organizing **Resistance movement** activities during the Second World War. Appointed Deputy Chief of Police in 1945 and Minister of the Interior in 1949, he was later arrested by order of **Rákosi** in April 1951, and tortured and imprisoned until 1954. When popular unrest and Soviet pressure forced Rákosi's resignation in July 1956, he was readmitted to the party executive and appointed Secretary-General in October, sharing political power with the new Prime Minister, **Nagy**. At first he supported Nagy's reform programme but soon became concerned that it was going too far too quickly. He left Budapest for Eastern Hungary, returning on 4 November with Soviet forces which crushed the **Hungarian Revolution**. Assuming also the office of Prime Minister, he reintroduced rigid Communist control. After 1959 he began to permit a limited degree of individual expression, and in the 1960s accepted a cautious liberalization and economic reform, but nevertheless supported the **Warsaw Pact** repression of the **Prague Spring** in 1968. In the 1980s he accepted a limited degree of political liberalization at the local level. However, despite his relatively more relaxed regime, pressure for change increased steadily throughout the decade both within and outside the party, and he was replaced as party leader in May 1988, moving instead to the titular position of head of state.

Kalinin, Mikhail Ivanovich. (1875–1946) Soviet head of state 1919–46. A member of the Bolshevik faction since 1903, he was appointed mayor of Petrograd in the October 1917 Revolution. In 1919 he became head of state, though the exact title changed several times. A loyal supporter of **Stalin**, he survived the purges, but was never anything more than a reliable and colourless figurehead.

Kaliningrad. A city and region (*oblast*) in **Russia**, formerly the city of Königsberg in East Prussia, it was annexed by the **USSR** in 1945, and the German population was expelled. It was developed as a major military and naval base closed to outsiders. After the collapse of the USSR in 1991 it remained part of Russia, but was separated from the rest of the country by

241

Poland and **Lithuania**. Still a heavily garrisoned province and the principal base of the former Soviet fleet, but otherwise experiencing severe economic stagnation, it voted heavily for the nationalistic **Liberal Democratic Party** in 1993. Tension increased after 1991 because of the settlement in the region of numbers of ethnic Germans returning from Siberia.

Kania, Stanisław. (1927–) Leader of the **Polish United Workers' Party** 1980–81. After playing an active role in the war-time **Resistance movement**, he joined the party in 1945, working thereafter as a party administrator, mainly within its youth movement. He was promoted to the Central Committee in 1968 and the **Politburo** in 1975. During the political crisis of 1980 caused by the rise of **Solidarity** and a wave of strikes, he successfully argued against the use of force against the workers, gaining a reputation as something of a moderate, which was a factor in his later nomination to replace **Gierek** as party leader. Vaguely sympathetic towards reform, he found it difficult to balance pressure from Solidarity and the hard-line position of members of his own party. His position steadily weakened and he resigned in October 1981, two months before **Jaruzelski** imposed military rule upon **Poland**.

Karadžić, Radovan. (1945–) Bosnian Serb politician. A practising psychiatrist specializing in the treatment of neuroses and depression, he was elected as leader of the new **Serbian Democratic Party (SDS)** which emerged as the major voice of the Serb communities in **Bosnia-Hercegovina**. In December 1992 he was elected President of the self-proclaimed Serbian Republic which seized control of large areas of Bosnia. Directing a government from the small town of Pale, he was the public face of Bosnian Serb defiance of the United Nations in the Bosnian civil war.

Karamanlis, Konstantinos. (1907–) Prime Minister of **Greece** 1955–63, 1974–80, and President 1980–85, 1990–95. A lawyer, he entered Parliament for the Populist Party in 1935, serving in several government positions 1946–55. After the death of **Papagos**, he was appointed Prime Minister by King Paul, who encouraged him to form a new conservative party, the National Radical Union. He successfully gained international aid to help the weak economy, but failed in his bid to join the **European Economic Community (EEC)**. He returned to opposition after the 1964 election, and when power was seized by the **Greek Colonels** in 1967 he refused to collaborate with the new regime, going into voluntary exile in Paris. Invited back after the collapse of the military junta in July 1974 to rebuild parliamentary democracy, he created a new party, **New Democracy**, and in June 1975 introduced a new republican constitution. In 1980 he stood down in order to contest the presidency. Serving with a Socialist government after 1980 he maintained a strictly constitutional interpretation of the presidency, but resigned in 1985 as a protest against the removal by the government of the President's discretionary executive powers. He easily won re-election as President in 1990.

Kardelj, Edward. (1910–1979) Yugoslav politician. A Communist since the 1920s and a close associate of **Tito**, he was the chief theoretician of **Yugoslavia**'s national road to socialism, developing the ideological basis of the social self-management system and the notion of a collegiate presidency to cope with the country's multi-ethnicism. He served as Vice-President 1946–53 and Foreign Minister 1948–53.

Karelia. An autonomous region within **Russia**. Part of **Finland** after the fourteenth century, the eastern areas were mainly lost to Russia in the eighteenth century, but they remained a focus of Finnish nationalist senti- ment after independence in 1917. Finland's rejection of Soviet demands in 1939 for territorial concessions in Western Karelia was a factor in the Soviet invasion that led to the Winter War. Karelia was seized by the **USSR** in 1940 under the Treaty of Moscow and constituted as a Soviet republic. In 1956 it was made an autonomous region within the Russian Soviet Republic. Finnish claims to the area have lapsed, though sentimental attachment to it as a historic Finnish region remained evident, while Karelian exiles and their descendants have called for the restitution of their land and property.

Kekkonen, Urho Kaleva. (1900–1986) Prime Minister of **Finland** 1950–53, 1954–56, and President 1956–81. Entering Parliament in 1935 for the Agrarian Union, he held ministerial office 1936–39, and again in 1944. After leading four government coalitions in the early 1950s, he was elected President in February 1956 in succession to **Paasikivi**. Like his predecessor, he attempted to strike a balance between Finland's independence and links with Western Europe, and assuring the **USSR** that these did not constitute a threat to it or a breach of the 1948 treaty between the two countries. He successfully became a trusted visitor to Moscow and often acted as a conduit to the West for Soviet ideas and proposals about international affairs when the Soviet leadership wished, without committing itself in public, to gauge what the Western reaction might be. In 1980 the USSR awarded him the Lenin Peace Prize. A constitutional amendment was passed in 1970 to enable him to continue as President until 1984, mainly because of his successful relationship with the USSR. While that may have been profitable in foreign affairs, his rather autocratic personality and his attempts to ensure the formation of governments that would be acceptable to the USSR led in the 1970s to greater discontent and a loss of popularity, and he chose to retire in 1981 rather than serve to the end of his term.

Kelly, Petra. (1947–1992) West German politician. Born in **Bavaria**, at the age of 13 she moved with her mother to the USA, where she worked for Hubert Humphrey. Returning to Europe she was employed for a while at the **Commission** in **Brussels**, an experience which hardened her dislike of bureaucracy. She joined the **Social Democratic Party (SPD)** in 1972, but resigned in 1978 because she opposed the pragmatic moderate style of its leader, **Schmidt**. In 1979 she was a co-founder of the **Green Party** and rapidly became internationally known as its major figure. While a drafter of the rotational leadership principle, she turned to oppose it after her election to Parliament in 1983, arguing that it prevented the party from acquiring a base of political experience, and attempts were made to remove her from the party executive. She became steadily more disillusioned with what she regarded as the amateurish and sectarian behaviour of the party, while still trying to hold it together. She lost her parliamentary seat in 1990 and was found, alongside her companion and ex-party colleague, **Bastian**, shot dead in a Bonn apartment in October 1992 in what appeared to be a suicide pact.

Kennedy Round. The sixth series of negotiations on tariff reductions held by the **General Agreement on Tariffs and Trade (GATT)** 1964–67, named in memory of President John F. Kennedy. It was the first time GATT attempted to move beyond manufactured products, and its major European significance was that it marked the emergence of the **European Communities (EC)** as a major economic actor, with the **Commission** serving as the sole representative of and mouthpiece for the EC Member States.

Keynesianism. An economic theory and practice based upon the writings of the British economist, John Maynard Keynes (1883–1946), who in the 1930s had attacked the conventional view that a modern economy would naturally adjust to an operational level of full employment. Keynes argued that aggregate demand (that is, total spending by governments, producers and consumers) was the basic determinant of national income and employment levels and that therefore governments could combat economic depression by encouraging spending, even if this meant they ran deficits. It gave a theoretical rationale and justification for an activist government role in the management of the economy, and after 1945 became almost an article of faith of government thinking in liberal democracies as the key to preventing unemployment. It fell into greater disrepute in the 1970s and 1980s as countries began to experience greater inflation and unemployment simultaneously, with governments seemingly unable to halt the trend. For a while its place seemed to have been taken over by **monetarism**, and it never regained its former undisputed predominance.

KGB. (*Komitet Gosudarstvennoi Bezopasnosti*) The Committee of State Security in the **USSR**, established in 1954 and the last of several name changes to the Cheka secret police established by Lenin in 1917. It was responsible for investigating domestic 'crimes against the state', internal counter-intelligence, and external espionage. Under the leadership of **Andropov** in 1964–82, it developed a highly sophisticated system of control within the USSR and espionage system abroad, and was much feared. After

Gorbachev became Soviet leader in 1985, some of its operations were made public and its range of arbitrary powers restricted. Its senior personnel were divided over Gorbachev's reforms. It was formally dissolved after the disintegration of the USSR, though many of its personnel seemingly continued to perform the same function in **Russia**.

Khrushchev, Nikita Sergeyevich. (1894–1971) Secretary-General of the **Communist Party of the Soviet Union** 1953–64. An active party member since 1919, he rose through its ranks to become premier of the Ukrainian Soviet Republic 1943–47. In 1949 he was appointed by **Stalin** to reorganize and strengthen Soviet agriculture. Within the collective leadership that was established after Stalin's death, he was appointed Party Secretary in September 1953. He used the post to strengthen his own position against **Malenkov**, and placed his own nominee, **Bulganin**, in the premiership in February 1955. He dismissed Bulganin in 1958, assuming the premiership himself. His definition of an **Anti-party group** was a manoeuvre to weaken and destroy possible opponents of his undisputed control. In January 1956 he attacked Stalin and his 'cult of personality' at the **Twentieth Party Congress**, a speech seen abroad as indicative of a willingness to consider some form of **détente**. While willing to seek a relaxation of tension, his peaceful gestures alternated with aggressive threats. Détente did not mean any softening of the division of Europe. While restoring **Gomulka** to power in **Poland**, he reasserted Soviet control and military strength in quelling the 1956 **Hungarian Revolution**. After issuing several threats about the untenable status of West **Berlin**, he endorsed the construction of the **Berlin Wall** in 1961. In October 1962 he came close to war with the USA over the installation of Soviet missiles in Cuba, and after 1961 began a serious ideological dispute with China. At home he attempted some economic modernization, closed some prison camps and introduced regional administrative reforms, but his most ambitious programme of agricultural self-sufficiency was a failure. By 1964 his erratic behaviour, which had threatened war with both the USA and China, combined with Soviet economic problems, led his colleagues, many of whom were resistant to the notion of change, to remove him from office. Stripped of all public and party posts, he lived in retirement outside Moscow until his death.

Kiesinger, Kurt-Georg. (1904–1988) Chancellor of the **Federal Republic of Germany** 1966–69. A lawyer, he joined the Nazi Party in the 1930s, but refused membership of the Guild of National Socialist Lawyers in 1938. Briefly interned by American troops in 1945, but cleared by a denazification court, he was a founding member of the **Christian Democratic Union (CDU)**, representing it in Parliament 1949–58. He then moved to regional politics to become, 1958–66, Minister-President (premier) of his native Baden-Württemberg. Identified with the liberal wing of the CDU, he replaced **Erhard** as Chancellor in 1966. To meet economic problems and the potential challenge of a new extreme right-wing organization, the **National Democratic Party**, he negotiated a **grand coalition** with the **Social Democratic Party (SPD)**. A conciliator rather than an innovator, he led the party into opposition after the 1969 election produced, for the first time since 1949, the possibility of a government without the CDU. He resigned as party leader in 1971.

Kiessling Affair. A political controversy in the **Federal Republic of Germany**. In December 1983 the deputy commander of the **North Atlantic Treaty Organization (NATO)**, General Gunther Kiessling, was dismissed from his posts by the Minister of Defence, **Wörner**, after several counter-intelligence reports suggested that his homosexuality made him a serious security risk. Severe doubts were later placed upon the veracity of the reports, with claims that Kiessling had been framed by rivals within the military. Despite demands for his resignation, Wörner remained in office, and in April 1984 Kiessling was publicly exonerated and reinstated, but subsequently took early retirement with full military honours.

Kinnock, Neil. (1942–) British politician. Entering Parliament in 1970 as a representative of the **Labour Party**, he quickly acquired a reputation as one of the leading representatives of the party's left-wing. Elected party leader in 1983, he subsequently attempted to weaken left-wing influences within the party through organizational reform and policy changes. While the restructuring of the party was largely successful, it failed to bring electoral victory, and after two defeats in 1987 and 1992 he resigned the leadership. In 1994 he was nominated to be a member of the **Commission**.

Klaipeda. *See* MEMEL.

Klaus, Václav. (1941–) Prime Minister of the **Czech Republic** from 1992. An economist and critic of the Communist regime, he was dismissed from his public sector position in 1970 because of his reformist views. He was a member of **Civic Forum**, acting as chair of the organization 1990–91, after which he led it as the reconstituted Civic Democratic Party. After democratization he was appointed vice-premier of **Czechoslovakia** 1989–92. A keen supporter of market reform, he urged a rapid liberalization of the Czechoslovak economy, and was impatient with Slovak concerns about the effect of the reform upon the regional economy and national identity. He led the Czech delegation in the negotiations on the divorce of the two regions of the country, and after 1992 as leader of the Czech Republic he continued his strategy of aligning it politically and economically with the West as quickly as possible.

Klerides, Glavkos. (1919–) President of **Cyprus** from 1993. A lawyer who served with the British Royal Air Force 1940–45, he became a minister in the 1959–60 transitional government, serving after independence as

President (Speaker) of the legislature until 1976, and was also acting President in 1974. He led several Greek Cypriot delegations in discussions with Turkish Cypriots to seek a solution to the island's ethnic problems. He founded the **Democratic Rally** in 1976 as an opposition to **Makarios**, but re-entered Parliament only in 1981. Pro-Western in orientation, he made unsuccessful bids for the presidency in 1983 and 1988 before winning the 1993 election.

Klessheim Declaration. *See* EUROPEAN DEMOCRATIC UNION.

Kohl, Helmut. (1930–) Chancellor of the **Federal Republic of Germany** from 1982. A career politician and member of the **Christian Democratic Union (CDU)**, he entered the regional state legislature of Rhineland-Palatinate (Rheinland-Pfalz) in 1959. He served as chairman of the state CDU 1966–76, and after 1969 was elected premier of the state government. In 1976 he was selected by the national CDU as its candidate for the Chancellorship, effectively becoming nominal leader of the party. Although the CDU lost the election, he entered the national parliament and survived a challenge from the right, led by **Strauss**, who attacked his leadership as colourless. A realignment to the right by the small **Free Democratic Party (FDP)** in 1982 enabled him to become premier of a coalition government. He supported progress towards European integration, often calling for action to establish European union, and built a close working relationship with President **Mitterrand** of **France**.

After the collapse of the Communist regime in the **German Democratic Republic (DDR)** in 1989, he moved quickly, against the doubts and opposition of many, to seek rapid German reunification. In 1990 he secured from the **USSR** an agreement that a united Germany could remain within the **North Atlantic Treaty Organization (NATO)**, and unified the currencies of the two Germanies on a one-to-one basis. The all-German election of 1990 was a personal triumph in the ex-DDR, but his party fared less well in West Germany. Leading the largest democracy in Europe after 1990, his influence became potentially more important, but after establishing a close relationship with the USA, his hesitant stance over the Gulf War, due partly to constitutional limitations on German military involvement abroad, weakened his position. He continued to urge political union in Europe as a way of assuaging worries about German power, and was instrumental in the development of the 1991 **Treaty on European Union**. A convivial yet somewhat remote figure who had successfully neutralized internal challenges to his party leadership, his domestic standing began to erode after 1992 because of the escalating costs on West Germany of reunification, high unemployment in the ex-DDR and a resentment there against a perceived West German takeover, his hesitant response to outbreaks of neo-Nazi violence, and popular worries about some of the implications of European union.

Koivisto, Mauno Henrik. (1923–) President of **Finland** 1981–94; and Prime Minister 1968–70, 1979–81. A banker and a member of the **Finnish Social Democratic Party**, he entered politics in 1957, serving as a government minister 1966–70 and 1972–81, including two spells as premier of centre-left coalition administrations. In September 1981 he was nominated as interim President following the resignation of **Kekkonen**, and won the presidential election the following year despite indications from the **USSR** that he was not its preferred candidate. His election marked the beginning of a change in Finnish foreign policy as he began to follow a more independent line vis-à-vis the USSR, a trend that he could accelerate after 1985. He easily won re-election for a second term in office.

Komarno Declaration. A petition signed by some 3,000 leaders of the Hungarian minority in **Slovakia** in January 1994. It set down the goal of greater autonomy for the minority and outlined proposals for the creation of distinct provinces differentiated along ethnic lines along the southern rim of the country. It created a backlash among Slovak nationalists and was strongly criticized by the government.

Kommandatura. *See* ALLIED KOMMANDATURA.

Koniev, Ivan Stepanovich. (1897–1973) Marshall of the **USSR**. A professional soldier who joined the Bolsheviks in 1917, he survived the military purges of the 1930s to command several army groups during the Second World War, playing a major role in the capture of **Berlin**. In 1946 he was made Commander-in-Chief of Soviet land forces before becoming the first overall commander of the **Warsaw Pact** upon its creation in 1955, a position he held until his retirement.

Kopp Affair. The forced resignation of a government minister in **Switzerland** in December 1988. Elizabeth Kopp of the **Radical Democratic Party** had become the first woman government minister in October 1984. Her resignation followed allegations that she had violated official secrecy by warning her husband, a leading businessman, that a company he was associated with was possibly involved in the laundering of drug money. A special commission was appointed to investigate the allegations, and her parliamentary immunity from prosecution was lifted. She was acquitted in February 1990. The affair involved a widespread discussion on the role of the state, as reports issued in 1989 indicated that some Swiss banks had been unwittingly involved in money laundering and that the government held secret files on almost one million people deemed to be possible threats to state security. In 1993 an investigative commission reported that the security agencies had engaged in surveillance, but almost exclusively against the political left, and that on occasions they had been over-zealous and had conducted themselves unprofessionally.

Koskotas Affair. A banking scandal in **Greece**. In October 1988 Giorgios

Koskotas, the owner of the Bank of Crete, was charged with forging accounts. He escaped to the USA where he was arrested pending extradition. Under questioning about the bank's liabilities, some of his business associates alleged that ministers of the socialist government had accepted bribes to cover up the embezzlement. A more extensive government involvement was alleged by Koskotas in March 1989, when he claimed that **Papandreou** had endorsed a scheme for diverting public funds into party coffers. The scandal split the **Panhellenic Socialist Movement (PASOK)**, seriously damaging its credibility and the reputation of Papandreou. After the June 1989 election a new right-wing government passed a special law in ministerial culpability, and several PASOK ministers, including Papandreou, were indicted. The trials began in 1991, but Koskotas was unable to substantiate most of his allegations. The following year he was sentenced to five years imprisonment, but Papandreou was acquitted.

Kosovo. A region of **Yugoslavia**, and after 1992 of **Serbia**. A semi-autonomous province of Serbia within Yugoslavia, it was an area of some tension. Of symbolic importance to Serbs as the original centre of a Serb state and their ancestral home, its population was primarily Albanian. After riots in 1968 by the Albanian majority against perceived discrimination, the Yugoslav government pursued a policy of promoting ethnic Albanian interests. This in turn provoked resentment among the native Serbs and in the rest of Serbia. Increasing discontent led to further ethnic violence in 1981: the province was placed under military control and the regional Communist leadership was purged. As central Yugoslav authority began to weaken in the late 1980s, the rise to power in Serbia of **Milošević** and his appeal to Serb nationalism led to a stronger emphasis upon Serb interests in the area. He changed the Serb constitution, reducing the powers of the autonomous provinces, and in 1989 forced the Kosovo legislature to cede its powers to Serbia, an act which led to extensive Albanian rioting. In response the Democratic League of Kosovo (*Demokratski Savez Kosovo/Lidhja Demokratike e Kosovës*) was formed as a voice of the Albanian majority. It demanded full autonomy for the region. In 1991 Kosovo voted overwhelmingly in a referendum for independence, and nationalists overwhelmingly won the election of the same year. Both results were declared illegal by Serbia and what remained of federal Yugoslav authority. The hardline Serbian position and military power effectively precluded any attempts by the Albanian population to benefit from the disintegration of Yugoslavia after 1991. The Albanians boycotted the elections organized by Serbia after 1992, and the 'unofficial government' elected in 1991 called for passive resistance to Serb authority and attempted to construct a parallel system of public services.

Kostov, Traicho. (1900–1949) Secretary-General of the **Bulgarian Com-**

munist Party 1940–49. After joining the party in 1920, he spent much of the next 20 years in prison or working underground for the party. Appointed party secretary in 1940, he was later arrested, and in 1942 was imprisoned for life. Partially disabled as a result of his lengthy imprisonments, he was freed in 1944 after the seizure of power by the **Fatherland Front**. Although a close associate of **Dimitrov**, he was suspect in the eyes of many Moscow-trained Communists because he had spent his entire life within **Bulgaria**. After Dimitrov's death, his power began to wane, and he was an early victim of the Stalinist purges conducted by **Chervenkov**. Arrested in 1949 on charges of being an agent of **Tito** and an imperialist spy, he was the only leading Communist to withdraw his confession later in open court and plead not guilty. He was executed in December 1949. He was exonerated and rehabilitated in 1962.

Kosygin, Alexei Nikolayevich. (1904–1980) Soviet Prime Minister 1964–80. Joining the Communist Party in 1927, he became a specialist in industrial economics. Mayor of Leningrad in 1938–39, he was later promoted to the party's Central Committee and appointed Commissar for the Textile Industry. After 1945 he held a variety of official positions before becoming head of the State Economic Planning Commission in 1960. Aligning himself with the opponents of **Khrushchev**, he succeeded the latter as premier in October 1964, collaborating closely with **Brezhnev** and **Gromyko**. His major areas of responsibility were in domestic policy, but his main efforts to decentralize industry and agriculture and to increase the production and availability of consumer goods had only limited success. A loyal party man and follower rather than leader, he eventually retired from public life in October 1980 because of ill-health.

Krajina. An area of southern **Croatia**, bordering **Bosnia-Hercegovina**, possessing a predominantly Serb population. Of strategic importance in that the Serb enclave effectively divided Croatia into two, it held a referendum in August 1990, as Yugoslav authority began to wane, which endorsed autonomy for the area. This claim was rejected by Croat nationalists, and war between the two groups erupted after the declaration of Croat independence. The Serbs, backed by the federal Yugoslav army, successfully resisted Croat forces and declared an independent republic whose ultimate objective was reunion with other Serb states. In July 1995 Croat forces invaded the region. Serb resistance collapsed within a few days. Most of the Serb population fled from the area, which was quickly reintegrated with Croatia.

Kravchuk, Leonid. (1934–) President of **Ukraine** 1991–94. A career party functionary who rose to become Communist leader of the Ukrainian Soviet Socialist Republic, he led the territory to independence after the disintegration of the **USSR**. Involved in disputes with **Russia** over the disposition of ex-Soviet military resources and the secessionist demands of the **Crimea**, and under pressure from the USA to engage in **disarmament** talks because of his inheritance of a large nuclear arsenal, his relatively high external profile was not matched internally. His economic policy was largely a failure, and his attempts to emphasize a separate Ukrainian identity were met with suspicion by the more nationalist western areas, which remembered his Communist past, and with hostility by the more Russified east which wanted reconciliation with Russia. By 1994 his original base in the east had eroded, and although he was successful in attracting western support in the presidential election, he lost to a more pro-Russian candidate, Leonid Kuchma.

Krefeld Appeal. A mass petition in the **Federal Republic of Germany**. Initiated by left-wing groups opposed to the decision by the **North Atlantic Treaty Organization (NATO)** to install intermediate-range nuclear missiles in Western Europe, including in West Germany, it was launched in the city of Krefeld in November 1980. It demanded that the Federal Republic reject the NATO decision, but was drafted in such a way as not to seem openly anti-American. It gained some respectability from the fact that one of the drafters had been **Bastian**, a leading military figure. The most prominent expression of the West German peace movement, by April 1982 it claimed to have almost three million signatures, but its demands were largely ignored by the government.

Kreisky, Bruno. (1911–1990) Chancellor of **Austria** 1970–83. Briefly imprisoned and persecuted for his Jewish origins, he escaped to **Sweden** in 1938, returning to Austria only in 1950 when he renewed his activities in the **Social Democratic Party (SPÖ)**. He served as Foreign Minister 1959–66 in a **grand coalition** government. Appointed party leader in 1967, he became premier of a majority government in 1970. He pursued a foreign policy of active neutrality, easing relationships with his several Communist neighbours, and became a highly respected international statesman who also enjoyed huge prestige at home. In domestic politics he sought to consolidate and expand a comprehensive welfare state system with full employment, wage and price restraint, and market controls. Highly successful in the 1970s, the policies later became more difficult to sustain. Increasing disillusion with the government led to declining support for the party. He chose to retire from politics after a disappointing election in 1983 which forced the party to accept coalition government as the only way of retaining office. In retirement he was an occasional critic of government and party policy.

Kremlinology. A name given to the problem of interpreting Soviet politics from a variety of indirect sources and allusions. Given the secrecy surrounding Soviet decision-making, foreign commentators had to read between the lines to understand the reality of politics, noting, for example, changes in the manner and coverage of a particular politician's speeches, the seating or placement arrangement of leaders at major public occasions, or the coded terminology used by Soviet representatives and leaders.

Krenz, Egon. (1937–) Head of State of the **German Democratic Republic (DDR)** 1989. After a career as an organizer of the youth movement of the **Socialist Unity Party (SED)**, he was admitted to the **Politburo** in 1983, and for a while was widely regarded as the probable successor to **Honecker**. A hard-liner publicly opposed to any relaxation of Communist control, he was nevertheless involved in the moves in the summer of 1989 to remove Honecker from office. Appointed DDR leader in November as someone who might stem the tide of popular protest, he will probably be chiefly remembered as the man who ordered the opening of the **Berlin Wall**. His concessions were not sufficient to satisfy the mounting pressure for change, and doubts about his trustworthiness remained because of his previous reputation. He was forced to resign after only one month in office, and in January 1990 he was expelled from the party, and retired to private life. In 1994 he was indicted on charges relating to the DDR's border and refugee policy.

Kurdistan Workers' Party. (*Partîya Karkerên Kurdistan – PKK*) An extreme left-wing ethnic guerilla organization in **Turkey**. Formed in 1974, its objective was the establishment of an independent and socialist state of Kurdistan which would incorporate all the traditional Kurdish areas of Iran, Iraq, Syria and Turkey. It began a more systematic campaign of bombings, assassinations and abductions in 1984. The object of several major Turkish government offensives, it was exposed to the more intensive Turkish military counter-attacks in 1995.

Kyprianou, Spyros. (1932–) President of **Cyprus** 1977–88. An economist, lawyer and journalist who worked for Cypriot independence in the 1950s, he was a close ally of **Makarios**. After independence he served as Foreign Minister until 1972. A strong critic of the **Greek Colonels** regime and its policies towards Cyprus, after the Turkish invasion of the island he formed the **Democratic Party**. He successfully contested the presidency in 1977, but his personal appeal declined in the 1980s, in part because of opposition to his attempts to pursue a conciliatory line that might end the partition of the island, and he was eventually defeated in 1988.

L

Labour Party. A small left-wing party in **Ireland**. Its ability to consolidate itself was limited initially by the hostility of the powerful Catholic Church to socialism and by the domination of issues of nationalism. Until 1992 its presence in government was as a junior partner in coalition governments with the conservative **Fine Gael** party. From 1992 to 1994, partly as a result of increased electoral strength, it was accepted for the first time as a coalition partner by the largest party, the centre-left **Fianna Fáil**.

Labour Party. (*Partit tal Haddiema*) A major left-wing party in **Malta**, founded in 1921. It formed single party governments 1947–50, 1955–58 and 1971–87. Under the strong leadership of **Mintoff** 1950–84 it was firmly anti-colonialist and hostile to continued British influence in the island, seeking a more neutralist position and cultivating relationships with the Communist world and with Libya. By the 1990s it had shifted position to accept more readily a future in Europe.

Labour Party. (*Partij van der Arbeid – PvdA*) A major left-wing party in the **Netherlands**. Founded in 1946 as the successor to the pre-war Social Democratic Workers' Party (founded in 1894), it was the major alternative to the domination of Dutch politics by religious parties. It was widely regarded as a key element of the Dutch version of **consociational democracy** and a frequent participant in coalition governments. When the religious parties began to decline in the 1960s, it adopted a more radical stance in order to serve as the locus of a broad left-wing coalition, but this led to a secession of moderate members, and it subsequently returned to a more centrist and consensual orientation.

Labour Party. (*Det Norske Arbeiderpartiet – DNA*) The major political party in **Norway** since the 1930s. In power 1935–63, it built up a welfare state and largely determined the post-war agenda of Norwegian politics. Despite a wariness of international ties, it committed Norway to membership of the **North Atlantic Treaty Organization (NATO)**, in the 1950s expelling members opposed to the Atlantic alliance. It lost its absolute majority in 1961, but refused to consider coalition with other parties. After 1971 the inability of the non-socialist parties to collaborate on a long-term basis enabled it to form several minority administrations. In 1972 and again in

1994 the leadership's commitment to joining the **European Communities (EC)** was rejected in referendums by many of its supporters.

Labour Party. (*Partei der Arbeid/Parti Suisse de Travail – PdA/PST*) A small left-wing party in **Switzerland** formed in 1944 by a merger of the previously illegal Communist Party with left-wing Socialists. It failed to command significant support and found itself confined primarily to some French-speaking areas.

Labour Party. The major left-wing party in the **United Kingdom**, formed in 1900 and adopting its present name in 1906. After forming minority governments in 1924 and 1929–31, it won a large majority in 1945, proceeding to introduce widespread socio-economic reforms. In opposition 1951–64 it began to experience internal tensions between moderates and those more committed to socialism, though the main area of contention was unilateral disarmament. In power 1964–70 it failed to remedy economic problems though passing much social legislation. Returning to government in 1974 as a minority administration, it had to struggle with severe economic and financial problems, and the leadership faced strong left-wing challenges over internal party democracy, socialist measures, and disarmament. Its loss of influence over the trade unions and the so-called **Winter of Discontent** of union action cost it the 1979 election. In 1980 the left-wing won control of the party, leading to the defection of some right-wing leaders to form the **Social Democratic Party (SDP)**, and in 1983 to its worst electoral performance since 1931. Under the leadership of **Kinnock** the party slowly began to control left-wing influences and underwent a re-examination of its principles and commitments, but this was insufficient to gain electoral victory. The push towards the centre was continued in the 1990s by Kinnock's successors, John Smith and Tony Blair.

Labour Union. (*Unia Pracy – UP*) A political party in **Poland**. With roots in the political wing of **Solidarity**, it was formed in 1992 as a merger of several smaller groups. It presented a moderate left profile that urged caution in the move towards a market economy, with a greater stress upon social welfare, but it remained a minor force in the fragmented system.

Lafontaine, Oskar. (1943–) West German politician. Joining the **Social Democratic Party (SPD)** in 1966, he became party leader in the **Saarland** in 1977 and premier of the province in 1985. Identified as a member of the New Left of the party and a supporter of environmental protection, disarmament and abandonment of a nuclear energy programme, he was seen as the standard-bearer of the party left, whose support gained him nomination as the SPD Chancellor-candidate in 1990, but his controversial pronouncements limited his appeal outside left-wing circles. He was critical of the headlong rush towards speedy reunification, but his warnings went largely unheeded and he failed to reverse the party's fortunes in the 1991 all-German elections.

Lambsdorff, Otto Graf. (1926–) West German politician. Joining the **Free Democratic Party (FDP)** in 1951, he entered Parliament in 1971 after a career in banking and insurance. In 1977 he was appointed Minister of Economics. In 1982 he openly criticized the economic policies of the major coalition partner, the **Social Democratic Party (SPD)**, in a letter to the Chancellor, **Schmidt**, and set down conditions that the SPD should accept. When the conditions were rejected by Schmidt, the FDP switched to support a centre-right government, with Lambsdorff continuing in office. After allegations implicating him in the **Flick Affair**, he resigned his office in 1984, but was cleared of all impropriety at a subsequent trial. A strong supporter of free market principles and on the right of the FDP, he served as party leader 1988–93.

Landsbergis, Vytautas. (1932–) President of **Lithuania** 1990–92. A musicologist who had also published biographies of several Lithuanian composers, he joined the new **Sąjūdis** in 1988, rapidly becoming its major representative and leader, and the symbol of Lithuanian nationalist determination to break free of the **USSR**. Elected president of the regional parliament after the 1990 multi-party elections, he became the first leader of an independent Lithuania in 1991. His unyielding nationalist stance and unsuccessful economic policy produced defeat in 1992. The following year he became leader of the Homeland Union, which succeeded Sąjūdis.

Lange, Halvard. (1902–1970) Norwegian politician. He worked as a full-time administrator for the **Labour Party** after leaving university. Active in the **Resistance**, he was arrested in 1940 and again in 1942, being sent to a prison camp in Germany. In 1945 he was appointed Foreign Minister in succession to **Lie**, a position he held for the next 20 years. Initially favouring neutrality for **Norway** and the role of a bridge-builder between East and West, he soon became alarmed by a possible Soviet threat and argued that membership of the **North Atlantic Treaty Organization (NATO)** was essential. Very much the strong man of the party, aligned with its dominant moderate wing, he retired from politics in 1969.

Laniel, Jean. (1889–1975) Prime Minister of **France** 1953–54. A businessman, he first entered Parliament in 1932 for the **Radical Republican and Radical Socialist Party**. During the Second World War he worked for the **Resistance movement**. Relatively unknown outside the legislature, he was appointed premier of a coalition government after a five-week parliamentary crisis which had led France to be called 'the sick man of Europe'. He encouraged investment in industrial development and stabilized the ailing currency, but his premiership coincided with the crisis in **French Indo-China**, and he was forced to resign three days after the fall of **Dien Bien Phu**.

La Rete. (*The Network*) A protest party in **Italy**. It was formed in 1990 by a splinter group of the **Christian Democratic Party (DC)** in Sicily, to mobilize 'civil society' against political corruption and the criminal activities of the **Mafia**. Its founder and inspiration was the former Mayor of Palermo, Leoluca Orlando, who had led a personal crusade against the network. Supported by liberal elements of the Catholic Church and other reformers, Orlando attempted to establish it as a national party in 1992, but it failed to advance much beyond its original core areas.

Latvia. A **Baltic state** annexed by **Russia** in the eighteenth century. It declared its independence in April 1918, gaining international recognition in 1921. Its economy suffered from the loss of the Russian market and with the great depression Karlis Ulmanis of the leading Agrarian Party suspended the constitution and established an authoritarian dictatorship. After the 1939 Nazi–Soviet Pact Latvia was occupied by the **USSR** in June 1940. Captured by Germany in 1941 and held until October 1944, it was retaken by the USSR which declared it a constituent Soviet republic. Latvian nationalism was suppressed and large-scale Russian immigration encouraged, especially after the 1960s. The Soviet claims to sovereignty were never recognized by the West. One of the more prosperous regions of the USSR, in the late 1980s it began to experience a resurgence of national sentiment, expressed at first in Lutheran church services. More open demonstrations broke out in 1989, and the following May the Latvian Supreme Soviet demanded independence from the USSR and the restoration of the 1922 Latvian constitution. After tense negotiations, and with strong opposition from the substantial Russian population in Latvia, the USSR was forced to cede independence in 1991 after an abortive coup by Communist hardliners. The new state introduced market reforms and sought to strengthen economic and political ties with Western Europe, but problems arose because of Latvian determination to deny citizenship to almost the whole of the large Russian minority, a policy which strained further relationships with Russia. The final withdrawal of Soviet troops from Latvia was completed in August 1994.

Latvian Way. (*Latvijas Ceļš – LC*) A centre-right party in **Latvia**, formed in 1993 out of the reformist and pro-independence Popular Front which had won the 1990 multi-party Soviet elections in the region. It became the government party after the 1993 election.

League for Economic Co-operation in Europe. *See* EUROPEAN LEAGUE FOR ECONOMIC CO-OPERATION.

League of Communists of Yugoslavia. (*Savez Komunista Jugoslavija – SKJ*) The ruling party of **Yugoslavia**. Founded as the Communist Party in 1919, the League title and structure were introduced in 1982 to reflect the ethnic diversity of the country and the federal structure set up earlier by **Tito** to compensate for the end of his personal rule which would come with his death. It was also intended to mark a change in the relationship between party and state, with the former giving up direct responsibility for running the country. Party members were to be responsible primarily for education rather than direction. The party was divided into eight regional organizations with a collective leadership, the head of which would rotate across the regions. Rather than providing cohesion, the structure encouraged fragmentation and inter-ethnic disputes, since personal party careers became dependent upon regional power bases rather than a national organization. After several years of quarrelling, tensions heightened when the League in **Croatia** openly espoused Croatian nationalism. The end of the SKJ as an effective organization came in 1990 when the party in **Slovenia** walked out of the organization and declared for independence. The crumbling of the party heralded the disintegration of the state.

Lecanuet, Jean François. (1920–) French politician. A **Resistance** activist, in 1944 he joined the new **Popular Republican Movement (MRP)**, serving as a parliamentary deputy 1951–55. In 1965 he put himself forward as a presidential candidate, hoping to rally what was left of a decaying MRP to act as the focus of a centrist coalition against **de Gaulle**. He later formed the Centre Democrats with the same centrist objective in mind. While failing in his purpose, he laid some of the groundwork for the later alliance led in the 1970s by **Giscard d'Estaing**.

Lefèvre, Théo. (1914–1973) Prime Minister of **Belgium** 1961–65. A lawyer who worked for the **Resistance movement**, he entered Parliament in 1946 for the **Christian Social Party**, becoming party leader in 1950. Strongly pro-European, he supported the integration moves of the 1950s, and as premier was a leading critic of the European policy followed by **de Gaulle**. His premiership coincided with the escalation of linguistic problems. Committed to the preservation of the unitary state, he attempted to defuse the issue by accepting the notion of linguistic frontiers and restrictions on the expansion of **Brussels** into the Flemish countryside. He also reinforced the teaching of Flemish as well as French in schools and the right to use either language in the public service. His policies were the first of several which, over the coming decades, failed to halt the politicization of the language divide.

Left Party–Communists. (*Vänsterpartiet-Kommunisterna – VpK*) A small left-wing party in **Sweden**. Originally the Communist Party, it changed its name in the late 1950s in order to become more attractive to left-wing Socialists, and after 1970 was willing to support minority **Social Democratic Labour** governments. In 1990 it voted to drop 'Communist' from its title.

Left Radical Movement. (*Mouvement des Radicaux de Gauche – MRG*) A centre-left party in **France**, founded in 1972 by left-wing members of the **Radical Republican and Radical Socialist Party** who supported the common programme of government of the left. It aligned itself with the

Socialist Party (PS) in 1981 and gained some ministerial positions in PS governments in the 1980s, which gave it a greater influence than its weak electoral support would merit.

Left Unity (CG). A cross-national **party group** in the **European Parliament (EP)**. It was formed after the 1989 EP elections as a result of a split in the **Communist and Allies** group. It consisted of those members who rejected **Eurocommunism** and insisted upon loyalty to Marxist-Leninist principles. It was dominated by members of the **French Communist Party (PCF)**. In 1994 its survivors reformed as the **Confederal European United Left**.

Left-Wing Alliance. (*Vasemmistoliitto*) A small left-wing party in **Finland**. It was formed in April 1990 as an attempt to reunite Communists and left-wing Socialists. It was a merger of the **Finnish Communist Party** (including the dissident Finnish Communist Party-Unity), the **Finnish People's Democratic League**, and the **Democratic Alternative**, but scars left by earlier ideological arguments and conflicts hindered its effectiveness and appeal.

Legal Personality. A legal concept meaning that a collective body has the right under international law to take autonomous actions rather than relying upon governments to act on its behalf. The **Treaty of Rome** conferred legal personality upon the **European Communities (EC)**, giving them the right to act in law as an independent authority and to enter into legally binding agreements.

Lemass, Sean. (1899–1971) Prime Minister of **Ireland** 1959–66. An active participant in the struggle for independence and involved in the 1916 Easter Uprising, he joined the **Irish Republican Army (IRA)**. He sided with **de Valéra** in rejecting the Irish Free State, and in 1932 became the youngest member of the **Fianna Fáil** government. The unanimous choice to succeed de Valéra in 1959, he sought a more pragmatic policy, diluting his predecessor's insistence upon economic self-sufficiency and directive economic programmes, agreeing to establish the Anglo-Irish Free Trade Area. He also sought to open a dialogue on **Northern Ireland**, meeting with his **Stormont** counterpart, **O'Neill**. He resigned as premier and party leader in 1966, retiring from politics in 1969.

Leningrad Case. A purge in the **USSR** in 1949 of former associates of **Zhdanov**. It resulted in the execution of almost all the previous Communist leadership of the Leningrad region, as well as of many others associated in some way with the region. In 1956 **Khrushchev** declared that the purge had been organized on the basis of evidence fabricated by **Beria**, but in 1961 it was claimed that the action had been initiated by **Malenkov** who had been Zhdanov's main rival for the position as heir-apparent to **Stalin**.

Leone, Giovanni. (1908–) President of **Italy** 1971–78. A founder member of the **Christian Democratic Party (DC)** and co-author of the post-war Constitution, he was elected to Parliament in 1946. A conservative identified with the right-wing of the party, he served briefly as Prime Minister in 1963 and 1968 before being elected to the presidency in 1971. His election was contentious, breaking previous traditions of seeking a broad consensus for the ceremonial but politically sensitive office, since his nomination was opposed by all the left of centre parties. He resigned in 1978 after newspaper allegations that he had accepted bribes from officials of the American Lockheed company who were trying to sell their new Hercules aircraft to the Italian airforce.

Leopold III. (1901–1983) King of the Belgians 1934–51. During the Second World War he took command of the Belgian army in May 1940, ordering a cease-fire. When the Prime Minister called upon Belgians to continue to resist, he refused to follow the government into exile. Imprisoned by the German occupation authorities, he was subsequently released, and went to **Switzerland** in May 1945. He denied allegations that he had been a collaborator, and rejected the several calls that he should abdicate. In January 1946 the government turned down his request for a referendum on the question of him retaining the crown. The royal crisis persisted for several years. The political right and **Flanders** were broadly in favour of his return, while the left and **Wallonia** wished his abdication. He returned to **Belgium** in July 1950 after a narrow referendum victory in his favour, but the resulting riots were so serious that within a week he announced his intention to abdicate. In July 1951 he was succeeded by his son, Baudouin.

Le Pen, Jean-Marie. (1928–) French politician. A paratrooper who had served in **French Indo-China** and in Algeria, he was the youngest deputy when he entered Parliament in 1956 as a **Poujadist**. He later founded the National Front for French Algeria in 1960, but left the legislature in 1962. After a decade of relative obscurity, he founded the **National Front (FN)** in 1972, putting himself forward as a presidential candidate in 1974 and 1988. He returned to Parliament 1986–88, and was elected to the **European Parliament (EP)** in 1989, where he became the leading force of the **European Right**. The leader and dominant personality of the FN, he preached a consistent extreme right-wing philosophy, including strong racialist attacks on immigrants and ethnic minorities. Ostracized by most mainstream politicians, he became for many the major symbol of a perceived resurgence of neo-Fascism in Europe.

Liberal Alliance of Montenegro. (*Liberalni Savez Crne Gore – LSCG*) A political party in **Yugoslavia**, formed in 1990 as a regionalist movement in **Montenegro**. Centrist in orientation, it argued for a rapid transformation to a fully market-based economy.

Liberal, Democratic and Reformist Group (LDR). A cross-national **party group** in the **European Parliament (EP)**. Formed in 1974 as a broadly centrist grouping, it was a heterogeneous formation of moderate conservatives and progressives, a marriage that made it one of the least cohesive groups in the EP.

Liberal Democratic Party. An extreme right-wing populist party in **Russia**. Founded in 1992 by the flamboyant demagogue, **Zhirinovsky**, its electoral popularity surprised and alarmed many people. Zhirinovsky preached a message of Slavic supremacy, demanding the Russian reconquest of all former Soviet and Tsarist territories and the elimination of all alien influences and foreigners from Russia. Its nationalist appeal proved electorally attractive.

Liberal Democratic Party. (*Liberalna Demokratična Strana – LDS*) A political party in **Slovenia**, founded in 1990. It came out of the youth section of the Slovenian **League of Communists**, which had agitated for political reforms since the early 1980s. It established itself as the largest party in the new state in 1992, and in 1994, after absorbing several small centre-left parties, it renamed itself the Liberal Democratic Party of Slovenia (*Liberalna Demokracija Slovenije*).

Liberal Democratic Party of Germany. (*Liberal-Demokratisch Partei Deutschlands – LDPD*) A small party in the **German Democratic Republic (DDR)** allied to the **Socialist Unity Party (SED)**. Founded in 1945 as a liberal grouping, it was soon subordinated by the SED, and survived only as a means of organizing white collar and professional groups behind the SED and the regime. In 1989 its leader, Manfred Gerlach, was one of the first politicians in the DDR to argue for reform, but the party was too compromised by its past to be successful after Communist rule collapsed. In 1990 its remnants moved towards becoming part of the West German **Free Democratic Party (FDP)**.

Liberal Forum. *See* FREEDOM PARTY OF AUSTRIA.

Liberal Party. (*Venstre*) A centre-right party in **Denmark**. For much of its history it was dominated by, and was the mouthpiece of, agricultural interests, and was widely regarded as an agrarian party. The farming influence within the party began to decline after 1970. It generally favoured collaboration with other non-socialist parties.

Liberal Party. (*Venstre*) A small centrist party in **Norway**. The survivor of the great nineteenth century liberal coalition, it saw itself after 1945 as the hinge of the party system, but its support was never required by the major **Labour Party**. Its collaboration with other non-socialist parties and participation in coalition governments after 1963 was not liked by many members. It split into two independent factions in 1972 over the issue of **European Communities (EC)** membership, declining rapidly to lose all parliamentary representation by 1985, although the two factions reunited in 1988. It returned to Parliament in 1993.

Liberal Party. A small centre-left party in the **United Kingdom**. Once the major alternative to the **Conservative Party**, it declined rapidly after 1918 to third party status. Under the leadership of Jo Grimond, it attempted after the mid-1950s to redefine itself as a moderate left-wing alternative to the **Labour Party**, with which it formed a pact in March 1977, agreeing to support the minority **Callaghan** government in return for prior consultation over policy. Never popular with many members, the pact was abandoned the following May. In 1981 it accepted an electoral alliance with the new **Social Democratic Party (SDP)**, and the two amalgamated in 1988 as the **Social and Liberal Democratic Party**.

Liberal Party of Switzerland. (*Liberale Partei der Schweiz/Parti Libéral Suisse – LP/PL*) A small centre-left party in **Switzerland**. It adopted its present name in 1977, but has always been essentially an alliance of regional liberal parties in only a few western cantons, and it has argued strongly for the defence of cantonal and linguistic rights.

Liberal Reform Party. (*Parti Reformateur Libéral – PRL*) A centre-right party in **Belgium**, representing the French-speaking segments of the old Belgian Liberal Party. It was formed as a separate organization in 1974 by a merger of the regional Liberal organizations in **Brussels** and **Wallonia**, and in 1979 absorbed some elements of the former Walloon Rally. While it supported a federal structure for Belgium, it wanted a single regional legislature to represent both Brussels and Wallonia, something which other French-speaking parties tended to reject. It continued to collaborate on many issues with its Flemish counterpart.

Lie, Trygve Halfdan. (1896–1968) Secretary-General of the United Nations (UN) 1946–53. A lawyer, he joined the Norwegian **Labour Party** in 1913, eventually becoming its chief legal adviser, and holding several government positions 1935–46, including the foreign ministry during the Second World War. He was a compromise choice as the UN's first Secretary-General in 1946. He had to struggle against Soviet hostility, especially after he took the lead in June 1950 to organize UN forces for the defence of South Korea. Although re-elected in 1951 for a second term of office, he chose to resign in March 1953, returning to domestic Norwegian politics. His resignation created a constitutional crisis in the UN, which took seven months to agree upon a successor.

Liechtenstein. A constitutional and hereditary principality established in 1719. Part of the German Confederation 1815–68, it then opted for permanent neutrality. A democratic system was established in 1921, but women were not granted the right to vote until 1984. After 1918 responsibility for its diplomatic relations passed from **Austria** to **Switzerland**, with which it developed a **customs union** and common currency in 1923. In 1992 it voted to become part of the **European Economic Area (EEA)** after the latter had been rejected by a Swiss referendum, an act which would lead to a revision of the 1923 union. Since 1938 it has been governed by a permanent coalition of the **Fatherland Union** and the **Progressive Citizens' Party**.

Ligachev, Yegor. (1920–) Soviet politician. He joined the Communist Party in 1944. Trained as an engineer, he worked as a party and state administrator after 1949. In the late 1980s he acquired a reputation as a defender of Communist orthodoxy, emerging as the leading critic of the reforms proposed by **Gorbachev**. Although his views were shared by many in the party, he did not enjoy much personal popularity, and in 1990 he retired from political life, leaving Moscow to live in Tomsk, Siberia.

Lilov, Aleksandur Vasilev. (1933–) Bulgarian politician. Becoming Secretary of the Central committee of the **Bulgarian Communist Party** in 1972 and a **Politburo** member in 1974, he was widely regarded as a possible heir to **Zhivkov**, despite having acquired a liberal reputation. He was abruptly dismissed from his posts in 1983, seemingly for criticizing Zhivkov's cult of personality. He was reappointed in 1989 after Zhivkov's dismissal, and in February 1990, as a reformer relatively untainted by the past, was made party leader. He then tended to oppose rapid economic reform and party restructuring, and was replaced as leader in December 1991.

Lingua. A programe for supporting and developing the teaching of **European Communities (EC)** languages to schoolchildren as part of a strategy for increasing European cultural cohesion and unity. First proposed in 1984, it was adopted in 1989, but the **United Kingdom** refused to participate in the programme on constitutional grounds.

Lisbon Force Goals. A decision by the **North Atlantic Treaty Organization (NATO)** in Lisbon in 1952 to increase its conventional forces to a level capable of repelling a Soviet invasion of Western Europe. It was in line with NATO's original assumptions in 1949, and envisaged a planned doubling of NATO forces within two years. The European members were reluctant to divert resources from economic investment and social welfare provisions, and in 1953 the incoming Eisenhower administration in the USA feared that the scale of increase in conventional armaments would produce inflationary pressures, and the Goals were abandoned. NATO then switched to an emphasis upon nuclear defence and the adoption of **massive retaliation** in 1954. NATO's conventional forces were thereafter viewed more as a symbolic warning to the **USSR** of the risks of an invasion of Western Europe.

Lithuania. A **Baltic state** annexed by **Russia** 1793–1917. It declared its independence in 1918, but lost its historic capital, Vilna, to **Poland**. An authoritarian government under Antanas Smetona seized power in 1923. A mutual assistance pact with the **USSR** in October 1939 permitted the return of Vilna on condition that the city house a Soviet garrison. Continued Soviet pressure led the national assembly to vote for incorporation into the USSR in July 1940, and in August it was declared a constituent Soviet republic, although it was occupied by Germany from 1941–44. Despite Soviet control, national sentiment, identified with the Catholic religion, persisted, and there were serious riots in 1956 and 1972 demanding religious and political freedom. Dissident movements survived throughout the 1960s and 1970s, but became more outspoken in the late 1980s, and in October 1988 widespread demonstrations demanded greater autonomy, leading to the formation of a nationalist movement, **Sąjūdis**. The nationalists won a majority of seats in the March 1990 regional elections, and unilaterally declared independence. The USSR rejected the claim as illegal, and responded with an economic blockade and threat of military intervention. In December the Lithuanian Communists broke with the **Communist Party of the Soviet Union**, criticizing past Soviet policies, and the following year renamed itself the Lithuanian Democratic Labour Party (*Lietuvos Demokratinė Darbo Partija – LDDP*). After negotiations had reduced the level of tension, in 1991 the USSR was forced to accept the secession of Lithuania. The Sąjūdis government struggled to maintain its unity and to introduce a range of market reforms. Internal disarray and popular discontent with economic dislocation led to electoral victory in 1992 for the reformed Communists under **Brazauskas**, who stressed their commitment to economic reform.

Live Differently. (*Anders Gaan Leven – AGALEV*) A small and mainly urban environmentalist party in **Belgium**. It was founded in 1982 as a Flemish organization, but was prepared to contest elections jointly with the French-speaking **Ecology Party**.

Lombardy League. (*Lega Lombarda*) A populist protest movement in **Italy**. Founded in 1979 by **Bossi**, who became its Secretary and leader, and Luigi Moretti, it attacked government centralization, inefficiency, and subsidization of the South. It demanded the extensive federalization of Italy, and even independence for the northern provinces. Its support increased substantially in the late 1980s, becoming a major political force in Piedmont and the Veneto as well as Lombardy, and it formed the core of the **Northern League** after 1991.

Lomé Convention. An economic trading agreement between the **European Communities (EC)** and the group of developing countries, all ex-colonies of EC states, known as the **African, Caribbean and Pacific (ACP) States**. Signed in 1975, it replaced the earlier and more limited **Yaoundé Convention**. It allowed most ACP exports duty-free access to the EC on a non-reciprocal basis, though textiles and agriculture were excluded, and it created a mechanism for development aid to be given to the ACP states in the form of grants from the **European Development Fund (EDF)** and low-interest loans from the **European Investment Bank (EIB)**. A **Centre for the Development of Industry (CDI)** was also established to assist ACP industrial development. The Convention was renewed and modified in 1979, 1984 and 1989.

London Agreement. An agreement in June 1961 whereby those members of the **European Free Trade Association (EFTA)** which had declared an intention to apply for membership of the **European Communities (EC)** pledged to take the interests of their EFTA partners into account in the negotiations and to reject terms of entry unless satisfactory safeguards were offered to the remaining EFTA states. No mention of the Agreement was made when the applications for EC entry were renewed in 1967 and 1970.

London Club. *See* PARIS CLUB.

London Declaration. A statement issued in July 1990 after a meeting of the government leaders of the members of the **North Atlantic Treaty Organization (NATO)**. It stated that in light of the events in Eastern Europe and the **USSR**, NATO would offer friendship to, and establish diplomatic links with, Eastern European countries. It also called upon all members of the **Conference on Security and Co-operation in Europe (CSCE)** jointly to affirm a commitment to non-aggression.

London Six-Power Conference. A series of meetings between February and June 1948, between representatives of **Belgium**, **France**, **Luxembourg**, the **Netherlands**, the **United Kingdom**, and the USA. Its objective was to conduct a broad review of economic, military and political questions within the context of American–European relations. It laid the groundwork for a Western strategy to counteract possible threats from the **USSR**, and agreed on measures to stimulate Western European economic recovery. In March it accepted the creation of a West German state, and the European participants signed the **Treaty of Brussels**.

Long-Term Defence Programme. An abortive policy adopted by the **North Atlantic Treaty Organization (NATO)** in 1977. Its objective was to offset the conventional arms superiority of the **Warsaw Pact**, with NATO members agreeing to commit themselves to an annual increase in defence expenditure of 3 per cent in real terms through to 1985. It failed because most countries did not honour the commitment, with only the **United Kingdom** and the USA attempting to sustain the increases.

Lottizzazione. (Allocation) A word describing the system of patronage in **Italy** in which senior positions in the public sector – one of the largest in Western Europe – were distributed to members and nominees of the political parties. Its heyday was in the 1980s. It was a major target of the wave of anti-corruption sentiment which in the 1990s destroyed the traditional party system. (*See also* CLIENTELISM, PARTITOCRAZIA.)

Lubbers, Rudolphus Francescus Maria. (1939–) Prime Minister of the **Netherlands** 1982–86, 1989–94. An economist and businessman who entered government in 1973, he was one of the political leaders responsible for a merging of the three major Dutch religious parties, becoming leader of the resulting **Christian Democratic Appeal (CDA)** in 1978. Active in European integration, he also advocated a **European Energy Charter** to assist the new democracies of Eastern Europe. In 1991 he was responsible for organizing the agenda and the meeting of the **European Council** that adopted the **Treaty on European Union**. In 1991 he became the longest-serving Dutch premier, but stood down from Parliament in 1994.

Lübke, Heinrich. (1894–1972) President of the **Federal Republic of Germany** 1959–69. He first entered politics in 1931 as a representative of the Catholic Centre Party in the Prussian Parliament. Arrested several times by the Nazi regime, he founded the Westphalian branch of the **Christian Democratic Union (CDU)** after 1945. From 1947 to 1952 he remained in regional politics before serving as a government minister 1953–59. As President he was criticized for being too partisan on occasions, but in 1965, when he was re-elected for a second term, he indicated his strong preference for a **grand coalition** government.

Luca, Vasily. (1898–1963) Romanian Communist. He joined the party in 1922 and spent much of the inter-war period in prison. Released by the Soviet army in 1940 when it occupied Northern **Bukovina**, he went to Moscow. He returned to **Romania** in 1944 to become, along with **Gheorghiu-Dej** and **Pauker**, one of the ruling Communist triumvirate. But after greater power had been gathered by Gheorghiu-Dej, he was suddenly stripped of all offices in 1952, arrested and sentenced to death. In 1954 the sentence was commuted to life imprisonment. He was rehabilitated in 1968, five years after his death.

Lucona Affair. A political scandal in **Austria**, arising from the sinking of the Lucona freighter in 1977. Its charterer, Udo Proksch, a close friend of **Socialist Party of Austria (SPÖ)** ministers and leaders, claimed it contained a uranium treatment plant. It was later discovered that the ship had only a cargo of scrap metal, and in 1985 Proksch was arrested for making a fraudulent insurance claim. He was released after producing satisfactory documentation, but was re-arrested in 1989 when this too was found to have been falsified. A parliamentary inquiry in June 1989 criticized the role of leading SPÖ politicians for hindering the police investigations, suppressing relevant files, providing incomplete information to Parliament, and disciplining officials working on the inquiry. Some party leaders resigned as the result of a scandal that damaged government and political stability. Proksch was found guilty in March 1991.

Lukanov, Andrei Karlov. (1938–) Prime Minister of **Bulgaria** 1990–92. After a career as an administrator in the foreign trade sector, he acquired a reputation for pragmatism and flexibility, and was promoted to a deputy premiership in 1976. In 1989 he became Minister of Foreign Economic Relations, aligning himself with the faction in the **Bulgarian Communist Party** opposed to **Zhivkov**. His appointment as premier was regarded by reformist and dissident groups as an indication that the party was changing course away from Communist orthodoxy, although he strove to maintain the supremacy of the party. He was arrested in July 1992 and accused of misappropriating public funds.

Luns, Joseph Marie Antoine Hubert. (1911–) Secretary-General of the **North Atlantic Treaty Organization (NATO)** 1971–84. A long-serving (1952–71) Foreign Minister of the **Netherlands**, he had supported a broadly based European integration and argued that Western Europe must retain a close relationship with the USA. He was the most forthright opponent of the views of **de Gaulle** on political union, rejecting the **Fouchet Plan** and attacking the French veto of the British application to join the **European Communities (EC)**. As NATO Secretary-General during a period of continued Soviet military build-up, he committed himself to persuading the NATO states to strengthen, and collaborate more closely on, their defence capacity, including the deployment of intermediate nuclear missiles in Western Europe.

Lustration. (*Lustrace*) A word used in **Czechoslovakia**, and later employed in other former Communist countries to describe the process of exposing people who had collaborated with the security services of the Communist regimes between 1948 and 1989. The term derives from the Latin word, *lustratio*, meaning a sacrificial purification.

Luxembourg. A Grand Duchy in Western Europe, established as an independent state in 1815. During the Second World War it was incorporated into Germany 1942–45. It developed close economic links with **Belgium** after 1921, which were extended in the post-war **Benelux** structure. A strong supporter of European integration, it was a founder member of the **European Communities (EC)**, for which it became a major administrative centre. It was the home of the High Authority of the **European Coal and Steel Community (ECSC)**, and since 1958 the **Council of Ministers** has continued to meet there once a year. It was also made the home of the Secretariat of the **European Parliament (EP)**, the **Court of Justice**, and the **European Investment Bank (EIB)**.

Luxembourg Compromise. An agreement by the six Member States of the **European Communities (EC)** in January 1966 which resolved the six-month dispute of the **empty chair crisis** between **France** and its partners. It dealt with the rights of states within the EC **Council of Ministers**, accepting that they had a right of veto on proposals where they believed their own national interests might be adversely affected. It largely vindicated the French position in the dispute. Although it had no legal force and was not regularized in later EC constitutional revisions, it decisively changed the direction of the EC, strengthening the role of national governments and stalling developments in integration until the late 1980s.

Luxembourg Declaration. A joint statement in 1984 by the **European Communities (EC)** and the **European Free Trade Association (EFTA)** that they would co-operate closely in economic matters. It became irrelevant in 1990 when the two bodies agreed to establish the **European Economic Area (EEA)**.

Luxembourg Socialist Workers' Party. (*Letzeburger Sozialistesch Arbeiterpartei/Parti Ouvrier Socialiste Luxembourgeoise – LSAP/POSL*) The major left-wing party in **Luxembourg**. Founded in 1902 as the Social Democratic Party, it changed its name after 1945. It has been a frequent and pragmatic participant in centrist coalition governments since 1947.

Lynch, John. (1917–) Prime Minister of **Ireland** 1966–73, 1977–79. A lawyer and distinguished athlete, he entered Parliament in 1948 as a **Fianna Fáil** representative. He served as a government minister 1951–54 and 1957–66 before becoming party leader and premier. He attempted to establish a dialogue with **Northern Ireland** which, by raising Catholic expectations in the province, contributed in part to the hardening of the community divide after 1969. He resigned the leadership after losing the 1973 election, though returning later as premier.

M
___

Maastricht Summit. A meeting of the **European Council** in December 1991. It had been preceded by two intergovernmental conferences which had discussed and drawn up proposals for political and monetary union within the **European Communities (EC)**. These provided the agenda for the summit which, after extensive and often acrimonious argument, agreed upon a fundamental revision of the **Treaty of Rome** in the form of the **Treaty on European Union**.

Maastricht Treaty. *See* TREATY ON EUROPEAN UNION.

MacDougall Report. A report on the role of public finance in **Economic and Monetary Union (EMU)**. It was published in 1977 by a committee, headed by Sir Donald MacDougall, appointed in 1972 by the **European Communities (EC)**. It argued that EC public expenditure could aid EMU by redistributing wealth, but that it would need to be set at a specific and rising level of Gross Domestic Product (GDP). No action was taken on the report since by 1977 EMU had largely been abandoned. In the 1988 budgetary settlement designed to prepare the way for the 1992 **internal market** and a new attempt at EMU, the levels set for EC funding for the next few years were still significantly lower than the MacDougall recommendations, and further increases were rejected by the member states in 1992.

Macedonia. A region of the Balkans absorbed by the Ottoman Empire in 1380, and after the late nineteenth century disputed by **Bulgaria**, **Greece** and **Serbia**. The 1919 Treaty of Neuilly gave most of the region to **Yugoslavia**, and this was later reconfirmed by the 1947 **Paris Peace Treaties**. In January 1946 Yugoslavia created a constituent federal republic of Macedonia, with Skopje as the regional capital. The poorest region of Yugoslavia, it experienced significant emigration to other areas of the country. Nationalist sentiment began to emerge in 1989, and in December 1990 regional elections rejected Communist rule. Led by the former Communist leader, **Gligorev**, it formally seceded from Yugoslavia in September 1991. Its independence remained precarious, with the possibility of ethnic tensions because of unrest among its large Albanian minority, and because of possible claims on part of its territory by **Albania** and Bulgaria. Above all, its economy and future was challenged by the hostility of Greece to the new state calling itself

Macedonia, which Greece claimed was a term which historically referred to part of Greece, and that its use indicated that Macedonia had claims on Greek territory. An unsatisfactory compromise was reached in 1993 whereby it was admitted to the United Nations as the Former Yugoslav Republic of Macedonia (FYROM) pending resolution of the argument by international mediators. While it did not halt further deterioration of relations with Greece, by 1994 many Western governments had recognized it.

Macmillan, Maurice Harold. (1894–1986) British Prime Minister 1957–63. Elected to Parliament in 1924, he was identified with the left-wing of the **Conservative Party**. During the Second World War he served in several government positions, and later held several Cabinet posts 1951–57. Appointed as the successor to **Eden**, his immediate task was to repair the damage to the party caused by the **Suez Crisis**. He won a large majority in the 1959 election, but in 1963 retired on health grounds, although his authority and prestige had already begun to weaken because of the **Profumo Affair** and growing economic problems. The first years of his premiership were a period of rising affluence, but more unemployment and balance of payments problems appeared later. In 1960 he acknowledged the irreversability of decolonialization and condemned South African apartheid in his famous 'winds of change' speech. By accepting the American Polaris missile in the 1963 **Nassau Agreement** he ended Britain's role as a fully independent nuclear power. In July 1961 he reversed British post-1945 European policy by declaring an intention to apply for membership of the **European Communities (EC)**. After resigning the party leadership, he declined a peerage in 1963, but was created Earl of Stockton in 1984.

Mafia. A collective term used to describe those responsible for organized crime in the south of **Italy**. Originally referring only to groups in Sicily, it came to be used more generally to describe networks of criminal groups, locally organized and based upon personal allegiances and family ties, rather than a single organization. The groups became politically involved in order to protect and pursue their criminal activities, building up complex systems of corrupt relationships in local government, most prominently in public procurement. The subject of periodic attacks by Italian governments, it was more systematically prosecuted after the early 1980s through the High Commission for the Fight Against the Mafia, but responded to arrests and trials of its leaders with a campaign of intimidation, including bombing attacks and assassination attempts. A more determined anti-Mafia campaign was launched after December 1992, with the formation of a new and more powerful Anti-Mafia Investigation Directorate (*Direzione Investigativa Anti-Mafia*), and in 1993 many of its alleged leaders were placed on trial for murder and other crimes.

Magic Formula. (*Zauberformel*) A common name for the 2-2-2-1 formula by which the four largest parties in **Switzerland** have shared the positions in the seven-member government since 1959.

Major, John. (1943–) British Prime Minister from 1991. A banker, he entered local politics in 1968 as a member of the **Conservative Party**. He entered Parliament in 1979, holding a number of junior government positions before becoming a minister in 1987. In 1991 he won the party election held to find a successor to **Thatcher**. Although winning the 1992 election, he faced major economic problems, and had severe difficulties in maintaining authority over a party whose internal divisions had deepened over several issues, but especially that of British involvement in further European integration. In an attempt to reassert his authority over his party, he resigned the leadership in 1995, decisively winning the subsequent election.

Makarios III, Archbishop. (1913–1977) President of **Cyprus** 1960–77. Born Mihail Christodoulou Mouskos, he was ordained into the Orthodox Church in 1946, and elected Archbishop of Cyprus in 1950. A supporter of **enosis**, he became a symbol for those who wished for the end of British colonial rule. Suspected by the British military authorities of having direct links with the **National Organization of Cypriot Fighters (EOKA)**, he was deported to the Seychelles in March 1956. He was allowed to return after renouncing enosis and accepting a British offer of Cypriot independence. He was elected President of the new republic in December 1959, taking up office the following August. He followed a broadly moderate line on the issue of Greek–Turkish relations on the ethnically divided island. In July 1974 Greek officers in the National guard occupied his palace and forced him into exile. The attempted coup, engineered by the **Greek Colonels** regime in Athens, failed, and part of the island was occupied by Turkish armed forces. He returned to the presidency five months later, but failed to persuade **Turkey** to relinquish its control of one-third of Cyprus. He died in office of a heart attack.

Malenkov, Georgy Maksimilianovich. (1902–1988) Soviet Prime Minister 1953–55. He joined the Red Army in 1917 and the Communist Party in 1920, becoming a close associate of **Stalin** in the 1930s. He was elected to the **Politburo** in 1946, and in 1948 was designated by Stalin as his chosen successor. After Stalin's death he became both Party Secretary and Prime Minister, but was not strong enough to resist pressure from all his rivals. Within two weeks he was forced to yield the secretariat to **Khrushchev**. He proclaimed the notion of peaceful co-existence with the West, and sought to reduce arms production in order to release more resources for improving the standard of living. His policies met with strong opposition, and lacking a firm power base within the party he was forced to resign in 1955, stating as his reason that he was too inexperienced to undertake the required level of responsibility. His fall was completed in July 1957 when he was denounced by Khrushchev as a member of the **anti-party group** and expelled from the party. He subsequently was allowed to work as a minor provincial administrator. The fact that his disgrace did not lead to trial and execution was interpreted abroad as a sign of a greater self-confidence among the Soviet leadership.

Malfatti, Franco Maria. (1927–1993) President of the **Commission** 1970–72. A member of the Italian **Christian Democratic Party (DC)** who entered Parliament in 1958, he held only junior ministerial office in Rome. A relative unknown before his appointment as Commission President, his term of office was dominated by the negotiations with applicant states and the **enlargement** of the **European Communities (EC)**. He lacked the authority and strength to re-establish the influence of the Commission on EC developments, and resigned prematurely in 1972 to return to a domestic political career in **Italy**.

Malta. An island in the Mediterranean, annexed by the **United Kingdom** in 1814. An assembly was established in 1921, but there were periodic demonstrations and riots against the colonial administration, and the constitution was suspended in 1933. Britain's main Mediterranean base, the island was besieged and severely bombed during the Second World War. Its resistance was honoured by the collective award of the George Cross in April 1942. In 1947 internal self-government was restored, but riots broke out again in 1956 after a referendum in which a majority had voted for integration with Britain on terms similar to those of **Northern Ireland**. Because of British hesitation over the proposal, support for full independence began to grow, and this was accepted in 1964. As Britain began to abandon its naval bases on the island, the government negotiated an agreement with the **North Atlantic Treaty Organization (NATO)** in return for promising that it would not offer naval concessions to **Warsaw Pact** countries. In 1989 the Constitution was amended to ban any foreign military base or nuclear vessels. Although an agreement with the **European Communities (EC)** was signed in 1970, subsequent **Labour Party** governments pursued a non-aligned foreign policy, looking more to Third World countries. In 1990 a **Nationalist Party** government formally applied for EC membership. Domestic politics after independence were characterized by bitter conflict between the Labour and Nationalist parties, peaking in the 1980s over a Labour government's proposal to expropriate over 75 per cent of the assets of the Catholic Church as a means of funding universal free education.

Manifest Crisis. *See* EUROPEAN COAL AND STEEL COMMUNITY.

Maniu, Iuliu. (1873–1953) Prime Minister of **Romania** 1928–33. Leader of the National Peasant Party, he aligned himself with Fascist groups in the late 1930s, and in 1940 backed the military dictatorship of Ion Antonescu.

He later switched his position and headed a resistance movement which participated in the overthrow of Antonescu in August 1944. A forthright opponent of the Communist influence in post-war politics, his background hindered his attempts to present himself as a democratic spokesman after 1945. He was arrested by the Communist regime on charges of espionage and imprisoned in 1947. He died in prison.

Mannerheim, Carl Gustav Emil. (1867–1951) President of **Finland** 1944–46. A distinguished general in the Tsarist army, he later led the anti-Communist White forces in the 1917–18 civil war which established Finnish independence. In 1920 he was appointed head of the Finnish Defence Council. He negotiated an anti-Soviet alliance with Germany in 1941, but with the country facing defeat by the **USSR** in 1944 he insisted that Finland must surrender and sue for peace immediately, no matter what the cost. He was appointed President in March, and the following September successfully negotiated an armistice. He argued that future Finnish independence could only be preserved by cultivating Soviet friendship and trust, a line that was pursued by his presidential successors. He retired on health grounds in March 1946.

Mansholt Plan. *See* COMMON AGRICULTURAL POLICY; MANSHOLT, SICCO LEENDERT.

Mansholt, Sicco Leendert. (1908–1995) President of the **Commission** 1972–73. A farmer, he was a leading member of the Dutch **Labour Party**, and first became a government minister in 1945. He was appointed as a founder member of the Commission in 1958, being made responsible for agriculture. He had long had an interest in a **Common Agricultural Policy (CAP)**, and had argued for one in the **Council of Europe** in 1950. The most complete version of his ideas was the 1968 Mansholt Plan, which outlined both a system of price guarantees and protection for farmers, and a scheme for agricultural rationalization and modernization. It was criticized at the time by most farming organizations in the **European Communities (EC)**. The version adopted by the EC in 1972 was much less comprehensive in scope, especially in placing little emphasis upon rationalization. After 14 years on the Commission, he served briefly, following the resignation of **Malfatti**, as its interim President 1972–73 before retiring from public life.

Marchais, Georges René Louis. (1920–) Leader of the **French Communist Party (PCF)** 1970–93. Trained as a mechanic, he joined the PCF in 1947, being admitted to the leadership group in 1956. He did not enter Parliament until 1973. Although as leader he agreed to an electoral alliance with the **Socialist Party (PS)**, flirted briefly with **Eurocommunism**, and took the party into a coalition government with the PS in 1981, he was a Marxist-Leninist loyalist, and was happier holding the party to a strict isolationist line. His complete control of the party meant that no internal dissent or debate was tolerated, with expulsion from the party the penalty. His unwillingness to adapt to changing circumstances led to many defections and expulsions from the PCF at the same time as its mass support began to erode in the 1980s. Despite the collapse of Communist regimes in Eastern Europe, he continued to reject liberalization after 1989, but in 1990 did indicate that he and the PCF had been misled for many years by the **USSR**. Still in full control of a truncated party, he eventually retired in January 1994.

Marković, Ante. (1924–) Prime Minister of **Yugoslavia** 1989–91. Joining the Communist Party as a **Resistance movement** partisan in 1940, he worked as an engineer before entering politics in the 1960s. He served as premier of the Croatian Republic 1982–86, where he acquired a reputation as a political liberal and economic pragmatist. These qualities were partly responsible for his appointment in 1989 as national premier, but the processes of disintegration over the next two years were too strong to be overcome, and when he resigned in December 1991 Yugoslavia had effectively ceased to exist.

Marshall, George Catlett. (1880–1959) American Secretary of State 1947–49. A distinguished soldier and general, Chief of Staff of the American Army 1939–45, he played a decisive role in the post-war organization of Western Europe, initiating massive aid to **Greece** and **Turkey** to enable them to resist Communist pressure, and proposing an ambitious aid programme, the **Marshall Plan**, to assist European economic reconstruction. He uncompromisingly opposed the Soviet **Berlin Blockade** and laid much of the groundwork for the establishment of the **North Atlantic Treaty Organization (NATO)**.

Marshall Plan. A proposal for an extensive programme of American aid to assist and stimulate economic reconstruction and recovery in Europe after the Second World War. Outlined by **Marshall** in June 1947, it was immediately welcomed by most Western European countries. Because the **USSR** and the countries subject to Soviet influence rejected the Plan, it could not be channelled through the **Economic Commission for Europe (ECE)**. A Committee for European Economic Co-operation (CEEC), restricted to Western European countries, was formed to discuss how, in terms of the needs of each participant, aid could be most effectively distributed over a four-year period. The Plan became the European Recovery Programme (ERP), launched in 1948. In the USA the 1948 Foreign Assistance Act created the Economic Co-operation Administration (ECA) to supervise it. The USA insisted that its operation and the allocation of priorities had to be a European responsibility, and the CEEC was transformed into the **Organization for European Economic Co-operation (OEEC)**. When the Plan ended in 1952, some $17,000 million in Marshall Aid had been given to

Western Europe, giving the latter a considerable financial and psychological boost. Along with the **Truman Doctrine** and the **North Atlantic Treaty Organization (NATO)**, it symbolized the American commitment to Western Europe, where it also helped to foster a better culture and level of inter-state co-operation.

Martens, Wilfried. (1936–) Prime Minister of **Belgium** 1979–80, 1981–92. A lawyer from **Flanders**, he became president of the youth wing of the **Christian People's Party (CVP)**. He was elected CVP leader in 1972 and entered Parliament in 1974. A skilled negotiator, he had had no ministerial experience before accepting the premiership in 1979. Heading several coalition governments with various partners, he lent his support to efforts for further European integration and in domestic politics worked for a satisfactory solution to Belgium's linguistic problems through economic reform and a constitutional decentralization of the state.

Masaryk, Jan. (1886–1948) Foreign Minister of **Czechoslovakia** 1945–48. Son of Tómás Masaryk, the founder and first president of Czechoslovakia, he pursued a diplomatic career after 1918, but resigned in 1938 in protest at the Munich Agreement. He later became Foreign Minister and deputy leader of the government in exile in London. After liberation he continued as Foreign Minister in the Communist-dominated government of **Gottwald**. He soon became disillusioned with the government's pro-Soviet policy. but remained in office after the February 1948 coup which effectively created a one-party state, at the request of President **Beneš**. On 10 March 1948 he fell to his death from a window in the Foreign Ministry building in Prague. The exact circumstances surrounding the fall – accident, suicide or murder – were never determined.

Massive retaliation. A strategic doctrine adopted in 1954 by the USA and **North Atlantic Treaty Organization (NATO)**. It stated that the response to an invasion of Western Europe by the **USSR** would be the use of nuclear weapons. NATO's original assumption had been that a European conflict would be a conventional war, but the failure of the **Lisbon Force Goals** indicated that the cost of matching the conventional strength of the USSR was more than the NATO states were willing to bear. Regarded as a cost-effective defence, massive retaliation meant a large-scale nuclear response against Soviet territory. Its major problem was its credibility, since there were doubts as to how far the USA, controlling NATO's nuclear capacity, would be willing to risk a major war and possible Soviet counter-strikes against its own cities on the basis of what might be a relatively minor incident in Europe. It was abandoned in 1967, being replaced by the doctrine of **flexible response**.

Massu, Jacques. (1908–) French general and paratrooper. A professional soldier, he joined the Free French Forces in 1940, later serving in **French Indo-China**. He was military commander in Algeria 1957–60. His hard-line approach had some success against the Algerian nationalists, but alienated the Muslim population. Fearing that the politicians in Paris would capitulate to Algerian demands, he was the instigator of the military rebellion in Algiers which formed a Committee of Public Safety, and called for the return to power of **de Gaulle**. He later served as Commander-in-Chief of the French forces in Germany.

Maudling Committee. A committee of the **Organization for European Economic Co-operation (OEEC)** established in 1957 to seek a **free trade area** agreement for the whole of Western Europe. Named after its British chairman, Reginald Maudling, it was a reaction to the impending establishment of the **European Economic Community (EEC)** and a fear in the OEEC that this might create a fatal economic division and trade war in Europe. The Committee failed to secure agreement between the supporters of a broad free trade area and those who wanted a more comprehensive **common market**, and it was wound up in 1959. Its failure was one factor that led to the transformation of the OEEC into the broader **Organization for Economic Co-operation and Development (OECD)**.

Mauroy, Pierre. (1928–) Prime Minister of **France** 1981–84. A teacher, he joined the old Socialist Party (SFIO) in 1950, occupying a variety of party posts over the next two decades. He worked closely with **Mitterrand** in reconstructing a new **Socialist Party (PS)** in 1971, and as its general secretary until 1979 was largely responsible for the development of an effective organization. The first Socialist premier of the **Fifth French Republic**, his tenure was marked by economic problems as his government, which for a while included Communist participants, was forced to reverse its attempts to pursue an expansionist economic policy and adopt a policy of retrenchment. He later served as first secretary of the PS 1988–92.

May Events. A series of large-scale demonstrations, riots and strikes in **France** in 1968 which threatened to topple the **de Gaulle** regime. They began with student protests, mainly in Paris, about the antiquated system of higher education and inadequate provisions, though radical student leaders also sought to use the protests as a vanguard of a social and political revolution. The protests became full-scale riots, which also spread to the provinces, after violent police counter-measures. One week later the trade unions called a one-day strike as a gesture of solidarity, but lost control of their members who effectively established a general strike. The protests were unable to sustain their momentum. De Gaulle sought and obtained the support of the army, and the Prime Minister, **Pompidou**, bought peace by promising educational and economic reforms. Although the Gaullists won a huge majority at the subsequent general election, the episode weakened the prestige and authority of de Gaulle, and created inflationary problems which persisted for a number of years.

Mazowiecki, Tadeusz. (1927–) Prime Minister of **Poland** 1989–91. A lawyer and a Catholic activist, editing several Catholic magazines 1948–81, he acted as a mouthpiece in May 1977 for members of the **Committee for the Defence of Workers (KOR)**, and in 1980 as a negotiator with the government in talks on permitting trade union pluralism. He later acted as an adviser to **Solidarity**. Interned 1981–82 after the military seizure of power by **Jaruzelski**, he continued to collaborate with the banned Solidarity movement, and in 1989 was appointed to be the country's first post-war non-Communist premier. He formed and led the **Democratic Union** after 1990. His objective was to transform Poland as quickly as possible into a liberal democracy and capitalist market economy, but his broad coalition government lacked cohesion and he failed to secure a clear support in the fragmented party system that emerged after the fall of Communism. After his bid for the presidency failed, his position deteriorated further and he resigned in 1991. In 1994 he became leader of the Freedom Union, the successor to the Democratic Union.

Mečiar, Vladimir. (1942–) Prime Minister of **Slovakia** from 1992. After working for several years as a party administrator, he was expelled from the Czechoslovakian Communist Party in 1970 for holding 'progressive opinions', subsequently working as a labourer before becoming a lawyer. A founder member of the **Public Against Violence (VPN)**, the Slovak equivalent of **Civic Forum**, he was elected as premier of the Slovak Republic in 1990, adopting a hard line on Slovak autonomy, which led to his dismissal in 1991 after accusations that he had abused his power by obtaining access to secret police files. He left the VPN to form the **Movement for a Democratic Slovakia (HZDS)**. Although challenged by a more extreme Slovak nationalism, he remained the major standard bearer of Slovak rights and possible independence, winning the 1992 election. Emphasizing nationalism, economic protectionism and a distaste for moving quickly to a market economy, he remained at odds with his Czech counterparts, who accepted the secession of Slovakia at the end of 1992. During the next 15 months increasing economic problems and political factionalism seemingly weakened his authority, and the Parliament dismissed him as premier in March 1994. Taking his campaign to the electorate, he was a convincing victor in the September election, returning to the premiership.

Mediterranean Action Plan. *See* BARCELONA CONVENTION.

Meinhof, Ulrike. *See* BAADER-MEINHOF GROUP.

Melilla. *See* CEUTA AND MELILLA.

Memel. (Klaipeda) A German-speaking Baltic port, once part of East Prussia but assigned to **Lithuania** in 1919. It rejected Lithuanian claims and authority and, strongly pro-Nazi in the 1930s, was seized by Germany in

March 1939. Recaptured by the **USSR**, it was incorporated after 1945 into the Socialist Republic of Lithuania within the USSR. Its name was changed to Klaipeda and its German residents arrested or expelled.

Mende, Erich. (1916–) West German politician. He was born in **Silesia**, which was incorporated into **Poland** after 1945. A decorated war veteran, he was one of the founders of the **Free Democratic Party (FDP)**, and in 1949 was elected to the West German Parliament. Originally identified with the liberal wing of the party, he shifted to the right to become its major conservative representative. He was elected party leader in 1960, and after the 1961 election made it a condition of the FDP joining a coalition government with the **Christian Democratic Union (CDU)** that **Adenauer** retire within two years. His insistence upon holding the party to a conservative right-wing position came under attack in the 1960s, and an internal rebellion forced his resignation as leader in 1967. His departure marked a complete change of direction in the FDP, which then sought to portray itself as a liberal centrist party and the hinge of the party system. He left the FDP in 1970 and joined the CDU.

Menderes, Adnan. (1899–1961) Prime Minister of **Turkey** 1950–1960. A lawyer, he entered politics in 1932. A critic of the founder of modern Turkey, Mustapha Kemal Atatürk, he established the **Democratic Party** in 1945, leading it to victory in 1950. He continued the previous pro-Western policy, taking Turkey into the **North Atlantic Treaty Organization (NATO)** in 1952, and in 1959 he accepted the idea of independence for **Cyprus**, on condition of safeguards for its Turkish minority. His domestic policies were more contentious, and increasingly repressive in the late 1950s. His power base was among the peasantry, and his opponents feared that he was seeking to mobilize and advance Islamic interests. To quell the mounting opposition he assumed dictatorial powers in April 1960. One month later he was deposed by the army. Charged with breaking the Constitution, he was sentenced to death after a long trial and executed in September 1961.

Mendès-France, Pierre. (1907–1982) Prime Minister of **France** 1954–55. Joining the **Radical Republican and Radical Socialist Party** in 1923, he entered Parliament in 1932. During the Second World War he served with **de Gaulle** in London, representing France at the 1944 **Bretton Woods** conference. After 1945 he opposed the right-wing trend of Gaullist policy and became a persistent critic of successive governments. In June 1954 he was invited to head a coalition government in the aftermath of the fall of **Dien Bien Phu**. It was hoped that he would regenerate, and bring a new stability to, the **Fourth French Republic**. He launched an anti-inflation policy, negotiated independence for **French Indo-China**, and removed the contentious **European Defence Community (EDC)** treaty from the political agenda. His dispatch of additional troops to the new conflict in Algeria was opposed by his coalition partners, and he resigned in February 1955. Although in 1956 he briefly served in the **Mollet** government, he soon resumed his role as critic, and in 1959 resigned from the Radical Party. He disliked the constitutional structure of the **Fifth French Republic** and attacked de Gaulle's autocratic presidency. In 1965 he backed the presidential bid of **Mitterrand**. He retired from politics in 1973.

Merger Treaty. A document which formally integrated the executives of the **European Atomic Energy Community (EURATOM)**, the **European Coal and Steel Community (ECSC)** and the **European Economic Community (EEC)**. It created a single **Commission** and a single **Council of Ministers**. Signed on 8 April 1965, it came into effect on 1 July 1967.

Messina Conference. A meeting of the foreign ministers of the six members of the **European Coal and Steel Community (ECSC)** in June 1955. Its purpose was to revive a momentum for integration after the collapse of the planned **European Defence Community (EDC)**. An invitation to attend was declined by the **United Kingdom**. The meeting agreed to a new integrationist start and to plan for a **common market** and a nuclear energy community. The Belgian minister, **Spaak**, was appointed to head a committee which would draft a detailed plan for the new bodies that would be considered by the six national governments. The Spaak Report was the basis of the **Treaty of Rome**.

Messmer, Pierre Auguste Joseph. (1916–) Prime Minister of **France** 1972–74. In active service 1939–46 he then followed a career in the diplomatic and colonial service until 1959. He served as a government minister under **de Gaulle** 1960–69, but entered Parliament only in 1968. He was appointed to the premiership by **Pompidou** in 1972, but resigned as a result of the 1974 election. He continued in Parliament until 1986.

Mezzogiorno. An Italian term meaning 'mid-day', applied to the southern half of **Italy**. The region has been a persistent economic problem, with an absence of economic development and extensive underemployment. The recipient since 1950 of huge public investment, which showed little in return, the area was politically conservative and developed a dependency culture built around public funding, welfare, and **clientelism**, characteristics which intensified its distinctiveness from northern Italy and generated steady criticism from the latter about the economic burdens it imposed upon the state.

Mielke, Erich. (1907–) East German politician. A shipping clerk, he joined the German Communist Party in 1925. He lived in exile in the **USSR** 1939–45. A close associate of **Ulbricht**, he helped create the **Socialist Unity Party (SED)** in 1946. After a variety of party positions he was appointed head of the **Stasi** in 1957, building it up to become an active and influential secret state police force. Much feared, he was removed from his position in November 1989 by **Krenz** after SED rule had already begun to crumble in an attempt to demonstrate a new Communist start. He was later accused of corruption, especially rigging soccer matches to enable his sponsored team, Dynamo Berlin, to win. After German reunification he was arrested on several charges, including manslaughter, embezzlement and espionage. The real charge was that of being head of the Stasi and the man responsible for its repressive actions. In 1992 a court ruled that he was too ill to stand trial, but the following year he was found guilty of complicity in the murder of two police officers in 1931.

Mifsud Bonnici, Karmenu. (1933–) Prime Minister of **Malta** 1984–87. A lawyer, he became leader of the **Labour Party** in 1982 and was subsequently co-opted into Parliament. He sought to moderate the non-alignment policies of his predecessors, and to pursue a more consensual style of government, seeking reconciliation with the Catholic Church. While largely successful in his objectives, he lost the 1987 election, and after further defeat in the 1992 election resigned as party leader.

Mihailovich, Draza. (1893–1946). Yugoslavian Resistance leader. A professional soldier, after 1941 he headed the royalist nationalist Chetnik guerillas, who failed to gain as much popular support as the Communist partisans of **Tito**. The **United Kingdom** withdrew its support of him in 1944 after allegations that he was collaborating with German military forces against Tito. He continued to wage a guerilla campaign against the new Yugoslavian regime after the end of the war until captured by police in March 1946. Charged with collaboration and war crimes, he was executed in July.

Mikolajczyk, Stanisław. (1901–1966) Polish politician. A farmer, he was elected to Parliament in 1930 as a member of the Peasant People's Party, becoming party leader in 1937. He was a member of the government in exile in London during the Second World War, succeeding General Sikorski as premier in 1943. He resigned the premiership in November 1944 after failing to persuade the Allied leaders to alter their views on the future of **Poland**. He returned to his home country in 1945 and joined the new Soviet-sponsored provisional government as Minister of Agriculture, but attempted in the face of increasing Communist pressure to preserve the independence of the reconstituted Peasant Party. Under constant criticism from the regime, he protested against its undue influence in the 1947 elections and attempted a trial of strength against the Communists, a move which only split his own party. Receiving warnings of his imminent arrest, in October 1947 he fled abroad to live in exile in the USA.

Mikoyan, Anastas Ivanovich. (1895–1978) Soviet politician. Born in **Armenia**, he joined the Bolsheviks in 1915. He worked in a variety of party administrative posts after 1921, becoming a **Politburo** member in 1935 and a Deputy Prime Minister in 1937. After the death of **Stalin** he supported the principle of collective leadership, and endorsed the 1956 denunciation of Stalin by **Khrushchev**. He later became the principle Soviet negotiator and troubleshooter with the Eastern European Communist regimes, and in 1964 served briefly as President of the Praesidium of the Supreme Soviet before his retirement from public life in 1965.

Milošević, Slobodan. (1941–) President of **Serbia** from 1989. After working in law and banking, he was elected leader of the Serbian **League of Communists** in 1987 on the basis of a strong advocacy of Serbian interests within **Yugoslavia**. His support for a more overt and aggressive Serbian nationalism and his demands for greater Serbian rights in and control of the autonomous provinces of **Kosovo** and **Vojvodina** attracted massive popular support, and was a significant factor in the further weakening of the already enfeebled national Yugoslav leadership. After the break-up of Yugoslavia in 1991 he consolidated his authority in Serbia, and provided aid to Serb groups in **Bosnia-Hercegovina** and **Croatia**. Although he later distanced himself from these groups, at least in public, he was suspected of attempting, in defiance of world opinion and sanctions, to establish a Greater Serbia.

Mindszenty, József. (1892–1975) Catholic Primate of **Hungary** 1945–48. Born József Pehm, and ordained in 1915, he became Bishop of Veszprém in 1944. He was later arrested after the German invasion of Hungary for his outspoken anti-Nazi views. After his release he was made Archbishop of Hungary in October 1945 and a Cardinal in 1947. He clashed with the Communist-dominated government on several occasions, and was arrested in December 1948 after returning from a visit to the USA. Charged with treason and currency offences, he used his February 1949 trial as an opportunity to attack Communism and urge the restoration of the Habsburg monarchy. The sentence of life imprisonment was later commuted to house detention. Released during the 1956 **Hungarian Revolution**, he was allowed to return to Budapest and to broadcast to the country. When Soviet forces crushed the uprising he took refuge in the American Embassy, where he stayed until 1971, consistently refusing to accept the reconciliation negotiated between Hungary and the **Vatican**. In 1971 he was persuaded to go to Vienna, from where he travelled on to Rome. His uncompromising stand made him, in the eyes of many, a symbol and martyr of the **Cold War**. In May 1991 his remains were returned from **Austria** to be reinterred in his home land.

Mines Safety and Health Commission. An agency inherited by the **European Communities (EC)** from the **European Coal and Steel Community (ECSC)**. It was formed to initiate proposals on, and supervise, health and safety conditions in all branches of mining and quarrying activities, with a membership drawn from representatives of governments, employers' associations and trade unions.

Mintoff, Dominic. (1916–) Prime Minister of **Malta** 1955–58, 1971–84. Playing an active role in the reorganization of the **Labour Party** after 1945, he became its leader in 1949. As premier after 1955 he sought integration with the **United Kingdom**, but British doubts about the idea led to his resignation in 1958, and he later developed anti-British views. The experience made him more wary of relying solely upon Western links. Returning to power in 1971 he pursued a more neutralist policy, seeking in particular closer links with the Arab world. His strong personality helped to polarize Maltese society, and in his latter years he came into conflict with the Catholic Church over his plans to expropriate much of its property. He resigned as premier and party leader in 1984, retiring from public life.

Mitsotakis, Konstantinos. (1918–) Prime Minister of **Greece** 1990–93. A **Resistance movement** activist during the Second World War, he entered Parliament in 1949 as a Liberal, later joining the leftist Centre Union of **Papandreou**. He broke with Papandreou in 1965, and later spent the years of the **Greek Colonels** in exile in Paris. Upon his return he formed the New Liberal Party, but merged it with the conservative **New Democracy** in 1978. He was elected leader of New Democracy in 1984, and both in opposition and in government after 1990 had to struggle to maintain party unity. Deep economic problems and a party split cost him the 1993 election. In 1994 the new Socialist government placed him under investigation in connection with allegations of illegal phone tapping and bribery, but the charges were later dropped.

Mitteleuropa. (Central Europe) A concept first developed in the nineteenth century in the German-speaking areas of the Habsburg Empire to describe an area possessing an identity distinct from both Prussian and Russian Slav traditions and culture. It later came to be used to indicate a 'natural' region of German political and economic hegemony lying between Germany and **Russia**. It fell into disuse after 1945 because of its association with Nazi aggression, expansion and racism. It was revived after 1989 in the former Communist states of Eastern Europe as a symbol of their wish to establish an identity distinctive from that of both Russia and Western Europe.

Mitterrand, François Maurice Marie. (1916–) President of **France** 1981–95. Becoming a socialist as a law student after 1936, he was captured by German troops in 1940. Escaping from captivity, he joined the **Resistance movement**. He entered Parliament as a Socialist deputy in 1946 and apart from three years (1959–62) in the Senate, remained a deputy until 1980. He held several government positions during the **Fourth French Republic**, developing a reputation as a shrewd tactician. In the 1960s he sought to unify and revivify the demoralized non-Communist left, contesting the 1965 presidential election against **de Gaulle** and forming the **Federation of the Democratic and Socialist Left**. After the latter had crumbled, at the Socialist congress in Épinay in 1971 he restructured the old party as a new **Socialist Party (PS)**. He lost the 1974 presidential election to **Giscard d'Estaing**, but gained revenge in 1981, winning re-election in 1988. With the PS also winning the 1981 parliamentary election, he launched an interventionist programme of radical reform, raising basic wages and social benefits and nationalizing key industries. It led to high inflation and currency pressures, and had to be abandoned in 1983. He also shelved his promises to decentralize government. In foreign policy he followed the lines developed by his predecessors, pushing for European integration while preserving French interests and seeking to increase French influence in European organizations. He constructed a close relationship with the **Federal Republic of Germany**, and sought to reduce American influence in Europe, especially through a greater European defence co-ordination exclusive of American involvement. These concerns were maintained after German reunification and the ending of the **Cold War** which he believed had made the preservation of French influence over Germany within European integration even more imperative. A skilful manipulator of French politics in the 1980s, his prestige began to decline after 1990. He only barely won a 1992 referendum held to approve the **Treaty on European Union**, and in 1993 the PS, already badly divided, suffered a humiliating electoral defeat. The last years of his presidency were marred by accusations of corruption within the PS and among people close to him.

Mladenov, Petur Toskev. (1936–) President of **Bulgaria** 1990. After working in the youth section of the **Bulgarian Communist Party (BKP)**, he became a youthful Minister of Foreign Affairs in 1971, serving until 1989. Appointed to the **Politburo** in 1977, he was, despite his record, something of a surprise choice as General Secretary of the party in 1989 after the dismissal of **Zhivkov**. He promised democratic reforms, giving concessions on human rights and an amnesty for political prisoners, and removing hard-liners from important party positions. In February 1990 he was replaced as party leader by **Lilov**, who was seen as a more genuine reformer, but in April was elected to the presidency by the National Assembly. Although the BKP, reorganized as the Bulgarian Socialist Party, narrowly won the June elections, problems of and accusations about his past persisted, and he was forced to resign. He was later accused of racial discrimination.

Mladić, Ratko. (1943–) Bosnian Serb soldier. A professional soldier who became a lieutenant-colonel in the federal Yugoslav army, he was commander in the **Krajina** region in 1991, and supported local Serb forces when **Croatia** declared independence. In May 1992 he was promoted to general, and placed in charge of the Bosnian Serb forces in the civil war in **Bosnia-**

Hercegovina. A skilful and hard-line commander, he was prepared to defy totally the United Nations and was an advocate of the merging of all Serb areas into a Greater **Serbia**.

Moderate Unity Party. (*Moderata Samlingspartiet – M*) The major conservative party in **Sweden**. Founded in 1904 as the Right Party (*Höger-partiet*), it was displaced by the **Liberal Party** as the leading non-socialist party in 1948. In opposition until 1976, when it participated in a non-socialist coalition government, it experienced greater popularity after 1982, becoming Sweden's second largest party and, under the leadership of **Bildt**, heading a coalition government after 1991.

Modrow, Hans. (1928–) Prime Minister of the **German Democratic Republic** 1989–90. Drafted into the German army, he was captured by Soviet troops and remained a prisoner of war until 1949. He joined the **Socialist Unity Party (SED)** in 1949, working within the party's youth organization 1952–61. He was admitted to the central committee in 1967, and in 1973 was made secretary of the regional party in Dresden where he established a reputation for honesty and sympathy for liberal reformism. These qualities made him disliked by **Honecker** and distrusted by the party leadership, and he was reprimanded by an investigative commission for pursuing mistaken strategies. When the removal of Honecker in 1989 failed to halt the tide of popular protest against the regime, he was recalled to **Berlin** and made premier. He began to plan for democratization and free elections. After the SED defeat in the March 1990 election, he was replaced as Prime Minister, retiring from political life. In 1993 he was charged with fraud in connection with local elections, and the following year with perjury in connection with anti-Communist demonstrations in 1989.

Mogadishu Raid. A rescue operation on 18 October 1977 by a West German anti-terrorist police squad (*Grenzschutzgruppe*) at Mogadishu airport in Somalia. They freed hostages held by members of the Red Army Faction (*see* **Baader-Meinhof Group**) aboard an airliner hijacked five days previously on a flight from Palma to Frankfurt. When news of the successful raid was announced in the **Federal Republic of Germany**, Andreas Baader and two of his associates committed suicide in their prison cells.

Moldova. A successor state of the **USSR**. Consisting mainly of the historic province of **Bessarabia** ceded to **Russia** in 1815, but returned to **Romania** in 1918, it was claimed by the USSR in June 1940 and incorporated in March 1944 as the Moldavian Socialist Republic. The majority of the population were Romanian speakers, and nationalist sentiment, fuelled by language disputes, re-emerged after 1988 with the decline of Soviet authority. A newly formed Moldavian National Front captured more than one-third of the seats in the 1990 regional Soviet election. In 1991 independence was declared and the Communist Party banned. The declaration was rejected by the Russian minority clustered mainly in the north of the province. Armed conflict and sporadic military skirmishes followed the demand of the Russian areas for reincorporation with Russia or recognition of a separate state of **Trans-Dnestria**. A truce and compromise was reached in 1992, with the acceptance of a special status for the minority area. Despite previous nationalist sentiment, a 1994 referendum decisively rejected a proposal that Moldova should rejoin Romania, and in elections later in the year the pro-Romanian parties were routed.

Mollet, Guy. (1905–1975) Prime Minister of **France** 1956–57. From a working-class background, he was a teacher but his career was disrupted by the Second World War. Captured by German troops in 1940, he was later released in a prisoner exchange and became active in the **Resistance movement**. He was a Socialist Party (SFIO) delegate at the 1945 Constituent Assembly. In 1946 he was elected SFIO leader, serving until it collapsed as an organization in 1969. A member of several earlier coalition governments, in 1956 he headed the longest-lived government of the **Fourth French Republic**. His premiership was dominated by foreign policy problems: the 1956 **Suez Crisis** and an escalation of the **Algerian War of Independence** distracted him from important domestic issues. His increasingly ineffectual government was eventually defeated on a financial issue in 1957. After 1958 he attempted unsuccessfully to build a unified democratic opposition to **de Gaulle** and the **Fifth French Republic**, but with his influence heavily constrained he saw his party decline to the point of extinction. In 1969 he resigned as leader, and retired from politics in 1971.

Mölln Killings. The murder of members of an ethnic Turkish family in their home in an arson attack in Mölln in the **Federal Republic of Germany** in October 1992. Young extreme right-wing nationalists were arrested for the crime, which highlighted the small but vociferous and dangerous right-wing extremism and neo-Nazi views which became more prominent after German reunification. It forced more decisive government measures, and several small extreme right-wing groups were banned. But a worse racial attack on ethnic Turks occurred in the city of Solingen the following May. One consequence of the racial tension was the implementation of restrictive amendments to the hitherto liberal right of asylum in Germany.

Molotov, Vyacheslav Mikhailovich. (1890–1986) Soviet Foreign Minister 1939–49, 1953–56. He joined the Bolsheviks in 1905 and was one of the leadership group that planned the 1917 October Revolution. He joined the **Politburo** in 1921, and served as Prime Minister 1930–41. An utterly loyal lieutenant of **Stalin**, he was the latter's closest adviser at the **Yalta** and **Potsdam Conferences**, and played a leading role in developing the hard-line Soviet position in the late 1940s. Although he was re-appointed Foreign Minister after Stalin's death, his influence declined with the rise of **Khrushchev**, and he was dismissed from office in June 1956. The following year he was accused of belonging to the **anti-party group** and was stripped of all party positions. Banished to become Ambassador to the Mongolian People's Republic 1957–60, he continued to be publicly criticized for his loyalty to Stalin, and in 1960 he was expelled from the party, retiring from public life. He was rehabilitated within the party only in 1984.

Momper, Walter. (1945–) German politician. An archivist, he joined the **Social Democratic Party (SPD)** in 1967, and in 1974 was elected to the West **Berlin** city council. In 1986 he became SPD leader in the city and as mayor after the January 1989 city elections formed a controversial coalition administration with the **Green Party**. After the crumbling of Communist authority in the **German Democratic Republic (DDR)** in late 1989, as mayor of West Berlin he had an important role in considering the possible consequences of the opening of the **Berlin Wall** and the place of the city in a united Germany. He resigned as mayor in 1992.

Monaco. An enclave city state within French territory on the Mediterranean, ruled by the Grimaldi dynasty since the thirteenth century. It was placed under French protection in 1861. A 1918 treaty accepted policy conformity with **France**, and a further treaty in 1919 provided for incorporation into France if a reigning prince had no heir. The relationship was redefined and tightened in 1963 after French complaints about Monaco's status as a tax refuge. Under the 1962 Constitution the prince shares power with a minister of state approved by France, which in practice directly administers several policy areas within the principality. For much of the post-1945 period it has effectively been a one-party system, with political competition dominated by the National and Democratic Union (*Union Nationale et Démocratique*).

Monetarism. An economic theory which argues that inflation and economic output can be managed only through control of the money supply. Associated in particular with the American economist, Milton Friedman, it rejected the principles and domination of **Keynesianism** and its associated policies by which governments had sought to reflate their economies through public spending, since this only increased the money supply. The perceived inability of Keynesian policies to resolve the economic problems of the 1970s made it attractive to several right-wing politicians, but no government persistently and comprehensively adopted it. The first **Thatcher** government in the **United Kingdom** introduced monetarist policies in 1979, but rising unemployment and other problems led to them being largely abandoned by 1981. In the 1980s, however, some of its ideas, if not the general principles, took root in many governments.

Monetary Compensation Amounts (MCAs). *See* GREEN CURRENCIES.

Monetary Policy Committee. *See* ECONOMIC AND FINANCIAL COUNCIL OF MINISTERS.

Monnet, Jean. (1888–1979) French economist and administrator. Largely self-educated, he followed a distinguished business and diplomatic career before 1945, being a consultant economist at the 1919–20 peace conferences and later a Deputy Secretary-General of the League of Nations. In 1939–40 he was a member of a committee in London working on economic collaboration between **France** and the **United Kingdom**, and was attached 1940–43 to the British Supply Council in Washington DC before being charged by **de Gaulle** with preparing plans for French post-war economic reconstruction. He returned to France in 1945 to head a new Planning Commission, but became convinced that no single European country could effectively plan for growth and prosperity by itself. He saw integration as the alternative, with eventual union being built upon an accumulation of co-operative ventures in specific economic sectors. He persuaded **Schuman** of the benefits of **sectoral integration**, producing the draft of the **Schuman Plan** and the later Pleven Plan. In 1952 he was appointed as the first President of the High Authority of the **European Coal and Steel Community (ECSC)**. After the plans for a **European Defence Community (EDC)** collapsed, he refused re-appointment in 1955, instead forming the **Action Committee for a United States of Europe (ACUSE)** as a pro-integration pressure group. He successfully argued the case for a nuclear energy community. He was a critic of French policy under de Gaulle in the 1960s, regarding an integrated Europe without Britain as unthinkable, but accepted that the core of integration had to be a Franco-German alliance. He resigned from ACUSE in 1975 and retired from public life. His activities led him to be widely regarded as the architect of European integration, and his efforts were commemmorated by the **European Communities (EC)** in a variety of ways, mainly in the field of education.

Montebello Decision. An agreement by the defence ministers of the **North Atlantic Treaty Organization (NATO)**, meeting as the **Nuclear Planning Group**, in October 1983. Named after the town in Canada where the meeting was held, its aim was to reduce the stockpile of battlefield nuclear weapons. While presented as a contribution to **arms control**, it was meant to sharpen NATO's defences since most of the affected warheads were obsolete, and also because the meeting further agreed to upgrade and modernize the remaining stockpile.

Montenegro. (Crna Gora) A mountainous region of **Yugoslavia**. An independent principality which had successfully resisted incorporation by the Ottoman Empire, its dynasty was deposed in 1918 by an assembly at Podgorica which voted for union with **Serbia**. After 1946 it was constituted as a republic within the Yugoslav federation. When central political authority collapsed in 1990, it elected to maintain the link with Serbia in a truncated Yugoslavia, being the only republic not to opt for independence. Because of concerns about Serb nationalism and the economic consequences of the war in **Bosnia-Hercegovina**, some popular doubts about continuing the union began to emerge after 1993.

Morgenthau Plan. A policy adopted officially by the USA and the **United Kingdom** in September 1944. Developed by the American Secretary of the Treasury, Henry J. Morgenthau, it defined Germany as inherently evil and aggressive, and sought a solution to the German threat through permanent partition of the country. It also proposed ending all higher education and the destruction and prohibition of all heavy industry. Its desire for revenge and punishment made it unrealistic and impractical, and it was abandoned early in 1945.

Moro, Aldo. (1916–1978) Prime Minister of **Italy** 1963–68, 1974–76. A prominent member of the anti-Fascist Catholic student movement when he was a law student, he later participated in the 1946 constituent assembly and was elected to Parliament for the **Christian Democratic Party (DC)**. Identified with the liberal wing of the party, as Minister of Justice 1955–57 he reformed the prison system. In addition to his terms as premier, he served as Foreign Minister 1965–66, 1969–72 and 1973–74. In 1976 he was willing to consider some kind of co-operation with the **Italian Communist Party (PCI)** after the latter's declaration of the **historic compromise**. He was kidnapped in a car ambush in Rome on 17 March 1978 by **Red Brigade** terrorists. The ransom they sought for his release was freedom for terrorists held in custody or prison. Despite impassioned pleas from his family and close friends, the DC coalition government rejected the kidnappers' demands. He was murdered and his bullet-riddled body was found in a car near the DC headquarters in Rome on 9 May. In later years rumours persisted that the kidnapping and murder had been arranged in conjunction with right-wing groups which wished to prevent any kind of alliance between the DC and PCI, though no proof of this was forthcoming.

Mother and Child Affair. A political controversy in **Ireland**. In 1951 Noel Browne, the **Fine Gael** Minister of Health in the coalition government led by his party decided to implement elements of a health bill which had first been drafted by the previous **Fianna Fáil** government in 1946. Browne proposed free medical care for all children and for pre- and post-natal mothers, without a means test. His proposal, and the original general principles, were attacked by the powerful medical association as 'socialized medicine' and by the Catholic Church, which was concerned about the absence of a means test and the possibility of Catholics receiving instruction from non-Catholic sources. The resulting furore ended with the withdrawal of the proposed legislation and the resignation of Browne. Although the controversy was generated by a series of personal conflicts and political coincidences, it was widely seen as a straightforward conflict between church and state and as an affair epitomizing the political influence of the Catholic Church in Ireland.

Mother Croatia. (*Matica Hrvatska*) A cultural and political organization in **Croatia**, founded originally in 1842 and playing an important role in the development of Croatian national consciousness in the nineteenth and twentieth centuries. Tolerated for a while after 1945, it was finally banned in 1971 and its leaders imprisoned for espionage and separatist agitation. It was reconstructed in 1990 and developed a close liaison with the dominant right-wing Croatian Democratic Union.

Motherland Party. (*Anavatan Partisi*) A political party in **Turkey**. Based upon political traditions developed by the earlier **Democratic Party** and **Justice Party**, it was constructed as a conservative movement by **Özal** in 1983 after the country was returned to civilian rule by the military. Moderately nationalist, it was pro-Western and favoured a liberal economic policy but insisted that closer ties with the Islamic world were also desirable. Under Özal's leadership it formed the government through to 1991 when it went into opposition. It later suffered from internal factionalism and secession.

Mother Slovakia. (*Matica Slovenská*) A cultural and political organiz-ation in **Slovakia**. It developed after 1860 to mobilize Slovak nationalism. Banned in **Czechoslovakia** after 1948, it re-emerged in 1990 as a large-scale mass movement. Strongly nationalistic, with close links to right-wing nationalist parties, it demanded the denial of special rights for the country's ethnic minorities, especially the substantial Hungarian population.

Movement for a Democratic Slovakia. (*Hnutie za Demokratické Slovensko – HZDS*) A nationalist party in **Slovakia**. It was formed by **Mečiar** in 1991 after his break with the **Public Against Violence**, and was in the vanguard of the push for Slovakian independence. Although failing to win a majority in the 1992 election, it headed a coalition government. During the next two years it experienced considerable internal tension and faction-alism before Mečiar reasserted his control in 1994. After 1993 groups opposed to Mečiar seceded to form rival organizations.

Movement for Rights and Freedoms. (*Dvizhenie za Prava i Svobodi – DPS*) A political party in **Bulgaria**. Its roots lay in the ethnic Turk protest groups of the 1980s against the **Zhivkov** regime's policy of **Bulgarization**. It was constituted as a party in 1990, claiming to represent the Turkish minority and campaigned for equal rights, but denied that it had any separatist aspirations.

Multi-Fibre Arrangement (MFA). An international agreement to control imports of low-cost textiles in a way that in theory would both assist the growth of textile exports from developing countries and enable Western textile industries to plan for an orderly contraction and reconstruction. More properly the Agreement Regarding International Trade in Textiles, it was negotiated in 1973 within the **General Agreement on Tariffs and Trade (GATT)** and later renewed on several occasions. In practice it worked more to restrict imports from developing countries, as Western states adopted steadily stricter import quotas and until the **Uruguay Round** excluded textiles from general discussions on trade liberalization. The **European Communities (EC)** applied MFA rules even within the **Lomé Convention**.

Multilateral Force (MLF). A proposal by USA President, John F. Kennedy, in 1961 for the creation within the **North Atlantic Treaty Organization (NATO)** of international units jointly staffed by nationals of all NATO countries. It was in part a response to the longstanding NATO concern of how to reconcile its collective reliance upon nuclear defence with the exclusive American control of its nuclear capacity. Europeans were concerned that in the event of a European war the USA might not be prepared to use the nuclear option if that meant risking Soviet retaliation against American territory, or that for its own strategic reasons the USA might pull Western Europe into a nuclear war against its will. Several ideas on a collective NATO control had been expressed since the mid-1950s. The attractions of the MLF, as opposed to a Multi-National Force (MNF), were that the mixing of personnel would prevent any unit being unilaterally withdrawn or controlled by a single country, and that it would hinder a possible proliferation of independent European nuclear forces. The USA did not spell out its ideas in detail, suggesting initially that the MLF would apply to submarines, but later referring only to surface ships. It was dropped by President Johnson in 1964. The USA was not willing to give up supreme military control to a veto from any MLF participant, while the **United Kingdom** and **France** were reluctant to cede whatever nuclear independence they possessed.

Munich Olympic Killings. An attack by Palestinian guerillas of the Black September movement on 5 September 1972 on the living quarters of the Israeli team participating in the Twentieth Olympiad in Munich. Two athletes were killed and nine others taken hostage. A rescue bid by West German units at Munich airport resulted in the death of all the hostages and five terrorists. The surviving terrorists were flown to Libya, but were released five weeks later in response to the hijacking of a West German airliner.

Mutual and Balanced Force Reductions (MBFR). A series of attempts in the early 1970s by the **North Atlantic Treaty Organization (NATO)** and the **Warsaw Pact** to secure a limitation on the number of land-based troops deployed along the **Central Front**. Talks began in Vienna in October 1973. Differences of opinion within NATO made a common negotiating position difficult, but the two sides could not agree on the level of forces actually deployed in Europe or on how reductions, if agreed upon, could be enforced and verified. In 1985 NATO proposed that if agreement on cuts in troop levels could be reached, the reductions could be phased in prior to any agreement on what the existing level of deployment actually was, but this was rejected by the Warsaw Pact. In February 1989, with no agreement after 16 years of talks, the two sides agreed to wind up the MBFR and to reconvene in Vienna as the **Conventional Forces in Europe (CFE)** forum.

Mutual Recognition. The principle in the **European Communities (EC)** that Member States recognize each other's rules, regulations and standards in situations relating to the development and operation of an **internal market**. It was originally defined as the principle that goods legally manufactured in one Member State should be allowed free entry, without discrimination, into another Member State. With the 1987 **Single European Act (SEA)**, its definition was extended to cover other forms of economic activity such as services, in addition to implying that the mutual recognition of national regulations should apply in situations where EC rules had yet to be developed.

N

Naboland Boards. Delegations for Nordic Economic Co-operation established in 1934 by each of the Nordic countries. The idea came from the **Norden Associations**. They were expected to consider how the Nordic countries might grant reciprocal preferential tariffs and other trade concessions. After 1952 their activities were subsumed within the broader structures of the **Nordic Council**.

Nagorno-Karabakh. A Caucasian territory disputed by **Armenia** and **Azerbaijan**. Largely Armenian speaking, it was ceded to Azerbaijan by the 1920 Treaty of Kars between the **USSR** and **Turkey**. Unrest began to emerge after **Gorbachev** became Soviet leader. In 1987 a popular petition for the area to be transferred to Armenia was rejected by the USSR which said that such a transfer would require the agreement of both populations. Riots erupted in February 1988, and inter-ethnic violence spilled over into other parts of both Armenia and Azerbaijan. In December leading Armenian activists in Nagorno-Karabakh were arrested, and the following month the USSR imposed direct rule on the province. This failed to stop the escalation of conflict into an undeclared civil war, and direct rule was ended in November 1989 when the USSR decreed that the province should remain part of Azerbaijan. Conflict continued, and in September 1991 the Armenian population unilaterally declared the territory to be an independent republic. As Soviet authority crumbled, Armenia and Azerbaijan entered into a full-scale conflict which soon led to an Armenian victory and effective control over the province.

Nagy, Imre. (1896–1958) Prime Minister of **Hungary** 1953–55, 1956. He became a Communist after his capture by Russian troops while serving on the Eastern Front in the First World War. He returned to Hungary in 1921, but fled in 1928, living in exile in Moscow 1930–44. Appointed Minister of Agriculture upon his return to Hungary after its liberation by Soviet forces, he introduced a major programme of land reform. Briefly Minister of the Interior, he was dismissed from office by **Rákosi** who regarded him as ideologically unsound. In the 1953 party shake-up, with the support of the new Soviet premier, **Malenkov**, he replaced Rákosi as Prime Minister and introduced a more liberal regime, relaxing censorship, slowing the pace of agricultural **collectivization**, and encouraging the production of consumer goods. With the fall of Malenkov, he was dismissed from office in February 1955. Accused of Titoist deviation, he was expelled from the party in November. After the widespread demonstrations of October 1956 that marked the beginning of the **Hungarian Revolution**, he was recalled to lead the government. He attempted to accelerate the pace of change, included non-Communists in his government, and announced that Hungary would leave the **Warsaw Pact**. The speed of his reforms alarmed both the USSR and the Party Secretary, **Kádár**, who used Soviet troops to quell the revolution. Nagy took refuge in the Yugoslav embassy. Believing that he had a pledge of safe conduct out of the country from the Soviet forces, he left the embassy after 18 days, but was arrested and handed over to the Hungarian authorities. He was tried in secret and executed on 18 June 1958. In June 1989 he was fully rehabilitated and was given a reburial with full state honours.

Nassau Agreement. An agreement between USA President Kennedy and the British Prime Minister, **Macmillan**, at Nassau in the Bahamas on 18 December 1962. It confirmed that the USA would provide Polaris missiles for the British navy operating under the command of the **North Atlantic Treaty Organization (NATO)**, effectively ending British nuclear independence. It was criticized by the French President, **de Gaulle**, and deepened his hostility towards both countries. Four weeks later de Gaulle vetoed the British application to join the **European Communities (EC)**, citing the Agreement as proof that the **United Kingdom** was not wholly committed to Europe.

National Action for People and Homeland. (*Nationale Aktion für Volk und Heimat/Action Nationale pour la Peuple et la Patrie – NA/AN*) A small extreme right-wing protest party in **Switzerland**. Founded in 1961, it campaigned almost exclusively on immigration, demanding a ban on and repatriation of all immigrants. It renamed itself the Swiss Democrats (*Schweizer Demokraten/Démocratiques Suisses*) after 1990.

National Action Party. (*Milliyetçi Hareket Partisi – MHP*) A right-wing Islamic party in **Turkey**. Founded as the Nationalist Party in 1948, it was dissolved in 1953 because its advocacy of the creation of an Islamic state had been declared unconstitutional. It suffered from internecine factionalism after the 1960s before being banned in 1980 by the military regime. It was reformed as the Conservative Party in 1983, renaming itself the National Labour Party in 1985 before adopting the present title in 1992.

National Alliance. *See* ITALIAN SOCIAL MOVEMENT.

National Coalition Party. (*Kansallinen Kokoomus – KK*) The main conservative party in **Finland**, founded in 1918. Its strong association with Finnish nationalism made it suspect in the eyes of the **USSR**, and Soviet disapproval helped to prevent it being a possible element of coalition governments for much of the post-1945 period. It began to expand its electoral support after the late 1970s to become one of the largest parties in the country. Its claims to be a potential government partner could not so easily be denied and it entered a coalition in 1987.

National Democratic Party. (*Nationaldemokratische Partei Deutschlands – NPD*) A small extreme right-wing party in the **Federal Republic of Germany**. It was formed in November 1964 in Hanover by Adolf von Thadden as a merger of several extremist groups. It denied accusations that it was a neo-Nazi organization and was careful in its pronouncements in order to avoid a constitutional ban. Its brief but strong electoral performance in regional elections 1966–68 was perhaps due as much to economic problems, but it alarmed the political elites and its rise was one factor that persuaded the two major parties to form a **grand coalition**. It suffered from internal tension, and declined and fragmented after 1970.

National Democratic Party. (*National Demokratische Partei Deutschlands – NPDP*) A political party in the **German Democratic Republic (DDR)**. It was founded in 1948 by the **Socialist Unity Party (SED)** as an auxiliary organization for the mobilization of soldiers and ex-Nazis not accused of serious war crimes. Part of the SED-dominated National Front, and effectively controlled by the SED, it served only as a mouthpiece for the official state ideology. After the March 1990 elections it decided to merge with the **Liberal Democratic Party (LDPD)**.

National Front. (*Front National – FN*) A small extreme right-wing party in **France**. Founded in 1972 by **Le Pen** and used by him as a personal vehicle, it campaigned almost exclusively on an anti-immigration platform, linking the issue with problems of public safety, law and order, and unemployment. Although its success was limited and variable, the appeal of its platform was more widespread and forced the major conservative parties to take a stronger line on immigration.

National Front of the Czechoslovakian Socialist Republic. The governing coalition in **Czechoslovakia** 1945–89. Originally formed as a forum for the development of common policies in the wake of liberation, after 1948 it was effectively controlled by the **Communist Party of Czechoslovakia**. It served more as a forum for the expression of different views briefly during the **Prague Spring**. It contained four other small parties and several socio-economic organizations as well as the Communists.

National Harmony Party. (*Tautas Saskaņas Partija – TSP*) A political party in **Latvia**, formed in 1994 as a reconstruction of Harmony for Latvia–Economic Rebirth. Presenting a centre-left profile, it supported a gradual transition to a market economy, and also supported the granting of full citizens' rights to the country's large Russian minority.

Nationalist Party. (*Partit Nazzjonalista – PN*) The major conservative party in **Malta**, representing itself as a Christian Democratic organization. Founded in 1880, it played a central political role before independence. After returning to government in 1987 after 16 years in opposition, it sought to move Malta closer to Europe and pursued a policy of economic liberalization after the years of protectionism.

National Organization of Cypriot Fighters. (*Ethniki Organosis Kyprion Agoniston – EOKA*) The militant arm of the **énosis** movement in **Cyprus**. Led by **Grivas**, it waged a guerilla war against the British administration and army 1954–59, not for independence but for union with **Greece**. After the granting of independence in 1960 it returned underground, continuing to operate as EOKA-B. In 1974 its surviving elements collaborated with the **Greek Colonels** regime in Athens to engineer a pro-union coup on the island. The failure of the coup and the consequent Turkish invasion of the island, along with the collapse of the Greek military regime, largely discredited it and greatly weakened it as an effective underground revolutionary force.

National Party. (*Ethniko Komma*) A small right-wing party in **Greece**, and the successor of the earlier National Political Union. Both parties endorsed extremist policies and campaigned for the release from prison of the leaders of the 1967–74 military regime.

National Party of Montenegro. (*Narodna Stranka Crne Gore – NS*) A right-wing political party in **Montenegro** formed in 1990 to support a centralized state for and a closer union between **Serbia** and Montenegro.

National People's Liberation Army (ELAS). An organization created in **Greece** during the Second World War as a partisan force by the Communist-controlled National Liberation Front (EAM). In 1945 it controlled much of Greece after the withdrawal of German forces. It opposed the restoration of the monarchy endorsed by a 1946 plebiscite, and launched upon a civil war. Support for the government from the **United Kingdom** and, later, the USA, along with the unwillingness of **Stalin** to back it directly, handicapped its activities. It was forced to admit defeat in 1949 after a series of military reverses and the loss of its bases and refuges in neighbouring **Albania** and **Yugoslavia** after **Tito** broke with the **USSR**.

National Salvation Front. A political party in **Romania**. A hastily-formed organization of various groups that took power after the fall of the **Ceauşescu** regime in December 1989, it declared that it would act only as an interim government during the transition to democracy, but under the leadership of **Iliescu** later constituted itself as a party. Successful in the 1990 election, it attracted much criticism for containing many people belonging to or associated with the previous regime. In 1992 a conservative faction of former Communists seceded to form the National Salvation Front 22

December Group (eventually the Social Democracy Party). Adopting a broadly centre-left programme and a commitment to a free market economy, in 1993 the Front changed its name to the Social Democratic Party of Romania, and then to the Democratic Party (*Partidul Democrat – PD*).

National Salvation Party. (*Milli Selâmet Partisi – MSP*) An Islamic party in **Turkey**. It was founded in 1972 as a successor to the earlier National Order Party which had been banned by the courts for using religion for political purposes. It was the first Islamic party to co-operate in a coalition government since the establishment of the secular state in 1923. Banned after the 1980 military coup, it was succeeded in 1983 by the Welfare Party (*Refah Partisi – RP*) as the country's major fundamentalist Islamic group.

National Service. The official name of the system of **conscription** operated by the **United Kingdom** from 1939 to the early 1960s.

National Unity Party. (*Ulusal Birlik Partisi – UBP*) A centre-right party in the **Turkish Republic of Northern Cyprus**. It was founded by **Denktash** in 1976 out of the earlier National Solidarity (*Ulusal Dayanişma*) movement. Dominant since 1976, though weakened by a 1992 secession of a Democratic Party which cost it government power in 1993, it advocated the idea of a bicommunal confederal state of **Cyprus**, but later shifted to accept the possibility of two separate states.

Nations of Europe. A cross-national **party group** in the **European Parliament (EP)**. It was formed in 1994 as a conservative group largely opposed to any further extension of supranationalism in the **European Union (EU)**. Its core was the newly-created Another Europe (*L'Autre Europe*) in **France**.

NATO. *See* NORTH ATLANTIC TREATY ORGANIZATION.

Natolin Group. A faction within the **Polish United Workers' Party**. Named after the location near Warsaw where it held its meetings, it consisted of Communists who opposed the reform proposals put forward by **Gomulka** in 1956, and who wanted to reassert a Stalinist influence within the party leadership.

NATO Military Committee. The highest military organ within the **North Atlantic Treaty Organization (NATO)**, with the task of planning and co-ordinating defence strategy. Made up of the national Chiefs of Staff, it was not given any command functions. Meeting at least twice yearly, it made recommendations to the higher civilian and political NATO structures, as well as providing guidance to the principal NATO commanders. Its presidency rotated annually across the Member States.

Natta, Alessandro. (1918–) Secretary-General of the **Italian Communist Party (PCI)** 1983–88. An anti-Fascist activist after 1936, he was arrested and deported to Germany in 1941. He joined the PCI in 1945 and entered Parliament in 1948. Admitted to the party leadership in 1968 he was made leader after the death of **Berlinguer**. Rather more cautious than his predecessor, he saw PCI support begin to decline. After 1988 he criticized the change of direction pursued by his successor, **Occhetto**, and opposed the decision to change the party's name. He retired from active politics in 1990.

Near abroad. (*Blizheye zarubezhe*) A term widely used in official and popular circles in **Russia** after 1991 to describe the successor states of the **USSR**. It reflected a belief that these states were of major interest to Russia, which at the least had a right to seek to influence their policies, or even to reincorporate them into a new Russian empire. It was essentially a new version of the concept of sphere of influence.

Neman. A border dispute between **Lithuania** and **Russia**. The Neman (Nemunas) river was the border between Lithuania and the **Kaliningrad** region of the **USSR** after the territories were first incorporated into the USSR in 1940, with the border being drawn along the Lithuanian bank. The Neman is a navigable river, and hence of economic value, and after 1990 Lithuania argued that according to international law the boundary should follow the middle of the river.

Németh, Miklós. (1948–) Prime Minister of **Hungary** 1988–90. A lecturer and economist, he worked in the National Planning Office after 1977. He joined the **Hungarian Socialist Workers' Party** in 1968, leading its economic policy section after 1984. He was promoted to the **Politburo** in May 1988 after the removal of **Kádár**. He was appointed premier in November, and in March 1989 broke with **Nomenklatura** practice by reorganizing the government without first seeking clearance from the Politburo, and introduced a programme of reform. He resigned from the party in December 1989 when it reconstituted itself as the Hungarian Socialist Party because of its refusal to support his austerity programme. In 1991 he was appointed as a Vice-President of the **European Bank for Reconstruction and Development (EBRD)**.

Nenni, Pietro. (1891–1980) Italian politician. The long-time leader of the **Italian Socialist Party (PSI)** 1944–63, he took the party into an alliance with the Communists, which led to a right-wing faction seceding from the party in 1948. In the 1950s he began to steer the party more towards the centre, arguing that the ruling **Christian Democratic Party (DC)** should accept an 'opening to the left'. Due in part to his efforts, the two parties reconciled most of their differences, and he served as Deputy Prime Minister in coalition governments 1963–68. After the 1966 merger with the **Italian Social Democratic Party (PSDI)**, he was elected leader of the unified organization, serving until 1969 when the PSDI reasserted its independence.

Netherlands. A constitutional kingdom in Western Europe existing within its current boundaries since 1839. Neutral in the First World War, it was invaded and occupied by Germany in 1940. Its experiences during the Second World War persuaded it that neutrality was no longer an option. It was a signatory of the 1948 **Treaty of Brussels** and the following year became a founder member of the **North Atlantic Treaty Organization (NATO)**. A strong supporter of European integration, its entry into **Benelux** was followed after 1950 by participation from the outset in the **European Communities (EC)**. The third largest colonial power before 1940, the end of its empire after 1945 caused some domestic social and political problems, mainly arising from the loss of the Dutch East Indies, with South Moluccan exiles being held responsible for terrorist attacks in 1975 and 1977. The Dutch political system was held to be an example of **consociational democracy**, with politics dominated by a plurality of highly organized subcultures, and the interactions between them, structured broadly around religious differences. The organizational networks and structures, particularly that of the Catholic population, began to disintegrate after the mid-1960s, but the consensual style of elite co-operation and decision-making which the old structures were said to have engendered continued to characterize the system.

New Community Instrument (NCI). A fund established by the **European Communities (EC)** in 1977 to supplement the work of the **European Investment Bank (EIB)** in assisting industrial projects. Known also as the Ortoli Facility, it was directed more towards helping small and medium-sized companies, usually within the context of the EC's regional policy.

New Dawn Party. (*Yeni Dogus Partisi – YDP*) A centre-right party in **Cyprus**. It was formed in 1984 mainly to represent those people who had moved from **Turkey** to the area of the island occupied by Turkish forces in 1974. It first entered the government in 1986, and in 1993 merged with the **Democratic Party**.

New Democracy. (*Néa Dimokratía*) A conservative party in **Greece**. It was formed in 1974 by **Karamanlis** as a broad centre-right movement, pro-Western in orientation and in favour of a liberal free market economy. It formed the first government after the fall of the **Greek Colonels**, but suffered leadership problems and internal disputes in the 1980s. These were intensified after 1991 with difference in particular over policy towards **Macedonia**, and in 1993 a faction seceded from it, bringing down the government headed by **Mitsotakis**.

New Democracy. (*Ny Demokrati – ND*) A small right-wing populist party in **Sweden**. Formed in 1990, it adopted a rather satirical stance in its critiques of the political establishment and the bureaucratic state. Its programme stressed law and order, the reduction of immigration, government reform and reduction of the welfare state, and **privatization**. It enjoyed modest but surprising electoral success in 1991 and 1994.

New Economic Mechanism. The central element of the economic reform programme in **Hungary** proposed by **Kádár**. Intended to promote more consumerism as a way of securing greater legitimacy and support for the regime, it was largely in place by 1968. Although there were some reverses in the 1970s, it was reasserted in 1979. The objectives included introducing self-management in production and marketing in the collective farms, breaking up monopolistic state enterprises, permitting some private ownership, and linking prices to world markets. It helped to put Hungary in a better position to cope with economic change after the fall of the Communist regimes in 1989 than most Eastern European countries.

New Forum. (*Neues Forum – NF*) An opposition group in the **German Democratic Republic (DDR)**. It was formed in 1989 not as a party, but as a forum for discussions on socialist and humanitarian values which it wished the regime to adopt. It sought the liberalization of the regime rather than its destruction. When the Communist regime collapsed later in the year, its loose structure and more limited objectives prevented it from competing effectively with new political formations, and it disintegrated in 1990.

Night frost crisis. A phrase used by **Khrushchev** to describe relationships between the **USSR** and **Finland** in 1958. The crisis began with a shift of power within the **Finnish Social Democratic Party** in April and a party split occasioned by the leadership victory of the veteran Väinö Tanner. Under Soviet pressure Tanner had been imprisoned in 1946 on dubious charges of war crimes. The split led to increased government instability and after the 1958 election the USSR was greatly concerned that the Tanner party might be included in the next government. It openly warned other Finnish parties about such collaboration and halted all trade negotiations between the two countries. It took the skills of **Kekkonen** to restore confidence between the two states, appointing a coalition government acceptable to the USSR in January 1959. Normal relations were restored immediately afterwards. The crisis confirmed and consolidated the role of the Finnish presidency and emphasized that the USSR claimed a right to influence the make-up of Finnish governments.

Night of the Long Knives. A phrase that was sometimes used to describe the first meeting of a newly appointed **Commission** when the major item of business was the allocation of policy portfolios among the Commissioners. Many regarded its use as being in bad taste, given that it was first used by Hitler to describe the night of 29/30 June 1934 when under his orders the SS murdered the leaders of the SA and other potential opponents of the Nazi regime.

NKVD. The Soviet People's Commissariat for Internal Affairs, the secret police agency of the **USSR**. It was established in 1934 after a reorganization of its OGPU predecessor. In 1946 it was restructured by **Beria** and merged with the Ministry of Internal Affairs (MVD), responsible for the police and prison camps, and the Ministry of State Security which had also supervised the police forces in the Eastern European satellite states. After the elimination of Beria in 1953, the new more comprehensive body was reorganized and strengthened as the **KGB**.

Noel, Émile. (1922–) Secretary-General of the **Commission** 1958–87. The first appointee to the position, his long tenure as the most senior administrative officer of the **European Communities (EC)** enabled him to play an important role in shaping their administrative ethos and practices. His involvement in European affairs had begun in 1949, working for the **Council of Europe** until 1954.

Nomenklatura. Formally the list of positions, and of the people who were candidates for them, in the **USSR**. Appointments to all public positions at all levels were the prerogative of the **Communist Party of the Soviet Union**. One of the principal criteria for public eligibility was political reliability. Never officially acknowledged, the nomenklatura system gave the party full control of career advancement and of recruitment to elite positions. It eventually created a distinct privileged social caste of party members and their dependants. The system was also adopted by the Communist regimes of Eastern Europe.

Norden Associations. A network of national organizations in Scandinavia established after 1919 to promote cultural links between the Nordic states. They remained independent of each other until the formation of an international League of Norden Associations in 1965. Their campaign for a Nordic forum was realized in 1952 with the establishment of the **Nordic Council**.

Nordic Council. An inter-governmental and inter-parliamentary association of the Nordic states established in 1952. While informal collaboration had existed since 1918, attempts to create a more structured co-operation had failed. In 1951 the Danish premier, **Hedtoft**, took up the idea of a Council which had first been put forward by the **Norden Associations** in 1938. The Council was established not by treaty, but by a common statute adopted by the national parliaments, as an annual gathering of legislators which would advise governments on matters of common concern and recommend co-ordinated policy actions and administrative procedures. A high degree of collaboration, including a common labour market, transfer of pension rights and abolition of currency controls, was soon achieved, but more contentious issues such as defence and foreign policy were never raised or discussed. Several efforts to achieve economic integration also failed. Some formalization was introduced with the 1962 Treaty of Nordic Co-operation (the

Helsinki Convention) which specified major areas of co-operation to cover the eventuality of some members joining the **European Communities (EC)**. A more institutionalized structure was introduced in 1971 because of renewed applications to the EC and as a result of the 1969–70 failure to create a **Nordic Economic Union (NORDEK)**. The reforms established a Council of Ministers, with a supporting secretariat, to operate alongside the legislators' assembly. In 1986 the Council's secretariat was merged with the Copenhagen secretariat of the Nordic Cultural Council, an agency formed in 1972 after a 1971 Nordic Cultural treaty. After 1971 the Council of Ministers, representing national governments, became the focal point of co-operative proposals and activity. Its decisions had to be unanimous and were usually regarded as binding. The structures were reviewed and reorganized in 1993, making them more like those of the EC. In 1991 the newly independent **Baltic States** expressed an interest in joining the Council.

Nordic Council of Ministers. *See* NORDIC COUNCIL.

Nordic Cultural Council. *See* NORDIC COUNCIL.

Nordic Economic Union (NORDEK). Abortive discussions by the Nordic states 1969–70. A desire for Nordic economic union had been expressed since the nineteenth century, but without result. Proposals in the late 1940s for a customs and economic union also failed. They were revived in 1962 as a result of Nordic applications to join the **European Communities (EC)**. The 1969 proposals were partly stimulated by the fact that renewed applications to the EC were likely to succeed after the retirement of **de Gaulle**. The discussions implied a limited institutional framework, a common agricultural policy, and a **common external tariff**, but the states failed to reach agreement on almost every point. The negotiations were abandoned in 1971, with the countries settling instead for a modest strengthening of the Nordic Council that had little or no economic implications.

Nordic Inter-Parliamentary Union. The Scandinavian section of the Inter-Parliamentary Union, founded in 1907. It worked for Nordic co-operation and the adoption in the area of common legislation. Much of its importance declined after 1952 with the formation of the **Nordic Council**.

Nordic Investment Bank. Established by the **Nordic Council** in 1976 to finance projects within the Nordic area and to promote exports. Based in Helsinki, it was modelled upon the **European Investment Bank (EIB)**. After 1982 it also began to finance projects in developing countries.

NORTHAG. The more widely used acronym for Northern Army Group, Central Europe, the more northerly of the two **Central Front** land forces of the **North Atlantic Treaty Organization (NATO)**. Under the command of NATO's Allied Forces Central Europe (**AFCENT**), it was usually headed by a British general since it covered the Front sector where the **British Army of**

the Rhine (BAOR) would operate. Its responsibility was defence of the North German Plain, a historic invasion route from east to west.

North Atlantic Co-operation Council. A body linking the North Atlantic Treaty Organization (NATO) with the new democracies of Eastern Europe and the Commonwealth of Independent States (CIS). Established by NATO in 1992, its purpose was to help NATO define a new role for itself in the post-Cold War world, especially possible intervention outside its traditional territory. It was seen as a means of providing some stability for Eastern Europe and a mechanism for providing peace-keeping forces in more localized conflicts in the former USSR and Eastern Europe. Its formation was criticized for duplicating and confusing the role of the Conference for Security and Co-operation in Europe (CSCE), and France in particular voiced suspicions that it was merely an American strategy for retaining influence in Europe.

North Atlantic Fisheries Organization (NAFO). An association of countries possessing a major interest in the deep-sea fishing areas of the North Atlantic. Its purpose was to seek agreement on fishing limits and zones, permissible quotas and catches, and stock conservation, but consensus was difficult to achieve.

North Atlantic Marine Mammals Commission. An inter-governmental organization established in April 1992 by the Faroe Islands, Greenland, Iceland and Norway, all countries with major whaling interests which had opposed the 1991 decision by the International Whaling Commission (IWC) to uphold the ban on commercial whaling introduced in 1985. Their argument was that the IWC had been persuaded by ethical considerations rather than by any concern with stock conservation and management. The 1991 decision had already led Iceland to leave the IWC, and in 1993 Norway announced, to considerable international hostility, that it would resume the commercial hunting of minke whales.

North Atlantic Treaty. See NORTH ATLANTIC TREATY ORGANIZATION.

North Atlantic Treaty Organization (NATO). The major defensive organization of Western Europe, established on 4 April 1949 by the North Atlantic Treaty signed in Washington DC. It linked the USA and Canada with Western European countries in a system of mutual defence. Its formation was the result of Western European fears after 1945 of Soviet intentions and ambitions. Its core principles was that an attack upon one member would be regarded as an attack upon all, but it was never clear how members were expected to respond to such a situation, being obliged only to take such action as they deemed necessary. The vagueness was due to the USA which did not wish to be forced to respond in any conceivable circumstance. The obligation applied only to the territories of the members and to their ships and aircraft when operating north of the Tropic of Cancer. An elaborate political and military structure, its military head is **SACEUR**, a position always filled by an American general. A North Atlantic Council presided over by a Secretary-General, always a European, was set up as the supreme decision-making authority, defining arms policies and defence strategies. Underneath it there emerged a complex network of collaborative bodies such as a Defence Planning Committee (DPC) of defence ministers, the **Nuclear Planning Group (NPG)**, the **Eurogroup**, the **Independent European Programme Group**, and a North Atlantic Assembly of parliamentarians. Its headquarters were in Paris 1949–66, moving to **Brussels** when **France** withdrew from the military organization.

NATO always suffered from internal tensions. Within Europe the greatest problems were between **Greece** and **Turkey**, but tensions between Europe and the USA were more important. There was persistent European unease about American domination of NATO, but whenever questions were raised in the USA about the costs of its involvement in NATO, Western Europe became insistent upon the American commitment, as it did at times of super-power crisis. In periods of relative calm or **détente**, it was more concerned that the two super-powers might strike a deal that would adversely affect its own interests and security. The USA was further irritated by a European reluctance to bear a greater share of the costs of defence. NATO's original strategy was to prepare for a conventional war in Europe. Because of the greater conventional superiority of the **USSR** and its **Warsaw Pact** allies, and the Western European refusal to increase defence expenditure, it switched to a nuclear defence strategy, **massive retaliation**, in 1954, modifying it to **flexible response** after 1967.

With the ending of the Cold War after 1989, NATO was left without a readily identifiable enemy or purpose, though all argued that the alliance should be maintained. Its aims and objectives were amended by the 1991 **Rome Declaration on Peace and Co-operation**. Discussions on its future focused upon developing a small rapid deployment force that could be used outside the traditional NATO area, and on extending its membership into Eastern Europe. Agreement on a Rapid Reaction Corps was reached in May 1991. The Corps was inaugurated in October 1992, with full operationalization scheduled for the end of 1995. The 1992 creation of the **North Atlantic Co-operation Council** was a first step in the direction of extending NATO membership, but despite requests from several Eastern European governments, it delayed indefinitely any decision about accepting them as direct members. Instead they were offered association with NATO through a planned agreement on Partnership for Peace. Most had accepted the proposal by 1994, although **Russia** expressed considerable reservation about it.

North-East Atlantic Fisheries Commission (NEAFC). An inter-governmental body established in 1980. Its objective was to develop co-operation with fishing interests to manage the conservation of fish stocks.

Northern Epirus. A southern region of **Albania** possessing an ethnic Greek majority. The Albanian Communist regime had always officially denied the existence of a Greek population within its borders. The rights of the ethnic Greeks were taken up after 1990 by **Greece**, which expressed concern about possible violations of human rights by Albania, but it did not reject the boundary between the two states which had been established in 1925.

Northern Flank. A term describing the northernmost reach of the **North Atlantic Treaty Organization (NATO)**. It normally referred only to northern **Norway**, where NATO territory adjoined the **USSR** and the important Soviet military bases on the Kola peninsula. It was given its own NATO command, Allied Forces Northern Europe (AFNORTH).

Northern Ireland. The six north-eastern counties of **Ireland** that remained within the **United Kingdom** after Irish independence in 1922. Established as a self-governing province by the 1920 Government of Ireland Act, its govern-ment was dominated by the majority Protestants, with extensive discrimina-tion against the minority Catholic population. Protests against discrimination in jobs and housing broke out in 1968, spreading to become more extensive civil rights demonstrations. The government failed to control the emergence of violence, and in April 1969 British troops were sent to police the province, but they were soon caught in the middle between the terrorist campaigns of the **Irish Republican Army (IRA)** and Protestant paramilitary groups. After troops fired on a Catholic demonstration in Londonderry on 30 January 1972 (Bloody Sunday), Britain suspended the Northern Ireland Constitution and imposed direct rule from London. Its attempts after 1972 to establish a political settlement acceptable to both communities failed. An assembly elected in June 1973 collapsed because of Protestant objections to power-sharing within a non-sectarian executive, and a constitutional convention in 1976 failed to reach an agreement. After 1979 Britain and Ireland began to collaborate more closely, signing the **Anglo-Irish Agreement** in 1985, but the two communities could not be brought to agree upon a system of provin-cial government, and terrorists from both sides continued to wage war. A new attempt was made with the 1994 **Downing Street Declaration**. Although it resulted in a ceasefire of all paramilitary groups, the consequent framework document, which outlined possible cross-border institutions, was greeted with some scepticism and hostility. Arguments over what steps should be taken, in particular the decommissioning of arms, stalled further progress.

Northern League. (*Lega Nord*) A populist protest movement in **Italy**. Formed in 1991 as an alliance of several regional anti-centre movements in Northern Italy, clustering around the **Lombardy League** of **Bossi**, it demanded at the least a federalization of the country, with some activists desiring the creation of a separate northern state on fiscal and cultural grounds, as well as extensive institutional reform, an end to government waste and political corruption, and strict controls on immigration. It enjoyed considerable electoral success in 1994 after the collapse of the traditional party system. It entered a coalition government under **Berlusconi**, but it was an unruly partner and it was Bossi who brought the government down a few months later. His actions split the League, as many of its members opted to continue to support Berlusconi.

Norway. A constitutional monarchy in Western Europe, independent since 1905 after previously belonging to **Denmark** and, from 1814 to 1905, in a union with **Sweden**. It adopted a policy of neutrality, but was invaded and occupied by German forces in 1940. After 1945 concerns about security, especially the fact that it was strategically important and shared a border with the **USSR**, led it to become a founder member of the **North Atlantic Treaty Organization (NATO)**, but it consistently refused to permit nuclear weapons within its territory. It was sceptical about European integration, but joined the **European Free Trade Association (EFTA)** in 1960. Economic considerations later led governments to seek membership of the **European Communities (EC)**, but in 1972 and again in 1994 the agreement signed with the EC was narrowly rejected in a popular referendum. Since 1935 politics have been dominated by the **Labour Party**. Forming single-party majority governments 1945–61, the party carried out a programme of economic redistribution and constructed an extensive welfare system, largely setting an agenda for national politics which other parties had to accept. Since 1961 government has alternated between non-socialist coalitions and minority Labour administrations within a broad framework of national consensus on most issues other than that of European integration.

Note campaign. A diplomatic move by the **USSR** in 1952. **Stalin** sent two notes to Western governments offering the possibility of discussions on a peace treaty on Germany, suggesting reunification of the two German states, the withdrawal of all foreign armed forces, free elections, and a neutral Germany which would be permitted to have its own armed forces. The offers were rejected by the Western states and by the **Adenauer** government in the **Federal Republic of Germany**. The West saw the notes as being tactical moves which, by creating differences of opinion within the West, might prevent the strengthening of the **North Atlantic Treaty Organization (NATO)** agreed upon in the **Lisbon Force Goals**, and the rearming of West Germany within the proposed **European Defence Community (EDC)**. In addition, there were concerns that a neutral Germany might easily fall within the Soviet sphere of influence.

Note crisis. A crisis in relations between the **USSR** and **Finland** in 1961. It was occasioned by the planned presence of West German forces in **North**

Atlantic Treaty Organization (NATO) exercises in the Baltic. The USSR claimed this was a threat to its own security and proposed that it and Finland should hold joint consultations on defence, invoking the terms of the 1948 **Treaty of Friendship, Co-operation and Mutual Assistance**. In addition, the USSR seemed to be concerned that **Kekkonen**, with whom it had established a good relationship, might be defeated in the forthcoming Finnish presidential election. Kekkonen, who was in Hawaii when the note was issued, met **Khrushchev** a month later and persuaded him to drop the demand. The issue indicated that the USSR had an interest in who became the President of Finland. Kekkonen was subsequently re-elected unopposed.

Nouvelles Équipes Internationales. *See* EUROPEAN UNION OF CHRISTIAN DEMOCRATS.

Nouvelles Frontières. The name of a French travel agency that challenged the price-fixing regulations of the French Civil Aviation Code. In April 1986 the **Court of Justice** ruled in favour of the agency, declaring that air transport was not exempt from **European Communities (EC)** competition policy, and that the Member States were not permitted to approve air fares which resulted from agreements between air lines. It was the first major challenge to air fare cartel arrangements.

Noviks Affair. A political controversy in **Latvia**. Alfons Noviks, an ethnic Latvian, had joined the Soviet secret police after the annexation of Latvia by the **USSR** in 1940, rising to become head of the secret police in the region and retiring in the 1980s. After independence in 1991 calls were made for his arrest on charges of involvement in the mass deportations of Latvians to Siberia in 1941 and of personally ordering the torture and execution of political prisoners. Despite his advanced age (86) he was arrested in March 1994 and placed on trial.

Novotný, Anton. (1904–1975) President of **Czechoslovakia** 1957–68. He joined the Communist Party in 1921 and became a party activist. Confined in a concentration camp in 1941, after his release in 1945 he rose through the party ranks to be appointed First Secretary in 1953 after the **Slansky Trial**, retaining the office until 1968 when he was replaced by **Dubček**. A committed Stalinist, his hostility to the attempts by **Khrushchev** to adopt a more liberal line for the Communist bloc made him a highly unpopular figure. He assumed the presidency in 1957 and his insistence upon developing heavy industry caused an economic recession and consequent student demonstrations after 1961. His authority was weakened by widespread protests by students and intellectuals in 1967. In an attempt to block change, in February 1968 he asked the army to occupy Prague. When it turned him down, he was forced to resign his offices in disgrace. Although officially back in favour by 1971, he played no further political role after the crushing of the **Prague Spring**.

Nuclear Energy Agency (NEA). An autonomous agency associated with the **Organization for Economic Co-operation and Development (OECD)**. Established in April 1972 with an expanded non-European membership, it replaced the earlier **European Nuclear Energy Agency (ENEA)**. Its brief was to promote technical and economic studies of nuclear development, and collaboration on the use of nuclear energy for peaceful purposes.

Nuclear-free zone (NFZ). An area where the manufacture, storage and deployment of nuclear weapons would not be permitted. There have been two types of NFZ proposals. Many local government authorities made NFZ declarations, but these were largely symbolic since no local area could be insulated from national policies or the effects of nuclear conflict. Other proposals looked for the establishment of NFZs by international treaty. The first was the 1957 **Rapacki Plan** for an NFZ in Central Europe. A similar proposal was made by **Sweden** in 1983, based upon the report of an Independent Commission on Disarmament and Security headed by **Palme**. In 1963 and again in 1978 the Finnish President, **Kekkonen**, backed by the **USSR**, proposed a Nordic NFZ to be confirmed by treaty. More tentative suggestions for a Balkan NFZ were raised by **Romania** in 1957 and **Greece** in 1982. None of the proposals bore fruition. The NFZ idea was largely irrelevant to both national and international politics, being largely a reflection of the desires of anti-nuclear groups in Western Europe. It was supported on occasions by the USSR, which saw it as a way of weakening and confusing the Western defence commitment.

Nuclear Non-Proliferation Treaty. An agreement signed in July 1968 by the **United Kingdom**, USA and **USSR** who agreed that from 1970 they would not aid other states to obtain or produce nuclear weapons. More than 100 countries subsequently signed the treaty. The **Federal Republic of Germany** was required to sign it by the USSR as a precondition of Soviet participation in the **Ostpolitik** discussions. **France** did not sign it, but applied its prohibitions on the sale of nuclear arms. The treaty also provided for quinquennial reviews of its clauses.

Nuclear Planning Group (NPG). A committee of the **North Atlantic Treaty Organization (NATO)** dealing with nuclear aspects of defence planning and strategy. It was formed in 1967 after the failure of the **multilateral force (MLF)** proposals as a response to European concerns about the American monopoly on the nuclear guarantee within NATO. It was not intended to be a decision-making body but a forum for general discussion on modernization and deployment, and the USA never felt totally bound by its recommendations.

Nuclear Test Ban Treaty. *See* COMPREHENSIVE TEST BAN TREATY.

Nuclear Umbrella. A popular phrase describing the nuclear guarantee and protection provided by the USA to Western Europe. It was never clear what level of Soviet action or threat would trigger the American nuclear response.

Nuremberg Trials. A series of 13 trials of major Nazi figures accused of war crimes and crimes against humanity, held in Nuremberg 1945–47. They were presided over by American, British, French and Soviet judges, and 177 Germans and Austrians were indicted: 25 were given the death penalty, 20 life imprisonment, 97 prison sentences, and 35 were acquitted. While the trials were conducted under principles of international law governing the conduct of war, there was criticism that the trials were little more than the military victors trying the defeated, something which it was claimed could set a dangerous precedent for all future conflicts.

Nyborg Agreements. A decision by the finance ministers of the **European Communities (EC)** in November 1987 to ease some of the problems created by the **Exchange Rate Mechanism (ERM)**. Meeting in the Danish town of Nyborg, they agreed to allow bilateral currency adjustments within the permissible limits of the ERM to be made without the consent of the other country, and that repayment of short-term national central bank credits should be in **European Currency Units (ECUs)**.

O

Occhetto, Achille. (1936–) Italian politician. Elected to Parliament for the **Italian Communist Party (PCI)** in 1976, he replaced **Natta** as party leader in June 1988. He directed his attention towards reorganizing the party structure. The need to initiate policy changes became more urgent after the collapse of Communism in Eastern Europe after 1989, and he sought, against some strong opposition, to recast the party in a social democratic mould. In 1991 he pushed through a change of name to the Democratic Party of the Left at the cost of a secession of hardliners, and in 1994 forged a broad left-wing alliance. He was forced to accept much of the blame for the defeat of the left in the 1994 election, and resigned the leadership.

Oder–Neisse Line. The post-1945 boundary between Germany and **Poland**, following the line of the river Oder from the Baltic Sea to its confluence with the river Neisse, then following the Western Neisse to the Czechoslovakian border. It was provisionally agreed, until ratification by a peace treaty with Germany, by the Allies at the **Yalta** and **Potsdam Conferences**, and was a consequence of the seizure by the **USSR** of pre-war Polish territory in the east and the need to compensate Poland for this loss. No peace treaty was signed because of the **Cold War** and the division of Germany. The **German Democratic Republic (DDR)** recognized the boundary in 1950, but the **Federal Republic of Germany** refused to do so on the grounds that only a unified Germany could ratify the boundary. It was formally recognized by West Germany in 1972 as part of the **Ostpolitik** treaties. After reunification in 1990 the German government was initially hesitant about Polish and Soviet demands that the line be reconfirmed as an international boundary, but it later formally renounced all claims to the ex-German territories east of the line.

Official Ulster Unionist Party (OUP). The larger of the two Protestant parties in **Northern Ireland** demanding that the province remain part of the **United Kingdom**. Founded in 1905 as the **Ulster Unionist Party**, a name it still prefers to use, it dominated the **Stormont** system of devolved government until the imposition of direct London rule in 1972. It became more widely known as the OUP after the secession of more hard-line Protestant activists after 1969 who formed the **Democratic Unionist Party**.

Olivier, Borg. (1911–1979) Prime Minister of **Malta** 1950–55, 1962–71. The long-time leader of the **Nationalist Party**, in the 1950s he opposed the proposal that the island should become part of the **United Kingdom**. In the 1960s he presided over the British withdrawal from Malta, but his inability to attract sufficient industry and investment for a reconstruction of the island's economy cost him the 1971 election. He retired from politics in 1977.

Ollenauer, Erich. (1901–1963) West German politician. He joined the **Social Democratic Party (SPD)** in 1916, and worked as a party administrator. Entering Parliament in 1949, he was the automatic choice to succeed **Schumacher** as party leader in 1952. He argued for a European security system involving demilitarization in Central Europe in place of the two power blocs. The last SPD leader of the pre-Hitler generation, he strove domestically to sustain the party's ideological heritage and purity. An uninspiring leader, his party and foreign policy stands were out of tune with the mood of the time, and he was replaced as leader in 1960.

OMON. (*Otryad Militsii Osobogo Naznacheniya*) An elite armed unit, the Special Purpose Police Squad, in the **USSR**. Controlled by the Ministry of the Interior, it was established in 1987 as a crime investigation unit, but was more generally used to maintain law and order and to counteract anti-government demonstrations and regional separatist movements. It was particularly active in the **Baltic States** until they gained their independence in 1991.

O'Neill, Terence. (1914–1990) Prime Minister of **Northern Ireland** 1963–69. An army officer, he entered the **Stormont** Parliament in 1946. As leader of the **Ulster Unionist Party** after 1963, he attempted to follow a more moderate line on the issue of civil rights for Catholics in the province, and on relations with **Ireland**. His policies and his meeting with the Prime Minister of Ireland provoked resentment and a challenge to his leadership from Protestant hardliners. In an attempt to gain support for his policy, he called an election in February 1969, but when it failed to produce the desired result, he was obliged to resign, retiring from politics.

Open Barracks. An agreement reached by several post-1989 democratic regimes in Eastern Europe to exchange information on troop levels and deployments, and to permit the mutual inspection of army bases. Modelled on the **Open Skies Agreement**, the measures were intended to secure a reduction of tension.

Open Skies Agreement. A **Confidence-Building Measure (CBM)** signed at the 1992 Helsinki session of the **Conference on Security and Co-operation in Europe (CSCE)**. It was the outcome of negotiations begun in Vienna in 1989 at meetings of the **Conventional Forces in Europe (CFE)** forum. It overcame the problem of verification that had hindered previous

arms control talks, allowing unarmed low-flying surveillance to ensure that there was compliance with arms control agreements. The concept had been first proposed by the USA in 1955.

Operational Manoeuvre Group (OMG). A key component of **Warsaw Pact** planning for a war on the **Central Front**. The Pact's strategy called for a relatively wide dispersal of troop concentrations to avoid presenting an easy target for **North Atlantic Treaty Organization (NATO)** nuclear forces, with its armies approaching the battle zone in staggered echelons. These were to be reinforced by OMGs, a series of compact and highly mobile units which would exploit weaknesses in NATO's defences to penetrate and operate far behind them.

Operation PHARE. Officially the Poland and Hungary Assistance for Economic Restructuring Programme, it was a programme of economic aid proposed in 1989 by Western countries to assist the democratization process in Eastern Europe. The lead was taken by the **Organization for Economic Co-operation and Development (OECD)** which offered aid to **Hungary** and **Poland**. In 1990 it was extended to other Eastern European countries. An additional programme, PHARE Democracy was established in July 1992 to support the political reform process in Eastern Europe. *See also* CENTRE FOR CO-OPERATION WITH EUROPEAN ECONOMIES IN TRANSITION, GROUP OF TWENTY FOUR.

Opt out. Within the **European Union (EU)** a dispensation by which a Member State is not bound by specific provisions of the founding treaties and their amendments. The first opt outs, granted to **Denmark** and the **United Kingdom**, occurred during the discussions on further integration that culminated with the ratification of the **Treaty on European Union**.

Opus Dei. A secret conservative Catholic sect. Founded in Madrid in 1928 by Escriva de Balaguer, it spread to some 20 countries, eventually receiving the approval of **John Paul II**. It insisted upon doctrinal authoritarianism and strict internal discipline, preaching that its lay and clergy members should both preach and practise the Catholic gospel through all aspects of their working lives. Its major political impact was in **Spain**, where its founder was associated with the **Franco** regime. Frequently accused of elitism, Fascism and intolerance, its influence waned sharply after the reintroduction of democracy in Spain.

Organisation de l'Armée Secrète (OAS). A terrorist organization in Algeria and **France** seeking to overthrow **de Gaulle** and the **Fifth French Republic**. Its formation was the result of de Gaulle's conclusion in 1959 that the **Algerian War of Independence** could not be won militarily by France. The OAS leader was General **Salan**, and most of the activists were army officers or former white settlers in Algeria. In April 1961 it attempted a coup in Algeria, and during the negotiations that led to the **Évian Agreements** it waged a bombing campaign in France and made several attempts upon de Gaulle's life. Salan and most of its leaders were captured in 1962, and it soon collapsed as an effective organization.

Organization for Economic Co-operation and Development (OECD). An economic forum of advanced industrial democracies formed in 1961. A reconstitution under American leadership of the **Organization for European Economic Co-operation (OEEC)**, it was a result of the recognition that the OEEC had achieved all it could usefully do, and of American concern about the division of Western Europe between the **European Economic Community (EEC)** and the **European Free Trade Association (EFTA)**. Its brief went beyond Europe with the aims of promoting economic growth, employment and standards of living, developing non-discriminatory multilateral trade, and helping economic development in the Third World. Based in Paris, it developed into a respected body whose reports and recommendations were highly regarded.

Organization for European Economic Co-operation (OEEC). A body established in April 1948 by Western European countries as an agency for the administration of American aid under the **Marshall Plan**. It was the result of American insistence that Europe had to take the responsibility for allocating funds in a way that would achieve the maximum economic effect across and within the participating countries. It was formed by those states which had been involved in the planning sessions of the Committee for European Economic Co-operation established in July 1947 to discuss the Marshall Plan with the USA. It set up a consultative and administrative structure headed by a Council of Ministers whose decisions were binding upon all members. For the first three years it administered Marshall aid according to agreed guidelines, establishing an infrastructure of generalized boards and expert groups. After American aid ended, it continued to work for the liberalization of European trade, and by the late 1950s had achieved almost all that was possible within its limited terms of reference. In 1958 it failed to reconcile the arguments between those who wished to establish a **customs union** and **common market** and those content with a **free trade area**. After the collapse of the **Maudling Committee** talks, the USA took the lead in reconstituting it in 1961 into a broader **Organization for Economic Cooperation and Development (OECD)** in which non-European countries would become full members.

Organization for International Economic Co-operation (OIEC). *See* COUNCIL FOR MUTUAL ECONOMIC ASSISTANCE.

Organization for Postal and Telecommunications Administrators (OSS). An inter-governmental association of the national administrations of the Communist regimes in Eastern Europe. After 1988 it began to seek ways of possible collaboration with the Western **European**

Conference of Postal and Telecommunications Administrations (ECPT).

Organization for Security and Co-operation in Europe. *See* CONFERENCE ON SECURITY AND CO-OPERATION IN EUROPE.

Organizations for the Promotion of Energy Technologies (OPET). *See* EUROPEAN ENERGY CHARTER.

Ortoli, François-Xavier. (1925–) President of the **Commission** 1973–77. A long-serving French administrator before moving to **Brussels**, he had to cope with the 1973 **enlargement** of the **European Communities (EC)**, monetary difficulties arising from floating exchange rates, and economic recession, but his cautious approach to issues failed to halt a decline in the momentum for integration. His major initiative was the **New Community Instrument (NCI)**, sometimes known as the Ortoli Facility.

Oslo Convention. An international agreement, formally the Convention for the Prevention of Marine Pollution by Dumping from Ships and Aircraft, signed in 1972 by the European Atlantic littoral states, on preventing the dumping of waste from airplanes and ships into the north-east Atlantic. It came into force in 1974, administered by an Oslo Commission, with a secretariat in London. *See also* PARIS CONVENTION.

Oslo Declaration. A statement in March 1990 by the heads of government of the **European Free Trade Association (EFTA)** agreeing to strengthen their linkages with the **European Communities (EC)** and to seek access to the EC's planned **internal market** through collective negotiations rather than separate bilateral talks. EFTA's objectives were largely met by the 1991 agreement to create a **European Economic Area (EEA)**.

Ossetia. An ethnically distinctive region of the Caucasus divided in the **USSR** between the Russian Federation (North Ossetia) and **Georgia** (South Ossetia). As Soviet authority began to decline, demands began to be made in 1989 for more autonomy and reunion between north and south. The problem became more acute in South Ossetia after the declaration of Georgian independence, and armed conflict broke out with demands from the region to be reunited with the north within **Russia**. The demand was confirmed by a referendum in January 1992, but this was rejected by Georgia. When the faltering Georgian authority was bolstered by Russian support, a ceasefire was accepted in South Ossetia in July 1992: it was monitored jointly by Georgian and Russian observers.

Ostpolitik. A reorientation of **Federal Republic of Germany** foreign policy and a series of treaties negotiated with several Eastern European countries 1970–72. It was launched by the 1969 **Brandt** government, and marked the final abandonment of the policy of strength pursued earlier by **Adenauer** and reflected in the **Hallstein Doctrine**. It was an acceptance of the fact that German reunification could only be achieved at the European level and not as the result of a separate West German policy. Its core was three treaties, with **Poland** and the **USSR** in 1970, and with the **German Democratic Republic (DDR)** in 1972. They confirmed the existing territorial structures in Central Europe – the status of the two German states and the **Oder–Neisse Line** – but without conceding anything of West Germany's legal position. They opened up a direct relationship between the two Germanies, although in practice it was the DDR which benefited more. While West Germany agreed to accept the existence of the DDR, it continued to reject recognizing it as a foreign state, and the 1972 treaty was officially described as a Basic Agreement. As part of Ostpolitik the four wartime Allies signed a separate **Quadripartite Agreement** on the status of **Berlin** and their rights in the city.

Outer Seven. A phrase often used in the 1960s to describe the Member States of the **European Free Trade Association (EFTA)**.

Overseas Countries and Territories (OCTs). An arrangement under the **Treaty of Rome** to accommodate mainly French colonies or overseas possessions within the **European Economic Community (EEC)**. OCT products were given access to the EC market on the same terms as those of the Member States, with customs duties to be removed gradually over a five-year period and aid to be provided from an **Overseas Development Fund (ODF)**. In 1963 the OCTs were absorbed into the broader agreement of the **Yaoundé Convention** which in turn was replaced by the 1975 **Lomé Convention**.

Overseas Development Fund (ODF). Established in 1958 as a means of linking the **European Economic Community (EEC)** with its **Overseas Countries and Territories (OCTs)** for an initial five-year period, financed by the EEC Member States. It was superseded in 1963 by the **Yaoundé Convention**.

Owen, David Anthony Llewellyn. (1938–) British politician. A doctor, he entered Parliament in 1966 for the **Labour Party**, serving in government after 1968. He was Foreign Secretary 1977–79. On the right of the party, he rejected its radicalization in the late 1970s, and in 1981 he left it to be a co-founder of the **Social Democratic Party (SDP)**. He later refused to accept a merger with the **Liberal Party** in 1987, continuing to lead a tiny SDP rump until 1992 when he stood down from Parliament. He was made a peer, Lord Owen of Plymouth, in 1992, and the following year was invited by the **European Communities (EC)** to act as their chief negotiator in seeking to achieve a solution to the armed conflict in **Bosnia-Hercegovina**, giving up the position in 1995.

Owen–Stoltenberg Plan. A proposal for a resolution of the civil war in **Bosnia-Hercegovina**, put forward in July 1993 by the **European Communities (EC)** and United Nations (UN) mediators, **Owen** and Thorvald

Stoltenberg. It accepted the earlier notion of cantonization, a territorial division along ethnic lines, and suggested a territorial division along ethnic lines within a union of three republics, with the UN being responsible for a ceasefire and demilitarization. While the principle of partition was accepted by all three warring factions – Croat, Muslim and Serb – the subsequent negotiations broke down on several points of detail, and the plan had to be abandoned by the end of the year. The search for a solution was then taken up by the **Contact Group**.

Own resources. A term referring to the possession by the **European Communities (EC)** of financial resources which belong to them as of right. They were made up of customs duties on imports, levies on agricultural imports, a proportion of the value-added tax levied by Member States, and contributions from Member States based upon each one's share of EC gross national product.

Özal, Turgut. (1927–1993) Prime Minister of **Turkey** 1983–89, and President 1989–93. An engineer, he became an associate and protégé of **Demirel** during the 1960s. When the Demirel government was removed by the military in 1971, he went to the USA, where a spell at the World Bank converted him to the idea of the free market. With a new Demirel government in power in 1979 he returned to Turkey where he authored the January 1980 austerity programme designed to restore the country's credit with the international community, later becoming its chief administrator. He remained in office after the military coup of September 1980, serving until 1982 as Deputy Prime Minister with special responsibility for economic policy. He formed the **Motherland Party** which, aided by a military ban on the political old guard, won a narrow majority in 1983. As premier he struck a balance with the military, and successfully curbed the various political and religious strands of his umbrella party, undertaking an ambitious programme of economic and monetary reform. The stability and prosperity he brought to Turkey was offset by criticisms of the network of favours and patronage that came with it. His economic reforms failed to reduce inflation, and after disappointing local elections in 1989, he became President. His domination of Turkish politics, already in decline, was weakened in 1991 when his party lost the premiership. He died in office of a heart attack.

P

Paasikivi, Juho Kusti. (1870–1956) President of **Finland** 1946–54. He began his long political career in 1906 as a Senator of the Grand Duchy of Finland. Involved in almost all negotiations with the **USSR** after 1920, he was Prime Minister on several occasions during the inter-war period, and was reappointed again in 1944 when, along with **Mannerheim**, he strove to alleviate the political consequences of Finland's defeat by the USSR. Succeeding Mannerheim as President in 1946, he advocated a line of strict neutrality between East and West and adopted a policy of cultivating and consulting the USSR to demonstrate that a non-Communist Finland would not be a threat to Soviet interests. This also meant acknowledging that the USSR had a legitimate interest in domestic Finnish politics. Although a conservative, he came to be trusted in Moscow, and his strategy was maintained by his successor, **Kekkonen**, becoming popularly known as the Paasikivi–Kekkonen line.

Pacifist Socialist Party. (*Pacifistisch Socialistische Partij – PSP*) A small left-wing party in the **Netherlands**. It was formed in 1957 as a radical secession from the **Labour Party (PvdA)** on the issue of Dutch membership of the Western European security alliance. Mainly on the fringe of politics, in 1989 it joined forces with three other small left-wing groups in a **Green Left** alliance.

Paisley, Ian Richard Kyle. (1926–) **Northern Ireland** clergyman and politician. Ordained a Presbyterian minister in 1946, he formed his own church in 1951, quickly building up a mass following. By the 1960s he was the recognized leader of hard-line Protestant opinion, accusing the **United Kingdom** of unduly placating the Catholic community. In 1966 he was imprisoned for 'unlawful assembly', and in 1969 broke with the **Ulster Unionist Party**. He formed a Protestant Unity Party (PUP), winning election to the British Parliament in 1970. In 1972 he reconstituted the PUP as the **Democratic Unionist Party (DUP)**, becoming its leader. He sat in the short-lived Northern Ireland Assembly 1973–75, and was elected to the **European Parliament (EP)**. He resigned his British seat in 1985 in protest at the **Anglo-Irish Agreement**, but returned the following year. Rejecting Irish reunification, he persistently refused to compromise on his basic demand for a return to self-government for Northern Ireland within the United Kingdom, and in 1994 attacked the **Downing Street Agreement** and its subsequent framework document.

Palach, Jan. (1947–1969) Czechoslovakian student. He burnt himself to death in Wenceslas Square in Prague in January 1969 as a protest against the 1968 Soviet invasion and crushing of the **Prague Spring**. His death made him a martyr and national hero.

Palme, Olof Joachim. (1927–1986) Prime Minister of **Sweden** 1969–76, 1982–86. A member of a prominent banking family and a law graduate, he became a personal assistant to **Erlander**, the **Social Democratic Labour Party** leader and Prime Minister in 1953. Entering Parliament in 1957 he held various government offices after 1963 before succeeding Erlander as premier and party leader in 1969. Under his leadership the party shifted slightly to the left, making traditional Swedish consensus politics more difficult. His minority governments had to rely primarily upon support from the **Left Party–Communists**. After losing the 1976 election, when the party left office for the first time in 40 years, he became more active internationally. He led a fact-finding mission to South Africa in 1977, served as a member of the Brandt Commission on the world economy, and chaired an Independent Commission on Disarmament and Security, which reported in 1982. Prominent in advocating peace initiatives in Europe, he was assassinated in Stockholm in February 1986. The killer was never identified.

Pan-European Union. An organization urging European union. Founded in 1923 by **Coudenhove-Kalergi**, it was the most well-known pro-union group of the inter-war years, although its influence waned in the 1930s. It failed to re-establish an impetus and prominence after 1945, contracting rapidly to have little influence or activity outside **Austria**.

Panhellenic Socialist Movement. (*Panellínion Sosialistikón Kínima – PASOK*) The major left-wing party in **Greece**. Founded in 1974 out of the Panhellenic Resistance Movement (PUK) which had advocated the violent overthrow of the **Greek Colonels** regime, it was an alliance of centrists, social democrats and Marxists. Very much dominated by its leader, Andreas **Papandreou**, who used it as a personal vehicle, it was initially hostile to pro-Western links, but moderated its position slightly after 1985.

Papadopoulos, Georgios. (1918–) Prime Minister of **Greece** 1969–74. A serving army officer and one of the architects of the 1967 **Greek Colonels** coup, he was the most forceful personality in the military junta government, quickly taking command of overall policy. In 1972 he declared himself regent and in 1973 Greece a republic with himself as President. He failed to control growing popular discontent and after the brutal suppression of riots in November 1973 handed the presidency to General Gizikis. After the restoration of civilian government in 1974 he was arrested, and in August 1975 condemned to death, but the sentence was commuted to life imprisonment.

Papagos, Alexander. (1883–1955) Prime Minister of **Greece** 1952–55. A professional soldier and general, he entered politics in the 1930s. Upon returning to Greece after imprisonment in Germany 1941–45 he was promoted to marshal and made commander-in-chief of the royalist forces during the **Greek Civil War**. In 1951 he resigned from the army and founded the Greek Rally which won the November 1952 election. His government was authoritarian and right-wing, but his strong anti-Communist attitude gained him American support and aid. He died in office in October 1955, being succeeded by **Karamanlis**.

Papandreou, Andreas. (1919–) Prime Minister of **Greece** 1981–89, and from 1993. Son of **Georgios Papandreou**, he pursued an academic career in the USA before returning to political life in Greece. After the 1967 **Greek Colonels** coup he was detained in custody until January 1968 when he was allowed to leave for the USA. He returned in 1973 and after the fall of the military regime formed a new left-wing party, the **Panhellenic Socialist Movement (PASOK)**. After winning the 1981 election he headed a government which attempted to push through a controversial programme of radical reform. In foreign policy his abrasive statements often irritated other Western leaders. His reputation and support eroded in the late 1980s because of personal scandal and allegations of involvement in financial corruption, but he survived to lead the party to victory in 1993, having been acquitted of all charges in January 1992.

Papandreou, Georgios. (1888–1968) Prime Minister of **Greece** 1944, 1963, 1964–65. Entering politics as a socialist republican, he served in several governments 1923–35. He escaped from Greece in 1942, returning in 1944 to head briefly a coalition government. His left-wing views made him unacceptable to the army, and he remained in opposition until 1963. In 1961 he founded the Centre Union Party, an alliance of republicans and democratic socialists. In February 1964 he became Prime Minister, pledged to a programme of progressive reforms, but the continuing **Cyprus** problem, hostility from the army, and a dispute with **Constantine II** forced his resignation in July 1965. It was widely expected in 1967 that he would win the scheduled election. It was to prevent his probable victory that the **Greek Colonels** staged their military coup. He was briefly detained, but with his health failing he died the following year.

Paris Agreements. *See* ALLIED CONTROL AUTHORITY.

Paris Club. An international forum for the negotiation, rescheduling and consolidation of debts given or guaranteed by official bilateral creditors. It was established in 1956 by a group of Western European countries initially seeking agreement on a multilateral trade and payments system for Argentina and its external debt. It was open to any creditor government willing to accept its rules and practices, and did not possess an institutional framework or fixed membership. Private banks were excluded from the Club, handling their credit negotiations instead through a parallel and similar London Club, but they were expected to offer terms identical to those of the Paris Club.

Paris Convention. An international agreement, formally the Convention for the Prevention of Marine Pollution from Land-Based Sources, adopted by the European Atlantic states in 1974 on preventing the dumping of waste into the North-East Atlantic. It came into force in 1978, and a revision in 1992 imposed stricter conditions and controls on the signatories. It was to be administered by a Paris Commission, with a permanent secretariat based in London. *See also* OSLO CONVENTION.

Paris Peace Accords. A series of agreements signed in Paris in January 1973 by China, **France**, North Vietnam, the **United Kingdom**, the USA and the **USSR**, along with representatives of the Vietnamese National Liberation Front. They concluded five years of negotiations on peace in Vietnam. They were rejected by President Thieu of South Vietnam who, after American withdrawal from the war, fought on alone until 1975.

Paris Peace Treaties. The result of meetings in Paris between June 1946 and February 1947 to prepare peace terms for the allies of Germany during the Second World War, namely **Bulgaria, Finland, Hungary, Italy** and **Romania**. Partly because all had broken with Germany before the end of the war to sue for a separate peace, the terms were reasonably moderate. The major conditions involved territorial adjustments.

Partial Test Ban Treaty. *See* COMPREHENSIVE TEST BAN TREATY.

Partitocrazia. ('Partyocracy'). A term widely used in **Italy** to describe the system of political control exercised by the ruling **Christian Democratic Party (DC)** and its allies from the 1950s to the 1990s. A consequence of the practice of **clientelism** associated particularly with the DC, and extended and refined by the **Italian Socialist Party (PSI)** after 1980, it involved extensive patronage, bribery and the appointment of party members to key public positions throughout the whole of society. It was most pronounced in the **Mezzogiorno**, the southern stronghold of the DC.

Partnership for Peace. *See* NORTH ATLANTIC TREATY ORGANIZATION.

Party for Democratic Prosperity–National Democratic Party. (*Partija za Demokratski Prosperitet–Nacionalna Demokratska Partija*) An alliance of political parties in **Macedonia** claiming to represent the minority ethnic Albanian community. Formed in 1991, the merger came to an end in 1994 in a dispute over how much autonomy should be sought from the government, but in July both began a boycott of politics in protest against the conviction of ten Albanians accused of conspiring to overthrow the government.

Party groups. The basic organizational feature of the **European Parliament (EP)**. They are cross-national groupings of Members of the European Parliament (MEPs) that some have seen as prototypes of supranational political parties. The groups themselves have been only alliances of representatives of national political parties. Criteria relating to minimum size, variable depending upon the number of countries the relevant MEPs come from, were set in 1979. Recognition of a group was important because the groups were permitted to regulate the working of the EP, nominating and electing its officers and committee memberships, and to be the basis of secretarial funding and other forms of assistance.

Party of Democratic Socialism (PDS). *See* SOCIALIST UNITY PARTY.

Party of Labour. (*Partia e Punës e Shqipërisë*) The Communist party of **Albania**. It was founded as the Albanian Communist Party in 1941 under Yugoslav sponsorship. It changed its name in 1948 when the pro-Communist elements within the party were purged by **Hoxha** who retained personal control of it until his death. After the disintegration of Communist rule, it changed its name in 1991 to the Socialist Party of Albania (*Partia Socialiste e Shqipërisë*), but was defeated in the 1992 election.

Party of Slovak Renewal. (*Strana Slovenskej Obrody*) One of the two non-Communist Slovak parties within the **National Front of the Czechoslovakian Socialist Republic**, founded in 1948 to mobilize Slovaks for the Communist Party. In December 1989 it voted to revert to the pre-1948 name of the Democratic Party, and declared it would follow a programme based upon Christian values.

Party of the Social Democratic Centre. (*Partido dos Centro Democrático Social – CDS*) A conservative party in **Portugal**. With right-wing movements banned after the 1974 revolution, it was the most conservative party when it was founded in 1974 by Diogo Freitas do Amaral, a former **Salazar** aide. Christian Democratic in orientation, it entered a **Socialist Party** coalition in 1978, but left the following year to form part of a Democratic Alliance led by the **Social Democratic Party**. Its appeal was limited to the northern regions of the country, and during the 1980s it adopted a more right-wing profile.

Pauker, Ana. (1893–1960) Romanian Communist. A member of the Communist Party since 1921, she spent most of the inter-war period working underground or in Moscow. She was imprisoned in 1935, but released in 1940, returning to the **USSR**. A protégé of **Stalin**, she returned to **Romania** in 1944 with the Soviet army to become one of the ruling Communist triumvirate, along with **Gheorghiu-Dej** and **Luca**. Despite her credentials, she was accused of deviation by Gheorghiu-Dej in 1952, partly perhaps because of her Jewish background, and dismissed from all party and public positions. She disappeared from public view and her death was reported unofficially in 1960.

Paul VI. (1897–1978) Pope 1963–78. Born Giovanni Battista Montini, he was ordained in 1920, working mainly in the **Vatican** until made Archbishop of Milan in 1954. Created a cardinal in 1958, he succeeded **John XXIII** as Pope. He continued the ecumenical policy of his predecessor, reconvening the Second **Vatican Council** 1963–65, but was a strict believer in personal morality and hostile to anything that might undermine the Church's authority. His support of the use of vernacular languages in the Mass offended conservative traditionalists. He was the first Pope to travel widely outside **Italy**, undertaking several world tours.

Peace Dividend. A phrase used first in 1989 to describe the perceived economic benefits that would come from the ending of the **Cold War** through a reduction in defence spending and the redirection of resources from military to civilian objectives. While defence cuts were introduced by all European governments, the expected benefits did not materialize. Defence reductions acted adversely upon employment, and a general economic restructuring proved much more costly than anticipated during a period when a widespread economic depression further constrained governmental financial freedom.

Pentagonale. A regional initiative launched by **Italy** in November 1989 originally to develop co-operation in South-Central Europe across the East–West divide. **Austria**, **Czechoslovakia**, **Hungary** and **Yugoslavia** were the other members. When **Poland** joined in 1992, the name was changed to Hexagonale. Italy's objective was to boost its own influence in the area, and all saw it as something that might aid economic development in the area and also help limit German economic expansion and influence in Eastern Europe. In 1992 the group renamed itself the Central European Initiative as a loose inter-governmental structure. The membership of the rump Yugoslavia was suspended in 1992 because of its involvement in the civil war in **Bosnia-Hercegovina**.

Pentapartito. The five-party coalition that formed the basis of all Italian governments from August 1983 until the breakdown of the system in the 1990s. Its members were the **Christian Democratic Party (DC)**, **Italian Socialist Party (PSI)**, **Italian Republican Party (PRI)**, **Italian Social Democratic Party (PSDI)**, and **Italian Liberal Party (PLI)**. All five were discredited and swept away by the revelations after 1992 about illegal party funding and other forms of political corruption.

People's Alliance. (*Althydubandalag*) A left-wing party in **Iceland**. It was formed in 1956 as an alliance between the Communist Party and left-wing Social Democrats, constituting itself as a party in 1968. It pursued pragmatic policies and participated in several government coalitions. In 1991 it redefined itself as a left-socialist party.

People's Forces of 25 April. (*Forças Populares de 25 Abril – FP25*) An extreme left-wing group in **Portugal**. Taking its name from the date of the 1974 revolution, it was formed in 1980 as an extra-parliamentary opposition, but most of its activities were restricted to bank raids, bombing campaigns and extortion. Many of its alleged leaders, including Lieutenant-Colonel Otelo Sariva de Carvalho, a major protagonist in the 1974 revolution, were arrested in 1984 and by 1987 all had been sentenced to terms of imprisonment. Carvalho, who received a 15-year sentence, was released in 1989 after a retrial, and in February 1990 he publicly renounced the armed struggle.

People's Party. (*Folkpartiet – FP*) A small centre party in **Sweden**. Founded in its present form in 1934, it is a liberal party with nineteenth century roots and since 1976 has been prepared on occasions to collaborate with other non-socialist parties.

People's Party for Freedom and Democracy. (*Volkspartij voor Vrijheid en Democratie – VVD*) The main conservative party in the **Netherlands**. It was founded in 1948 as a successor to the pre-war Liberal Union. Identified primarily with secular middle-class interests, it argued for free trade economic policies, but accepted more liberal social policies. It has frequently been in government, usually in alliance with and subordinate to religious parties, but in 1994 it formed a 'purple coalition' government with the **Labour Party (PvdA)**.

People's Union. (*Volksunie – VU*) A centre-right party in **Belgium**. Founded in 1954 as a flagbearer of Flemish nationalism, it demanded extensive autonomy for **Flanders** within a federal state. Centrist on economic questions, but socially conservative, it participated in the discussions after 1970 on the regionalization of the country. Its willingness to consider compromise and rejection of secession led to challenges from more extreme Flemish nationalist groups.

People's Unity. *See* HERRI BATASUNA.

Perestroika. A Russian word meaning restructuring. It was used by the Soviet leader, **Gorbachev**, in a speech in February 1986 to the 27th Congress of the Soviet Communist Party in connection with the socio-economic reform programme he wished to introduce. It was seen abroad as a term which also reflected what he was seeking in international affairs. While Gorbachev argued that it was an updating of Leninist theory and of the role of the Communist Party that would enable necessary economic development to occur, the popular interpretation of it within the **USSR** was that it permitted pluralist discussion, debate and criticism, something which contributed to the further weakening of Communist authority and the disintegration of the Soviet state.

Permanent representation. The delegation of diplomats and administrative officials which each Member State of the **European Communities (EC)** maintains in **Brussels**. The delegations are headed by ambassadorial Permanent Representatives who meet collectively as the **Committee of Permanent Representatives (COREPER)**.

Pertini, Alessandro. (1896–1990) President of **Italy** 1978–85. Joining the **Italian Socialist Party (PSI)** in 1918, he was arrested by the Fascist regime in 1926 but escaped, fleeing to **France**. He was re-arrested after his return to Italy in 1929 and not released until 1943 when he joined the **Resistance** partisans. He was sentenced to death after capture by German forces, but again escaped. He became PSI secretary in 1945, entering Parliament in 1946 and later serving as its speaker 1968–76. His offer of resignation after the 1969 breakdown of the merger of the PSI and **Italian Social Democratic Party (PSDI)** was unanimously rejected. He was elected to the presidency in 1976 with an unprecedented level of support. He was the first President to utilize the right to speak as 'the representative of national unity' to comment critically on controversial issues, public institutions and the political parties, a practice extended by his successor, **Cossiga**.

Petersberg Agreement. An agreement signed in November 1949 between the new **Federal Republic of Germany** and the Western occupying powers. It defined the terms of the relationship more precisely than the original Occupation Statute, listing in particular the rights and obligations of the occupying powers. It was, in a sense, West Germany's first international treaty, one involving the recognition of its independence by its former enemies.

Petkov, Nikola. (1889–1947) Bulgarian politician. The leader of the Bulgarian Agrarian Party, he was the most forthright opponent of the Communists and the **Fatherland Front**. He was dramatically arrested on the floor of the Parliament in April 1947. Accused of being an American and British agent and reported to have made a signed confession, he was found guilty and hanged.

Petöfi Club. A group of Hungarian intellectuals whose demonstrations in June 1956 led to mass protests against the regime and to the **Hungarian Revolution**. It took its name from a revolutionary poet who was celebrated as a national hero during the 1848–49 revolt against the Habsburg Empire.

Petsamo. A former Arctic region of **Finland**. Strategically important, it was ceded to the **USSR** after the Finnish defeat in the 1939–40 Winter War. After the collapse of the USSR in 1991, some small nationalist groups in Finland called for its return, but no major party supported the demand.

Petseri. A former area of **Estonia**. Lying east of the Narva river, it was ceded by the **USSR** to the Russian Federation in 1945. After 1991 some Estonian nationalist groups called for its return.

Pflimlin, Pierre. (1907–) Prime Minister of **France** 1958. Entering Parliament for the **Popular Republican Movement (MRP)** in 1945, he became party leader in 1956. In 1958 he became the last premier of the **Fourth French Republic**, serving for only 17 days. Failing to re-establish government authority in the face of the military revolt in Algeria, he accepted the return of **de Gaulle** and the end of the Republic rather than risk a civil war. After June 1958 he served briefly in de Gaulle's first government, but saw his party collapse.

Pieck, Wilhelm. (1876–1960) President of the **German Democratic Republic** 1949–60. Joining the **Social Democratic Party (SPD)**, he entered Parliament in 1905. In 1915 he broke with the party leadership over its support for the government in the First World War, and helped form the *Spartakusbund*. In 1921 he joined the Communist Party. In exile 1933–45, he was a co-founder of the **Socialist Unity Party (SED)**. A loyal party functionary and supporter of **Ulbricht**, as President he was very much a figurehead. After his death the office was abolished, with Ulbricht taking over its functions.

Pieds Noirs. A collective name in **France** for the large number of white settlers in Algeria who returned to France after Algerian independence in 1962. Most settled in the southern part of the country where they sought to preserve a distinctive identity, regarding themselves as exiles rather than expatriates. They proved receptive to the appeals of extreme right-wing groups, most recently the **National Front**. The name (black feet) derives from the nickname given in North Africa to French soldiers, who wore black boots.

Pinay, Antoine. (1891–1994) Prime Minister of **France** 1952. A businessman, he entered local politics in 1929 and Parliament in 1936. Not closely identified with any political party, he was one of the few conservatives elected to the 1946 Constituent Assembly. He was the first premier of the **Fourth French Republic** who had been a supporter of the 1940 Vichy regime. In his brief tenure he was credited with restoring French monetary confidence, and became widely acknowledged as the leader of the moderate right. He later served as the first Finance Minister of the **Fifth French Republic** 1958–60 where his policy of austerity laid a stable financial foundation. He left office, having refused to resign, because of disagreements with **de Gaulle** over the latter's policy of moving France away from a relationship with the USA. Although he no longer played an active political role, his views were widely solicited, and in 1965 he was strongly urged to become a centrist candidate for the presidency. In 1973 he was chosen as the first French Ombudsman, though it was an office with very limited authority.

Pius XII. (1876–1958) Pope 1939–58. Born Eugenio Maria Giuseppe Pacelli, he was ordained in 1899. He spent most of his life before 1939 in the papal diplomatic service, becoming a cardinal in 1930. He attempted to remain politically impartial during the Second World War, but was later severely criticized for his ambivalent attitude towards and at least tacit condonement of Nazi activities. After 1945 he strongly attacked Communism, and his *Apostolica Acta* excommunicated those Catholics who knowingly joined a Communist organization.

Plaid Cymru. (Party of Wales) A small minority nationalist party in the **United Kingdom**. Founded in 1925 as the party of Welsh nationalism, it became closely identified with the Welsh language and culture. While its final objective was independence for **Wales**, it concentrated more on demands for extensive self-government. It consolidated itself only in the 1960s as a major force in Welsh-speaking rural areas, but failed to advance in the populous urban regions. It gradually adopted a social democratic stance.

Pleven Plan. *See* EUROPEAN DEFENCE COMMUNITY.

Pleven, René. (1901–1993) Prime Minister of **France** 1950–51, 1951–52. After a career in banking and industry, he joined forces with **de Gaulle** in 1940, being given responsibility for various aspects of colonial affairs. A co-founder with **Mitterrand** of the Democratic and Socialist Union of the Resistance, he was elected to the 1945 constituent assembly and Parliament in 1946. Between 1946 and 1958 he served in various ministerial positions in several governments. A pragmatic politician who was never quite able to come to grips with the tortuous and shifting party politics of the **Fourth French Republic**, he was best known for the Pleven Plan, a proposal for a European army which led to the draft **European Defence Community (EDC)**.

Plogoff. The site in **Brittany** of a proposed nuclear power station. It was the scene of large and violent demonstrations in the 1970s. After its electoral victory in 1981, the new **Socialist Party (PS)** government decided not to proceed with construction of the plant and announced a halt on other nuclear projects still in the planning stage.

Podgorny, Nikolay Viktorovich. (1903–1983) Soviet politician. A commissar in the **Ukraine** 1939–45, he was appointed to the Ukrainian Council of Ministers in 1946, but entered the party's Central Committee only in 1963. In 1965 he became Chairman of the Praesidium and nominally the ceremonial Head of State. He was removed from the post in 1977 by **Brezhnev**, who assumed the position himself. A rather colourless loyal, and therefore safe, administrator, he lived in retirement after 1977.

Poland. A state in Eastern Europe. A traditional kingdom, it was partitioned after 1772 between Prussia and the Russian and Habsburg Empires. An independent state was reconstructed only in 1918. The democratic republic succumbed to military dictatorship in 1926, and in 1939 was subjugated by the **USSR** and Germany. A Communist-dominated government was established in 1944. By 1948 it had passed under one-party Communist rule under **Bierut**, and a Soviet-style constitution was introduced in 1952. Popular discontent over the cost of living and political restrictions erupted into riots in 1956. For a while more liberal policies were pursued by **Gomulka**, but demonstrations and discontent persisted in the 1960s and 1970s to plague all future Polish leaders. The powerful Catholic Church continued to act as a symbol of national identity and a focal point of opposition to the regime. A new wave of protest in 1980 was centred around a new trade union movement, **Solidarity**. As conditions of stability deteriorated martial law was declared by **Jaruzelski** in 1981. Economic problems continued to mount in the 1980s, with the government also experiencing severe international debt problems. The principle of some limited decentralization for economic enterprises was accepted in 1987, and Solidarity was legalized in January 1989. The following month the regime entered into discussions with the Catholic church, Solidarity and other groups, leading to constitutional revision. Multi-party elections were held in the summer, but by the end of the year the Communist regime had collapsed. A new democratic system was instituted, with **Wałęsa** being elected as President. The new parliament was dominated by a fragmented party system which, along with opposition to what was seen as an authoritarian presidential style, contributed towards instability. Popular unhappiness with the harsh economic conditions produced by a rapid move towards a free market economy enabled the reformed Communists to regain popularity, winning the 1993 election. The new regime, to improve its economy and ensure its security, pressed for early membership of both the **European Communities (EC)** and the **North Atlantic Treaty Organization (NATO)**.

Poland and Hungary Assistance for Economic Restructuring Programme. *See* OPERATION PHARE.

Polish Peasant Party. *See* UNITED PEASANT PARTY.

Polish United Workers' Party. (*Polska Zjednoczona Partia Robotnicza – PZPR*) The Communist party of **Poland** 1948–89. It was formed in 1948 by a merger of the Polish Worker's Party (formed in 1942 after the 1938 dissolution of the Communist Party) and the Polish Socialist Party. While it modelled itself on the Soviet Communist Party, it suffered from several internal strains, with reformist, revisionist and Polish nationalist tendencies always present, and in many ways, especially after the death of **Stalin**, it had to accommodate itself to the popular influence of the Catholic Church. Its authority was reduced after the 1981 military takeover by **Jaruzelski**. After democratization it dissolved itself in January 1990, reforming as the Social Democracy of the Republic of Poland (*Socjalde-mokracja Rzeczypospolitej Polskiej*). Briefly out of favour, public discontent at the pace and costs of enforced economic liberalization enabled it to make a come-back and, as the dominant element after 1991 of the Alliance of the Democratic Left (*Sojusz Lewicy Demokratycznej*), it emerged from the 1993 election as the largest party, campaigning on a social democratic programme and providing the Prime Minister by 1995.

Politburo. The political bureau of a Communist party central committee and the authoritative decision-making body of Communist regimes. The Soviet Politburo was formed in 1917 to provide leadership and direct all aspects of Soviet life. Its influence was reduced during the later years of **Stalin** because of his increased dictatorial rule. It was abolished in 1952 and replaced by a Praesidium of the Central Committee, but the name was reinstated by **Brezhnev** in 1966. Other Communist regimes adopted a similar institution to head their party structure.

Political Committee. A body within the **European Union** established by the **Treaty on European Union** as part of the **Common Foreign and Security Policy (CFSP)**. Composed of the **Political Directors**, its purpose was to advise the **European Council** on foreign and security policy, and to assist in the implementation of policies.

Political Directors. Senior diplomats who collectively were made responsible to the foreign ministers of the member states of the **European Communities (EC)** for the co-ordination and implementation of foreign policy initiatives within the framework of **European Political Co-operation (EPC)**. They were provided with a secretariat in **Brussels** in 1986. The position of chair of the group rotates across its members. Their immediate subordinates, who organized the daily routine of EPC, were known as the European Correspondents. With the **Treaty on European Union**, they were to form the **Political Committee**, an advisory body within the EPC replacement, the **Common Foreign and Security Policy (CFSP)**.

Political Reformed Party. (*Staatkundig Gereformeerde Partij – SGP*) A small religious party in the **Netherlands**. Formed in 1918, it became the largest of the several small fundamentalist Calvinist parties, successfully maintaining parliamentary representation, although its support was confined to a few rural areas. In 1993 it passed a resolution, against the wishes of its leadership, that women should be banned from politics on the grounds that the Bible indicated that God never wanted women in politics.

Political Spring. (*Politikí Ánixi – POLA*) A right-wing populist party in **Greece**. It was formed in 1993 by Antonis Samaras, who had been foreign minister in the **New Democracy (ND)** government of **Mitsotakis**. Its secession, which reflected dissent in the ND over its leadership and policies, brought the government down. Its major concern was to ensure that governments followed a strong nationalist line in foreign policy, especially on the issue of the recognition of **Macedonia**.

Polycentrism. *See* EUROCOMMUNISM, TOGLIATTI, PALMIRO.

Pompidou, Georges Jean Raymond. (1911–1974) President of France 1969–74. A schoolteacher, he joined the **Resistance movement** in the Second World War and became an adviser to **de Gaulle**. After 1945 he pursued a career in banking before becoming de Gaulle's chief administrative adviser in May 1958, negotiating the **Évian Agreements**. A parliamentary deputy in 1958, he was appointed Prime Minister in 1962, loyally pursuing Gaullist policy. Although he demonstrated skill in handling the 1968 **May Events**, he was subsequently dismissed by de Gaulle. He immediately declared himself a future contender for the presidency, winning the election after de Gaulle's resignation in April 1969. He moved decisively on economic policy, devaluing the franc and imposing a price freeze. In general he accepted his predecessor's foreign policy, but was more flexible on most issues. He was the instigator of the 1969 **Hague Summit** and believed that frequent summit meetings of heads of government would provide the best direction for the **European Communities** (**EC**), but his proposals for summits were not always accepted by his partners. His health began to fail in 1973 and he died of cancer in April 1974.

Pompidou Group. An informal system of inter-governmental collaboration established in 1971 to develop and co-ordinate a European approach to combatting the growth in drug trafficking and drug abuse. The initiative came from **Pompidou**. After 1980 its work was done under the aegis of the **Council of Europe**.

Popieluszko, Jerzy. (1947–1984) Polish priest. An outspoken supporter of the banned **Solidarity** movement, he openly held masses for it in Warsaw. In October 1984 he was abducted, tortured and murdered. His death aroused widespread anger, restrained only by appeals for calm from **Wałęsa** and the Catholic Church. Police agents were subsequently arrested and sentenced for the crime in February 1985. The case was reopened in 1990 after one of the convicted men alleged that senior government officials had been involved in the affair, as well as in other murders. Two former generals who had headed the security service and the religious affairs section of the Ministry of the Interior were subsequently charged with planning Popieluszko's murder, but they were acquitted in August 1994 after a two-year trial.

Popular Front. (*Rahvarinne*) A political organization in **Estonia**, founded in 1992 as a centre-left alliance. Its core was the Estonian People's Centre Party (*Eesti Rahva-Keskerakond*), the descendant of the reformist Popular Front movement established in 1988 which had led the demands for independence from the **USSR**.

Popular Party. (*Partido Popular – PP*) A conservative party in **Spain**. It began as the Popular Alliance (*Alianza Popular*), founded in 1976 by **Fraga Iribarne** as a coalition of several right-wing groups led by ex-ministers of the **Franco** regime. The past associations of its leadership and its conservatism limited its appeal. It aligned itself with other conservative groups, but then began to adopt a more centrist Christian Democrat position, which was formalized by its 1989 congress. In 1986 it headed a broad alliance, the Popular Coalition (*Coalición Popular*), but continued failure to achieve an electoral breakthrough provoked a leadership crisis and its reconstitution as the PP in 1989. In the 1990s it absorbed several smaller parties to become a major force in Spanish politics.

Popular Republican Movement. (*Mouvement Républicain Populaire – MRP*) A Christian Democratic party in **France**, founded in 1944. Unlike most Christian Democratic parties, it adopted a more left-wing radical profile, being part of the **tripartism** governments 1945–47. Its electoral support declined steadily in the 1950s, with recurring tensions between its left and right wings. It collapsed as a meaningful organization after the formation of the **Fifth French Republic**. The attempt by **Lecanuet** to revivify it in 1965 through a merger with other small groups in a **Democratic Centre** failed, and in 1967 the surviving rump voted to disband the party.

Portugal. A state in Western Europe. It was a traditional monarchy until 1910, when a bloodless revolution established an unstable and violent republic. In 1926 a military coup established a new regime which came to be dominated by **Carmona** and **Salazar**. Supported by the Catholic Church and the army, Salazar established a corporatist New State (*Estado Novo*), which persisted until 1974. The regime rejected any form of political liberalization and strove, despite huge economic costs, to contain wars of liberation in its African colonies. The economic and human losses of the wars radicalized and politicized elements of the army, and in April 1974 the **Armed Forces Movement** overthrew the regime in a military coup. The next two years were a period of considerable political confusion, with several competing radical military and political groups vying for political power, though a new Constitution was approved. Stability began to return after 1976 under the presidency of **Eanes** who neutralized or expelled the more radical elements from the army. Although it was a founder member of the **North Atlantic Treaty Organization (NATO)** in 1949 and the **European Free Trade Association (EFTA)** in 1960, its authoritarian regime meant that Portugal played only a peripheral role in European affairs until it reverted to democracy. It joined the **European Communities (EC)** in 1986.

Portuguese Communist Party. (*Partido Comunista Português – PCP*) A left-wing party in **Portugal**. Founded in 1921, it remained an underground movement from 1926 until 1974 and the collapse of the regime established by **Salazar**. It participated in interim governments 1974–76 while simultaneously seeking to radicalize the military and escalate the revolutionary atmosphere in order to establish a Communist regime. Lacking a large popular support, its ambitions were blocked by the reassertion of authority by **Eanes** after 1976, and it fell back to being a minor and peripheral political force. In the 1980s it formed a Popular Unity Alliance (APU) and in 1987 a Unitary Democratic Coalition (*Coligação Democrática Unitária*) with other left-wing groups, but without increasing its support. In the 1970s it rejected the validity of **Eurocommunism**, and in 1990 ignored demands for internal change after the collapse of the Communist regimes in Eastern Europe, reaffirming its commitment to **democratic centralism** and the principles of Marxist-Leninism.

Potsdam Conference. The first conference, in July 1945, of the Allies after the surrender of Germany. Its purpose was to confirm the decisions taken at the previous **Yalta Conference**, and to prepare for a peace treaty with Germany. It also established a Council of Ministers to handle peace treaties with Germany's allies. Of the personnel involved, only **Stalin** provided continuity with the past. President Roosevelt had died three months earlier, to be succeeded by Truman. **Churchill** had to withdraw shortly after the sessions began, after losing the British election, and was replaced by **Attlee**. With the war over, the meeting was characterized by a heightened mutual suspicion between the **USSR** and the Western Allies, who were concerned about Stalin's actions in Eastern Europe. Its major theme was Germany, and agreement was reached on a zonal military occupation which would work for the reconstruction of a democratic Germany. It agreed to begin a process of denazification and that the country would be treated as a single economic unit. The final communiqué was vaguely worded, and the commitments were broken almost immediately. The military zones operated independently of each other, the USSR began to dismantle economic assets in its zone for removal to its own territory, and the two sides moved quickly into the rigid opposition of the **Cold War**.

Poujadism. A right-wing populist movement in **France** 1954–58 which engaged in sometimes violent direct action. It was formed in November 1953 by Pierre Poujade, a bookseller, who had previously organized a series of violent anti-tax demonstrations. Entitled the *Union de Défense des Commerçants et Artisans*, it appealed strongly to small shopkeepers and other minor entrepreneurs affected by post-war scarcity and inflation. Stridently anti-socialist, anti-European and anti-intellectual, it enjoyed electoral success in January 1956, but lacking an effective organization and discipline, it was little more than a disruptive force in Parliament that soon began to disintegrate, disappearing in 1958. It became regarded as a symbol of negative demogogic rebellion lacking any coherent political objective.

Pozsgay, Imre. (1933–) Hungarian politician. A teacher, he joined the

Communist Party in 1950. He held various party positions, mainly working in its ideology and propaganda divisions. In the 1970s he emerged as the leading reformist within the party. Appointed Minister of Culture in 1976, he was dismissed in 1982, but continued to argue for reform. He was brought back into the government in 1987 where he promoted a re-appraisal of the events of 1956 and persuaded the **Hungarian Socialist Workers' Party** to accept multipartyism. He was nominated by the party as its presidential candidate in 1989. He subsequently broke with the reformed Hungarian Socialist Party in 1990, and in 1992 formed the Association of National Democrats (*Nemzeti Demokrata Szövetség*).

Prague Spring. The popular name for the brief period of liberalization in **Czechoslovakia** 1967–69. It began with the refusal of the army to support the request by **Novotný** that it suppress popular demonstrations and his replacement by **Dubček**. The new government outlined a reform programme which, emphasizing 'socialism with a human face', would restore individual freedoms and multi-party politics. Alarmed by the speed of events, the **USSR** sent **Warsaw Pact** forces to occupy Czechoslovakia. The reform programme was abandoned, and Dubček was removed from office in April 1969, after which a new government restored Communist orthodoxy.

Preferential Trade Agreements. Agreements by two or more countries freeing trade between them from their normal regulations governing imports and exports. The principles under which they are permissible were defined by the **General Agreement on Tariffs and Trade (GATT)**. The most important agreements in Europe have been those signed by the **European Communities (EC)** with several other countries in and beyond Europe.

Prison Camps. A penal labour system in the **USSR**. A tradition of exiling political dissidents to Siberia was well-established in imperial **Russia**. The USSR continued it after 1919, but during the **Stalin** regime it became more organized, and affected millions of people, including peasants and religious adherents as well as intellectuals and political protesters. After 1930 it became an institutionalized forced labour camp system administered by the Main Administration of Corrective Labour Camps (**Gulag**). The number of prisoners was estimated variously at between 6 and 15 million. After the execution of **Beria** and the denunciation of Stalin by **Khrushchev** in 1956, some of the worst excesses of the system were reformed, but it was not until after 1987 that a run-down of the system began, with most prisoners being released.

Privatization. A process involving the denationalization of public control, involving the sale of state-owned companies and public utilities through a share issue on the stock market. The term was first used in 1959 to describe the post-1949 policy of the **Federal Republic of Germany**. After 1979 it became a major element of **Conservative Party** governments in the **United**

Kingdom. Similar policies, though less extensive, were introduced later or promised in many other Western European countries. Privatization schemes were also developed in the 1990s in the former **USSR** and Eastern Europe as part of the post-Communist change from a command to a market economy.

Profumo Affair. A political scandal in the **United Kingdom** in 1963. It referred to the involvement of the Minister of War, John Profumo, with a call-girl who had also had a relationship with a Soviet naval attaché based in London. When the relationship came to light, Profumo resigned from the government in June after admitting that in earlier denying the affair he had lied to the House of Commons. While a subsequent inquiry concluded that national security had not been endangered by Profumo's liaison, the publicity surrounding the affair and the subsequent suicide of one of the other major protagonists damaged the reputation of **Macmillan** and his government, which had seemingly been taken by surprise by the episode.

Progress Party. (*Fremskridtspartiet – FP*) A populist right-wing party in **Denmark**. It was founded in 1972 by **Glistrup** and declared an anti-bureaucracy, anti-tax platform, also demanding the abolition of the military forces and the diplomatic corps. Under Glistrup's controversial leadership during a period of instability in party politics, it quickly emerged as the second largest party in the country, but acted as a negative force, shunned by other parties. It failed to sustain its early electoral momentum, and in the 1980s expelled Glistrup, seeking to present a more acceptable facade. In 1991 it declared an intention to be an ordinary party and not, as it had earlier claimed to be, a protest movement.

Progress Party. (*Fremskrittspartiet – FP*) A populist right-wing party in **Norway**. It was founded by the veteran conservative politician, Anders Lange, in 1973 in the aftermath of the contentious referendum on **European Communities (EC)** membership. Originally known as the Anders Lange Party Against Taxes and Public Expenditure, it changed its name in 1975 after Lange's death. It broadened its anti-tax platform to incorporate advocating free market economic policies, and in the late 1980s began to demand greater controls on immigration, but its electoral appeal began to weaken in the 1990s.

Progressive Citizens' Party. (*Fortschrittliche Bürgerpartei – FBP*) A conservative party in **Liechtenstein**. Formed in 1918, it has governed the country in coalition with the centre-right **Fatherland Union** since 1938.

Progressive Democratic Party. A small centre-left party in **Ireland**. It was formed in 1985 as a result of a secession from **Fianna Fáil**. The cause of the split was disagreement over economic policy and personal antagonism towards the leadership of **Haughey**. The new party argued for free enterprise policies and a more moderate line on **Northern Ireland**. In 1989 it agreed to enter a coalition with the more conservative **Fine Gael**.

Progressive Organizations of Switzerland. (*Progressive Organisation der Schweiz/Organisations Progressistes Suisses – POCH*) A small left-wing party in **Switzerland** founded in 1971 by dissident Communists and student radicals. It pursued a strict Marxist-Leninist line, but was predominantly a German-speaking organization. After 1979 it sought to persuade similar groups to join a left-wing alliance, and in 1987 joined the **Green Alliance**.

Progressive Party. (*Framsóknarflokkurin*) A centrist party in **Iceland**. established in 1916 essentially to defend rural and agrarian interests, it developed to become the second largest party in the country, and after 1945 was a member of most government coalitions.

Progressive Party of the Working Class. (*Anorthotikón Kómma Ergazómenou Laou – AKEL*) The Communist party of **Cyprus**. Formed in 1941, it was declared illegal by the British authorities in 1955. The ban was lifted shortly before independence, and it was able to enjoy considerable electoral support. Though espousing orthodox Communist rhetoric, it was willing to consider alliances with other left-wing movements and backed most winning presidential candidates. It was more willing than other Greek Cypriot parties to accept that Turkish Cypriot concerns had to be taken into account, and was prepared to accept a federal solution to the division of the island.

Proletarian Democracy. (*Democrazia Proletaria – DP*) A small left-wing party in **Italy**. It was founded in 1977 out of an electoral alliance formed the previous year by radical Marxists dissatisfied with the more accommodative line pursued by the **Italian Communist Party (PCI)** with the **historic compromise**. It was able to carve a limited electoral niche to the left of the PCI.

Propaganda Due (P-2). A secret Masonic lodge in **Italy**. With a membership drawn primarily from the Italian elite, in May 1981 it was alleged to have been involved in several seditious and criminal activities. After popular pressure, the Prime Minister, **Forlani**, authorized the release of a list of its members, who included government ministers, other senior politicians, and high-ranking members of the security forces, obtained in a police raid on its premises. Other documents implicated many of its members in several scandals, including organized tax evasion and links with right-wing terrorists. The Forlani government was forced to resign, several arrests followed, and some senior military officers were suspended, leading to a major reorganization of the armed forces. The lodge leader, Licia Gellia, had been abroad when the scandal broke. He was tried in absentia on charges of political conspiracy and anti-state activities. He was later imprisoned after being extradited from **Switzerland** in 1988. In 1984 a parliamentary inquiry claimed that the P-2 membership lists were authentic, and the other documents reliable. The scandal discredited and weakened the political establishment, and presaged the later more widespread allegations of conspiracy and fraud. Trials of people associated with P-2 continued into the 1990s.

Proportionality. The principle in the **European Union (EU)** that the EU or the Member States should use appropriate means to achieve specific aims. It implies that measures deemed to be excessive in terms of what is strictly necessary may be declared illegal by the **Court of Justice**.

Proportional representation (PR). A system of voting and method of election which endeavours to distribute parliamentary seats or other units of legislative representation among political parties or other bodies putting forward candidates in an election in a way that is proportionate to their share of the votes. The method of allocation is based upon a predetermined mathematical formula. There are many different kinds of PR systems and formulas, but none can achieve pure or exact proportionality. They became the norm for democracies outside the Anglo-Saxon world.

Proporz. (Proportionality) A term referring to the distribution of public and political positions negotiated by the **grand coalition** in **Austria** after 1945. In a series of pacts the two major parties agreed to partition between themselves the distribution not only of government posts but also of all public sector positions at the national, regional and local levels, as well as those in the nationalized banks and industries. The ratio or *proporz* for each party was determined by the result of the previous general election. The practice to a large extent survived the ending of the grand coalition in 1966.

Proporzpaket. *See* ALTO ADIGE.

Public Against Violence. A dissident movement in **Czechoslovakia**, and the Slovak counterpart of **Civic Forum**, formed in 1989. It had rather less impact than its counterpart, and in 1991 split over the issues of the speed and nature of economic reform and the future constitutional structure of the Czechoslovakian state. Its most significant successor was the **Movement for a Democratic Slovakia**.

Pujol i Soley, Jorge. (1933–) Prime Minister of **Catalonia** from 1980. A banker, he was a long-time opponent of the **Franco** regime, and was imprisoned for his views. He founded Democratic Convergence in 1976 and later became the leader of **Convergence and Union (CiU)**. The dominant figure in Catalan politics after 1980, with independence as an ultimate goal, after 1992 he agreed to support a minority government in Madrid in return for further concessions to Catalonia.

Q

Quadripartite Agreement. A document signed in 1971 by the four Second World War Allies as part of the **Ostpolitik** process. It confirmed the rights of the Allies in **Berlin**, something long sought by the Western powers, and recognized that West Berlin had special links with the **Federal Republic of Germany**. The settlement of the principle between the Western Allies and the **USSR** essentially eliminated Berlin as a major flashpoint of the **Cold War**, guaranteeing the rights of West Berlin as an enclave within the **German Democratic Republic (DDR)** and the right of transit between it and West Germany. It was formally abrogated by the Allies in 1990 as part of the process of German reunification.

Queuille, Henri. (1884–1970) Prime Minister of **France** 1948–49. A doctor, he entered Parliament in 1922 and joined the **Radical Republican and Radical Socialist Party**. In all he held ministerial office on 30 occasions, serving in 12 successive **Fourth French Republic** governments 1948–54. His premiership was one of the longest of the republic, surviving primarily because he avoided all positive action. Described at the time as 'the father of immobility', his behaviour and the lack of action typified the problems of coalitions and government ministers in the fourth Republic.

Quick Reaction Consultation Centre. A body established in June 1991 by the **European Communities (EC)** as a mechanism that would provide a co-ordinated response by the Member States to sudden and large-scale immigration pressures. It was a consequence of EC concerns about migratory flows that might result from the political and territorial changes in Eastern Europe.

R

Raab, Julius. (1891–1964) Chancellor of **Austria** 1953–61. An engineer, he was a parliamentary deputy of the Christian Social Party 1927–34, retiring from politics after the Anschluss with Germany. In 1945 he was a co-founder of the **Austrian People's Party (ÖVP)**, emerging as the strong man of the party. He was its parliamentary leader until 1953 when he assumed the premiership. A strong supporter of the **social market economy**, he maintained the **grand coalition** and played a leading role in the negotiations on the **Austrian State Treaty**.

Radical Democratic Party. (*Freisinnig-Demokratische Partei/Parti Radical-Démocratique – FDP/PRD*) A centre-right party in **Switzerland**. Founded in 1894 out of an earlier Radical grouping that emerged in 1848, it has remained a major political force and a member of the four-party coalition that has been in office more or less continuously since the 1940s. In one form or another Radicals have been permanently in government since 1848.

Radical Liberal Party. (*Det Radikale Venstre – RV*) A small centrist party in **Denmark**. It was formed in 1905 by urban dissidents from the agrarian-dominated **Liberal Party**. Until the 1960s it possessed a left-wing orientation, often supporting the **Social Democratic Party**. It later became more centrist, willing to support centre-right governments on economic issues, although not on defence, foreign policy and environmental questions, where it maintained a left-wing stance.

Radical Party. (*Partito Radicale – PR*) A small left-wing party in **Italy**. It was formed in 1955 by left-wing dissidents from the **Italian Liberal Party (PLI)**, but did not gain parliamentary representation until 1976. It stressed human and civil rights, opposition to nuclear energy, and liberalization of moral questions such as divorce. Its political impact was greater than its support would merit because of its extensive use of the constitutional provision which permitted large petitions to lead to a referendum, using the device as a tactic to force political debate on controversial issues. In the 1980s it became better known for the esoteric character of several of its representatives. It ceased contesting elections in 1987.

Radical Political Party. (*Politieke Partij Radikalen – PPR*) A small left-wing party in the **Netherlands**. It was formed in 1968 by dissidents breaking away from the moderate **Catholic People's Party**. It advocated extensive democratization of public life and protection of the environment. In 1989 it joined forces with three other radical groups in a **Green Left** alliance.

Radical Republican and Radical Socialist Party. (*Parti Républicain et Radical Socialiste*) A centrist party in **France**. The dominant influence in the pre-1940 Third Republic, after 1945 it enjoyed an influence in the **Fourth French Republic** in excess of what its size would merit. Generally conservative on economic issues, it was strongly anticlerical. It was less an organized party than a collection of *notables* possessing their own local power bases. Its proneness to internal dissension led to weak leadership and several secessions on both left and right, and its support declined to the point of extinction in the 1960s.

Radikalenerlass. (Radicals' Decree) A joint statement issued in January 1972 by the **Brandt** government and the regional premiers within the **Federal Republic of Germany**. It reminded those people responsible for recruitment to any level of public employment that all appointees should promise to support the Basic Law (constitution). It was a response to the worries of the political leadership about the perceived threat to democracy of the **extra-parliamentary opposition (APO)** and other groups (including the **Baader-Meinhof Group**) seeking to undermine stability and public confidence from within the state institutions. Although not a law – an attempt to give it a legal basis failed in 1976 – it was widely perceived as such. Its critics described it as a *Berufsverbot* (employment ban) directed specifically at people who held left-wing beliefs. Although it was applied more to left-wing rather than right-wing individuals, very few people were affected by the consequences of the statement, though it became a highly contentious and symbolic issue in West German politics. Never formally renounced, it gradually disappeared from public prominence in the 1980s, but after German reunification in 1991 it was used in the former East German territories to remove members of the former Communist elite from public office.

Rainbow Group. A **party group** in the **European Parliament (EP)**. It was formed after the 1984 elections by representatives of Green and small regional-nationalist parties who did not feel able to join the established party groups. A disparate alliance, in general it lacked a coherent policy line or unity, and this did not improve when the Greens left after the 1989 elections to form their own party group. After the 1994 elections, its survivors joined the new **European Radical Group**.

Rajk, Laszlo. (1909–1949) Hungarian Communist. Joining the Communist Party in 1931, he enlisted in an International Brigade during the Spanish Civil War. In 1938 he returned to **Hungary** where he sought to rebuild the party underground. He was interned in 1941 and moved to a German concentration camp in November 1944. Released the following May, he was appointed party leader in Budapest, and in 1946 was made Minister of the Interior, moving to the Foreign Ministry in 1948. In May 1949 he was suddenly arrested and charged with Titoist and Trotskyite deviation, and of acting as a secret police agent of the conservative regime in the 1930s. He admitted the charges in his trial in September, and was executed. The evidence was clearly fabricated. It was widely assumed that the arrest had been ordered by **Stalin**, for whom he was guilty of being a home-grown Communist without any links with the **USSR**. Rajk was also thought to be too liberal, having expressed concern about the pace of Stalinist change being enforced by **Rákosi**. He was rehabilitated in 1956.

Rákosi, Mátyás. (1892–1971) Hungarian Communist leader 1944–56. A member of Béla Kun's 1919 Communist government, he fled to **Austria** after the regime was overthrown, later moving to Moscow. He returned secretly to **Hungary** in 1928, but was arrested and imprisoned for eight years. Although released early, he was re-arrested in 1935, receiving a life sentence. He was freed in November 1940 in exchange for the return of Hungarian memorabilia from the **USSR**, and went to Moscow. He returned to Hungary with the Soviet Army in 1944 and took charge of the Hungarian Communist Party, presiding over the construction of a rigid Stalinist regime, purging party dissidents as well as other possible opponents. Although serving only briefly as Prime Minister 1952–53, his absolute power rested in his control of the party and the secret police. By the mid-1950s his ruthlessness had persuaded the post-**Stalin** leadership in the USSR that he should be replaced, and he was removed from his offices in 1956. The severity of his rule contributed to the dissent which led to the 1956 **Hungarian Revolution**. He played no role in the quelling of the Revolution. Expelled from the party in 1962, he died in Moscow in 1971.

Rakowski, Mieczyslaw Franciszek. (1926–) Prime Minister of **Poland** 1988–89. Joining the **Polish United Workers' Party** in 1946, he worked as a journalist and editor, gaining a reputation for holding liberal views. In 1981 he was appointed Deputy Prime Minister by **Jaruzelski**, with responsibility for trade union policy, but he failed to establish a working relationship with **Solidarity**, and resigned in 1985. He was promoted to the **Politburo** in 1987. As premier he supervised moves towards liberalization, but failed to win a seat in the June 1989 multi-party election. He subsequently became Party General Secretary, presiding over its dissolution in January 1990, but refused to be considered for the leadership of the new party structure that replaced it.

Rally for the Republic. (*Rassemblement pour la République – RPR*) A conservative party in **France**. Founded in 1976 it was the heir to the Gaullist tradition and became the major right-wing party. It was used by its leader,

Chirac, as a vehicle for his presidential ambitions as the undisputed leader of the French centre and right. His leadership was not challenged until the 1990s. While it continued to emphasize Gaullist principles, in the 1980s it came to favour more deregulation and **privatization**.

Rally of the French People. (*Rassemblement du Peuple Français – RPF*) A populist right-wing party in **France**. It was founded in April 1947 to aid **de Gaulle** in his bid for power after emerging from retirement. It attacked party rule and behaviour, and sought a more authoritarian form of government. Strongly nationalistic, it attacked parliamentary domination, European involvement, the USA, and Communism. It became the largest party in the 1947 local elections, but failed to maintain its momentum and went into sharp decline after 1951. De Gaulle, who kept it at arm's length, broke with it in 1953, and its survivors reconstituted themselves in 1954 as the Republican and Social Action Union (*Union Républicain et d'Action Sociale*).

Ramadier, Paul. (1888–1961) Prime Minister of **France** 1947. A lawyer, he entered Parliament in 1919 for the Socialist Party (SFIO). His brief premiership was marked by the fact that it ended the period of government **tripartism**. He refused to bend to **French Communist Party (PCF)** demands, and skilfully stalled them until they 'voluntarily' walked out of the government. He resigned six months later. He later served in the **Mollet** government 1956–57. In 1958 he openly opposed the return of **de Gaulle**, but failed to gain any popular support.

Rankovic, Aleksandar. (1903–1983) Yugoslav Communist. After joining the party in 1928, he spent most of the 1930s in prison. A partisan leader during the Second World War, he was made Minister of the Interior and police chief in 1945, helping to consolidate Communist rule. After his appointment as Vice-President in 1953 he was widely regarded as the recognized successor to **Tito**. An orthodox Communist, his opposition to reform and decentralization led in 1966 to his dismissal from office. He was accused of endorsing illegal secret police activity and of obstructing democratic and economic reforms.

Rapacki Plan. A proposal in October 1957 for a **nuclear-free zone (NFZ)** in Central Europe. It was made by the Foreign Minister of **Poland**, Adam Rapacki (1909–1970), at the General Assembly of the United Nations (UN), and amplified the following February in a memorandum sent to foreign diplomats in Warsaw. It envisaged a ban on the manufacture, storage and deployment of nuclear weapons in an area covering the two Germanies, **Czechoslovakia** and Poland, as well as proposing negotiations on German reunification, with the NFZ being jointly monitored by the **North Atlantic Treaty Organization (NATO)** and **Warsaw Pact**. Rapacki hoped it would lead to similar schemes elsewhere in Europe and to a reduction in conventional arms. It was endorsed by **Khrushchev** but rejected by Western countries which feared that it would give strategic advantage to the Warsaw Pact because of the latter's great superiority in conventional forces. The linkage of an NFZ to German reunification also aroused Western suspicions.

Rau, Johannes. (1931–) West German politician. A publisher, he joined the **Social Democratic Party (SPD)** in 1957, and was elected to the regional parliament of North Rhine-Westphalia (NRW) the following year. He served as a regional minister 1970–78 before becoming NRW premier. Admitted to the national party leadership in 1978, he became deputy chairman in 1982. On the moderate wing of the party, he was selected as the party's chancellor candidate and hence nominal party leader in 1987, in the hope that he would revive the party's fortunes, but he failed to remove the more left-wing image the party had acquired and lost the 1987 election.

Red Army Faction (RAF). *See* BAADER-MEINHOF GROUP.

Red Brigades. (*Brigate Rosse – BR*) A left-wing terrorist organization in **Italy**. Formed in 1969 by a former Catholic student activist, Renato Curcio, it had links with other radical groups such as Front Line (*Prima Linea*), Proletarian Autonomy (*Autonomia Proletaria*) and Armed Proletarian Nuclei (*Nuclei Armati Proletari*). It launched a series of kidnappings, moving on in 1974 to murder and assassinations. Its actions became more ruthless after its leader, Curcio, was captured and imprisoned in 1976. Its most well-known exploit was the 1978 kidnapping and murder of **Moro**. Security operations were intensified after the incident, and by 1980 many of the organization's leaders had been captured. Its challenge to the state declined in the 1980s although several offshoots were responsible for continued acts of violence. From prison, Curcio renounced violence and the end of the revolution in 1988, but in 1985 some of the surviving activists had regrouped as the Union of Fighting Communists (*Unione dei Comunisti Combattenti*). A further splinter group, the Fighting Communist Party (*Partito Comunista Combattente*), emerged in 1988, but the levels of violence of the 1970s were not repeated. Yet another descendant, the Fighting Communist Nuclei (*Nuclei Comunista Combattente*), became active in the 1990s.

Reder Handshake. A political scandal in **Austria**. In 1985 the Minister of Defence, a member of the conservative **Freedom Party of Austria (FPÖ)**, laid on an official welcome at Vienna airport for Walter Reder, a former member of the SS. Reder, who had been given a life sentence in **Italy** for shooting civilian hostages towards the end of the Second World War, had recently been pardoned and deported to Austria. The welcome and the publicized handshake between the two men aroused widespread domestic and international protest. Many leading members of the major government party, the **Socialist Party of Austria (SPÖ)**, threatened to resign. While no immediate action was taken, the incident contributed to the collapse in 1986 of the coalition between the two parties, damaging the support and reputation of the SPÖ. It was one of several episodes that weakened the public credibility of the political elite.

Referendum. A procedure whereby a political issue or proposal is submitted for approval or resolution to a direct popular vote by the entire electorate. The alternative name of plebiscite, which serves the same function, is sometimes used. A constitutional requirement and part of normal legislative procedure in **Switzerland**, it is used to a lesser extent in many European countries, usually for issues deemed to be of great significance.

Reformed Political Federation. (*Reformatorische Politieke Federatie – RPF*) A small fundamentalist Protestant party in the **Netherlands**. It was formed in 1975 partly as a reaction to the proposal of the three major Dutch religious parties to join together in an inter-confessional **Christian Democratic Appeal (CDA)**.

Reformed Political Union. (*Gereformeerd Politiek Verbond – GPV*) A small fundamentalist Protestant party in the **Netherlands**. Formed in 1948, it resisted incorporation by other Protestant parties, and criticized the 1975 decision of the three major Dutch religious parties to merge together in an inter-confessional party.

Renner, Karl. (1870–1950) President of **Austria** 1945–50. A lawyer and member of the Social Democratic Party, he was first elected to Parliament in 1907. Briefly Chancellor 1919–20, he was arrested at the end of the 1934 civil war. Soon released, he lived in retirement, but was interned during the Second World War. After the occupation of Vienna by the Soviet army in 1945, he was selected by the **USSR** to head a provisional government, a decision later endorsed by the Western Allies. He formed a broad-based coalition, but believed that future stability and the regaining of full independence depended upon reconciliation between the Catholic and Socialist blocs and the isolation of the small Communist Party. His strategy laid the foundations of the **grand coalition** that ruled Austria until 1966. After the 1945 election he resigned as premier and was elected to the largely ceremonial presidency, holding office until his death.

Reparations. Compensation for damage done in a war to its victors, extracted from the defeated enemy. A traditional military and political practice, the scale of reparations demanded of Germany after 1918 was held to have contributed to its political problems in the 1920s and the rise of Adolf Hitler. A European Reparations Commission was established in 1945 as part of the military occupation of Germany, but it was agreed that reparations would involve payment in kind through a transfer of capital equipment, with the largest shares going to **France** and the **USSR**. The three Western Allies abandoned collection in 1952, but **Stalin** continued to insist upon reparations in kind. After 1953 the **Federal Republic of Germany** paid large sums of money to Israel as reparations for the persecution and murder of Jews under the Nazi regime.

Republican Party. (*Republikaner*) A small extreme right-wing party in Germany. It was founded in 1983 by Franz Schönhuber and dissidents from the Bavarian **Christian Social Union (CSU)**. A first electoral success in West **Berlin** in 1989 was not repeated elsewhere until after German reunification. Its 1987 programme stressed nationalist themes, and it attacked the liberal asylum laws of the **Federal Republic of Germany**, demanding strict controls on immigration, although it was careful in its use of language and references to the German past in order to avoid a possible legal ban being imposed on it. Its ability to attract substantial electoral support in the 1990s worried many politicians, but it reflected the popular unease arising from problems of reunification. Internal factionalism led to Schönhuber being briefly expelled from the party in May 1990, but he quickly regained authority and control. By 1994 its electoral challenge seemed to have faded.

Republican People's Party. (*Cumhuriyet Halk Partisi – CHP*) A political party in **Turkey**. Founded by Kemal Atatürk in 1923, it was led by **Inönü** until 1972. Totally dominant before 1950, it was traditionally based upon an urban elite and public officials, with a secular and paternalistic style. Its support began to decay after the 1950s, and under the leadership of **Ecevit** after 1966 it moved sharply to the left to become a socialist movement, but this failed to halt its decline. Dissolved in 1981 after the military takeover, it later reappeared as a much smaller Social Democratic Populist Party, but in 1992 a faction seceded to resurrect the old CHP title.

Republican Turkish Party. (*Cumhuriyetei Turk Partisi – CTP*) An ethnic Communist party in **Cyprus**, founded in 1970. After the partition of the island it increased its support substantially, entering the Turkish Cypriot assembly, but boycotted the legislature 1991–93 in protest against the introduction of a new electoral law. It supported a federal solution to the division of the island.

Resistance movements. Extensive underground movements engaged in guerilla warfare and sabotage against Nazi Germany in the occupied countries of Europe during the Second World War. In addition to their military and espionage activities, they prepared plans for the post-war structure of Europe. Although in each country the Resistance was mainly a loose amalgam of different politically oriented groups, there was a general consensus that because of its war-time role it had earned the moral right to direct post-war affairs, and that the main objective had to be the establishment of a united Europe. Declarations in favour of a federal union in Europe were made in several countries during the war, and a major meeting of

Resistance representatives in July 1944 issued the Geneva Declaration which urged a federal United States of Europe. Few Resistance activists, however, were able to make the transition and survive in the post-war political world, which was soon dominated by traditional political parties and more experienced politicians, and governments tended to ignore the call for a federal Europe. In 1951 the survivors of some national groups formed the International Federation of Resistance Movements in Vienna, but it was a body with no political influence.

Restitutions. The controversial export subsidies or refunds in the **Common Agricultural Policy (CAP)** that permitted **European Communities (EC)** agricultural produce to be priced competitively on the world markets.

Rete. *See* LA RETE.

Reuter, Ernst. (1889–1953) German politician. Born in Silesia and joining the **Social Democratic Party (SPD)** in 1912, he was captured on the Eastern Front in the First World War. As a prisoner of war in **Russia**, he became involved in the Russian Revolution. He joined the Bolsheviks and was appointed by Lenin as Commissar for the German Volga territory. Returning to Germany he became general secretary of the German Communist Party in 1921, but soon left to rejoin the SPD. After the Nazi seizure of power he emigrated to **Turkey** in 1935, returning to live in **Berlin** in 1946. Elected mayor of the city, he headed the SPD faction that refused to amalgamate with the Communists. During the 1948 **Berlin Blockade** he became the German symbol of resistance against the **USSR**, gaining a high profile in the West. He also moved the city administration from its traditional site in the Soviet zone of the city to a new location in the Western zone. After 1949 he and his aides (who included **Brandt**) supported the pro-Western policy of strength of **Adenauer**, and he was very critical of the emphasis of the West German SPD leader, **Schumacher**, on the need for German neutrality.

Revisionism. A term broadly used to attack attempts to revise accepted ideological beliefs. It was particularly employed by orthodox Marxists against reassessments of revolutionary socialism as that had been defined by Lenin. It was the basis of the accusations by **Stalin** against **Tito** and of the Stalinist purges in Eastern European Communist regimes in the late 1940s and early 1950s.

Revolutionary Anti-Racist Action. (*Revolutionaire anti-Racistische Actie – RARA*) A left-wing terrorist group in the **Netherlands**. It claimed to be acting on behalf of all asylum seekers, but tended to support all left-wing causes. Uniquely among terrorist groups, it pledged that it would not kill people in furtherance of its cause, but did claim responsibility for several attacks on property. In 1992 it announced that it intended to widen its range of potential targets.

Revolutionary Left. (*Devrimci-Sol*) A Marxist and nationalist terrorist group in **Turkey** active since the late 1970s. Most of its original members were arrested or killed in the 1980s, with no less than 723 receiving the death penalty or lengthy prison sentences in 1989. But this did not prevent the emergence of a new group of activists who waged bombing campaigns and assassination attempts against security personnel and foreign, especially American, military and business people.

Revolutionary People's Struggle. (*Epanastatikó Laïkó Agónas – ELA*) A shadowy terrorist group in **Greece** which after 1976 claimed responsibility for several bombing campaigns.

Rey, Jean. (1902–1983) President of the **Commission** 1967–70. An experienced Belgian politician, he took over leadership of the Commission from the activist **Hallstein** in an atmosphere soured by the **empty chair crisis**, and also had the task of consolidating the Commission's role as a result of the merger of the three executives of the **European Communities (EC)** in 1967. Tactful and cautious, he acted more as a broker, seeking less to initiate action than to strike a balance between national viewpoints, but his approach failed to revive the prestige and dynamism of the Commission.

Reynaud, Paul. (1878–1966) Prime Minister of France 1940. A lawyer, he entered Parliament in 1919 for the conservative Democratic Alliance, holding various government offices in the 1930s. A consistent opponent of Nazi Germany, he resigned as premier when Marshal Pétain negotiated an armistice. Interned by the Vichy regime and imprisoned in **Austria**, he returned to parliamentary politics in 1946, serving later as a minister in a few **Fourth French Republic** governments. Although regarded as a kind of elder statesman in the Fourth Republic, he failed to secure a parliamentary majority when invited to become premier in 1953. An early supporter of **de Gaulle**, he headed the committee in 1958 charged with preparing a new constitution, and later acted as chairman of the parliamentary finance committee before breaking with de Gaulle and retiring from politics.

Reynolds, Albert. (1932–) Prime Minister of **Ireland** 1992–94. A businessman and member of **Fianna Fáil**, he entered parliament in 1977 and government in 1979. Dismissed later by **Haughey**, he became a rival of the latter, succeeding him as party leader and premier in 1992. He negotiated the **Downing Street Declaration** with **Major** shortly before a political crisis over public appointments forced his resignation.

Rijeka. *See* FIUME.

Robinson, Mary. (1944–) President of **Ireland** from 1990. A lawyer active in the areas of human rights and civil liberties, and a member of the Senate, she resigned from the **Labour Party** in 1985 in protest at the exclusion of **Northern Ireland** Protestant interests and concerns from the discussions on the **Anglo-Irish Agreement**. Backed by an alliance of left-wing groups, she defeated the **Fianna Fáil** candidate in the 1990 presidential election, attributing her success to the women of Ireland who 'instead of rocking the cradle, rocked the system'.

Rocard, Michel. (1930–) Prime Minister of **France** 1988–91. A professional politician and leader of the small Unified Socialist Party 1967–73, he contested the 1969 presidential election. In 1974 he joined the **Socialist Party (PS)** of **Mitterrand**, serving on its executive 1975–81 and again after 1986. A government minister in 1981, he resigned in 1985 in protest against the decision to reform the electoral system in favour of **proportional representation**. A long-time opponent of and potential rival to Mitterrand, he nevertheless was appointed premier in 1988. He increasingly tended to question socialist policies, especially in the economic area, and Mitterrand demanded his resignation in 1991. As the PS began to collapse in 1993 he argued that it should disband itself in order to permit the establishment of a new and more effective social democratic organization, a process he subsequently launched as part of his bid to be a contender in the 1995 presidential election. Very poor election results in 1994 led to a vote of no confidence in him, and he resigned as party leader in 1994.

Rockall. A small and remote rock outcrop in the North Atlantic. Its annexation by the **United Kingdom** in 1955 was disputed by **Denmark**, **Iceland** and **Ireland**. At issue was whether it was part of the continental shelf, an island or merely a rock. Under international law this affected rights to territorial and economic jurisdiction over its surrounding waters and sea-bed, rich in fish and minerals. Ireland and the United Kingdom signed a partial boundary agreement in 1988.

Rokossovsky, Konstantin Konstantinovich. (1887–1968) Prime Minister of **Poland** 1952–56. Born in Warsaw, he joined the Bolsheviks in 1917 and became a professional soldier in the Soviet army. Imprisoned in the 1938 Great Purge until 1941, he then commanded the defence of Moscow and took part in the Battle of Stalingrad. Still retaining a Soviet military rank, he returned to Poland in 1945, serving as defence minister 1945–56 and premier 1952–56. He directed the suppression of demonstrators in Poznań in June 1956. A deeply unpopular figure in Poland, he was recalled to Moscow after **Gomulka** was installed in power, serving as deputy Soviet Minister of Defence until his retirement in 1962.

Roldán Affair. A political scandal in **Spain**. Luis Roldán, leader of the paramilitary Civil Guard 1986–93 was accused of embezzlement. In reply he laid allegations of corruption and abuse of power against several government ministers. In April 1994 he failed to respond to a court summons to answer charges that he had used his position to amass personal wealth through a misuse of public funds. He later claimed that the premier, **González**, had ordered secret investigations of political opponents, and that several government ministers had appropriated public funds for personal use. Although the various accusations were not fully resolved, several senior politicians and police officers resigned or were dismissed, and a series of new anti-corruption measures were introduced. The controversy was one of several corruption scandals that weakened the credibility of the ruling **Spanish Socialist Workers' Party**.

Romania. A state in Eastern Europe. The modern state was established as a kingdom in 1878, after an earlier 1859 union of Moldovia and Wallachia. Further territory was acquired or annexed in 1918. Economic problems persisted under a primarily royal dictatorship, which was superseded by a military dictatorship 1940–44 under Ion Antonescu allied with Germany. The dictatorship was overthrown by a broad alliance headed by the monarchy, but the Communist party steadily increased its influence in government and administration, and the king was forced to abdicate in December 1947. The following year the Communists, firmly in control, declared the establishment of a People's Republic. The dominant personality was **Gheorghiu-Dej**, who by the early 1950s had purged the party of his potential rivals. Although he emphasized Romanian nationalism, the country was economically subservient to the **USSR** until the 1960s. Under the long rule of **Ceauşescu**, nationalism was re-emphasized and economic development plans established independent of Soviet wishes. Ceauşescu also pursued an independent foreign policy line, especially in terms of developing trading links with the West, criticizing the 1968 **Warsaw Pact** invasion of **Czechoslovakia** and joining the International Monetary Fund in 1971. Liberalization did not extend to domestic policy, and when the economic plans failed to bring prosperity, popular disillusionment sparked a draconian intensification of an already repressive and increasingly pesonalized regime. It failed to follow the more liberal moves of the USSR after 1985, becoming even more isolated. The regime had successfully prevented the existence of opposition groups and dissidents, but it was toppled within three days by a mass revolt in December 1989. Ceauşescu and his wife were executed. Authority was taken over by a hastily assembled **National Salvation Front**, consisting mainly of previous Communist administrators. The extent of democratization and movement towards a free market economy after 1989 were slower than in most other ex-Communist countries, and a deteriorating economy led to mass demonstrations 1993–94. Relations with **Hungary** remained strained after 1989 because of Romanian policy towards the Hungarian minority in **Transylvania**.

Romanian Communist Party. (*Partidul Comunist Român – PCR*) The single legal party in **Romania** 1948–89. Founded in 1921, it was banned in 1924, holding its meetings abroad. In 1944 it was a minor partner in the overthrow of the Antonescu military dictatorship. It steadily accumulated power before merging with the Social Democrats in 1948 to form the

Romanian Workers' Party. It reverted back to its original name in 1965. After a massive purge of members after 1948, it became very much the personal vehicle of **Gheorghiu-Dej** (whose personality cult it denounced in 1968) and later of **Ceauşescu**. The increasing harshness and arbitrariness of Ceauşescu's rule limited the party's structure and organization, and in 1989 there were few dissident groups or reformist Communists to fill the vacuum after his fall. Although the party disappeared in 1990, several of its leading activists were to the fore in the **National Salvation Front**.

Romanian Hearth. (*Vatră Românească*) A cultural and political organization in **Romania**. It was founded in 1990 originally to defend the rights of ethnic Romanians in **Transylvania**, rejecting any concessions to the region's Hungarian population. Its electoral wing was the extreme right-wing Romanian National Unity Party (*Partidul Unităţii Naţionale Române*).

Rome Declaration on Peace and Co-operation. An international agreement signed by members of the **North Atlantic Treaty Organization (NATO)** in November 1991. It amended the aims and objectives of the alliance in order to take account of the post-**Cold War** situation in Europe. It attempted to define the future role of NATO in terms of continent-wide security structures and a partnership with the countries of Eastern Europe.

Rossem. An idiosyncratic protest party in **Belgium**, founded in 1991. Named after its founder, Jean-Pierre van Rossem, it defined itself as an ultra-liberal movement, demanding, *inter alia*, the **privatization** of the social security system and the abolition of marriage. It surprisingly gained parliamentary representation in 1991.

Round Table. (*Runder Tisch*) A discussion forum in the **German Democratic Republic (DDR)**, formed in December 1989. It met on a frequent but irregular basis to review the political failure of the DDR regime and what might replace it. Its membership came from all political parties except the ruling **Socialist Unity Party (SED)**, various interest groups and new opposition political movements. Its heterogeneous composition prevented it from developing any coherent structure or policy line, and in the face of competition between the political parties and the growing momentum for German reunification, which it opposed, it failed to make a persuasive case for the political reconstruction of the DDR, and was disbanded in March 1990.

Round Table Agreement. An agreement in **Poland** signed in April 1989 between representatives of the government and several opposition groups. Its origins lay in renewed contacts between the government and **Solidarity** representatives who agreed to hold talks on general socio-economic issues as well as the legal recognition of Solidarity and trade union pluralism. After repeated postponements, the discussions, broadened to incorporate representatives of other opposition groups, began in February 1989. The Agreement laid down a framework for multi-party elections and the transformation to, and structure of, a democratic system.

Rukh. A political party in **Ukraine**. Founded in September 1989, and calling itself the Popular Movement for the Restructuring of the Ukraine, it argued for a reassertion of Ukrainian nationalism within a democratic and liberal framework. Its core lay in the more religious (Uniate) areas of Western Ukraine where it did well in the 1990 regional elections, but failed to attract support in the more populous and Russified eastern areas. This regional pattern of support was repeated after Ukrainian independence. It formally turned itself into a political party in 1993, but soon found itself challenged in the west by more extremist nationalist groups.

Rumor, Mariano. (1915–) Prime Minister of **Italy** 1968–70, 1973–74. A **Resistance** activist and founder member of the **Christian Democratic Party (DC)**, he entered Parliament in 1948. Serving in various government positions after 1951, he became Party Secretary in 1964. A supporter of the opening to the left, an alliance with the **Italian Socialist Party (PSI)**, he resigned as premier in 1970 because of the split in the PSI which destabilized the government coalition. He was accused of being implicated in the financial scandal of the Lockheed Affair, but was eventually cleared by a parliamentary investigation in 1978. He resigned from the legislature the following year.

Russia. A new state in Eastern Europe. By the twentieth century the Russian Empire extended, under the Romanov dynasty, from the Baltic to the Pacific. After the 1917 Russian Revolution this vast territory was inherited by the **USSR**. Within the USSR Russia was the largest republic, with some 70 per cent of the Soviet population, although made up itself as a federation of several autonomous republics, provinces and territories which reflected the existence of numerous ethnic minorities. Although Russian influence was powerful within the USSR, its interests were checked by the supremacy of the Communist party. As liberalization began after 1985, a greater emphasis upon Russian interests and nationalism began to emerge. In September 1989 it was agreed that the 1978 constitution should be revised. The reforms were introduced in March 1990, with a Congress of People's Deputies and a Supreme Soviet, with multi-party elections permitted. **Yeltsin** was elected Chairman of the Soviet (equivalent to President of the Republic) on a platform of Russian nationalism and political and economic reform. As the USSR disintegrated, a new Russian state was established. It adopted a presidential form of government, with Yeltsin easily winning the election. The new political system drifted towards greater instability, with a vast political pluralism of weak and disorganized political parties and unstable coalitions jostling for influence in a rapidly declining economic situation, with high budget deficits, inflation and rising crime rates. Abroad, the new state attempted to retain influence over the other successor states of the USSR, which collectively it defined as the **near abroad**. The major institutional vehicle for influence was the **Commonwealth of Independent States (CIS)**. It also faced unrest from several of its ethnic minorities, most seriously in **Chechnya** where its strong military response indicated that it was prepared totally to resist challenges to its territorial integrity.

Russian Democratic Movement. (*Vene Demokraatlik Liikumine/Rossiyskoye Demokratskoye Dvizheniye – VDL/RDD*) A political organization in **Estonia**. It was formed in 1990 to represent the interests and concerns of the large ethnic Russian minority, and after independence it registered itself as a political party. Its major objective was to secure equal rights for Russian speakers, especially the granting of citizenship, but it did not contest the 1992 election.

Russian Unity. A reformist political party in **Russia** formed in Novgorod in 1993 shortly before the parliamentary elections. It wished to see a more cautious and slower programme of economic reform than that pursued by the **Yeltsin** government, and argued that the interests of the regions ought to be better represented at the centre. These positions prevented it from co-operating easily with **Russia's Choice**, but it fared badly in the elections.

Russia's Choice. A reformist political party in **Russia** formed in 1993 by supporters of **Yeltsin**. More an alliance of groups than an organization, it was committed to extensive economic reform and the establishment of a market economy. The unpopularity of the government's economic programme limited its appeal and electoral success in 1993.

Ruthenia. A region of the **Ukraine**, also known as Subcarpathia or Transcarpathia. A small area with a primarily Ukrainian population, but with Slovak and Hungarian minorities, it was incorporated into **Czechoslovakia** in 1920. The **USSR** annexed it in 1945, making it part of the Ukrainian Soviet Socialist Republic. After 1991 it was one of the more nationalist areas of the Ukraine.

S

Saarland. A small industrialized region of Germany bordering **France**, and a source of dispute between the two countries. To meet French security concerns and **reparations** demands after the First World War, it was detached from German political control and placed under the League of Nations, but with French control of its coal mines. A 1935 plebiscite voted overwhelmingly in favour of a return to Germany. After 1945 and the military occupation of Germany, it was made a French responsibility, but was not treated as part of the French zone of occupation. In 1947 it was given some local autonomy within a form of economic union with France, which hoped ultimately to incorporate it completely. With the creation of the **Federal Republic of Germany**, France demanded that the region be excluded from the new state, but after 1949 West Germany claimed the territory. With the plans in 1951 for a **European Political Community (EPC)**, it was proposed that the Saarland become a special autonomous or 'European' region directly administered by the EPC. When the EPC plans collapsed in 1954, the European option for the region was retained within the proposed **Western European Union (WEU)**. A Franco-German agreement of 1954 decided that the WEU option be placed before the Saarland electorate for approval. It was decisively rejected in the 1955 referendum which voted strongly in favour of rejoining West Germany. The region was formally incorporated into the Federal Republic in January 1957, with the remaining economic concessions to France ending in 1959.

SACEUR. (Supreme Allied Commander Europe) The most important senior command in the **North Atlantic Treaty Organization (NATO)**, established in 1950. Always filled by an American general, the post was responsible for all NATO land and air forces in Western Europe. Its second in command was usually a British or West German officer. The position was somewhat ambiguous: under the control of NATO, SACEUR was a serving officer who would be expected to take orders from the American president. While responsible for training programmes, during peacetime he had command only of those national units directly assigned to NATO. Its role during the **Cold War** was primarily political, with the major responsibilities of pressing

NATO members to maintain their defence expenditure and of recommending priorities for the alliance.

SACLANT. (Supreme Allied Command Atlantic) The senior naval command in the **North Atlantic Treaty Organization (NATO)**, always held by the Commander-in-Chief of the American navy based in Norfolk, Virginia. No forces were attached to it in peacetime, but all NATO members with deep sea naval forces had units temporarily seconded to it for training exercises.

Sąjūdis. A nationalist party, the Movement for Reconstruction, in **Lithuania**. Founded in 1988 as a protest group by dissidents and intellectuals who wished to reorganize Communist society and to gain sovereignty for Lithuania, it organized mass demonstrations over the next year to become the leading manifestation of pressures for decentralization in the **USSR**. It led the first independent government and attempted to institute a programme of rapid economic reform, but poor economic policy and internal factionalism led to its electoral defeat in 1992 and a consequent split in the party. After 1992 it co-operated with several other centre-right parties in a Homeland Accord (*Tėvynės Santara*), and in 1993 it renamed itself the Homeland Union (*Tėvynės Sąjunga*).

Sakharov, Andrei Dimitrievich. (1921–1989) Soviet nuclear physicist and dissident. As the director of the Soviet nuclear programme, he publicly called for a test ban treaty in 1961. A supporter of the **Prague Spring**, his view of 1968 helped him to become a human rights activist, and in 1970 he co-authored an open letter to **Brezhnev** calling for the democratization of the **USSR**. His campaign received wide publicity and respect abroad, and in 1975 he was awarded the Nobel Peace Prize, but was not allowed by the Soviet authorities to go abroad to receive it. He was associated with the **Helsinki Human Rights Group** in 1976, criticizing their later persecution, and in 1979 condemned the Soviet invasion of **Afghanistan**. In January 1980 he and his equally active wife were exiled to the closed city of Gorki, where he went on hunger strike. Released in 1986, his return to Moscow in 1987 was regarded as a test of the **glasnost** policy advocated by **Gorbachev**. In 1989 he won election as an independent to the Congress of People's Deputies, where he was a constant critic of government policy, urging greater liberalization. He died suddenly in December, and was given an official lying-in-state where Gorbachev publicly paid his respects. In 1987 the **European Communities** (**EC**) honoured his courageous stand by creating the Sakharov Prize for Defence of Human Rights.

Salami Tactics. A phrase often used to describe the method by which the Soviet-backed Communist parties of Eastern Europe gained power after 1945. It referred to a 'slicing off', one at a time, of other parties and groups occupying positions of authority in the coalition governments of national unity that were formed after 1945. The Communists had usually insisted upon being given the Defence and Interior ministries in the coalition governments. This enabled them to control the police and army, which were used along with strikes, demonstrations and campaigns of political intimidation to force the other parties out of the coalition or to merge with the Communists, leaving them eventually with the choice of conforming or being eliminated.

Salan, Raoul Albin Louis. (1899–1984) French general. A professional soldier, he was part of the Free French Movement of **de Gaulle** after 1940, and later a commander in **French Indo-China** 1945–53. In 1956 he was made the senior officer in Algiers, and Commander-in-Chief in Algeria in 1958. His hard-line repressive policies contributed to the intensification of the **Algerian War of Independence**, and he was recalled to **France** to become Military Governor of Paris. Opposing de Gaulle's efforts to secure a political solution in Algeria, he resigned in 1960 and moved to **Spain** where he established the **Organisation de l'Armée Secrète (OAS)**. His attempt to launch a military and white settler revolt in Algeria in 1961 failed. Arrested the following year, he was sentenced to death for treason. He was formally pardoned by de Gaulle and released from prison in 1968.

Salazar, António de Oliviera. (1889–1970) Prime Minister of **Portugal** 1932–68. Trained for the priesthood, he became an academic, and entered politics in 1928, being made Minister of Finance. His successful handling of economic problems led to his appointment as premier in July 1932, with almost dictatorial powers. He introduced a new constitution in 1933, creating a new state (*Estado Novo*) along Fascist lines and outlawing all political parties except his own National Union. He ruled as virtual dictator until 1968. He maintained Portuguese neutrality during the Spanish Civil War and the Second World War. While he later introduced some limited social and economic reforms, he was hostile to political change and democratization. After the 1950s his determination to retain Portugal's African colonies at any cost placed a great burden upon the society and economy, eventually generating opposition among his military leaders. Incapacitated by a stroke in 1968, he was succeeded by his long-time lieutenant, **Caetano**.

Saltsjöbaden Agreement. An agreement on wages in **Sweden** in 1938 between the national employers' and trade union federations. It provided for annual negotiations on wages, the results of which would be binding throughout much of the Swedish economy and which were accepted by governments. It was the basis of an effective system of industrial relations, and was often held to be a key factor in the success of the **Swedish model** of government. A series of unofficial strikes in 1969 and 1970 marked the beginning of a decade of pressure on the Agreement. It eventually collapsed with a general strike in 1980, after which argument rather than consensus marked industrial relations.

Sami Council. An association of the Sami (Lapp) communities of **Finland**, **Norway** and **Sweden**, founded at Karasjok, Norway, in 1956. It joined the World Council of Indigenous Peoples (WCIO) in 1975. Its objectives were to protect Sami economic interests, to develop cultural co-operation, and to act as a forum for placing demands before national governments. It was particularly concerned about the erosion of Sami culture and the traditional nomadic way of life. A national Sami consultative assembly was formed in Finland in 1976, and in Norway in 1987.

Samizdat. Literally, self-publication, the hand-to-hand distribution in the **USSR** of manuscripts which had failed to receive or which could not obtain state approval. It operated on the chain letter principle, with individuals passing copies to friends, who in turn repeated the process. While the production of a samizdat was legally not a crime, those caught in possession of one were invariably arrested and charged with distributing anti-Soviet propaganda. When the practice began to be widespread in the early 1960s, the material was largely literary and works of fiction, but under **Brezhnev** it became more political. Similar practices were pursued in the Communist states of Eastern Europe where the material was more overtly political.

San Marino. A small independent republican enclave within **Italy**. Reputedly established as a political entity in 301, it was given papal recognition in 1631. After the 1861 *Risorgimento* it declined to join the unified Italian state, in 1862 signing instead a treaty of friendship and co-operation, which has been renewed and amended at varying intervals. It has operated internally as an independent government and political system, with elections and its own party system, but has had an economic union and a single customs area with Italy which collects all customs duties and pays a subsidy to it. It was the first Western state after 1945 to elect a Communist-led government, with a Communist–Socialist alliance 1945–57, and again 1978–86. After 1986 the Communists formed an alliance with the Christian Democrats, an arrangement that failed to be realized in Italy. It joined the United Nations (UN) in 1992.

Santer, Jacques. (1937–) President of the **Commission** from 1995. A lawyer from **Luxembourg** and a member of the **Christian Social People's Party** since 1966, he served as Party Secretary 1972–74. Elected to Parliament in 1974, he was appointed Prime Minister in 1984. In 1994 he was a compromise choice for the Commission presidency, but after his election declared his intention of following the drive towards closer European integration, albeit in a more consensual manner, pursued by his predecessor.

Saragat, Giuseppe. (1889–1988) President of **Italy** 1965–71. A journalist, he joined the **Italian Socialist Party (PSI)** in 1922. He spent most of the Fascist period abroad, returning to Italy in 1943. Uneasy about the close collaboration of the PSI with the **Italian Communist Party (PCI)**, he led a right-wing secession in January 1947 to found the **Italian Social Democratic Party (PSDI)**, remaining its leader until it merged with the PSI in 1966. He participated in a number of coalition governments with the **Christian Democratic Party (DC)** after 1947. His election as president was due to a broad alliance of secular parties which wished to break the domination of the office by the DC. As President he accepted the convention of avoiding partisan involvement and refusing to make statements on current issues and policies.

Sarajevo. The capital of **Bosnia-Hercegovina**. The site in June 1914 of the assassination of Archduke Franz Ferdinand, the heir to the Habsburg throne, an act which was the catalyst of the First World War. It reacquired international prominence in 1992 as a focal point of the civil war that raged in the province between Bosnian, Croat and Serb forces. Held by Bosnian forces and declared to be the capital of the new state, it was completely surrounded by Serb-held territory and under a state of permanent siege. Several cease-fires were negotiated by United Nations forces who provided the only guarantee of esssential requirements reaching the city.

Sardinia. An island in the Mediterranean with a distinctive culture and history, incorporated into **Italy** in 1861. Economically backward, it never lost its reputation for lawlessness and banditry, especially in the interior where traditional semi-tribal customs prevailed. A statute of autonomy was introduced in 1948, but was largely ineffective. After the 1970s extreme nationalist groups carried out acts of violence against Italian-owned property. Neither the major legitimate face of nationalism, the Sardinian Action Party (*Partidu Sardu/Partito Sardo d'Azione*), founded in 1921, or other groups, which tended to support the notion of independence within a federal Europe, were able to command substantial electoral support.

Scalfaro, Oscar Luigi. (1918–) President of Italy from 1992. A lawyer, he was elected to Parliament for the **Christian Democratic Party (DC)** in 1946, serving as a government minister on several occasions after 1954. Widely respected and one of the few DC politicians untouched by the allegations of corruption that swept the country in the 1990s, he was elected President in 1992 after the sudden resignation of **Cossiga**, and scrupulously maintained an impartial but authoritative stance during the radical transformation of the Italian system after 1993.

Scheel, Walter. (1919–) President of the **Federal Republic of Germany** 1974–79. Entering Parliament in 1953 for the **Free Democratic Party (FDP)**, he served as minister in the 1961 **Adenauer** coalition government. A leading member of the party left, he was a major actor in the removal of

Mende as party leader and the subsequent liberal realignment of the party. He was Party Chairman 1968–74, and in 1969 became Foreign Minister in the **Brandt** government, and instrumental in the **Ostpolitik** process. He resigned his other offices upon election to the ceremonial presidency in 1974.

Schengen Agreement. An agreement by some member states of the **European Communities (EC)** to create a border-free zone among themselves. Named after the town in **Luxembourg** where the first meeting was held in June 1985, a first draft agreement was not produced until March 1989, but its scheduled acceptance the following December was delayed because of problems arising from the opening of the border between the two Germanies. The final version was signed in June 1990, but its planned introduction in January 1992 was further delayed because of concerns over control of illegal immigration and asylum-seekers. By 1994 it was finally introduced but it had not been fully implemented in 1995, with some states still refusing to sign it. Its introduction was marred by some confusion and inadequate provisions, with doubts over its potential effectiveness and survival persisting.

Schiller Plan. A 1970 document on **Economic and Monetary Union (EMU)** put forward by the West German finance Minister, Karl Schiller, as a result of the decision of the 1969 **Hague summit** to set 1980 as the deadline for EMU. It argued that the EMU could only be achieved if the **European Communities (EC)** accepted that economic co-ordination and harmonization must be the first step and the precondition of any monetary union. *See also* BARRE PLAN, WERNER REPORT.

Schleswig. (Slesvig) A border region between **Denmark** and the **Federal Republic of Germany**. Annexed by Prussia in 1866, plebiscites after 1918 gave much of northern Schleswig to Denmark, but small ethnic minorities remained on both sides of the border, giving rise to some tension between the wars. Uneasiness persisted after 1945, but the boundary remained unchanged, and by the 1950s each state had given guaranteed rights to its minority, especially in local government.

Schlüter, Poul. (1929–) Prime Minister of **Denmark** 1982–93. Elected to Parliament in 1964 for the **Conservative People's Party (KF)**, he became party leader in 1974, overseeing a rise in party support. In September 1982 he became the first KF premier for 81 years, surviving as head of several minority coalitions for 11 years. Because of the lack of a majority, he accepted that defeat for the government in Parliament would be a frequent occurrence and not necessarily a matter of resignation. He was a skilful operator in a difficult situation, and prepared, as with the issue of ratification of the **Single European Act (SEA)**, to make a blunt appeal to the electorate through a referendum. Although the KF's popular appeal was beginning to decline, his resignation in January 1993 was the result of the implication of the government and party in the **Tamilgate** immigration and refugee scandal. He resigned as party leader the following September.

Schmidt, Helmut. (1918–) Chancellor of the **Federal Republic of Germany** 1974–82. Joining the **Social Democratic Party (SPD)**, he worked in the Hamburg city administration 1949–53. Elected to Parliament in 1953 he served as Minister of Defence 1969–72 and Minister of Finance under his friend, **Brandt**. In 1974 he succeeded Brandt as premier and party leader. He sought to continue the **Ostpolitik** process, although he was less trusting of the **USSR** and the **German Democratic Republic (DDR)**, with whom relations became more strained after the Soviet invasion of **Afghanistan** in 1979. An influential figure in international politics, he forged a close personal friendship with the French President, **Giscard d'Estaing**, and the two men dominated the **European Council** in the 1970s. His approach to European integration, while positive, was pragmatic, and he evaluated new initiatives also in the context of their practicality and financial cost. In the late 1970s he became concerned by a continued Soviet military build-up. He argued for a modernization of the **North Atlantic Treaty Organization (NATO)**, and was a major advocate for the interim installation in Western Europe of American intermediate range nuclear missiles. The weapons issue was a major factor in his loss of political support at home, where his popularity had been adversely affected by his seemingly more austere and aloof style of leadership. In particular, he failed to stem a radicalization of his party, and his growing isolation within a more left-wing dominated SPD helped to persuade the junior partner in his coalition, the **Free Democratic Party (FDP)**, to leave the government in 1982. The Schmidt government was consequently defeated in Parliament. He resigned his office, also retiring from active party politics. He later, through his writings and speeches, became a kind of international elder statesman.

Schools Pact. A political agreement in **Belgium** in 1958. The schools issue, the role and rights of the Catholic Church in education, had first been raised in the 1870s, but the presence in government from 1880 to 1954 of a Catholic or Christian Democrat party had kept it off the agenda. It arose again in 1954 when a new secular government of Liberals and Socialists proposed a reduction in state subsidies for Catholic institutions and an increase in the number of state schools. A large-scale mobilization by the Church led to the defeat of the government coalition in the 1958 election. The resulting Schools Pact was signed by all three parties. Although a compromise and signed initially for only 12 years, it largely safeguarded the Church's existing position and educational rights and effectively removed the one major religious issue from the political agenda, and the Church hierarchy ceased to play a direct political role. The success of the Pact opened the way for language issues to dominate politics.

Schröder, Gerhard. (1910–1990) West German politician. After active service in the Second World War, he joined the **Christian Democratic Union (CDU)** and was elected to Parliament in 1949. He first served in government in 1953 and later became Foreign Minister 1961–66 before moving to the Ministry of Defence. A prominent member of the Protestant wing of the CDU, he was an Atlanticist and advocate of a broad Western alliance, and was hostile to the pro-French stance of **Adenauer** after 1961, believing that a European policy based solely or primarily upon a relationship with **France** could not provide West Germany with the necessary level of security commitment. He also believed that Adenauer's policy of strength needed to be amended to incorporate a West German national interest and in 1965 took the first steps to alter the **Hallstein Doctrine**, suggesting it was wrong to expect West Germany's allies to honour it, but even this was still too radical for the CDU to accept. In 1969 he became the party candidate for the presidency, but his defeat by **Heinemann** and the departure of the CDU from government effectively brought his political career to an end.

Schumacher, Kurt. (1895–1952) West German politician. A member of the **Social Democratic Party (SPD)**, he served in the Württemberg regional parliament 1924–31, also being elected to the national legislature in 1930. He was arrested in 1933 and sent to a concentration camp. Released in 1944, he lived in Hanover from where he declared the reconstitution of the SPD as soon as the city was liberated by the Western allies. He was a forceful and dogmatic personality, and his pre-war experiences in the Weimar Republic and under the Nazi regime had left him with a deep distrust of Communism. Quickly establishing himself as party leader in Western Germany, his views brought him into conflict with the SPD leadership in the Soviet zone under **Grotewohl** which was willing to enter into an alliance with the Communists, and he bitterly attacked the 1946 merger there of the two parties to produce the **Socialist Unity Party (SED)**. As SPD leader he led the parliamentary opposition after 1949 to the coalition government of **Adenauer**. He was critical of Adenauer's pro-Western policy and advocacy of West German rearmament within the Western alliance, believing that they would hinder the primary goal of German reunification which, he argued, would be more possible if the country accepted a position of neutrality in international affairs. His unbending character and principled opposition ignored the realities of the period, and proved not to be attractive to the electorate. Plagued by ill-health since his long imprisonment, he died in 1952, to be succeeded as SPD leader by **Ollenauer**.

Schuman Plan. A proposal in 1950 for the pooling of coal and steel resources in Western Europe. Named after the French Foreign Minister, **Schuman**, it had been drafted by **Monnet** as part of his strategy for European integration. It was supported by **France**, which saw it as a way of retaining influence over West German economic policy after the formation of the **Federal Republic of Germany** and the failure of the **International Ruhr Authority (IRA)** to realize French objectives. Unveiled at a press conference on 9 May, it outlined a plan of co-operation as a first step towards a European federation, with France and West Germany as its core. The responses from governments to the proposal reflected and confirmed the existing national differences on the value and nature of European integration. Only six countries were prepared to accept the offer and begin negotiations. These resulted in the **Treaty of Paris** which established the **European Coal and Steel Community (ECSC)**.

Schuman, Robert. (1886–1963) Prime Minister of **France** 1947–48, and Foreign Minister 1948–53. Born in **Luxembourg** and brought up in Lorraine, then part of Germany, he served in the German forces in the First World War. Acquiring French citizenship in 1918 when Lorraine was returned to France, he was elected to Parliament in 1919 as a moderate conservative. Arrested by the Gestapo in September 1940, he escaped from prison in 1942 and joined the **Resistance movement**. In 1944 he joined the newly formed **Popular Republican Movement (MRP)**, representing the party in Parliament 1945–62. Briefly Prime Minister, his major political influence was as Foreign Minister. A strong supporter of European integration, he believed it had to be based upon a lasting reconciliation between France and Germany. He accepted the arguments of **Monnet** about the value of a strategy of **sectoral integration**, and in May 1950 proposed the **Schuman Plan**. He later supported the proposed **European Defence Community (EDC)**, but strong opposition to it eventually forced his resignation in 1953. Central to the first stages of integration, his pioneering work was honoured at the first meeting of the Parliamentary Assembly of the **European Economic Community (EEC)** in 1958, which elected him as its president in preference to the nominee of the foreign ministers of the Member States. In 1986, to mark the centenary of his birth, the **European Communities (EC)** made 9 May, the date of the Schuman Plan, Europe Day.

Schwarzenbach, James. (1911–1994) Swiss politician. A publicist and journalist, he entered Parliament in 1967 as a non-partisan member of the **National Action for People and Homeland**. He achieved notoriety, and ostracism, for his arguments in favour of strict immigration controls and a savage reduction of the numbers of foreign workers already in the country. He successfully forced a referendum on the issue in 1970, losing it only narrowly.

Scotland. A territory within the **United Kingdom**. An independent kingdom, it joined with England in 1707, but retained its own legal system, educational system, and religion, an institutional infrastructure which helped the retention of a strong sense of Scottish identity and the maintenance of a Scottish elite. Nationalist sentiment against the Union began to emerge in the 1880s, but although a nationalist party was formed in 1925, political nationalism did not appear to pose a threat until the mid-1960s. The **Scottish National Party (SNP)** consolidated itself as a meaningful political presence, but in 1979 only some one-third of the electorate, albeit a majority of those who voted, supported a proposal for devolution and a Scottish assembly. However, of the main political parties, only the **Conservative Party**, steadily reduced to become a rump by the 1990s, argued for the *status quo*. The others promised some form of extensive devolution as opposed to the SNP commitment to independence.

Scottish National Party (SNP). A nationalist party in **Scotland**. It was founded in 1934 by a merger of the National Party of Scotland and the Scottish Party. Internal disputes between those who found some form of home rule within the **United Kingdom** an acceptable goal and those who insisted on nothing less than full independence were resolved in the latter's favour by the 1950s. It achieved an electoral breakthrough in the 1960s, winning almost one-third of the Scottish vote in 1974. In the 1980s it attempted to present a more specific social democratic profile in addition to its nationalist commitment as it moved to become the major challenger in Scotland to the dominant **Labour Party**.

Second Economy. A phrase frequently used by economists to describe various forms of private economic activity pursued in the **USSR** and the Communist systems of Eastern Europe. In addition to black market dealings in goods and currency speculation, it referred to independent entrepreneurial activity condoned by the state, as well as bribery and official corruption. Alternative terms sometimes used included the shadow economy and the informal economy.

Sectoral integration. A strategy for European integration involving a step-by-step approach of unifying single economic sectors. It was advanced after 1945 primarily by **Monnet** as a more realistic route to union than the dominant federalist theme of the time. It took a more long-term view, arguing that political union would be stronger if built upon an effective economic base of co-operation and harmonization. As more and more economic sectors were integrated, the strategy assumed that movement towards political union would accelerate. The **European Coal and Steel Community (ECSC)** was to be the first integrated segment of a rolling programme, but the defeat of the **European Defence Community (EDC)** meant it was also the last. The establishment of the **European Economic Community (EEC)** in 1957 short-circuited the concept by proposing to move immediately to a **common market**.

Securitate. The state secret police of Communist **Romania**. Heavily armed, it was developed by **Ceauşescu** into an effective and much feared instrument of state terror and oppression. Many of its leaders were personally loyal to Ceauşescu, and opposed the popular and military forces that sought to overthrow him in 1989. Many senior officials were subsequently arrested and imprisoned after the fall of the regime, and the organization was officially disbanded. A large number of lower ranking members were retained in a reconstructed intelligence service or were transferred to the police forces.

Segni, Mariotto. (1939–) Italian politician. A lawyer and academic, he entered Parliament for the **Christian Democratic Party (DC)** in 1976. After holding junior government posts in the early 1980s, he became a major critic of the system and its corruption and inefficiency, and a protagonist of electoral reform. He resigned from the DC in 1992 and the following year successfully sponsored a referendum on electoral reform. He failed to establish a base for himself in the reformed system, but won election to the **European Parliament (EP)**.

Serbia. A state in Eastern Europe and former constituent republic of **Yugoslavia**. The modern sense of identity dates from the 1804–13 revolution, but full independence was not gained until 1882. A disruptive element in Balkan imperial politics, in 1918 it formed part of Yugoslavia. The most populous, but not the most economically advanced, area of the new state, its political preponderance was increasingly rejected by other areas, especially **Croatia** and **Slovenia**. Inter-ethnic rivalry continued after 1945, but were largely contained until the death of **Tito**. A new expression of Serb nationalism emerged in 1987 when **Milošević** became leader of the Serb Communist Party. He adopted a more aggressive line within Yugoslavia, but particularly against the Albanian population in **Kosovo**. In 1991 the Yugoslav army, whose officers were primarily Serbs, failed to stop the secession of Croatia and Slovenia. Serbia backed the Serb populations in Croatia and **Bosnia-Hercegovina** in their attempts to seize control of territory. Its seeming endorsement of aggressive policies by these minorities revived the traditional fears of Serbian expansionism, and led to the imposition of international sanctions. While these produced great economic hardship and inflation, it did not diminish the Serb position. Milošević consolidated his authority through his reconstitution of the Communist organization as the Socialist Party of Serbia (*Socijalistička Partija Srbije*), and the major opposition to him was an even more extreme version of nationalism, especially the **Serbian Radical Party**, which kept alive the international worry that Serbia might again prove to be the spark of a more general Balkan conflict.

Serbian Democratic Party. (*Srpska Demokratska Stranka – SDS*) A political party in **Bosnia-Hercegovina**, founded in 1990. Led by **Karadžić**, it established itself as the main voice of the Bosnian Serb population. Its objectives were the unification of the Serb-populated areas with **Serbia**, and it was the prime mover of the formation of a Serbian Republic within Bosnia.

Serbian Radical Party. (*Srpska Radikalna Stranka – SRS*) An extreme right-wing nationalist party in **Serbia**. Advocating the integration of all Serb territories in a Greater Serbia, it modelled itself on the Fascist parties of the 1930s, using their leadership principle, and established itself as a major alternative to **Milošević** and his Socialist Party of Serbia. It formed a paramilitary group, the Serbian Chetnik Movement (*Srpski Četnicki Pokret*) which acted as an auxiliary to the Serb military forces in **Bosnia-Hercegovina** and **Croatia**.

Serbian Renewal Movement. *See* DEMOCRATIC MOVEMENT OF SERBIA.

Seventeenth November Revolutionary Organization. (*Dekaeptá Noémvris Epanastatikó Orgánosi*) A left-wing terrorist group in **Greece**. Named after the day in 1973 of a brutal repression of a student protest in Athens by the **Greek Colonels** regime, it claimed to be the true voice of socialism. After its formation in 1975 it claimed responsibility for several assassinations and numerous bombings, but no member of the shadowy group was identified or arrested.

Seveso. The site in **Italy** of an environmental disaster caused by an explosion at a chemicals factory in 1976. The explosion released into the atmosphere a cloud of toxic gas which contaminated a large area of the countryside, forcing the evacuation of local populations and the destruction of livestock. The most serious accident of its kind in Western Europe, it led to a review by the **European Communities (EC)** and national governments of their regulations governing the use of hazardous materials.

SHAPE. (Supreme Headquarters Allied Powers Europe) The headquarters of the European military command of the **North Atlantic Treaty Organization (NATO)**. Outside war-time conditions it was essentially an administrative institution rather than a command post. Originally based at Versailles, it was moved to near Mons (Bergen) in **Belgium** in 1966 after **France** withdrew militarily from NATO. In the event of a European war, it was to move to a secret and highly fortified location.

Shatalin Plan. A proposal for economic and political reform in the **USSR**. Advanced by Stanislav Shatalin in 1990, it envisaged an 'Economic Union of Sovereign Republics' where an extensive devolution of authority to the constituent republics would be accompanied by radical economic reform through the privatization of many industrial and commercial enterprises. It was rejected by **Gorbachev** who regarded it as too much of a risk.

Shehu, Mehmet. (1913–1981) Prime Minister of **Albania** 1954–81. A long-time lieutenant of **Hoxha** who had served in the International Brigades in the Spanish Civil War, he was widely regarded as Hoxhas's presumed heir. As the long-serving head of government he had acquired a reputation for orthodoxy and repression at least as great as that of his mentor. He was dismissed from office without reason in 1981, but it was widely believed that Hoxha thought his unpopularity would destabilize the state if he became the party leader. A few months later it was reported that he had been killed in a shooting accident, with suicide being the implication. Shortly afterwards there was a purge of his family and followers.

Shevardnadze, Eduard Amvrosievich. (1928–) President of **Georgia** from 1992. He joined the Communist Party in 1948, working for the party's youth movement before moving into party administration and the regional government in Georgia in 1961. Largely unknown elsewhere in the **USSR** and abroad, and with no experience of international politics, he was the surprise choice for Foreign Minister by **Gorbachev** in 1985. An earlier advocate of reforms in the party and state structure, he was a firm ally of Gorbachev in the pursuit of **glasnost** and **perestroika**, and followed an activist foreign policy of **détente**. He restructured the foreign ministry and insisted that all foreign policy-making should be publicly visible and accountable. During the abortive 1991 coup against Gorbachev, he appeared in public at the side of **Yeltsin** and denounced the conspirators. After the disintegration of the USSR he returned to Georgia where in 1992 he was invited to assume the presidency after a military coup had ousted the **Gamsakhurdia** government. He struggled, mainly unsuccessfully, to reverse the breakdown of law and order and to maintain Georgian territorial integrity, but by 1993 had lost control of the rebellious province of **Abkhazia**. With his army demoralized and in danger of disintegrating, and faced also by the challenge of rebel forces loyal to Gamsakhurdia, he was forced to turn to **Russia** for military aid. While this stabilized the internal situation, it also reduced his freedom of action.

Silesia. A multi-ethnic region of Central Europe, mostly given to Prussia in 1815. After a series of plebiscites in 1918 the more industrial Upper Silesia was awarded to **Poland**, with Germany retaining Lower Silesia. German army units occupied Polish Silesia in September 1939, but the Allies decided at the 1945 **Potsdam Conference** that the whole region should go to Poland. The German population was expelled, settling mostly in the **Federal Republic of Germany** where they formed influential interest groups demanding the right to return to and live in their homelands. In 1990 the reunified Germany formally renounced all claims to the territory.

Simmenthal SpA v. Commission. A 1980 ruling by the **Court of Justice** that national governments must apply **European Communities (EC)** law in full, and that where this is not done, individuals have a right to appeal against a government to the Court.

Sinatra Doctrine. A humorous phrase describing the new policy of non-intervention in the domestic affairs of Eastern Europe announced by the **USSR** in November 1989. The statement was made in Warsaw at a meeting of the **Warsaw Pact**, and it effectively marked the Soviet abandonment of the **Brezhnev Doctrine**. It accepted that every state had the right to determine the course of its own social and economic doctrine and policy. The term derived from comments made on American television by the Soviet Foreign Ministry spokesman, Gennady Gerasimov, who said, quoting a popular song associated with Frank Sinatra, that the Warsaw Pact countries had decided to 'do it their way'.

Single Administrative Document (SAD). A **European Communities (EC)** decision in January 1988 relating to the implementation of a single **internal market**. Its objective was to simplify or abolish some frontier controls by having only one composite document to replace the hundred or so forms relating to import/export and transit required by drivers of commercial vehicles for crossing national borders within the EC.

Single European Act (SEA). A major revision in July 1987 of the **Treaty of Rome**. It was the outcome of a decision in June 1985 of the **European Council**. It had three major themes: the establishment of an **internal market**, the strengthening of **European Political Co-operation (EPC)**, and reform of the institutional structures of the **European Communities (EC)**. It extended EC competence in a range of policy areas, and obliged the member states to work for **harmonization** across a range of differing national standards and regulations. The institutional reforms restricted the veto power of national governments by reducing the range of decisions requiring unanimous consent, as well as increasing the role of the **European Parliament (EP)**. It also created a **Court of First Instance** to ease the workload of the **Court of Justice**.

Single European Market. *See* INTERNAL MARKET.

Sinn Féin. (Ourselves Alone) A small republican and nationalist party in **Ireland**. Founded in 1902, it developed after the 1916 Easter Uprising into a mass movement pressing for Irish independence. It was split by the 1922 decision to accept an Irish Free State, with the moderates leaving the movement. After **De Valéra** broke with it to form **Fianna Fáil** and pursue full independence by constitutional means, it declined to a small rump which was soon outlawed. After years of a shadowy existence, it re-emerged with some popular appeal in **Northern Ireland** as the political front of the Provisional **Irish Republican Army (IRA)**, regarding IRA acts of violence as legitimate acts of war. In 1994 after some hesitation it accepted the terms of the **Downing Street Declaration** and agreed to be part of the talks on the future of Northern Ireland. It also survived in Ireland, but with minimal support and little electoral activity.

Six. A popular term, alternatively the Europe of the Six, often used to refer to the six founding members of the **European Communities (EC)**, and also before 1973 to the EC.

Slansky Trial. The trial in **Czechoslovakia** of the vice-premier, Rudolf Slansky, and other leading Communist officials in November 1952. The Secretary of the Party, Slansky was arrested by the security police on charges of treason. Among the other 13 people arrested was Vladimir Clementis, who had been Foreign Minister 1948–50. All those arrested were Jews. In a show trial, they were all accused of being Trotskyist, Titoist, Zionist, bourgeois nationalist traitors. Slansky and ten others were found guilty on all charges and executed in December. The other three were given long prison sentences and were pardoned only in 1963. It was the most significant Communist purge outside the **USSR**, and was thought to have been ordered by **Stalin**, whose **anti-semitism** had become obsessive. The evidence seems to have been totally fabricated. As a bizarre ending, after the execution the bodies were cremated and the ashes used as filler material in a road construction scheme outside Prague.

Slavonia. An eastern region of **Croatia**. Bordering **Serbia**, its population was an ethnical mix of Croats and Serbs. When Croatia declared its independence from **Yugoslavia** in 1991, the region erupted into civil war between the ethnic communities. Much of the territory was captured by Serb forces, with the Croats fleeing or being expelled. While the Serb intention was for their areas of Slavonia to be united with Serbia, the international community regarded the area as part of Croatia. In 1995 Western Slavonia was recaptured by Croat forces.

Slavonic Commonwealth. *See* COMMONWEALTH OF INDEPENDENT STATES.

Slesvig. *See* SCHLESWIG.

Slovakia. A component region of **Czechoslovakia**, declaring itself independent in 1992. A strong sense of Slovakian identity persisted after the creation of the Czechoslovakian state in 1918, and after 1938 a separate Slovak state was established under German tutellage. Resentment at perceived Czech domination endured after 1945, and in 1968 a new federal structure with separate Slovak institutions was introduced. After democratization in 1989, Slovak nationalism was re-emphasized, with considerable opposition to the Czech insistence upon a rapid transition to a market economy. The Slovak claims were spearheaded by **Mečiar**, leading to an amicable divorce in 1992, after which Slovak politics were dominated by competition between various forms of nationalism, and many of the earlier market-oriented reforms were halted or reversed.

Slovenia. An ethnically homogeneous region in Central Europe, part of the Habsburg Empire from the fourteenth century to 1918 when it was incorporated into the new state of **Yugoslavia**. The most highly developed economy in Yugoslavia, its Catholic population resented Serbian domination of the state. It became a republic in federal Yugoslavia after 1945. Nationalist sentiment remained strong and reasserted itself as a political force in 1989. In January 1990 the Slovene delegation walked out of a congress of the **League of Communists** after their proposals for reform of the federal party and the granting of more autonomy to its regional bodies had been rejected. Elections later in the year resulted in a non-Communist regional government, which in June 1991 declared the secession of Slovenia from Yugoslavia. Attempts by the Serb-dominated Yugoslav army to prevent the breakaway failed, with military action ending after only a month, and it was formally recognized as an independent state which was able to stay apart from the conflicts that afflicted other parts of the former Yugoslavia.

Smithsonian Agreement. An attempt by Western countries in 1971 to retain some of the stability of fixed exchange rates believed to have been provided by the 1944 **Bretton Woods Agreement**. Its objective was to impose limits on how far floating currencies could move against each other, but failed to cope with persisting currency crises, especially of the American dollar. It was effectively destroyed by the 1973 oil crisis and was more or less abandoned within a year.

Snake. An agreement by several Western European countries in 1972 to establish their own system of exchange rates within the parameters of the **Smithsonian Agreement**. For its participants the permitted range of currency fluctuation was reduced by one-half, allowing, it was said, the European currencies to wriggle like a snake within the broader Smithsonian limits. It faced problems from the outset, particularly in its inability to overcome difficulties associated with the great disparity in strength of the various currencies. Many governments found it impossible to stay within its limits without endangering their own economies, and left the system. By 1976 it was largely discredited, confined to only a few currencies, and collapsed. Its end was a severe blow to the **European Communities (EC)** which had seen it as a core component of their plan to achieve **Economic and Monetary Union (EMU)**.

Soares, Mário Alberto Nobre Lopes. (1924–) President of **Portugal** from 1986. A lawyer and teacher, he was imprisoned 12 times by the **Salazar** regime for his opposition to the system before being deported to Sao Tomé in 1968. He founded Portuguese Social Action in 1964, and in 1973 transformed it into the **Socialist Party (PS)** during his exile in Paris 1970–74. He returned to Portugal after the 1974 revolution as PS leader. Appointed Foreign Minister 1974–75 he negotiated independence for Portugal's colonies. In the revolutionary atmosphere of post-1974 politics he strove to establish a stable democratic system, playing a major role in the consolidation of democracy. He served as a minority Prime Minister 1976–78 and again 1983–85, in between serving as a minister in various coalition governments. The best-known and one of the most popular politicians in the country, he was elected to the presidency in February 1986 by a substantial majority, resigning the leadership of his party.

Social Action Programme. A 1974 **European Communities (EC)** programme intended to cope with the prevailing economic problems. The Member States undertook to implement some 40 measures relating to employment and working conditions, and to involve workers and employers in their socio-economic conditions.

Social and Liberal Democratic Party. A political party in the **United Kingdom** founded in 1988 by a merger of the **Liberal Party** and the bulk of the **Social Democratic Party (SDP)**. Its programme and objectives were largely those of the Liberal Party, and it became more commonly known as the Liberal Democrats.

Social Charter. *See* CHARTER OF FUNDAMENTAL SOCIAL RIGHTS.

Social Democratic and Labour Party (SDLP). A major political party in **Northern Ireland**. Founded in 1970, it was the first systematic attempt to mobilize and organize the Catholic minority. It rejected political violence and repudiated the activities of the **Irish Republican Army (IRA)**. It sought the implementation of equal rights in the province and the reunification of the island, but stressed that reunification had to be achieved by democratic means and hopefully with the involvement of the Protestant majority in the province.

Social Democratic Labour Party. (*Socialdemokratiskar Arbetarparti – SAP*) A major left-wing party in **Sweden**. Founded in 1889, it became the largest party in 1914. After forming three short-lived minority governments in the 1920s, it governed continuously 1932–76, as either a majority or a minority administration supported by either the **Centre** (Agrarian) **Party** or Communist Party. Through its long tenure in office, it shaped society in what was often called the **Swedish model,** linking the free play of market forces in manufacturing to a voluntary but tight regulation of the labour market, close consultation with major social interests, extensive redistribution policies, and a comprehensive welfare system. Losing power in 1976, it returned to government 1982–91 and after 1994. Its attempts after the 1960s to move on from political and social democracy to forms of economic democracy pushed it in a more radical direction, but in the late 1980s the increasing gap between the costs of social provision and the ability of the economy to pay for it led most of the leadership to accept that the agenda had to be changed to incorporate some reduction in the cost and extent of public provision.

Social Democratic Party. (*Social-Demokratiet – SD*). A major left-wing party in **Denmark**. Founded in 1881, it became the largest party in 1924, but was never able to win a majority. From the 1920s to the 1960s it tended to form an alliance with the small **Radical Liberal Party**, the two forming coalition governments for most of the period. After 1964 its continued frequent presence in government was as a single party minority administration relying upon the support of the more left-wing **Socialist People's Party**. A more pronounced radicalism led to a right-wing secession in 1973. The weakened party could continue as a minority government 1975–78, 1979–82, and after 1993, but was forced to rely upon *ad hoc* support from various parties on a more or less issue-by-issue basis, which hindered it in developing and implementing a coherent party programme.

Social Democratic Party. (*Sozialdemokratische Partei Deutschlands – SPD*) A major left-wing party in the **Federal Republic of Germany**. Founded in 1875 as the German Socialist Workers' Party, it adopted a Marxist programme, retaining the associated doctrines until 1957. Quickly emerging after 1875 as the largest socialist party in Europe, after 1918 it faced a powerful challenge from a strong Communist movement with which it was in deep and bitter conflict. It voted against Hitler's 1933 Enabling Act which suspended the Weimar Republic and abolished political parties. It quickly re-established itself in 1945 after the defeat of Germany. In the Soviet zone of occupation many of its leaders were in favour of an alliance with the Communists, and in 1946 the two were merged as the **Socialist Unity Party (SED)** which after 1949 became the official party of the **German Democratic Republic (DDR)**. Ex-SPD members were soon removed from leading positions in the SED. In the Western zones of occupation the SPD, led by **Schumacher**, rejected any association with the Communists. After the 1949 formation of the Federal Republic the party remained in opposition until 1966. Under Schumacher it rejected the pro-Western policy of **Adenauer**, believing that reunification could best be achieved through neutrality, and it remained wedded to a Marxist vocabulary. In 1959 party reformers forced through the **Bad Godesberg Programme**, attempting to turn the SPD into a more broadly based centre-left party. Its electoral performances began to improve. It entered into a **grand coalition** 1966–69, and under the leadership of **Brandt** and **Schmidt** led coalition governments 1969–82. Left-wing sentiment within the party gained more influence after the late 1970s, generating internal tensions which damaged its electoral appeal and created a persisting problem of leadership. In the DDR a new Social Democratic Party (SDP) was constituted in October 1989 as an illegal organization. It changed its name to SPD the following January in order to develop links with the western party with which it subsequently merged.

Social Democratic Party. (*Althyduflokkurinn – A*) A small left-wing party in **Iceland**. Founded in 1916, its support declined markedly after the formation in 1956 of the rival and more radical **People's Alliance**. Moderate in outlook and policy, it was a member of several centrist or conservative-oriented coalition governments after 1945.

Social Democratic Party. (*Partido Social Democratico – PSD*) A centrist party in **Portugal**, founded in 1974 as the Popular Democratic Party and adopting its present title in 1976. Initially left of centre, it moved to the right in 1977. It opposed efforts by left-wing groups to maintain a radical and revolutionary momentum 1975–76, and backed the presidency of **Eanes**. It formed part of a moderate coalition government 1979–83 with the **Party of the Democratic Centre**, but its leader (and Prime Minister) Francisco Sá Carneiro was killed in a plane crash in December 1980. Under the later leadership of **Cavalco Silva**, it grew in strength, forming a minority government in 1985 and winning a majority in 1987. Its centrist position made it prone to factional and personality disputes between its left and right wings.

Social Democratic Party. (*Sozialdemokratische Partei/Parti Socialiste – SP/PS*) The major left-wing party in **Switzerland**, founded in 1988. Despite still professing a revolutionary Marxist creed, in 1943 it became the fourth party of the permanent coalition that governs Switzerland. Leaving the coalition in 1953, it returned in 1959 and abandoned its original ideological programme and emphasis upon class conflict, making theory conform to practice.

Social Democratic Party (SDP). A small centre-left party in the **United Kingdom**. In January 1981 four leading members of the **Labour Party**, including **Jenkins** and **Owen**, disillusioned by what they saw as a militant radical takeover of the party, formed a Council for Social Democracy. In March they launched the SDP as a centrist party that would 'break the mould' of British politics. It enjoyed some initial popularity, especially in local elections, but its momentum began to decline after 1982. It formed an electoral alliance with the **Liberal Party** in 1983 and 1987, but won few seats. The tensions between the parties were more serious for the smaller SDP, and after 1987 a majority supported a merger with the Liberals. The merger produced the **Social and Liberal Democratic Party** in 1988, but this was rejected by **Owen** who led a tiny rump SDP until its disbandment in 1992. The initial successes of the SDP were one factor that led to a reassessment by Labour of its policies and practices.

Social Democratic People's Party. (*Sosyal Demokratik Halkçi Parti – SHP*) A left-wing party in **Turkey** formed in 1985 as a merger of several successor groups to the disbanded **Republican People's Party (CHP)**. It became an important political actor, but in 1992 a significant minority seceded to form a reconstituted CHP.

Social dumping. A phrase used after the late 1980s in the **European**

Communities (EC) to describe the process whereby, under the greater freedoms of the **internal market**, manufacturers shift their production sites from high to low wage areas. Critics of the practice argued that it constituted unfair competition and that it would lead to an erosion of welfare provisions and workers' rights.

Socialist Alliance of the Working People of Yugoslavia. (*Socijalistička Savez Radnog Naroda Jugoslavija*) A popular front grouping for the Communist Party. Originally called the People's Front, it was renamed in 1952. It had the task of controlling electoral procedures, but was less subservient to the Communist party organization than similar fronts in other Communist regimes.

Socialist Group. Since 1973 the largest **party group** in the **European Parliament (EP)**. Formed by representatives of national socialist and social democratic parties, it often found its cohesion weakened by conflicting ideological and national party perspectives. To counteract this tendency, it sought, with some success, to develop a common line on issues by pursuing consensus and compromise in working groups and caucuses before formal EP plenary or committee sessions.

Socialist Left Party. (*Sosialistisk Venstrepartiet – SV*) A small left-wing party in **Norway**. It was formed in 1975 by the **Socialist People's Party** and dissident members of the **Labour Party** who, along with the Communist Party, had opposed Norway's proposed entry into the **European Communities (EC)** on ideological grounds. They had first joined forces to campaign against entry in the 1972 referendum, and in 1973 formed a Socialist Electoral Alliance. The more adamant socialist position of the SV and its demands for a non-aligned foreign policy enabled it to secure an electoral base to the left of Labour.

Socialist Party. (*Sozialistische Partei Österreichs – SPÖ*) A major left-wing party in **Austria**. Formed in 1945 as a reconstruction of the pre-war Social Democratic Party, it retained a programmatic commitment to Marxism until the late 1950s, but in practice abandoned the strong ideological line of its predecessor. Entering a **grand coalition** with the **Austrian People's Party (ÖVP)**, it was in opposition only between 1966 and 1970. It reached the peak of its popularity under the leadership of **Kreisky**, but its appeal declined in the 1980s because of growing economic problems arising partly from the cost burden of the huge public sector, which it was reluctant to reduce, and because of several political and financial scandals. In 1986 it invited the ÖVP to rejoin it in a grand coalition. In 1991 it changed its name to the Social Democratic Party and agreed to enter into an extensive review of possible reforms.

Socialist Party. (*Parti Socialiste – PS*) A left-wing party in **Belgium**. It was established in 1978 as one of the successors to the Belgian Socialist

Party (PSB), based in **Wallonia** and representing the French-speaking community. The leading party in Wallonia, it was stronger than its Flemish counterpart. It supported the federalization of Belgium, believing that devolution was the best way for Wallonia to halt and reverse its relative economic decline, but generally continued to be willing to collaborate with other parties.

Socialist Party. (*Parti Socialiste – PS*) A major left-wing party in **France**. The party was originally founded in 1905 as the French Section of the Workers' International (*Section Française de l'Internationale Ouvrière – SFIO*), and first entered government in the 1936 Popular Front coalition. Active in the war-time **Resistance movement**, it was a member of the 1945–47 **tripartism** coalition governments, but soon found itself over-shadowed by a more powerful **French Communist Party (PCF)**. Its support, already in decline, collapsed to the point of extinction in the 1960s. Under the direction of **Mitterrand**, its remnants merged with other groups at the 1971 Épinay congress to form the PS. In 1972 it forged an alliance – the Union of the Left (*Union de la Gauche*) – with the PCF which, despite strains and disruptions, survived until the early 1980s. It formed a majority government 1981–93 apart from the 1986–88 period of **cohabitation**, but after 1988 internal dissension became more prominent. The increasing lack of internal cohesion, symbolized by feuding among its leaders, contributed to a decisive electoral defeat in 1993. Several of its leaders later were placed under investigation in connection with several cases of financial fraud and corruption.

Socialist Party. (*Partido Socialista – PS*) A major left-wing party in **Portugal**. Formed in exile by **Soares** in 1973, it was a descendant of the 1875 Portuguese Socialist Workers' Party and the 1964 Portuguese Social Action. After the 1974 revolution it established itself as a major force in Portugal, participating in the first radical interim governments and emerging as the largest party in 1975. After a brief flirtation with revolutionary ideas, it supported **Eanes** in 1976 and re-entered government. Failure to resolve economic problems, secessions, and conflict between Eanes and Soares led to the loss of some support, and in 1979 it returned to opposition. It only briefly made up the lost ground in the mid-1980s, although in 1986 Soares was elected to the presidency. In 1986 it also officially declared itself to be a non-Marxist party.

Socialist Party of Albania. *See* PARTY OF LABOUR.

Socialist Party of Serbia. (*Socijalistička Partija Srbije – SPS*) A political party in **Serbia**, founded in 1990 as a successor to the Serbian **League of Communists**. Led by **Milošević**, it adopted a democratic socialist programme, but the former communist leadership remained more or less intact.

Socialist People's Party. (*Socialistisk Folkeparti – SF*) A small left-wing party in **Denmark**. It was formed in 1958 by ex-Communists disillusioned by the 1956 Soviet invasion of **Hungary** and left-wing dissidents from the **Social Democratic Party** opposed to Danish membership of the **North Atlantic Treaty Organization (NATO)**. Although it supported Social Democratic minority governments in the 1960s, it maintained its commitment to non-alignment, and later remained opposed to Danish membership of the **European Communities (EC)**.

Socialist People's Party. (*Sosialistisk Folkepartiet – SF*) A small left-wing party in **Norway** formed in 1957. Its core were left-wing dissidents expelled from the **Labour Party** for their opposition to membership of the **North Atlantic Treaty Organization (NATO)**. Its entry into Parliament in 1961 ended Labour's majority position, and in 1963 it helped to bring to an end 28 years of Labour rule by supporting a vote of no-confidence. It opposed entry into the **European Communities (EC)**, and in 1973 formed the bulk of a Socialist Electoral Alliance which in 1975 was turned into the **Socialist Left Party**, with the SF disappearing as a separate organization.

Socialist Unity Party. (*Sozialistische Einheitspartei Deutschlands – SED*) The governing party of the **German Democratic Republic (DDR)**. It was formed in 1946 in the Soviet occupation of Germany by a merger of the Communist Party and the **Social Democratic Party (SPD)**. Most ex-members of the SPD were soon moved from positions of authority within the SED, which from 1950 followed a pro-Soviet line under the Stalinist leadership of **Ulbricht**. Other legally permitted parties and organizations were made subservient to it within a National Front structure, and it controlled all aspects of life in the DDR. In the late 1980s it rejected the reformist tendencies emerging in the **USSR**, but was unable to resist popular pressure and its leaders were forced to resign in late 1989. In 1990 a new leadership under **Gysi** attempted to reconstruct it as the Party of Democratic Socialism (PDS) and it began to enjoy some electoral success after 1993 in the former DDR territories.

Social market economy. (*Sozial Marktwirtschaft*) A term used to describe the economic policies of the **Federal Republic of Germany**. Frequently claimed to have been the basis of the West German economic miracle (**Wirtschaftswunder**) – the rapid growth of the 1950s and 1960s – it lay at the heart of economic policy through to the 1990s. It consisted of a combination of a free market economy within a framework of **Concerted Action** that defined the limits of unrestrained competition along with an extensive network of social benefits designed to support national economic competitiveness as well as the redistribution of public resources.

Social partnership. A concept linking democratic principles with structures of **corporatism**. It took the institutionalized corporatist co-operation between governments, employers and trade unions as the basis of a proper system of economic democracy. Historically, it was an important element of Catholic social doctrine, but after 1945 was also supported as a necessary political reform by many social democratic parties. Its institutionalization was possibly greatest in post-1945 **Austria**.

Socio-Economic Council. (*Sociaal-Economische Raad*) A tripartite body of experts appointed by the government and representatives of employers' and trade union federations in the **Netherlands**. Formed in 1950, and reflecting the religious basis of political competition between the parties, its purpose was to advise the government on social and economic issues, but in practice, because it represented all the major strands of Dutch politics, governments tended to drop proposed legislation which met with strong reservations in the Council. It was widely held to be a key institution in the Dutch version of **consociational democracy**.

Sokolovsky, Vasily. (1897–1968) Soviet Marshal. A professional soldier, he replaced **Zhukov** as the Soviet military governor in Germany in 1946. When he heard of the impending currency reform in the western zones of occupation, he initiated the action that led to the **Berlin Blockade**, shutting off the overland transit routes to the city. His actions marked the end of attempts by the Allies to secure agreements on Germany, and the hardening of the **Cold War**.

Solemn Declaration on European Union. A statement issued by the **European Council** in June 1983. It outlined how far the potential for integration of **European Communities (EC)** institutions had been realized, and reviewed possibilities for new developments. It set no timetable and was more a statement of beliefs than a call for action.

Solidarity. (*Solidarnosc*) A strongly Catholic trade union movement in **Poland**. Formed in August 1980 and led by **Wałęsa**, it emerged out of a wave of strikes in the **Gdansk** shipyards which sought the right to establish trade unions independent of the **Polish United Workers' Party**. It rapidly acquired a mass membership and reached an agreement with the government on a reduction of the working week, improved food supplies, and greater freedom in broadcasting. It began to act almost as an opposition party. Further popular discontent in 1981 over food distribution problems caused by a poor harvest brought it into further political conflict with the government. In December martial law was imposed by **Jaruzelski**, and its leaders were imprisoned or interned. The organization was banned, but continued to operate underground. Wałęsa was released from prison in November 1982. In October 1984 a pro-Solidarity priest, **Popieluszko**, was murdered by police agents. His death generated considerable public anger, held in check only by Wałęsa and other Solidarity leaders, as well as provoking a strong reaction from the Catholic Church. Solidarity banners were openly displayed again in 1988 during renewed economic problems in Gdansk. In 1989 its leaders were invited to participate in a series of discussions on the worsening economic crisis, and it was relegalized. Its candidates were successful in the June 1989 multiparty election, and in September it joined the non-Communist coalition government of **Mazowiecki**, whom it had nominated for the premiership. After the re-establishment of democracy, its effectiveness and cohesion began to decline. Restructured as the Civic Parliamentary Forum, it disintegrated after 1991 into several competing groups as tensions between its various strands, ranging from devout Catholic to secular radical, became more visible in the new pluralist climate.

Solingen Killings. *See* MÖLLN KILLINGS.

Solzhenitsyn, Aleksandr. (1919–) Russian writer and dissident. Imprisoned 1945–53 for alleged anti-Soviet agitation and propaganda, and exiled to Siberia 1953–56, where he worked as a teacher, his first novel, *A Day in the Life of Ivan Denisovich*, published in 1962, was praised by **Khrushchev** for its exposé of life in the prison camps under **Stalin**. After Khrushchev's dismissal as Soviet leader, his later novels, which continued to attack Soviet authoritarianism and corruption, were banned in the **USSR**, which criticized his award of the Nobel Prize for Literature in 1970. In 1974 he was stripped of his Soviet citizenship and expelled from the USSR, settling in the USA. In 1990 he was restored to favour and invited to return to his homeland. He rejected the invitation, but in 1993 decided to return to **Russia**.

Soustelle, Jacques. (1912–1990) French politician. An early supporter of **de Gaulle** during the Second World War, in 1947 he organized the Gaullist **Rally of the French People (RPF)**, serving as its Secretary until 1952. He was appointed Governor-General of Algeria in 1955, but his outspoken support for the white settlers led the following year to his recall to Paris. He strongly supported de Gaulle's return to power in 1958 and became a government minister, but was dismissed in January 1960 because of his outright rejection of independence for Algeria. In May he joined the executive of the **Organisation de l'Armée Secrète (OAS)**. He was exiled in September 1962, returning to **France** in 1968 after de Gaulle pardoned former OAS leaders, but played no further role in political life.

South Tyrol. *See* ALTO ADIGE.

Soviet. An elective governing council. A soviet of workers' deputies was first formed in St Petersberg in 1905 to co-ordinate strikes and protests. It was the model for the 1917 Petrograd Soviet which the Bolsheviks sought to control. During the Russian Revolution local soviets were formed in many cities and villages, and came to form the basis of the institutional structure of the **USSR**. At the apex of the system was the Supreme Soviet of the Union, consisting of delegates from the constituent republics of the USSR, which in turn had their own supreme soviets composed of delegates from local soviets.

Soviet Union. *See* USSR.

Spaak, Paul-Henri. (1899–1972) Prime Minister of **Belgium** 1938–39, 1947–49. A member of the Belgian Socialist Party (PSB), he entered Parliament in 1932, becoming the country's first socialist premier in 1938. In exile in London during the Second World War, he was one of the architects of the **Benelux Economic Union,** and he later presided over the first session of the General Assembly of the United Nations. Returning as Prime Minister in 1947, he played a major role in the 1948 **Congress of Europe** and became one of the international patrons of the **European Movement.** In July 1948 he invited the Movement to prepare a plan for a European assembly. This was the basis of the **Council of Europe**, where he was elected as the first president of its consultative assembly. He resigned the office in 1951 because its limited capacity to effect change and sponsor closer integration was less than he wished. He supported the ideas of **Monnet**, and was the initiator of the plans that produced a draft **European Political Community (EPC)**. As Foreign Minister 1954–57, he attended the 1955 **Messina Conference** which nominated him to chair a committee that would develop the proposal for a **common market** into a concrete plan. The Spaak Report was the basis of the **European Economic Community (EEC)**. From 1957 to 1961 he served as Secretary-General of the **North Atlantic Treaty Organization (NATO)** before a final spell as Belgian Foreign Minister 1961–66 and his retirement from political life. His persistent efforts on behalf of European co-operation and integration, and the roles he played in the pursuit of this goal, earned him the popular title of Mr Europe.

Spaak Report. *See* MESSINA CONFERENCE, SPAAK, PAUL-HENRI.

Spadolini, Giovanni. (1925–1994) Prime Minister of **Italy** 1981–82. An academic historian and journalist, he entered politics only in 1972 being elected to the Senate for the **Italian Republican Party (PRI)**. Appointed as a government minister in 1974, he was elected PRI leader in 1979. Following the forced resignation of the **Forlani** government and disarray in the dominant **Christian Democratic Party (DC)**, he was appointed to head a coalition government, becoming the first post-war premier not to come from the DC. He later served as Minister of Defence 1982–87, before being elected President (Speaker) of the Senate.

Spain. A constitutional monarchy in Western Europe. Spanish history in the nineteenth and early twentieth centuries had been one of almost continuous tension between liberals and authoritarian monarchists. The monarchy ended in 1931 but the consequent republic erupted in the Spanish Civil War 1936–39. The nationalist victory resulted in the dictatorship of **Franco**, who dominated politics until his death in 1975. Franco abolished all political groups except the **Falange**, and pursued a policy of repression against ethnic minorities, especially the **Basques** and in **Catalonia**. He kept Spain neutral in the Second World War, though sympathizing with the Axis powers. His regime was largely ostracized by other Western democracies, but by the early 1950s his strong anti-Communism led relationships to be established with the USA. Economic development by the 1960s led to some cautious but very limited liberalization, but the regime still reacted strongly to popular demands for greater political rights, leading to an increase in acts of violence, especially by the terrorist **Euskadi ta Askatasuna (ETA)**. In 1969 Franco nominated Prince **Juan Carlos** as his successor as head of state. After Franco's death, Juan Carlos accelerated the pace of liberalization. Political parties were legalized and a new government under **Suárez** introduced a constitutional democracy with a multi-party system. Extensive decentralization was offered to the Basques and Catalonia, though this continued to be rejected by the more extreme forms of Basque nationalism. The regime survived attempted coups by right-wing army officers in 1978 and 1981. In the 1980s Spain's international isolation ended when it became a member of several European organizations, including the **European Communities (EC)** and the **North Atlantic Treaty Organization (NATO)**.

Spandau. A prison in West **Berlin**. After 1945 it was used solely by the occupying military powers to house those Nazis sentenced to imprisonment for war crimes at the **Nuremberg Trials**. The four occupying powers rotated control of the prison and guard duty on a monthly basis. After 1966 **Hess**, sentenced to life imprisonment, was the sole inmate. The **USSR** refused to consider proposals for his release. After his death in 1987 the prison was closed and plans were laid to demolish the complex.

Spanish Socialist Workers' Party. (*Partido Socialista Orero Español – PSOE*) The major left-wing party in **Spain**. Founded in 1879, it retained a strong Marxist emphasis. After playing a major role in the 1931–36 Second Republic, it was banned by **Franco**. In exile its ageing leadership consistently refused to consider co-operation with other anti-Franco groups. A reformist faction gained control of the party in 1972, and one of its leaders, **González**, was elected leader in 1974. After democratization it emerged in 1977 as the largest left-wing party, successfully absorbing some smaller socialist formations. In 1979 González persuaded the party to abandon its Marxist commitment, and it formally redefined itself as a democratic socialist party. Its electoral support grew, and it came to power with an absolute majority in 1982, losing overall control only in 1993. Its long tenure of office was aided by a divided opposition and the identification of the Spanish right with the Franco regime. It pursued a more right-wing economic policy which by the 1990s had produced a series of protests from trade unions and workers, as well as from its own left-wing. Its prestige also declined dramatically by revelations of the involvement of some of its leaders in financial scandals and covert anti-terrorist activities.

Special Relations Agreements. Agreements signed by the **European Communities (EC)** with Western European countries which did not regard themselves as potential applicants for EC membership. They were signed in the early 1970s with members of the **European Free Trade Association (EFTA)**. They offered a phased introduction of industrial free trade, and provided a much greater degree of trade reciprocity than was found in other kinds of agreements signed by the EC. After 1988 all the countries which had previously signed an agreement revised their earlier position and either applied for EC membership or indicated that they might be interested in doing so.

Spillover. A term used in the 1950s to describe how **sectoral integration** would lead to an economic and political union in Europe. Functional spillover described how, as more economic sectors became integrated, they would affect and place pressure upon the remaining sectors. Political spillover referred to the belief that the benefits derived from integrated sectors would lead interest groups and other organizations to look to the supranational level for the realization of their demands. The term was abandoned as an explanation of and strategy for integration after the formation of the **European Economic Community (EEC)**.

Spinelli, Altiero. (1907–1986) Italian federalist. Arguably the leading advocate of European federalism, he disliked the more gradualist approach to integration that dominated after 1950, distrusting the motives of national governments. A member of the **Italian Communist Party (PCI)**, he was imprisoned by the Mussolini regime. His federalist views were first expressed in the 1941 Ventotene Manifesto which, smuggled out of prison, became the basis of most of the proposals prepared by federalist activists in the various **Resistance movements** on the post-war reconstruction of Europe. After 1945 he remained on the fringes of political developments, with his activities confined mainly to several non-governmental organizations, including the **European Union of Federalists**. After years in the wilderness he was appointed to the **Commission** 1970–76, and in 1979 was elected to the **European Parliament (EP)** as an independent on the PCI ticket. He founded the **Crocodile Club** in 1980 and was the major architect of the **Draft Treaty on European Union**.

Spinola, Antonió Sebastiao Riberio. (1910–) Portuguese soldier. His military career culminated with his appointment as General in 1969 and Vice-Chief of the General Staff 1973–74. His dismissal from the latter as a result of the failure to quell rebellion in **Portugal's** African colonies made him a hero to many younger officers. He did not take part in the April 1974 **Carnation Revolution**, but joined the rebels later and accepted the leadership of the military junta. Out of sympathy with the radical tendencies of the **Armed Forces Movement**, he resigned in September, retiring also from the army. In March 1975 he headed an abortive conservative coup against the regime. After its failure he fled to **Spain** where he remained in exile until 1977. His rank was restored in 1978.

Spitsbergen. (*Svalbard*) A group of islands in the North Atlantic. The 1920 Treaty of Paris awarded sovereignty over the archipelago to **Norway**, which formally took them over in 1925. The Treaty also permitted any of its signatories to establish bases on the islands for economic exploitation of their resources, but only Norway and the **USSR** developed mining interests after 1930. After 1945 the USSR persistently sought to pressure Norway and other countries to discuss the defence status of the islands. The West always rejected the USSR's overtures, pointing to their status under the 1920 Treaty as a non-military area where no military bases or fortifications were to be permitted.

Sputnik. The name given by the **USSR** to its first space satellites. Sputnik I, the first manufactured object in space, was launched into orbit on 4 October 1957, circling the Earth for 95 minutes, and confounding the alleged technological superiority of the West. On 3 November Sputnik II carried a dog into space. The sputniks raised Soviet prestige in the world.

Stalin, Josef Vissarionovich. (1879–1953) Soviet dictator 1923–53. Born Djugashvili in **Georgia** and originally intended for the priesthood, he joined the Social Democratic Party in 1898, aligning himself with the Bolsheviks in 1903. He was banished to Siberia on several occasions for his political activities. After the 1917 Russian Revolution he emerged as Lenin's major lieutenant. He gained control of the Communist party machine at its 12th congress in 1923, using it to consolidate his grip on the country. In 1928 he launched a series of Five-Year Plans to achieve 'Socialism in one country' through extensive and rapid heavy industrialization, and in the 1930s extended his removal of rivals through a series of ruthless purges of the party, army and other potential opponents, creating a vast network of forced labour camps (the **Gulag**) in Siberia. In 1941 he extended his formal titles beyond the party to become also Prime Minister and marshal. With victory in the Second World War he sponsored and supported Communist regimes in Eastern Europe for both ideological and security reasons, exporting to them his brand of state repression and terrorism to eliminate potential opponents. His subjugation of Eastern Europe and the consequent fears in the West of his intentions and territorial ambitions helped to fuel the **Cold War** and freeze the division of Europe until 1989. His major European failures were in Germany, where the Western powers hindered his efforts to bring the whole country under Soviet influence, and in **Yugoslavia**, where **Tito** refused to accept his diktats and survived Soviet attempts to discredit and remove him from power. In his later years Stalin became increasingly paranoiac and anti-semitic, with his behaviour and actions more irrational and unpredictable. He died on 9 March 1953. In 1956 **Khrushchev** attacked the personality cult and savagery of Stalinism, but the true extent of the damage done to Soviet society and the number of lives lost under his personalized dictatorship only became known after **glasnost** and the more open climate that emerged in the late 1980s.

Stasi. The nickname for the Ministry of State Security (*Ministerium für Staatssicherheit*) and its personnel in the **German Democratic Republic (DDR)**. Founded in 1950 as a secret police agency, it was headed by **Mielke** from 1957 until its abolition in 1989. It established a huge network of espionage, based partly upon bribery and blackmail, both within the DDR and abroad, as well as pursuing a harsh policy of suppression against dissidence with the regime. Popular hatred of it was such that with the crumbling of the regime at the end of 1989, it was one of the first DDR institutions to be abolished, with Mielke and other leaders arrested. After reunification in 1990 individuals were given the right of access to Stasi files in order to clear their names of any slanders or wrongful allegations. Revelations and allegations about politicians and other prominent individuals in several walks of life who had acted as Stasi informers or agents continued to rock Germany long after reunification.

Stepinac, Aloysius. (1898–1960) Primate of **Croatia** 1937–60. Ordained in 1918, he supported the creation of a unified **Yugoslavia**, but by the late 1920s was critical of Serbian domination of the state and discrimination against Croatia. He was appointed Archbishop of Zagreb in 1937, and in 1941 welcomed the establishment of Croatian independence under the Fascist **Uštaše**, but in 1943 attacked its leader, Ante Pavelić, for the regime's atrocities against the Serb minority and in **Bosnia-Hercegovina**. In 1945 he met with **Tito** to seek an agreement on church–state relations, but a year later was arrested on charges of war-time collaboration with Germany and sentenced to 16 years imprisonment. Released in 1951, he was allowed to resume duties as a priest, but not his function as archbishop and primate. The Catholic Church regarded him as a martyr of Communism, and **Pius XII** made him a cardinal in 1952. He was refused a visa by Tito and so declined to go to Rome to receive his red hat for fear that he would not be allowed to re-enter Yugoslavia. He maintained his forthright opposition to Communism until his death from leukaemia in 1960. A reconciliation between the state and the Catholic Church was achieved by his successor, Archbishop Seper.

Stockholm Accord. An agreement of 21 September 1986 that the **North Atlantic Treaty Organization (NATO)** and the **Warsaw Pact** would provide each other with advance notice of planned troop exercises, manoeuvres or movements. It was hoped that this would reduce the risk of a European war breaking out accidentally through misunderstanding or misinterpretation, and was an outcome of the 1984 **Conference on Security and Confidence-Building Measures and Disarmament in Europe (CDE)**.

Stockholm Convention. The document signed in November 1959, and taking effect in May 1960, which formally established the **European Free Trade Association (EFTA)**. Its aim was defined as the elimination of tariffs on industrial goods on the basis of fair and free trade in a way which would not disadvantage the less economically developed signatories. It contained no implications for national political sovereignty. *See also* FINEFTA.

Stoph, Willi. (1914–) Prime Minister of the **German Democratic Republic (DDR)** 1964–89. A construction worker, he joined the German Communist Party in 1931. Serving in the armed forces during the Second World War, he resumed political activities in 1946 as a member of the **Socialist Unity Party (SED)**, being promoted to the government in 1952 and the **Politburo** in 1953. In addition to serving as premier, he was also appointed President after the death of **Ulbricht** in 1973, serving until 1976. A loyal party functionary, he had little impact upon policy, since his positions were subordinate to those of the party. He briefly survived the fall of **Honecker**, but his government was forced to resign on 7 November 1989. He was later expelled from the SED and arrested on charges of corruption, though soon released. Re-arrested in 1991 over the shooting policy employed by the DDR at its borders, he was released in 1992, without coming to trial, on grounds of ill health.

Stormont. A suburb of Belfast and the seat of the **Northern Ireland** Parliament 1920–72. Established by the Government of Ireland Act as a subordinate body to the Westminster Parliament, the Protestant majority had an in-built majority in it, strengthened by a gerrymandering of constituencies. It was suspended in March 1972 when the **United Kingdom** imposed direct rule on the province following Stormont's inability to maintain law and order. The province was then administered by bureaucrats of the Northern Ireland Office based at Stormont Castle, which previously had been the official residence of the Northern Ireland Prime Minister.

Strasbourg. A city in **France** and one of the centres of the **European Communities (EC)**. The largest city in **Alsace-Lorraine**, it was offered by France in 1949 as a home for the **Council of Europe**. When the **European Coal and Steel Community (ECSC)** was established in 1951, its Assembly was formed by the delegates of its Member States who already sat in the Council of Europe. This agreement was repeated in the later Communities, and after their merger the city continued to be the base for the plenary sessions of the **European Parliament (EP)**. France rejected all proposals to relocate the EP to **Brussels**, and in 1993 began construction of a new parliamentary building.

Strauss, Franz-Josef. (1915–1988). West German politician. Becoming politically active in 1945, he was a co-founder of the **Christian Social Union (CSU)** in his native **Bavaria**, serving as its general secretary 1949–52. He was elected to Parliament in 1949, serving until 1978. He entered the government in 1955 and served as Minister of Defence 1956–62. He was forced to resign over the **Der Spiegel Affair**, but later served as Finance Minister 1966–69. Strongly conservative and regionalist in his views, he dominated the CSU and after 1959 consolidated its organization to make it a hegemonic force in Bavarian politics. A powerful opponent of Communism, he attacked the **Ostpolitik** process of the 1970s and what he described as 'socialist legislation'. In 1976, disillusioned with his more moderate ally, the **Christian Democratic Union (CDU)**, and critical of its electoral campaign, he threatened to turn the CSU into a national conservative party in direct competition with the CDU. While he later withdrew the threat, he was nominated as the joint CDU/CSU Chancellor candidate for the 1980 election. The result was disastrous. A flamboyant character, disliked by the centre and left, his personality was the dominant electoral issue, and the result demonstrated his limited appeal outside Bavaria. He subsequently returned to Bavarian politics, becoming Prime Minister of the state until his death. He was offered a national government position by **Kohl** in 1983, but declined as he was willing to accept only the Foreign Ministry.

Structural Funds. The major expenditure funds of the **European Communities (EC)** intended to foster socio-economic development through the elimination of regional disparities within and between the Member States, consisting of the **European Regional Development Fund (ERDF)**, **European Social Fund (ESF)**, and the Guidance Section of the **European Agricultural Guidance and Guarantee Fund (EAGGF)**. All are expected to focus their spending on projects which have a regional focus.

Suárez González, Adolfo. (1932–) Prime Minister of **Spain** 1976–82. He entered public service under the **Franco** regime, becoming a regional governor in 1969 and then director of the state broadcasting service. After Franco's death, he was appointed Prime Minister at the instigation of King **Juan Carlos**. Despite suspicions and doubts about his democratic credentials, he successfully and forcefully presided over the transition to democracy, and in 1977 founded the **Union of the Democratic Centre (UCD)** as a vehicle for himself. Elected to Parliament in 1977 as part of a UCD majority, he was reappointed premier, implementing policies of economic and regional reform. He resigned the government leadership in 1981, and in July 1982 the party leadership, because of growing tensions and factionalism within the UCD. In October 1982 he founded a new party, the **Democratic and Social Centre**, but was unable to repeat his successes of the 1970s and he resigned as party leader in 1991.

Subsidiarity. A principle stating that policy problems and issues should be handled at the lowest possible level of government, and that only where this is not possible should a higher level of government become involved. The term was first used by Pius XI in the context of the Lateran Treaty between the **Vatican** and **Italy**, and expressed his preference for federalism and decentralization. It gained currency within the **European Communities (EC)** after the late 1980s to allay fears that further integration would radically diminish national sovereignty and concentrate decision-making at the supranational level. It was defined in the 1991 **Treaty on European Union** on the basis of the principles that the EC can act only when they possess legal powers to do so, that the EC should act only when an objective can be better achieved at the supranational level, and that the means employed by the EC should be proportional to the desired objective. Theoretically implying that national powers would be the norm, with EC action the exception, it remained ambiguous in practice with EC institutions seeming to assume that they would make the decision on which level of government would be appropriate for any one issue.

Suchocka, Hanna. (1946–) Prime Minister of **Poland** 1992–93. A lawyer and academic, she entered Parliament in the 1970s as a representative of the **Democratic Party**. She resigned from the party in 1981 in protest against the imposition of martial law by **Jaruzelski**. Associated with the reform movements, she was re-elected to Parliament in 1989 on the **Solidarity** ticket, subsequently joining the new centre-left **Democratic Union**. She was appointed premier of a centrist caretaker coalition in July 1992, which succeeded in surviving for 15 months before losing a vote of confidence on its economic policies.

Sudetenland. An industrialized region in western **Czechoslovakia**. Before 1945 the majority of its population was German, and in the 1935 election the region strongly supported the Nazi party. Under the 1938 Munich Agreement it was annexed by Germany, but the 1945 **Potsdam Conference** returned it to Czechoslovakia which expelled more than three million Germans. The expellees formed active interest associations in the **Federal Republic of Germany** which agitated for the right to return to the lost territories, but West Germany subsequently renounced all claims on the region.

Suez Crisis. A conflict in 1956 arising from Egypt's appropriation of the Suez Canal Company. The canal was built in 1869, with British troops stationed along it in 1882. Under an Anglo-Egyptian Treaty of October 1954 the troops were withdrawn in June 1956. One month later President Nasser of Egypt nationalized the Suez Company, whose shares were mainly held by the British government and French investors, arguing that unrestricted transit would be maintained and that he needed the passage levies to finance the Aswan Dam project on the Nile, which the **United Kingdom** and the USA had been unwilling to fund. Britain and **France** secretly discussed an invasion of Egypt to depose Nasser. They were also aware of a plan by Israel, alarmed by the appropriation, to invade Egypt and occupy the Sinai. The Israeli attack was launched on 29 October. Britain and France issued an ultimatum that hostilities should cease. When this was rejected by Nasser, they began an airborne operation to occupy the Canal Zone, ostensibly to restore order in the region, on 5–6 November. The action was condemned by other Western countries, especially the USA, and by the **USSR**. American hostility and a sterling crisis led to an immediate halt in the operation, and the Anglo-French forces were withdrawn in December, to be replaced by a United Nations (UN) peace-keeping force. Israeli troops were withdrawn in March 1957. The crisis strained Anglo-French relations, as France had been more willing to defy world opinion. The French military regarded it as a further humiliation and lack of political resolve, contributing to its later politicization in Algeria. It fatally weakened the British Prime Minister, **Eden**, who had likened Nasser to Hitler and who had staked his personal reputation on the operation, and he resigned on health grounds two months later. The crisis marked the end of the ability of Western Europe to wage gunboat diplomacy in other parts of the world without American approval and support. It also distracted Western attention from the simultaneous Soviet suppression of the **Hungarian Revolution**.

Svalbard. *See* SPITSBERGEN.

Svoboda, Ludvik. (1895–1979) President of **Czechoslovakia** 1968–75. A professional soldier, he escaped to the **USSR** in 1939 and led the Czech army corps which liberated Prague in 1945. He served as Minister of Defence until 1950, joining the Communist Party in 1948. His huge prestige and popularity aroused the suspicion of **Stalin**. Removed from public life, he was briefly imprisoned before being exiled to a collective farm. He was rehabilitated during the **Khrushchev** period and made a Hero of both the Czechoslovak Republic and the USSR. His image as a kind of father figure made him a safe choice in March 1968 to succeed **Novotný** as President. He accepted the reforms of the **Dubček** government and the **Prague Spring**, and attempted to persuade the USSR to be more conciliatory towards them, personally leading a delegation to Moscow. After the USSR invasion he refused to accept a government hand-picked by Moscow, which enabled the Dubček government to continue for another eight months. He continued in office after the reimposition of an orthodox Communist regime under **Husák**, accepting that it was futile to resist the USSR and that accommodation with its demands was the only realistic policy.

Sweden. A constitutional monarchy in Northern Europe. An imperial power in the Baltic in the seventeenth and eighteenth centuries, the present monarchy dates from 1810. Sweden has avoided involvement in all international conflicts since 1814, with a foreign policy based upon neutrality and, since 1945, strong commitment to the United Nations, although it has been keen to pursue closer collaboration with its Nordic neighbours. It was a founder member of the **European Free Trade Association (EFTA)** in 1960, but expressed disinterest in closer European integration, in part because of its neutrality policy. It had to re-evaluate its policy of non-involvement as a consequence of the decision of the **European Communities (EC)** to establish an **internal market**, and the ending of the **Cold War**. In 1995 it formally entered the EC. Domestic politics were dominated by the **Social Democratic Labour Party** after the 1930s. Because of its long tenure of office, the party essentially constructed and determined the political agenda, building a strong economy and an extensive welfare state, but with very high levels of taxation. The **Swedish model** of socio-economic policies was often put forward as an example which other countries ought to consider, but by the 1980s some of its key conditions were beginning to unravel, and governments were forced to question the viability of sustaining the high levels of provision of public goods and services.

Swedish model. A phrase often used to describe the socio-economic strategy pursued in **Sweden** as an example of success and as a model for other states to follow. The strategy, developed by the **Social Democratic Labour Party**, possessed several principal features. It accepted that capitalism and market forces should prevail in the productive sectors of the economy, with governments not intervening to save bankrupt companies, but that this should be combined with an active labour market policy in which governments would provide training and other resources to enable workers to move from one industry to another. Other major features were a centralized pay bargaining structure (the **Saltsjöbaden Agreement**) which set wages in line with what the country could afford, and a comprehensive welfare system. By the 1980s some of the key elements had disintegrated and there were questions about whether the model could survive without, at the least, extensive reform.

Swedish People's Party. (*Svenska Folkpartiet – SFP*) A small party in **Finland**. It was founded in 1906 to protect and advance the rights of the Swedish-speaking minority. Centre-right in orientation, after principles of bilingualism had been laid down in the 1922 Language Acts it was prepared to participate in most coalition governments in return for reassurances that language rights would continued to be respected. A steady reduction in the number of Swedish speakers led to a continuing decline in its level of electoral support after 1945.

Swiss People's Party. (*Schweizerische Volkspartei/Parti Suisse de l'Union Démocratique du Centre – SVP/UDC*) A centrist liberal party in **Switzerland**. It was formed in 1971 by a merger of the Farmers', Traders' and Citizens' Party (BGB) with the smaller Swiss Democratic Party (founded in 1942). The BGB had been formed in 1921 as a primarily agrarian secession from the **Radical Democratic Party**. Confined mainly to a few German-speaking cantons, it was admitted to the government in 1929 and has remained a member of the country's permanent governing coalition. The merger was an attempt to compensate for a declining rural base and to extend its territorial appeal, but it remained primarily a German-speaking party.

Switzerland. A federal republic in Western Europe existing in its current format since 1848, having previously been a much looser confederation of autonomous cantons. A multi-ethnic society, with German, French, Italian and Romansch speakers, it is also religiously divided between Protestant and Catholic, but religious and linguistic dividing lines cut across each other. Political change has been slow and limited. The four major parties have formed a permanent coalition government for almost the whole of the post-1945 period, although extensive use is made of referendums, which has helped other groups to force issues on to the political agenda. At the federal level women were not allowed to vote until 1971, and the final voting restrictions on women in some cantons were not ended until the 1990s. The 1815 Congress of Vienna accepted the principle of 'perpetual neutrality' for the confederation, and this has been maintained by Switzerland ever since. It has not been involved in any wars since 1815 and has stayed apart from all alliances, remaining neutral in both World Wars. After 1945 it reaffirmed its neutrality, even staying outside the United Nations until after the ending of the **Cold War**. It did join the **European Free Trade Association (EFTA)** in 1960 as an organization that had no political or strategic implications, but in the 1990s government wishes to consider becoming part of the **European Communities (EC)** were dashed by a referendum rejection of membership of the **European Economic Area (EEA)**.

Systemization. (*Sistemizaţie*) The policy of forced rural resettlement in **Romania** pursued by the **Ceauşescu** regime in the 1980s. It involved the destruction of hundreds of villages and the removal of their populations to new agro-towns. Intended to contribute towards agricultural and industrial development, it was deeply resented. It was abandoned immediately after the overthrow of the regime in December 1989.

T

Tamilgate. A political scandal in **Denmark**. It arose from a decision by the Minister of Justice, Erik Ninn-Hansen, in 1987 that relatives remaining in Sri Lanka of Tamil refugees would no longer be allowed to join their family in Denmark. The decision was attacked for being in breach of Danish law, and was later reversed. A judicial inquiry was established, especially to determine whether the **Schlüter** government had misled Parliament in 1989 when it claimed that nothing surrounding the affair had been concealed. The inquiry reported in January 1993: it was of the view that Parliament had been misled by the Prime Minister. Schlüter accepted the verdict of the report and resigned, but expressed his disagreement with its conclusions. Ninn-Hansen was impeached in 1994.

Tangentopoli. (Bribe City) The name widely used to describe a series of political and financial scandals in **Italy** in the 1990s. The name derived from the original investigation of numerous allegations of corruption and under-the-counter payments by contractors to members of political parties in Milan in the 1980s in order to secure public contracts. While all parties were implicated to some extent, the most severely affected was the **Italian Socialist Party (PSI)** and its leader, **Craxi**. A travel company even offered a Tangentopoli tour of Milan: an unwanted additional lane of a motorway, an unfinished theatre complex, a superfluous addition to a football stadium, an unbuilt training centre. The network of allegations marked the beginning of a nation-wide judicial investigation of political corruption, to which the term was then applied, that resulted 1993–94 in the destruction of the post-1945 Italian party system. *See also* CLEAN HANDS.

Tereshkova, Valentina Vladimirovna. (1937–) Soviet cosmonaut. She was the first woman to fly in space, piloting the Vostok 6 satellite for 48 orbits of the Earth in 1963. Her achievement underlined the Soviet lead in space development and further enhanced Soviet prestige.

Ter-Petrosian, Levon. (1945–) President of **Armenia** from 1991. A linguist and academic, he emerged as a leading nationalist dissident in the late 1980s, forming the Armenian Pan-National Movement in 1989. After winning a majority in the 1990 regional elections, he declared Armenian independence from the **USSR** the following year. His major foreign policy concern was the war with **Azerbaijan** over **Nagorno-Karabakh**, which was largely successful. However, he failed to stop the rapid downward slide of the domestic economy.

Teschen. A small industrial region in Central Europe. A Grand Duchy of the Habsburg Empire after 1772, it was claimed by both **Czechoslovakia** and **Poland** in 1918. After a brief conflict, a 1920 international conference in Paris partitioned it between the two states. In 1938 Poland collaborated with Hitler in order to gain the whole area. The dispute resurfaced in 1945, but the Czech and Polish foreign ministers were summoned to Moscow where **Stalin** and **Molotov** unilaterally reimposed the pre-1938 boundary.

Thatcher, Margaret Hilda. (1925–) British Prime Minister 1979–90. Trained as an industrial chemist, and then a barrister, she was elected to Parliament for the **Conservative Party** in 1959, holding government positions 1961–64 and 1970–74. In 1975 she successfully challenged **Heath** for the party leadership, becoming the first European woman premier in 1979. Under her direction the Conservatives adopted many right-wing populist policies and she led the party to three successive electoral victories, becoming in 1988 the longest continuously serving British Prime Minister of the twentieth century. Her principal domestic objectives were to reduce inflation and the size and costs of the public sector, and to improve industrial efficiency through a rolling back of the state. A severe policy of **monetarism** was abandoned by 1981 when it failed to reduce inflation, but not before it had contributed to a significant diminution of Britain's industrial base. She successfully introduced legislation curbing trade union activities and rights, encouraged greater home ownership through the sale to tenants of public housing, restricted the freedom of local authorities, and introduced a massive **privatization** of public agencies. She later launched reform programmes in education, health and law in the face of the professionals employed in those areas. Although she partially realized her aim of reducing the role of government in society, persisting high unemployment and pressure on the social services meant that public spending continued to rise, while restrictions on local authorities led to a greater centralization of decision-making.

Her foreign policy reflected a suspicion of other countries and was in part meant to reassert British pride and influence. She refused to compromise over the 1982 **Falklands War**, declaring that the sovereignty of the islands was not negotiable. Suspicious of moves to promote European political unity, she preferred to strengthen an Atlantic commitment with the USA, forging a close personal relationship with President Ronald Reagan. Deeply hostile to Communism and the **USSR**, which dubbed her the 'iron lady', she nevertheless welcomed **Gorbachev** as a man with whom she could do business. In 1979 she engaged in a long-running dispute with the **European Communities (EC)**, primarily over the size of the British contribution to the

EC budget, eventually gaining concessions in 1984. She later welcomed the moves by the EC to establish an **internal market**, but resisted and denounced its political implications. Her aggressive and autocratic style of government, along with unease over her attacks on Europe and a disastrous attempt to reform local government finance, led to a challenge to her party leadership in November 1990. She subsequently withdrew from the electoral contest and resigned as Prime Minister. Her tenure in office radically transformed British society and politics, and she was arguably the dominant Western European political personality of the 1980s. In 1992 she was created Baroness Thatcher of Kesteven.

Thatcherism. A term that appeared in the 1980s to describe the ideological thrust of the British governments led by **Thatcher**, and was primarily employed by her critics. It referred among other things to an emphasis upon **monetarism**, **privatization**, and regulation of trade union activity. Although she was a conviction politician, her actions were not always consistent with her rhetoric, and it is difficult to relate all her behaviour to a single coherent ideological belief system. From a political theory viewpoint, it refers more to a core commitment to *laissez-faire* and the free play of the market, and to notions of individual freedom and responsibility, both more reminiscent of classical liberalism than right-wing thinking.

Thorez, Maurice. (1900–1964) Leader of the **French Communist Party (PCF)** 1930–64. A founder member of the PCF in 1920 and imprisoned on several occasions, he became its Secretary-General in 1930, serving until his death, even though a semi-invalid after 1950. He was elected to Parliament in 1932, and in 1936 agreed to support the Popular Front government of **Blum**. Conscripted into the army in 1939, he deserted and fled to Moscow. He returned to **France** in 1945, becoming a parliamentary representative 1945–58, and briefly serving as vice-premier 1946–47 during the period of **tripartism**. In 1948, under orders from the **USSR**, he used the PCF control of the largest trade union federation to launch a general strike in order to destabilize and topple the **Fourth French Republic**. Its failure effectively isolated the PCF and confirmed its inability to carry through a revolution, although it retained a large voting support. Although introducing a resolution supporting de-Stalinization at the 1956 party congress, he loyally followed a Stalinist line to the end, maintaining a rigid control over the party and refusing to tolerate any expressions of dissent or competing opinions.

Thorn, Gaston. (1928–) President of the **Commission** 1981–85. A lawyer and member of the **Democratic Party**, he served as Prime Minister of **Luxembourg** 1974–79 before his move to **Brussels**. Less dynamic than his predecessor, he failed to maintain or develop any momentum, and his Commission struggled without much success to deal with a growing backlog of unresolved issues that confronted the **European Communities (EC)**.

Threshold Test Ban Treaty. *See* COMPREHENSIVE TEST BAN TREATY.

Tiedge Scandal. A spy scandal in the **Federal Republic of Germany**. To respond to the problem of espionage directed by the **German Democratic Republic (DDR)**, West Germany established a large counter-intelligence agency. One of its key sections in the early 1980s was headed by Hans-Joachim Tiedge. An alcoholic, and suffering from massive financial debts after the death of his wife in mysterious circumstances in 1982, he suddenly fled to the DDR in August 1985, taking with him intelligence information and lists of agents. His defection led to an intensive investigation by West German counter-intelligence which unearthed an extensive network of DDR agents across several important government departments. The scandal was one of the most serious espionage affairs in West Germany since 1949, but the government resisted demands for the dismissal of the Defence Minister.

Tindemans, Leo. (1922–) Prime Minister of **Belgium** 1974–78. Entering Parliament in 1961 for the **Christian People's Party**, he first served as a government minister in 1968 before being appointed premier in 1974. He supervised discussions on the development of new federal structures for a decentralized Belgium, and later served as Foreign Minister. A committed supporter of European union, in 1974 he prepared a report on integration for the **European Council**. He left national politics in 1989 and was elected to the **European Parliament (EP)**.

Tindemans Report. A document commissioned by the government heads of the member states of the **European Communities (EC)** in 1974. They requested the Belgian premier, **Tindemans**, to consult with the national governments on the degree of political co-operation they thought possible or desirable. The report was published in 1976. It recommended a common foreign policy and defence collaboration, more common policies, and a popularly elected legislature. It also suggested that more might be achieved with a two-speed route to integration, where all members were not obliged to move in tandem on all policies. It was never formally discussed by the **European Council**, despite being on the agenda of all its meetings until 1978. Many of its ideas were repeated in later reviews of the EC's future.

Tiso, Josef. (1887–1947) President of the Slovak Republic 1939–45. Ordained a Catholic priest in 1910, he helped after 1918 to form the Slovak People's Party, which demanded Slovak autonomy within **Czechoslovakia**. He became party leader in August 1938, and premier of the autonomous Slovak government set up after the Munich Agreement. In March 1939 he declared Slovak independence, although his republic was essentially a German protectorate. With the Soviet invasion of Czechoslovakia and the collapse of the regime, he fled to **Austria**, but was arrested in hiding in May 1945. Accused of collaboration, he was sentenced to death in April 1947.

There were numerous appeals made for a reprieve, but these were rejected by the **Gottwald** government and he was immediately executed. Demands for Slovakian autonomy and independence resurfaced after the collapse of the Communist regime in 1989, and he became regarded as something of a hero by many Slovak nationalists.

Tito, Josip Broz. (1892–1980) Prime Minister of **Yugoslavia** 1945–53, and President 1953–80. Born in Habsburg **Croatia** and serving in the imperial army, he was captured by Russian troops in 1915. He escaped captivity to join the Petrograd revolutionaries in 1917. He returned to Croatia in 1920, where he helped to form an illegal Communist party. Imprisoned in 1928, he went to Moscow after his release in 1934, where he became Secretary-General of the Yugoslav Communist Party. He returned to Yugoslavia in 1941 and organized a partisan resistance movement. In 1943 the Communist **Jacje Congress** declared him Marshal of Yugoslavia, and the Western Allies recognized his partisan movement rather than the royalist-nationalist Chetnik guerillas. Leader of the Communist-controlled federal republic after 1945, he refused to follow policies imposed by **Stalin**, who denounced him as a revisionist and expelled Yugoslavia from the **Communist Information Bureau (COMINFORM)**. His assertion of independence from Moscow enabled him to introduce a structure of workers' self-government and to pursue a foreign policy of non-alignment. He was reconciled with the **USSR** in 1955, but criticized the Soviet interventions in **Hungary** in 1956 and in **Czechoslovakia** in 1968. A new constitution in 1963 made him President for life. His creation of a federal Yugoslavia under Communist control had been an attempt to hold in check the mutual hostility of its ethnic communities. Enjoying good relations with the West, he was also able to attract substantial Western investment for economic growth. After his death the presidency was replaced by a collective leadership of the six constituent republics, but ethnic conflict and discontent against perceived Serbian domination reappeared, and in 1991 the country collapsed into civil war.

Togliatti, Palmiro. (1893–1964) Leader of the **Italian Communist Party (PCI)** 1926–64. He began his political life as a member of the **Italian Socialist Party (PSI)**, but left in 1921 to form the PCI, becoming its Secretary-General in 1926. When the PCI was banned by Mussolini, he went abroad, living mostly in Moscow. He returned to **Italy** in 1944 and served briefly as a government minister during the **tripartism** period. He built up the PCI to make it the largest Communist party in Western Europe, and for a few years after 1945 maintained a close relationship with the PSI. In 1948 he attempted to use the PCI and its associated trade unions to force, through a general strike, the government to resign. He later became more pragmatic, accepting the importance of the Catholic Church in Italy and rejecting the demands of **Stalin** for an uncritical obedience to Soviet leadership. He developed the notion of polycentrism, an early forerunner of the ideas of **Eurocommunism**, arguing that there could be several different national routes to Communism: his own contribution was the development of a mass PCI designed to fit with Italian conditions. After 1953 he remained critical of several Soviet policies and actions, but retained the loyalty and control of his party until his death.

Total Allowable Catch (TAC). The core element of the **Common Fisheries Policy (CFP)** of the **European Communities (EC)**. TACs were defined as overall quotas, fixed annually, for species of fish under threat from overfishing in EC waters. Each state was to receive its own quota within each TAC. A team of inspectors answerable to the **Commission** was made responsible for monitoring and documentation, with the right to impose financial penalties upon Member States for infringements of the quotas. They were highly controversial, and deeply resented by national fishers' organizations.

Touvier Affair. A political controversy in **France**. Paul Touvier had been head of the pro-German Militia in Lyon 1943–44. He was arrested after the Liberation but escaped from police custody in 1947 and went into hiding. He was aided by some conservative Catholic organizations. He was tried in his absence and sentenced to death for treason, but was pardoned in 1971. Jewish organizations and **Resistance** groups protested the decision, and in 1989 he was arrested and charged with crimes against humanity, specifically for ordering the execution of seven Jewish hostages. He was found guilty in 1994 and sentenced to life imprisonment. The case was controversial because it stirred up memories of a bitter and divisive period of French history, underlining the reluctance of the state to prosecute alleged collaborators, and because it was the first time that the charge of crimes against humanity had been laid against a French citizen.

Transatlantic Declaration. A document signed in November 1990 by the **European Communities (EC)** and the USA. It was intended to place the relationship between the two on a more regularized basis, with from 1991 a framework within which consultations could be held on political and economic issues of interest to both sides.

Trans-Dnestria. A small region of **Moldova**. Its mainly Russian population began in the late 1980s to express a wish to be part of the Russian Federation within the **USSR**, and as Soviet authority began to crumble the region unilaterally declared its secession from the Moldovan republic in September 1990. Armed conflict with Moldova broke out in December 1991 when Moldova declared its independence. The survival of the small Trans-Dnestrian republic was aided by the presence there of Russian troops. In 1992 negotiations led to agreement on a special status for the region within

Moldova. After Moldova had rejected union with **Romania**, and with little indication within the region of support for union with **Russia**, the 1992 agreement was reconfirmed in 1994.

Trans-European Networks. A concept introduced into the **European Communities (EC)** by the 1991 **Treaty on European Union**. It committed the EC to a series of continental infrastructural projects to achieve an integration of national networks in energy, telecommunications and transport in order to maximize the benefits of the **internal market**.

Transparency. A term relating to the **European Communities (EC)** in the 1990s. It referred to the need for more openness in, and greater public access to, the operations of EC institutions. The **Council of Ministers** prepared a code for the disclosure of EC documents in 1993.

Transylvania. A region of the Carpathian Mountains disputed by **Hungary** and **Romania**. In 1918 it was taken from Hungary and given to Romania. The frontier, which left a large Magyar population in Romania, was later confirmed by the 1947 **Paris Peace Treaties**. In 1952 a constitutional revision created a Magyar Autonomous Area within Transylvania, but a reorganization in 1960 introduced a much greater degree of central control. The notion of autonomy was finally abolished in 1967. Under the **Ceauşescu** regime a harsh policy of forced Romanian assimilation was increasingly pursued, intensified greatly in the 1980s with the announcement of plans to relocate the Magyar minority and concentrate it in limited areas. Relations with Hungary steadily worsened, as protests against the Romanian government increased. Violent demonstrations against the regime in 1989 were brutally suppressed by the **Securitate**. Discontent and riots continued up to the fall of the Ceauşescu regime in December 1991. Few concessions to the minority were offered by the post-Communist regime which tolerated strong expressions of Romanian nationalism. The new democratic government in Hungary declared it had a duty to help and protect Magyar populations in other states, and the region remained a symbol of nationalist aspirations in both countries.

Treaty of Accession. The document signed by the **European Communities (EC)** and an applicant state once the terms of its entry to the EC have been agreed. Each treaty must also be ratified by the national legislatures of all the existing Member States and, since 1986, by the **European Parliament (EP)**.

Treaty of Brussels. A 50-year agreement signed in March 1948 by **France**, the Low Countries and the **United Kingdom**. Officially the Treaty of Economic, Social and Cultural Collaboration and Collective Self-Defence (also known as Western Union), it was Western Europe's first post-1945 collective security agreement, with promises of mutual aid should any one signatory be attacked. It offered protection against 'a renewal by Germany of an aggressive policy', but because of the onset of the **Cold War** many believed it to be equally a pact against the potential aggression of the **USSR**. A Consultative Committee of the five foreign ministers, with a permanent commission based in London, was responsible for implementing it. It became militarily redundant in 1949 with the establishment of the **North Atlantic Treaty Organization (NATO)**. The non-military treaty provisions remained undeveloped, although in 1950 the signatories agreed to pursue closer political and economic co-operation. The treaty was resurrected in 1954 after the collapse of the **European Defence Community (EDC)**. With some amendments to accommodate the entry of the **Federal Republic of Germany** and **Italy**, it became the basis of **Western European Union (WEU)**.

Treaty of Dunkirk. The first post-1945 bilateral treaty in Western Europe, signed in 1947 by **France** and the **United Kingdom**. Its major purpose was defence security, but it also agreed to economic assistance and co-operation. It was a specific guarantee of mutual aid against any future German aggression. It served as a basis for, and was superseded by, the broader security agreement of the 1948 **Treaty of Brussels**.

Treaty of Friendship. A document signed on 22 January 1963 by the **Federal Republic of Germany** and **France**. It provided for institutional co-operation in defence, foreign policy, education, and cultural affairs. Criticized at the time by several other European countries, it became the foundation of a strong liaison between the two states through regular bilateral meetings of political and administrative representatives, and of the Franco-German axis that was central to Western European politics and integration after 1970.

Treaty of Friendship, Co-operation and Mutual Assistance.
A document signed on 6 April 1948 between **Finland** and the **USSR**. In September 1944 Finland had sued for peace and agreed to an armistice with the USSR, the terms of which were incorporated into the 1947 **Paris Peace Treaties**. In February 1948 **Stalin** proposed that the two countries sign a mutual assistance treaty similar to those which the USSR had already signed with some Eastern European states. The resultant treaty was, however, rather different. It committed Finland to remaining neutral in power bloc politics, stipulated bilateral consultation and co-operation, and allowed for reciprocal military assistance in the event of invasion. The treaty provided the basis for the concept of **Finlandization**, although it did not provide for unilateral Soviet intervention in Finnish affairs. However, Finnish politics were largely constrained, in any given situation, by what they imagined the Soviet view might be, and whether the USSR might use the treaty to justify pressure upon Finland, as it did with the **Note Crisis**. The treaty was renewed on several occasions, but the 1991 revision deleted the clause on military assistance and

consultation in the event of aggression. In June 1992 Finland signed a new treaty with **Russia**. It was identical to the 1948 version except for the omission of the former military and defence references.

Treaty of Guarantee. An international agreement signed by **Cyprus**, **Greece**, **Turkey** and the **United Kingdom** in August 1960 when Cyprus became independent. The other three signatories undertook to protect the independence of the island and to preserve its territorial integrity.

Treaty of Luxembourg. An amendment to the **Treaty of Rome**. Signed in April 1970, its most important consequence for **European Communities** **(EC)** structures was the incorporation of a new budgetary system for funding the organization.

Treaty of Nordic Co-operation. *See* NORDIC COUNCIL.

Treaty of Osino. *See* TRIESTE.

Treaty of Paris. A 50-year treaty signed on 18 April 1951 to establish the **European Coal and Steel Community (ECSC)**. It committed the signatories to work for economic growth. Countries which subsequently joined the **European Communities (EC)** had to accept its terms and obligations.

Treaty of Rome. A document signed on 25 March 1957 formally establishing the **European Economic Community (EEC)**. Concluded for an unlimited period of time, it was the most important of the founding treaties of the **European Communities (EC)**. A complex document, its basic intent was to establish a **common market** in three stages, each of four years duration. Within 12 years the common market would have a **common external tariff**, the free movement of capital, labour, goods and services, and a **Common Agricultural Policy (CAP)**. For supporters of the Treaty these economic objectives were to be a prelude to closer political integration. EC institutions and the Member States were bound by its provisions, which were to take precedence over national law. It was subsequently amended on several occasions, most importantly by the 1991 **Treaty on European Union**. **Italy** was appointed guardian of the Treaty, and the original copies of it along with those arising from a **Treaty of Accession** with a new Member State have been deposited in Rome. A second Treaty of Rome was signed on the same day in 1957 establishing the **European Atomic Energy Community (EURATOM)**.

Treaty of Westminster. *See* COUNCIL OF EUROPE.

Treaty on European Union. A treaty accepted by the **European Council** at its meeting in Maastricht in December 1991 for further integration within the **European Communities (EC)**, involving a radical revision of the **Treaty of Rome**. It confirmed the **internal market** with an opening of internal borders, and the implementation of the **Charter of Fundamental Rights**, although because of British objections the latter was a separate protocol. It also committed the EC to **Economic and Monetary Union**

(EMU) by 1999 at the latest, a more integrated foreign and security policy as a prelude to a common defence policy, greater governmental co-operation on judicial and police matters, and a strengthening of the EC's supranational structures. The EC also became the central pillar of a **European Union (EU)**, buttressed by two inter-governmental pillars, the **Common Foreign and Security Policy (CFSP)** and **Justice and Home Affairs (JHA)**. The **United Kingdom** refused to endorse some elements of the treaty and gained exemption from them. Popular opposition and concern grew in 1992: in June a referendum in **Denmark** voted against ratification, while in September a referendum in **France** recorded only a narrow endorsement. Further opposition was expressed in the **Federal Republic of Germany**. Denmark gained substantial concessions and exclusions in subsequent renegotiations. The disruptions in the **Exchange Rate Mechanism (ERM)** in 1992–93 also placed doubts about the timetable set for EMU. After several delays in the ratification process, the EU was formally inaugurated in November 1993. The treaty was due to be reviewed and possibly amended in 1996.

Treaty on the Final Settlement with Respect to Germany. *See* TWO PLUS FOUR TALKS.

Treuhandanstalt. (Trusteeship Authority) An agency (*Bundesanstalt zur treuhänderischen Verwaltung des Volkseigentums*) in the **Federal Republic of Germany**. Established in March 1990 by the **Modrow** government in the former **German Democratic Republic (DDR)**, it was charged with managing the restructuring and **privatization** of some 8,000 (growing later to some 14,000) state enterprises. After reunification it became an agent of the federal government. After an initial spurt of enthusiasm, its task became increasingly difficult as the extent of the economic problems of the former DDR became more widely known. Germany's move into economic recession also made it difficult to attract Western buyers: several West German companies pulled out of previous agreements, and many other enterprises were liquidated on the grounds that they were not sellable. These and other problems, including accusations of asset-stripping and allegations of corruption, made it extremely unpopular in the former DDR territory where many blamed it for the huge increase in unemployment. The programme was extended beyond its original termination date of 1993, but the agency was eventually wound up at the end of 1994, with its balance showing a massive deficit that had to be borne by taxpayers.

TREVI. The more common French acronym for *Terrorisme, Radicalisme, Extrémisme, Violence Internationale*, an agency established by the **European Communities (EC)** in 1975 as a forum for inter-governmental co-operation and co-ordination on matters relating to internal security, organized crime, terrorism, drug trafficking, and asylum and immigration policy. It formed the basis of the more formal **Justice and Home Affairs (JHY)** pillar of the **European Union (EU)** set up by the **Treaty on European Union**.

Trieste. A city on the Adriatic Sea and its hinterland, the Istrian peninsula, disputed after 1918 by **Italy** and **Yugoslavia**. Awarded to Italy in 1919, it had a large Slovene and Croat population. In June 1945 it was temporarily partitioned. Zone A, mainly the city, was placed under Allied military government, with the remainder, Zone B, allocated to Yugoslav administration. A 1946 proposal to make it a neutral and demilitarized Free Territory was rejected by both countries, and the 1947 peace treaty failed to resolve the sovereignty issue. On occasions continuing hostility led to riots until a memorandum of understanding was reached in October 1954 by the two claimants, along with the **United Kingdom** and the USA, whereby Trieste was allocated to Italy and almost the whole of Istria to Yugoslavia. The issue was finally settled by the Treaty of Osino in November 1975 which, with a few minor boundary adjustments, confirmed the 1954 partition. In 1963 the Italian area, Friuli-Venezia Giuliu, was given the status of an autonomous region. After the break-up of Yugoslavia in 1991, Istria became part of **Croatia**. A new party, the Istrian Democratic Assembly (*Istarski Demokratski Sabor*) emerged to campaign for regional autonomy, subsequently gaining a dominant electoral position in the area.

Tripartism. A term referring to the period of three-party coalition government in **France** and **Italy** 1945–47. In both countries the three parties concerned represented the major strands of the **Resistance movements**: Communists, Socialists and Catholics. The coalitions were continually under strain, with the parties increasingly expressing mutual hostility. In both states the end came in May 1947. In France the **French Communist Party (PCF)** left the government, to the relief of the other two parties who accused it of fomenting anti-government strikes. The PCF believed that no government could function without it, but this was not to be the case, and it was left totally isolated. In Italy the **Christian Democratic Party (DC)** was in a much stronger position, but its leader, **de Gasperi**, waited until the close alliance between the two Marxist parties caused moderate Socialists to break away to form the **Italian Social Democratic Party (PSDI)**. He then dissolved Parliament and constructed a broad centrist coalition government.

Truce of Varkiza. *See* GREEK CIVIL WAR.

True Path Party. (*Doğru Yol Partisia – DYP*) A centre-right secularist party in **Turkey**. It was established in 1983 by **Demirel**, acting behind the scenes, as a successor to the banned **Justice Party**. In opposition during the Özal period, it won control of the presidency and the government after 1991. After the ban on former politicians was lifted in 1987, Demirel took over formally as leader. It became the major alternative to the **Motherland Party**.

Truman Doctrine. A declaration on 12 March 1947 by the American President, Harry Truman, that the USA would 'support free peoples who are resisting attempted subjugation by armed minorities or by outside pressures'. It was spurred by the British decision that it could no longer militarily support the government in the **Greek Civil War**. The USA had to accept the risk of **Greece** (and **Turkey**, also under pressure from the **USSR**) falling within the Soviet sphere of influence, or replace the **United Kingdom** as the military guarantor in the Eastern Mediterranean. The Doctrine committed the USA to support democratic governments under threat from Communism, and became the cornerstone of American foreign policy. All subsequent American administrations accepted it, at least implicitly.

Tudjman, Franjo. (1922–) President of **Croatia** from 1991. A Second World War partisan, he served in the Yugoslav army until 1961, working later as a historian. He was dismissed from his academic position in 1967 and expelled from the **League of Communists** for his Croat nationalist views. He was imprisoned in 1972 and again in 1981 for dissident activity. He was the founder of the Croat Democratic Union (*Hrvatska Demokratska Zajednica*) in 1989. After the party's domination of the Croat Assembly after 1990, he declared secession from **Yugoslavia**, surviving an assassination attempt in March 1990. His assertion of independence and advocacy of a Greater Croatia alarmed the Serb minority, and armed conflict led him to lose parts of Croat territory in **Krajina** and **Slavonia**. He refused to accept the loss of the regions, and was often in conflict with the United Nations peace-keeping forces there. Originally praised by the West for his democratic credentials, after 1992 he was criticized for introducing a more authoritarian style of government.

Turkey. The successor state to the Ottoman Empire after 1918. A secular state was established by Mustafa Kemal Atatürk in 1923, with a centralized system of control and active economic direction under the domination of his party, the **Republican People's Party (CHP)**. Although sympathizing with the West, Turkey remained neutral in the Second World War. The CHP lost power in 1950 to a more conservative **Democratic Party** whose increasingly authoritarian style of government led to a military coup in 1960, with the army claiming its actions were necessary to protect Atatürk's secular state. A reconstructed democratic system was permitted in 1961 but for the next two decades political life was marked by intense conflict between the major political groups and leaders, and by increasingly unstable and short-lived governments. The military intervened again in 1971 to halt escalating violence by the political extremes, imposing martial law until 1973, but continuing political violence, instability and economic problems led to further intervention in 1980, when the army abolished the constitution and replaced it with a quasi-presidential system. The military regime stabilized law and order, but at the expense of transgressing human and civil rights. The existing political parties were dissolved and ex-politicians disqualified from political life for between five and ten years. Civilian government was reintroduced in 1983, but a consensual system still proved difficult to achieve, and governments continued to be criticized for flouting international conventions on human rights, especially against the country's Kurdish minority. Turkey became a member of the **North Atlantic Treaty Organization (NATO)** in 1952, where its geographical situation bordering the **USSR** gave it great strategic importance. It was perpetually in dispute with **Greece**, most particularly over **Cyprus**, after 1974 because of its support for the **Turkish Republic of Northern Cyprus**. Its application to join the **European Communities (EC)** has been stalled, primarily because of Greek objections.

Turkish Republic of Northern Cyprus. A self-proclaimed state that resulted from the Turkish invasion of **Cyprus** in July 1974 after the right-wing coup that deposed **Makarios** and sought union with **Greece**. The successful invasion effectively partitioned the island, with **Turkey** rejecting all later concessions offered by the Greek Cypriots, being willing only to accept a bicommunal federal state in Cyprus. The leaders of the Turkish Cypriot community declared a Turkish Federated State in the one third of the island controlled by Turkish army units, and in 1983 reconstituted as the Turkish Republic of Northern Cyprus, but it was recognized as a sovereign unity only by Turkey.

Twentieth Party Congress. A meeting of the **Communist Party of the Soviet Union** in Moscow in February 1956, when **Khrushchev** attacked the dictatorial methods of his predecessor, **Stalin**, and the cult of personality. He also stressed the need for, and desirability of, peaceful co-existence and acknowledged that there could be different roads to socialism. The speech encouraged a belief in Eastern Europe that the **USSR** was willing to relax its rigid control of the region, with changes in political structures being permitted. While Khrushchev did not react to minor reforms in several countries, he was not prepared to relinquish overall control of the area as an ideological and security bloc. This was emphasized by the Soviet suppression of the **Hungarian Revolution** later in the year. Within the USSR the speech heralded that there would be a modification of some of the worst excesses of the Stalin period.

Two Plus Four Talks. A series of discussions between the two Germanies and the four Second World War Allies on a territorial settlement, held after the collapse of the Communist regimes in Eastern Europe. An international meeting in Ottawa in February 1990 had concluded that the German question and reunification could not be left to the Germans alone. A preliminary meeting of foreign ministers in Bonn in May then agreed on a schedule of further talks and their agenda. There were two major issues. One was the Western insistence that a reunited Germany must be part of the **North Atlantic Treaty Organization (NATO)**, a demand eventually conceded by the **USSR**. In return it was agreed that no NATO forces would be stationed in the territory of the **German Democratic Republic (DDR)**. The second issue was the German–Polish border, since the West had never formally accepted the post-1945 **Oder–Neisse Line**. This was eventually accepted and the **Federal Republic of Germany** renounced any claims to the lands east of the Line. A Treaty on the Final Settlement with Respect to Germany was signed by the six foreign ministers in Moscow on 12 September. It provided for the staged withdrawal of Soviet forces from DDR territory by the end of 1994, and imposed limits on the size of German armed forces and the kinds of weapons they could possess. West Germany also signed four further bilateral treaties with the USSR relating to economic co-operation and German payments to assist the upkeep of Soviet forces in Germany and the costs of their relocation to the USSR. The issue of **Berlin** was settled in New York on 1 October when the four war-time Allies signed an agreement that ended their rights and responsibilities in Germany. It was the last act of the Second World War.

U

Ukraine. A new state in Eastern Europe. The descendant of the Kievan Rus state which collapsed in the thirteenth century, its eastern areas were ruled by **Russia** after 1654. It proclaimed independence in 1918, but by 1922 had been reconquered by the Soviet army. As the Ukrainian Socialist Soviet Republic it was one of the first four constituent states of the **USSR**. After 1945 Soviet territorial gains reunited all the historic and ethnic Ukrainian territory, and the Republic was given separate representation at the United Nations. The more liberal policies of **Gorbachev** were resisted in the Ukraine by the Communist leader, Volodymyr Sheherbilsky, but as the USSR began to decline in 1990 nationalist sentiment began to reassert itself. The Communist monopoly of power was abolished, and elections resulted in a victory for **Kravchuk**, a reformist Communist. After the failure of the coup in Moscow against Gorbachev in 1991, the Communist Party was banned and independence declared. The new state was in dispute with Russia over the **Crimea**, with its large Russian population, and distribution of former Soviet resources, especially the Black Sea fleet. The location of much former Soviet nuclear hardware, the government pledged itself by 1994 to initiate a programme of nuclear disarmament. Nationalist sentiment was much stronger and anti-Russian in Western Ukraine, while in the east Russian minorities were discontented with the new state. The economic problems and failures of the Kravchuk government led to its electoral defeat in 1994 by groups which wished to forge closer political and economic ties with Russia.

Ulbricht, Walter. (1893–1973) Leader of the **Socialist Unity Party (SED)** 1950–71 and President of the **German Democratic Republic (DDR)** 1960–73. He joined the German Communist Party in 1919, and was a Member of Parliament 1928–33. After Hitler came to power, he left for the **USSR**, returning to Germany in 1945 where he reorganized the Communist party in **Berlin**. He was the major architect of the forced merger in the Soviet zone of occupation of the Communists and the **Social Democratic Party (SPD)** to form the SED. He dominated the party and the DDR until his death. A loyal disciple of **Stalin**, he resisted and rejected shifts in Soviet policy after Stalin's death. He ruthlessly suppressed workers' riots in 1953 with the aid of Soviet troops, and successfully argued with the USSR for the building of the **Berlin Wall** to seal the border with the West and block the flow of refugees from the DDR. An austere and cold personality, he was succeeded as DDR supremo by **Honecker**.

Ulster. A historic province of **Ireland** compromising the nine northernmost counties. In 1920 six counties (Antrim, Armagh, Down, Fermanagh, Londonderry and Tyrone) formed the province of **Northern Ireland** within the **United Kingdom**. The remaining three counties formed the province of Ulster within the Irish republic.

Ulster Defence Association (UDA). An umbrella paramilitary group in **Northern Ireland**. Formed in 1971 as an association of Protestant 'defence associations', it became the largest Protestant organization of its kind in the province. While rejecting the use of violence and denying involvement in it, it was widely believed to be linked to active terrorist groups. In 1994 it accepted a ceasefire on the basis of the **Downing Street Declaration**.

Ulster Peace Movement. A spontaneous mass movement in **Northern Ireland** that emerged in August 1976 after an incident involving the **Irish Republican Army (IRA)** in which three children were killed. It was organized by a group of Protestant and Catholic mothers in Belfast, and spread throughout the province. Two of its leaders, Mairead Corrigan and Betty Williams, were awarded the 1976 Nobel Peace Prize. It failed to sustain its momentum or to reduce the level of violence in the province, and soon disappeared.

Ulster Popular Unionist Party (UPUP). A small Protestant party in **Northern Ireland**. Formed in 1980, it generally co-operated with the **Official Ulster Unionist Party**, but adopted a more liberal position on social issues.

Ulster Unionist Party (UUP). A Protestant party in **Northern Ireland**. It emerged out of the Protestant resistance in the 1880s to Irish Home Rule, and was established as a party after the division of **Ireland** in 1921. It formed the government of Northern Ireland until the imposition of direct rule from London in 1972. For long the official voice of the Protestant community, after **Paisley** and other dissidents seceded in 1969, it was renamed the **Official Ulster Unionist Party**, remaining hostile to British concessions to the Catholic minority.

Unified Democratic Union of Cyprus. (*Ethniki Demokratiki Énosi Kyprou – EDEK*) A small left-wing party in **Cyprus**. Founded in 1969 as the Democratic Centre Union, it adopted a socialist programme of radical socio-economic change. After 1974 it demanded the end of the Turkish occupation and the international implementation of United Nations resolutions on Cyprus.

Union for French Democracy. (*Union pour la Démocratie Française – UDF*) A centre-right coalition in **France**. It was founded in 1978 by several small groups which supported **Giscard d'Estaing**, who later became its leader in 1988. Although it agreed to co-operate with the Gaullist **Rally for the Republic (RPR)** in 1986, the two were rivals for the leadership of the French right. It was weakened in 1988 by the withdrawal of the **Centre of Social Democrats**, but in 1990 agreed to form a confederative alliance with the RPR, the Union for France (*Union pour la France*).

Union for the New Republic. (*Union pour la Nouvelle République – UNR*) A political party in **France**. It was hastily established in 1958 as a loose amalgam of various groups which supported **de Gaulle**. Until 1965 de Gaulle discouraged efforts to turn it into a disciplined organized party. In 1967 it was reorganized as the Democratic Union of the Republic (*Union Démocratique pour la V*ᵉ *République – UDR*). Despite its electoral successes in the 1960s, it remained a collection of different factions and groups, and these became more pronounced after de Gaulle's retirement. In 1976 it was restructured by **Chirac** as the **Rally for the Republic**.

Union of Democratic Forces. (*Soyuz na Demokratichni Sili – SDS*) A political alliance in **Bulgaria**. It was founded in December 1989 after the removal of **Zhivkov**, to act as an umbrella organization of several opposition groups and press for immediate democratization. Differences of opinion among its components prevented it from developing an effective cohesion. Although enjoying initial electoral success, heightened factionalism after 1992 helped to produce defeat in 1994 and a breach between it and the president, **Zhelev**.

Union of Fighting Communists. *See* RED BRIGADES.

Union of Industrial and Employers' Federations of Europe (UNICE). The umbrella organization of Western European business, representing over ten million companies. It was accepted by the **European Communities (EC)** as the official voice of European business, with representation in several EC agencies and committees. It has opposed too much intervention in the economy of either national governments or the EC, but its effectiveness has been hindered on occasions by conflicts of interest between its various economic and national components.

Union of the Democratic Centre. (*Unión de Centro Democrático – UCD*) A political party in **Spain**. It was formed in 1976 by **Suárez** as an amalgam of several small centre-right groups. It won the first free elections after the end of the **Franco** regime, but failed to establish an effective and disciplined organization. Already riven by intense factional disputes, it collapsed after Suárez resigned the party leadership in 1982.

Uniscan. An agreement on economic co-operation between the **United Kingdom** and the Nordic countries in 1950. Since 1947 the Nordic states had unsuccessfully attempted to establish some form of Scandinavian economic co-operation, and in 1949 they accepted a British proposal to explore ways of establishing a few limited and specified measures of economic and financial collaboration. All of the countries involved were hostile to the current proposals for European integration, rejecting anything that went beyond limited inter-governmental co-operation. A plan was drawn up in December 1949, and Uniscan was formed the following month. It was little more than an Anglo-Scandinavian committee of officials who met occasionally to discuss various economic issues. Its impact was negligible and it disappeared with the formation of the **European Free Trade Association (EFTA)**.

Unitarian Socialist Party. (*Partito Socialista Unitario – PSU*) A small left-wing party in **Switzerland**. It was formed in 1988 by a merger of two radical socialist groups in the Italian-speaking canton of Ticino, but failed to attract support elsewhere.

United Kingdom. A major state and parliamentary monarchy in Western Europe, developing over several centuries on the basis of constitutional practice, statute law and common law, with no written constitution, and consisting since 1923 of England, **Scotland**, **Wales** and **Northern Ireland**. A major world power in the nineteenth and early twentieth centuries, with a large empire, its post-war history was one of contraction, with government being contested by the **Conservative** and **Labour** parties. The 1945 Labour government nationalized key industries and launched a major welfare programme that after 1951 was largely accepted by Conservative governments 1951–64. By the early 1960s the phrase, **Butskellism**, had been coined to describe the apparent lack of differences of principle between the two major parties. Labour governments were dominant in the 1960s and 1970s, but with a small or no overall majority. The collapsing economic structure and trade union militancy led to a Conservative victory in 1979. The subsequent **Thatcher** governments were a watershed. Committed to free market policies, they initiated a radical programme of **privatization**, deregulation, tax reform and trade union reform. By the 1990s the Conservative governments were becoming unpopular, but in transforming the face of British politics, they had forced the Labour Party to move to the right and accept many of the reforms introduced in the 1980s. The dismantling of the colonial empire, begun in 1947 and more or less complete by the 1970s, was largely peaceful, with most ex-colonies joining the **Commonwealth of Nations**. A founder member of Western defensive alliances, Britain became a nuclear power in 1952, but escalating costs forced it after the early 1960s to become dependent upon American-constructed missiles. It rejected all forms of European integration other than inter-governmental co-operation, but in 1961 and in 1967 it sought to join the **European Communities (EC)**, but the applications were vetoed by **France**. It joined the EC in 1973 but thereafter often found itself isolated from its partners on a range of issues, which partially reflected a continuing distrust of and reluctance to be involved in extensive integration and any further loss of sovereignty.

United Left. (*Izquierdaa Unida – IU*) An alliance of three left-wing parties in **Spain**. It was formed in 1986 after a national referendum accepted a government proposal to join the **North Atlantic Treaty Organization (NATO)**. The largest component was the Communist Party of the Peoples of Spain (PCPE), a strongly pro-Soviet faction which had seceded from the **Communist Party of Spain** in 1984. It joined forces with the Republican Left, a small group which had adopted the name of a major pre-war party, and dissidents from the **Spanish Socialist Workers' Party** who had founded a Socialist Action Party (PASOC) in 1983.

United Nations Peace-Keeping Force in Cyprus (UNFICYP).

An international military force established under a United Nations (UN) mandate in 1964. Its objective was to preserve law and order in **Cyprus** by halting the outbreaks of violence between the Greek and Turkish Cypriot communities. After the 1974 Turkish invasion which led to the partition of the island, it supervised the ceasefire and patrolled the buffer zone between the two parts of the island.

United Nations Protection Force (UNPROFOR).

The collective name for the international military forces, mandated by the United Nations (UN) in 1992 as peace-keeping agents in the former **Yugoslavia**. The Force had three separate components: one deployed in Serb-populated areas of **Croatia**, one in **Bosnia-Hercegovina**, and the third in **Macedonia**. By 1995 the failure of UNPROFOR to halt the violence, especially in Bosnia, led to increasing calls for its withdrawal.

United Nations Relief and Rehabilitation Administration (UNRRA).

A specialized agency of the United Nations (UN), uniquely established and operative before the UN had been formally inaugurated. It was established in November 1943 to prepare the groundwork for handling the social and economic dislocations in Europe caused by the Second World War once peace had been secured. Countries possessing colonies were assumed to be able to draw upon the resources of their overseas possessions and were excluded from its brief. The bulk of its funding was spent on relief programmes in **Italy** and in Eastern Europe. It fell victim to the **Cold War**, and the USA withdrew its substantial financial support in 1947. It was abolished in March 1949, with some of its activities passing to other specialized UN agencies.

United Nations War Crimes Commission for Former Yugoslavia.

An international judicial body established by the United Nations (UN) in October 1992 to examine alleged breaches of humanitarian law and the

Geneva Conventions in the civil wars that raged in **Yugoslavia** after the disintegration of the state in January 1991.

United Peasant Party. (*Zjednoczone Stronnictwo Ludowe – ZSL*) A political party in **Poland**. It was founded in 1949 by a merger between a small pro-Communist Peasant Party and the Polish Peasants' Party, which in 1945 had been the leading opponent of Communism but which by 1947 had been taken over by a faction which looked for an alliance with the Communists. Its major purpose was to serve as an ancillary body of the **Polish United Workers' Party** to secure agrarian support for the regime. In November 1989 it sought to assert some independence, reconstituting itself as the Polish Peasant Party – Rebirth (*Polskie Stronnictwo Ludowe – Odrodzenie*). It survived into the post-Communist period and, led by Waldemar Pawlak, it entered into a government coalition with the ex-Communist party in 1994.

Urba. A political scandal in **France**. The name derived from Urba-Gracco, one of a number of dummy consulting agencies set up in the 1980s by local branches of the **Socialist Party (PS)**. Businesspeople sympathetic to the PS were charged for non-existent reports supplied by printers and advertising agencies who had produced campaign material. Charges were brought in 1993 against several members of the party, including ex-ministers and the former Speaker of the National Assembly.

Uruguay Round. The eighth series of negotiations on world trade under the auspices of the **General Agreement on Tariffs and Trade (GATT)**. The sessions began in September 1986 in Punta del Este in Uruguay. Previous GATT rounds had focused primarily upon manufactured goods. This time 15 different trade areas were debated, including agriculture, copyright, services and textiles, and success depended upon agreement on the Round as a whole. Due to be completed by the end of 1990, the talks were interminably extended and hovered on the brink of collapse on several occasions. One major stumbling block was a series of disagreements between the USA and the **European Communities (EC)**. That on agriculture was eventually resolved by the 1993 **Blair House Agreement**. After several further threats of collapse, the Round was eventually concluded by the end of 1994, with the further agreement that GATT would be transformed into a World Trade Organization.

USSR. (Union of Soviet Socialist Republics) The Communist state founded by Lenin after the 1917 Russian Revolution. Originally consisting of four republics, it grew to be a union of 15 socialist republics, of which the largest by far was **Russia**. Under the increasingly personalized and brutal dictatorship of **Stalin** 1926–53, it engaged in a programme of enforced industrialization, emerging after the Second World War as a major political and military power. After 1945 it created a network of satellite Communist states in

Eastern Europe, forming with them the **Warsaw Pact** in 1955. Soviet forces quelled attempts at liberalization in **Hungary** in 1956 and **Czechoslovakia** in 1968. Elsewhere in the world the USSR gave financial and military aid to pro-Soviet regimes, and in 1979 were sent into **Afghanistan** where their attempts to sustain a Communist regime became bogged down in a costly war. Within the USSR itself, although the harsh excesses of the Stalin period were not repeated, control was strictly held by the Communist party through practices such as **democratic centralism** and the **nomenklatura**. The **KGB** maintained an extensive system of internal surveillance, and all forms of dissidence were firmly suppressed. Within the party, despite the post-Stalin acceptance of a collective leadership, power tended still to reside in one individual, first **Khrushchev** and then **Brezhnev**.

The appointment of **Gorbachev** as Soviet leader in 1985 marked a fundamental change in government policies. More willing than his predecessors to accept the major economic weaknesses of the USSR, Gorbachev attempted, through his policies of **glasnost** and **perestroika**, to secure a programme of economic and technological modernization that would involve some degree of internal liberalization and a more genuine international **détente** and **arms control**. His reforms met with strong resistance from within the Communist Party, and in an effort to speed up the process he initiated extensive constitutional reform, making himself President in 1990 and introducing multi-party elections. The liberalization led to a more open debate on the future of the USSR, with independence movements emerging in many of the constituent republics, especially the **Baltic States**. Hard-line opponents of the reform process attempted a coup in 1991, but this was successfully resisted by forces loyal to Gorbachev and **Yeltsin**. By the end of 1991 it was clear that Gorbachev's attempt to introduce economic reform while maintaining Communist supremacy had failed. The implication of the party in the failed coup accelerated its rejection by the population, and by the end of the year the regime collapsed, with its constituent republics all becoming independent states.

Uštaše. An independence movement in **Croatia**. The name had traditionally been used by rebel patriots, and in 1929 was revived by the nationalist Ante Pavelić for a secret terrorist organization which later formed the German puppet government in Croatia 1941–45. Proscribed in **Yugoslavia** after 1945, it survived abroad as an anti-Communist separatist terrorist group. It waged a bombing and assassination campaign in other countries, especially the **Federal Republic of Germany** and **Sweden**, in the late 1960s, and was alleged to have been implicated in the murder of **Palme** in 1986.

V

Val d'Aosta. An Alpine region of **Italy** granted a statute of autonomy in 1948. Primarily French-speaking, its claims for linguistic rights and some form of autonomy were expressed by a successful regional party, the *Union Valdôtaine (UV)*, which after 1978 became the largest in the region. Some further limited autonomy was granted in the 1960s.

Vance–Owen Plan. A proposal for a settlement to the civil war in **Bosnia-Hercegovina** developed by the mediators appointed by the United Nations (UN) and the **European Communities (EC)**, Cyrus Vance and **Owen** in October 1992. It envisaged a division of the country along ethnic lines to take account of the territorial gains already achieved by the Bosnian Serbs. While it was accepted by the Bosnian Croats and Muslims, the Serbs rejected it in April 1993. A new attempt was made with the later **Owen–Stoltenberg Plan**.

Van den Boeynants, Paul. (1919–) Prime Minister of **Belgium** 1966–68, 1978–79. A leader of the **Christian Social Party**, he was later convicted of fiscal fraud in 1986. In January 1989 he was kidnapped, but was released the following month upon payment of a ransom. There did not appear to be a political motive, and the kidnappers were arrested shortly afterwards.

Van Gend en Loos. (Van Gend en Loos v. Nederlandse Administratie der Belastingen) A 1963 ruling by the **Court of Justice** that **European Communities (EC)** law was a new legal order, directly applicable in the Member States.

Variable geometry. A phrase referring to the possibility of common policies being developed and implemented at different rates by members of the **European Communities (EC)**. It referred back to the idea of a two-speed Europe contained in the 1976 **Tindemans Report**. It was coined by **Delors** and subsequently used by **Mitterrand**. It reflected discontent among pro-unionists that the EC's rate of progress towards integration tended to be dictated by the more reluctant Member States. It was criticized by the latter, who feared that they would be sidelined by it, and also by those who believed that it would hinder economic **harmonization** and political integration. It seemed to be given some credence in the **Treaty on European Union**, and by subsequent developments in the 1990s.

Vassilou, Georgios. (1931–) President of **Cyprus** 1988–93. A business-man with limited political experience, he declared himself an independent presidential candidate in 1988, and was backed by the Communist **Progressive Party of the Working Class**. He failed to resolve the division of the island, and after defeat in 1993 formed a Free Democratic Movement.

Vatican City. A city state in **Italy**. In 1870 the former Papal States were absorbed into the Italian state. The Holy See in the Vatican City was eventually recognized by Italy as sovereign and the government of the Roman Catholic Church in the Lateran Concordat of 1929, which was revised in 1985. Within the Vatican the Pope has had absolute political power, but his temporal authority extends over an area of only some 45 hectares in and around Rome, primarily the area around the Basilica of St Peter. After 1978 **John Paul II** instituted major administrative reforms which devolved most of the temporal powers to the Papal commission and the Secretariat of State.

Vatican Council. The second council meeting of the hierarchy of the Catholic Church 1962–65, the first being in 1869–70. It was summoned by **John XXIII** in January 1959 to discuss renewal of the faith and Christian unity. Opening in October 1962, it was attended by over 8,000 bishops, along with observers from other Christian communions. The first sessions (1962–63) resulted in 16 decrees which accepted a more tolerant approach to other churches and proposed more informality in church services, including the use of vernaculars rather than Latin. After the death of John, it was reconvened 1963–65 by his successor, **Paul VI**, and proposed further liturgical reform.

Velvet Revolution. The popular name given to the period of peaceful anti-regime demonstrations and the cautious process of democratization in **Czechoslovakia** in and after 1989 that brought about the end of Communist rule and the introduction of democracy.

Virgin Lands. An ambitious project in the **USSR** to increase the acreage of land available for agriculture. It was part of the plans of **Khrushchev** to improve Soviet agricultural output by developing idle or unproductive land. Announced in 1954, it was a major policy failure. Productivity and crop yields were poor, and the strategy of seeking to develop more acreage was abandoned in 1965. The failure of the programme was an important factor that contributed to Khrushchev's fall from power.

Visegrad Triangle. An association formed in February 1991 by **Czecho-slovakia**, **Hungary** and **Poland**. Named after the town where representatives of the three countries first met, its major objectives were declared to be co-operation in economic affairs, especially in adapting to a market economy, and also in security, and to co-ordinate their plans to seek membership of the **European Communities (EC)**. In December 1992 they signed a Central

European Free Trade Agreement, with the aim of removing most of the tariff barriers between them by 2001, and the following year the foreign ministers formed the Central European Co-operation Committee.

Voeren. (Fourons) A small area of **Belgium**. A group of mainly French-speaking villages, it was transferred in 1962 from the French-speaking province of Liège to the Flemish province of Limburg. This placed it on the 'wrong' side of Belgium's internal language boundary, since its administration was to be conducted in Flemish. Objections to the transfer persisted after 1962, but controversy emerged more strongly in 1986 with the election as mayor of **Happart**, who refused to take a test of competence in Flemish. It became a national issue and in 1987 forced the resignation of the **Martens** government. Although the immediate crisis was resolved in January 1989 with the election of a bilingual mayor, the problem remained as French-speakers continued to object to being part of **Flanders**.

Vojvodina. An autonomous province, since 1962, of **Serbia** within **Yugoslavia**. Previously part of the Habsburg Empire, it was incorporated into Serbia in 1918. An autonomous province within Serbia after 1946, its relative freedom was effectively abolished in 1990. After the disintegration of Yugoslavia in 1991 it remained with Serbia, but the rise of a more aggressive Serb nationalism that sought to restrict the rights of minorities alarmed its substantial Magyar minority. In 1990 the Democratic Union of Vojvodina Hungarians (*Vajdasádi Magyarok Demokratikas Közössége*) was formed to act as the voice of the ethnic Hungarian community to argue for autonomy for the region.

Voluntary Export Restraints (VERs). Bilateral agreements signed by the **European Communities** (**EC**) and its Member States with other countries, under which the latter agreed to limit the volume of their exports of particular products to the EC. They were not really voluntary, as the restrictions were accepted by the exporting countries in preference to the probability of more severe restraints being imposed.

Von Weizsäcker, Richard. (1920–) President of the **Federal Republic of Germany** 1984–94. A lawyer and practising member of the Evangelical Church, he joined the **Christian Democratic Union (CDU)** in 1950. Elected to Parliament in 1969, he served until 1981 when he went to West **Berlin** as mayor of the city. He was the CDU candidate for the presidency in 1974. Elected in 1984 and re-elected in 1989, he received widespread acclaim and respect for his careful and dignified statements on Germany's past and his outright criticisms of political extremism. After 1991 he visibly sought to use the presidency as a symbol of a united Germany.

Voroshilov, Kliment. (1881–1969) Soviet head of state 1953–60. A Bolshevik since 1903, he served as Commissar for Defence 1925–39, and was created a marshal in 1935. A loyal supporter of **Stalin**, he was appointed to the largely ceremonial position of Head of State after the latter's death, retiring in 1960 on grounds of ill-health. In 1961 he was accused of being a member of the **anti-party group** and charged with complicity in Stalin's purges of the 1930s. The charges were later dropped after the intervention of **Khrushchev**, and he lived in retirement until his death.

Vranitzky, Franz. (1937–) Chancellor of **Austria** from 1986. A successful banker and financier, he was appointed by **Kreisky** as a government economic adviser 1970–76. He joined the **Socialist Party of Austria (SPÖ)** and served as Minister of Finance 1984–86. He replaced Fred Sinowatz as Chancellor in 1986, the first SPÖ premier to come from a working-class background, and in 1988 also took over the party leadership. He sought to restore the party's prestige after a number of damaging scandals, and to wean it away from its commitment to public ownership.

Vyshinsky, Andrei Yanuarievich. (1883–1955) Soviet politician. A previous supporter of the Mensheviks, he switched to the Bolsheviks and served in the Red Army 1918–21 under Trotsky. After an academic career as Professor of Law in Moscow 1921–35, he was appointed Soviet state prosecutor in 1935, putting into practice the legal doctrine he had taught at university that a prisoner's guilt is absolute once a confession has been made. He became notorious as the public prosecutor in the Great Purge (*Yezhovshchina*) trials. In 1940 he was transferred to the legal section of the foreign ministry, becoming deputy Foreign Minister. He was the chief Soviet delegate to the United Nations 1945–49 and 1953–54, serving in between as Foreign Minister. A loyal and unquestioning Stalinist, he was noted for his cold and negative personality and for his unflinching application of policies.

W

Wackersdorf. The site in **Bavaria** of a proposed nuclear reprocessing plant. After construction began in 1982 it became the focus of continuous opposition from anti-nuclear groups, with several direct confrontations between demonstrators and police. The mounting pressure eventually persuaded the government to abandon the development in 1989.

Waldheim, Kurt. (1918–) President of **Austria** 1986–92. A diplomat, he served as Foreign Minister 1968–70, before running unsuccessfully as the **Austrian People's Party (ÖVP)** candidate in the 1971 presidential election. Between 1971 and 1982 he served as Secretary-General of the United Nations: his term of office was a time when the Security Council was frequently deadlocked, limiting his efforts to secure reconciliation in international disputes. He retired to Vienna in January 1982, and in 1986 was elected to the presidency as the ÖVP candidate. The campaign and his term of office were marred by allegations that during his war-time military service in the Balkans 1942–44 he had been involved in or had first-hand knowledge of atrocities committed by German forces against civilians. Although he sought to refute the allegations, with no conclusive proof of the accusations being demonstrated, he was declared *persona non grata* by the USA and several other countries, which effectively ostracized him internationally. An independent commission of historians cleared him of complicity in war crimes but claimed that he had known about them and had not been wholly honest about his military service. Primarily because of his isolation and the damage his election had done to Austrian prestige, he declined renomination in 1992.

Wales. A constituent country of the **United Kingdom**, formally incorporated with England in 1536. It has had no distinctive political status, but was given some decentralized administrative capacity through the Welsh Office. The main focus of nationalist sentiment, expressed politically through **Plaid Cymru**, has been the preservation of the Welsh language and culture. In a 1979 referendum it rejected proposals for a devolved assembly with limited powers.

Wałęsa, Lech. (1943–) President of **Poland** from 1990–95. An electrician, he worked in the **Gdansk** shipyards 1967–76, but was dismissed for drawing up a list of grievances that criticized the management. Unemployed, he began to develop an independent trade union movement, setting up a strike committee 1979–80 to seek higher wages and greater civil rights. After a total industrial stoppage in all Baltic cities, the government conceded the right of workers to organize themselves independently in the August 1980 Gdansk Agreement. He became chairman of the new **Solidarity** movement. After the military coup by **Jaruzelski**, he was arrested in December 1981, and interned until the following November. In 1983 he was awarded the Nobel Peace Prize. Subsequently allowed greater freedom of movement, he travelled widely and sought to moderate some of the more extreme demands of Solidarity, now a proscribed organization. After it was relegalized in January 1989, he played a leading role in discussions with the government on political reforms, and helped to organize Solidarity's publicity campaign for the June 1989 elections. Re-elected as Solidarity leader in April, he demanded the withdrawal of Soviet forces from Poland, but refused to be a candidate for the premiership. On the right-wing of Solidarity and a devout Catholic, he was criticized by radicals for his cautious approach to reform. After his victory in the November 1990 presidential election, he continued to urge reform, but was increasingly accused from all sides of the political spectrum, including many of his previous Solidarity colleagues, for adopting an authoritarian and unpredictable style of leadership, and he was defeated by an ex-communist in the November 1995 Presidential election.

Wallenberg Case. A controversy surrounding the disappearance of the Swedish businessman and diplomat, Raoul Wallenberg, towards the end of the Second World War. He had acted as a special envoy in **Hungary** 1944–45, saving many Jews from deportation to Nazi camps by issuing them with Swedish passports. He was arrested for espionage by the Soviet army after it occupied Budapest in January 1945. The **USSR** refused to reveal his fate, but eventually conceded that he had died in custody of a heart attack in 1947. Over the next three decades several prisoners freed from Soviet labour camps claimed that they had seen him alive in prison. Soviet documents released after 1991 indicated that he had been executed in 1947, but his family and others rejected the evidence as inconclusive.

Wallonia. A region of **Belgium**. Almost exclusively French-speaking, it had been the original heartland of Belgian industrialization, but after the 1950s entered into severe economic decline. In the 1960s, with increasing pressure from the majority Flemish population for extensive decentralization, a similar sentiment was expressed in Wallonia, where the Walloon Rally (*Rassemblement Wallon*) emerged to demand autonomy for the province as the best way of achieving control over economic policy and development. Walloon wings of the national parties also took up the call for autonomy and federalization, and in the constitutional reform of 1980

Wallonia was defined as an autonomous unit within a newly federal Belgian state which was fully implemented by 1994. By 1985 what was left of the Walloon Rally, which had fragmented after 1974, had joined forces with other groups into the left-wing Walloon Party (*Parti Wallon*) to demand independence.

War crimes. *See* NUREMBERG TRIALS.

Warsaw Pact. A co-operative defence and security agreement, formally the Eastern European Mutual Assistance Treaty, signed on 14 May by the **USSR** and the Communist regimes of Eastern Europe (except **Yugoslavia**). **Finland** declined an invitation to join the Pact, while assuring the USSR of its intention to remain neutral and non-aligned. **Albania** ceased its collaboration in 1961 and formally withdrew from the Pact in 1968. Partly a response to the admission of the **Federal Republic of Germany** into the **North Atlantic Treaty Organization (NATO)**, the Pact largely confirmed a defence arrangement that was already in place. It was superimposed upon and strengthened by a network of similar bilateral treaties among its signatories. It created a unified military command with a political and military structure, but in practice few of its institutions met regularly. The USSR was totally dominant. The Pact's headquarters in Moscow was a departmental section of the Soviet High Command, and virtually all senior positions were filled by Soviet officers. In the field the role of Pact forces was to support Soviet military deployments, and all non-Soviet forces were linked to a particular Soviet command and exercised regularly with it. A Soviet military mission was also attached to, and effectively supervised, every non-Soviet army. Apart from joint manoeuvres, Pact forces (bar those of **Czechoslovakia** and **Romania**) collaborated only once, in the subjugation of the **Prague Spring** in 1968. The early attempt by **Hungary** in 1956 to leave the Pact was crushed by Soviet forces, and proposals from Eastern Europe for reform were consistently rejected by the USSR. The cohesion of the Pact was weakened in the late 1980s by the more liberal policies of **Gorbachev**. At its annual summit in July 1989 its leaders declared that no member had the right to dictate events in another country. This implicit rejection of the **Brezhnev Doctrine** was confirmed in October at a meeting of the Foreign Ministers. By the time of the 1990 summit non-Communist governments were in place throughout Eastern Europe, and they agreed to dismantle the military structure of the Pact by April 1991, with political dissolution by March 1992. The collapse of the USSR at the end of 1991 confirmed the end of the Soviet-controlled security system. By 1994 all Russian troops had departed from the former Pact territories.

Wehner, Herbert. (1906–1990) West German politician. He joined the Communist Party in 1927, going into exile after the Nazi accession to power. Moving to Prague in 1935, he worked in the Communist International under

Dimitrov. He was sent to Stockholm in 1941, but was arrested the following year for espionage. Becoming disillusioned with Communism, he returned to Germany in 1946 and joined the **Social Democratic Party (SPD)** in Hamburg. Entering Parliament in 1949 he became one of the major supporters of party reform in the 1950s, arguing that the SPD had to shed its Marxist ideology and image. One of the forces behind the **Bad Godesberg Programme**, he remained until his retirement perhaps the principal party strategist and ideologue. A close ally of **Brandt** and a proponent of **Ostpolitik**, he served in government only during the 1966–69 **grand coalition**. After 1969 he served as SPD parliamentary leader until his retirement in 1983.

Welfare Party. *See* NATIONAL SALVATION PARTY.

Werner Report. A report on **Economic and Monetary Union (EMU)** commissioned in December 1969 by the heads of government of the **European Communities (EC)** and published the following year. The leaders had set 1980 as the deadline for EMU, and invited Pierre Werner, the Prime Minister of **Luxembourg**, to chair a committee to investigate the practicalities and set a timetable. The Report recommended that the EC should proceed simultaneously in harmonizing and co-ordinating both economic and financial policy, with EMU being completed in three stages, the first to be in place by 1973. Although accepted in 1971, the Report was not implemented, being derailed by the turmoil in the world economy and the effects of the 1973 oil crisis. The EC did not return to the question of EMU until 1988.

West Berlin. *See* BERLIN.

Western Economic Summits. *See* GROUP OF SEVEN.

Western European Union (WEU). A collaborative defence agreement and extension of the 1948 **Treaty of Brussels**, signed in 1955 and intended to resolve some of the fears aroused by the rearmament of the **Federal Republic of Germany**. After the collapse of the proposed **European Defence Community (EDC)** in 1954, the British Prime Minister, **Eden**, suggested that the Brussels treaty, extended to include West Germany and **Italy**, could meet the American demand for German rearmament and European concerns about it. Apart from the general declaration of promoting European unity and accommodating West German rearmament, WEU was designed as a means of checking West German military strength and as a guarantee that the **United Kingdom** would maintain a military presence in West Germany. It had very little infrastructure and was rarely activated in the 1950s. West Germany became a direct member of the **North Atlantic Treaty Organization (NATO)**, and the presence of British troops in Germany was integral to NATO strategy. The social and cultural responsibilities WEU inherited from the Treaty of Brussels were handed over to the

Council of Europe in 1960. Occasional attempts to revive it were made after 1960, but reactivation came only in 1984. This was partly a reflection of European concerns about the possible adverse effect of a rapprochement between the USA and **USSR**, and it became seen as a possible vehicle for a distinctive European voice on defence and security issues. There were several collaborative initiatives after 1984, and it was agreed in 1989 that its role as the sole Western European institution competent in the defence area should be strengthened. The new possibility for WEU was confused after 1989 with the ending of the **Cold War** and an argument, put most strongly by **France**, that it should become the defence and security arm of the **European Communities (EC)**. While the argument was not totally acceptable to other member states, the **Treaty on European Union** made it part of the **European Union (EU)** within the new security pillar. WEU subsequently moved its headquarters to **Brussels** and granted observer status to other Western European countries. Several Eastern European countries became associate partners of WEU in 1994.

Western Union. *See* TREATY OF BRUSSELS.

Wiesenthal, Simon. (1908–) Austrian war crimes investigator. A Jewish architect who lived in **Poland** until 1941, he spent the next three years in Nazi labour and concentration camps. After 1945 he dedicated his life to tracking down Nazi war criminals. He and his associates in the Jewish Documentation Centre in Vienna, established in 1961, have exposed over 1,000 war criminals.

Wilson, James Harold. (1916–1995) British Prime Minister 1964–70, 1974–76. Elected to Parliament in 1945 for the **Labour Party** after an academic career, he served as a junior government minister 1947–51, resigning in protest over the imposition of health charges. Identified as sympathizing more with the left wing of the party, he succeeded **Gaitskell** as party leader in February 1963, and narrowly won the 1964 election. As Prime Minister he pursued a non-doctrinal programme that attempted to revive the economy. He resolved the balance of payments problem, but devalued sterling in 1967. He imposed restrictions on immigration, unsuccessfully attempted to regulate the trade unions, and in 1967, in a reversal of party policy, submitted the second British application to join the **European Communities (EC)**. He also lifted the party's ban on proscribed organizations, opening the way for radical left-wing groups to infiltrate the party, something which became a severe problem in the late 1970s. In opposition after 1970 he opposed the terms of entry to the EC negotiated by the **Heath** government and pledged to seek a satisfactory renegotiation. Returning as premier in March 1974 he persuaded the EC to renegotiate the terms, and the following January recommended that the revisions be accepted, submitting them to a referendum for approval. His 1974 government did not possess a clear majority. It struggled to cope with a weak economy and a severe balance of payments problem through an unsuccessful social compact with the trade unions. With his health failing, and with inflation running at over 20 per cent, he suddenly resigned in April 1976, being succeeded by **Callaghan**. He was created a life peer, Baron Wilson of Rievaulx, in 1983.

Wine Lake. A phrase, similar to that of the **butter mountain**, employed to symbolize the consequences of the price guarantee and intervention element of the **Common Agricultural Policy (CAP)**. It referred to the large stores of surplus wine generated by over-production.

Winter of Discontent. A popular phrase used to describe the winter months of 1978–79 in the **United Kingdom**. The period was characterized by a declining ability of the minority **Callaghan** government to manage the economy and by a wave of both official and wild-cat strikes, primarily in the public sector, against the the government's wages policy. The unrest discredited both the trade union movement and the **Labour Party**. The gravity of the situation was a major factor in the 1979 electoral victory of the **Conservative Party** under **Thatcher.**

Wirtschaftswunder. (Economic Miracle) A phrase describing the post-war economic recovery of the **Federal Republic of Germany** from the devastation of 1945. The recovery was aided by the 1948 currency reform introduced by **Erhard**, the **Marshall Plan**, and the adoption of a **social market economy** in which the principles of a market economy, with little involvement by the state in direction or planning, was linked with extensive welfare and social security provisions.

Wolf, Markus. (1923–) East German spymaster. His family left Germany for the **USSR** in 1933 after the Nazi accession to power. He studied at the Communist International (Comintern) training school in Moscow, and in 1945 became an administrator in the Soviet zone of Germany. He headed the **German Democratic Republic (DDR)** intelligence service 1953–87, building up a large spy network in West Germany and other Western countries. He went to the USSR in 1990 after the collapse of the DDR, but returned in 1991 and was arrested. In December 1993 he received a prison sentence for several counts of treason and corruption.

Women's Alliance. (*Samtök um Kvennalista – K*) A feminist political party in **Iceland**. It was founded in 1983 with the objectives of increasing the parliamentary representation of women and improving their socio-economic position. It adopted a collective leadership and also argued for a decentralization of government and a withdrawal from military alliances.

Women's Employment and Equality Office. An agency established by the **Commission** as part of a **European Communities (EC)** commitment to the promotion of equal rights and opportunities for women. It was given the responsibility for developing and implementing EC policy on women's rights, and for ensuring that these were taken into account across a broad range of policy fields.

Women's Information Service. An agency established by the **Commission** to liaise between the **European Communities (EC)** and women's organizations in the Member States. It was intended to provide information about all aspects of EC policy that might affect the role and place of women in society.

Worker-priests. Catholic priests in **France** who worked incognito in industrial factories. It was an experiment introduced in 1946 as a means of reconverting the working classes to Catholicism and counteracting the appeal of Marxism. Once they were accepted as equals by their work colleagues, it was believed that the priests could then reveal their true identity and begin their missionary work. In 1951 several worker-priests were arrested by police in a general operation against Communist-inspired riots in Paris, and subsequent questioning revealed that some had become, if not Marxists, then sympathetic to Marxist ideas. Although the French Catholic hierarchy was willing to permit the experiment to continue, it was overruled by **Pius XII**, and in 1959 **John XXIII** declared that factory work and the mission of the clergy were incompatible.

Workers' Party. (*Pairté na nOibré*) A small left-wing party in **Ireland**. It emerged out of a split in 1969–70 in the nationalist **Sinn Féin**, representing the socialist faction, and attempted to establish itself as an independent Marxist group that demanded Irish reunification within the framework of a socialist republic. In 1992 it split into two factions as a result of an argument as to whether it should accept principles of democratic socialism. The larger reformist segment, committing itself to Irish reunification by peaceful means, formed the Democratic Left Party.

World Trade Organization (WTO). *See* GENERAL AGREEMENT ON TARIFFS AND TRADE, URUGUAY ROUND.

Wörner, Manfred. (1934–1994) Secretary-General of the **North Atlantic Treaty Organization (NATO)** 1988–94. A lawyer, he joined the West German **Christian Democratic Union (CDU)** in 1956 as a party administrator and policy adviser. He entered Parliament in 1965, and served as Minister of Defence 1982–88. The first German to occupy the most senior NATO post, he argued for caution in winding down Western defence networks after the ending of the **Cold War**. While interested in establishing some kind of relationship with the new democracies of Eastern Europe, he stressed the importance of maintaining the transatlantic link and of a continuing American military presence in Europe. He died in office after a long illness.

Wyszynski, Stefan. (1901–1981) Catholic Primate of **Poland** 1949–81.

Entering the priesthood in 1925, he was made Bishop of Lublin in 1946 and Primate in 1949. The increasing hostility between the Catholic Church and the Communist regime led to his arrest in 1953 and confinement in various monasteries. After **Gomulka** came to power in 1956, he was allowed to resume his office. He worked thereafter to establish a better relationship between Church and state. The relationship remained uneasy, and in 1966 he was refused permission to travel to Rome to participate in the papal celebrations of a millenium of Polish Christianity. While continuing to be willing to collaborate with the regime in order to gain further concessions for the Church and Catholics, he remained a forceful critic of much Communist policy until his death.

Y

Yabloko. (Apple) A liberal party in **Russia**, founded and led by the reformist economist, Grigori Yavlinsky. Originally a supporter of **Yeltsin**, it later adopted a more critical stance towards the democratic credentials of the regime, and also argued for a more cautious and measured programme of transformation to a market economy.

Yalta Conference. A meeting of the Second World War Allies in February 1945. They met at Yalta in the **USSR** to consider the structure of the post-war world. They reached a consensus on Germany, agreeing to a requirement for its unconditional surrender to all the Allies, and to the complete disarmament and military occupation of the country. The **United Kingdom** and the USA refused to accept the Soviet demand for recognition of the **Oder–Neisse Line** as Germany's new eastern boundary, and deferred the Soviet demand for **reparations** until their next meeting, which took place later in the year, after the German surrender, at **Potsdam**.

Yaoundé Convention. An agreement signed in 1963 by the **European Economic Community (EEC)** with 18 developing countries, all ex-colonies of the Member States and collectively known as the **Associated African States and Madagascar (AASM)**. It fulfilled the obligations of the **Treaty of Rome**, giving duty-free access to the EEC for most products on a non-reciprocal basis, and the opportunity to receive loans and grants from the EEC. It was renegotiated in 1969, but in 1975 was replaced by the more comprehensive **Lomé Convention**.

Yeltsin, Boris Nikolaevich. (1931–) President of **Russia** from 1990. After working in the building industry, he joined the Communist Party in 1961, occupying various party administrative positions after 1968. In 1985 he was brought from Sverdlovsk to Moscow by **Gorbachev** and made party head in the capital. His attempts to reform the city party caused much resentment, and he was dismissed in November 1987 for his criticisms of party conservatism. In 1988 he was removed from the **Politburo** for his continuing criticism of the party leadership and the limited nature of Gorbachev's reform programme. His stand had enabled him to build up a considerable popular following in Moscow, and in March 1989 he easily won election to the new multi-party Congress of People's Deputies against the official Communist candidate. Increasingly seen as a rival to Gorbachev, in March 1990 he was elected to the Supreme Soviet of the Russian Federation and then as Federation President, giving himself a very important power base within the **USSR** that was demonstrably based upon popular appeal. He dramatically announced his resignation from the Communist party and from all Soviet positions at a session of the Congress in 1991. He was the rallying point of the opposition to the abortive coup against Gorbachev later in 1991, and his uncompromising stand gained him more domestic popularity and new respect abroad. After the collapse of the USSR he continued as Russian President, but became increasingly frustrated by a conservative Communist and nationalist majority in the Russian Parliament which resisted his plans for radical economic reform. In 1993 he unilaterally and unconstitutionally dissolved the Parliament, and when resisted by his opponents, who attempted to establish their own regime from within the Parliament building, he used military force to end their defiance. His actions did not heal the rifts within Russia, and the new Parliament elected a few months later was fragmented and equally resistant to his economic programmes, which were becoming increasingly unpopular, and to the accumulation of power within the presidency. His use of Russian troops in 1994 to quell the rebellion in **Chechnya** was equally unpopular.

Youth Exchange Scheme for Europe (YES). A programme established by the **European Communities (EC)** in 1987 to foster a sense of European identity and mutual understanding among young people who were not in full-time education. It enabled young people to visit and spend some time in another Member State. It was inspired by a successful bilateral youth exchange programme operated by the **Federal Republic of Germany** and **France** since the 1950s.

Yugoslavia. A state in Eastern Europe. Founded in 1918 as the Kingdom of Serbs, Croats and Slovenes, it adopted the title of Yugoslavia in 1929. Its democratic system proved extremely fragile, dominated by conflicts and mutual suspicions between its constituent ethnic groups, especially between Serbs and the rest. A royalist dictatorship was established in 1929. Generally pro-Serb, it pursued an autocratic line, and in the 1930s came increasingly under German and Italian influence, signing the Anti-Comintern Pact in March 1941. Two days later a military coup established a more pro-Western regime, but the country was immediately invaded and occupied by German forces. The country was dismembered and in **Croatia** a puppet Fascist regime was established. Resistance was carried out by two rival groups, the royalist and nationalist Chetniks led by **Mihailovich**, and the Communist partisans of **Tito**. Allied support was switched to the Tito group, which at the 1943 **Jajce Congress** established a government. A Socialist Federal Republic was formally declared in November 1945: it consisted of the regional units of **Serbia**, Croatia, **Slovenia**, **Bosnia-Hercegovina**, **Macedonia** and **Montenegro**.

While single party and centralized Communist rule was imposed upon the country, Tito was not prepared uncritically to follow every edict of the **USSR**, and in 1948 he publicly broke with **Stalin** and advanced Yugoslavia as a champion of non-alignment and 'positive neutrality'. While the rift with the USSR was healed in 1955, Tito continued to be a critic of Soviet foreign policy, especially in Europe. After 1948 the original programme of forced industrial and agricultural **collectivization** was relaxed, and a system of workers' councils was gradually developed which allowed employees to participate in the management of economic enterprises, leading after 1965 to a removal of many economic controls in a move towards a form of market economy. Tito, who was elected President for life in 1974, remained in firm control until his death in 1980. Thereafter the **League of Communists** established a collective leadership with a rotating annual presidency. This gave more prominence to the constituent republics, all of which were ethnically distinctive, and during the 1980s ethnic and cultural differences began to be more openly and violently expressed, especially in the more economically advanced units of Croatia and Slovenia, and among the Albanian majority within the Serb province of **Kosovo**. Within Serbia itself, a more hard-line Serb nationalism emerged, symbolized by **Milošević**, which favoured the *status quo*, especially with regard to the Serb minorities in Bosnia and Croatia. The federal system, which had been designed to allay fears of Serb domination, also provided the basis for pressures for secession.

The sweeping away of the Soviet-backed Communist regimes elsewhere in Eastern Europe also impinged upon Yugoslavia. In January 1990 the League of Communists agreed to give up its monopoly of power, but the reforms failed to dampen ethnic pressures, and the first multi-party elections later in the year brought non-Communists to power in Croatia and Slovenia. However, even regional Communist parties had been converted to the cause of regional nationalism, and with nationalistic sentiment dominating in all the constituent republics there was no agreement on what the future shape of Yugoslavia should be. In June 1991 Slovenia and Croatia unilaterally declared their independence, precipitating a brief conflict in Slovenia and the occupation of Serb areas of Croatia by local Serb forces and Yugoslav army units. Macedonia and Bosnia-Hercegovina declared independence later. Serbia and Montenegro remained linked together, and in April 1992 declared the constitution of a rump Federal Republic of Yugoslavia. The secessions were not peaceful. While the Slovene issue was quickly settled, Croatia suffered severe conflict between its Croat and Serb populations, and the loss of considerable territory in **Krajina** and **Slavonia** to Serb groups. By 1993 an uneasy peace prevailed, but an even more severe conflict endured in

Bosnia-Hercegovina with a three-sided contest for control of territory between Bosnians, Croats and Serbs. At a peace conference in November 1995 in Dayton, Ohio, the Presidents of Bosnia, Croatia and Serbia agreed to a settlement of the territorial disputes between them and a territorial solution for Bosnia.

Z

Zápotocky, Anton. (1884–1957) Prime Minister of **Czechoslovakia** 1948–53, and President 1953–57. Jailed in 1905 and again in 1920 for fomenting strikes by workers, he was a founder member of the Communist Party in 1922, and worked as a trade union organizer and party administrator until 1938. Interned in a concentration camp 1940–45, after his release he became a close ally of **Gottwald**, taking charge of the trade union movement. He played a central but supporting role in the consolidation of Communist power after 1945.

Zero Option. The name given to the **arms control** proposals of President Reagan as a way of resolving the **Euromissile** issue. When talks on intermediate nuclear forces (INF) between the USA and the **USSR** began in **Geneva** in 1981, the USA put forward the zero option, a proposal that INF deployment by the **North Atlantic Treaty Organization (NATO)** would not take place if the USSR removed its own intermediate missiles from Europe. The proposal was not taken seriously by the USSR, and it was not entirely acceptable to America's European allies. It was dropped in November 1983 when the Geneva talks were abandoned. The USA reintroduced the idea at the 1986 Reykjavik summit between Reagan and **Gorbachev**, but met with the same response. As a counter-proposal Gorbachev responded with the **Double Zero Option**.

Zhdanov, Andrei. (1896–1948) Soviet politician. Joining the Bolsheviks in 1915, he played an active role in the 1917 Revolution. In 1924 he was made party leader in Novgorod, moving to Leningrad in 1934. He was appointed to the **Politburo** in 1939 and made responsible for the ideological reinforcement of Stalinism. He ruthlessly enforced social realism in the arts as well as a Bolshevik historiography, and regularly inveighed against Western decadence. He became widely regarded as a rival to **Malenkov** as the heir of **Stalin**, but died suddenly in 1948. Shortly before his death he had helped establish the **Communist Information Bureau (COMINFORM)**.

Zhelev, Zhelyu. (1935–) President of **Bulgaria** from 1992. A philosopher and dissident, he was expelled from the Communist party and the University of Sofia in 1965, and banned from employment in his occupation until 1972 for his views. He was the leader of the **Club for the Support of Glasnost**

and Perestroika, and in 1990 was made leader of the loose anti-Communist **Union of Democratic Forces**. In August 1990 he was appointed interim President by the Communist-dominated legislature, and was formally re-elected in 1992. Strongly committed to the establishment of a working democracy, he also argued that there was no alternative to **privatization** and a market economy. After 1992 he became more alienated from, and a critic of, his own party.

Zhirinovsky, Vladimir. (1946–) Russian politician. Trained as a linguist and interpreter, he worked in several occupations before entering politics in 1990. He formed and led the right-wing populist **Liberal Democratic Party**. His extreme right-wing and Russophile views, which envisaged the reincorporation of all pre-1917 imperial lands under Russian leadership, led him to attack the **Yeltsin** regime. His demagogic stand and views struck a chord among the Russian electorate, but alarmed other countries, especially those which had recently emerged from the ending of the **USSR**.

Zhivkov, Todor Kristov. (1911–) Prime Minister of **Bulgaria** 1962–71, and President 1971–89. A printer, he joined the youth section of the outlawed Communist Party in 1931, holding various party offices and later helping to organize a **Resistance movement** during the Second World War. He was appointed party leader in Sofia in 1944, and the following year, as head of the militia, he directed the arrest and elimination of thousands of political opponents. Appointed Party Secretary by **Chervenkov**, he used the office to build a power base for himself, successfully marginalizing Cherven-kov and other potential rivals. By the mid-1950s he was the undisputed ruler of the country, though not emerging to take public office until 1962. He easily disposed of an attempted coup against him in 1968 and remained thereafter unchallenged until ousted from office in November 1989 as Communist rule began to crumble. He was charged in 1991 with embezzle-ment and a year later with introducing forced labour camps and inciting racial discrimination, receiving a prison sentence despite his strong denial of the charges.

Zhukov, Georg Konstantinovich. (1896–1974) Soviet Marshal. Join-ing the army in 1918, he became a regular soldier, rising through the ranks to receive prominence by his defeat of Japanese infiltrators in Mongolia in 1939. During the Second World War he became the most prominent Soviet commander, leading the invasion of Germany. After 1945 he commanded the Soviet occupation zone in Germany, but in 1947 was recalled and demoted by **Stalin**. Very much a folk hero, his popularity made him suspect in Stalin's eyes. Back in favour after Stalin's death, he was appointed Minister of Defence in 1955, but was suddenly removed from all his positions in October 1957 and accused of encouraging a cult of personality and of hindering the work of the party in the army, but was not arrested. He was reinstated in rank in 1964 after the fall from power of **Khrushchev**, but continued to live in retirement until his death.

Published by ECW Press
665 Gerrard Street East
Toronto, ON M4M 1Y2
416-694-3348 / info@ecwpress.com

Editor for the press: Michael Holmes
Cover design: Michel Vrana
Cover image: Ryan Stimson
Cartoon illustrations: Joshua Smith

LIBRARY AND ARCHIVES CANADA
CATALOGUING IN PUBLICATION

Vollman, Rob, author
A fan's guide to hockey analytics / Rob Vollman.

(Stat shot ; 2)
Issued in print and electronic formats.
ISBN 978-1-77041-412-9 (softcover)
ISBN 978-1-77305-250-2 (HTML)
ISBN 978-1-77305-251-9 (PDF)

1. Hockey—Statistics. 2. Hockey—Statistical
methods. I. Title.

GV847.V64 2018   796.96202'1   C2018-902547-6
C2018-902548-4

The publication of *Stat Shot: A Fan's Guide to Hockey Analytics* has been generously supported by the
Government of Canada. *Ce livre est financé en partie par le gouvernement du Canada.* We also acknowledge
the contribution of the Government of Ontario through the Ontario Book Publishing Tax Credit and the
Ontario Media Development Corporation.

Ontario
Ontario Media Development
Corporation

Canada

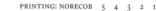

PRINTED AND BOUND IN CANADA   PRINTING: NORECOB   5   4   3   2   1

MIX
Paper from
responsible sources
FSC
www.fsc.org   FSC® C103560

At ECW Press, we want you to enjoy this book in whatever format
you like, whenever you like. Leave your print book at home and take
the eBook to go! Purchase the print edition and receive the eBook free.
Just send an email to ebook@ecwpress.com and include:

**Get the
eBook free!***
*proof of purchase
required

- the book title
- the name of the store where you purchased it
- your receipt number
- your preference of file type: PDF or ePub

A real person will respond to your email with your eBook attached.
And thanks for supporting an independently owned Canadian publisher with your purchase!

Stat Shot

A FAN'S GUIDE TO HOCKEY ANALYTICS

ROB VOLLMAN